FINANCE & FINANCIAL MARKETS

'This comprehensive, student-friendly text ... provides a terrific introduction for students on economics, finance and business programs.' John Goddard, *Professor of Financial Economics, Bangor University, UK*

'A comprehensive textbook that will skilfully guide students through the essential building blocks of modern finance. Beginners' appetite for numerical examples and graphical demonstrations will certainly find satisfaction here. Given its well-proportioned balance between intuitive thinking and analytical rigour, this book will also prove to be a precious reference book for more advanced students.' Gabriele M. Lepori, *Assistant Professor, Department of Finance, Copenhagen Business School, Denmark*

'An excellent intermediate-to-postgraduate-level text that explores the differences across the main financial centres of the world, utilising innovative examples and real-world tables and figures, helping to bring alive many difficult financial theories to the non-mathematical financial specialist. His approach offers a readable way to understand the complexities behind the current financial crisis in explaining different financial instruments and the time-line of the world-wide credit crunch.' Richard Simper, *Senior Lecturer in Economics, Loughborough University, UK*

'This book provides financial services students with a concise and easily understandable review of financial institutions and markets, and its updates in the light of the Credit Crunch help to create awareness in students of the potential impact of financial innovation.' Claire McCann, *Lecturer in Finance, University of Ulster, UK*

'This book provides an excellent introduction to the role and operation of financial markets, instruments and institutions. It is written in a clear and accessible style, with plenty of illustrative diagrams and worked examples. Given its comprehensive and up-to-date coverage of the subject area, I have no hesitation in recommending this book.' Jackie Harvey, *Professor of Financial Management, Risk and Performance, Department of Accounting and Financial Management, Newcastle Business School, UK*

FINANCE & FINANCIAL MARKETS

THIRD EDITION

Keith Pilbeam

Professor of International Economics and Finance,
City University, London, UK

palgrave
macmillan

First edition 1998
Reprinted six times
Second edition 2005
Reprinted nine times
Third edition 2010
Published by
PALGRAVE MACMILLAN

Palgrave Macmillan in the UK is an imprint of Macmillan Publishers Limited,
registered in England, company number 785998, of Houndmills, Basingstoke,
Hampshire RG21 6XS.

Palgrave Macmillan in the US is a division of St Martin's Press LLC,
175 Fifth Avenue, New York, NY 10010.

Palgrave Macmillan is the global academic imprint of the above companies
and has companies and representatives throughout the world.
Palgrave® and Macmillan® are registered trademarks in the United States,
the United Kingdom, Europe and other countries

ISBN 978-0-230-23321-8   paperback

This book is printed on paper suitable for recycling and made from fully
managed and sustained forest sources. Logging, pulping and manufacturing
processes are expected to conform to the environmental regulations of the
country of origin.

A catalogue record for this book is available from the British Library.

A catalog record for this book is available from the Library of Congress.

10   9   8   7   6   5   4   3   2   1
19   18   17   16   15   14   13   12   11   10

Printed in China

To Suzie

CONTENTS OVERVIEW

CONTENTS

LIST OF TABLES

LIST OF FIGURES

LIST OF BOXES

PREFACE

The importance of financial markets, institutions and instruments to the successful operation of a modern economy has grown markedly during the last five decades. Indeed, the world of finance has itself undergone remarkable changes during this period. Financial institutions have become less regulated and increasingly international in their outlook. Markets are less segmented, with money markets, foreign exchange, bond markets, stockmarkets and derivative markets becoming ever more inextricably linked. Moreover, domestic and foreign markets are increasingly interdependent, with movements in foreign financial markets exerting significant impacts on domestic markets. More recently, the range of international financial markets has increased, with developing countries such as China and India experiencing very high rates of economic growth and attempting to improve the functioning of their financial institutions and markets. Likewise, the Eastern-bloc countries have been keen to develop their financial services sectors. Finally, the range of financial instruments that are traded has mushroomed, with investors and borrowers being able to choose from an ever-increasing range of risk–return products. A good example of this phenomenon has been the exponential growth of trading in derivative instruments such as options, futures and swaps. Even more recent financial innovations have included collateralized debt obligations and credit default swaps, which played a crucial role in the credit crunch.

The increasing importance of finance has inevitably been reflected in the popularity of courses dealing with finance theory, financial markets and financial instruments at both the undergraduate and postgraduate level. Indeed, these days virtually all MBA programmes have finance-related core or elective courses. This third edition of *Finance and Financial Markets* is designed to be a comprehensive, and at the same time accessible, introduction to financial institutions, markets and instruments for undergraduate and MBA students. I hope that it builds upon the success of the first two editions. Many excellent books on finance are written to quite an advanced level and tend to adopt a relatively technical approach to the topic. The aim of this book is to provide a less technical and more practically oriented introduction to the field of finance whilst maintaining a reasonable degree of rigour. The book provides enough coverage to satisfy most introductory courses; however, it is hoped that the book will also serve as a springboard to the more advanced texts.

The opening five chapters provide an introduction to the world of finance and cover the basic theory relating to the operation of financial institutions and the domestic and offshore (Eurocurrency) money markets. Chapters 6 to 10 deal with both the theory and practice relating to capital markets. The theory covers areas such as portfolio diversification, the capital asset pricing model, the Gordon growth model and the efficient market hypothesis, while the practice looks at the domestic and international bond markets and equity markets.

Chapters 11 and 12 are devoted to the foreign exchange market. Chapter 11 provides an introduction to the spot and forward markets and Chapter 12 presents an analysis of the purchasing power parity theory and more modern theories of exchange rate determination. Chapters 13 to 16 are concerned with derivative instruments. Chapter 13 looks at forwards and futures contracts, and specific examples of currency, bond and equity index contracts are included. Chapters 14 and 15 look at options. Chapter 14 examines what options are, how they can be used for speculative and hedging purposes and at various option strategies, while Chapter 15 focuses on the more complex issue of option pricing and in particular the Black–Scholes option pricing formula. Chapter 16 looks at the swap market, which since the first swaps agreements were made in the 1980s has become increasingly important to the operation of domestic and international bond markets. Chapter 17 is a brand new chapter entitled 'Financial Innovation and the Credit Crunch'. It looks at two of the crucial financial innovations that played a significant role in the crisis, namely collateralized debt obligations (CDOs) and credit default swaps (CDSs) and argues that these financial innovations were 'misunderstood, misrated, mis-sold and mispriced' by financial market participants. The chapter looks at the causes of the crisis, its evolution and the policy response as well as some of the lessons that will hopefully be learnt. Finally, Chapter 18 provides an analysis of the crucial issue of regulation of the financial sector. It has been extensively rewritten to reflect issues arising from the credit crunch.

The first two editions have undergone substantial change to create this third edition, including the addition of a significant amount of new data and extensive rewriting, along with the incorporation of more worked examples. The new chapter on the credit crunch makes this one of the first texts to include an extensive and up-to-date analysis of the crisis and to give detailed coverage of financial instruments such as collateralized debt obligations and credit default swaps. Another major addition for the new edition are 26 boxed features covering a large variety of subjects related to the real world of finance. The boxes cover such diverse topics as the collapse of Lehman Brothers and American International Group, the carry trade, initial public offerings and the dot com bubble, Islamic finance, Sovereign Wealth Funds, behavioural finance, the TED spread, the VIX index, bankers' bonuses and other areas of current interest. The aim of these boxes is to provoke class discussion and to remind students that finance is not just about equations and statistics – it includes other dimensions such as human psychology, politics and error.

A significant feature of this book is the inclusion of revision questions at the end of each chapter. The aim of these questions is to enhance student understanding and to give lecturers the chance to see the type of questions that they might set for students to test their understanding of the material covered in the book. Multiple choice questions and their solutions, as well as answers to the revision questions, can be found on the website: www.palgrave.com/business/pilbeam.

One final point about this book is that the rapid changes in the world of finance make it hard for any author to keep abreast of all developments. To this end, the present book is not heavy on institutional detail, preferring to concentrate on the key theories and underlying principles. A thorough understanding of these should enable the reader to understand and interpret developments for themselves.

KEITH PILBEAM

ACKNOWLEDGEMENTS

In writing this book, I have been extremely fortunate to have had valuable discussions and receive comments on various draft chapters from numerous people. This third edition builds upon the second edition and I should like to thank Professor John Cubbin, Professor David Mayes, Professor Peter Howells, Professor David Greenaway, Professor John Thompson, Professor Ali El-Agraa, Professor Johannes Fedderke, Dr Alan Webber, Dr Everton Dockery, Dr Dimitrios Asteriou, Dr Andy Adams, Dr Jose Olmo and Dr Jason Laws for comments and suggestions on one, two or, in some cases, all three editions. In addition, I benefited greatly from anonymous reviewers of the second edition, who made very useful suggestions for the new edition. At the same time, I should make clear that any errors or shortcomings are entirely those of the author! In addition, many thanks are due to students at City University, Cass Business School and Boston University, as well as participants in various executive and banking courses held at the Executive Development Centre. They were subjected to the contents of the book and have had a significant impact upon the final product.

I would like to thank *Financial Times*, Bank for International Settlements, Euronext.Liffe, International Financial Services London, and Chicago Mercantile Exchange for allowing me to use their financial data and the *Financial Analysts Journal* for permission to adapt materials for Figure 7.6.

I would also like to thank Rakesh Jilka for technical assistance and the commissioning people at Palgrave Macmillan, Stephen Rutt (first edition), Stephen Wenham (second edition) and the ever-patient and humorous Martin Drewe (third edition) for their enthusiastic and excellent support throughout the duration of the project. Finally I should like to thank Ann Edmondson for excellent assistance at the production phase.

KEITH PILBEAM

1

THE WORLD OF FINANCE

Learning objectives

In this chapter you will learn about:

- the various statistics on international financial markets
- the various forces for change in international financial markets
- the role of financial centres such as London, New York and Tokyo
- the globalization of financial markets
- the various types of financial innovation
- the growing importance of emerging markets

1.1   Introduction

The world of finance has changed beyond all recognition over the last few decades, and among the most important changes have been:

1   the so-called globalization of the world of finance with literally trillions of dollars swirling around the global financial markets;
2   the unprecedented increase in the volume of funds and the size of the financial services industry;
3   the growing institutionalization of markets with funds increasingly managed on behalf of individual investors by pension funds, unit trusts/mutual funds, insurance companies, hedge funds and the like;
4   the range of new instruments traded such as junk bonds, collateralized debt obligations (CDOs), credit default swaps (CDS) and derivative instruments such as futures, options and swaps;
5   the use of new technology;
6   the development of the internet, enabling retail customers to access online dealing, extensive information and banking services;
7   increased pressures on banks as they have seen corporate lending fall dramatically due to the development of new forms of corporate finance such as Eurobonds;
8   the trend towards deregulation of the financial sector;
9   the use of the Euro in financial markets following the creation of a European Monetary Union in January 1999 and its introduction at street level in January 2002;
10   the increased importance of so-called emerging markets and their economies;
11   the impact of the so-called 'credit crunch', which started on 9 August 2007 and was ongoing in 2010, and its effect on the financial sector which will take many years to become fully known.

emerging market the market of a country which is experiencing rapid economic growth but whose income per capita usually makes it a low to middle income economy

These changes have not taken place in isolation, rather they have fed off each other, and interacted in a dynamic self-reinforcing manner. The credit crunch mentioned in point 11 was the culmination of many years of debt build-up, deregulation, financial innovation and other forces that were not fully understood by market participants.

In this opening chapter we attempt to give an overview of the world of finance. We look at some of the factors that have influenced the development of the financial services industry from the 1980s up to the present. In particular we focus upon four factors: the globalization of financial markets; the impact of technology; the deregulation of the financial services industry and the importance of product innovation. We then proceed to a brief look at the so-called emerging markets which are becoming more important to the global financial system, and some of the issues and obstacles that these markets will have to tackle as they develop. The chapter concludes with a rather speculative gaze into the financial crystal ball.

1.2   Financial centres

Most developed countries of the world have a major financial centre that meets much of the demand for financial services of the domestic market, and these centres compete to various degrees for international business. Inter-market competition is on the increase. New York, London and Tokyo vie with each other for recognition as the foremost financial centre. At the European level, London is the pre-eminent financial centre but in some areas it faces healthy competition from Paris and Frankfurt. In Southeast Asia, although Tokyo is the dominant financial centre it finds itself increasingly in competition with Shanghai, Singapore and Hong Kong. Qatar and Dubai have become important regional centres serving the specific needs of the Middle East region, and have begun to make an impact at the global level. Financial centres, whether major or relatively minor, increasingly find themselves competing in a global marketplace, both to retain their domestic market and for international business. Many governments have sought to enhance the status of their financial centres, especially since a competitive financial centre can prove to be an important foreign exchange earner and provide employment for substantial numbers of people. A healthy financial centre can also aid an economy by channelling investors' funds into the best-performing investments and businesses.

1.3   The role of a financial centre

A financial centre has a number of diverse and important roles to play. Perhaps the most important is to recycle funds from surplus to deficit agents as efficiently as possible. This process is illustrated in **Figure 1.1** which shows surplus agents, made up of individuals, companies and public/private bodies including central government, with surplus funds that they wish to invest. On the other hand, there are individuals, companies and public/private bodies including central government that need to borrow money and do not have sufficient current funds themselves. A key role of a financial centre is to channel funds from the surplus agents to the deficit agents in as efficient a manner as possible. However, it must be recognized that there is an enormous amount of heterogeneity within the two groups. Agents with surplus funds vary enormously, with some individuals saving only for the short term, some for the long term, for retirement and the like. Similarly, companies with excess money balances might wish to invest only for the short run or in some cases for the long term. When it comes to the deficit agents, their needs are again very varied, with some individuals requiring just short- or medium-term loans to solve a short-term cash problem, whereas others borrow long-term, for example by taking out a mortgage to finance a house purchase. Similarly, some companies need to borrow only short-term to iron out certain cash-flow problems, while others need to borrow long-term to undertake new investment.

Figure 1.1   The role of a financial centre

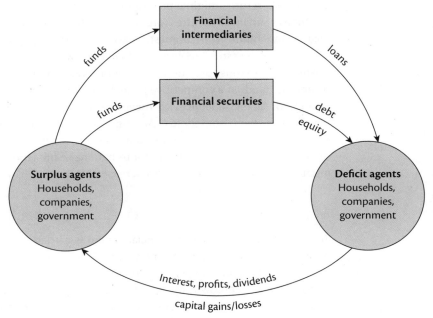

Notes:
Surplus agents are generally risk-averse, with relatively short-term horizons.
Deficit agents are generally risk-taking, with medium- to long-term horizons.

One of the prime functions of a financial centre is to facilitate the transfer of funds from surplus to deficit agents. For this purpose, a financial centre will have a range of what are known as financial intermediaries that design products/ securities to facilitate the exchange of funds between the surplus and deficit agents. In designing such products/securities, financial intermediaries must recognize that there are significant problems to overcome. In general, surplus agents tend to be risk-averse, that is only willing to take increasing risks with their surplus funds so long as there is a sufficient increase in expected return to compensate them for those risks. Because they are risk-averse, surplus agents tend to want to invest in fairly low-risk financial instruments. Also, surplus agents in general have quite short-term time horizons and usually require the ability to access their funds at very short notice. By contrast, in general the deficit agents frequently require funds to undertake risky ventures – for example, a company may borrow money to set up a new factory that may or may not succeed, an individual may borrow to set up a company that may or may not succeed. Also, the time frame of deficit agents is typically longer than that of surplus agents, they require funds normally for the medium- to long-term time horizon. The heterogeneity within the two groups and the different risk and time preferences of deficit and surplus agents need to be somehow reconciled if there are to be economically significant transfers of funds between the two groups. As we shall see in Chapter 3, there exists a wide range of financial intermediaries with niches that try to meet the varying needs of both surplus and deficit agents. In much of this book we shall also be looking at a range of financial securities such as Treasury bills,

risk-averse an investor that will only take on increased risk if there is sufficient prospective return to compensate

commercial bills, Treasury and corporate bonds and equities that exist to meet the varying risk–return and time preferences of both surplus and deficit agents.

Today's financial centres are increasingly global, concerned not only with channelling funds from domestic savers to domestic borrowers but also from international investors to international borrowers. In transferring these funds a financial centre must provide a range of products to meet investors' and borrowers' diverse demands at a competitive price. In addition, a financial centre should provide a range of financial services to meet the demands of investors, borrowers, firms, governments and households. Among the services most in demand are foreign exchange, risk management, insurance, swaps, secondary and primary markets in bonds and equities, domestic and international bank lending, a range of derivative instruments and research/advisory services.

Risk management
the process of identifying and reducing risks facing an institution or individual. The aim is to quantify the risks and take action to achieve a target risk–return trade-off

1.4   Money markets, capital markets and the banking system

Capital market
a market in which individuals and institutions trade financial securities of greater than one year to maturity such as stocks and bonds

The transfer of funds in the financial system is carried out by several means, three of the most important being money markets, capital markets (bond and equity markets) and the banking system. There are considerable differences in the relative importance of these as a means of recycling funds between economic agents. In **Table 1.1** we present the figures for stockmarket capitalization in July 2009, which shows the importance of the stockmarket particularly for the United States and the

Table 1.1   Global stockmarkets 2009 in US$ billions

Stockmarket	Listings	
	Capitalization	Domestic/Foreign
NYSE Euronext (US)	9,829	5,448/792
Tokyo	3,331	2,373/16
NASDAQ	2,812	2,714/294
London	2,416	2,399/673
NYSE Euronext (Europe)	2,196	1,013/0
Shanghai	2,724	244/2
Hong Kong	2,052	2,399/673
Deutsche Borse	1,195	742/90
BME Spanish Exchanges	1,211	3,517/40
Bombay Stock Exchange	1,072	4,925/0
National Stock Exchange India	1,004	1,405/0
World	40,555	

Notes:

Figures at at July 2009

1 The USA has two national exchanges: the New York Stock Exchange and the National Association of Securities Dealers Automatic Quotations (NASDAQ). The NYSE Euronext took over the AMEX exchange in 2008.

2 The NYSE Euronext Europe is a merger of the Paris, Lisbon, Brussels and Amsterdam exchanges.

Source: World Federation of Exchanges

United Kingdom. In those economies there has been a long tradition of firms relying on stockmarkets as a source of finance. This is much less the case in countries like Germany and Japan which have tended to rely on their banking systems as a means of recycling finance.

Debts markets are another key means of deficit agents raising finance through the issue of short-term debt instruments like Treasury and commercial bills (less than a year) or Treasury and corporate bonds (usually 1 to 30 years). As **Table 1.2** shows, there are considerable differences in both the size of the debt markets and the balance between government and private-sector debt issuance. In the United States there is also huge use by corporations of the debt markets to raise finance. In Europe the corporate bond market is less developed and is much more extensively used by governments to finance their fiscal deficits, and this has also been true of Japan where since the collapse of its bubble economy in the early 1990s the government has made frequent recourse to debt finance to prop up its economy.

bubble a rapid and substantial rise in equity prices that is not warranted by the economic fundamentals; it is ultimately followed by a dramatic price decline when the bubble bursts

Table 1.2   Global debt securities 2008 in US $billions

	Public	Private financial	Private corporate	Total debt
USA	7,888	13,819	2,914	24,622
Japan	9,113	1,197	767	11,077
Italy	1,780	1,055	427	3,262
France	1,437	1,160	324	2,921
Germany	1,364	929	300	2,593
Spain	540	543	663	1,746
UK	827	378	19	1,223
Canada	670	254	110	1,035
Belgium	373	144	36	553
Others	5,795	3,795	1,045	10,634
World	29,787	23,274	6,605	59,666

Source IFSL, Bank for International Settlements

Countries like Germany and Japan have traditionally relied on close relationships between their banking systems and corporations as a means of financing their corporations, and banks have been allowed to have stakes in companies – a situation not normally allowed in the USA or the UK. As **Table 1.3** shows, the Japanese banking system, despite Japan's much smaller economy, has assets which are actually not far behind those of the US banking system. In fact, it can be seen that the US banking system's assets are significantly lower as a percentage of gross domestic product (GDP) compared to the other economies listed in **Table 1.3**. Interestingly, there is a significant difference in the importance of the banking system in terms of GDP between the USA and the UK despite their similarities with respect to the importance of stockmarkets and debt securities.

Table 1.3   Bank deposits 2005

	Bank deposits ($ billions)	Number of banks	Banking assets % GDP
USA	5,153	7,526	41.5
UK	4,555	335	206.9
Japan	4,442	1,771	98.0
Germany	3,071	2,344	109.9
France	1,519	318	71.4
Italy	1,159	784	65.8
Switzerland	926	337	252.3

Source: European Banking Federation, US Federal Reserve, Bank of Japan

1.5   Services of a financial centre

To stake a claim to being a key international financial centre, a centre should have some or all of the following characteristics and offer the following kinds of services:

- There should be a large number of both domestic and foreign banks, and the centre should have a reasonable share of international bank lending.
- A substantial amount of foreign exchange business should be conducted.
- There should be a significant offshore market; that is, deposit and lending markets that deal in currencies different from those of the financial centre.
- The stockmarket should be well capitalized and offer investors a high degree of liquidity.
- The centre should be a major market for corporate bond finance, be it with domestic bond issues, foreign bond issues or Eurobond issues.
- There should be a range of financial institutions and associated services other than commercial banks, such as merchant/investment banks, insurance companies, securities houses, brokers, accountancy firms, commercial law firms and consultancy services.
- The centre should have a significant presence in derivative markets such as future and forward contracts, options and swaps.

In **Table 1.4** we present some comparative statistics on three key financial centres of the world, namely London, New York and Tokyo, and, for comparative purposes, those of France and Germany. London differs from the other two key financial centres in one very important respect: its claim to be a pre-eminent financial centre is heavily dependent on international business. New York is supported in its claim of being a pre-eminent financial centre by the huge size of the US economy, and Tokyo's claim is similarly supported because Japan has the second largest global economy. These two financial centres are much more domestically oriented in their business than London. The international nature of the UK financial sector is amply illustrated by the high number of foreign firms listed on the UK stockmarket (see **Table 1.1**), the large share

Table 1.4   The importance of different financial centres (2007/8) (percentage shares)

	UK	USA	Japan	France	Germany	Others
Cross-border bank lending	18	8	8	8	11	47
Foreign equities turnover	22	67	–	–	2	9
Derivatives turnover						
Exchange traded	6	39	2	1	12	40
Over the counter	43	24	4	7	4	18
Marine insurance net premium income	20	10	11	6	8	45
International bonds secondary market	70	na	na	na	na	na
Foreign exchange	35	16	6	na	na	43
Hedge fund assets	18	69	2	1	na	10
Private equity investment value	7	71	na	2	1	10
Securitization issuance	14	55	2	na	3	26

Notes: Mixture of 2007/2008 data

Source: IFSL, BIS

Over-the-counter derivatives 'tailor made' derivative contracts that are not traded on organized exchanges but between banks and other financial institutions/dealers and with their clients

of cross-border bank lending shown in **Table 1.4** and its 70% share of international bond issues, that is bonds issued by foreign entities or denominated in a currency other than the domestic currency. In addition, London is by far the biggest centre for foreign exchange trading and for trading in over-the-counter derivative contracts, that is, non-exchange traded derivatives.

Table 1.5 shows that the insurance industry is also a significant part of the financial services sector, with the United States and Japan by far the largest markets followed by the UK. However, in terms of insurance premiums per capita, the UK is in fact a more significant market with premiums per capita being significantly lower in France, Germany and Italy. In **Table 1.6** we can see that in terms of institutional funds under management, the US market is clearly a dominant player, with its pension funds and mutual funds of roughly equal significance as institutional investors. By contrast, in Japan mutual funds are less significant as institutional investors, while the insurance industry is more significant. **Table 1.6** shows that the balance of funds between these different forms of institutional investors varies significantly between countries. **Table 1.7** presents some statistics on three of the key global derivatives markets, with the Chicago Mercantile Exchange being followed by Eurex and Korea Futures Exchange. NYSE Euronext-LIFFE exchange, a merger of the London, Amsterdam, Brussels, Lisbon and Paris exchanges, comes fourth in terms of volume of contracts traded annually.

Table 1.5   World's largest insurance markets in 2007

	Gross insurance premiums (in US$ billions)	Premium per capita	World percentage share
USA	1,230	$4,087	30.3
UK	464	$7,114	11.4
Japan	425	$3,320	10.5
France	269	$4,148	6.6
Germany	223	$2,662	5.5
Italy	142	$2,322	3.5
South Korea	117	$2,384	2.9
Others	1,191	na	29.3
World	4,061	$608	100.0

Source: Swiss Re

Table 1.6   Sources of global assets under management at the end of 2007

	Pensions ($billions)	Insurance ($billions)	Mutual funds ($billions)	Total ($billions)	Share (%)
USA	17,205	6,324	12,012	35,541	48
Japan	3,161	2,862	945	6,968	9
UK	1,803	2,839	714	4,636	6
France	167	2,230	1,990	4,387	6
Germany	563	1,880	372	2,814	4
Netherlands	999	493	114	1,606	2
Switzerland	491	395	176	1,061	1
Other	4,463	2,813	9,877	17,153	23
World	28,228	19,836	26,200	74,264	100

Source: IFSL

Table 1.7   Derivative exchanges 2008, annual number of contracts traded in millions

Chicago Mercantile Exchange	3,278
Eurex	3,173
Korea Futures Exchange	2,865
NYSE Euronext-Liffe	1,674
CBOE Holdings	1,195

Notes:
Eurex is a merger of the German and Swiss derivatives exchanges.
NYSE Euronext includes NYSE Liffe markets in London, Amsterdam, Paris, Brussels and Lisbon.

Source: IFSL, Futures Industry Association

1.6 The growth of the financial services industry

The financial services sector has expanded since the 1980s to become important both in terms of employment and as a percentage of GDP. In the UK, employment in the financial services industry rose from 782,000 in 1981 to over one million in 2007. Not only that, but in 2008 it is estimated that the sector was a net exporter for the British economy to the tune of £43.3 billion and accounted for 7.6% of UK GDP. A number of influences have led to the rapid expansion of the financial services industry since the 1980s, in particular the continued globalization of finance, the adoption and impact of new technology, government deregulation of financial services, and an unprecedented amount of financial innovation resulting in a range of new financial instruments and products. Given that there were so many positive influences combining at the same time, and to a large extent feeding off each other, it is not surprising that the sector grew and changed so dramatically. We now briefly examine some of the major forces for change since 1980.

1.7 The globalization of financial markets

Bretton Woods a fixed but adjustable exchange rate regime (1947–71) whereby the major currencies were pegged to the US dollar within a ±1 per cent band; the dollar was pegged to gold at $35 per ounce

Globalization the tendency of financial institutions and their customers to move beyond their domestic markets to other markets around the globe

The term 'globalization' was one of the buzzwords that characterized the financial services industry in the 1980s. In the modern world people communicate with one another almost instantaneously and at low cost, information is speedily disseminated, and governments have greatly reduced, and in many cases removed, controls on the movement of funds. The growth of international trade has outpaced the economic growth rates of most countries, making them more trade-dependent. In turn, these factors have stimulated the demand for trade-finance products, such as foreign exchange management and borrowing and lending facilities in foreign countries and currencies. The breakdown of the Bretton Woods system of pegged exchange rates in the early 1970s made currencies more volatile both in the short and medium term. At the same time businesses have become more global and so too have international investors who have sought the benefits of international portfolio diversification. All these factors have contributed to the phenomenon of the 'globalization' of financial markets.

Globalization is a loose term capturing the idea that the world of finance has become a globalized industry; national financial markets are increasingly integrated into a globally integrated network of markets. In layman's terms the concept is about the ability to 'do anything anywhere'. Globalization has many characteristics. Borrowers seeking to raise funds are no longer limited purely to their national markets, they can raise funds on the financial markets of other countries. Similarly, investors with surplus funds are no longer restricted to the investment opportunities of their national markets but can increasingly take advantage of investment opportunities in other nations. Financial institutions seek to have a global presence both as a means of expansion and to retain their existing customers who are ever more reliant on trade and economic interactions with foreign residents. By abolishing exchange controls, as the Conservative government did on coming into office in the United Kingdom in 1979, or by relaxing controls, governments have enabled financial capital to seek out investment opportunities in other countries.

moratorium
a situation in which
a debtor declares
that it is suspending
repayments of
principal and interest

subprime mortgages
mortgages made
to people with a
poor credit rating;
they have a higher
rate of interest
than conventional
mortgages to
compensate for the
higher risk of default

ponzi scheme
a fraudulent
investment scheme
offering a high rate
of return which is
financed by payments
made by newly
acquired investors;
eventually the
scheme will collapse
with large losses for
the late joiners

Globalization is not always beneficial. One problem is the loss of local knowledge – do bankers in London really know the best firms to lend to or the best banks to buy in the United States? In the 1970s and early 1980s huge sums of money were lent to countries in Latin America, and Mexico's moratorium on its debt repayments in 1982 sparked off an international debt crisis as the Mexicans were quickly followed by Brazil, Argentina and Venezuela. More recently, the American subprime problem was exported around the world as foreign banks and other investors invested heavily in securities made up of subprime mortgages. Globalization has also led to problems in detecting wrongdoing. The main operations of Bank of Commerce and Credit International (BCCI) were based in the UK, but its headquarters was in Luxembourg. In 1995, Barings Bank was brought to the brink of collapse by the infamous Nick Leeson operating on behalf of the bank on the SIMEX exchange in Singapore. Wealthy investors around the world also faced huge losses in 2008 when they learnt that their investments held by Bernard Madoff were in fact invested in a huge ponzi scheme.

Globalization has also brought with it increased interactions and spillovers between markets, amply illustrated during the Asian financial crisis of 1997 when investors decided to pull out of Asian stocks and currencies almost indiscriminately. This led to large falls in the values of some Asian currencies and stockmarkets and caused major economic disruption to their economies. The credit crunch has amply demonstrated the interlinked nature of today's Global financial system, as problems in the US subprime mortgage market and housing market got transmitted around the world leading to large falls in global equity markets and huge bank losses worldwide. In general, across the globe it seems to be the case that stockmarkets and bond markets move increasingly in synch with each other and, as we shall see, this reduces the potential for investors and fund managers to reduce risks to their portfolios.

1.8 Technology

The 1980s witnessed an unprecedented increase in the use of new technology, and especially the widespread use of computers in the financial services industry. New technology has enabled some markets such as the London Stock Exchange to switch over to screen-based trading. Improved information systems mean the almost instantaneous transfer of price-sensitive information around the globe, and computers have enabled the industry to store and analyze masses of information. More importantly, computers have enabled new complex products to be devised and priced in real time. The complexity of some of these products has meant that higher skills are required than those of traditional traders, and many advertisements for trading positions in the financial services industry require PhDs in mathematics, engineering and physics.

Technology has also had a dramatic effect on the way banks conduct their business, process and dispense payments. Automatic telling machines (ATMs) have reduced the need for cashiers and the increased use of debit cards has dramatically reduced the cost of processing payments – the marginal cost of making a transfer made by a debit card is less than 5 per cent of processing a cheque payment. Technology has enabled retail banks to offer a wider range of services, including internet banking which gives customers the ability to examine their balances and make transfers speedily. The use of sophisticated databases means that new services can be targeted at the customer, rather than waiting for customers to enter branches.

The adoption of new technology has enabled the financial services industry to become more efficient and offer its clients a better range of products and quality of service. Many back-room operations and processing operations can now be carried out in cheaper locations than traditional, more expensive, financial centres, and in recent years many banks have relocated some of their information technology (IT) functions to India where labour costs are significantly cheaper. Technological advances have greatly reduced communication costs and improved the speed and capacity to act because information is rapidly transmitted from one financial centre to another, reducing the cost of executing orders and enhancing the ability of financial markets to monitor and analyze financial, political and economic developments.

Nonetheless, new technology has not always been viewed as purely advantageous by the industry. New technology can be very expensive to implement and some extremely costly mistakes have been made. For example, the London Stock Exchange had to abandon a planned paperless trading system called TAURUS in 1995 at an estimated cost of £400 million due to problems with the system. Another problem with new technology is that, while it can bring cost savings, there can be increased costs in the way of expensive IT staff. In addition, new hardware and software are very expensive. The need for backward compatibility with previous systems means that it is often very difficult for existing firms to take full advantage of the latest developments, while being less so for new entrants, who can in some cases quickly establish significant market shares.

There are also issues of security and reliability associated with new technology; cases of 'hacking' and people gaining access to confidential client information are big worries for many companies. New technology also increases the mobility and demands of customers who shop around for the best quotes. In sum, many financial institutions that have invested heavily in new technology find it difficult to earn an adequate return on their capital investments, especially as any advantage they may gain is usually transient, lasting only until their competitors catch up. One very important aspect of new technology is that it has changed the balance between fixed and variable costs, and in so doing has made market share an increasingly important issue. For example, new ATMs and debit payments systems are extremely costly to install and set up, but the marginal operating costs are relatively low. This has tended to mean that firms require a large and increasing market share to cover the high initial investments and to reap rewards from their investment.

backward compatibility
the need for new information technology, such as computers and software, to work with older technology in order to service existing clients

1.9 Deregulation

deregulation
the reduction or elimination of regulations designed to increase competition and reduce prices facing consumers

Governments have always intervened to regulate the financial services industry, but since the 1980s there has been a fundamental shift towards less regulation by many governments. This shift is known as the process of deregulation.

Government policies in the 1980s were particularly favourable for the development of the financial services industry, as deregulation in the UK was followed by deregulation on the continent. The UK government introduced a range of tax breaks for savers such as TESSAs (tax exempt special savings accounts) and personal equity plans (PEPs), and shifted the tax structure from taxes on income to taxes on expenditure, which left consumers with larger disposable incomes. While indirect taxes were increased on goods and services, financial products remained largely exempt, which increased their relative attractiveness.

The UK government adopted a privatization programme that benefited the financial services through advice, consultancy and underwriting fees. The programme also increased public interest in shares in general. While technology may have been the driving force enabling firms to offer a wider range of financial services, deregulation has been essential in permitting financial institutions to offer the new services. There are numerous arguments in favour of and against regulation and these are worth reviewing.

One of the major arguments in favour of regulation is the need for investor protection. Investors need to be protected from misinformation which encourages them to invest in products that are unsuitable, and they need to be protected against the misuse of their funds once they have been handed over (for example, fraud). However, many in the financial services industry oppose regulation which they argue increases costs to meet compliance. In addition, regulation can prevent the introduction of new innovative products. Another problem is that financial centres around the world find themselves in competition with one another for business, and for this reason centres are especially keen to avoid heavy-handed regulations which drive business away to other centres that adopt a more light-handed approach. This is one of the lessons to be learnt from the Eurodollar market in which US regulations clearly stimulated the development of the market.

Another problem of regulation is that too much investor protection can create a problem known as moral hazard. Moral hazard occurs when insuring against an event makes the insured-against event itself more likely to occur. For example, if governments guarantee investors' money this may encourage investors to place their money in institutions offering the highest return because, regardless of the risks involved, investors know that their principal is safe. Overall, this can then lead investors to place too much of their funds with high-risk institutions resulting in a misallocation of savings. This factor undoubtedly played a significant part in the savings-and-loans fiasco in the USA at the end of the 1980s. In the early 1980s, the savings-and-loans business was deregulated and competition for funds led to many institutions offering high rates of interest. Most investors' deposits were insured by the Federal Deposit Insurance Corporation (up to $100,000), and investors consequently placed their funds with the highest-interest-paying institution. In a bid to meet these interest payments many savings institutions lent money to increasingly risky ventures, a large number of which subsequently failed, making those savings-and-loans institutions insolvent. The result was that the Federal Deposit Insurance Corporation was required to pay out far more than it had received in premiums. Ultimately, the US taxpayer had to foot a bill which is estimated to be close to $300 billion spread over 30 years.

It is clear that most governments need to strike a balance between regulation and the need to allow their financial services industry to develop without over-burdensome restrictions. The 1980s witnessed considerable financial deregulation. London experienced the 'big bang' in 1986, which involved ending the broker–jobber divide and fixed commissions for share-dealing. The reform was motivated by the desire to improve

privatization the sale of state-owned enterprises to the private sector, often through the sale of shares to the public and institutions

regulation the set of rules or laws governing the conduct of financial institutions, markets and instruments

moral hazard the existence of an insurance policy makes the insured event more likely to occur than in the absence of the insurance policy

Federal Deposit Insurance Corporation (FDIC) a US corporation that insures US bank deposits up to the value of $250,000; it was created in 1933 to maintain public confidence in the banking system

Basel Accords
two agreements,
emanating from the
Bank for International
Settlements in 1988
and 2004, that require
large international
banks to set aside
capital reserves
against potential
losses equivalent to
8% of their
risk-adjusted assets

the competitiveness of London share-dealing, and has been considered important in maintaining London's competitiveness as an international financial centre.

However, although there was a general trend towards deregulation of national financial systems, there was one clear exception to this trend at the global level in the Basel Accord of 1988. During the 1980s regulators and central banks had become increasingly concerned that the process of globalization had led to increased interactions between banks from different countries, with a perceived danger that a banking crisis in one country could transmit itself to other countries. Hence there was an attempt to ensure that banks had sufficient capital to absorb potential losses, which resulted in the Basel Accord of 1988. As we shall see in Chapter 17, this first initiative in global regulation inevitably encountered much criticism and the Basel II Accord, which came into force in 2006, was negotiated to address these problems.

1.10 Financial innovation

financial innovation
the design of new
financial securities
and methods of
delivering financial
services

By financial innovation we mean the design of new financial instruments or the packaging together of existing ones. There are two main views on why financial innovation occurs. One cynical view is that innovations are primarily designed to overcome the effects of regulations and to exploit tax loopholes, whilst the more positive view is that they are all about designing products to meet the wide variety of needs of investors and to improve the efficiency with which they can achieve those objectives. Since the 1980s we have witnessed the rapid development and widespread availability of a whole range of financial products; examples include the proliferation of new types of options and futures contracts, warrants, swaps, junk bonds, index-tracking unit trusts, exchange traded funds (ETFs) and secondary markets in third-world debt. The greater availability and wider financial product range means that firms and investors are better able to achieve their risk–return investment objectives,. In addition, the wider range helps to attract new custom.

There were a number of forces in the 1970s and 1980s that lay behind the rapid pace of financial innovations. One was the greater volatility in both goods and financial markets. The early 1970s witnessed the breakdown of the Bretton Woods system of fixed exchange rates and witnessed high exchange rate, stockmarket and interest rate volatility. Following the first oil price shock of 1973 when the price of oil was quadrupled by the OPEC cartel, many countries suffered high and volatile inflation rates. The more turbulent environment greatly increased the demand for financial products to protect investors' and borrowers' interests.

The 1980s witnessed the widespread introduction of highly sophisticated computers and the development of appropriate software, enabling new and more complex products to be brought to the marketplace. Deregulation and greater competition in the financial sector undoubtedly had the effect of increasing both the range and quality of financial products offered. Information flows greatly improved and this led customers to demand products that enabled them to cope with rapidly changing forces. The 1990s witnessed the rise of the internet and the ability of retail customers to buy and sell shares, access financial information, and carry out their banking online. The impact and implications of all of this are still being felt by the financial services industry.

Box 1.1	Securitization

One of the biggest innovations in the debt markets during the 1980s to the present has been the process of securitization. In its simplest form the idea of securitization is to turn relatively illiquid assets with cash flows into a liquid asset by combining the cash flows from the illiquid assets into a security to investors. The basics of securitization can be illustrated with an example. Imagine that Bank ABC wishes to raise $1 billion to take over Bank XYZ. The problem Bank ABC has is that it does not have any spare cash – it could of course undertake a rights issue, that is sell new shares to its existing shareholders or perhaps increase its debt burden by issuing a corporate bond. Alternatively, it could consider turning some of its illiquid assets, such as loans and mortgages which generate a cash flow to the bank, into an asset backed security (ABS). The cash flows of the ABS can be bought by investors which will then give Bank ABC the money it requires to complete the takeover of Bank XYZ. The process of securitization is illustrated in **Figure 1.2**.

Figure 1.2 The process of securitization

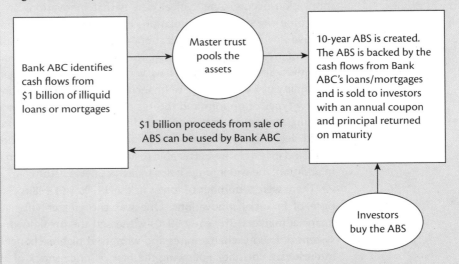

As can be seen in **Figure 1.2** Bank ABC identifies a pool of loans or mortgages on which it is currently receiving interest and principal payments and it packages them together. A master trust is set up to manage the cash flows from the loans to ensure payments are made to investors in the ABS. In return for giving up the cash flows from the loans and mortgages Bank ABC receives $1 billion cash from the sale of the ABS to fund its takeover of Bank XYZ. The process of securitization has enabled Bank ABC to turn some relatively illiquid assets into cash for operational purposes today.

The process of securitization can be used to turn existing assets such as loans and mortgages into cash but it can also be used to turn prospective future cash flows into cash today. In a famous issuance the UK rock star David Bowie raised $55 million in 1997 by selling an ABS, the cash flows for which were financed by

Box 1.1	Securitization – *continued*

future sales and royalties from 25 of the albums he produced prior to 1990. The so-called 'Bowie Bond' paid a rate of interest of 7.9% per annum, and the Prudential Insurance Corporation bought the entire issue. The ABS matured in 2007 and Bowie once again collects the royalties from sales of 25 of his early albums.

Securitization is a vital part of the modern financial landscape enabling banks and firms to generate cash based on their existing assets or prospective future cash flows. The construction of many commercial properties is financed by issuing ABSs based upon future cash flows likely to be generated by renting out the property over the years. Without securitization of future cash flows many projects might not go ahead, to the detriment of the economy, society and jobs.

As we shall see later in the book, securitization has been taken even further than our simple examples. This occurs when the ABS is in effect divided up into various tranches with different risk return characteristics.

1.11 Types of financial innovations

Examples from the wide range of innovations include the following:

1. Market-broadening innovations – these work to increase the liquidity of markets by attracting new investors and providing new opportunities for borrowers.
2. Risk-management innovations – these have the effect of redistributing financial risk exposure from agents that are risk-averse to agents that are willing to undertake the risks.
3. Arbitraging innovations – in these agents exploit arbitrage opportunities either within or between different markets, often to take advantage of loopholes in the regulatory or tax framework.
4. Pricing innovations – these seek to reduce the cost of achieving a specific investment objective.
5. Marketing innovations – in addition to innovative financial instruments, financial markets are also adept at finding innovative methods of selling and distributing financial products.

1.12 Emerging markets

Since the 1980s there has been a rapid rise in the significance of financial markets in most of the so-called emerging market countries. Countries in Southeast Asia and Latin America have increasingly found themselves attracting the interest of investors from the industrialized nations, this interest being very much spurred on by the rapid rates of economic growth of these countries. In more recent years, the newly independent countries of Eastern Europe that have emerged since the break-up of the Soviet bloc in the 1990s have also attracted the interest of international investors. In particular, countries like Poland, Hungary and Russia have attracted significant capital inflows. Many of these Eastern-bloc countries joined the European

| Box 1.2 | The growth of Islamic banking and finance |

The credit crunch which started in August 2007 led many to question the foundations of the Western banking system. By contrast, Islamic banking and finance was far less severely impacted by the crisis than its Western counterpart. Islamic banking is a system of banking that is consistent with the principles of Sharia law (or Islamic law) whose primary sources are the Koran and the sayings of the Prophet Muhammad. The rules of Islamic commercial jurisprudence are known as *fiqh al-mu'amalat*. *Fiqh al-mu'amalat* focuses on what contracts are permissible and desirable (*halal*) and which are prohibited and undesirable (*haram*). A small group of Islamic scholars in each country determine whether a product is Sharia compliant. Sharia law prohibits the payment of interest (*riba*) on the borrowing of money and also forbids the investment of money in businesses that provide goods or services that are contrary to its principles, such as alcohol, tobacco, gambling or pornography, or companies that have too high debt levels (typically meaning more than 33% of stockmaket capitalization). In addition, the use of money to finance speculation (*qimar*) or gambling (*maysir*) is prohibited, as are contracts involving ambiguity as to subject matter (*gharar*). There can be differences between national jurisdictions – a product deemed Sharia compliant in more liberal Malaysia may not be deemed compliant in more conservative Saudi Arabia.

In the late 20th century a number of Islamic banks were formed to offer banking services based on Sharia principles to personal and corporate entities within the Muslim community. The first experiment with modern Islamic banking started in Egypt in 1963, led by Ahmad Elnaggar who set up a form of a savings bank based upon profit sharing. In 1975 the Islamic Development Bank was set up to provide funding for member countries. Today Islamic banking has more than 300 institutions in more than 50 countries and some 250 mutual funds with over $500 billion of assets under management according to Islamic principles (see **Table 1.8**). Many Western banks such as Citibank, Goldman Sachs and Standard Chartered also offer Sharia compliant products. The basic principle of Islamic banking is that profits and losses are shared (*mudharabah*, which means profit sharing). Other useful terms are *wadiah* (meaning safekeeping), *murabahah* (meaning cost plus) and *ijarah* (leasing/rent).

Table 1.8 Sharia compliant assets 2007

	$billions		$billions
Iran	154.6	Brunei	31.5
Saudi Arabia	69.4	Bahrain	26.3
Malaysia	65.1	Pakistan	15.9
Kuwait	37.7	Lebanon	14.3
United Arab Emirates	35.4	Britain	10.4

| Box 1.2 | The growth of Islamic banking and finance – *continued* |

Because interest cannot be charged, a typical house purchase can be financed by the bank purchasing a house on behalf of a buyer and then selling the house to the buyer at a higher price. The bank allows the buyer to pay it back in instalments under a contract known as a *musharakah mutanaqisah partnership*. Similarly, a car purchase can be financed by the bank buying the car, then selling it on to the buyer at a higher price and allowing payment by instalments, with the bank retaining ownership of the vehicle until the final instalment is paid. Such a contract is known as *murabaha*. In a business transaction an Islamic bank may lend money to the company based on a certain percentage of the company's profits. Once the principal amount of the loan plus cost is repaid, the cost plus contract, which is known as *mudarabahah*, ends. A partnership or joint venture, namely *muskarakah*, is an arrangement whereby an entrepreneur provides labour and the bank provides financing so that both profits and losses are shared. The sharing of the capital provided by the bank and the labour by the business reflects the Islamic view that the borrower must not bear all the risk and cost of a failure. This results in a balanced distribution of income and means that the lender is not allowed to monopolize the economy. Depositors in Islamic banks keep their money in *mudoraba* or *wakala* accounts and receive a percentage of the profits rather than a given rate of interest, although most Islamic banks maintain 'profit equalization reserves' to ensure minimum payments even if losses are made. More recently Islamic finance has developed Sharia compliant bonds called *sukuks* which have been used to finance companies and development in Islamic countries. A typical *sukuk* is based upon an asset backed *ijarah* structure, which is an asset backed bond on a sale and leaseback arrangement that uses revenue from an asset, usually a property, to pay investors. These payments are based on rent or profits which are not considered to provide a guaranteed return as the property could fall in value, although investors invariably get their principal back. While a conventional bond is a promise to repay a loan, purchasing a *sukuk* constitutes partial ownership of a debt, asset, project, business or investment.

Sharia principles meant that Islamic banks did relatively well compared to their Western counterparts during the financial crisis which started in 2007. They had low amounts of leverage, little exposure to the toxic subprime mortgages and a relatively stable deposit base. The main hit to the Islamic banks was their exposure to the real estate market in the Middle East which had boomed prior to the outbreak of the crisis but was significantly hit during the downturn. There are still some problems that confront Islamic banks. One particular problem is that they cannot access the interbank market because they are not allowed to pay interest, so short-term liquidity has to be managed by other means. The use of derivatives may be sanctioned if they are used to hedge risk, but not for speculative purposes. The future development of the Islamic finance sector will depend on its ability to innovate and offer wider ranges of products and services at competitive prices so as to be able to compete with Western-based banks.

Union in April 2004. This will, over time, no doubt lead to further strengthening of their economies and lead them to further develop their financial systems, including measures to attract foreign investment. The emerging markets' stockmarkets have often offered spectacular returns, but also on many occasions the falls have led to equally large losses such as during the Mexican crisis of late 1994–early 1995 and the East Asian financial crisis of 1997. During this crisis markets like Hong Kong fell from 16,500 to a low of around 6,500, although by late 2009 the Hong Kong index had recovered to above 20,000. One of the lessons for investors is that overexposure to a single emerging market is a risky business, but this does not necessarily apply to exposure to a portfolio of emerging markets.

1.13   Problems concerning investment in emerging markets

Although there is a strong theoretical case for international portfolio diversification, there are a number of reasons why investment managers in developed countries are reluctant to invest more significant amounts of money in emerging markets, and why investors are often warned to be wary of investment in such markets. These reasons include:

- Poor accounting standards. In developed financial markets there are usually strict regulations and standards regarding reporting the financial positions of companies. In many emerging markets, however, standards are often relatively poor making it extremely difficult for investors to ascertain a clear picture of the financial worth of a company.
- Governance of companies. In developed financial markets companies are run by directors who act as agents for shareholders. In theory, at least, directors are selected on merit and can be replaced if performance is unsatisfactory. In many emerging markets, control of companies is often exerted by a board made up of founding family shareholders who are not necessarily best suited to the job.
- Information costs. In developed financial markets, most quoted companies are subject to detailed financial analysis and the costs of acquiring good quality information are relatively low. When investing in emerging markets, however, there are language barriers and also far less dissemination of information, which means that the costs of acquiring good quality information are relatively high.
- Political risks. In developed financial markets governments are relatively stable and the election of the opposition to government does not necessarily have any significant influence on financial markets. In emerging markets, however, foreign investors face the risk of controls being imposed which will restrict the outflow of their investments, and often face withholding taxes (that is, taxes on dividends and interest paid to foreign investors) or the threat of such taxes. There are some tax treaties between countries that enable investors to gain a credit for the payment of such taxes so that they do not pay double taxation, but this is not always the case and the process of claiming the tax credit can be cumbersome. In extreme instances, foreign investors face the risk of expropriation of their assets and even nationalization of the enterprises they have invested in.

witholding tax
a tax on investment income aimed specifically at foreign investors

- Foreign exchange risk. Investment in emerging markets may result in a capital and income gain measured in the currency of the emerging market economy. However, these investments need to be converted back into the developed country's currency for a comparison to be made with domestic investments. The currency change may provide a gain or loss representing an additional risk that is not present with domestic investments.
- Controls on foreign investments. In many emerging markets, governments can impose costly restrictions on how foreigners can invest and manipulate their investments. For example, foreign investors may only be allowed a certain proportion of investment in domestic companies, or allowed shares that have more limited voting rights than domestic investors.
- Higher transaction costs. In developed financial markets, deregulation and greater competition have had the effect of greatly reducing brokerage commissions. In most emerging markets these costs are significantly higher, and there are also additional costs associated with foreign exchange commissions and communication for the execution of orders.

frontier markets
countries with stockmarkets that are less developed than emerging markets

More recently there has been a growth of interest in what are known as frontier markets which refers to a subset of emerging markets that have low market capitalizations, relatively low turnover and poorer liquidity conditions than other emerging markets. While there is no decisive means of classifying frontier markets as distinct from other emerging markets a country may be classified as a frontier market due to its relatively small size, its lower level of development compared to other emerging markets and also higher level of investment restrictions. The countries classified by MSCI Barra as frontier markets are Argentina, Bahrain, Bangladesh, Botswana, Bulgaria, Croatia, Cyprus, Estonia, Ghana, Jamaica, Jordan, Kazakhstan, Kenya, Kuwait, Lebanon, Lithuania, Mauritius, Nigeria, Oman, Pakistan, Qatar, Romania, Saudi Arabia, Serbia, Slovenia, Sri Lanka, Tunisia, Ukraine, United Arab Emirates and Vietnam.

1.14 The future

Predicting the future is a hazardous business. Looking back over the last 40 years many of the important events for financial markets have been shocks that were largely unforeseeable. The oil-price hike of 1973–74 meant that huge OPEC (Organization of Petroleum Exporting Countries) surpluses were placed on the international money markets, much of which was then lent on to Latin America. In 1982, a moratorium on Mexico's debt repayments triggered off the international debt crisis. By then many major international banks had heavy exposure to the Latin American countries, and were preoccupied by the crisis throughout the 1980s. The global 1987 stockmarket collapse hit trading volumes on stockmarkets overnight. The reunification of East and West Germany in 1990 led to Germany becoming a big borrower of funds on global financial markets. Similarly, the Asian financial crisis of 1997 was largely unforeseen, yet it was undoubtedly one of the most turbulent events to ever affect global financial markets. The disintegration of the Soviet empire provided new opportunities and risks as witnessed by the 1998 Russian default. Likewise, stockmarkets went into a major downswing following the 11 September 2001 attacks on the twin buildings of the World Trade Center, a single shock that was totally unforeseen. Barely any commentators predicted the size and extent of losses and seize-up of the financial system that started in August 2007. Major financial institutions such as Citigroup, American International Group, Bank of America, Lehman Brothers, Merrill Lynch, Fannie Mae and Freddie Mac, the Royal Bank of Scotland Group, Halifax Bank of Scotland, Lloyds Bank and countless other financial institutions from around the world were drawn into the biggest financial crisis since the 1930s banking crisis. To some extent the future of the financial system will for many years to come be shaped by policy response and lessons to be learnt from the credit crunch.

Nonetheless, there are a number of trends that will undoubtedly have a major impact. One is that financial technology will continue to penetrate the home consumer market. The internet enables consumers to manage their bank accounts and make payments for goods and services directly from home. People in more and more countries will be able to trade stocks, bonds and other financial securities from their homes. Retail banking will increasingly become a tough commodity business, with consumers allocating more of their money to deposit accounts and less to current accounts. On the loan side, the ability to easily search the market for the most competitive loan rates will further erode profit margins.

Technology is also likely to impact heavily upon the way many financial instruments are traded. In New York and Tokyo, shares are still traded on the stock exchange floor and futures and options contracts involve traders gathering around a pit. The plain fact is that technology makes such arrangements an anachronism and it is only a matter of time before screen-based trading becomes the norm. The experience of London is instructive in this regard. When screen-based trading was first introduced following the big bang in 1986, it was supposed to complement trading on the stock exchange floor. However, within two weeks trading on the floor ceased and screen trading became the London norm. Electronic exchanges such as the NASDAQ in the United States have tended to gain share over rivals that do not fully utilise the benefits of modern technology.

In Europe the successful introduction of monetary union in 1999 and the euro at street level in 2002 had a profound effect, with mergers between the Amsterdam, Paris, Lisbon and Brussels stock exchanges to form the Euronext exchange. Since its introduction, the euro has proven to be a sound low-inflation currency and it may eventually emerge as a major reserve currency to rival the US dollar. The euro is leading to greater demands for a truly single market in the European financial services industry, and the removal of national governments' ability to unilaterally print money has led to a greater focus on economic reforms of social security and pension systems.

The regulatory environment in Europe is also changing rapidly, and the ability of financial firms to sell their services in other European Union (EU) countries is increasing. European policy is based on the concept of 'mutual recognition' and the so-called 'passport' principle. The concept of mutual recognition is that countries in the EU agree on the minimum standard for an insurance company or bank, and once this standard is agreed the financial institution is free to sell its services in all the EU countries. In effect, once a licence to operate is obtained in one EU country, the financial institution has a 'passport' to operate in every other EU state. This new regulatory environment contrasts with the old days when attempts to agree on full standards never got anywhere, and financial institutions required a separate licence to operate in each EU member country.

The significance of emerging market economies will no doubt be one of the biggest events over the next few decades. Countries like China and India have relatively low GDPs per capita and underdeveloped financial systems, but they have rapidly growing economies and their demands for finance and financial products will grow significantly. There is no doubt that they will look to developed capital markets such as the USA, UK and Japan for sources of finance and for models on which to develop their own financial services industries. The demand for Indian and Chinese investment bankers can be safely predicted to rise! Similarly, the Eastern-bloc economies can be expected to grow rapidly over time and they too will seek to further develop their own financial sectors.

1.15 Conclusions

The world of finance like the global economy has undergone major changes since the 1980s and many further changes can be expected in the future. To quote an old adage, 'the only constant is change'. Present-day financial institutions and the way of doing business today are likely to look very outdated in 30 years' time. Nonetheless, there are some fundamental principles of finance that do not change; one is that higher return is usually associated with higher risk, and another is that financial instruments and financial institutions will only survive in a marketplace if they are able to meet clients' needs at a competitive price. In the rest of this book we shall be looking in more detail at the role played by the financial sector of the economy, and the various financial instruments that exist.

Further reading

Bain, K. and Howells, P. (2007) *Financial Markets and Institutions*, 5th edn, Financial Times/Prentice-Hall.

Bodie, Z., Kane, A. and Marcus, A. (2008) *Investments*, 6th edn, McGraw-Hill.

Buckle, M. and Thompson, J. (2004) *The UK Financial System: Theory and Practice*, 3rd edn, Manchester University Press.

Valdez, S. (2010) *Introduction to Global Financial Markets*, 6th edn, Palgrave Macmillan.

Chapter 1	**Revision questions**

1 What are the key roles of a financial centre and to what extent is London a different financial centre than New York?

2 Discuss the pros and cons of the use of new technology in financial institutions.

3 What is meant by securitization?

| Chapter 1 | Revision questions – *continued* |

4   Discuss what is meant by financial innovation. What are the five types of financial innovation that can occur?

5   What is meant by 'globalization of financial markets'? Discuss the pros and cons of the globalization process in the world of finance.

6   Briefly describe five reasons why emerging markets may not prove popular with international investors.

Multiple choice questions available at **www.palgrave.com/business/pilbeam**

2

FINANCIAL INTERMEDIATION AND FINANCIAL MARKETS

Learning objectives

In this chapter you will learn about:

- what is meant by financial intermediation
- Type I, II, III and IV financial liabilities
- risk and maturity transformation
- the economic roles played by financial institutions
- the difference between primary and secondary markets
- hedgers, speculators and arbitrageurs

2.1 Introduction

Financial intermediation is the process of transferring sums of money from economic agents with surplus funds to economic agents that would like to utilize those funds. The key to understanding the process and the range of financial instruments available lies in recognizing that economic agents are a heterogeneous bunch having very different financial positions, investment, business and financial needs. For this reason, there are a wide range of financial intermediaries and financial instruments servicing these needs.

In this chapter we look at the various types of economic agents, making a crucial distinction between surplus and deficit agents. Money is transferred from one economic agent to another by a financial intermediary by means of the issuance of a financial security. The financial security is an asset for one party and a liability for the other party. As we shall see, financial intermediaries play a very important economic role in facilitating the transfer of funds between deficit and surplus economic agents, in large part because they are able to reconcile the often-conflicting needs of the two types of agent.

The chapter then proceeds to look at financial markets, where the financial securities are bought and sold, as well as the different types of players that operate in these markets. We look at various classifications that have been applied to financial markets, making the important distinction between primary and secondary markets. We then also look at the various players in financial markets that ultimately determine the prices of financial securities, that is, the hedgers, speculators and arbitrageurs.

financial intermediation
the process of transferring funds from economic agents with excess funds to those that need to acquire funds

2.2 Surplus and deficit agents

At any moment of time, in an economy, one can observe two distinct groups of economic agents: those that have surplus funds due to their expenditure being less than their income, and those that require funds to finance expenditure which exceeds their income. The former are referred to as surplus agents and the latter are deficit agents.

Surplus agents may be individuals or firms and have a wide variety of motives for saving surplus funds. There may be a need to meet unforeseen contingencies, firms save money to finance future investment, people save to finance future purchases, some investors save simply hoping to making a good return and some save for retirement, school fees, a deposit for house purchase and so forth. Generally speaking, surplus agents will want a range of savings products that provide them

surplus agents
economic agents with excess funds to invest as their expenditure is less than their income

deficit agents
economic agents that need to borrow funds as their expenditure is greater than their income

with a desirable mixture of liquidity (the ability to transform their savings into cash), return and protection against the effects of inflation.

Deficit agents may be individuals, firms or government agencies and have a wide variety of motives for borrowing funds. Many firms wish to borrow funds to finance investment, and because it takes time for investments to yield profits, they are particularly keen to obtain long-term finance. Since the returns on investment projects have a high degree of uncertainty, many firms are keen to raise equity finance whereby the holders of the equity have a return that is related to the eventual profitability of the investment. Individuals borrow to finance expenditure above current income, particularly major purchases such as a car or a house. Clearly there is potential for surplus funds to be transferred to deficit agents, and this is done with the help of financial intermediaries and through a variety of financial securities.

2.3   What is a financial security?

A financial security is simply a legal claim to a future cash flow. Financial securities are often called financial instruments, financial assets or financial claims, and throughout this book we shall use these terms interchangeably. Each financial security has an issuer that agrees to make future cash payments to the legal owner of the asset; the legal owner of the asset is referred to as the investor or holder. Consider the following examples of financial securities:

1. A $10,000 loan by Bank of America to Mr Jackson. The issuer in this case is Mr Jackson and the owner of the financial security (asset) is Bank of America. Mr Jackson agrees to pay Bank of America a specified amount of interest and principal repayments over an agreed time horizon.

2. A $500 million corporate bond issue by Sony Electronics group. In this instance, the issuer is Sony, which will agree to pay investors in the bond interest during the life of the bond and the principal upon maturity.

3. A $200 million issue of 10-year government bonds by the US Treasury. In this instance the issuer is the US Treasury, which will pay investors in the bond issue interest and principal.

4. A £400 million issue of ordinary shares by company XYZ. In this instance the issuer is Company XYZ, and investors in the share issue will be entitled to receive dividends distributed by the company. In addition, they also possess a claim on the net asset value of the company should it go into liquidation.

2.4   Types of financial claims: debt and equity

There are two distinct types of financial securities – debt claims and equity claims. With a debt claim the holder (investor) has a predetermined cash claim via the rate of interest charged which may be fixed or variable. With an equity claim the holder (investor) is only entitled to a cash payment in the form of dividends once holders of debt claims have been paid. A holder of an equity claim therefore has no guarantee that any cash flow will be paid. Many financial claims are a mixture of debt and equity; for instance, a preference share entitles the holder, once other debt holders

debt an amount of money borrowed by one party from another; government debt is borrowed via the issue of Treasury bonds and bills while corporate debt is borrowed from financial institutions via the issue of corporate bonds or commercial paper

have been paid, to both a predetermined payment and a share in any distributed dividends.

The distinction between debt and equity is of fundamental importance. Holders of debt instruments typically face relatively low risks compared to holders of equity. For example, when a bank lends to a firm it typically faces default risk, that is the risk that the firm will not repay part or all of its obligations. To reduce this possibility, there is usually a covenant in the loan agreement that entitles the bank to full repayment if the firm fails to meet the interest rate and capital repayments specified in the loan contract. In addition, the loan contract is often secured against specific assets of the firm, so that if the firm defaults the bank will usually be able to recuperate a significant part of the debt. By contrast, equity holders have a much more risky asset since the income stream and value of the equity are uncertain. The return to equity holders is not easy to predict and is mainly determined by the profitability and success of the firm in which the equity is held.

equity a share representing an ownership stake in a company; the holder is entitled to periodic dividends and can sell the shares to other parties at the prevailing market price

Firms regard the distinction between debt and equity as one of great importance. Investment by its nature is highly risky and this may be reflected in a firm's preference for equity as opposed to debt finance, since dividends will only have to be distributed if the project yields sufficient profit. At other times firms prefer to finance investment through sales of debt, especially when they are confident that the investment will produce sufficient yield to finance the debt or they regard borrowing costs as particularly attractive. Sometimes, however, firms are so concerned about the riskiness attached to the investment that they are undertaking that they prefer to raise equity finance. With equity finance, if the firm's investment is unsuccessful then this will be reflected in lower dividend payments.

Types of financial liabilities

A financial institution will have a stock of financial liabilities, falling within four categories known as Type I, Type II, Type III and Type IV liabilities (see **Table 2.1**).

Consider some examples of the various liabilities. A commercial bank may have a £1 million deposit that it will have to pay with a fixed interest payment of 8 per cent one year from now; this is an example of a Type I liability because the eventual outlay and time are both known. With a life assurance policy, the assurance company knows that it will have to pay a given amount of money upon the death of the assured, but the timing of the payment is uncertain, making this a Type II liability. A bank may have deposits on which it has to pay every six months a variable rate of interest according to market conditions; whilst the timing of the payment is known the actual amount to be paid is not, making this a Type III liability. Finally, many insurance companies

Table 2.1   Types of financial liabilities

Type of liablity	Amount of liability	Timing of liability
Type I	Known	Known
Type II	Known	Uncertain
Type III	Uncertain	Known
Type IV	Uncertain	Uncertain

have issued insurance policies for health, housing and motoring on which both the timing and eventual outlay are uncertain, and these are Type IV liabilities.

Although many financial intermediaries possess an uncertain liability structure, they can nonetheless use forecasting tools to estimate their likely cash outlays over a given time horizon. On the basis of these estimates the financial institution should maintain sufficient liquidity to satisfy its contractual obligations. If it fails to maintain sufficient liquidity, it may be forced to borrow funds at unfavourable interest rates.

2.5   The role of financial intermediaries

Financial intermediaries are predominantly concerned with the recycling of funds from surplus to deficit agents; that is, facilitating the transfer of funds from those that wish to save to those that wish to borrow. A financial market is defined as a market where financial assets are traded and exchanged. Financial assets are predominantly exchanged for other financial assets or money. However, they can be and frequently are exchanged for commodities or even goods and services.

> **financial market**
> a generic term describing a marketplace for the buying and selling of financial securities/assets such as equities, bonds, foreign exchange and derivative instruments

The most important function of a financial intermediary is to assist in the transfer of funds from surplus agents to deficit agents, and in assisting this process a financial intermediary undertakes several economic functions:

1   the provision of a payments mechanism;
2   maturity transformation;
3   risk transformation;
4   liquidity provision; and
5   reduction of transaction, information and search costs.

2.6   Provision of a payments mechanism

In many industrialized countries, most payments no longer involve the direct exchange of cash between agents. Certain financial intermediaries, especially commercial banks, facilitate the payments of funds by non-cash means such as cheques, credit cards, electronic transfers, debit cards and so forth. Increasingly, many of these services are offered by non-bank financial intermediaries that can compete both on price and quality with commercial banks. There is little doubt that the provision of an effective payments system is essential to the health of a modern economy. These days, economic transactions involve very significant transfers not only between domestic agents but also between domestic and foreign residents.

2.7   Maturity transformation

Surplus agents typically wish to have their surplus funds redeemable at short notice, while deficit agents typically wish to borrow funds over much longer-term horizons. A financial intermediary such as a commercial bank typically accepts investors' funds on a short-term basis of less than a year, and transforms these liabilities into longer-term assets such as loans. The process of converting short-term liabilities into longer-

maturity transformation
the process of transforming of short-term liabilities, such as deposits, into medium- to long-term assets, such as loans

term assets is known as maturity transformation. One of the most important reasons why financial institutions are able to perform maturity transformation is that they deal with a large number of deficit and surplus agents. This means that their inflow and outflow of funds is fairly predictable, so they can operate with a relatively low level of liquid reserves.

The maturity transformation process is vital since it provides both surplus and deficit agents with a greater choice in how to save and borrow funds. In the absence of a financial intermediary there would be less exchange between surplus and deficit agents since the short-term liquidity requirements of surplus agents would fail to coincide with the long-term capital requirements of deficit agents. Were there no financial intermediaries, it is likely that the borrowing requirements of deficit agents could be met only by paying a higher rate of interest to induce agents with surplus funds to lend long. Consequently, financial intermediaries help to increase fund transfers and reduce the cost of long-term capital for an economy.

2.8 Risk transformation

risk transformation
the process of transforming low-risk deposits into bundles of risky loans/assets

Agents with surplus funds typically have a high preference for safety in their investments; they often require complete protection for their capital although they may be prepared to accept some degree of risk if there are sufficient prospective returns to compensate. This contrasts with the requirements of many borrowers who require finance for inherently risky investment projects. A surplus agent could lend directly to a deficit agent; however, this would leave the surplus agent heavily exposed to the risk of default by the deficit agent. In principle this problem could be overcome by lending to a number of deficit agents. However, for the vast majority of surplus agents this is not a feasible option as the sums of money they possess are too small to make diversification a realistic cost-effective option. In the absence of financial intermediaries, firms might find it very difficult to obtain the risk finance that they require, as savers would be reluctant to put their funds at risk. Financial intermediaries can play an important part in transforming the low-risk requirements of savers into meeting the risk-finance requirements of firms.

A financial intermediary that receives funds from many surplus agents can pool these funds for on-lending to a large number of deficit agents. Via this diversification of funds a financial intermediary can considerably reduce its risk exposure. Effective risk reduction is achieved by making a relatively large number of small loans rather than a small number of large loans. In addition, a financial intermediary will tend to lend funds to different sectors of the economy, so that it will not be unduly affected by problems in any particular sector. Another way in which financial institutions can reduce risk is through specialist risk management. Since financial intermediaries have considerable experience in dealing with borrowers, they are then better equipped than individual agents to screen out high-risk cases. A financial intermediary can obtain information on the purpose of the loan and better relate the size of the loan to the ability to repay. In addition, a financial intermediary is likely to be more skilled in charging an appropriate rate of interest to compensate for the risk involved.

Financial intermediaries also have their own capital base which provides investors with a protective barrier for their savings should the institution's activities incur losses. Intermediaries maintain, or are required to maintain, some ratio of capital to their asset portfolio, and this ratio will usually rise according to the riskiness of their asset portfolio. The 1988 Basel Accord (see Chapter 18), for instance, requires banks to maintain a minimum of 8 per cent capital in relation to their risk-adjusted asset portfolio (made up principally of loans).

Another important role played by financial institutions in relation to risk management is formal insurance provision. Most economic agents are concerned about the effects of unforeseen, quite low probability events inflicting a significant negative effect on their wealth and/or income stream. Hence, they are willing to pay a fee premium to an agency prepared to insure them to some degree against such eventualities. Although the fee premium will exceed the expected payout (that is, the payout times the probability of the insured-against event occurring), risk-averse economic agents are usually prepared to undertake some degree of insurance protection provided the price is reasonable.

2.9   Liquidity provision

Surplus agents usually require a high degree of liquidity; that is, the ability to convert their savings in financial assets into money at short notice at low cost and at a fair price. The provision of liquidity is one of the key tasks performed by financial intermediaries and financial markets. Many savings assets, for example corporate and government bonds, have a long term to maturity and in the case of equity no term to maturity. Surplus agents would not be willing to hold these assets unless they also have the ability to on-sell them at short notice at a fair market price. Financial intermediaries and markets bring together numerous potential buyers and sellers of a financial asset, enabling those who wish to sell to obtain a best price according to market conditions. In addition to agents wishing to buy, some financial intermediaries, known as market-makers, will continuously quote prices at which they will either buy (bid price) or sell (ask price) a security. Competition for business between market-makers helps ensure that savers are able to sell their securities speedily, and with confidence that they are not being taken advantage of.

In the case of deposit-accepting institutions such as banks and building societies, savers demand highly liquid access to their savings. Deposit-taking institutions ensure almost instant access to their funds, although penalties are applied if savings are withdrawn before a deposit reaches its term to maturity. Deposit-accepting institutions are able to provide liquidity by maintaining liquid balances after forecasting their net outflow/inflow of funds. Since they have a large number of depositors, the withdrawal of funds is reasonably predictable and the inflow of funds is also reasonably predictable based on the maturity structure of their loan portfolio. Deposit-taking institutions are therefore able to ensure liquidity provision without maintaining large balances in relation to total deposits.

2.10   Reduction of contracting, search and information costs

Most surplus agents lack the time, skill and resources to find and analyze prospective deficit agents and draw up and enforce the necessary legal contracts. Financial intermediaries provide a convenient place of business for both borrowers and lenders of funds. In addition, financial intermediaries benefit from considerable economies of scale; because they are looking for many prospective investment opportunities, they can devote resources to recruiting and training high-quality staff to assist in the process of finding suitable deficit agents. They draw up standardized contracts and can devote the time and resources to monitor and enforce them. Through reducing the search, contracting and information costs, a financial intermediary reduces the costs and risk for surplus agents and also the borrowing costs for deficit agents. Both borrowers and lenders of funds can feel confident that the intermediary will fulfil its side of the contract, whereas less confidence would exist in direct contracts between surplus and deficit agents.

There can be little doubt that maturity transformation, risk transformation, liquidity provision, pricing, reduction in transaction, information and search costs are important roles performed by financial intermediaries. They encourage greater amounts of saving and investment over the longer term. It is true that greater deregulation can in general improve the access of people to credit facilities and reduce savings in the short term – a phenomenon observed in the mid to late 1980s in the United Kingdom. However, over the longer term the better functioning of financial intermediaries encourages people to save by increasing the range of products available so that savers' preferences are better met.

2.11 Types of financial markets

primary market
a market which both issues and prices new securities which raise funds for individuals, financial institutions, companies and governments

There are a wide variety of markets that serve differing needs. The money market deals in short-term assets that can be quickly transformed into money; the securities market deals with the raising of new capital and the trading of existing shares and bonds; the foreign exchange market is where differing currencies are traded for one another; while the derivatives market is where future obligations to buy/sell, or options to buy/sell, underlying financial assets are traded.

A distinction can be made between primary and secondary markets: in secondary markets existing issues are traded, whilst new securities are traded in primary markets.

Primary markets

underwriting the process by which investment banks guarantee that companies and governments will obtain the funds that they are seeking when issuing debt and equity securities

A primary market deals in issues of new securities, which include government bonds, local authority bonds, and shares in new public corporations. Among the most active market participants in underwriting and distributing new issues are investment and commercial banks and investment firms. These firms provide advice on the terms and timing of an offering and they might underwrite the issue and assist in the marketing of the issue to the public and financial institutions. An important part of the marketing process involves the production of a prospectus in which the nature of the business is described, and the record, risks and prospects for the company outlined. Regulations require that the prospectus be accurate and disclose all relevant material on the issue. A copy of the proposed prospectus is normally sent to the regulatory authorities for their comments and approval. Underwriting is a potentially risky business and because of the sums involved is usually undertaken by an underwriting syndicate of several investment firms under the direction of a firm that acts as the lead underwriter. The underwriting syndicate will guarantee the issuer a minimum price for the security and will then offer the security at a higher price to the public and institutional clients. Once the issue has been successfully sold, the investment firms are usually expected to ensure that there is an active secondary market in the issue.

There are number of methods by which new issues can be underwritten. The aim of these various methods is to minimize the costs for an issuer of debt as compared to the traditional underwriting process whereby a fee is paid to a syndicate for underwriting an issue. One method is the bought deal whereby a lead firm or syndicate offers a potential issuer of debt a firm bid to purchase an issue. The potential issuer will then have a short space of time to accept or reject the bid. If the bid is accepted, the lead manager or syndicate has bought the deal. The syndicate is then free to on-sell the securities wholly or in part to clients. Another method of selling a new issue is via an auction; the issuer announces the terms of the issue and then asks for bids to be submitted. Various syndicates will then tender bids for the issue and the syndicate that offers the best price wins the entire issue. Once its bid is accepted the syndicate can then on-sell the securities wholly or in part to clients. Other auction processes permit the issue to be sold to a number of bidders on the basis of the price bid and quantity tendered for.

Other methods of selling new issues include a pre-emptive rights offering to existing shareholders, offering them the right to buy new shares at a subscription price below the market value of their existing shareholding, where, if they do not exercise their rights, an underwriting syndicate picks up the remaining stock; or a private placement where securities are placed with a number of institutional firms such as investment funds, pensions and insurance companies.

Primary markets are concerned with raising new funds for ultimate borrowers by various methods, including the sale of shares, Treasury bills, commercial bills and bonds. Investment banks and other specialist financial institutions advise on the most appropriate ways to raise funds and are involved in the process of designing the issue and distributing it to potential clients. Competition for such business is very strong. For a financial institution responsible for distributing an issue, success is related to the quality of its database of prospective clients and depends upon having a good network of contacts.

Secondary markets

secondary market
the market for buying and selling a security that has already been issued on the primary market

A secondary market deals in financial securities that have already been issued, which means that the issuer of the asset does not receive any proceeds from the sale of the security. The secondary market is nonetheless important to the original issuer. The price of an issuer's shares on the secondary market will indicate the value of the company, and this in turn will help to indicate how the market would respond to any rights issue by the company. The secondary market is also vital for investors as it provides the liquidity that enables them to sell their shares. Without a healthy secondary market for shares there would be only a limited market for new issues. Further, if a secondary market lacks liquidity then the issuer of the shares will have to pay a liquidity premium to compensate investors for the lack of liquidity. A secondary market brings together buyers and sellers of a security, thus reducing search costs, and ideally enables deals to be completed at low transaction costs.

Increasingly important to the operation of secondary markets are market-makers that quote buy and sell prices for existing stock, and are prepared to buy or sell quite large amounts of stock in response to market demand and supply. This willingness to hold or be short of a particular stock at any given moment is vital in providing the market with liquidity and enabling large stock trades to be negotiated.

Secondary markets come in many forms and have diverse market structures. In a screen-based market, trading is undertaken by geographically dispersed market participants that are linked via telecommunications systems. Good examples of this type of market are the International Stock Exchange in London and the Paris Bourse. In a call market, orders are batched together at certain intervals throughout the day (or once a day), and a market-maker holds auctions for the stock either orally or in writing. The auction determines the market price at which trades are conducted. A good example of the call technique is the London gold bullion market where prices are determined twice a day, in the 'morning fix' and 'afternoon fix'. Some stock exchanges use the call technique for trading purposes. On a continuous market, prices are quoted continuously by market-makers throughout the trading day, such as on the London Stock Exchange and Paris Bourse. The New York Stock Exchange uses a mixed system, in which the call technique is used to determine the opening prices and then a continuous trading technique is used for trades throughout the day.

2.12 The classification of financial markets

There are a number of ways in which financial markets can be classified:

1 The *type* of asset traded. A market may deal with debt instruments or equity instruments or some combination of the two.
2 The *maturity* of the asset traded. If the market deals with debt instruments that have a term to maturity of less than a year, it is referred to as a money market. If the debt instruments have more than one year to maturity then the market is referred to as a capital market.
3 The *date of issue* of the assets traded. As already discussed, a primary market deals in newly issued financial assets, an example of which is the new issues market. A secondary market deals with financial assets that have been previously issued, an example of which is the stockmarket. A key distinction between primary and secondary markets is that in a primary market the issuer of the financial claim receives the funds, while in the secondary market the seller of the claim receives the funds.
4 The *means of settlement*. Some markets deal on the basis of immediate settlement, while in others settlement is adopted at some time in the future. If the settlement is for immediate delivery the market is referred to as a cash market, if settlement is for some time in the future it is referred to as a forward or futures market.
5 The *type of financial asset* traded. Some markets trade in assets in which the counterparties must exchange on an immediate or future basis, such as the spot and forward markets, respectively. In other markets, such as the options market,

---

market-maker
a broker or dealer that will quote bid–offer prices on securities; in so doing, the market-maker is prepared to take long and short positions in the securities

---

money market
a market dealing with short-term securities and the transfer of funds with a time horizon of one year or less, such as Treasury bills, commercial paper and short-term bank deposits

---

capital market
a market dealing with long-term securities and the transfer of funds with a time horizon greater than one year, such as equities and bonds

the holder buys the right but not the obligation to buy or sell an underlying asset at a given date and price in the future.

6   The *organizational structure* of the market. This is another key way in which financial markets can be classified. Some markets, like the swap market, are known as over-the-counter markets. These markets are based upon tailor-made products which have been specifically designed by individual banks to meet individual needs. Other markets are organized on the basis of broker–jobber relationships, with clients passing buy/sell instructions to their brokers who then seek the best price for their clients from jobbers/brokers. Some markets, such as the foreign exchange market, are based upon screen-based trading whereby banks buy and sell over computer networks.

7   The *method of sale/pricing*. A financial asset can be sold by various methods. The London Stock Exchange is primarily based upon a system of market-makers that both quote prices and buy or sell shares. The London International Financial Futures Exchange (LIFFE) and Chicago Mercantile Exchange (CME) are partly based upon a system of pit trading whereby traders set prices and buy and sell futures and options around a pit. In an over-the-counter market, the product is tailor-made and pricing is determined directly between buyers and sellers.

2.13   The role played by financial markets

Pricing of financial assets

Undoubtedly one of the key roles performed by financial markets is to provide, on a continuous basis, a price at which buyers and sellers are happy to conduct trade. If buyers exceed sellers of an asset, this will push it up in price, whereas if sellers exceed buyers the price will be driven down. According to the efficient-market hypothesis, the market price of a financial asset will quickly move to reflect all available information. This means that buyers and sellers can be confident that the price they trade at is fair and reasonable.

The discipline function

An important but often overlooked function of financial markets is that of helping to ensure prudent financial discipline on the part of both corporations and the government. The presence of financial markets that trade in corporate debt/equity and government debt means that both corporations and the government have to implement programmes with at least one eye upon how the financial markets will react to it. A corporation that tries to take over another corporation or engage in a rapid phase of expansion will have to bear in mind the possible reaction of the markets to this programme. If the market thinks the programme is financially unsound, then the company will find it faces an increased cost of borrowing and/or its share price will suffer. Similarly, if the financial markets do not believe that the government has a sound fiscal and monetary policy stance, the government will find that its borrowing costs are forced up. In this way financial markets provide an important discipline on both the public and private sector.

2.14 Participants in financial markets

Modern financial markets are characterized by the involvement of a variety of participants with a wide range of motivations. These include individuals, commercial and investment banks, financial institutions, investment companies, insurance and pension funds, businesses, multinationals, local and central government, and international institutions such as the European Investment Bank (EIB) and the World Bank, treasuries and central banks.

There are also brokers who act on behalf of a third party and regulators who seek to ensure the smooth functioning of market activity. The relative importance of the various market participants can vary greatly from one financial centre to another. Over the years, however, there has been a pronounced increase in the relative importance of institutional investors, a process known as the institutionalization of financial markets. Institutional investors, because they buy and sell large volumes of securities, require a high degree of liquidity so that their trades do not adversely affect the share prices in which they deal.

Brokers and market-makers

A broker acts as an intermediary on behalf of investors wishing to conduct a trade; the broker is the legal agent of the investors. In return for executing a client's instructions, a broker obtains a commission for his services. Many brokers offer additional services such as investment advice, research, custody and other services. A market-maker acts as a dealer in a financial security, quoting both a price at which he is willing to buy the security (the bid price) and a higher price at which he is willing to sell the security (the ask price). The difference between the bid and ask prices – the bid–ask spread – represents a profit margin. Market-makers provide liquidity for the market, a set of prices for investors and reliable price information.

Arbitrageurs, hedgers and speculators

In any financial market there are generally three different and important participants distinguished by their motivation for trading in the market.

arbitrage
the process of exploiting a pricing anomaly to make riskless guaranteed profits

Arbitrageurs – Arbitrage has a very specific meaning within the context of financial markets; it is the process of exploiting a price anomaly in order to make riskless guaranteed profits. Arbitrageurs are economic agents that buy and sell financial securities to make such profits. For example, if security A trades at a higher price on market 1 than on market 2, then arbitrageurs will buy the asset in market 2 at the cheap price and immediately sell it in market 1 at the higher price. The very act of arbitrage has the effect of lowering the price of security A in market 1 and raising the price in market 2, and this process continues until the price differential and arbitrage opportunity is eliminated. The potential for a riskless guaranteed profit to be made means that arbitrage opportunities are relatively rare in today's financial markets. Even when they exist, they usually do so only for a very short space of time.

hedging
the undertaking of a transaction to reduce or eliminate risk

Hedgers – Hedging is the process of buying or selling a financial asset in order to reduce or eliminate an existing risk. A hedger is a participant in financial markets who seeks to reduce or limit some risk by engaging in the purchase or sale of a financial security.

speculation
the undertaking of a
long or short position
in the financial
markets in the hope
of making a profit

Speculators – Speculation is the process of taking on risk in the hope of making a profit. A speculator is a participant in financial markets that assumes a risky or 'open' position in financial securities in the hope of making a profit. For example, if a speculator thinks security A is underpriced and likely to go up in price, he will purchase the security today and if the security goes up in price as he expects he will be rewarded with a profit. However, speculation is a risky business and security A may actually fall in price, in which case the speculator will have to 'close' his position at a loss.

2.15 Conclusions

Financial intermediation is a crucial function for the healthy operation of a modern economy. Financial markets and institutions provide this service by offering a range of financial products that are closely matched to the preferences of both borrowers and lenders of funds. Transferring funds from deficit to surplus agents involves a process of maturity and risk transformation. In addition, financial institutions and markets enable surplus agents, through the liquidity that they create, to speedily and easily convert their financial assets into cash should the need arise. It is vital to the healthy functioning of an economy that the transfer process from surplus to deficit agents is carried out in both a secure and cost-effective manner.

Further reading

Buckle, M. and Thompson, J. (2004) *The UK Financial System: Theory and Practice*, 3rd edn, Manchester University Press.

Falaschetti, D. and Orlando, M. (2008) *Money, Intermediation and Governance*. Edward Elgar.

Mayer, C. and Vives, X. (1995) *Capital Markets and Financial Intermediation*, Cambridge University Press.

Mikdashi, Z. (2001) *Financial Intermediation in the Twenty-first Century*, Palgrave Macmillan.

Spajic, L.D. (2002) *Financial Intermediation in Europe*, Kluwer Academic Press.

Thakor, A. and Boot, A. (eds) (2008) *Handbook of Financial Intermediation and Banking*, Elsevier.

Chapter 2	**Revision questions**

1   Briefly describe the key functions of a financial system with regard to surplus and deficit agents.

2   Briefly describe five types of product innovation that can occur in financial markets.

3   Which is the riskier claim, equity or debt issued by a company? What are the implications for the required rate of return on the two types of claim?

Chapter 2   **Revision questions** – *continued*

4   Explain the difference between Type I, Type II, Type III and Type IV liabilities.

5   Explain the difference between maturity transformation and risk transformation.

6   What is meant by the term 'liquidity' when applied to financial markets? How might it be measured?

    Multiple choice questions available at www.palgrave.com/business/pilbeam

3

FINANCIAL INSTITUTIONS

Learning objectives

In this chapter you will learn about:

- the various roles played by central banks
- the importance of capital adequacy
- the distinctions between commercial and investment banking
- the insurance industry and different types of insurance
- mutual finds, investment companies and exchange traded funds
- the importance of other institutional investors such as pension funds, hedge funds and private equity

3.1 Introduction

Individuals and businesses have various motives for saving and a wide variety of financial requirements. Individuals save for retirement, house purchase, future consumption, to meet future payments and insurance against loss of life or loss of property and so forth. Businesses put aside cash to meet unexpected contingencies, to finance investment, takeovers or for future development of the enterprise generally. Both individuals and businesses place many demands on financial institutions; they may require short-term borrowing facilities and may have a strong demand for long-term capital to finance projects. In addition to meeting the varied needs of businesses and individuals, financial institutions also face demands from governments that typically wish to borrow funds to meet various commitments as well as finance for capital projects.

A variety of financial institutions exist to meet these demands. Some institutions offer a wide variety of fairly standard services, while others provide more specialist products and services. In this chapter we look at various types of important financial institutions and the services that they offer. We first look at the central bank which has a number of important functions, one of which is overseeing the proper functioning of the banking system. We then proceed to look at deposit-accepting institutions that accept deposits and lend these directly to final borrowers. These bodies include the banking sector and other savings institutions. We also look at other types of financial intermediaries.

3.2 The central bank

The central bank is a key financial institution involved in setting the monetary framework within which both the economy and financial institutions operate. Among the best-known central banks are the Federal Reserve of the USA, the Bundesbank of Germany, the Bank of England, the Bank of Japan, the Bank of France and the Bank of Italy. Since the advent of European Monetary Union in January 1999, the European Central Bank has become the major central bank of Europe, such that national central banks like the Bundesbank and Bank of France are far less significant. Central banks have a crucial role in determining the monetary framework, although they differ in their degree of independence from central government and the ways in which they tend to operate. Nonetheless, central banks usually have a significant say in the design and implementation of monetary and exchange rate policies. A central bank will also advise on policy, current market conditions and the state of financial institutions. Typically the central bank has a number of important functions including:

1 the implementation of monetary and exchange rate policy;
2 the management of the national debt;
3 the supervision of the banking sector;
4 acting as the banker to the central government and the commercial banks;
5 acting as the lender of last resort.

3.3 The implementation of monetary policy

The central bank can influence the monetary base by conducting open market operations. Purchases of Treasury bills and other money market instruments from the private sector increase the money supply held by the private sector and raise the price of bills, thereby lowering short-term interest rates. Conversely, sales of Treasury bills and other money market instruments to the private sector decrease the money supply held by the private sector and lower the price of bills, thereby raising short-term interest rates. This control of short-term interest rates is one of the major tools of government economic policy designed to influence the level of economic activity.

3.4 Management of the national debt

Most governments end up spending more than they have raised through taxation. This being the case, a government has to borrow from domestic residents or overseas investors to finance the difference between its income and expenditure. The summation of all the past borrowing requirements of central and local government is known as the National Debt. Each year, part of the outstanding debt in the way of Treasury bills and bonds matures, and the central bank is responsible for ensuring that holders are repaid. This is usually done by issuing new debt.

National Debt
the total value of outstanding government debt

When deciding how to finance the maturing debt and raise new funds to finance the budget deficit, the central bank has to decide on the maturity structure of the new issue. The decision on the maturity structure can exert a significant effect on the structure of interest rates, that is, on the yield curve (short-, medium- and long-term interest rates). If the bank decides to sell more short-term debt such as Treasury bills rather than long-term bonds, then short-term interest rates will tend to rise relative to long-term rates. If, however, the bank decides to sell more long-term debt than short-term instruments, then long-term yields will rise relative to short-term yields.

3.5 Supervisory function

A central bank will usually be involved in licensing deposit-taking institutions and monitoring how well they are managed. This usually involves requiring licensed institutions to make statistical returns to the central bank. Overall, in its supervisory role of the banking system, the central bank is concerned with three key issues:

1 capital adequacy – does the bank have sufficient capital to cover the risks being undertaken in its business?
2 liquidity – does the bank have sufficient recourse to funds to meet the needs of depositors?
3 risk profile – is the bank engaged in excessive risk-taking that could endanger the safety of its deposits?

We now proceed to examine these issues in more detail.

Capital adequacy

capital adequacy a measure of the amount of capital reserves a bank holds to absorb potential losses

All banks need some degree of capital backing for the conduct of their business. This capital consists primarily of equity in companies (both financial and non-financial), holdings of Treasury bills and bonds, buildings, information technology, capital reserves and working capital. The capital reserves and working capital are extremely important since they provide a vital form of security for depositors. Should the bank make a loss on its operations, depositors need to be confident that their own funds will not be placed at risk, and the capital reserves of a bank are the principal means of protection against this.

Banks earn their money primarily by lending money, and, therefore, like to hold as little in the way of capital reserves as possible. The amount of reserves they hold should ideally be related to the size and risk attached to their loan portfolio.

Liquidity

Banks require a reasonable degree of liquidity to meet investors' demands for funds. Since liquid assets generally earn less interest than loans, banks usually prefer to maintain low liquidity ratios. The precise amount of liquidity required will be determined by the maturity structure of a bank's liabilities, the shorter the maturity structure of deposits then the greater the need for liquidity. In addition, a bank has to consider the volatility of its assets (loans) and liabilities (deposits), the more volatile these are then the greater the need for liquidity to meet unforeseen contingencies. In practice, the amount of liquidity held by banks is also heavily influenced by loan demand. If demand for loans is weak, then banks tend to hold more liquid assets (that is short-term assets) whereas, if demand for loans is high, they tend to hold less liquid assets since long-term loans are generally more profitable.

Risk profile

off-balance-sheet exposure the build up of risk which is not reflected in a bank's balance sheet that shows primarily its deposits (liabilities) and loans (assets)

Banks are generally allowed to lend money for legitimate purposes whenever there are potential profits to be made. Nonetheless, there needs to be some reasonable degree of risk management by a bank. Too much lending exposure to a particular firm or particular sector of an economy can make a bank vulnerable should there be problems with that firm or sector. In addition, many banks have non-traditional exposures such as off-balance-sheet exposure; for example, underwriting business that could result in losses, potential exposure to interest rate and exchange rate movements, and positions in derivative instruments and so forth.

3.6   Types of financial intermediaries

Financial institutions are like most other businesses in that they exist to make a profit and this is maximized by minimizing their costs and maximizing their revenue. Like most firms they can only survive if they design and sell products and services that can meet demand at a reasonable profit level.

We now proceed to look at some of the key types of financial institutions that are involved in the process of financial intermediation; that is, the transfer of funds between surplus and deficit agents. We distinguish between deposit-accepting institutions, such as banks and savings institutions, and other types of financial intermediaries, such as insurance companies, mutual funds/unit trusts, pension funds, hedge funds and private equity and the like.

3.7   Deposit institutions

deposit institution an institution such as a bank or savings institution that accepts cash deposits which can be either sight or term deposits

Deposit institutions accept deposits from economic agents. These funds become their liabilities which they then on-lend to make direct loans or investments, which become their assets. Deposit-taking institutions aim to make a profit in the way of 'spread income' between the cost of the deposits that they accept and other sources of funding, and the return that they receive on their investment portfolio in the way of loans, equity stakes and other investments. Examples of deposit institutions include commercial banks, savings banks and building societies. The deregulation trend in the 1980s meant that in many countries there was increasing overlap between various deposit-taking institutions.

default risk the risk that governments, companies or individuals who owe money will default on their repayments of principal and/or interest

In conducting their business, deposit-taking institutions face a number of risks. A major concern is the 'funding risk'; that is, the risk that interest rate movements may move in such a manner that profits will be adversely affected. For example, a commercial bank may pay its depositors a variable rate of interest which is currently 6 per cent, and on-lend the funds at a fixed interest rate of 8 per cent. If the variable rate of interest the bank has to pay becomes 9 per cent, it will be paying more for its funds than it is receiving and therefore be incurring losses. Another important concern is default risk; that is, the risk that borrowers from the institution will default on their obligations. A further concern is regulatory risk, which is the risk that regulators will change the regulatory framework in a manner that will adversely affect the profitability of the institution.

regulatory risk the risk that a change in regulations or the law will adversely impact upon the profitability of a financial institution or market participant

liquidity risk the risk that the market in a security will dry up such that it is difficult to turn it into cash without taking a substantial loss

All deposit-taking institutions are also concerned with liquidity risk. Deposit institutions generally accept short-term deposits and transform much of these into longer-term investments; this means that there is a mismatch between the maturity structure of the institutions' liabilities and their assets. Should there be unexpectedly large withdrawals by depositors, the deposit-taking institution could find itself short of funds and might be forced to borrow the funds at penal rates of interest from the central bank. There are a number of ways in which liquidity risk can be managed; for example, by holding sufficient cash reserves and investments in liquid securities which possess low price variability; by raising interest rates to discourage deposit withdrawals; or by attracting new deposits. There are limits to the amount of liquid reserves that banks will wish to hold, and short-term securities typically earn lower returns than long-term securities.

3.8   The banking sector

universal banking
banking that offers a broad range of financial services such as insurance, investment services in addition to basic banking services such as deposit taking and loan making

Banks are the major type of deposit-taking institution. They make their living predominantly by taking deposits which represent their liabilities and making loans of these funds to borrowers, which represent their assets. They loan out funds at a higher interest rate than that at which they raise the funds, and the difference represents their gross profit margin before expenses and tax. In addition, banks can earn commissions and fees by selling various products such as foreign exchange services, safe custody services, advice, account management charges, credit card facilities, insurance and so forth.

Despite common features, there are a variety of different types of bank. There are so-called universal banks which offer not only traditional deposit and lending facilities but also a whole range of financial services, while other types are more specialized, offering a more limited range of services and catering for particular types of clients. The commercial or retail banks tend to raise their deposits from the public and loan these funds out to individuals and companies. They also provide the principal means for clearing payments between economic agents. Commercial banks tend to raise their funds either through sight (current) or time (deposit) accounts. A perennial problem facing most commercial banks is that the way they raise funds is quite expensive; for example, most current accounts are relatively small in size and they are also quite active, imposing processing and transaction costs on the banks. In recent years, commercial banks have been keen to widen the range of services that they offer to their customers in order to improve the profitability of each customer; examples of services offered include credit cards, insurance, financial advice, pensions, share purchase and custody services.

commercial banking
typical banking, dealing with the taking in of deposits and making of loans in the form of personal, business and mortgage loans

investment banking
banking dealing with the raising of funds in the wholesale money and capital markets; investment banks deal with takeovers, mergers, buy outs, corporate finance, advisory work, the issuance of new securities, underwriting, market-making and proprietary trading

Investment banks (or merchant banks) traditionally specialized in financing trade by guaranteeing bills of exchange between traders (merchants) of different countries, but have subsequently widened the range of services they offer to meet other demands of the corporate sector. For example, they provide advice on all aspects of corporate finance, privatization, mergers, takeovers, corporate bond and equity issues. Due to their traditional experience in trade finance, many investment banks have considerable expertise in foreign exchange and are also significant players in the Euromarkets. Unlike the commercial banks that raise their funds from companies and the public, investment banks tend to raise their funds on the wholesale money markets and then on-lend these funds to the corporate sector.

3.9   Savings institutions

Like banks, savings institutions accept deposits and make loans. However, their historical origins, role and the regulatory regime under which they operate have traditionally clearly distinguished them from banks. For example, in the UK a prime example of a savings institution is a building society. Building societies began in the 18th century as friendly/mutual societies. Members would make periodic payments into the society to finance local house building and they could also draw on the funds to finance house purchase. Prior to 1986, building societies were only allowed to issue deposit accounts paying interest and were not allowed to issue cheque

Box 3.1	Bank risk management – value at risk and black swans

One of the key jobs of a bank is to manage its risk so as to reduce the possibility that it would suffer such large losses that it would run the risk of failure. Banks have many different ways of modelling their risk exposures but since the mid 1990s by far the most popular method of expressing risk is value at risk (VaR). The VaR concept was developed in the early 1990s by a small group of mathematicians and statisticians ('Quants' in the finance industry jargon) working for the investment bank JP Morgan. While the calculation of VaR is extremely complex it became very popular as a means of expressing the risk faced by the bank.

VaR measures the risk of a given dollar loss on a specific portfolio of assets for a given probability and a given time frame. For example, a bank may hold $5,000 million of assets and report that it has a daily VaR of $100 million at the 95 per cent confidence level. This means that over the course of the next 24 hours there is a 95 per cent chance that the bank will lose less than $100 million. This is equivalent to stating that there is only a 5 per cent chance that the bank will lose more than $100 million in the next 24 hours, or that it can expect to lose more than $100 million on 1 in 20 days. What VaR does not tell you is how much the bank may expect to gain or lose on the other 19 trading days, or what the bank can expect to lose on the 1 in 20 days when losses are expected to be above $100 million. The same bank might also calculate its weekly VaR as $300 million at the 95 per cent confidence level. This means that over the course of the next week there is a 95 per cent chance that the bank will lose less than $300 million. Or equivalently, there is only a 5 per cent chance – that is, for 1 in 20 weeks – that it will lose more than $300 million. Note that the VaR calculation requires that the portfolio of assets and trading positions held by the bank are assumed to be fixed. Most banks, of course, are changing the composition of assets on a daily basis and for this reason VaR calculations need to be updated daily.

VaR modelling became popular in the early 1990s when the Securities Exchange Commission required banks to disclose market risks they were undertaking to assist investors, and most banks chose to use VaR. This widespread usage of VaR was further validated when the Basel Committee on Banking Supervision introduced a 1996 Market Risk Amendment to the Basel Accord allowing banks' VaR calculations to influence the amount of regulatory capital they were required to hold, with a higher VaR raising the required capital holding. Many methods are used to calculate VaR, and the calculation requires a bank to take account of many variables such as the dollar value it holds in each asset class, the volatility of each asset class, the degree of diversification of the bank between the assets (that is, the weights in each asset class), correlations between bank assets and the degree of leverage being used. The VaR calculation will cover a wide range of positions held

| Box 3.1 | Bank risk management – value at risk and black swans – *continued* |

by banks in money market instruments, foreign exchange, bonds, loans, equities, derivatives and so on. A key reason for the popularity of VaR is that it is a single, easily understood concept and it can be applied to just about any portfolio of assets. Indeed, VaR can be applied to measure the amount of risk undertaken by a single trader, a bank's exposure to a particular asset class (for example, its bond or equity exposure) and also the total risk facing a bank. Usually a bank's chief risk manager will know its VaR within minutes of the markets closing.

Following the disastrous losses faced by both commercial and investment banks as a result of the 2007 credit crunch the widespread usage and usefulness of the VaR approach was called into question. According to David Einhorn, a prominent hedge fund manager, VaR is 'relatively useless as a risk-management tool and potentially catastrophic when its use creates a false sense of security among senior managers and watchdogs. This is like an air bag that works all the time, except when you have a car accident.' Nassim Nicholas Taleb, the author of the best-selling book *The Black Swan*, is heavily critical of the VaR approach which he calls 'a fraud'. The key point of Taleb's critique is that rare or extreme events (the so-called 'black swans') are impossible to predict, with regards to both timing and the size of losses that will occur, thereby making VaR a meaningless concept. If a bank has a daily VaR of $100 million at the 95 per cent confidence level and it makes a loss bigger than $100 million it might lose $101 million but on the other hand it might lose $2 billion. VaR cannot tell you what losses will occur and what magnitude they will be. Some risk managers still defend the usefulness of VaR, arguing that increases in VaR can be interpreted as an increase in riskiness. However, most risk managers accept that the VaR modelling is only as good as the assumptions and historical data used by the people that do the VaR modelling. It is now acknowledged that risk managers' use of only relatively recent data from when times were good and over-optimistic assumptions led banks to significantly underestimate the risks they were undertaking prior to the start of the 2007 credit crisis. One risk manager has made the analogy to using historic weather data that only has rainstorms – and then a tornado came along. In particular, VaR measurements missed the massive drying up of liquidity that was a key feature of the credit crunch. It also seems that bank traders may have been gaming with their bank's VaR system. Traders were rewarded for the profits they could generate and also for anything that reduced the bank's VaR. This led them to take positions or make trades which generated small profits for the vast majority of the time but would eventually, with only a small probability, produce massive losses when things went wrong.

accounts with cheque guarantee cards or offer overdraft facilities like the commercial banks. However, since 1986, there have been a number of regulatory changes that have made the traditional distinction between banks and building societies more blurred.

3.10　Insurance companies

Insurance companies are financial intermediaries that in return for payments, generally referred to as premiums, will make a payment to a policy-holder should an insured-against event occur whilst insured. The premiums paid to the insurance company reflect two key variables: (i) the likelihood of the insured-against event occurring, that is, the risk of a claim being made, and (ii) the payments to be made to the policy-holder in the event of a valid claim.

Insurance companies make their profits by charging for assuming risks on behalf of their policy-holders, and also through the investments they make with the assets under their control. The premiums paid provide a pool of funds from which payments can be drawn to meet valid claims. By their nature, insurance companies therefore exist by assuming risks; an unexpectedly large number of claims or a poor performance of funds under management can call into question the solvency of an insurance company.

There are two main types of insurance business – life insurance (often referred to as long-term insurance) and general insurance. Life insurance deals with death, illness/disablement and retirement policies. General insurance deals with theft, property, house, car and general accident insurance. Property insurance is normally divided into personal and commercial. There are also commercial insurance policies for dealing with product liability, malpractice, negligence and commercial property.

The distinction between life insurance and general insurance is of significance because the differing nature of their businesses leads to different investment strategies with respect to the premium income and assets under their control. Life insurance dealing with death is also referred to as 'assurance', and is based upon the fact that death is certain but the age at which it occurs is not. This uncertainty means that people wish to insure themselves to provide benefits for their family should they die prematurely. Life insurance companies provide a wide variety of products which include:

- *Term insurance policies* – which make a payment if the insured dies within a specified period of time, but which pay nothing if the insured lives beyond the contract. Term insurance, therefore, has no element of savings and is a pure insurance product.
- *Whole of life insurance policies* – which make a payment whenever the insured dies. Such policies can generally be surrendered prior to maturity but usually at a significant discount to the premiums paid.
- *Endowment policies* – which pay a fixed sum at a specified future date or upon death should the insured die prior to that date. Endowment policies are often taken out in conjunction with mortgage business. Upon advancement of a loan, a customer

may take out an endowment policy with the same date to maturity as the loan. The customer then repays the lender (for example, a bank) only the interest on the loan and makes separate payments for the endowment policy. At the end of the loan the principal becomes due and hopefully the endowment policy has made sufficient growth in profits to pay off the principal due. An endowment policy also generally provides life cover, enabling full repayment of the mortgage if the policy-holder dies.

- *Annuities* – which provide the policy-holder with regular income payments usually for the remainder of their life, and typically provide some minimum period of payments if the annuitant dies before the policy is due to commence payments. Premium payments for annuities are made either by regular premium contributions over a number of years or by one large capital payment.

General insurance companies need to hold fairly substantial amounts of short-term assets to enable them to speedily meet policy claims which can fluctuate considerably from one year to the next. For instance, unusually bad weather can lead to large claims for property damage. Reasonable levels of reserves are therefore needed to meet unexpectedly high losses that occur from time to time. Most insurance premiums are invested either in equities, property investments or government bonds, and the success of investments is crucial in enabling a company to keep its premiums competitive.

Insurance companies have very significant amounts of assets under their control and they have been significant investors in stockmarkets, government and corporate bonds. Were an insurance company unable to meet its obligations there is no guarantee that a government would step in. In deciding on the appropriate premium to insure a risk, actuaries are employed to calculate the probabilities of an event occurring. Life insurance companies tend to invest a higher proportion of their assets in long-term investments, such as government and corporate bonds, than do general insurance companies which have a far greater need for liquidity to meet claims.

3.11 The phenomenon of Bancassurance

In Europe, the 1980s and 1990s were a period of deregulation and liberalization of the financial services industry that permitted banks to diversify into insurance products. Many banks resorted to selling insurance policies to boost their profitability as increased competition and third-world debt write-offs impinged on profitability. In addition, banks were suffering severe competition for customers' deposits from insurance companies offering attractive alternative investments.

In many instances, banks set up insurance subsidiaries or formed partnerships with insurance companies, which has led to the term Bancassurance. The phenomenon is less widespread in the USA and Japan where strict regulations have clearly delineated the activities that can be undertaken by banks from those that can be undertaken by insurance companies. Insurance companies in Europe are increasingly taking advantage of European directives that permit cross-border activities, and this has resulted in merger activity and the setting up of new foreign branches.

3.12 Mutual funds or unit trusts

mutual fund
in the USA a fund
that pools funds from
a variety of investors
and invests them in
shares and/or bonds;
in the UK it is known
as a unit trust

A mutual fund (in the USA) or unit trust (in the UK) raises funds from the public and invests them in a variety of financial assets, mostly equity both domestic and overseas, and also in liquid money and capital market instruments. Unit trusts and mutual funds grew enormously in both number and value of assets under management in the 1980s and 1990s. In the UK unit trusts are based largely upon equity investment, whereas in the USA mutual funds are also extensively involved in bonds and money market instruments.

The growth in the popularity of mutual funds/unit trusts can be explained by the fact that as incomes have grown investors have been more willing to consider alternative forms of financial investment to traditional savings accounts. Another reason for their popularity is that they provide a relatively low-cost method for private investors to achieve portfolio diversification because the fund can reduce contracting and information costs. In addition, investors know that the fund is being professionally managed and the composition of shares is constantly adjusted to reflect new profit opportunities. Fund managers make money on the bid–ask spread, which is usually well below 5 per cent, and on the basis of an annual management fee, which is typically in the region of 0.5–1 per cent of the funds under management. The loss of deposits to many unit trusts has encouraged many commercial banks to set up their own mutual funds/unit trusts. According to the Investment Company Institute (www.ici.org) the initial upfront fee for a stock-based mutual fund fell from 2.32 per cent in 1980 to 0.99 per cent in 2008 while for bond funds it fell from 2.05 per cent to 0.75 per cent.

Investors in a mutual fund/unit trust have the potential to gain in two ways: (i) they are entitled to a share in the capital appreciation of the underlying assets, and (ii) they have a claim on the income generated by the underlying assets of the fund. Another attraction of investing in unit trusts is that they are run by professional fund managers who constantly monitor investment opportunities and adjust the composition of their portfolio to reflect this.

A typical mutual fund/unit trust is set up via a sale of units to the public, and the advert for the sale will specify the objectives of the fund. These vary; some funds seek high yield but are relatively risky, others seek lower but more stable yields; some are concerned with income generation while others aim for capital growth. There is an enormous variety of mutual funds/unit trusts and many have specialist interests such as investment in emerging markets, for example East Asian funds, Latin American funds, European funds, South Korean funds and so on. Another popular theme has been the emergence of sectoral funds that track a portfolio of firms in a particular sector of the economy; for example, technology stocks, smaller company stocks and so on. There are also index-linked funds which closely track the returns of a specific index such as the FTSE 100, or Standard & Poor's 500. Since mutual funds/unit trusts need to be valued on a daily basis, they restrict the vast majority of their investments to listed securities whose value is publicly listed each day.

Units are typically advertised at a certain price, for example £1 per unit. If £10 million of stock is applied for then the £10 million is raised and invested in assets and each shareholder receives a number of units; someone who subscribes £5,000 will be given 5,000 units and someone who subscribes £20,000 will receive 20,000 units. As the value of the fund's assets changes, then so do the unit prices which are calculated (approximately) as the total value of the fund divided by the number of units issued. Income received from ownership of the underlying assets in the way of dividends, interest and so on is then paid out to unit-holders in accordance with the number of units owned.

Most mutual funds/unit trusts are 'open ended', that is, new investors can join the fund at any time. If the inflow of funds from new investors exceeds the outflow of funds due to sales by existing investors, then new units are created at the existing market price. For example, if the current market price of units is £2 and £100,000 of net funds is received, then 50,000 new units are created. One important aspect of mutual funds/unit trusts is that investors can only sell their holding back to the fund management company at the current market price; there is no secondary market in unit trusts.

3.13 Investment companies and investment trusts

investment company
in the USA a company that holds stakes in the form of shares in other companies which can engage in takeovers and breakups; if it is publicly owned then its shares trade on the Stock Exchange. In the UK it is known as an investment trust

Investment companies (in the USA) and investment trusts (in the UK) are publicly quoted companies that specialize in the buying and selling of financial securities such as equities and bonds. Investors buy shares in the investment company. The success of the company in buying and selling stocks and shares in other companies and related activities will in turn affect the perceived profitability of the investment company, and hence the value of its own shares. Unlike unit trusts and other financial intermediaries which are 'open ended', allowing new savers to invest new capital without affecting the original savers, investment companies are 'closed' funds. Savers can only invest in the trust by purchasing stock from current stockholders of the company. The total amount of shares in the investment company is fixed unless it issues new stock. Unlike mutual funds and unit trusts where the value of the units is determined by the value of the underlying stock held by the trust, the value of shares in an investment company, which are fixed in supply at any point in time, is determined primarily by demand. Of course, this demand is in large part determined by the value of the underlying assets held by the investment company, but other factors such as the quality of management and possible activities of the fund can be important.

In effect, investment companies are financial intermediaries that sell shares to the public and invest the proceeds in a diversified portfolio of shares. The type of shares invested in depends upon the objectives set out in the prospectus of the company. Investors in investment companies benefit from portfolio diversification and the professional management of funds. Many investment companies have substantial overseas stock holdings and this enables private shareholders to gain access to overseas investment opportunities at a relatively low cost.

Since investment trusts are limited companies they fall within the ambit of the UK legislation relating to limited companies. They are also subject to corporation tax on profits made. The Stock Exchange imposes certain conditions relating to the nature of investments that the firm can undertake and merger/takeover activity should the company seek a listing. In addition, an investment trust must meet certain criteria set by the tax authorities to qualify for favourable tax treatment, especially in relation to capital gains tax on assets sold. An investment company has a board of directors that decides on the general investment strategy and objectives, the implementation of which is then often carried out by specialized investment management companies.

All in all, investment companies are an unusual type of financial intermediary, and indeed we might ask if they really are financial intermediaries in the sense that there is not a continuous flow of new savers whose funds are then channelled to new borrowers. Nonetheless, when an investment trust is newly established, new savers are attracted and consequently new funds are channelled to ultimate borrowers. Established investment companies can also attract new savings via rights issues which in turn are then channelled to borrowers. Finally, investment companies earn income in the form of interest, dividends and capital gains from their investments, a proportion of which is not immediately returned to investors but retained in the reserves for new investment purposes.

The fact that investment companies do not have to worry about attracting continuous inflows of capital and continuous redemptions by savers means that they do not have to maintain so much of their funds in money market instruments as unit trusts. However, managers do have to be concerned about a fall in the value of the investment company's shares which could make it a takeover target.

3.14 Exchange traded funds

exchange traded funds (ETFs)
investment vehicles made up of assets such as shares, bonds, commodities or currencies that trade on an exchange on a continuous basis with the price of the ETF trading very close to the value of the underlying assets that make up the ETF

In recent years, especially in the USA, there has been a rapid growth in exchange traded funds (ETFs). The first ETF traded in the USA in 1993 and they commenced trading on European exchanges in 1999. An ETF is an open ended investment vehicle which invests in a variety of securities. Its creation is very different from that for a mutual fund. A sponsor or ETF manger files a plan with a relevant body (for example, the Securities Exchange Commission in the USA). Following approval, the sponsor forms an agreement with an authorized participant such as an institutional investor who has authority to create or redeem ETF shares. The authorized participant will then borrow or buy shares from pension funds and other institutional investors, typically in bundles of 10,000 to 500,000 shares. These shares are then divided up to form creation units; for example, a bundle of 50,000 shares might represent 1 creation unit. As such, a creation unit represents a claim on some underlying assets. The creation units are then divided up by the sponsor into individual shares – or ETFs – which are traded on stock exchanges like an ordinary share although they represent a claim on a bundle of shares.

When shares in the ETF are bought and sold the underlying assets that were borrowed to form the creation units remain in the trust account. The trust sponsor will pay out dividends from shares held by the ETF to holders of ETF shares. A holder of an ETF will typically redeem their holding by selling the ETF at the prevailing market price to another party. If an institutional investor buys enough ETF shares they can then approach the ETF trust for the return of shares equivalent to one creation unit, and when they do so that creation unit no longer exists. More creation units can be formed if the sponsor obtains more shares. Originally ETFs were traded by institutional investors such as mutual funds, but they have become very popular with retail investors.

The crucial thing about an ETF is that the shares that make up a creation unit can be bought and sold on a continuous basis and the price of the share will move up or down in line with the value of the underlying securities that are held by the ETF sponsor. As such, it is vital that the investor knows the particular composition of the shares that make up the ETF. There are a wide range of ETFs on the market sponsored by various institutions such as Barclays ishares, Vanguard, Fidelity Investments and the like. One large advantage over mutual funds is that the transaction costs for ETFs are much lower. Also, you can buy as little as one ETF rather than a minimum commitment of capital, as required for a mutual fund. ETFs are classified as passive managed investments in that their composition is pretty much fixed, although there can be occasional changes in the underlying shares. This makes them quite similar to certain index tracking mutual funds but very different from actively traded mutual funds. ETFs come in many forms. Some are made of shares that track particular stock exchange indices, like the so-called 'spiders' – Standard & Poor Depository Receipts (ticker symbol SPY) – that track the prices of shares in the S&P 500. If each share of a spider represents one-tenth of the S&P index and the S&P 500 reads 1000 then the SPDR I is priced at $100. Other index-tracking ETFs are 'diamonds' (ticker symbol DIA) that track the Dow Jones Industrial Average or the Nasdaq 100 Tracker Fund (ticker symbol QQQQ) that tracks 100 of the most prominent NASDAQ shares.

ETFs have become so popular with investors that there are now hundreds available, and they cover not just ownership of shares comprising well known stock indices but also particular sectors such as technology or media shares or small cap stocks. According to the Investment Company Institute, in May 2009 there were 712 ETFs in the USA and the total value of assets held by ETFs was $582 billion. There is also a proliferation of ETFs which represent ownership of bonds, commodities, foreign stocks, and even foreign currencies. For example, a bond ETF may invest in US Treasury bonds or perhaps a selection of high yield corporate bonds. With a currency ETF an investor can track the movement of an individual currency like the pound or the euro or a basket of currencies such as one composed of the yen, Swiss franc and the euro. Similarly with a commodity ETF investors can go long or short on a particular commodity such as oil or gold or a basket of commodities. Since mid 2006, investors have been able to buy long or short leveraged ETFs that track a particular stock index – in a 2:1 leveraged ETF if the stock index rises by 2 per cent then a buyer of the leveraged ETF will experience a return of approximately 4 per cent, whereas if it falls by 2 per cent the buyer will lose approximately 4 per cent.

Another big advantage of ETFs is that unlike a mutual fund it is possible to short an ETF if the investor thinks that the stocks (or assets) that comprise the ETF are overvalued. If the ETF is sold short and the price falls the investor will make a profit by buying it back at the lower price. It is also possible to have options contracts based on ETFs giving the buyer the right to buy or sell the ETF at a particular price at a particular date in the future. All in all, ETFs offer private investors the possibility of diversification and ability to invest in a wider range of investments at relatively low cost as well as the ability to bet on price falls. It is no wonder that ETFs are classed as one of the greatest financial innovations of the past two decades.

3.15 Pension funds

pension fund
a fund established by
an employer which
pools contributions
from the company
and its employees
to be invested for
the purposes of
providing a pension
to employees upon
their retirement;
pension funds in the
USA and the UK are
among the largest
institutional investors
in the financial
markets

Pension funds are now significant institutional investors in today's financial markets; in the USA, for example, the amount of pension funds under management was estimated to be in the region of $15 trillion in 2007. Pension fund assets have grown substantially since the 1980s for a number of reasons. The most important is that greater economic prosperity has given people greater incomes, part of which can be devoted to securing their financial future. In addition, the demand for pension products has grown with greater life expectancy. Another factor fuelling the growth of pension funds has been that they usually attract significant tax concessions compared to other savings products. For example, in the UK contributions are made out of pre-tax income and the return made by the pensions fund is usually free of income and capital gains tax. These tax concessions mean that HM Revenue & Customs has to approve pension schemes, and places limits on the benefits such schemes can provide.

Pension schemes come in many forms and are run by both the state and private sector. In the UK there is a general state pension which applies to all citizens who reach retirement age. This is a universal scheme which is paid at a flat rate to all pensioners out of receipts from general taxation. There are also numerous special state pension schemes for the civil service, members of the armed forces, and employees of the National Health Service which are also guaranteed by the state and are also paid for out of general taxation, although employees may be required to make some payments towards these schemes. These pension schemes differ fundamentally from private-sector schemes in that the state will always raise taxation or borrow on a sufficient scale to ensure that the obligations of these schemes are fulfilled. With private-sector schemes there are no such guarantees; usually both employers and employees make contributions to a fund which is generally managed by a board of trustees which in turn invests these funds with the aim of paying out pensions in the future. The pension fund is legally separate from the company and therefore the contributions should be secure if the company itself becomes bankrupt or goes into liquidation.

Pension policies and contributions are by their nature long-term. The scale of contributions required from an individual reflects the benefit likely to accrue to an employee upon retirement. A typical pension policy will specify the maximum pension based on a certain percentage of 'final salary', and the employee may also be entitled to a capital sum upon retirement. The pension payable will usually rise in line with inflation or some other indexing formula, and the precise amount to be paid will depend upon the number of years an employee has made contributions to the scheme. Both pension fund obligations and contributions are relatively stable and predictable. Contributions of both employees and employers are prespecified by the pension contract and, since pensions are usually linked to final salary contributions, they usually rise in line with the employee's salary. The obligations are also relatively easy to predict since the number of members, their age distribution and future life expectancy upon retirement are all fairly easy to calculate. Nonetheless, it is vital that the pension funds are wisely managed in order to ensure that the fund will be able to meet its future pension obligations.

It should be noted that since pension schemes have both inflows of funds from contributions and income earned on investments and outflows to pay pensions, they only provide net savings to the extent that the former outweigh the latter. Although most funds currently receive contributions exceeding benefits paid, a decline in the working population relative to those retired will imply smaller surpluses and even deficits in the future unless income earned rises or contributions are raised. Since pension funds have long-term liabilities they tend to hold assets which do well over the longer run; the vast majority of their funds are held in domestic and overseas equities, with much of the remainder in government securities. Pension funds are currently one of the most important sources of long-term savings. Pension fund managers are, however, careful to manage their risk exposure via diversification and relatively safe investments as security of the funds is considered to be of prime importance.

3.16 Hedge funds

Hedge funds are funds that seek to make investors money regardless of the direction in which markets are moving. It must be recognized, however, that these funds are extremely diverse in their investment strategies, the markets in which they specialize and the size of funds under management – there is no such thing as a 'typical' hedge fund. There are, nonetheless, some common characteristics. A hedge fund is usually run by a number of partners that form the fund, and they typically seek to raise capital from wealthy individuals or, increasingly, institutional investors prepared to put in around $500,000 to $10 million of risk capital. The hedge fund partners will also be expected to put some of their own capital into the fund so that should they perform poorly then they themselves will participate in any losses. The hedge fund managers will usually make an annual charge of around 1–2 per cent of money under management, and in addition take a 15–25 per cent share of any profits made by the fund. Thus if the fund loses money, then fund managers' rewards are significantly affected.

Hedge funds will often use derivative contracts such as futures and options contracts to establish significant leveraged speculative positions on the direction of markets. For instance, should they think a particular equity market will rise, they may buy stock-index futures or call options on that market. If, however, they think that a market will fall, then they may sell stock-index futures or buy put options on that market. In this way they have the potential to make money whether markets are rising or falling. This differentiates hedge funds significantly from mutual funds/ unit trusts which, by holding shares and bonds, are 'long' on the markets, hoping that prices will rise. A hedge fund, however, as well as having long positions on a market will also take short positions on individual shares that they believe to be overpriced and likely to fall in price. If they are proved correct and the market or share falls in price, then they will make profits from such price falls.

It must be emphasized that there is an enormous variety of hedge funds pursuing very diverse investment strategies. There are, for example, so-called 'macro funds' that make major bets on certain economies. For instance, if a macro fund thinks that an economy is going to do well, then it may buy stock-index futures and currency futures on that country's currency in the hope of making a large gain should both the stockmarket and currency rise. Some funds specialize in buying or 'shorting' individual

Box 3.2	Hedge funds in the news

Hedge funds do occasionally hit the headlines for making either spectacular profits or spectacular losses. In September 1992 the Quantum Fund managed by George Soros made a huge speculative bet that the pound sterling would be devalued against the deutschmark and forced out of the exchange-rate mechanism. On this basis, the fund sold huge amounts of sterling (around £10 billion!) and bought huge amounts of deutschmarks. When the pound was subsequently devalued the fund made an estimated £1 billion on the so-called 'black Wednesday'. However, the Quantum Fund also lost $600 million on 14 February 1994 when it made a huge bet that the yen would depreciate against the dollar. In fact the yen appreciated, meaning that the fund suffered a huge loss, and this was termed the St Valentine's Day Massacre.

Another huge loss was made in 1998 by Long-Term Capital Management (LTCM), a fund run by John Meriwether with two Nobel prizewinners, Robert Merton and Myron Scholes, as directors. The fund took a massive bet that the yield spread between corporate and government bonds would narrow, purchasing some $2,120 billion worth of corporate bonds (which it thought would rise in price, reducing their yields) and short sold some $120 billion of US Treasury bonds (which they thought would fall in price, so raising the yield). LTCM was backed by just $2.3 billion of funds. A default by the Russian government in 1998 led to a 'flight to quality' in the capital markets, and corporate bonds fell in price while Treasury bonds rose in price. LTCM incurred huge losses and had to be rescued by a group of investment banks led by Merrill Lynch, Goldman Sachs and J.P. Morgan.

On 29 September 2006 Amaranth Advisors, a multistrategy hedge fund with $9 billion under management, collapsed in spectacular fashion after losing an estimated $6 billion on natural gas futures contracts. It seems that Amaranth's chief energy trader Brian Hunter, aged 32, placed huge spread bets with 8:1 leverage (that is, financed by borrowing $8 for every $1 of Amaranth's own capital) that the price of the March 2007 and March 2008 futures contracts would increase relative to the price of the April 2007 and April 2008 contracts; that is, the fund went 'long' on the March contracts and 'short' on the April contracts. The rationale for the spread trade was a forecast by Amaranth that the price of the March contract would rise, because March is the last month of winter with higher demand resulting in higher prices, and April prices would fall, as summer approached and a rise in supply would lower prices. Unfortunately for Amaranth investors, the trade went badly wrong. Rather than increase, the spread between March and April decreased dramatically within two weeks of the bet being placed. For example, the March and April 2007 spread fell from US$2.49 at the end of August 2006 to US$0.58 by the end of September 2006. A key lesson from the demise of Amaranth was not to put all your eggs in one basket – effectively the fund had placed a huge bet on natural gas prices and lost in spectacular fashion.

| Box 3.2 | Hedge funds in the news – *continued* |

Another lesson is not to borrow too much money to gamble in the marketplace because, while it increases your upside, it also dramatically increases your losses when you lose. Shortly after the collapse of Amaranth, Brian Hunter, despite his newly acquired nickname as the '$6 billion dollar' man, attempted to set up a new hedge fund, Solengo Capital Partners, but he was thwarted by regulatory agencies because of his previous questionable trading practices.

Of course, not all hedge funds get it wrong and lose massive amounts of money! John Paulson in 1994 set up a New York based hedge fund called Paulson & Co with $2 million of capital, which by June 2007 had grown to $12.5 billion of assets under management (some 95 per cent of it being institutional money). During 2007 Paulson & Co, foreseeing the collapse in the subprime market, took out a variety of contracts such as credit default swaps on mortgage backed securities and shorting subprime mortgage backed securities that would make huge profits if the subprime sector got into trouble. The trades proved to be extremely profitable and Institutional Investor calculated that Paulson earned $2.5 billion in 2008. His Paulson & Co hedge fund was also up 37 per cent in 2008, while the average hedge fund lost 19 per cent over the same period. Success also led to increased assets under management, which had grown to $36 billion by November 2008.

shares which they believe to be under/overvalued. Other funds specialize in bond prices, commodity prices and foreign exchange rates, while yet others have a broad mandate to speculate in a whole range of markets and instruments. It is commonly thought that hedge funds take enormous risks in order to make large profits but this is an exaggeration, there is a wide spectrum of investment strategies pursued by different funds. It is true that some funds aim to make very high percentage rates of return by taking on high-risk strategies that are highly leveraged, but there are also many funds that are less ambitious, seeking just to outperform the market at relatively low risk. Hedge funds also differ greatly in funds under management. The vast majority have between $200 million and $1 billion under management but some, such as the Quantum Fund and the Tiger Fund, have tens of billions under management.

3.17 Private equity

Private equity
a privately owned partnership which invests capital raised from individuals and institutions; usually used to purchase majority stakes in a variety of companies

Private equity firms are privately owned limited liability partnerships that raise funds which are invested in a variety of private companies and buy outs of publicly traded companies and in some instances commercial property and real estate. Capital for private equity is typically raised from a mix of institutional clients such as pension funds, insurance companies, banks, funds of funds, endowments, sovereign wealth funds and wealthy individuals. The capital raised is used to finance a range of investments including buying privately owned companies, management buy outs, leveraged buy outs, buying distressed debt and distressed companies and taking stakes in young and newly emerging companies that are in need of capital to finance their growth. There is, therefore, no such thing as a typical private equity fund as they pursue a wide range of investment strategies, with some specializing in particular areas while others specialize in a wider range of activities. The success of a private equity fund depends primarily on the quality of the investment decisions that its managers make and on its management and restructuring of the companies it acquires. In order to incentivize the management of the acquired company, the private equity group will typically provide a long-term incentive scheme for them. One claimed advantage of a private equity fund taking over a publicly traded company is that it relieves the management of the pressure to make short-term profits, thus enabling the management to take a longer-term perspective of the business even if this impacts on short-term profitability.

When investing in private equity investors need to realize that it is a relatively illiquid investment based on a medium- to long-term investment horizon of typically 5 to 12 years. In addition, a substantial amount of capital is normally required, with a minimum investment usually set as at least $1 million. Investors can only expect to realize cash from their investments when sales of acquired companies and assets are made or profits from investments are distributed by the management. An investment in private equity is classified as a passive investment in that the investor has no real control over the decisions made by the fund management. Also investors in private equity funds face a generally higher risk than investment in, say, a mutual fund due to the leverage employed by private equity and the nature of the companies in which private equity invests. The low liquidity, longer-term investment, use of leverage and riskiness of investments means that the expected rate of return on investment in private equity needs to be significantly higher than for mutual fund investments.

In a leveraged buy out (LBO) transaction a private equity firm will attempt to buy control of a mature company, raising the capital through the issuance of debt and bank borrowing. In a typical LBO, debt financing will be in the region of 60–90 per cent of the purchase price. The ability to raise debt financing is crucial to private equity as it enables the partnership to acquire relatively large companies and also to boost expected returns on equity. Once a company is acquired the private equity firm will typically seek to restructure the company to make it more profitable, with the aim of later selling the company at a profit compared to the acquisition price. The exit strategy will usually involve selling the company through an initial public offering whereby shares in the company are sold to investors or by selling the company to another company or breaking up the company, selling different parts of it to other companies. In recent years secondary buy outs, whereby the acquired company is sold onto another private equity group, have become quite popular.

Well known private equity firms include Texas Pacific Group (TPG), Goldman Sachs Capital Partners, the Carlyle Group, Kohlberg Kravis Roberts, Bain Capital, Blackstone Group, CVC Capital Partners, Warburg Pincus, Apollo Management, all of which run a variety of private equity funds with managed capital in the range of $20 billion to $100 billion under management. In recent years some private equity firms have realized money for their investors by going public. Most notably, the Blackstone group went public via an initial public offering raising $4.75 billion by selling shares in its management company. There are a number of examples of 'club deals' whereby

leveraged buy out
the takeover of a company primarily financed by the issuance of debt in the form of bonds or bank loans by the acquiring company; often the assets of the acquired company are used to finance the debt/loans

initial public offering
in the USA, the floating of a company on the stockmarket for the first time

groups of private equity firms pool their funds to finance an acquisition. For example, in 2007 TXU Energy was bought in a $48 billion transaction by Kohlberg Kravis Roberts, Goldman Sachs and Texas Pacific Group – the largest leveraged buy out in history.

Private equity boomed particularly in the period 2001–2007, the years prior to the break out of the credit crunch when debt finance was relatively easy to obtain and institutional investors had ample funds to allocate to private equity which was deemed to be an alternative asset class. A report by the World Economic Forum estimated that a total of $2.7 trillion of private equity deals were conducted over 2001–2007. The scope and scale of private equity has also been transformed with the private equity business moving from the USA and UK to Europe, Asia and other emerging markets where opportunities are deemed to be greater. In recent years concerns have been expressed about the role of private equity firms in the job losses that seem to occur once they acquire a company and the fact that less taxes are paid because interest on debt is a tax deductible expense.

3.18 Specialist financial institutions

A great deal of the financial needs of business and consumers is met by the banks, building societies, insurance companies, pension funds, investment trusts and so on. However, there are some areas where businesses and consumers have more specialized needs than these institutions can meet. In addition, there are niches in the market where more specialized institutions can provide a new or superior service at a more competitive price than the major types of institutions that we have so far looked at. We now briefly look at the services offered by these more specialist financial institutions which comprise venture capital companies, finance houses, leasing houses and consumer credit agencies, factoring and invoice discounting companies.

3.19 Venture capital companies

venture capital
private capital used to finance the growth of small companies that are generally risky and lack long-term trading records, making it difficult to secure finance from banks or capital markets

Venture capital companies (VCCs) are usually independent companies set up by professional venture capitalists with funds obtained from private investors or other financial institutions, such as pension funds and insurance companies. Some VCCs are subsidiaries of banks. Many start-ups or rapidly growing small companies find it difficult to raise finance from banks because they cannot provide sufficient asset security and are often regarded as highly risky. At the same time, they are usually either too small to seek equity finance and/or their trading record is not sufficient to meet listing requirements. These companies may offer high potential returns, but against this they usually have a high failure rate. Many of these companies need not only seed-corn capital to develop an idea, but also often require managerial expertise.

This is where VCCs come into the picture; they are prepared to invest in the company, usually for a limited period of typically 5 to 10 years, and provide some managerial expertise in return for a share (usually substantial) in the business. The vast majority of VCCs are interested in providing support for the company only for a limited period until the business is sufficiently mature that it can be floated on the stock exchange or sold off. The VCC aims to make a substantial capital gain from its investment via a flotation or sell off. This emphasis on capital gains arises from the fact that a rapidly growing company with low profitability in the initial years is unlikely to be in a position to pay dividends without constraining its growth.

VCCs are not involved exclusively with new companies; a major part of their business is concerned with management buy outs (MBOs). MBOs occur when the owners of existing companies decide to sell off part of their business. The existing management team in the part of the business for sale might feel that it is worth buying the business but usually they have insufficient capital for this purpose. The management may approach a VCC company and arrange a financial package in which their capital is supplemented by capital from the VCC. Many MBOs combine an element of debt finance arranged through banks in conjunction with finance arranged with the VCC. In return, the VCC usually obtains a substantial stake in the company. The control of the business remains with the existing management although they will be expected to meet performance targets set by the VCC.

management buy out managers and directors of a company buy a controlling interest in the company from the existing shareholders; often the buyout is financed by the issuance of debt

3.20 Finance companies or finance houses

Finance houses are either subsidiaries of banks or independent companies which raise funds on the wholesale money markets for the purpose of lending to businesses and consumers, and for the leasing of equipment, vehicles, plant and machinery and so on. The funds raised are usually surplus funds of the banking sector raised on the wholesale money markets or derived from the sale of commercial bills. Raising funds on the wholesale market tends to be a far cheaper means of raising funds than the deposit base of commercial banks. Apart from loans which compete directly with the banking sector, many finance houses offer a differentiated service. Particularly important is the practice of 'finance leasing' which is frequently used for capital investment; for example, land, vehicle, machinery or equipment purchases. Under a finance lease, the finance house purchases the investment asset, for example a machine, and then leases the asset to the firm. The ownership of the asset remains with the finance house, so that in effect the leasing agreement is a rental contract. A typical finance lease contract is of three to five years and the asset purchased usually has a reasonable secondhand market, thus providing some protection to the finance house should the lessee have financial problems. In many finance leasing contracts the finance house may also deal with aspects of maintenance.

A finance leasing contract can offer the lessee a number of advantages over taking a bank loan for direct purchase of equipment. One of the most important is that the leasing company usually provides the full cost of the equipment, whereas if the company took out a bank loan it might well have to finance part of the purchase from its own resources to provide the bank with some security. Another advantage is that, because the finance house retains ownership of the asset, it may be a cheaper way to obtain the use of the equipment than a bank loan which involves ownership of the asset by the firm. There may also be certain tax advantages; the firm can offset the rental payments directly against its profits which might be more advantageous than seeking capital allowances.

Hire purchase
a contract with a finance company that enables a consumer or business to purchase goods in return for an initial deposit and monthly payments; the good is legally owned by the finance company until the final payment is made

Another common form of finance provided by finance houses is hire-purchase contracts aimed at consumers or firms. Under a hire-purchase agreement, a consumer or firm buys a product or capital asset and obtains finance for the purchase from a finance house. The seller usually offers the financing facility at the point of sale, the offering of a finance package being viewed as a sales aid. A typical hire-purchase agreement involves the purchaser making equal payments for an agreed period of time, and on payment of the final instalment the purchaser becomes the legal owner of the item purchased. Most hire-purchase agreements are unsecured loans, and the main means of screening applicants is via a credit rating (usually based on filling out a questionnaire), although in instances where the purchase involves a large sum of money the purchaser may have to offer some security in case of default. Hire-purchase agreements are frequently used in connection with the purchase of a car or more costly consumer items such as furniture, consumer durables and so forth. Hire-purchase contracts are in close competition with personal or business loans offered by banks and other savings institutions. Finance houses are heavily dependent upon the efforts of vendors to introduce new customers, and usually offer a commission for each contract issued.

3.21 Factoring agencies

Factoring agencies and invoice discounting services are specialized agencies that are usually subsidiaries of banks or finance houses. Many businesses' cash flows suffer due to late payment of invoices and at times this can present a serious problem that could threaten an enterprise. In addition, there are usually substantial costs involved in chasing customers for money owed. This is where factoring agencies can be of use to small to medium-sized businesses. Such an agency will buy up invoices from a firm at a discount and then proceed to raise the face value of the invoice from the customer to which it was sent. The firm thus gets the vast majority of its funds immediately, reducing the need to take out loans and also reducing administration costs.

3.22 The role of financial institutions

Just like banks, other financial institutions assist in the transfer of funds from surplus to deficit units in the economy. They ensure that the costs and risks are lower than if the surplus and deficit agents dealt directly with each other, and thereby ensure that there is a greater flow than in the absence of financial intermediaries. Different types of financial institutions tend to differ in the types of surplus and deficit agents that they deal with. For example, savings institutions tend to draw upon personal customers for their deposits and also deal predominantly with such customers, especially in respect of mortgage business. Mutual funds/unit trusts draw upon the funds of the personal sector but then transfer these mainly into company shares and government bonds. Likewise, pension funds attract long-term personal-sector investment and place these funds into company stock and government bonds. Financial institutions are therefore distinguished by the type of liabilities they create and also the type of assets that they invest in.

| Box 3.3 | The rise of Sovereign Wealth Funds as global investors |

In recent years there has not only been a dramatic growth of private capital such as hedge funds and private equity looking to make returns from the global markets but also governments seeking out better returns for assets they hold on behalf of their citizens. A Sovereign Wealth Fund (SWF) is a state owned investment fund that invests its capital in a variety of financial securities, commodities and non-financial assets such as real estate around the globe. Some SWFs are run by the central bank while others are run by the state to manage its savings. Another related development has been the development of Sovereign Wealth Enterprises (SWEs) which are investment vehicles that are owned and controlled by SWFs.

The term Sovereign Wealth Fund is fairly recent, dating from an article by Andrew Rozanov (2005) entitled 'Who holds the Wealth of Nations?', but the first SWF was the Kuwait Investment Authority, set up in 1953 to invest some of Kuwait's surplus oil revenues. (It is now known as the Kuwait Reserve Fund.) Others have since been set up to manage some of Kuwait's foreign exchange reserves, pension assets and commodity related revenues (both oil and non-oil). Today other large funds include the Abu Dhabi Investment Authority of the United Arab Emirates (worth $875 billion in early 2008), Saudi Arabia's SAMA Foreign Holdings, Norway's Government Pension Fund, China's China Investment Corporation and SAFE Investment Company, Russia's National Welfare Fund, Singapore's Government Investment Corporation. The largest funds have hundreds of billions of assets under investment while smaller ones tend to have billions and tens of billions under management (see **Table 3.1**). The size and growth of SWFs mean that they now have considerably more funds under management than hedge funds and private equity combined, estimated to be at some $3.7 trillion in August 2009. Funds under management by SWFs are predicted to grow as large as $10 trillion by 2015.

The aims of SWFs vary greatly. Some, such as Norway's Government Pension Fund, are out to maximize long-term investment yield while others aim to promote regional development, ensure future prosperity when oil reserves run out, and others aim just to earn better returns than investing in US Treasury bonds or to seek to protect and stabilize the budget and economy from volatility in revenues and exports. There have been concerns about the growing power and influence of SWFs, especially in the USA where their attempts to acquire controlling stakes in strategic US companies have caused some alarm. In February 2006 when DP World, a port operator owned by the United Arab Emirates' government, sought to take over P&O ports in New York and New Jersey and four other US ports, concern was expressed over Arab ownership of strategic US infrastructure. Eventually the acquisition went through, but later in the year DP World sold its stake to an asset

| Box 3.3 | The rise of Sovereign Wealth Funds as global investors – *continued* |

Table 3.1 Top ten Sovereign Wealth Funds, August 2009

Country	Fund name	Assets ($billions)	Year set up	Ratio of assets to forex reserves
UAE	Abu Dhabi Investment Authority	627	1976	29.5
Saudi Arabia	SAMA Foreign Holdings	431	n/a	12.7
Norway	Government Pension Fund	397	1990	7.1
China	SAFE Investment Company	347	1997	0.2
China	China Investment Corporation	289	2007	0.1
Singapore	Government of Singapore Investment Corporation	248	1981	1.9
Kuwait	Kuwait Investment Authority	203	1953	12.7
Hong Kong	HKMA Investment Portfolio	193	1998	1.0
Russia	National Welfare Fund	179	2008	0.4
Singapore	Temasek Holdings	85	1974	0.8
China	National Social Security Fund	83	2000	<0.1
UAE	Investment Corporation of Dubai	82	2006	2.8

Source: swfinstitute.org

management company owned by American Investment Group. By contrast, during the 2007 credit crunch it was SWFs that came to the rescue of American banks such as Citigroup and Merrill Lynch and the UK bank Barclays with tens of billions of dollars of much needed capital. Nonetheless, there remain concerns about the lack of transparency of SWFs that tend not to disclose their portfolio holdings in any great detail. To some extent SWFs realize the concerns of American and European politicians and decide to limit the stakes they take in politically sensitive areas and also tend to take minority-only stakes in foreign companies.

Financial institutions aim to maximize the return on their investments for a given risk position. Managers are expected to take reasonable precautions to protect funds under management, for instance by spreading the financial institution's risks. These days financial institutions have enormous amounts of funds at their disposal and this gives private and public corporations the opportunity to raise new funds with a reasonable degree of confidence provided they can meet the risk–return criteria applied by the institutions.

The role of the financial sector in the success of an economy has always been a subject of considerable controversy. There are arguments that financial intermediaries are 'too short-term' in their investment strategies, implying that firms with longer-term investment objectives receive insufficient capital. Banks are often accused of starving small businesses and new and growing enterprises of funds because they have insufficient credit ratings and assets which banks can use as security for loans. There are frequently allegations that financial intermediaries such as pension funds invest too much in foreign companies and overseas to the detriment of the domestic economy. In addition, it is argued that banks and other financial institutions are often more interested in exciting projects offering high short-term gain, like takeovers and mergers, than investing in future production. Financial institutions are sometimes accused of only having short-term, fleeting interests and investments in companies, merely seeking to maximize the dividends and capital appreciation on their investments. As such they are only too pleased to sell their stakes in the companies which invariably appreciate following takeover bids. In addition, it is argued that financial institutions force companies to pay excessive short-term dividends at the expense of future investment.

The counter view is that financial intermediaries perform an important allocative efficiency role in the economy; monitoring the progress of companies and reallocating capital to the best-performing companies. New ventures with promising products are assessed and receive financial backing from risk-taking financial intermediaries such as venture capitalists; overseas investment ensures that savers are given opportunities to receive better returns than available in domestic investment which in turn leads ultimately to higher spending power and more demand for domestic production and investment. While banks are interested in takeovers and mergers, it is necessary to ensure that existing companies are efficiently run and the threat of takeovers and mergers helps to ensure this. Furthermore, ensuring that firms are kept on their toes in the short run is no bad thing, because the more they make in the short run the greater will be their productive potential in the longer run.

3.23 Conclusions

At the end of the day, economic agents with surplus funds have wide and varied needs, as do those economic agents that wish to borrow funds. The various types of financial institutions that we have looked at in this chapter reveal that there is plenty of room in the marketplace for a variety of specialist financial institutions to meet these differing demands.

Deregulation and greater competition in the financial services sector has meant that traditional boundaries between financial institutions are becoming increasingly blurred, with many banks offering insurance services and some insurance companies offering banking services. Competition between banks and savings institutions has made the two increasingly indistinguishable.

Further reading

Fabozzi, F., Modigliani, F. and Jones, F. (2009) *Foundations of Financial Markets and Institutions*, 4th edn, Pearson.

Madura, J. (2008) *Financial Markets and Institutions*, 7th edn, South Western College Publications.

Mishkin, F. and Eakins, S.G. (2008) *Financial Markets and Institutions*, 6th edn, Pearson.

Saunders, A. and Cornett M. (2009) *Financial Markets and Institutions*, 4th edn, McGraw-Hill.

Chapter 3	Revision questions

1   What is the difference between 'life insurance' and 'general insurance'?

2   What are the differences between an investment trust/investment company and a unit trust/mutual trust?

3   Briefly explain the main roles played by venture capitalists in the financial system.

4   Outline four types of risk that commercial banks face.

5   Explain some of the advantages to an employee of joining a company pension scheme over investing in the stock market directly.

 Multiple choice questions available at www.palgrave.com/business/pilbeam

4

MONETARY POLICY AND INTEREST RATE DETERMINATION

Learning objectives

In this chapter you will learn about:

- the differences between Treasury bills and Treasury bonds
- contractionary and expansionary open market operations
- the commercial banking system and the narrow and broad monetary aggregates
- the supply and demand for money
- the impact of inflation expectations and inflation risk on long-term interest rates
- the yield curve and what causes it to shift
- the various theories of the yield curve such as the expectations theory, liquidity preference theory and expectations theory

4.1 Introduction

The interest rate is the price that has to be paid by a borrower of money to a lender of money in return for the use of the funds. The rate of interest is a crucial economic variable which will affect the amount of consumption, saving and investment in an economy. It is a crucial part of the formula for pricing other financial assets such as forwards, futures, options and swaps, and for this reason a proper understanding of the factors that can cause interest rate changes is crucial to the study of financial markets.

Interest rates, whether short-term or long-term, are inextricably linked to the conduct of macroeconomic policy, especially monetary policy and future expectations about the conduct of economic policy. In this chapter we look at monetary policy and the fundamental forces that influence the general level of interest rates in an economy. We also make a crucial distinction between the nominal and real rates of interest. The chapter then examines the term structure of interest rates, or the yield curve, that is the plot of short-, medium- and long-term interest rates at any given point in time.

term structure of interest rates the yield to maturity on Treasury bills and bonds of different terms to maturity

4.2 The functions of money

Money is any generally accepted means of payment for delivery of goods or settlement of debt; it is the medium of exchange that facilitates transactions in an economy. It also serves as a common unit of account, enabling relative prices to be easily compared. Money also acts as a standard of deferred payment, enabling payments to be made in the future rather than today. Finally, to some extent money can act as a store of value over time, although the value of money is eroded by inflation. These useful properties of money and its integral role in a modern economy make monetary policy and the control of inflation key policy issues.

To understand the operation of monetary policy it is necessary to distinguish between bills and bonds. These are the securities that are bought and sold by the central bank when implementing its monetary policy. Crucial to understanding monetary policy is the relationship between the rate of interest and the price of bills and bonds.

4.3   Bills and bonds

Bills

Bills are financial assets with less than one year until the date that they will be redeemed by the original borrower. Treasury bills have a highly liquid secondary market and, because of their negligible risk and liquidity, they are highly attractive assets for institutions and investors to hold.

Treasury bills are sold at a discount to their face value, and the holder of a Treasury bill benefits entirely from capital appreciation. For example, if the government sells a three-month Treasury bill in April at £97 promising to repurchase it for £100 in 90 days' time in July, the holder of the bill will make £3 for three months' investment if the bill is held until maturity. If the government sells a three-month Treasury bill in April at £98 promising to repurchase it for £100 in 90 days' time in July, the holder of the bill will make £2 for three months' investment if the bill is held until maturity. It is easy to show that the lower the price of a bill the higher the rate of interest on the bill.

If a three-month £100 bill is sold at £97, the annual rate of interest at the time of issue is:

$$\frac{3}{97} \times 4 \times 100 = 12.37\%$$

If a three-month £100 bill is sold at £98, the annual rate of interest at the time of issue is:

$$\frac{2}{98} \times 4 \times 100 = 8.16\%$$

Hence, there is an inverse relationship between the price of bills and the short-term rate of interest. The higher the Treasury bill price, the lower the short-term rate of interest. Other things being equal, a Treasury bill will have a tendency to rise in price once issued, since it will eventually be redeemable at £100. For example, a 90-day Treasury bill sold at £97 will have a tendency to rise by slightly over 3 pence a day so that it eventually redeems at its face value. For example, a couple of days before it matures it may trade at say £99.94 since the holder knows that they will receive back £100 in two days' time. However, it should be noted that changes in short-term interest rates will have a strong effect on the secondary market price of bills: a bill sold at £97 will sell at £98 on the same day if, following issue, short-term interest rates were to dramatically fall from 12.37% to 8.16%. (Other things being equal, the bill will then rise by just over 2 pence a day until maturity.)

Bonds

Bonds are longer-term financial assets with a maturity of 1 to 30 years. They are issued at face value, and instead of capital appreciation the holder is entitled to a stream of coupon payments, for example the Treasury promises to pay £10 a year to the holder. The bond can be freely traded in the secondary bond market and the price of bonds once issued will fluctuate according to market conditions.

If a bond is originally issued at £100 and each year it makes an annual coupon payment of £10, then it is issued at an annual rate of interest of:

$$\frac{\text{Annual coupon payment}}{\text{Price of bond}} \times 100 = \frac{£10}{£100} \times 100 = 10\%$$

If immediately upon issue the price of the bond were to fall in the secondary market to £80, then the coupon rate of interest would be:

$$\frac{£10}{£80} \times 100 = 12.50\%$$

If immediately upon issue the price of the bond were to rise in the secondary market to £120, then the coupon rate of interest would be:

$$\frac{£10}{£120} \times 100 = 8.33\%$$

Hence, there is an inverse relationship between the price of bonds and the rate of interest. If bond prices fall then longer-term interest rates are rising, while if bond prices rise then longer-term interest rates are falling.

The inverse relationship between the rate of interest and bill and bond prices is crucial to the understanding of monetary policy. Rising Treasury bill prices imply falling short-run interest rates, while rising bond prices imply falling long-term interest rates. When both bill and bond markets are 'bullish', that is both Treasury bill and bond prices are rising, then both short- and long-term interest rates are falling.

4.4   The operation of monetary policy

Most countries have a central bank which is responsible for the operation of monetary policy; that is, changing the money supply held by banks and the public and targeting the short-term interest rates prevailing in the money markets. There are basically three types of monetary policy – neutral, contractionary and expansionary. An expansionary monetary policy involves cutting short-term interest rates and raising the money supply, while a contractionary monetary policy involves raising short-term interest rates and reducing the money supply. We now consider the effects of expansionary and contractionary monetary policies on both the domestic money and Treasury bill markets.

The effects of an expansionary monetary policy

expansionary OMO
an open market operation that increases the narrow money supply and lowers the short-term interest rate.

To increase the amount of money in circulation, the central bank will use an expansionary open market operation (OMO) in which it purchases short-term financial securities, usually Treasury bills. The result of an expansionary OMO is that the public holds more money but less bills, while the central bank has an increase in its liabilities (money in circulation with the public) but also a corresponding increase in its assets (bills). An expansionary OMO, by increasing the demand for bills, raises the price of bills and therefore lowers short-term interest rates. The effects of an expansionary OMO are depicted in **Figure 4.1**.

Figure 4.1   The effects of an expansionary OMO

(a) The money market

(b) The Treasury bill market

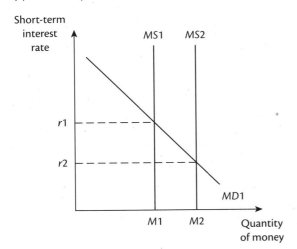

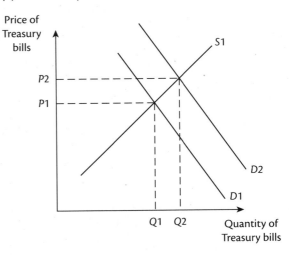

In **Figure 4.1**(a) the equilibrium short-term interest rate r1 is given by the intersection of the supply MS1 and demand MD1 for money in the money market. Note that the money supply schedule is vertical because we are referring to the monetary base which is determined exogenously by the central bank. The corresponding price of Treasury bills is given in **Figure 4.1**(b), where the price P1 is given by the intersection of the supply and demand for Treasury bills S1 and D1 respectively. If there is an expansionary OMO, the central bank will buy Treasury bills with its newly created monetary base and this will increase the money supply from MS1 to MS2 in the money market. However, it will also represent a rise in demand for Treasury bills from D1 to D2 in the Treasury bill market. The new equilibrium rate of interest in the money market will be r2 which corresponds to the new higher Treasury bills price of P2. It is quite evident that the central bank can lower short-term interest rates to very low levels since, as the creator of the monetary base, it can increase the money supply as much as it wants by buying as many Treasury bills as it wants.

The effects of an contractionary monetary policy

If the central bank wishes to tighten monetary policy it will use a contractionary open market operation. The central bank sells newly issued Treasury bills that are issued on behalf of the Treasury. The result of a contractionary OMO is that the public holds less money but more Treasury bills, the central bank has a decrease in its liabilities (money in circulation with the public) but also a corresponding decrease in its assets (Treasury bills). A contractionary OMO, by increasing the supply of bills, lowers the price of bills and therefore raises short-term interest rates. The effects of a contractionary OMO are shown in **Figure 4.2**.

In **Figure 4.2**(a) the equilibrium short-term interest rate r1 is given by the intersection of the supply MS1 and demand MD1 for money in the money market. The corresponding price of Treasury bills is given in **Figure 4.2**(b), in which the price

contractionary OMO an open market operation that decreases the narrow money supply and raises the short-term interest rate

Figure 4.2 The effects of a contractionary OMO

(a) The money market

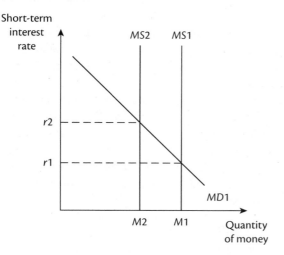

(b) The Treasury bill market

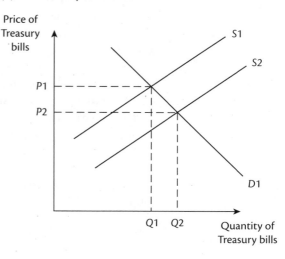

P1 is given by the intersection of the supply and demand for Treasury bills, S1 and D1 respectively. If there is a contractionary OMO, the central bank will sell Treasury bills in return for monetary base, which will increase the supply of Treasury bills from S1 to S2 and reduce the money supply from MS1 to MS2. The new equilibrium rate of interest in the money market will be r2 which corresponds to the new lower Treasury bills price of P2. It is quite evident that the central bank can raise short-term interest rates to very high levels since it can sell as many Treasury bills as it wishes, so reducing the money supply as much as it wishes. Economic agents will buy the Treasury bills being sold since the greater the sales, the lower the Treasury bill price and the higher the short-term rate of interest. The effects of expansionary and contractionary OMOs are summarized in **Figure 4.3**.

Figure 4.3   Summary of expansionary and contractionary monetary policies

An expansionary OMO

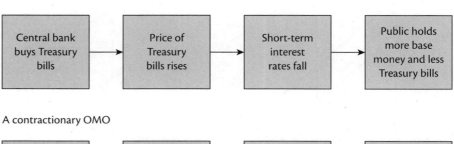

A contractionary OMO

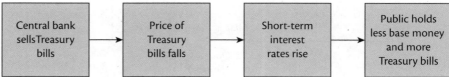

4.5　Monetary policy in practice and the announcement effect

The way we have described monetary policy can be misleading, although it follows the fairly standard textbook treatment. In practice, as we shall see, the power that central banks have to raise or lower short-term interest rates is such that merely stating their new target rate of interest will be sufficient to achieve their required rate of interest without actually having to buy or sell Treasury bills. In the USA, the Federal Reserve Open Market Committee meets every four to six weeks to discuss its target for short-term interest rates, and likewise in the UK the Monetary Policy Committee meets periodically to discuss its target short-term interest rate. These meetings are crucial to the implementation of monetary policy since at the end of the meeting the Committee will announce its target short-term rate which may be higher or lower than the market was expecting. To consider how policy announcements alone tend to achieve the desired short-term interest rate let us consider expansionary and contractionary OMOs that take the markets by surprise.

An unexpected cut in short-term interest rates

Suppose that the market is expecting short-term interest rates to remain at $r1$ and Treasury bills to remain at $P1$, and is happily trading at these levels prior to the announcement of an unexpected cut in interest rates to $r2$ by the central bank at the conclusion of its Open Market Committee meeting. The effects of this announcement are shown in **Figure 4.4**.

　　When the central bank surprises the market by announcing an unexpected cut in interest rates from $r1$ to $r2$, it is likely that the market will do the work for the central bank without it having to buy Treasury bills. To understand why this is the case, it is essential to understand that market participants, upon the announcement of the interest rate cut from $r1$ to $r2$, will know that Treasury bill prices must rise from $P1$ to $P2$. In such circumstances private agents will want to hold less money and more

Figure 4.4　The effects of an unexpected cut in the short-term interest rate

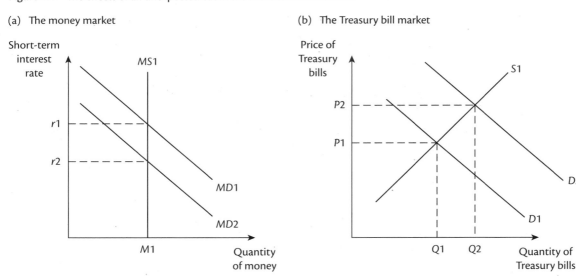

(a)　The money market

(b)　The Treasury bill market

Treasury bills in their portfolios, since they hope to make a capital appreciation from the rise in Treasury bill prices. As such, the money demand schedule will shift to the left from $MD1$ to $MD2$ and the demand for Treasury bills will increase, with a shift to the right from $D1$ to $D2$. This adjustment is likely to be instantaneous upon the announcement by the central bank of the new lower interest rate $r2$. Hence there is no need for the central bank to actually purchase Treasury bills with the newly created monetary base – the market will automatically move to the desired interest rate without an increase in the money supply. If the market does not move interest rates to $r2$ and the price of Treasury bills to $P2$, then it knows that the central bank will intervene with an open market purchase of Treasury bills and move the price of Treasury bills to $P2$ and the interest rate to the desired $r2$.

An unexpected rise in short-term interest rates

Suppose that the market is expecting short-term interest rates to remain at $r1$ and Treasury bills to remain at $P1$, and is happily trading at these levels prior to the announcement of an unexpected rise in interest rates to $r2$ by the central bank at the conclusion of its Open Market Committee meeting. The effects of this announcement are shown in **Figure 4.5**.

When the central bank surprises the market by announcing an unexpected rise in interest rates from $r1$ to $r2$, it is again likely that the market will do the work for the central bank without it having to sell Treasury bills. To appreciate why this is the case, it is essential to understand that market participants, upon the announcement of the interest rate rise from $r1$ to $r2$, will know that Treasury bill prices must fall from $P1$ to $P2$. In such circumstances private agents will want to hold fewer Treasury bills (which will fall in price) and more money in their portfolios since they hope to avoid a capital loss from the fall in Treasury bill prices. As such, the money demand schedule will shift from the right, $MD1$ to $MD2$, and the supply of Treasury bills increases with a shift to the right from $S1$ to $S2$. This adjustment is likely to be instantaneous upon the

Figure 4.5   The effects of an unexpected rise in the short-term interest rate

(a) The money market

(b) The Treasury bill market

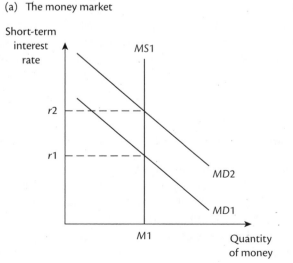

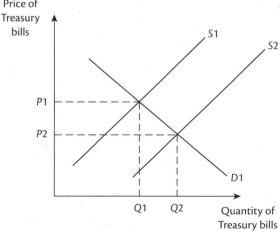

announcement by the central bank of the new higher interest rate $r2$. Hence there is no need for the central bank to actually sell Treasury bills and reduce the monetary base, the market will automatically move to the desired interest rate without a fall in the money supply. If the market does not move interest rates to $r2$ and the price of Treasury bills to $P2$, then it knows that the central bank will intervene with an open market sale of Treasury bills and move the price of Treasury bills to $P2$ and the interest rate to the desired $r2$.

4.6 The commercial banking system and the narrow and broad money supply

narrow money supply cash held by the non-bank public and cash reserves held by the banking system

Notes and coins held by the public and the banking system as reserves against withdrawals are known as the narrow money supply or the 'monetary base' (M0). However, the money supply consists not only of notes and coins, but also money which can be withdrawn upon demand from the banking system, and this measure of the money supply is known as the broad money supply (M1). There is a link between the narrow money supply and the broad money supply, and in order to understand this link it is necessary to examine how the commercial banking system operates.

broad money supply the narrow money supply plus demand deposits held by the banking system and certain interest rate yielding deposit accounts

Banks make money by taking deposits from the public and lending out these funds. Generally speaking the public places its funds on current account and these funds can be withdrawn on demand by means of a cheque or debit card or telephone/internet transfer. Demand deposits thus qualify as a form of money since they enable money holdings to be transferred from one agent to another. Banks can rely on the fact that depositors at any instant will only wish to withdraw a proportion of their deposits, which means that an initial deposit can be used by banks to create further deposits. To understand this process consider a simple example:

1   The public is assumed to hold a cash to deposit ratio (c) of 0.20; that is, for every £100 on deposit the public will hold £20 in cash.
2   The banks are assumed to hold a reserve to deposit ratio (r) of 0.10; that is, for every £100 of deposits they hold £10 of reserves against withdrawals.

Assume that there are only four banks – banks A, B, C and D – all of equal size. Consider what happens when an initial deposit of £25 million of notes and coins is made with each bank by the public. The combined balance sheet of the four banks is then:

Combined balance sheet of banks A, B, C and D

Liabilities		Assets	
Deposit 1	£100 million	Cash reserves 1	£100 million

From the initial deposit to each, the banking system will have a liability which is fully backed by its assets. The banking system can rely on the fact that only a fraction of these deposits, that is $c = 0.10 = $ £10 million, will be demanded by the public at any instant, enabling it to extend £90 million in loans. The loans will be an asset to the banking system but the additional deposits created will be a new liability. The combined balance sheet of the banking system will thus be:

	Liabilities		Assets
Deposit 1	£100m	Cash reserves 1	£10m
		Advances 1	£90m

The question now concerns what will happen when the £90 million of overdraft facilities is drawn upon. When this happens, there will be new receipts of money, part of which will be held (20 per cent = £18 million) and part of which will get redeposited with the banking system (£72 million). If each bank gets back an equal proportion, then the combined balance sheet of the banking system will look like:

	Liabilities		Assets
Deposit 1	£100m	Cash reserves 1	£10m
		Advances 1	£90m
Deposit 2	£72m	Cash 2	£72m

The banking system will now have £172 million in liabilities, and yet have total cash reserves of £82 million, which is above what is needed – £17.2 million (10 per cent of liabilities). This means that the banks will be in a position to lend out a further £64.80 million, and the combined balance sheet of the banking system will then look like:

	Liabilities		Assets
Deposit 1	£100m	Cash reserves 1	£10m
		Advances 1	£90m
Deposit 2	£72m	Cash reserves 2	£7.2m
		Advances 2	£64.8m

The new £64.8 million of advances will eventually be drawn upon, a proportion of which will be held by the public as cash (20 per cent = £12.96 million), and the remaining £51.84 million will be redeposited with the banking system so that the balance sheet of the banking system becomes:

	Liabilities		Assets
Deposit 1	£100m	Cash reserves 1	£10m
		Advances 1	£90m
Deposit 2	£72m	Cash reserves 2	£7.2m
		Advances 2	£64.8m
Deposit 3	£51.84m	Cash 3	£51.84m

The banking system will now have £223.84 million in liabilities, and yet have total cash reserves of £69.04 million which is above the £22.384 million that it needs. This means that the banks will be in a position to lend out a further £46.656 million so that the balance sheet of the banking system becomes:

	Liabilities		Assets
Deposit 1	£100m	Cash reserves 1	£10m
		Advances 1	£90m
Deposit 2	£72m	Cash reserves 2	£7.2m
		Advances 2	£64.8m
Deposit 3	£51.84m	Cash reserves 3	£5.184m
		Advances 3	£46.656m

Table 4.1   The relationship between base money, bank deposits and broad money

Bank reserves	Deposits	Cash held by non-bank public	Deposits of non-bank public	Base money	Broad money
10	100	90	450	100	190
20	200	80	400	100	280
30	300	70	350	100	370
33.33	333.33	66.67	333.33	100	400
40	400	60	300	100	460
50	500	50	250	100	550
60	600	40	200	100	640
70	700	30	150	100	730
80	800	20	100	100	820
90	900	10	50	100	910
100	1000	0	0	100	1000

The reader will note that at each stage the ability of a banking system to make new advances diminishes. The whole process will continue (see **Table 4.1**) in such a manner until the combined balance sheet of the banking system reads:

	Liabilities			*Assets*	
Deposits	£333.33 m		Cash reserves	£33.33m
			Advances	£300.00m

For a given monetary base of £100 million, the amount of bank deposits created must be consistent with both the banking system's cash reserve to deposit ratio ($r = 0.1$) and the public's cash to deposit ratio ($c = 0.20$). This occurs when the banking system is holding cash reserves of £33.33 million and the public is therefore holding £66.67 million as cash. Banks will have total deposits of £333.33 million, which means that their cash reserve ratio is 10 per cent as required. In addition, the public will hold cash of £66.67 million which is 20 per cent of their deposit holdings of £333.33 million. Finally, the deposits held by the banking system are exactly equal to the desired deposit holdings of the public. The broad money supply of £400 million in this example is four times the monetary base of £100 million.

4.7   Formula for the money multiplier

The link between the monetary base and the broad money supply is given by the money multiplier:

broad money supply = money multiplier × monetary base

The money multiplier can be derived algebraically by the following method.

The banks' desired ratio of cash reserves (R) to total deposits (D) is given by r:

$$r = R/D \tag{4.1}$$

The public's desired ratio of cash in circulation (C) to banks' deposits (D) is given by c:

$$c = C/D \tag{4.2}$$

The total reserves of the banking system (R) is given by the reserve ratio times the volume of deposits from equation (4.1):

$$R = rD \tag{4.3}$$

Also, the total cash held by the public is given by the volume of deposits times the cash holding ratio of the public, from equation (4.2):

$$C = cD \tag{4.4}$$

The monetary base is defined as cash held by the banks plus cash held by the non bank public:

$$B = C + R = (c + r)D \tag{4.5}$$

The broad money supply, M1, is currency in circulation plus banks' demand deposits; that is:

$$M1 = C + D = (c + 1)D \tag{4.6}$$

Thus

$$M1 = \frac{c + 1}{c + r} B \tag{4.7}$$

Equation (4.7) is the formula for the money multiplier. The value of the multiplier is $(c + 1)/(c + r)$, and since r and c are positive but less than one, the money multiplier exceeds unity.

An increase in the banks' cash reserve ratio (r) or in the public's desired cash to demand deposits ratio (c) will reduce the value of the money multiplier. Banks prefer to lend as much as they can but they nonetheless need to maintain some cash reserves rather than risk finding themselves short of funds; there may also be legal requirements for them to hold a certain reserve ratio (r). The value of c can be affected by financial innovations such as whether or not firms pay in cash and the growing use of credit cards may reduce cash holdings.

In our numerical example we assumed the monetary base was £100 million and that $c = 0.2$ and $r = 0.1$. Substituting these figures into equation (4.7) we obtain:

$$M1 = \frac{0.2 + 1}{0.2 + 0.1} \times £100 \text{ million} = £400 \text{ million} \tag{4.8}$$

In other words, the money multiplier is 4; that is, the broad money supply is four times the narrow money supply.

4.8   Controlling the money supply

Equation (4.7) shows that the value of the money supply can be affected by changes in either the money multiplier or changes in the money base. There are three main methods by which the authorities may try to control the money supply:

- *Contractionary open market operations.* A contractionary OMO occurs when the central bank reduces the monetary base by selling Treasury bills in the money market. The effect of selling Treasury bills is to reduce the public's holding of cash and thereby reduce the ability of banks to create advances. The public will have less cash holdings and therefore will have to reduce the amount of advances they make.
- *Raising the reserve requirement.* The required reserve ratio is a minimum ratio of cash reserves to deposits that the central bank requires commercial banks to hold. The effect of raising the cash reserve (*r*) above what the banks would have voluntarily held is to reduce the value of the money multiplier. In our example, if we raise *r* from 0.1 to 0.2, the old money multiplier was 1.2/0.3 = 4 but the new money multiplier would be 1.2/0.4 = 3.
- *Raising the central bank lending rate.* The central bank lending rate is the interest rate that the central bank charges banks who wish to borrow money. Commercial banks have to hold a prudent level of reserves against unexpected withdrawals; if they find themselves short of cash then they may have to maintain the minimum ratio by borrowing from the central bank. A higher central bank lending rate will have two effects: (i) it will encourage commercial banks to hold more cash reserves than they would otherwise, for fear of finding themselves short of cash, and (ii) banks are likely to raise their own interest rates in line with the central bank lending rate, which will discourage private sector borrowing.

4.9   The determination of interest rates

According to economic analysis, the rate of interest is the price of money and is consequently determined in the money market by the supply and demand for money. Money demand is of three types – transactions demand, speculative demand and precautionary demand.

In the simplified money market model, we assume that money is demanded for only two reasons; transactions purposes and speculative purposes. With the transactions motive people hold money because there is not normally a perfect synchronization between their receipt and expenditure of money. In general, it is postulated that the higher an individual's income the larger the amount of money that is held for transactions purposes. This is based on the presumption that the higher one's income the greater one's payments, and correspondingly the greater the desired holdings of money for transaction purposes. As such, the transactions demand for money is assumed to be a positive function of income. This is expressed algebraically as:

$$Mt = Mt(Y) \qquad\qquad (4.9)$$

where *Mt* is the transactions demand for money and *Y* is the level of national income.

Another reason for holding money is the speculative motive. It is assumed that any money balances held in excess of those required for transactions purposes are for speculative balances. If the rate of interest rises, then so does the opportunity cost of holding money. For instance, if the rate of interest is 5 per cent per annum the opportunity cost of holding £100 is £5 per annum, but if the interest rate is 10 per cent the opportunity cost is £10 per annum, and consequently the demand to hold speculative balances will fall as the rate of interest rises. This inverse relationship between the demand for speculative balances and the rate of interest is expressed algebraically as:

$$Msp = Msp(r) \tag{4.10}$$

where Msp is the speculative demand for money and r is the rate of interest.

In equilibrium, money demand (Md), made up of transactions and speculative balances, is equal to the money supply (Ms), which is expressed algebraically as:

$$Md = Msp + Mt = Ms \tag{4.11}$$

The supply of money is assumed to be exogenously determined by the authorities, and equilibrium in the money market is shown in **Figure 4.6**.

Figure 4.6 shows that the demand for ($Md1$) and supply of money ($Ms1$) determine the interest rate ($r1$) in equilibrium, with real money balances given by $M1$. According to this approach, changes in the rate of interest are caused by changes in the supply and demand for money. Interest rates will rise if money demand rises from $Md1$ to $Md2$ as in **Figure 4.7**(a) due, for example, to an increase in income. Conversely, interest rates will fall if the supply of money is increased by the authorities due, for example, to an expansionary OMO as in **Figure 4.7**(b).

Figure 4.6   The supply and demand for money

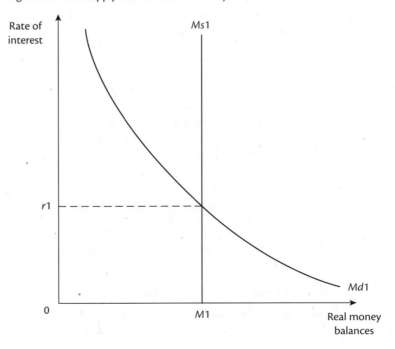

Figure 4.7   The effects of increases in money demand and money supply

(a) Increase in money demand

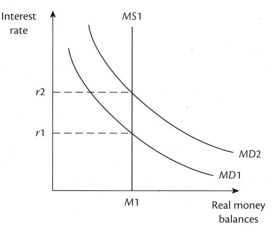

(b) Increase in money supply

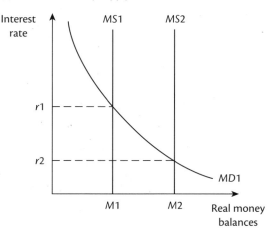

4.10 The loanable funds approach to interest rate determination

The loanable funds theory of interest rates looks at the rate of interest from another angle than the supply and demand for money approach. The approach argues that economic agents have a certain amount of financial wealth and they can choose to hold this wealth in the form of either interest-earning financial assets, or in money which earns no interest, or some combination of the two.

The supply of loanable funds

The stock of loanable funds is the stock of financial assets on which interest is paid, and is determined by three principal factors:

1 The amount of savings – this includes purchases of financial securities, mortgage repayments, business profits retained, funds set aside for capital replacement, and the savings of the central government and local authorities due to tax receipts greater than expenditure.
2 Switches from money holdings into savings products – there may be switches by private agents and business from holding financial wealth in the form of money into savings products.
3 An increase in loans made by financial institutions. With a given deposit base, deposit-taking institutions might be prepared to lend more funds; for example if business confidence improves, perhaps as an economy moves out of recession.

A rise in the interest rate will, other things being equal, lead to an increase in all of these three factors giving an upward-sloping supply of loanable funds schedule as shown in **Figure 4.8**.

The demand for loanable funds

The demand for loanable funds represents the demand for an increased stock of debt, to finance present aggregate demand in the form of consumption, investment

Figure 4.8   The demand for loanable funds

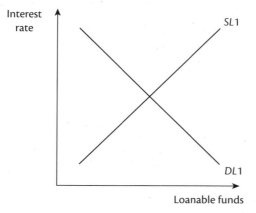

and government expenditure on goods and services. The demand for loanable funds is determined by a number of factors:

1   Investment demand – increases in investment are usually financed by borrowing. The investment demand may come from the private sector or the government sector, usually for capital projects like schools, housing, hospitals, road-building and so forth.

2   Borrowing for consumption – increases in consumer incomes or consumer confidence usually mean that people are prepared to consider increased borrowing.

3   Increases in money demand – many firms and individuals may want to increase their money holdings and therefore demand funds for this purpose.

A rise in the interest rate will, other things being equal, lead to a fall in all of these three factors, giving a downward-sloping demand of the loanable funds schedule in **Figure 4.8**. According to the loanable funds approach to interest rate determination, it is the intersection of the supply and demand for loanable funds that determines the interest rate as depicted in **Figure 4.8**.

The approach focuses on the factors that influence the supply and demand for loanable funds in order to predict the direction of interest rate movements. Firstly, in considering the demand for loanable funds there are several important factors that can lead to an increase in demand and a rightward shift of the loanable funds schedule:

(i)   an increase in expected future income will mean economic agents will be more confident about taking on more debt today;

(ii)   the prospect of future interest rate rises will also encourage economic agents to take on more debt at today's perceived lower rate;

(iii)   if consumers and firms are more confident about the future and they decide to borrow more this will be reflected in an increase in the demand for loanable funds.

The effects of an increase in the demand for loanable funds is depicted in **Figure 4.9**(a).

Figure 4.9   The effects of increases in demand and supply of loanable funds

(a) Increase in demand

(b) Increase in supply

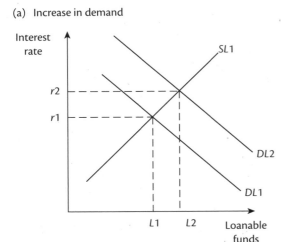

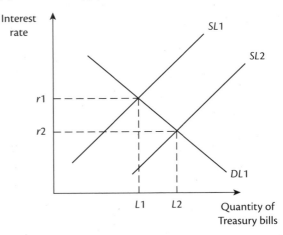

Correspondingly, there are again several important factors that can lead to an increase in the supply of loanable funds schedule (a rightward shift of the supply of loanable funds):

(i)   the level of savings in the economy – as incomes rise so does saving and the supply of loanable funds;

(ii) an increase in the proportion of savings held in the form of interest-earning assets compared to non interest-earning assets. Better financial intermediation is an important factor in this respect because it makes it easier for economic agents to hold funds in interest-earning assets; the more sophisticated financial intermediation process of developed countries is one reason why their real interest rates tend to be lower than in developing countries;

(iii) expectations about the future are extremely important – if economic agents become more pessimistic about the future they may well increase the amount they save, leading to a rightward shift in the supply of loanable funds.

The effect of such a rightward shift is depicted in **Figure 4.9**(b).

4.11   Money market or loanable funds theory?

According to the money market approach, it is the supply and demand for money that determines the rate of interest, whereas the loanable funds approach views the interest rate as being determined by the supply and demand for loanable funds. This raises the question as to which view is correct. In fact, the two views are complementary rather than alternatives. The supply and demand for money model looks at how the money market clears so that economic agents are satisfied with their holdings of non interest-earning money, while the loanable funds model looks at how the interest-earning asset market clears. The equilibrium interest rate has to clear both the money market and the loanable funds market.

Consider, for example, what happens if there is an increase in the money supply. According to the money market approach this leads to an excess of money balances and therefore a fall in the interest rate. With the loanable funds approach the increase in the money supply increases the amount of financial wealth held by economic agents and in so doing leads to an increase in the supply of loanable funds, resulting in a fall in the interest rate. Another example is when economic agents decide to increase their savings rate. According to the loanable funds approach the increased rate of savings is reflected in an increase in the supply of loanable funds and a fall in the interest rate. In the money market approach the increase in the rate of savings is equivalent to a fall in consumption which is reflected in a fall in income, a fall in the demand for money, and a fall in the interest rate. In other words the equilibrium rate of interest must be such that it clears both the money market and loanable funds market.

4.12 Inflation and interest rates

Before we look at an equation concerning the factors that determine the rate of interest, we must at least intuitively focus on the importance of the expected rate of inflation. For example, consider the case where a sum of £100 is being lent. The lender of the funds could purchase a basket of goods that cost £100 today or lend the funds to a borrower and therefore forgo current consumption of the basket of goods. If the expected rate of inflation is 10 per cent, then the basket of goods will be expected to cost £110 in a year's time. It would not make sense for the lender of funds to lend funds at less than 10 per cent per annum. If he charges 14 per cent interest than he gets back £114 which can then be used to buy the basket of goods at £110 with £4 left over. The £4 left over is an approximate real return of 4 per cent. If the funds had been lent at only 8 per cent, then, while the lender could have bought the basket of goods at the beginning of the year, at the end of the year he would expect the basket to cost £110 but would only get £108 back, and would not be able to buy the basket of goods.

Hence, it is clearly senseless to lend money at less than the expected rate of inflation. In our example, if the expected rate of inflation was only 5 per cent then a lender seeking a real rate of return of approximately 4 per cent would be willing to lend the funds out at 9 per cent. The lender expects the basket of goods to cost £105 at the end of the year but will have £109 back, so gaining £4 from lending the money. In sum, if the expected rate of inflation rises by 1 per cent then the nominal rate of interest needs to rise by 1 per cent, to maintain a given real rate of interest.

Clearly we need to examine the crucial role of the expected rate of inflation in more detail. For the purposes of our analysis we are going to divide the nominal interest rate into three components as given by equation (4.12).

$$r = i + \dot{P}e + RP \tag{4.12}$$

where r is the nominal rate of interest, i is the real rate of interest when agents forecast inflation with certainty, $\dot{P}e$ is the expected inflation rate, and RP is a risk premium reflecting inflation uncertainty.

According to equation (4.12), the nominal rate of interest has three components: the real rate of interest, which assumes that agents can forecast inflation with certainty, an additional premium to reflect the expected rate of inflation, and a risk premium component that reflects uncertainty about the inflation rate. To understand the economic reasoning behind this equation we need to understand that lenders of funds will require positive real expected returns from lending money, while borrowers will expect to pay a positive real cost for access to funds. This means that the expected inflation rate has to be incorporated into the actual rate of interest charged. Also, when inflation is uncertain then an additional rate of interest is required to reflect the risks run by lenders who are uncertain about what the inflation rate will actually be.

Consider two countries A and B. In country A

$$r_A = i_A + \dot{Pe}_A + RP_A$$
$$8\% = 2\% + 5\% + 1\%$$

whilst in country B

$$r_B = i_B + \dot{Pe}_B + RP_B$$
$$9\% = 2\% + 5\% + 2\%$$

In country A the nominal rate of interest is 8%. The first component is the real rate of interest of 2% – assuming with complete certainty that the expected inflation rate is 5%. The second component is the expected rate of inflation of 5% and the final component is an additional 1% risk premium because the inflation rate, while expected to average 5%, is not certain to be such. For example, the inflation rate may vary randomly in country A between the three values of 3%, 5% and 7%. The average is 5% but lenders of funds might find that inflation is 7%, which would reduce their real returns, so they charge a 1% inflation risk premium. If lenders were absolutely certain that the inflation rate would be 5% there would be no need to charge an inflation risk premium and the nominal rate of interest would only need to be 7%.

In country B the nominal rate of interest is 9%. The first component is the real rate of interest, which is 2% assuming the expected inflation rate known with certainty is the same as in country A. In this case it presupposes the expected inflation is 5% with complete certainty. The second component, the expected rate of inflation of 5%, is also the same as in country A, but the final component, an additional 2% risk premium, is higher than in country A. This may be the case because country B's inflation rate is much more variable than country A's, even though the inflation rate is expected to average 5%, which is the same as for country A. For example, country B's inflation rate may vary randomly between the three values of 2%, 5% and 8%, which is a greater range than the 3–7% of country A. Hence, in country B lenders of funds might find that inflation is 8%, which would reduce their real returns. They therefore charge a higher risk premium of 2% than country A's 1%, where the worst case scenario is 7% inflation. If lenders were absolutely certain that the inflation rate would be 5% there would be no need to charge a risk premium and the nominal rate of interest would then only need to be 7% in both countries.

From the preceding analysis it is clear that not only the expected rate of inflation but also its variability/predictability is extremely important in the determination of nominal interest rates. Interest rates and bond yields will be lower when inflation expectations are low and the inflation rate is predictable. This is the reason why many governments now set explicit target ranges for the inflation rate. For example, the Bank of England has a 2% central inflation target plus or minus 1%; that is, the Bank of England is expected to keep the inflation rate in the 1–3% range. One of the ideas behind this target range is that, by helping to keep inflation within a predictable range, the risk premium will be reduced, and so too the costs to the government of borrowing on the bond market when they issue bonds to finance their fiscal deficits.

In practice, it is not easy to observe the expected rate of inflation and many economists simply deduct the current rate of inflation from the current nominal rate of interest to arrive at an approximation to the current real rate of interest (inclusive of risk premium). Since the expected rate of inflation exerts such a powerful influence on interest rates, factors that influence the expected rate of inflation are crucial in determining interest rates at different time horizons. One of the most important factors in determining inflation expectations is the prospective monetary policy of the central bank. According to the simple version of the quantity theory of money, each 1 per cent rise in the money supply can be expected, other things being equal, to lead to a 1 per cent increase in the price level. Even if the link in practice is not so precise, the prospective rate of money supply growth will have a strong influence on the interest rate likely to be charged for a loan. Other factors likely to affect the future course of monetary policy include the outstanding amount of government debt, the fiscal policy, the degree of independence of the central bank from political interference, and the exchange rate policy pursued.

quantity theory of money a theory that an *x*% increase in the money supply will lead to an *x*% rise in prices

4.13 Fiscal policy and interest rates

Interest rates can be significantly affected by a government's fiscal stance, that is, its tax and expenditure policy. If a government spends more than it raises in tax revenue, that is it has a fiscal deficit, then it may well try to finance the difference by borrowing from the financial markets via Treasury bond sales. Treasury bond sales will initially reduce the money holdings of the public, but, provided the government uses the money raised to pay for part of its expenditure, then the money supply held by the non bank public will remain unchanged.

A fiscal expansion financed by borrowing will have the effect of raising aggregate demand. The increased government demand for goods and services will have the effect of raising real output although there will be some degree of crowding out due to the rise in the interest rate. This rise occurs for two reasons: (i) the increased bond sales to finance the increase in government expenditure depress bond prices and therefore raise the interest rate, and (ii) the increase in income raises money demand which for a given money stock requires a higher interest rate to clear the money market.

The national debt of a country is the outstanding stock of government bills and bonds in the market. The higher a country's national debt the higher the stock of bonds available on the market and, other things being equal, the higher the interest rate. Apart from this, governments with a high national debt tend to be distrusted by the financial markets. The markets may attach a higher risk to such countries for

crowding out the idea that the expansionary effects of an increase in government expenditure will to some extent be offset by a decrease in private consumption and investment and possibly exports

fear that the government may ultimately redeem the debt by printing money, which could lead to inflation. This extra inflation risk will tend to be priced into the rate at which the government can borrow.

4.14 Other factors influencing the interest rate

We have so far concentrated on the determination of interest rates by looking primarily at the role of government. For the private sector, such as companies and individuals, there are a few other factors that influence the rate of interest that a borrower may have to pay for funds.

- One of the most important factors is default risk, which is the risk that the borrower will default on all or part of the commitments in the loan contract. Highly rated companies with good credit ratings are generally able to borrow funds at a lower rate of interest than companies with poorer credit ratings. Loans to the government are generally regarded as risk-free, since a government is unlikely to renege on its obligations which can be met simply by printing money (although this may prove inflationary and be subject to inflation risk!).
- Another factor is the degree of liquidity, the ease with which a lender of funds can sell a security. The less liquid the security, the higher the rate of interest that will be charged by investors of funds.
- A final factor that is important in determining the rate of interest to be charged is the duration of a loan. The longer the duration then, generally speaking, the higher the risk that the company borrowing will run into difficulties and accordingly the higher the rate of interest that is likely to be charged.

4.15 Theories of the yield curve

In the real world there is no single interest rate charged to borrowers but a variety of interest rates depending upon numerous factors such as the length of the loan, risk assessment of the borrower and the expected rate of inflation. Interest rates vary from yields on Treasury bills and bonds to yields on deposit rates and interbank interest rates. The range of maturities is similarly large, from overnight money rates to 30-year government bonds. A plot of the interest rate charged against different terms to maturity for a bond that is identical in all other respects is known as a yield curve, a variety of which are shown in Figure **4.10**.

yield curve plots the yield to maturity of Treasury bills and Treasury bonds with different terms to maturity

Figure 4.10(a) shows a positively-sloped yield curve which indicates that borrowers who wish to borrow for long periods of time pay a higher rate of interest than medium-term borrowers, who in turn pay a higher rate of interest than short-term borrowers. **Figure 4.10**(b) shows a negatively-sloped yield curve which indicates that borrowers who wish to borrow in the short term pay a higher rate of interest than medium-term borrowers, who in turn pay a higher rate of interest than long-term borrowers. **Figure 4.10**(c) depicts a hump-shaped yield curve with borrowers that borrow medium-term paying higher rates of interest than those that borrow short-term or long-term. Finally, **Figure 4.10**(d) depicts a relatively flat yield curve with short-, medium- and long-term borrowers all borrowing at approximately the same rate of interest.

Figure 4.10 Various yield curves

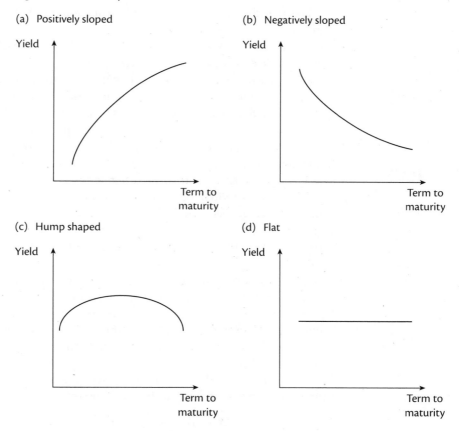

(a) Positively sloped

(b) Negatively sloped

(c) Hump shaped

(d) Flat

Yield curves can be quite volatile over time. Positively-sloped yield curves may become inverted yield curves, and yield curves can shift both upwards and downwards. Some economists have tried to examine the relationship between interest rates and the business cycle; while interest rates are usually high at the peak of the cycle, they sometimes peak before and sometimes after the start of a slowdown.

Since there are a variety of yield-curve shapes, any theory of interest rate determination needs to be able to explain these curves and why they may shift and change slope over time. A number of theories attempt to explain their shape: expectations theory, liquidity preference theory, the preferred habitat theory and the market segmentation theory.

4.16 Expectations theory

The main proposition of expectations theory is that long-term interest rates are determined by market expectations about the path of future short-term interest rates. According to the pure expectations theory, the entire term structure of interest rates reflects the market view about the path of future short-term interest rates. A positively-sloped yield curve would indicate that the market is expecting short-term interest rates to rise in the future, whereas a negatively-sloped yield curve indicates that the market is expecting short-term interest rates to fall. A flat yield curve indicates that the market expects short-term interest rates to remain fairly constant in the future.

Expectations theory works in the following fashion. Imagine that we currently have a flat yield curve with a short-term (one-year) interest rate of say 7 per cent and a long-term interest rate of 7 per cent, but then some economic news arrives that leads the market to expect a rise in interest rates in the future to, say, 10 per cent. This would have a number of effects on participants in the bond market. Long-term investors would be reluctant to hold long-term bonds at the current long-term interest rate of 7 per cent since they expect future short-term interest rates to be 10 per cent, which would involve capital losses on such long-term bond holdings; they will consequently wish to hold less long-term investments. Speculators will therefore sell long-term bonds today (or short them) so that they can buy them back in the future at a lower price and make a capital gain. This selling will continue until long-term bond prices fall to give a long-term yield of 10 per cent. Only when the long-term yield is 10 per cent would investors be prepared to hold the stock of long-term bonds.

According to the expectations view of interest rates, investors are completely indifferent to whether they hold a series of one-year bonds or long-term bonds. That is, short- and long-term bonds are perfectly substitutable. An investor is equally happy holding five one-year bonds one after the other as holding one five-year bond for five years. This means the expected return from these two investment possibilities should be equalized.

Let us imagine that the entire future path of interest rates is known with certainty. If this is the case then the long-term rate of interest is given by:

$$(1 + r_n)^n = (1 + r_0)(1 + r_1)(1 + r_2)\ldots(1 + r_{n-1}) \tag{4.13}$$

where r_n is the long-term interest rate on a bond with maturity of n years, r_0 is the current one-year interest rate, r_1 is the one-year interest rate expected in one year's time, r_2 is the one-year interest rate expected in two years' time, and r_{n-1} is the one-year interest rate expected in $n - 1$ years' time.

Equation (4.14) means that the interest rate on a five-year bond becomes the simple arithmetic average of all the future known interest rates, that is:

$$r_n = \frac{r_0 + r_1 + r_2 + r_{n-1}}{n} \tag{4.14}$$

Numerical example

Consider what the following set of expected interest rates implies for the interest rate on a five-year bond:

current one-year interest rate	$r_0 = 7\%$
one-year interest rate expected in one year's time	$r_1 = 8\%$
one-year interest rate expected in two years' time	$r_2 = 9\%$
one-year interest rate expected in three years' time	$r_3 = 10\%$
one-year interest rate expected in four years' time	$r_4 = 11\%$

Substituting these values into equation (4.14) yields:

$$r_5 = \frac{7 + 8 + 9 + 10 + 11}{5} = 9\%$$

which implies a five-year bond interest rate of 9.00 per cent.

Consider the term structure for the various five years assuming an investor has £100 to invest in bonds:

Year	Start of year capital	Expected interest rate	1-year interest	Expected end of year capital	Term structure
1	£100.00	7	£7.00	£107.00	7.0
2	£107.00	8	£8.56	£115.56	7.5
3	£115.56	9	£10.40	£125.96	8.0
4	£125.96	10	£12.60	£138.56	8.5
5	£138.56	11	£15.24	£153.80	9.0

The term structure for each year is found by taking the average of the expected interest rates. For example, the interest rate for year 2 is $(8 + 7)/2 = 7.5\%$, while the interest rate for year 3 is $(9 + 8 + 7)/3 = 8\%$ and so on. According to the expectations hypothesis the expected rates of interest are fully reflected in the term structure. For example, £100 locked away for three years at 8% interest will become $£100 \times (1.08)^3 = £125.97$ which coincides with the expected end of year capital at expected rates of interest of 7%, 8% and 9% respectively. Hence, according to the expectations hypothesis the term structure of interest rates is found by taking the simple arithmetic mean of all the relevant expected short-term interest rates.

4.17   Liquidity preference theory

In the real world, investors do not know with certainty the future course of interest rates; the estimates that they make will be subject to error, and the further into the future the more the scope for error in interest rate forecasts. Holding a short-term bond means that the investor will be subject to less uncertainty than a holder of longer-term bonds. According to the liquidity preference theory, bond holders are generally risk-averse in that they will wish to be compensated for the higher risk involved in holding long-term bonds by an appropriate risk premium on those bonds. According to the liquidity preference theory, the yield on longer-term bonds will therefore reflect not only market expectations, as outlined in the expectations theory, but also a liquidity premium.

liquidity premium the extra yield required to hold securities that are less liquid than securities with similar risk and maturity features

The liquidity premium theory therefore predicts a generally higher set of interest rates than the pure expectations theory. The basic idea underlying liquidity theory is that lenders of funds prefer to lend short, while borrowers generally prefer to borrow long. Hence borrowers are prepared to pay a liquidity premium to lenders to induce them to lend long. The size of the liquidity premium increases with the time to maturity.

4.18 Preferred habitat theory

The preferred habitat theory was first formulated by Modigliani and Sutch (1966). The theory argues that the term structure reflects both the expectations of the future path of interest rates and a liquidity premium. However, in the preferred habitat theory the liquidity premium does not have to rise uniformly with the maturity of the bond as assumed by the liquidity preference theory.

According to the preferred habitat theory, investors have specific objectives for their investments and this usually leads to specific time horizons (preferred habitats). For example, a person may be saving to purchase a house or a car, saving for retirement or saving to see offspring through university. If savers are risk-averse they will try to invest in bonds with the same term to maturity as required by their investment objective. Otherwise they will face reinvestment risk. For instance, someone saving to purchase a new car in five years' time will tend to invest in five-year bonds. If the investor invests in yearly bonds at the end of each year he faces the risk that a fall in interest rates will mean that he has insufficient funds at the end of five years to meet the investment objective. Similarly, if the saver invests in a 10-year bond then there is a danger that if interest rates rise the investor will not be able to sell the bond for a sufficient price to undertake the car purchase; that is, the investor would be assuming price risk.

Much investment is undertaken by financial institutions which also have specific investment objectives. Consider an institution that has issued a 10-year savings plan. The institution may be reluctant to invest in bonds of less than 10 years to maturity as it will face reinvestment risk, and it may be reluctant to invest in 20-year bonds because of the associated price risk.

In both of the previous cases there is a risk to the investor or financial institution of investing at a different investment horizon than their preferred habitat. According to the preferred habitat theory, risk premiums that exist to clear the bond market may be positive at certain time horizons in order to induce market participants to invest at different time horizons than their preferred habitat. For instance, if most investors have a preferred habitat of five-year investments, then short-term and longer-term interest rates may both be higher to induce investors to accept investments at these time horizons. Conversely, if both short- and long-term investments are preferred habitats, then medium-term interest rates may be higher to induce investors to undertake medium-term investments.

4.19 Market segmentation theory

The market segmentation theory was proposed by Culbertson (1957), and also assumes that investors have preferred habitats for their investments. However, the market segmentation theory assumes that there are barriers to switching between short-, medium- and long-term investments. These barriers may be due to the need to meet regulatory requirements, or they may be self-imposed regulations or even transaction costs. According to this theory the shape of the yield curve is determined by separate supply and demand forces in each particular maturity segment.

The theory presumes that changes in interest rates in a particular segment of the market will have relatively little influence on other segments of the market because investors do not shift funds between the various sectors. For instance, if demand for funds rises at the long end of the market, the theory predicts that there will be very little shifting of funds from the short end of the market to the long end of the market. The bond market in this view is divided up into different market segments and developments in one part of the market have relatively little effect on other parts of the market. While the theory can explain a wide variety of yield-curve shapes, it has fallen into disfavour since it is unlikely that investors and institutions will not move investments between different maturity horizons in response to changes in interest rates.

4.20 The importance of alternative views of the term structure

We have examined a range of different theories concerning the term structure of interest rates. The pure expectations theory assumes that the market is efficient in the sense that all available information is used and is incorporated into the term structure. A change at the short end of the market may well influence expectations at the long end of the market and thereby have a significant effect across the entire term structure of interest rates. This contrasts with the market segmentation viewpoint whereby changes at the short end of the market have little or no effect at the long end of the market. In between, we have the preferred habitat viewpoint whereby economic agents can be persuaded to switch funds from one part of the market to other parts provided there is sufficient inducement. The liquidity preference viewpoint argues that since investors are faced with uncertainty, which grows with time to maturity, then interest rates reflect not only market expectations but also market attitudes to risk.

These alternative viewpoints about term structure are of considerable importance for the implementation of monetary policy. Raising short-term interest rates may have the effect of reducing inflationary expectations. Within the context of the expectations viewpoint this will result in lowering of long-term interest rates which will then encourage greater investment. However, within the context of the market segmentation viewpoint, higher short-term rates will have relatively little effect on the long-term interest rate.

Also of considerable importance is the fact that the term structure can influence different institutions in different ways. The willingness and ability of banks to raise funds and to make loans is especially responsive to the level of the short-term interest rate. Pension funds are much more concerned about the influence of long-term interest rates, and changes in long-term interest rates tend to have a bigger effect on their investment strategies than changes at the short end of the market. The term structure can also be used by the authorities as a guide to the tightness or otherwise of monetary policy. If the yield curve is steeply upward-sloping, this can suggest that monetary policy is presently rather loose as inflation is expected to pick up significantly in the future. Whereas, if the yield curve is strongly negatively-sloped, this may indicate that monetary policy is currently quite tight, reflecting the fact that inflationary pressures in the economy are being brought under control.

4.21 Problems with monetary policy

In a modern economy there are many things that are close to fulfilling the role of traditional money (notes and coins); for example, current accounts, time accounts, certificates of deposit, credit cards, debit cards and so forth. In recent years, the pace of financial innovation has made it very difficult for central banks to decide precisely what the money supply is, and how to control it.

If the authorities decide to target a particular money-supply measure, the financial system is very good at producing close substitutes, making a nonsense of the monetary target. For example, if the authorities start controlling the supply of reserves to the banking system to stop it granting credit, borrowers may look elsewhere, for example to security markets, to raise finance. This process of disintermediation, that is the replacement of bank lending by other means, such as securitization.

> **disintermediation**
> the process of withdrawing funds from financial institutions so as to invest them directly in companies; it also involves companies raising funds directly from investors

Also, the authorities face a conflict between the control of the supply of money and the interest rate. In targeting the money supply the authorities give up control of the interest rate and *vice versa*. Another problem is that the demand for money is not necessarily stable and predictable in the short run, and hence the link between the money supply and prices may not be particularly powerful in the short run. For instance, an increase in the money supply which is matched by an increase in money demand may not be inflationary as the increased money supply will be willingly held.

Under fixed exchange rates the authorities cannot conduct an independent monetary policy, that is they give up control of the money supply due to the need to fix the exchange rate. They must sell domestic currency to purchase foreign currency when the domestic currency is under appreciation pressure (increasing the money supply held by the private sector and increasing the foreign exchange reserves of the country); and they must buy the currency when it is under depreciation pressure with foreign currency reserves (decreasing the money supply held by the private sector and decreasing the foreign exchange reserves of the country).

4.22 Conclusions

The factors determining short-term and long-term interest rates, as well as the position and slope of the yield curve, are both numerous and complex. The various factors include the credibility of a government's macroeconomic policy, the interaction between fiscal and monetary policies, the demand and supply of loanable funds on the part of the government and private sector, the rate of economic growth, inflationary expectations, risk perceptions, the creditworthiness of the borrower, political factors, economic agents' perceptions about the future, and international factors like interest rates in the rest of the world and the exchange rate regime adopted by the country concerned.

There are a number of competing theories concerning the shape of the yield curve. The most widely accepted is the expectations view of the term structure of interest rates in which the shape of the yield curve is determined by the expected future interest rate. Governments have the ability to exert a significant impact on short-term money market rates of interest through open market operations.

However, governments have relatively little control over medium- to long-term nominal interest rates which are determined predominantly by economic agents' expectations of inflation. To the extent that raising the short-term interest rate lowers economic agents' expectations about the future inflation rate, then this should enable a lowering of long-term interest rates. If, however, a rise in the short-term interest rate is seen as being 'too little and too late' as a response to inflationary pressure, it may even be accompanied by a rise in long-term rates!

Further reading

Mishkin, F. (2009) *Monetary Policy Strategy*, MIT Press.
Walsh, C. (2003) *Monetary Theory and Policy*, 2nd edn, MIT Press.
Woodford, M. (2003) *Interest and Prices: Foundations of a Theory of Monetary Policy*, Princeton University Press.

Chapter 4	Revision questions

1 Briefly explain with the aid of diagrams of the money market and Treasury bill market what happens when the central bank conducts a contractionary open market operation.

2 Explain with the aid of an equation the three factors that determine long-term interest rates.

3 Briefly explain what the yield curve is and draw a positively-sloped yield curve. Show the effect on the yield curve if the expected rate of inflation was to rise in both the short and the long term.

4 The narrow money supply is £100 million, the public's desired cash to deposit ratio is 0.15 and the banking system's reserve to deposit ratio is 0.1. What is the equilibrium value of the broad money supply?

5 Briefly explain the liquidity preference theory and discuss its implication for the slope of the yield curve.

 Multiple choice questions available at www.palgrave.com/business/pilbeam

5

DOMESTIC AND INTERNATIONAL MONEY MARKETS

Learning objectives

In this chapter you will learn about:

- Treasury bills and the relationship between Treasury bill prices and short-term rates of interest
- various other short-term securities such as commercial bills, certificates of deposit, repurchase agreements (repos) and bankers acceptances
- the history of the Eurodollar market and reasons for its continued growth
- the importance of dollar LIBOR ($LIBOR) to the interbank market
- note issuing facilities, Euro commercial paper and Euro medium-term notes

5.1 Introduction

Money market instruments are defined as securities that when issued have a year or less to maturity, and the market that trades in such instruments is known as the money market. Examples of money market instruments are Treasury bills, commercial paper, bankers' acceptances, certificates of deposit and Eurocurrency deposits. The money market is important because many of these instruments are held by banks as part of their eligible reserves, that is, they may be used (are eligible) as collateral if a bank wishes to raise funds from the central bank.

The money market is itself divided into two interrelated parts, the domestic money market and the international money market. The domestic market deals with short-term domestic currency deposits that are held in the country of issue. The international money market consists of national currencies that are held on short-term deposit in countries other than the country of issue of that currency. The international money market is referred to as the offshore market or Eurocurrency market.

> **money market**
> a market dealing with short-term securities and the transfer of funds with a time horizon of one year or less such as Treasury bills, commercial paper and short-term bank deposits

5.2 Types of domestic money market instruments

There are a number of domestic short-term money market instruments, and they vary in their degree of riskiness, return and liquidity. The most important is domestic Treasury bills since they provide the basis for all other short-term interest rates. The interest rate is normally expressed in basis points, where one basis point represents 1/100 of a per cent. For example, a movement in the rate of interest from 10 per cent to 10.20 per cent is a movement of 20 basis points. It should be noted that different markets have different market conventions: the Japanese and UK markets work on a 365-day year, while the US and European markets are based on a 360-day year.

5.3 Treasury bills

Treasury bills are issued by the treasury of the country concerned. They are generally regarded to be risk-free instruments since the government guarantees to pay their face value upon maturity, and because it can simply print the money to do this they are free of default risk. Another attractive feature of Treasury bills is that they are a highly liquid instrument with a well developed secondary market, which means that holders can easily convert their bills into cash if the need arises. A Treasury bill is a discount security, that is, upon issue the security is sold at a discount to its face value. Since a bill makes no coupon payments, the holder expects to gain from capital appreciation. The size of the discount determines the yield on holding the Treasury bill.

The current yield on a Treasury bill (assuming a 360-day year) is calculated as follows:

$$y = \frac{D}{P} \times \frac{360}{t} \times 100 \tag{5.1}$$

where y is the annualized yield, D is the discount to face value (that is the difference between the price and face value), P is the current market price, and t is the number of days remaining to maturity.

For example, on issue a six-month (180-day) Treasury bill with a face value of $100 is sold at $95. The current yield is calculated as:

$$y = \frac{\$5}{\$95} \times \frac{360}{180} \times 100 = 10.53\%$$

Treasury bills can be sold in a variety of ways to financial institutions, including:

1 A public issue, in which the central bank offers stock at a fixed price and hopes that financial institutions will purchase sufficient stock that there is little unsold stock left over.

2 A tender issue, in which the central bank sets a minimum tender price and then invites bids at or above this minimum price. Financial institutions and investors bid for the stock, and on the basis of these bids the minimum price at which the issue can be sold is calculated. Those that have bid above this price are entitled to a full allocation and the remainder of the issue is distributed on a pro rata basis to those bidding at the relevant bid price.

3 An auction issue, in which the central bank invites bids and sets no minimum price (although it reserves the right in exceptional circumstances to reduce the size of the issue). The issue is then sold to those that bid the highest price at the price at which they bid until all the stock is sold. The problem facing bidders in such circumstances is that they may find that they have over-bid in comparison to other bidders, and that when trading in the stock takes place they find it trades at a significant discount to their bid. This would discourage bidders, so to limit this risk the bank permits trading in the stock prior to the issue so that investors have a guide price upon which to base their bids. There are a number of advantages of the auction technique: the government can be sure of selling all the stock and revenue may be enhanced by selling the stock at different prices.

4 A direct placement, in which the central bank negotiates directly with financial institutions to sell the stock at an agreed price. The financial institutions then distribute the stock to clients and other investors.

5 Additional tranches of existing issues, in which the central bank offers additional tranches of stock that is already actively traded. Such issues can be useful in cases where the government's funding requirements are relatively small-scale, and the existence of an already liquid market means that appropriate pricing and success of the issue is assured.

The precise technique used depends on numerous factors such as the amount of funds to be raised, market conditions and the degree of certainty of sale required.

5.4   Commercial paper

A company that wishes to raise money for short-term purposes might obtain a bank overdraft. Alternatively, if the company has a good credit rating it could issue commercial paper. Commercial paper is an unsecured promissory note issued by a corporation into the money market. The issuer promises to pay purchasers of the issue the face value of the paper which is sold at a discount on the market. Most commercial paper has less than 360 days to maturity, and the typical maturity range is 30–60 days. The commercial paper market has grown enormously in the USA so that it is now bigger than the US Treasury bill market.

In the USA, most commercial paper is paid off by the issue of new commercial paper, and many banks hold commercial paper as part of their eligible assets to meet reserve requirements. The main risk faced by a holder of commercial paper is that the issuer will not be in a position to issue further paper upon maturity, but this risk is kept low by the fact that most commercial paper is backed up by the corporation's access to bank credit facilities. Issuers of commercial paper are also given credit ratings by credit-rating agencies.

A large proportion of commercial paper is issued by financial corporations who use the commercial paper market to raise funds to provide loans to customers. Some of these financial corporations are known as captive finance companies, and are basically subsidiaries of major corporations. The aim of a subsidiary is to raise and manage funds for the parent corporation; for example, in the USA the General Motors Acceptance Corporation issues commercial paper on behalf of General Motors. The commercial paper market was originally used only by corporations that had an excellent credit rating, but in recent years corporations with lower credit ratings have been able to enter the market. They have managed to sell their commercial paper by issuing paper that is backed by a letter of credit from a bank, in which the bank guarantees the commercial paper in the event of default by the issuer. In return for this the bank receives a fee from the issuer.

Commercial paper is either placed directly with the investor (direct paper), or is dealer-placed with investors (dealer paper) in return for an underwriting fee. Most direct paper is placed by financial corporations that are raising sufficient amounts of funds on a regular basis to justify the costs of maintaining a sales-force for their paper. Like Treasury bills, commercial paper is sold at a discount to face value based on a 360-day year. One interesting difference between the Treasury bill market and the commercial paper market is that most commercial paper is held to maturity, meaning that the secondary market in commercial paper is relatively thin compared to the high liquidity of the Treasury bill market. The discount on commercial paper is higher than the discount on Treasury bills principally due to the default risk involved and the fact that the secondary commercial paper market is less liquid than the Treasury bill market.

5.5   The interbank market

The interbank market is where commercial and investment/merchant banks (both domestic and foreign) as well as other non-bank financial intermediaries can lend and borrow money with each other. Banks with surplus funds can lend to banks which are short of funds. The market is predominantly a short-term market with most loans ranging from overnight to 14-day loans; on a much lesser scale some loans are for periods up to six months. The key rate of interest is the London Interbank Offered Rate (LIBOR), which is the rate charged on loans in the market. This forms the basis for the rates banks will charge for loans since it represents the likely cost of funds if they themselves are short of funds. Many variable-rate loan contracts are linked to LIBOR plus a margin.

There is a high degree of correlation between the LIBOR and the rate of interest prevailing in the Treasury bill market. LIBOR is usually marginally higher and more volatile than the Treasury bill market since all loans are unsecured and, unlike the Treasury bill market, the central bank will not act as a lender of last resort. If banks are suffering a shortage of funds they will tend to sell Treasury bills, thus raising the interest rate in that market. There will then be a shortage of funds in the interbank market, raising LIBOR. Conversely, if banks have a surplus of funds then they will tend to buy Treasury bills, leading to a lower rate of interest in the Treasury bill market. Funds will then be placed on the interbank market, so lowering LIBOR.

LIBOR (London interbank offered rate) a variety of short-term rates of interest at which one bank will lend to another bank in a given currency at given time horizons such as seven days, one month, three months, six months and one year; there are $LIBOR, £LIBOR €Libor and so on

5.6   Banker's acceptances

banker's acceptance a short-term draft by a company to pay a certain sum of money in the future; it is guaranteed for payment by a bank once it has been stamped 'accepted' and can thereafter be traded on the secondary markets at a discount to its face value

A banker's acceptance is simply a financial instrument that facilitates a commercial trade transaction. The financial instrument is called a banker's acceptance because a bank will guarantee the repayment of a loan to the holder. They are mainly used to facilitate trade of goods between companies of different countries, although they are occasionally used to facilitate trade between two companies within the same country. Bankers' acceptances help a country to export goods to, and import goods from, the rest of the world. In addition, third-country acceptances are used to finance storing and shipping of goods between two foreign firms.

An example of the role played by a banker's acceptance is as follows. A US car import company, 'Foreign Cars USA', that banks with Citigroup wishes to import in 60 days' time 50 British cars for $2 million for resale to its US customers. Assume that the British car manufacturer banks with NatWest. The British car manufacturer will be concerned at the risk of non-payment by Foreign Cars USA once the cars are shipped. To eliminate this concern, Foreign Cars USA will arrange for Citigroup to issue a letter of credit which will guarantee payment of the $2 million in 60 days' time. The letter of credit is forwarded to NatWest. Upon receipt the bank will notify the British car manufacturer which will then commence the shipment to Foreign Cars USA. Once the cars are shipped, the British car manufacturer will receive the present value of $2 million from NatWest. NatWest will present the shipping documents and letter of credit to Citigroup, which will stamp 'accepted' on the letter of credit which has now become a Citigroup banker's acceptance. This means that Citigroup will pay the holder of the banker's acceptance $2 million upon maturity. Citigroup will then pass on the shipping documents to Foreign Cars USA in return for an appropriate fee. NatWest will have the choice of holding onto the banker's acceptance or selling it at a discount to a third party. When the acceptance matures, Citigroup pays the holder the $2 million and recovers the funds from Car Imports USA plus a margin fee. The margins charged to customers for the issuance of bankers' acceptances typically range between 10 and 30 basis points.

5.7 Repurchase agreements

repurchase agreement (repo)
an agreement by the seller to buy back a security at a future date

A repurchase agreement (repo) involves the sale of a security with a commitment by the seller to repurchase the security at a specified price at a future date. The difference between the current market price of the security and the lower price at which it is sold is known as the 'haircut' in the repo. The amount of the haircut required will be determined by market conditions. In effect, a repurchase agreement is a collateralized loan with the seller handing over the security as collateral.

5.8 Certificates of deposit

certificate of deposit
a certificate which certifies that a deposit of a certain amount has been made at a bank and specifying the interest to be paid, usually issued by a commercial bank; can be used as collateral for a loan

A certificate of deposit (CD) is issued by a deposit-taking institution, usually a bank, to acknowledge that a specified sum of money has been deposited with the institution. CDs have a specified maturity date and attract a specified rate of interest. They come in two forms, negotiable and non-negotiable. A negotiable CD can be sold by the initial depositor on the open market before maturity, whilst a non-negotiable CD must be held by the depositor until maturity. The advantage of a negotiable CD for investors is that they have a tradable deposit paying a guaranteed rate of interest and liquidity should they require funds at short notice. The bank on the other side has attracted a deposit for a guaranteed fixed period and it can pay a marginally lower rate of interest for the negotiable CD, since the certificate gives the depositor a high degree of liquidity.

The vast majority of CDs are issued with less than a year to maturity, with three- and six-month deposits being the most common types, and the minimum term is seven days. There are two types of negotiable CD: large-denomination CDs with a value of £1 million or more, and retail CDs for which deposits can be as low as £50,000. The majority of large-value CDs are held by banks, investment funds, institutional investors and money market funds. CDs can be issued in any of the major currencies, and in the USA they are insured under the Federal Deposit Insurance Corporation scheme up to a maximum of $250,000.

There are also longer-term CDs issued for periods of one to five years known as term CDs, which pay interest semi-annually. Many term CDs are of the floating rate variety in which the rate of interest varies from time to time in accordance with changes in the base rate of interest. CDs are the basis of the Euromarkets (see below).

5.9 The international money market

The international money market is the market in which borrowers and lenders of funds from different countries are brought together to exchange funds. The main international money market is known as the Eurocurrency market, and since the early 1960s this market has grown at an astonishing pace. As we shall see, the development of the Eurocurrency market has had important implications for not only the international monetary system, but also for the development of domestic financial markets and the conduct of national macroeconomic policies.

5.10 Euromarkets

Eurodollar a short-term deposit or loan made in dollars outside the USA

Eurocurrency markets are defined as banking markets which are conducted outside of the legal jurisdiction of the authorities of the currency that is used for banking transactions. Examples of Eurodollar deposits are dollar deposits held in London and Paris, while examples for Eurosterling are pounds held in New York and Paris. The Eurocurrency market has two sides to it: the receipt of deposits and the loaning out of those deposits. By far the most important Eurocurrency is the Eurodollar which accounts for approximately 65 per cent of all Eurocurrency activity, followed by the Euroeuro(!), Eurofranc (Swiss), Eurosterling and Euroyen. The use of the prefix Euro is somewhat misleading because dollar deposits held by banks in Hong Kong or Tokyo, which are equally outside the legal jurisdiction of the US authorities, also constitute Eurodollar deposits. Similarly, euros and yen held in New York constitute Euroyen and Euroeuros. This more widespread geographical base means that Euromarkets are often referred to as 'offshore' markets.

Euromarkets are in many ways a phenomenon of the increasingly open world trading system; there is no reason why deposits and loans in a given currency need to be carried out exclusively in the particular country that issues the currency. The main reason for the rapid growth of Eurocurrency markets is that they provide better deposit and loan rates than those offered by domestic banks located in the country that issues the currency.

5.11 The origins and development of the Euromarkets

Since the 1960s the rate of growth of the Eurocurrency market has been remarkable (see **Table 5.1**). In 1963 the gross total value of Eurobank assets (a similar figure applies to deposit liabilities) was approximately $12.4 billion, but by the end of 2008 the Eurodollar market stood at $30,927 billion. This works out at an average growth

Table 5.1 The gross size of the Eurocurrency market in selected years

Year	US$ billions		Year	US$ billions
1964	14.9		1988	4,535.6
1966	26.5		1990	6,297.6
1968	46.4		1992	6,240.9
1970	93.2		1994	7,116.7
1972	149.9		1996	8,326.8
1974	248.0		1998	9,881.7
1976	341.7		2000	10,773.9
1978	893.6		2002	13,370.3
1980	1,321.9		2004	19,198.6
1982	1,695.2		2006	26,126.5
1984	2,168.8		2008	30,926.8
1986	3,289.8			

Source: Bank for International Settlements, *Annual Report Quarterly Review*, various years

rate of 18.95 per cent per annum over the 45 years! Measuring the actual size of the Eurocurrency market presents some difficulty because a distinction needs to be made between the gross and net size of the market. The gross measure includes both non-Eurobank and interbank deposits, while the net measure excludes interbank deposits. The gross measure gives an idea of the overall activity in the Euromarkets, while the net measure gives a better indication of the ability of the Eurobanking system to create credit.

The origins of the Euromarkets can be traced back to 1957. The Russians had acquired US dollars through their exports of raw materials and were, given the strong anti-communist sentiment prevailing in the USA and the 'cold war', reluctant to hold these funds with US banks. Instead, the funds were held in an account with a French bank in Paris, the cable address of which was EURO-BANK. Also in 1957, the Bank of England introduced restrictions on UK banks' ability to lend sterling to foreigners, and foreigners' ability to borrow sterling. This induced UK banks to turn to the US dollar as a means of retaining London's leading role in the financing of world trade. In 1958, the abolition of the European Payments Union and restoration of convertibility of European currencies meant that European banks could now hold US dollars without being forced to convert these dollar holdings with their central banks into domestic currencies. All these three factors provided the initial demand and supply of Eurodollars.

An important impetus for the rapid growth of the Eurodollar came from the increased regulation of domestic banking activities by the US authorities. Three measures are of particular note in this respect. In 1963 the US government introduced Regulation Q which imposed ceilings on the rate of interest that US banks could pay on savings and time-deposit accounts. (The idea was to prevent US banks pushing up interest rates in a competition for depositors' funds, which might then lead to risky lending policies.) Since the regulation did not apply to offshore banks, this encouraged many US banks to set up subsidiaries abroad in centres such as London. In the same year, the US authorities, concerned about the impact of capital outflow on the US balance of payments, introduced the interest equalization tax (IET). The IET raised the cost to foreigners of borrowing dollars in New York, which led them to borrow funds on the Eurodollar market. (The IET was abolished in 1974.) A further measure that restricted lending to foreigners by US banks was the Voluntary Foreign Credit Restraint Guidelines which were issued in 1965 and made compulsory in 1968.

This increased regulation of US domestic banks gave a boost to the development of Eurobanking activities to circumvent the effects of these controls, and many US banks decided to set up foreign branches and subsidiaries to escape the banking regulations. Indeed, since US banking law severely restricted US banks' ability to operate in more than one state, setting up subsidiaries abroad was an important means of expansion for many US banks. More importantly, it gave a competitive edge to Eurobanks which are not subject to such regulations.

Following the hike in oil prices in 1973/74 the oil petroleum export countries (OPEC) deposited large amounts of the resulting additional funds on the Euromarkets. The Eurobanks then on-lent much of the funds to oil-importing countries that faced balance-of-payments problems. The Eurobanks played an important intermediary role in recycling funds from the surplus OPEC countries to the deficit oil-importing countries. A similar role was performed by the Eurobanks following the second oil-price shock at the end of 1978, though on a lesser scale.

A final factor behind the growth of Eurobanking activity has been the rapid growth of world trade, which means that more companies have excess working balances in foreign currency and seek high rates of return or require borrowing facilities at competitive rates of interest.

In December 1981, the Federal Reserve, recognizing that many US banks had set up offshore branches to avoid US regulations in exotic locations such as the Bahamas and Cayman Islands, decided to legalize so-called international banking facilities (IBFs). IBFs essentially permit US banks to conduct Eurobanking business free of US regulations in the USA by maintaining a separate set of books for this business. IBFs can only accept deposits from non-US residents, and their loan facilities must be used for overseas purposes. Since IBFs are not subject to reserve requirements, interest rate regulations or deposit insurance premiums, their business is maintained on a separate book to the parent bank. IBFs have proved to be popular since their inception, and much business that was previously carried out in offshore offices has been relocated back to the USA.

> **international banking facility**
> a facility that enables short-term deposits and loans to be made, only for foreign residents and companies

5.12 The characteristics of the Eurodollar market

The centres which account for the majority of Eurobank activity are London, Paris, Luxembourg and Frankfurt. Offshore banking centres in Bahrain, the Bahamas, the Cayman Islands, Hong Kong, Panama, Netherland Antilles and Singapore account for a reasonable proportion of business, with North America and Japan accounting for the remainder. Eurobanks are generally free of government regulation, and, more especially, they do not face compulsory reserve requirements, interest ceilings or deposit insurance.

The main users of the Eurocurrency market facilities are the Eurobanks themselves, non-Eurobank financial institutions, multinational corporations, international institutions and central and local government. Multinationals are drawn by the attractive interest rates paid on their corporate funds and the competitive borrowing rates, while international organizations such as the World Bank frequently borrow funds from Eurobanks for lending to developing countries. A large proportion of Eurocurrency transactions are between Eurobanks themselves, those with surplus funds loaning to Eurobanks that have lending possibilities but are short of funds.

The pivotal rate of interest for the Eurocurrency markets is the London Interbank Offered Rate (LIBOR) which is the rate of interest that London clearing banks will charge for loans between themselves on the London interbank market. Non-bank borrowers then pay a spread above LIBOR depending on their credit rating and the banks' transaction costs; non-bank depositors typically receive a rate of interest on their deposits below LIBOR. In the early days of the Euromarket, the interest paid on deposits and charged for loans was usually fixed for the whole period of the deposit or loan. Increasingly, however, floating interest rates based on LIBOR have become the norm for medium- to long-term (above six months) deposits and loans. With floating rates, the interest charged on a medium- to long-term loan is adjusted every three or six months to stay within a fixed spread above LIBOR. In effect, many

| Box 5.1 | Stress in the money markets as indicated by the TED spread |

The TED spread stands for the Treasury Eurodollar spread and is measured by the difference between the 3-month dollar LIBOR and the 3-month US Treasury bill rate. For example, if the 3-month dollar LIBOR rate is 4.5 per cent and the 3-month dollar Treasury bill rate is 4.20 per cent then the TED spread is 0.3 per cent which is 30 basis points. The 3-month dollar LIBOR rate reflects the rate at which banks will lend dollars to each other while the 3-month dollar Treasury bill yield is the rate at which banks will lend to the US Treasury, and is regarded as risk-free. As such, increases in the TED spread can be taken as a sign of funding becoming more difficult in the interbank market and/or a sign that banks are becoming distrustful of each other. In effect, the TED spread represents a short-term 'risk premium' of lending to another bank as opposed to lending to the US government. The TED spread normally fluctuates in the region of 15 to 35 basis points but, as **Figure 5.1** shows, the TED spread widened dramatically in the summer of 2008 and peaked at a massive 463 basis points on 10 October 2008 following the collapse of Lehman Brothers and American International Group.

After its peak, the spread slowly fell as the Federal Reserve moved in to lend money and even guarantee interbank lending, and a series of measures were put in place to stabilize the financial system. As signs of financial stabilization occurred the TED spread fell back to much more normal levels by December 2009 indicating that the worst of the financial crisis was over.

Figure 5.1   The TED spread in basis points

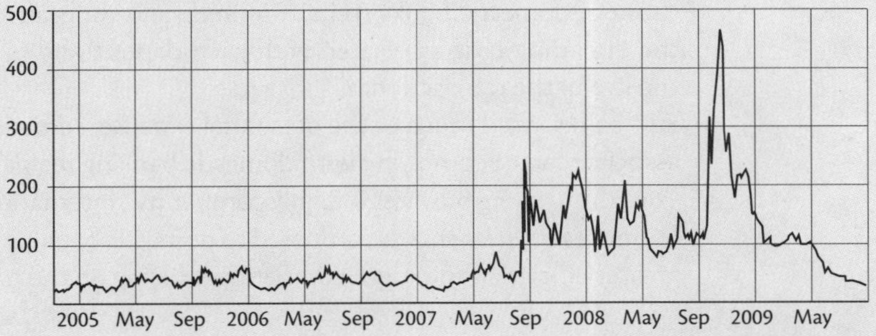

Source www.bloomberg.com

long-term loans are a succession of short-term loans that are automatically 'rolled over', but at interest rates that vary in line with changes in LIBOR. There are usually penalties to be paid if deposits are withdrawn before maturity.

One of the interesting characteristics of the structure of Eurobanks' assets (loans) and liabilities (deposits) is that they are predominantly of a short-term nature, with some deposits being as short as one day (overnight deposit) and the vast majority under six months. Furthermore, the maturity structure of deposits and liabilities is closely matched. Such a maturity structure stands in contrast to the balance sheets of domestic banks which usually accept short-term demand and time deposits and then engage in medium- to long-term lending.

5.13 The competitive advantage of Eurobanks

The main reason for the continuing success of Eurobanking despite the relaxation of regulation on US banks is their ability to offer higher deposit rates and lower loan rates than US banks. It is this competitive edge which is the fundamental reason for their continued popularity and growth. The competitive advantage of Eurobanks is illustrated in **Figure 5.2**.

The Eurobanks are generally able to pay a higher rate on deposits and charge a lower rate for loans than US banks for similar facilities. This implies that the interest rate spread, that is the difference between the rates paid on deposits and charged for loans, is lower for Eurobanks than US banks. The usual domestic interest rate used for the purposes of comparison with the Euro-interest rate is the interest on certificates of deposit. The difference between deposit rates on CDs and those on Eurodeposits fluctuates but the usual range is 10–40 basis points. The lower Euro-interest spread can be explained by a number of factors:

1   Eurobanks, unlike domestic banks, are free of regulatory control and in particular they are not required to hold reserve assets. This gives them a competitive advantage over domestic banks which are required to hold part of their assets in zero- or low-interest liquid funds to meet official reserve requirements. Since Eurobanks are not subject to reserve requirements, they are able to hold less money in the form of low-interest reserves enabling them to pay a higher interest rate on deposits and charge a lower rate on loans.

2   Eurobanks benefit from economies of scale. The average size of their deposits and loans (hundreds of thousands and millions of dollars) is considerably greater than those of domestic banks (tens, hundreds and thousands of dollars). This makes the operating cost associated with each deposit and loan smaller in relation to the size of the transaction.

3   Eurobanks avoid much of the personnel expense, administration costs and delays associated with complying with domestic banking regulations.

4   The Eurobanking business is highly competitive internationally with relatively easy entrance requirements as compared to domestic banking activity. This encourages greater efficiency and more competitive pricing on the part of Eurobanks.

Figure 5.2   Comparison of US CD and loan rates with Eurodollar deposit and loan rates

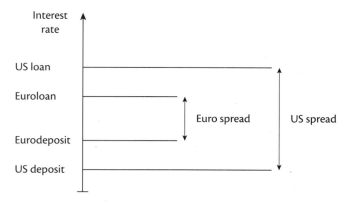

5 Eurobanks do not have to pay deposit insurance whereas US banks have to insure their deposit base with the Federal Deposit Insurance Corporation (FDIC).

6 Eurobank lending is almost exclusively to high-quality customers with a virtually negligible default rate. This contrasts with the relatively high default rate faced by domestic banks that have to charge an appropriate default-risk premium in their lending rates.

5.14 The coexistence of domestic and Eurobanking

Since Eurobanks generally pay higher interest rates on deposits and charge lower interest rates on loans, it is natural to ask why all borrowing and lending is not carried out via Eurobanks. The answer lies in the transaction costs for the parties involved. It usually pays a US firm to go to its local US bank for a loan because the local bank will have a record and understanding of the business. It will be able to assess more easily the risk of lending to the business, and to secure collateral and monitor the progress of the loan. If the firm were to go to a Eurobank the process of convincing the Eurobank that is was credit worthy and that the project was soundly-based could prove expensive. Similarly, it is not usually worth individuals and small enterprises holding a Eurodeposit because they rarely have sufficient surplus funds and prefer to use a bank which offers additional facilities such as cheque accounts, easy access to funds and so on.

5.15 The creation of Eurodeposits

Eurobanks are basically financial intermediaries whose function is channelling funds from a non-bank lender to a non-bank borrower. Between the deposit and the lending there may be a series of interbank transactions. To enhance our understanding of Eurocurrency markets we now examine, by means of a hypothetical example, how Eurocurrency deposits and loans are created.

We assume that a US multinational, SUPER Corp., starts off the process by transferring $50 million from its US bank account into a Eurodollar deposit account with EUROBANK A. EUROBANK A may not have an immediate use for these funds but EUROBANK B has a client, MINI Corp., which wishes to borrow $50 million. EUROBANK B is short of the necessary funds so it borrows the $50 million from EUROBANK A and then loans the funds to the ultimate borrower MINI Corp. A summary of these transactions is shown in **Figure 5.3**.

Figure 5.3   The creation of Eurobanking activity

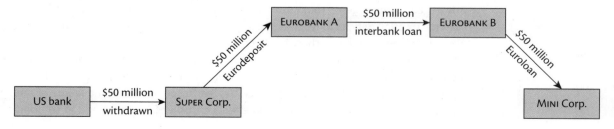

From these transactions we can see that what has basically occurred is that SUPER Corp. has switched a dollar deposit from a US bank to EUROBANK A. EUROBANK A has a new deposit liability to SUPER Corp., but also now holds increased funds which it can utilize for lending purposes. As far as the US banking system is concerned, the amount of deposits held by the non-bank public has fallen; however, these funds have been switched into the EUROBANKing arena. The transfer of funds from EUROBANK A to EUROBANK B constitutes an interbank transaction, the effect of which is to raise the total of Eurodollar deposits from $50 million to $100 million. We can now distinguish a difference between the effect on the net size of the Eurodollar market – the original $50 million deposit and the gross size of $100 million which includes the interbank transaction. With the loan to MINI Corp, the funds that were initially deposited by SUPER Corp have been given an ultimate use.

The Eurobanks are in effect acting as financial intermediaries ensuring that surplus funds from one organization (SUPER Corp.) are transferred to other organizations with borrowing requirements (MINI Corp.). When MINI Corp. starts to spend money, then the dollars have ultimately been derived from the US banking system not from the Eurobanks. Only the US banking system creates dollars, the Eurobanks create deposits which are not a means of payment. Eurobanks are essentially financial intermediaries, they accept deposits and then loan out these funds.

The real question which now arises is what MINI Corp. does with its borrowed funds. If it were to just redeposit them with another Eurobank then the whole process could be restarted. However, this is most unlikely to be the case. It is more likely that MINI Corp. will use the funds to pay various bills and will redeposit only a small fraction of its $50 million (for example, $1 million to $5 million) which will eventually end up back in the Eurobanking system to be used to create further credit.

This is a highly simplified example of the way the Eurobanking system creates credit, but there are some obvious limits to the amount of credit that can be created. In the first instance, EUROBANK A and EUROBANK B are unlikely to lend out instantly all the deposits they receive, and then MINI Corp. is likely to redeposit only a fraction of its money with the Eurobanking system. Most of the money received by MINI Corp. is likely to be re-injected into the American economy and thereby returned to the US banking system, from which there may be some further leakage back to the Eurocurrency markets.

5.16 The pros and cons of the Eurocurrency markets

There is no doubt that the Eurocurrency markets have increased the range of facilities available to both borrowers and lenders, and in addition they do so at very competitive rates of interest. They have not only facilitated financial transfers between private economic agents, but also between countries, enabling them to finance current account deficits with somewhat greater ease than before the Euromarkets existed. On the other hand, there has been much concern that Eurobanking activity is a ticking time-bomb underneath the world financial system. The fact that Eurobanks are not regulated and do not have access to lender-of-last-resort facilities, combined with the high degree of interbank activity, has led to concerns that the failure of one Eurobank would have serious knock-on effects on other Eurobanks and in so doing endanger the entire international financial system. Some authors have argued that Eurobanks and speculators with Eurobalances have used these masses of funds to mount speculative attacks on currencies and have increased currency volatility in general.

5.17 Syndicated loans

syndicated loan
a loan from a syndicate of banks/lenders to a single borrower

A syndicated loan is one of the most important forms of bank lending. It is a loan made by a syndicate of banks to a single borrower. The vast majority of such loans are made at a floating rate of interest based on a spread over LIBOR with the rate adjusted once every six to twelve months to reflect changes in LIBOR. Syndicated loans are usually for periods of three to eight years. Their main advantage is the opportunity for a bank to participate in a number of such loans allowing it to loan out large sums of money and diversify its loan book at relatively low cost. For borrowers, the main advantage of syndicated loans is that they can obtain larger sums of money than is possible from a single lender. The syndicated loans market used to attract multinationals and developing country governments. These days many multinationals prefer to raise money directly themselves from the Eurobond market, but their place has been taken up to some extent by Eastern European governments that have become significant borrowers. The market is extremely competitive and the profits generated by syndicated loans are generally speaking quite low, but managing banks that arrange syndicated loans view them as a useful means of generating new clients for other activities. **Table 5.2** shows the top ten arrangers of syndicated loans in the first half of 2009.

5.18 Euronotes

Euronote a short-term promissory note issued by a high quality corporate, financial or sovereign borrower

The Euronote market is basically a shorter-term borrowing market made up of three types of issue: note-issuing facilities, Eurocommercial paper and Euro medium-term notes.

Table 5.2   Global market syndicated loans, first half 2009

Bank	US$ million	Percentage share	Number of issues
JP Morgan	65,630	7.50	214
Mizuho	55,700	6.30	314
Bank of America Merrill Lynch	55,536	6.30	323
Mitsubishi UFJ Financial Group	49,788	5.70	444
Citi	49,274	5.60	157
Sumitomo Mitsui Banking Corp	48,889	5.60	336
BNP Paribas	34,188	3.90	216
Royal Bank of Scotland	28,198	3.30	163
Calyon	27,453	3.10	165
Barclays	24,863	2.80	124

Source: Dealogic

Note-issuing facilities (NIFs)

The original Euronotes were note-issuing facilities which are underwritten by syndicates of banks and which are medium-term. A NIF is essentially a guarantee by the syndicate for a predetermined length of time (usually 5–10 years) to underwrite a series of short-term bearer notes issued (usually every one, three or six months) by the borrower. If a borrower is unable to sell the notes at a given spread over LIBOR, then the syndicate of underwriting banks guarantees to purchase the issue. A NIF thus converts a series of short-term borrowing into a longer-term borrowing facility. The underwriting firms charge the borrower a fee for their underwriting services and, provided the notes are successfully placed, then the facility is treated as off-balance-sheet. NIFs were developed as an alternative to syndicated loans. Increased concern on the part of regulators about the obligations that NIFs might involve for the underwriting banks has led to pressure from central banks for banks with NIF commitments to raise their capital base, especially in instances where the borrower has a poor credit rating.

Eurocommercial paper

This is short-term borrowing, usually of less than nine months, that is not underwritten by syndicates of banks. Most Eurocommercial paper is credit-rated, and highly rated companies often find that Euronote issues enable them to borrow more cheaply than if they were to sell US commercial paper.

Euro medium-term notes (EMTNs)

These notes are issues above nine months and less than 10 years (although some issues are for longer periods). The medium-term note market has proved an increasingly popular means of raising finance for companies over the traditional bond market. This is because EMTNs are more flexible financial instruments due to the shorter maturity terms, and they have a relatively high degree of liquidity provided by the dealers in the instrument.

5.19 Conclusions

The growth of parallel money markets such as the Eurocurrency markets, certificates of deposit and the interbank market has made the process of monetary control more difficult for central banks, in stark contrast to the days when they themselves were the main source of liquidity for banks short of funds. Up to the early 1960s any shortage of liquidity by banks would have led to heavy calls for funds in the money market, and the central bank could then charge a high rate of interest in its capacity as lender of last resort. These days, if banks are short of funds they have alternatives other than the central bank, such as the interbank market and the Eurocurrency markets. The diminishing importance of the central bank is reflected in the fact that financial institutions increasingly use LIBOR as the key reference rate of interest rather than Treasury bill rates or central bank lending rates.

Nonetheless, central banks still maintain a high degree of influence over short-term interest rates through open-market operations. Indeed, if a central bank decides to create a general shortage of funds through large Treasury bill sales this is bound to eventually filter through to the other markets. The rates of interest in the Eurocurrency and offshore markets are ultimately linked to the domestic markets of the relevant Eurocurrency. For example, if the US Federal Reserve sells Treasury bills, short-term interest rates rise in the USA, and Eurobanks will find that they need to raise their Eurodollar interest rates in order to prevent a seepage of funds back to the US market. Conversely, if the US Federal Reserve conducts an expansionary open-market operation, it purchases Treasury bills, thus lowering the US interest rate and leading to a seepage of funds into the Euromarkets, and Eurobanks will find they are able to raise dollar funds at a lower cost, so lowering the Eurodollar rates.

Further reading

Buckle, M. and Thompson, J. (2004) *The UK Financial System: Theory and Practice*, 3rd edn, Manchester University Press.

Fabozzi, F., Mann, S. and Choudhury, M. (2002) *The Global Money Markets*, Wiley.

Miller, R. and Van Hoose, D. (2003) *Money Banking and Financial Markets*, 2nd edn, South Western College Publications.

Stigum, M. and Crescenzi A. (2007) *Stigum's Money Market*, 4th edn, McGraw Hill.

Chapter 5	Revision questions

1   Discuss the various methods by which a central bank might sell its Treasury bills to financial institutions and investors.

2   Explain what is meant by LIBOR and why it is such a pivotal rate of interest in the financial markets. Discuss the extent to which LIBOR will be affected by changes in dollar Treasury bill interest rates.

3   Explain what is meant by the TED spread. What does a rise in the TED spread signify on the interbank market?

4   Explain what is meant by a Eurodollar. Discuss the historical development of the Eurodollar market and the extent to which regulation played a role in its development.

5   Explain why Eurobanks based in London can offer more competitive deposit and loan rates on dollars than US-based banks.

6   Discuss the ways in which a Eurobank differs from a normal commercial bank.

7   Is Eurobanking activity a threat to the world financial system or does it provide much needed services?

6

THE DOMESTIC AND INTERNATIONAL BOND MARKET

Learning objectives

In this chapter you will learn about:

- the pricing of Treasury bonds and their relationship with long-term interest rates
- the meaning of yield to maturity
- bond price volatility and the meaning of duration
- the economic significance of the yield curve
- the role of credit rating agencies
- the difference between domestic, foreign and Eurobonds

6.1 Introduction

When lending funds the lender will want the principal to be returned (that is the original sum of money lent) and to receive interest, at a rate that is usually expressed as a percentage per annum of the principal loaned. Interest rates charged on loans reflect many factors, such as the length of the loan, the perceived risk attached to the borrower of funds, fundamental economic forces, the liquidity of the loan contact and expected inflation during the period of the loan. In this chapter we examine the fundamental forces that determine the price of bonds issued by governments, which in turn provides the benchmark for the cost of funds for corporations and other borrowers.

Government bonds are very important financial securities. They have a high degree of liquidity and transaction costs are much lower than for equities. In addition, settlement takes place the day after the transaction. Bonds are held by a variety of financial institutions including pension funds, insurance companies, banks and savings societies. Some financial institutions tend to invest in bonds for the whole life of the bond, especially pension funds and insurance companies, while others such as banks tend to on-sell much of their bond holdings prior to maturity in order to meet short-run liquidity demands. Government bonds are sometimes accorded special tax treatment to encourage investors to hold them.

6.2 Trading in government bonds

Trading in government bonds is usually restricted to certain licensed institutions, for example in the UK trading is carried out on the London Stock Exchange by authorized gilt edged market makers (GEMMs). The GEMMs buy and sell both new and existing government stock and have an obligation to provide continuous two-way prices (bid–offer) in government bonds. If GEMMS could only sell stock that they actually held this would severely restrict their ability to make a market. If they are short of bonds they can arrange to temporarily borrow bonds from institutional investors via the services of inter-dealer brokers, and conversely if they need funds to buy large amounts of bonds they can borrow funds from the brokers.

6.3 Determining the price of government bonds

A government bond provides a stream of income payments known as coupon payments (most coupon payments are twice yearly), and a payment upon the maturity of the bond that is equal to the face value of the bond. Government bonds have the advantage of being risk-free in the sense that the purchaser of the bond can be sure that the government will pay the coupon payments and maturity value. Ultimately the government could just print the money if it had to.

The basic principle underlying the price of any financial asset is that it should be determined by the present value of the asset's expected cash flow. By the expected cash flow we mean the expected stream of cash payments over the life of the asset. That is, assuming interest rates are known with certainty for periods 1, 2 . . . T to be $r_1, r_2 \ldots r_T$ respectively, the relevant formula for the price of a government bond is given by:

$$P_B = \frac{CF_1}{1 + r_1} + \frac{CF_2}{(1 + r_1)(1 + r_2)} + \ldots + \frac{CF_T}{(1 + r_1)(1 + r_2) \ldots (1 + r_T)} \qquad (6.1)$$

where P_B is the price of the security at time 0 with T periods to maturity; $CF_1, CF_2 \ldots CF_T$ are cash flows at the end of periods 1, 2 . . . T; $r_1, r_2 \ldots r_T$ are interest rates in periods 1, 2 . . . T.

In a more streamlined version of equation (6.1), splitting up the cash flows between coupon payments and principal repayment upon maturity produces the equation:

$$P_B = \sum_{t=1}^{T} \frac{C}{(1 + r)^t} + \frac{M}{(1 + r)^T} \qquad (6.2)$$

where M is the value of the bond upon maturity (all principal repaid only upon maturity); C is the annual coupon payment until maturity; t is the relevant time period 1, 2, 3 . . . T; and T is the time to maturity.

Each of the right-hand variables shows the present value of the relevant income streams. From equations (6.1) and (6.2) we can make the following observations about bond prices, other things being equal:

1 The bond price will be higher the greater the coupon payment attached to the bond.
2 The price of the bond will be higher the greater the maturity value of the bond.
3 The price of the bond will be more volatile with respect to a change in interest rates the longer the term to maturity of the bond.

Numerical example

Calculation of a bond price

Consider a five-year bond which has the following cash flows and assume interest rates are known and projected with certainty to be 7% ($r_1 = 0.07$) in year 1, 8% ($r_2 = 0.08$) in year 2, 9% ($r_3 = 0.09$) in year 3, 10% ($r_4 = 0.10$) in year 4, and 11% ($r_5 = 0.11$) in year 5.

Year	Coupon (C)	Principal (M)	Cash flow (CF)
1	7	0	7
2	7	0	7
3	7	0	7
4	7	0	7
5	7	100	107

$$P_B = \frac{7}{(1.07)} + \frac{7}{(1.07)(1.08)} + \frac{7}{(1.07)(1.08)(1.09)} +$$

$$\frac{7}{(1.07)(1.08)(1.09)(1.10)} + \frac{107}{(1.07)(1.08)(1.09)(1.10)(1.11)}$$

$P_B = \$92.78$

Effects of an interest rate rise

One interesting question is the appropriate price of the bond in the previous example if interest rates were to rise by 3 per cent for all years, that is:

$$r_1 = 0.10, \quad r_2 = 0.11, \quad r_3 = 0.12, \quad r_4 = 0.13, \quad r_5 = 0.14$$

$$P_B = \frac{7}{(1.10)} + \frac{7}{(1.10)(1.11)} + \frac{7}{(1.10)(1.11)(1.12)} +$$

$$\frac{7}{(1.10)(1.11)(1.12)(1.13)} + \frac{107}{(1.10)(1.11)(1.12)(1.13)(1.14)}$$

$P_B = \$82.48$

The effect of higher interest rates is to lower the price of the bond.

6.4 Clean and dirty bond prices

Since February 1986, the price quoted in the UK bond market is the clean price of the bond; that is, the price excluding accrued interest. The actual price paid for a bond in the market is known as the dirty price (or full price). The dirty price is the clean price plus the total accrued interest to which the bond holder would be entitled for holding the bond between coupon payments. The dirty price thus compensates the bond holder for holding the bond since the last coupon receipt. It increasingly exceeds the clean price as the next coupon payment becomes due. The day that the coupon payment is made means that the dirty price needs no premium over the clean price and the two prices coincide. The clean price is the most commonly used benchmark price for the calculation of yields.

6.5 The current yield

The most basic measure of the yield is the current yield, which is simply the coupon payment over the current price of the bond:

$$Y_C = \frac{C}{P_B} \times 100 \tag{6.3}$$

where Y_C is the current yield; C is the coupon payment; and P_B is the current clean price of the bond.

For example, consider a bond with an annual coupon payment of \$7 with a current market price of \$92.78. From equation (6.3):

$$Y_C = \frac{7}{92.78} \times 100 = 7.54\%$$

The current yield measure is only a very imprecise measure of the actual yield on a bond, since it takes no account of the potential capital gains or losses resulting from the difference between the current market price of the bond and its value upon maturity. Consequently, the current yield is a useful measure only if the bond has a long term to maturity, which has the effect of reducing the capital gain/loss element.

6.6   The simple yield to maturity

The simple yield to maturity takes into account capital gains and losses assuming that the capital gain or loss on a bond occurs evenly over the remaining life of the bond. The formula is given by:

$$Y_S = \left[\frac{C}{P_B} + \frac{(100 - P_B)/T}{P_B}\right] \times 100 \qquad (6.4)$$

where Y_S is the simple yield to maturity; C is the coupon payment; P_B is the current clean price of the bond; and T is the number of years to maturity.

Consider the same bond as in the current yield example, that is, paying a coupon of $7 per annum with 5 years until maturity:

$$Y_S = \left[\frac{7}{92.78} + \frac{(100 - 92.78)/5}{92.78}\right] \times 100 = 9.10\%$$

The second expression in the brackets, i.e. $[((100 - 92.78)/5)/92.78] \times 100 = 1.56\%$, gives an approximation to the annual capital gain from holding the bond to the bond holder. That is the bond holder will make 7.54% per annum from the coupon payment and 1.56% per year from a capital gain, given that the bond holder that invests $92.78 today will receive $100 when the bond matures in 5 years' time. So the total return per year is $7.54\% + 1.56\% = 9.10\%$.

The main problem with the simple yield to maturity measure is that it does not take into account the fact that coupon receipts can be reinvested and hence further interest gained. A measure which takes this factor into consideration is known as the yield to maturity measure.

6.7   Yield to maturity

An investor wishes to compare the rates of return on different government bonds which are all risk-free but have different coupon payments, different lengths to maturity and different current prices. The most commonly used measure for such comparisons is the yield to maturity. The yield to maturity measure (or bond equivalent yield or redemption yield) takes into account the cash flows, the bond's term to maturity and the potential capital gain or loss of holding the bond to maturity. In addition, unlike the simple yield to maturity measure it takes into account the fact that coupon payments that are received can be reinvested to earn additional interest.

yield to maturity (YTM) the rate of return on a bond expressed as a percentage per annum if it is held till maturity; the YTM takes account of all coupon payments and any prospective capital gains/losses as well as the term to maturity and assumes that future coupon payments can be reinvested at the YTM

The yield to maturity (y) is calculated as follows:

$$P_B = \frac{C}{(1+y)} + \frac{C}{(1+y)^2} + \frac{C}{(1+y)^3} + \cdots + \frac{C}{(1+y)^T} + \frac{M}{(1+y)^T} \qquad (6.5)$$

where P_B is the current (dirty) price of the bond; C is the coupon payment on the bond; M is the maturity value of the bond; y is the yield to maturity; and T is the number of years to maturity.

Equation (6.5) simplifies to:

$$P_B = \sum_{t=1}^{T} \frac{C}{(1+y)^t} + \frac{M}{(1+y)^T} \qquad (6.6)$$

The yield to maturity y is calculated by iteration; it is the average discount applied to the cash flows on the bond over the remaining life of the bond. The formula assumes that all coupon payments received are immediately reinvested in the bond.

Consider the example of a bond with an annual coupon payment of $7, a current market price of $92.78, a value at maturity of $100, with five full years to maturity. For simplicity, assume that the clean price and dirty price are the same since a coupon payment has just been made. The cash flows associated with the bond are 7, 7, 7, 7, 107. Thus, from equation (6.5):

$$92.78 = \frac{7}{(1+y)} + \frac{7}{(1+y)^2} + \frac{7}{(1+y)^3} + \frac{7}{(1+y)^4} + \frac{7}{(1+y)^5} + \frac{100}{(1+y)^5}$$

The relevant y is (0.088489 or 8.8489%). It can be calculated by using interpolation or more easily by using the YIELD function supplied with spreadsheets such as EXCEL. In other words, the cash flows on the bond represent an average return of 8.8489% over the remaining life of the bond on the $92.78 invested, assuming the bond is held to maturity and coupon payments are reinvested at the yield to maturity. The investor could invest the $92.78 at 8.8489% for five years and it would become with accrued interest $92.78 × 1.088489^5 = $141.77.

This is identical to placing $92.78 in the bond and making a capital gain of $7.22 upon maturity plus investing the $7 coupon payment at the end of the first year which will become $7 × 1.088489 = $7.62 by the end of the second year. The investor is then entitled to a further $7 coupon payment giving a total $14.62 which would become $14.62 × 1.088489 = $15.91 by the end of the third year. The investor is then entitled to a further $7 coupon payment giving a total $22.91 which would become $22.91 × 1.088489 = $24.94 by the end of the fourth year, when the investor also receives a $7 coupon payment. In the final year he has $31.94 which would become $31.94 × 1.088489 = $34.77. Upon maturity he also gets a further $7 coupon payment. The total from coupon payments with reinvestment interest is $41.77. Hence, in total, the $92.78 bond investment increases by $7.22 + $41.77 to become $141.77.

6.8   The par value relation

A commonly used measure used in talking about bond prices is the par value relation; this is simply the ratio of the current bond price to its maturity value, that is P_B/M. If this ratio is unity then the bond is selling 'at par'; if the ratio is greater than unity the bond is selling at a 'premium'; while if the ratio is less than unity the bond is selling at a 'discount'.

6.9   Bond price volatility

Interest rates in the future are not known with certainty, which means that the future price of bonds is also uncertain. A rise in interest rates will lead to a fall in bond prices, while a fall in interest rates will lead to a rise in bond prices. However, the amount by which bond prices are affected by changes in interest rates will be affected by the time to maturity of the bond.

Consider **Table 6.1** which shows the value of a $100 bond with an initial 7% yield based upon a $7 coupon payment with three different times to maturity: 5 years, 10 years and 20 years. The table shows indices of the price of the bond in relation to an issue price index of 100. In our earlier numerical calculations the $7 coupon bond with 5 years to maturity had a yield to maturity of 8.8849% and so traded at $92.78, that is fairly close to the 9% yield price for a 5-year bond of $92.22 in **Table 6.1**. From the table we can see that a given interest rate change has a more significant effect on the price the longer the term to maturity of the bond.

The relationship between yield and the price of the bond is both negative and convex as depicted in **Figure 6.1**.

There are two factors that determine the price volatility of a bond: the coupon payments and the term to maturity. The lower the coupon payments for a given

Table 6.1   Bond prices for different yields to maturity

Yield	$7 coupon 5-year	$7 coupon 10-year	$7 coupon 20-year	Yield change in basis points
4.00	113.36	124.34	140.77	−300
4.50	110.97	119.78	132.52	−250
5.00	108.66	115.44	124.92	−200
5.50	106.41	111.31	117.93	−150
6.00	104.21	107.36	111.47	−100
6.50	102.08	103.59	105.51	−50
7.00	100.00	100.00	100.00	0
7.50	97.98	96.57	94.90	+50
8.00	96.01	93.29	90.18	+100
8.50	94.09	90.16	85.80	+150
9.00	92.22	87.16	81.74	+200
9.50	90.40	84.30	77.97	+250
10.00	88.63	81.57	74.46	+300

Figure 6.1   The convex relationship between bond prices and yield

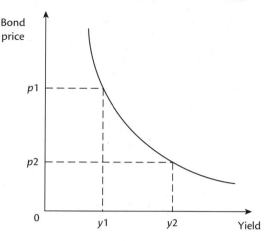

term to maturity the greater the volatility of price (measured by the percentage price change) in response to interest rate movements. With regard to the term to maturity, the greater the term to maturity with a given coupon payment the greater the price volatility.

6.10   Duration

Macaulay duration
the weighted-average term to maturity of the cash flows on a bond; the weight of each cash flow is determined by dividing the present value of the cash flow by the price of the bond

Portfolio managers and investors require a measure of bond price volatility to calculate the risk on their investments and to devise appropriate investment strategies. A commonly used measure of volatility is the so-called Macaulay duration, the formula for which is given by:

$$D = \frac{\dfrac{C \times 1}{(1+y)} + \dfrac{C \times 2}{(1+y)^2} + \dfrac{C \times 3}{(1+y)^3} + \ldots + \dfrac{C \times T}{(1+y)^T} + \dfrac{M \times T}{(1+y)^T}}{P_B} \qquad (6.7)$$

where D is the duration, C is the coupon payment on the bond; $C \times 1$ means coupon times 1, $C \times 2$ means coupon times 2 etc.; M is the maturity value of the bond; $M \times T$ is the maturity value of the bond times T; P_B is the price of the bond; y is the yield to maturity; and T is the number of years to maturity.

Note that this formula applies to a bond with a single annual coupon payment. In cases where the bond pays interest on a semi-annual basis, the Macaulay duration is adjusted to use semi-annual yield and coupon payments.

The Macaulay duration calculates a weighted average term to maturity of a bond with the cash flows calculated in terms of their present value rather than their nominal value. The larger the duration of a bond, the greater the sensitivity of the price of the bond to changes in its yield. The Macaulay duration has two important characteristics:

1   The Macaulay duration for a coupon bond is less than its term to maturity; and
2   The longer the term to maturity, the greater the Macaulay duration and price volatility.

Numerical example

Calculation of Macaulay duration for 5-year bond on issue

Assume that we have a newly issued 5-year bond with a coupon of $7 and a yield to maturity of 7%; so the bond is trading at its face value of $100:

$$C = \$7, \ y = 0.07, \ T = 5, \ P_B = 100, \ M = 100$$

t	C	$C/(1.07)^t$	$(C \times t)/(1.07)^t$
1	7	6.5421	6.5421
2	7	6.1141	12.2282
3	7	5.7141	17.1423
4	7	5.3403	21.3612
5	107	76.2895	381.4475
		$P_B = 100.0000$	438.7213

$$\text{The Macaulay duration} = \frac{438.7213}{100} = 4.3872$$

Assume that we have a bond with 5 years to maturity, a coupon of $7 and a yield to maturity of 8%, so the bond is trading at $96.01 (see **Table 6.1**).

$$C = \$7, \ y = 0.08, \ T = 5, \ P_B = 96.0073, \ M = 100$$

t	C	$C/(1.08)^t$	$(C \times t)/(1.08)^t$
1	7	6.4815	6.4815
2	7	6.0014	12.0028
3	7	5.5568	16.6704
4	7	5.1452	20.5808
5	107	72.8224	364.1120
		$P_B = 96.0073$	419.8475

$$\text{The Macaulay duration} = \frac{419.8475}{96.0073} = 4.3731$$

6.11 Modified duration

modified duration
a formula that measures the sensitivity of the price of a bond to changes in the rate of interest

To calculate the percentage change in a bond's price for a given change in yield, bond market participants use a measure known as the modified duration of the bond which is given by the formula:

$$\text{Modified duration} = \frac{\text{Macaulay duration}}{(1 + y)}$$

where y is the yield to maturity.

$$\text{Approximate change in bond value} = -\text{Modified duration} \times \text{Yield change in basis points}$$

Consider the $7 coupon 5-year bond selling at $96.01 with a current yield of 8%. The Macaulay duration is 4.3731. The modified duration is 4.3731/(1.08) = 4.0492.

Suppose that yields increase from 8.00% to 8.50%. The yield change is 0.50% so we would expect a price change of:

$$-4.0492 \times 0.5 = -2.0246\%$$

According to the modified duration measure the bond price can be expected to change from 96.01 to 94.10 (that is, 96.01/1.020246). From **Table 6.1** the actual price change is 94.09 and the actual percentage change is −2.03 per cent. Hence, for small changes in basis points the modified Macaulay duration measure gives a good approximation of the percentage price change. In effect, the modified duration measure gives the slope of the price–yield curve depicted in **Figure 6.1**. From this, we note that as yield increases then duration will decrease. If we take an initial yield y_1 and then take another yield y_2, the approximation of duration analysis will understate the actual price change. The accuracy of the approximation is best for small changes in yield and also depends on the degree of convexity of the price/yield relationship.

An alternative method of calculating the modified duration of a bond is:

$$\frac{\text{Price if yield is decreased} - \text{Price if yield is increased}}{\text{Initial price} \times (\text{Higher yield} - \text{Lower yield})}$$

The higher yield refers to the yield that is used to determine the price if the yield is increased. The lower yield is the yield used to determine the price if the yield is decreased.

For example, our 5-year bond with par value $100 and one $7 coupon payment per year is currently selling at $96.01 since the current yield is 8.00%. If the yield is increased by 50 basis points from 8.00% to 8.50% the price would be $94.09. Conversely, if the yield decreased from 8.00% to 7.50% then the price would rise to $97.98. This means that we have the following values:

Initial price = $96.01
If yield rises to 8.50%, price = $94.09
If yield falls to 7.50%, price = $97.98

The application of the above formula gives a duration of:

$$\frac{\$97.98 - \$94.09}{\$96.01 \times (0.085 - 0.075)} = 4.05$$

The modified duration measure increases with three factors:

1 the term to maturity of the bond, see **Table 6.2**. This accords with the fact that longer-term bonds fluctuate more in price for a change in yield than shorter-term bonds.
2 the lower the coupon payment, see **Table 6.3**. As the coupon falls then more of the relative weight of the cash flows is transferred to the repayment of principal on the maturity of the bond, so raising the duration of the bond.
3 the lower the initial yield, see **Table 6.3**. As yield falls the present value of all future cash flows increases but that of the most distant cash flows rises more than those of the nearest cash flows. This increases the weight of the more distant cash flows and so raises duration.

Table 6.2   Modified duration of a £7 coupon bond with par value of £100 and initial yield of 8%

	Number of years to maturity		
	5	10	20
Price at 7.5%	97.98	96.57	94.90
Price at 8.0%	96.01	93.29	90.18
Price at 8.5%	94.09	90.16	85.80
Modified duration	4.05	6.88	10.09

Table 6.3   Modified duration of bonds of differing coupon payments and different yields

		Number of years to maturity		
Coupon	Yield	5	10	20
£7	5%	4.20	7.34	11.67
£7	7%	4.10	7.02	10.59
£7	9%	4.00	6.71	9.57
£10	5%	4.05	6.92	10.93
£10	7%	3.94	6.61	9.91
£10	9%	3.84	6.30	8.96

6.12   The duration for a portfolio of bonds

One of the great properties of duration is that we can use it to measure the approximate change in the value of the portfolio of bonds. To calculate the modified duration of the entire portfolio we simply take the weighted average of the modified duration of the various bonds that make up the portfolio.

$$\text{Modified duration of portfolio} = D_p = \sum_{i=1}^{N} w_i D_i$$

where D_p is the modified duration of the portfolio
         D_i is the modified duration of the individual bond
         w_i is the weight of the individual bonds in the portfolio
         N is the number of bonds in the portfolio

Example

A bond fund manager has a $100 million bond portfolio invested 30% in 5 year bonds with a modified duration of 4 years, 25% invested in 10 year bonds with a modified duration of 7 years and 45% in 20 year bonds with a modified duration of 11 years. The yield curve is currently flat at 8% across all maturities (5 year, 10 year and 20 year). The bond manager believes that interest rates are likely to fall by 50 basis points to 7.5% and wishes to calculate the likely rise in the value of the bond portfolio.

The first step is to calculate the modified duration for the bond portfolio. In this case:

$$D_p = 0.3(4) + 0.25(7) + 0.45(11) = 7.9$$

As a result of the fall in bond yields of 50 basis points across the entire range you would expect the bond portfolio to rise in price by:

$$7.9(0.5) = 3.95\%$$

Hence if interest rates fall to 7.5% then the bond portfolio should be valued at approximately $103,950,000.

6.13 A formula to calculate duration

So far we have had to perform a number of discounting calculations in order to find duration. There is, however, a formula that can be used to directly calculate duration. This is given by equation (6.8):

$$D = \frac{1+y}{y} - \frac{(1+y) + T(c-y)}{c[(1+y)^T - 1] + y} \tag{6.8}$$

where y is the bond yield; c is the annual coupon yield on issue and T is the number of periods left on the bond.

Numerical calculation

Assume that we have a bond with 5 years to maturity, a coupon of $7 and a yield to maturity of 8%, so the bond is trading at $96.01.

$$D = \frac{1.08}{0.08} - \frac{1.08 + 5(0.07 - 0.08)}{0.07[(1.08)^5 - 1] + 0.08}$$

$$= 13.5 - \frac{1.03}{0.1128}$$

$$= 13.5 - 9.13$$

$$= 4.37$$

6.14 Duration and the problem of curvature of the bond–price relationship

The measure of duration that we have been using is in fact only an approximate measure of the degree to which the bond price will change and is valid only for small changes in interest rates of around 100 basis points. The problem is that the measure of duration will become increasingly imprecise as a guide to the actual price change of a bond as the change in yield becomes increasingly large. The problem is depicted in **Figure 6.2**.

The problem lies in the fact that the measure of duration we have been using is only a linear approximation. This approximation will become increasingly inaccurate

Figure 6.2   Duration and the problem of curvature

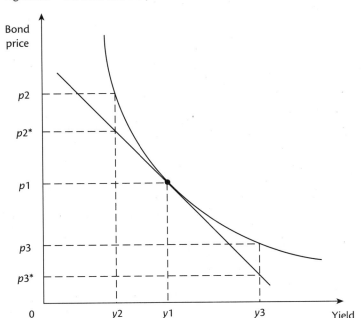

as a predictor of bond price changes as we increase the size of the yield change in basis points. The true price–yield relationship is given by the curved line. Hence, if yields fall from y1 to y2 the linear approximation suggests the bond price should rise to P2* whereas the true price rise will be to P2. Conversely, if yields rise from y1 to y3 the linear approximation suggests the bond price should fall to P3* whereas the true price fall will be to P3. Hence the linear measure of duration will under-predict a price rise in bonds and over-predict a price fall in bonds. In practice, we have more complicated formulas to correct for the problem of curvature.

6.15   The usefulness of the duration measure

Duration has its limitations and only serves as an approximate measure of bond price volatility requiring correction for curvature in the price–yield relation. Nonetheless, duration is extensively used by dealers and investment managers. It is especially useful for bond portfolio management since the duration measure can be combined across an entire portfolio. Since, as we have seen, the duration of a portfolio is equal to the market value weighted average of the duration of bonds in a portfolio, investment managers use duration analysis to measure interest rate risk and can adjust the duration of their portfolio to increase expected returns from anticipated changes in interest rates. For example, if interest rates are expected to rise, that is, bond prices are expected to fall, then an investment manager may try to decrease the duration of his portfolio so that the impact of any bond price falls will be limited. Conversely, if interest rates are expected to fall and bond prices rise, it will pay to be in long-term bonds which will rise proportionately more in price than short-term bonds.

Table 6.4   The yield curve, coupon payments and bond prices

Term to maturity	Yield to maturity	Coupon	Bond price
0.5	6.00	£0.00	97.11
1	6.30	£0.00	92.19
2	6.60	£6.00	99.91
3	7.00	£6.50	98.69
4	7.50	£6.50	96.65
5	7.60	£7.00	97.68
6	7.70	£7.00	96.73
7	7.90	£7.50	97.91
8	8.00	£8.00	100.00
9	8.20	£8.00	98.76
10	8.30	£7.50	94.70
11	8.60	£8.00	95.84
12	8.80	£8.50	97.83
13	9.00	£9.00	100.00
14	9.30	£9.50	101.53
15	9.50	£9.00	96.09
16	9.70	£9.50	98.41
17	9.80	£9.00	93.50
18	9.90	£8.50	88.44
19	9.90	£8.00	84.00
20	10.00	£7.00	74.46

6.16   Yield curves

The yield curve plots the term to maturity and the relevant yields. **Table 6.4** shows the relevant coupon payments and prices of bonds for a hypothetical yield curve given by the first two columns.

Having considered how to calculate yields and measure bond prices volatility we can now look at different types of bond other than Treasury bonds.

6.17   Corporate bonds

corporate bond
a bond issued by a company to investors, with the yield depending in part on the credit rating of the company

Corporate bonds are issued by corporations that wish to raise funds for various purposes. Corporate bonds come in many forms, such as medium-term notes and high-yield bonds commonly referred to as junk bonds. A typical corporate bond issue is usually of a substantial size and issues of $50–$300 million are commonplace. Most corporate bond issues promise to pay the holders a specified coupon payment at designated dates and then pay the face value of the bond upon maturity. Most corporate bond issues are for periods of 10 to 20 years, but there are some issues of 10 years or less that are referred to as medium-term notes. Some corporate bonds, known as serial bonds, pay both interest and part of the principal on a specified date.

| Box 6.1 | PIMCO – one of the world's largest bond funds |

Pacific Investment Management Corporation, PIMCO, was founded in Newport, California in 1971. It is one of the largest fixed income managers in the world with some $841 billion under management at 30 June 2009. It has offices around the world: Hong Kong, New York, London, Sydney, Tokyo. In 2000 PIMCO was acquired by the German financial services company, Alliance SE, for $3.3 billion. PIMCO employs over 1,200 people. Its fund deals with a wide range of clients including corporate and public pension funds, corporate treasury departments, foundations, financial intermediaries, sovereign wealth funds and high net worth individuals. It also deals with the huge variety of debt and related instruments such as interest rate swaps, mortgage backed securities (MBS), corporate bonds, commercial bills, emerging market bonds, real estate investment trusts, Treasury bonds and bills, global bonds, municipal bonds, high yield corporate bonds, collateralized debt obligations and credit default swaps. PIMCO has also been at the forefront of financial innovations with the creation of its PIMCO ETFs based upon movements in a variety of debt instruments.

The PIMCO investment fund tends to take a 3- to 5-year time investment horizon and it spends a lot of time thinking about the direction of short- and long-term interest rates and volatility in the bond markets. PIMCO's managing director is Bill Gross and dubbed by *Fortune* magazine the 'King of Bonds'. He manages the world's largest bond fund – the PIMCO Total Return Fund (ticker PTTRX) – which in December 2009 had $200 billion of assets, and has been among the top two performing bond funds in the last 10 years. Bill Gross' analysis and pronouncements on the bond market and prospective yield curve movements are carefully listened to by market participants around the world. More information on PIMCO, including much useful material in their education centre, can be found at www.pimco.com.

6.18 Credit ratings

The vast majority of corporate bond issues are undertaken by financial and non-financial corporations and attract investors such as insurance companies, pension funds, foreign investors and investment funds. Investors rely heavily upon the credit rating of the corporation when deciding whether or not to subscribe to an issue. In addition, domestic bonds are often secured against company assets (such as property, equipment or shares in subsidiaries) giving bond holders the legal right to sell company assets in instances of default by the issuer. Bond issues which are secured by a specific pledge against company assets are known as debenture bonds. Another type of corporate bond is a subordinated debenture bond which is a general claim on the assets of the company after the secured and debenture holders' claims have been met.

Often corporate bond issues have a call provision that permits the issuer to buy back part or all of the issue prior to maturity. A call provision is usually included

call provision
a clause giving the issuer of a security the right to redeem the security prior to maturity

because it gives the issuer the option to take advantage of a fall in interest rates by buying back the issue and undertaking a new issue at the lower rate of interest. If a corporate bond holder wishes to exercise a call provision, that is to redeem all or part of a bond issue, it usually has to pay a premium to the face value of the bond. The premium payable declines with the number of years the bond has been on the market. After a certain number of years the premium can vanish entirely. In instances where the bond issuer wishes to redeem only part of the issue, this is done either on a pro rata or random basis (using bond serial numbers) according to the provisions of the bond indenture.

Credit rating analysis is undertaken by companies such as Moody's Investors service and Standard & Poor's and other agencies. Credit rating agencies keep a careful watch on companies' balance sheets, cash flows and activities and sell these ratings to subscribers to their services. A high-grade company is one that is deemed to have a low credit risk, that is, a high probability of future repayment; whereas a low-grade company has a high credit risk compared to high-grade companies. The credit ratings attached to companies are vital in determining the rate of interest they will be expected to pay on their bond issues. The two major measures used are Standard & Poor's and Moody's.

Table 6.5 shows the credit rating system used by the two agencies. **Table 6.6** shows the corporate bond long-term yield averages for the period 1980–2004. As can be seen, a change from a AAA rating to a AA rating appears to add around 32 basis points to borrowing costs, a change from a AA to a A rating appears to add a further

Table 6.5   Credit rating systems on corporate debt

Moody's grade	Moody's	Standard & Poor's	Standard & Poor's grade
Best quality	Aaa	AAA	Highest rating
High quality	Aa	AA	Slightly below highest
Upper medium	A	A	Strong
Medium grade	Baa	BBB	Adequate protection
Speculative elements	Ba	BB	Potential vulnerability
Speculative	B	B	Greater vulnerability
Poor	Caa	CCC	Identifiable vulnerability
–	–	CC	Highly vulnerable
Highly speculative	Ca	C	Bankruptcy filed
Extremely poor	C	D	In payment default

Notes:
(a) Above the line are rated investment grade. Below the line are rated below investment grade.
(b) The table tries to show the comparable grade between the two systems, but can only be regarded as roughly comparable since the two agencies use their own separate methodologies to assess risk.
(c) Standard & Poor's ratings from AA to CCC may be modified by the addition of a plus (+) or minus (−) sign to show the relative standing within the major categories, while Moody's uses a 1, 2, 3 modifier.
(d) The verbal grades assigned in the above table are only illustrative of the actual meaning of the grade. More details are obtainable from the two agencies.

Table 6.6 Moody's corporate bond yield averages (long-term bonds), annual averages 1980–2008

Year	Aaa	Aa	A	Baa	Average
1980	11.9	12.5	12.9	13.7	12.7
1981	14.2	14.7	15.3	16.0	15.1
1982	13.8	14.4	15.4	16.1	14.9
1983	12.0	12.4	13.1	13.6	12.8
1984	12.7	13.3	13.7	14.2	13.5
1985	11.4	11.8	12.3	12.7	12.0
1986	9.0	9.5	9.9	10.4	9.7
1987	9.4	9.7	10.0	10.6	9.9
1988	9.7	9.9	10.2	10.8	10.2
1989	9.3	9.5	9.7	10.2	9.7
1990	9.3	9.6	9.8	10.4	9.8
1991	8.8	9.1	9.3	9.8	9.2
1992	8.1	8.5	8.6	9.0	8.5
1993	7.2	7.4	7.6	7.9	7.5
1994	8.0	8.1	8.3	8.6	8.3
1995	7.6	7.7	7.8	8.2	7.8
1996	7.4	7.5	7.7	8.1	7.7
1997	7.3	7.5	7.5	7.9	7.5
1998	6.5	6.8	6.9	7.2	6.9
1999	7.0	7.3	7.5	7.9	7.4
2000	7.6	7.8	8.1	8.4	8.0
2001	7.1	7.3	7.7	8.0	7.6
2002	6.5	6.9	7.2	7.8	7.1
2003	5.7	6.1	6.4	6.8	6.2
2004	5.4	5.8	6.0	6.3	5.9
2005	5.2	5.4	5.6	6.1	5.6
2006	5.6	6.0	6.2	6.5	6.1
2007	5.6	5.9	6.1	6.5	6.0
2008	5.6	6.2	6.7	7.4	6.5
Average	8.45	8.47	9.09	9.55	8.97

Source: Moody's

Table 6.7   Bond ratings and average yield spreads versus Treasuries

Rating	Spread
AAA	0.20%
AA	0.50%
A+	0.80%
A	1.00%
A–	1.25%
BBB	1.50%
BB	2.00%
B+	2.50%
B	3.25%
B–	4.25%
CCC	5.00%
CC	6.00%

Source: *Bond Buyer*

32 basis points to borrowing costs, while a move from A to BBB appears to add a further 46 basis points to borrowing costs. **Table 6.7** paints a fairly similar picture from a separate source but compares spreads of different bonds versus US Treasuries and also shows bonds with lower credit ratings.

Table 6.8 shows the actual default rates within the first year of issue and at the 10-year horizon on different grades of bonds during the period 1983–2006. For Aaa rated companies there were no cases of default in the first year of issue, while Ba rated companies had a default rate of 1.201% in the first year, and for B rated companies the default rate was as high as 5.334% in the first year of issue. Over the full 10-year investment horizon a mere 0.526% of Aaa rated companies defaulted, while 18.924% of Ba rated companies defaulted and for B rated companies the default rate was a high 43.696%.

quality spread the extra yield payable by a lower-rated issuer than a higher-rated issuer, other things being equal

flight to quality a term used to describe a situation in which investors decide to sell risky securities and use the proceeds to buy what are regarded as safer securities

The poorer a company's credit rating the more interest on average that a corporation will have to pay to sell its bonds. This reflects the fact that investors in corporate bonds face credit risk which is deemed to increase as the grading of the company diminishes. The difference in the yield between two issues that are identical in all respects except for the quality rating of the companies is known as the quality spread. The quality spread tends to vary with the business cycle. In times of recession there is an increase in the spread between high- and low-grade bonds which declines during economic recovery. The explanation is that, in times of recession, there is a perception that the lower-grade companies are even more likely to default compared to high-grade companies that are better equipped to survive. This results in a flight to quality and an increased spread. Conversely, in times of economic recovery there is the perception that all companies are much less likely to default but especially so for lower-grade companies. This results in a shift towards lower-grade companies and a consequent narrowing of the quality spread.

Table 6.8   Issuer weighted cumulative default rates for differently rated corporate and sovereign bonds for the period 1983–2006

Corporate issuers			
Grade of bond	Default rate 1 year horizon	Default rate 5 year horizon	Default rate 10 year horizon
Aaa	0.000%	0.101%	0.526%
Aa	0.008%	0.178%	0.524%
A	0.021%	0.474%	1.293%
Baa	0.177%	1.908%	4.613%
Ba	1.201%	10.149%	18.924%
B	5.334%	27.022%	43.696%
Caa–C	19.347%	52.596%	70.126%

Sovereign issuers			
Grade of bond	Default rate 1 year horizon	Default rate 5 year horizon	Default rate 10 year horizon
Aaa	0.000%	0.000%	0.000%
Aa	0.000%	0.000%	0.000%
A	0.000%	0.000%	0.000%
Baa	0.000%	3.018%	3.903%
Ba	1.302%	10.285%	23.690%
B	4.264%	13.934%	27.748%
Caa–C	22.901%	34.731%	n.a.

Notes: Historically sovereign ratings are more stable than their corporate counterparts. Sovereign default rates have been lower than their corporate counterparts with the differences widening at lower ratings and at longer-term horizons. The differences in default rates, however, are unlikely to be significant because default risk is highly correlated across emerging market sovereigns and the overall size of the sovereign sample is small.

Source: Moody's

6.19   Risks associated with corporate bonds

Investors in corporate bonds face a number of risks. Apart from the usual interest rate risk, reinvestment risk and inflation risk associated with Treasury bonds, there are a number of other risks associated with corporate bond issues. The most obvious is credit risk, that is the bond issuer may default on its debt-servicing obligations. Another is call risk, that is, the risk that a fall in interest rates will make it worthwhile for the bond issuer to exercise a call provision. If interest rates decline and a bond has a call provision then the price of the bond will tend to get closer to the call price; the more the interest rate falls the more likely it is that the issuer will redeem the issue at the call price. This means that a bond issued with call provision will not rise in price by as much as a similar bond issue that does not have a call provision. A final risk associated with corporate bond issues is known as event risk. This is the risk that some dramatic unexpected event will occur that will undermine the ability of the issuer to service the debt. Such events may be a major accident involving the company or a change in the regulatory environment that undermines the company's business. Alternatively, event risk may be caused by a debt-financed takeover by the firm. If a firm finances the takeover of another firm by issuing new debt this can potentially undermine the credit rating of the company and expose bond holders to more risk of default than they had anticipated. Other event risks involve the possibility of fraud or serious mismanagement.

6.20 Financial innovation and corporate bonds

The very first corporate bond issues were of a relatively simple nature, the bonds had a fixed coupon payment and a fixed maturity date. However, since the 1970s there have been numerous innovations in bond issues. In part, these innovations were required to meet the demands of both corporations and investors that were worried by the greater volatility of interest rates following the collapse of the Bretton Woods system of fixed exchange rates in 1971.

Convertible and exchangeable bonds

convertible bond a bond that can be converted into either shares or some other asset at some point

A convertible bond grants the bond holder and/or the issuer the right to convert the bond into a predetermined amount of ordinary stock of the issuing company. In effect, a convertible bond is a corporate bond with an option to convert the debt into equity of the company. An exchangeable bond grants the bond holder the right to convert the bond into a predetermined amount of ordinary stock of a specified company other than the issuing company. The amount of common stock that a bond holder can convert the bond into is determined by the conversion ratio which declines over the life of the bond.

One motive for a firm issuing a convertible bond is that it regards its stock valuation as too low and does not wish to raise a given amount of cash by a rights issue which would excessively dilute the equity interest of current stockholders. In such circumstances, it may decide to raise the money by a convertible bond sale so that if the price of its stock recovers it can then exercise its call option and convert the bonds into stock.

Bonds with warrants

warrant a medium- or long-term option attached to a bond that gives the holder the right to buy or sell a security at a given price; warrants can be detached from the bond and traded separately from the bond

A corporate bond may have a warrant attached to the offer. The warrant grants the bond holder the right to purchase a specified amount of a security at a predetermined price. In other words, a warrant is a call option that gives the bond holder the right to purchase ordinary shares in the issuing company or in a specified firm other than the issuer. A warrant may alternatively give the bond holder a right to purchase a debt obligation from the issuer at a predetermined price. The warrants can be detached and traded separately, in contrast to a convertible bond whereby the bond itself must be exchanged for equity.

Warrants are distinguished from most other types of options (see Chapter 14) in that they are longer-term, typically with expiry dates of five years or more, which contrasts with most options that have a life of less than one year. The attractiveness of adding a warrant to a bond from the issuer's viewpoint is that the possibility of a capital gain may mean that the firm is able to raise finance more cheaply than would otherwise be the case.

Putable bond

putable bond
a bond that allows the holder to force the company to repurchase the bond at par usually on certain fixed dates

A putable bond grants the bond holder the right to sell the bond back to the issuer at its par value on designated dates. The major advantage of this to the bond holder is that should interest rates rise, depressing the price of the bond, the bond holder will be able to exercise the right to sell back the bond to the issuer at its par value. This feature ensures that the bond will stay above its par value and the bondholder will have some degree of protection should the credit rating of the company deteriorate.

Floating rate notes

floating rate note
a bond (note) that has a variable coupon or rate of interest; for example, it may be expressed at 1% above $LIBOR and will fluctuate according to changes in $LIBOR

A floating rate note is simply a bond on which the coupon rate is reset periodically in line with some predetermined benchmark. For example, an AAA rated company might adjust its coupon rate every six months at a spread equal to 35 basis points above the corresponding six-month Treasury bill rate. Floating rate issues are particularly attractive to investors with liabilities that increase with rises in interest rates. In general, floating rate bonds tend to sell very close to their par value. If, however, the credit rating of the issuer declines such that the market would require a higher spread, then this is achieved by the bond selling at below par. Conversely, if the credit rating of the company improves then the bond may sell above its par value. Floating rate notes can prove a useful substitute to holding funds in short-term security instruments that have to be constantly 'rolled over' (that is, renewed) upon maturity, which involves time and resources. By contrast, holding a floating rate note means that the investor is holding an instrument that has its interest rate adjusted periodically and there are no rollover costs.

Floating rate securities can prove to be an attractive source of finance for corporations that wish to raise funds from investors rather than banks and use their credit rating to obtain relatively low-cost finance. In addition, the rate of interest payable is related to short-term interest rates, enabling the corporation to raise long-term finance at a cost related to short-term rather than long-term interest rates. This latter feature may prove especially attractive in periods of high inflation and uncertainty which may mean that long-term interest rates have a relatively high inflation premium. Many floating rate note issues have special features such as a put option, the possibility of convertibility after a specified time period (usually five years) into a fixed interest rate security, and minimum and maximum interest rate provisions.

6.21 Junk bonds

junk bond
a high-risk high-yield bond with a credit rating below BBB (Standard & Poor's) or Baa (Moody's)

A junk bond is a high-yield bond issued by a corporation that has a relatively low credit rating of less than BBB. In order to compensate investors for the higher risk of default the bonds have to be issued at significantly higher yields than other corporate bonds. The junk bond market was relatively small in the mid-1970s at roughly $15 billion; however, in the 1980s, it grew enormously with one US company, Drexel Burnham Lambert, dominating the market. The market was estimated to be worth some $200 billion by the end of the 1980s. However, following spectacular defaults on many of the issues and the collapse of Drexel Burnham Lambert the market has since declined dramatically.

The growth of the junk bond market enabled many firms to access capital at lower rates of interest than bank finance. Much of the growth of the junk bond market in the 1980s was merely a replacement for bank lending. Another attractive feature of the junk bond market is that some high-risk companies, especially those with relatively few assets, are able to gain access to funds that banks simply will not provide. In other cases, junk bonds enable companies to raise long-term funds in circumstances where banks would only be prepared to lend funds on a short-term basis. In some cases, the funds raised by junk bonds have been used to finance acquisitions, mergers, working capital and the retirement of debt from previous mergers and acquisitions.

One question that surrounds junk bonds which typically have spreads above Treasury bond interest rates of 300 to 700 basis points is whether the higher prospective yield represents a reasonable return for the risks associated with holding the bond. A default can involve the complete loss of capital invested in the bond, although holders of defaulted bonds frequently recover 30 per cent or more of the capital invested. The key question is whether holding a portfolio of junk bonds in which defaults can be expected provides a sufficient excess return above Treasury bonds to compensate for the additional risks involved. Academic studies have provided mixed results depending on the methodology employed, companies studied, time period considered and other factors. Drexel Burnham Lambert estimated that the annual default rate on junk bonds was 2.4 per cent, while other academic studies have put the annual default rate at 3–4 per cent. The studies seem to show that, while the total returns on junk bonds have exceeded those on Treasury bonds and good quality corporate bonds, the excess returns have been rather small and lower than the close substitute of investment in common stocks and shares.

6.22 Medium-term notes

Medium-term notes are corporate debt instruments that typically have less than 10 years to maturity. In fact, the vast majority of medium-term note issues have a term to maturity of 2 to 5 years. Most medium-term notes are issued at par and make specified payments to holders. The first medium-term notes were issued in 1981 by Merrill Lynch to fill a gap between commercial paper finance and long-term corporate bond finance. The annual US market for medium-term notes grew from less than $4 billion in 1982 to over $800 billion in 2009. Most are issued by companies with high credit ratings; however, recent financial innovations have opened up the market to lower-grade issuers via the use of guarantees by third parties. The yield offered on medium-term notes is determined by the yield on Treasury bonds of comparable maturity and the credit premium which is demanded by the market based upon the company's credit rating. Some medium-term note issues are at fixed rates of interest while others are made on a floating rate basis. While most involve the repayment of principal at the date of maturity, there are amortized issues which offer investors equal periodic payments of both principal and interest payments over the life of the loan.

6.23 The international capital market

Domestic bond
a bond issued in the domestic currency by a domestic entity

The international capital market is the market in which borrowers and lenders of funds from different countries are brought together to exchange funds. It is made up of three markets: the domestic bond market, the foreign bond market and the Eurobond market. A domestic bond is a bond issued in the currency of the country of issue by a domestic entity, for example a US dollar Treasury bond issued by the US Treasury or a dollar corporate bond issued by a US corporation in the USA. A foreign bond is a bond issued in the domestic currency of the country but by a foreign company – for example, a British company that issues a dollar bond in the US market. Foreign bonds have names symbolizing the country whose currency is being borrowed, such as Yankees for US dollar bonds, Bulldogs for sterling bonds, Samurais for yen bonds and Kangaroos for Australian dollar bonds. A Eurobond is a bond that is sold by a government, institution or company in a currency that is different from the country where the bond is issued. For example, a dollar bond sold in London is a dollar Eurobond and a sterling bond sold in Germany is a sterling Eurobond. In the following sections, we pay particular attention to the Eurobond markets.

foreign bond
a bond issued in the domestic currency of the country by a foreign entity

Eurobond
a bond that is sold by a domestic or foreign government, institution or company in a currency that is different from the country where the bond is issued

Since the early 1960s the international capital market has grown at an astonishing pace both in terms of the funds transferred and the volume of participants making use of the facilities offered. The development of various international capital markets has had important implications not only for the international monetary system but also for the development of domestic financial markets and the conduct of national macroeconomic policies. These days there is no need for securities markets to be restricted to national boundaries. Economic agents can raise funds in either the domestic or a foreign currency and in raising the funds at the cheapest possible cost they may seek the assistance of foreign financial institutions and foreign investors.

6.24 Motivations behind international capital flows

There are numerous participants in the international capital markets; these include national governments, local authorities, financial institutions such as banks, multinational firms, companies, and international institutions such as the International Monetary Fund, World Bank and European Investment Bank. Most industrialized countries participate both as lenders and borrowers of funds, while many developing countries use the markets almost exclusively for borrowing purposes. The various types of capital flows between economic agents of different countries are motivated by various factors which include:

1 A trade financing motive – much trade is financed by borrowing on international capital markets.

2 A borrowing/lending motive – many capital flows are simply motivated by the desire of savers to get the best possible return on their money, while borrowers are merely seeking to obtain the lowest possible interest rate. The Eurobond market is especially strong in this respect.

3 A speculative motive – much borrowing or lending is due to the taking of speculative positions based on profiting from prospective interest rate/exchange rate changes.

4 A hedging motive – some borrowing and lending is motivated by a desire to hedge positions, that is, to avoid losses resulting from prospective interest rate/ exchange rate changes.

5 A capital flight motive – many movements of capital are motivated by a desire to protect investors' funds from penal taxation, possible seizure by the domestic government, restrictions being imposed on convertibility or political risk.

6.25 The origins and development of the Eurobond market

The first Eurobond was issued in 1963 and since then the market has grown enormously, particularly during the 1980s. The Eurobond market dates back to the imposition of the Interest Equalization Tax by the US authorities on US citizens that held dollar bonds issued by foreign entities in the USA. The US authorities imposed the tax because of concern about the long-term outflow of capital on the US balance of payments. By reducing the attractiveness to US investors of investing in foreign bonds, the tax provided a stimulus for foreign entities to issue US dollar bonds outside of the USA. A further incentive for the development of Eurobond market was that the US authorities also imposed withholding taxes on foreign citizens that held US bonds and this meant that foreign citizens had a clear incentive to hold Eurobonds that could not be taxed by the US authorities. Although the IET was abolished in 1974 and withholding taxes removed in 1984, the Eurobond market continues to prosper because it generally means lower-cost finance for well known companies and imposes far less stringent regulatory and disclosure requirements on the corporate issuer. Also it allows for considerable financial innovation.

The Eurobond market growth in the 1980s was also stimulated by the fact that corporations found banks increasingly reluctant to lend funds due to problems stemming from the third world debt crisis. Furthermore, corporations with credit ratings often as good if not better than some of the banks increasingly deemed the rates of interest and security requirements of banks to be excessive. In addition, many corporations found banks were reluctant to lend at fixed rates of interest for the longer time horizons that corporations were interested in. A major advantage of a Eurobond issue over domestic and foreign bond issues is that the lower regulatory requirements enable borrowers to raise finance at lower rates than banks can offer. The Eurobond market has grown from its origins in the mid-1960s to such an extent that the value of outstanding Eurobonds issued significantly exceeds the issue of domestic corporate bonds.

witholding tax
a tax on investment income aimed specifically at non-residents (i.e. foreigners)

6.26 Typical features of a Eurobond

Dollar and Euro denominated Eurobonds are the most popular form of issue, as depicted in **Table 6.9**. The Euro has in recent years replaced the dollar as the most important currency of issue The main reason for this is that many corporations have been keen to attract savings from countries with high savings ratios, especially Japan and Germany, whose investors tend to be more keen to buy Eurobonds which are denominated in Euros due to dollar weakness.

Table 6.9   Characteristics of international bond issues

By currency		
	Rank	Amount outstanding ($ billions March 2009)
Euro	1	10,683.6
US dollar	2	8,569.5
Yen	3	682.8
Sterling	4	1,772.8
Swiss	5	322.1

By type of bond	
	Amount outstanding ($ billions March 2009)
Straight fixed rate	14,713.9
Floating rate notes	7,768.8
Equity-related*	386.7
Total	22,869.4

* Equity-related is made up of warrants and convertibles.

By issuer	
	Amount outstanding ($ billions March 2009)
Financial institutions	17,873.3
Governments	1,836.7
International organizations	662.7
Corporate issuers	2,496.7
Total	22,869.4

Source: Bank for International Settlements

Most Eurobond issues are undertaken by very highly rated issuers, with AAA and AA issuers accounting for approximately 75% of all issues. The market is used extensively by governments, international organizations such the World Bank, the European Investment Bank and multinational corporations. Some issuers use the market to raise funds in currencies they do not wish to ultimately hold but as part of a swap deal. The yield at which a borrower obtains funds will depend on market conditions and the credit rating of the issuer, with governments typically being able to raise funds at a lower cost than corporations with the same credit rating.

Eurobonds come in a variety of forms, and the most common type are known as straights which pay fixed rates of interest with repayment of principal upon maturity. Increasingly popular are floating rate notes which are Eurobonds on which the interest rate is adjusted every 3 to 6 months in line with changes in a key interest rate such as LIBOR. Floating rate issues are especially popular with banks since the floating rate of interest means that the capital value of the bond is largely unaffected

straight a bond with a fixed periodic coupon payment

floating rate note a bond (note) that has a variable coupon or rate of interest

by interest rate movement. A convertible bond issue gives the owner the right to convert the bond into ordinary shares in the issuing company at a predetermined price at some time in the future. Convertible bond issues usually pay a below market rate of interest with holders attracted by the potential gain on the possibility of a share price conversion. Some Eurobonds have a warrant attached that gives the holder the right to buy shares in the company at a predetermined price in the future. The warrants can be detached from the bond and traded separately.

The Eurobond market is primarily a medium-term borrowing market with the vast majority of issues (approximately 80 per cent) being for under 10 years, with many typically in the range 5–7 years. This contrasts with the domestic bond market which is generally speaking a longer-term market with most borrowing ranging from 10 to 30 years. Most Eurobonds are issued at fixed rates of interest and others are issued at floating rates of interest or are equity-related. Many issues are sold at short notice to take advantage of what are perceived to be favourable market conditions. **Table 6.10** summarizes the features of a typical dollar Eurobond issue.

Table 6.10   Features of a typical dollar Eurobond issue

Amount	$100 million - $2,000 million.
Issuers	Governments, international organizations, e.g. World Bank and European Investment Bank, banks/financial institutions and major corporations with AAA and AA credit ratings accounting for approximately 75% of all corporate issues.
Maturity	10 years or less. Most issues are in the 4–7 year range.
Principal	Typically repayable in full upon maturity ('bullet form'). Occasionally some issues have the principal repayable in stages over the life of the bond and sometimes the principal repayable linked to movements in a market index such as the Nikkei or S&P 500.
Coupon	Payable annually. Vast majority are 'straights', that is, at a fixed coupon. Approximately 30% of issues are at a variable coupon linked to a spread over LIBOR (or some other benchmark) known as floating rate notes.
Yield	Spread over US Treasury bonds depends on credit rating: AAA governments around 10–20 basis points AAA corporates around 20–40 basis points AA governments around 30–50 basis points AA corporates around 40–80 basis points A governments around 50–100 basis points A corporates around 80–110 basis points BBB around 120+ basis points The above margins are only indicative and can change significantly depending on market conditions and the date to maturity.
Security	Usually senior unsecured debt (i.e. high priority in case of closure of the business). In some instances, the bond is backed by letter of credit or other collateral such as outstanding company assets.
Form	Bearer form. Holder is deemed to be owner and the anonymity is one of the attractions to investors.
Tax status	The bonds are issued free of withholding taxes.
Listing	London or Luxembourg.
Denominations	$1000, $5000 or $10,000.
Special features	Many bonds have call back features typically after 5 years, some have warrants attached and others can be converted into equity at a predetermined price.

bearer form a bond that is not registered by the issuer; the bearer is taken to be the owner and entitled to the attached coupons

The bearer form of most Eurobond issues is a particular attraction for international investors that like to avoid open registration of their ownership. (Although they are legally obliged to reveal coupon earnings to their tax authorities, this may not always happen!) Another attraction of Eurobond issues for investors is that they are free of withholding taxes, and this means that investors can save on paperwork in trying to avoid double taxation on their interest income.

6.27 Control and regulation of the Eurobond market

Eurobonds are generally exempt from the rules and regulations that govern the issue of foreign bonds in the country; for example, the need to issue very detailed prospectuses and withholding taxes (taxes on non-residents which are deducted at source). However, Eurobond issues and trading do have to meet certain regulatory requirements, and a self-regulatory body known as the Association of International Bond Dealers sets rules and standards. Most Eurobonds are issued in bearer form which means that holders are able to avoid open registration of their ownership.

Despite the fact that the Eurobond market is by definition outside the legal jurisdiction of the country of the currency of issue, this does not mean that the national authorities of the currency in question are unable to exert significant influence on the Eurobond market. National governments have always exerted control on national capital markets for a number of reasons. The most important is that they are usually huge borrowers themselves, but they are also keen to encourage scarce domestic capital to be invested in domestic bond issues, and they are concerned about possible tax avoidance and excessive outflows of capital on the value of the currency. Governments still have a number of means of controlling the issue of Eurobonds in their national currencies. Firstly, most clearance of funds in Eurobonds is done through the clearing system of the domestic banking system of the currency in question, giving the central bank of that currency the ability to prohibit issues if it so wishes. Secondly, governments can exert pressure on both domestic investment banks and foreign investment banks not to participate in Eurobond issues with the implicit threat of losing government business and even ultimately their licence to operate in that country. The Swiss authorities have effectively controlled Eurobond issues in Swiss francs by requiring all Swiss franc issues to be done in Switzerland, and the Japanese have managed to exert strong control over Eurobond issues in yen.

The US authorities have generally had a concerned but tolerant attitude to the Eurobond market. The main concern has been that, because Eurobonds are issued in bearer form, the possibility of tax avoidance is high. Their other concern is to protect US investors from investment risk due to the looser regulatory and disclosure requirements. For these reasons, the US authorities prohibit the sale of Eurobonds by investment banks to US citizens with the Securities Exchange Commission requiring US investment banks to take measures "reasonably designed to preclude distribution or redistribution of the securities, within, or to nationals of, the United States." However, there is currently no law preventing US citizens purchasing Eurobonds on their own initiative although they would clearly be expected to reveal any coupon earnings in their tax declarations. The private placements rule 144A permits sophisticated US financial institutions to hold Eurobonds in their investment portfolio so long as they are held demonstrably for investment purposes.

6.28 The management of a Eurobond issue

A typical Eurobond issue is normally handled on behalf of a client by a lead or managing bank, the lead bank recruits other banks to form a syndicate which underwrites the issue and helps distribute it to clients.

A typical Eurobond issue involves talks between the borrower and the lead manager bank concerning the currency of issue, the amount and terms at which the borrower would like to raise funds. Once these talks are sufficiently advanced, the lead manager is appointed and where the deal involves a particularly large sum other co-managers may be appointed. The lead manager and co-managers together form the management group. The next stage involves appointing an underwriting syndicate of anything between 10 and 200 banks/securities houses to underwrite the issue so that the issuer is guaranteed the funds. The underwriting group, which includes the banks from the management group, also has the task of assisting in placing the issue with Eurobond investors. A final group, which comprises the management group and the underwriting syndicate plus other selected banks, forms the selling group whose task is to place the issue with Eurobond investors.

A typical Eurobond issue is partly placed with institutional investors and partly with private investors, with each sector usually accounting for around one-half of the value of the issue. A few weeks or sometimes days prior to the issue being placed on the market a 'red herring' prospectus is issued which sets out the likely features of the bond and is used by the selling group to canvass interest in the issue. In some cases the bond trades in a 'grey market,' which is a short-term forward market which gives prospective investors an opportunity to see the likely price of the issue and provide some confidence in it. On the basis of feedback from potential investors, the selling group will return to the issuer to 'fine tune' the issue adjusting its final terms to meet some of the prospective investors' demands. Once agreement is reached, the selling group will commit itself to buying the entire issue at a discount to the offer price and a final prospectus is printed and distributed to potential investors.

Competition between members of the selling group is fierce and it may well be the case that different investors are able to buy the bonds at different prices, often at a discount to the offer price in the prospectus. The lead manager is expected to ensure, using their own funds if necessary, an orderly primary and secondary market in the issue and failure to do so would adversely affect their reputation in the Eurobond market. Unlike domestic bond markets, the secondary market in Eurobonds is relatively 'thin' and most Eurobond investors tend to hold the issue right through to maturity. Nonetheless, for some of the very large issues with well known issuers, the secondary market can be reasonably active and Eurobond market-makers quote bid-offer prices. The bid-offer spread in the Eurobond market reflects the lower degree of liquidity and can typically range from 50 to 75 basis points, while for US Treasury bonds the spread because of the greater liquidity is typically less than 10 basis points.

Once an issue has been successfully placed the lead bank will usually act as a market-maker in the issue, ensuring that the issue has a secondary market. The lead bank and the syndicate charge the client for both managing, placing and underwriting the issue. On occasions, the syndicate will actually purchase part or all of the issue

Table 6.11   Top international bond lead managers 2008

Manager	Rank	Amount ($ billions)	Percentage share
Barclays Capital	1	368.8	8.3
JP Morgan	2	350.6	7.9
Deutsche Bank	3	252.9	5.7
Citi	4	250.6	5.7
RBS	5	217.2	4.9
Merrill Lynch	6	214.9	4.9
UBS	7	202.5	4.6
Goldman Sachs	8	187.0	4.2
Bank of America	9	182.8	4.1
Credit Suisse	10	180.2	4.1
Industry totals		4420.1	

Note: Fees fluctuate but are typically in the region of 0.2% to 0.3% of the funds raised.

Source: Dealogic

and then hopefully place it with clients at a higher price, thus making a profit. A typical fee structure involves 20 per cent of fees going to the management group, 20 per cent to the underwriting group and 60 per cent to the selling group. The fees and precise proportions between the groups are variable depending upon the complexity of the issue, the credit rating of the issuer, and how easy the issue is to place with investors. The total fee as a percentage of the value of the issue is usually in the range of 0.5 to 2 per cent with this again being dependent upon the complexity and degree of difficulty of placing the issue. The competition for Eurobond business is extremely fierce, particularly as banks are keen to appear highly placed in the Eurobond league tables, such as that shown in **Table 6.11**. In some Eurobond issues the management group may even confine all three tasks to itself so as to maximize its fee earnings.

6.29 Innovations in the Eurobond market

The first Eurobond issues were in the form of 'straights,' that is, borrowing at a fixed rate of interest. The Eurobond market has since developed so that many Eurobond issues have innovative features. These days a good proportion (around a quarter) of Eurobond issues are at floating rates of interest and are called floating rate notes. Another major innovation is that a higher percentage of Eurobond issues are in the Euro. Such bonds are attractive to international investors that wish to diversify away from the US dollar.

Other innovations include the issue of convertible Eurobonds whereby the investor has the right to convert the bond into shares in the company at a predetermined price. Some Eurobonds are issued with warrants attached which can be traded separately giving the holder the right to buy shares at a predetermined price. Many Eurobond issues also have a 'call back' feature which enables the issuer to buy back the issue should it wish to do so. This is a particularly useful feature if its cash flow turns out to be better than expected, or if interest rates decline sufficiently.

More recently, in some Eurobond issues the principal to be returned to the investor is linked to movements in a broad market index such as the Nikkei. An even more recent innovation is asset-backed Eurobonds; with these, illiquid assets such as the outstanding loans of a bank are sold in the form of a Eurobond promising to pay a given coupon based on the income from the outstanding loans. Such bonds can still have a AAA rating because the bond will typically be over-collateralized, that is, backed up by loans with a face value considerably higher than that of the bond, so even if allowance is made for default on some of the outstanding loans the Eurobond investor can expect to receive full payment.

In recent years, the Eurobond market has been opened up to governments from so-called emerging markets such as Argentina, Mexico, Venezuela, South Africa, China, Poland and South Korea. Some of the high-risk countries such as Argentina and Mexico were paying in 1996 as much as 500 to 600 basis points above the equivalent US Treasury bond rates; while other emerging countries such as China, Poland and South Africa can get away with borrowing at a spread of 150 basis points or less. In many ways the Eurobond market has the potential to provide a valuable source of funding for emerging-market governments, although such borrowers are of a higher risk than traditional Eurobond borrowers.

All of these innovative features, as well as the fact that interest is paid once a year and the lower liquidity of Eurobonds compared to Treasury bonds, make it quite difficult to compare the yields on Eurobonds with standard Treasury and corporate bonds. Nonetheless, a typical Eurobond offers a premium over the standard Treasury bond of between 30 to 150 basis points depending on the credit rating of the issuer. More importantly from the viewpoint of the issuer, the typical cost savings of a Eurobond issue compared to a domestic bond issue can range from 25 to 200 basis points.

6.30 Conclusions

Bonds come in a huge variety of different forms, varying in the credit rating of the issuer, the maturity of the issue, the liquidity of the secondary market, the currency of denomination, whether of a fixed or variable rate and in specific features. This makes comparing different bonds a complex issue. Nonetheless, the yield to maturity is a particularly useful measure, as is the modified Macaulay duration which captures the sensitivity of the price of a bond to changes in yield. The bond market is constantly evolving and innovating to meet the changing preferences of both borrowers and investors of funds. These days, with the abolition of exchange rate controls, the domestic capital market is in fierce competition with other markets such as the Eurobond market to attract scarce international capital. The Eurobond market has the advantage of lower regulatory requirements which reduce borrowing costs for issuers. Nonetheless, the domestic capital market still provides valuable access to longer-term corporate and government borrowing.

Further reading

Brown, P. (2006) *An Introduction to the Bond Markets*, Wiley.
Choudhry, M. (2006) *An Introduction to the Bond Market*, 3rd edn, Wiley.
Fabozzi, F. (2009) *Bond Markets, Analysis and Strategies*, Pearson.

Chapter 6	Revision questions

1   Explain the difference between a domestic bond, foreign bond and a Eurobond giving examples of each.

2   A Treasury bond with £100 maturity value has a £7 annual coupon and 10 years left to maturity.

   (i)   What price will the bond sell for assuming that the 10 year yield to maturity in the market is 4%, 7% and 10% respectively? (Show your calculations.)

   (ii)   What would be your answer to part (i) if the bond only had 8 years to maturity?

   (iii)   What would be your answer to part (i) if the bond had only 4 years to maturity?

   (iv)   What does your answer to parts (i) to (iii) tell you about the relationship of bond prices, term to maturity and changes in bond yields?

3   Currently the yields to maturity on 10 year bonds are as follows:

Bond type	Yield to maturity
Treasury	5.00%
AAA corporates	6.00%
BBB corporates	8.00%

You are a bond manager and currently have 33% of your portfolio in Treasuries, 33% in AAA corporates and 34% in BBB corporates. Your analysis of 'normal' yield spreads suggest that AAA bonds should offer about 150 basis points above Treasuries and BBB bonds should offer about 250 basis points over Treasuries.

   How will you adjust your portfolio and what does this involve you in doing? Suggest a new indicative weighting for your bond portfolio between the three classes of bonds.

4   (i)   Calculate the Macaulay duration for an £8 annual coupon bond with a face value of £100 and 5 years left to maturity if the bond's yield to maturity is 10%.

   (ii)   What is the modified duration of the bond?

   (iii)   If the 5-year yield to maturity were to suddenly increase from 10% to 10.30% and the bond in problem (i) was selling for £92.42 at 10% yield, what would you expect the bond price to be after the yield increases to 10.30%?

5   You currently have a £100 million bond portfolio invested 30% in 5 year bonds with a modified duration of 4.05 years, 25% invested in 10 year bonds with a modified duration of 6.88 years and 45% in 20 year bonds with a modified duration of 10.09 years. The yield curve is currently flat at 8% across all maturities (5 year, 10 year and 20 year).

   (i)   Calculate the modified duration for your entire bond portfolio.

| Chapter 6 | Revision questions – *continued* |

(ii) What will be the approximate value of your portfolio if the entire yield curve suddenly shifts down to yield 7.5% across all maturities?

(iii) What might you wish to do with the length of the duration of your portfolio in the light of a projected fall in bond yields from 8% to 7.5%? Suggest a new weighting for your portfolio to achieve this and what it would involve you doing.

6 Consider the following bond data:

Bond	Credit rating	Years to maturity	Annual coupon	Macaulay duration	Yield to maturity
1	A	8	£9	7.3	13.2
2	AA	5	£10	4.5	13.0
3	BBB	10	£10	?	14.0
4	BBB	10	£10	?	14.0
5	A	10	£11	7.1	13.2
6	B	7	£10	4.5	14.5

(i) Is the duration of bond 4 shorter or longer than bond 3 or can we not say? Explain your reasoning.

(ii) You expect bond yields to fall across all maturities by 1%. What strategy will you employ in respect of bonds 1 and 5?

(iii) If you expect a recession and fall in yields generally combined with a widening of the corporate bond spread, which of bonds 2 and 6 would you choose to buy? Explain your reasoning.

(iv) Consider bond 5. If the yield to maturity on this bond were to move downward because of a credit rating upgrade to 12% what would be the expected percentage price change in this bond?

7 Briefly explain what is meant by a warrant attached to a bond and the advantages/disadvantages to a firm of issuing a bond with a warrant attached.

8 A Treasury bond with £100 maturity value has a £6 annual coupon and 4 years left to maturity.

(i) What price will the bond sell for, assuming that the 4-year yield to maturity in the market is 7%? (Show your calculations.)

(ii) What would be your answer to part (i) if the 4-year yield to maturity in the market is 9%? (Show your calculations.)

(iii) What does your answer to parts (i) and (ii) tell you about the relationship of bond prices, term to maturity and changes in bond yields?

7

PORTFOLIO ANALYSIS: RISK AND RETURN IN FINANCIAL MARKETS

Learning objectives

In this chapter you will learn about:

- the trade-off between risk and return
- the difference between systematic and unsystematic risk
- the benefits from portfolio diversification
- the importance of the market portfolio
- the market price of risk and how to measure it
- important key equations relating to measuring the benefits of portfolio diversification

7.1 Introduction

One of the most important variables that investors have to confront when investing in financial assets is risk, and the proper definition, measurement and management of risk is essential to the study of financial markets. Investors in financial assets do not usually put all their eggs into one basket; that is, they are not usually content to place all their financial wealth into only one financial asset. Typically investors will hold a bundle of financial assets known as their asset portfolio. Generally speaking investors are concerned about two key variables, namely the risk and return on their asset portfolio. As we shall see, most investors will seek to hold what are known as efficient portfolios – portfolios that will maximize the expected return for any given level of risk, or equivalently minimize the risks for a specified expected return.

In this chapter we define risk and return, applying these concepts firstly to an individual security and then to a portfolio of securities. An important distinction is made between systematic (market) risk and unsystematic (diversifiable or specific) risk. We shall see that the latter can be eliminated through the process of portfolio diversification, while the former cannot.

7.2 Determining the price of a financial asset

A financial asset is simply a legal claim to a future cash flow. The basic principle underlying the price of any financial asset is that it should be determined by the present value of the asset's expected cash flow, by which we mean the expected stream of cash receipts over the life of the asset. Note that we are referring to the expected cash flow, and this may be known with a high degree of certainty both with regard to the timing of payments and their size, or may be highly uncertain, or somewhere between these extremes.

There are a number of factors that will influence the degree of certainty with which the cash flow is expected. One is the nature of the financial asset. In the case of debt security the cash flow is usually more certain with regard to both the timing and amount compared to an equity security (that is, shares). With shares both the timing and size of dividend cash flows will be very much affected by the future performance of the company. Another important factor that will influence the degree of certainty of cash flows is the nature of the issuer of the financial asset; Treasury bonds issued by governments are usually regarded as risk-free because a government is highly unlikely to renege on its commitments, since it can simply print the money to redeem the bond if need be. The same cannot be said of corporate bonds; a corporation may face financial difficulties that force it to renege on or reschedule part or all of its commitments.

debt security
a financial security that entitles the holder to a series of future cash flows and which has a high creditor status

equity security
a financial security that gives the holder an ownership stake and the rights to a share in the profits usually in the form of dividends, but it has a lower status than debt instruments in cases of default

Another important factor is that today many governments and corporations issue financial assets that are denominated in foreign currencies. In this case a domestic investor might know what the return is likely to be in the foreign currency, but the unpredictability of exchange rate movements will mean that the value of the payments when converted into the domestic currency is uncertain. The investor thus faces exchange-rate risk.

7.3   The rate of return on a security

The return on a security is made up of two components: the income stream attached to ownership of the financial asset, and any change in the value of the asset:

$$R_1 = \frac{P_1 - P_0}{P_0} + \frac{C_1}{P_0} = \frac{P_1 - P_0 + C_1}{P_0} \tag{7.1}$$

where R_1 is the return on a financial asset at the end of period 1; P_1 is the price of a financial asset at the end of period 1; P_0 is the price of a financial asset at the beginning of period 1; and C_1 is the income received on the asset at the end of period 1.

Numerical example 1

A security has a value of £1000 at the beginning of the year and the market value at the end of the year is £1100; the income on the security of £30 is also obtained at the end of the year. In this case the total rate of return on the security is:

$$\frac{£1100 - £1000}{£1000} + \frac{£30}{£1000} = 0.13$$

That is, the return is 13% over the holding period which in this case is one year.

The rate of return on a security is the percentage return on a security per annum. In our example the investor makes £130 return on a £1000 investment over one year, so the rate of return is:

$$\frac{£130}{£1000} \times 100 = 13\% \text{ per annum}$$

We usually refer to the rate of return on a per annum basis. Generally the expected rate of return on an asset is uncertain and the investor will have to attach a subjective probability to a range of possible returns. The expected rate of return on a security is given by:

$$E(R_i) = P_1 R_1 + P_2 R_2 + \ldots + P_N R_N \tag{7.2}$$

where $P_1, P_2 \ldots P_N$ is the probability of outcome 1, 2, $\ldots$ N occurring; and $R_1, R_2 \ldots R_N$ is the rate of return associated with outcome 1, 2, $\ldots$ N.

Equation (7.2) can be summarized as:

$$E(R_i) = \sum_{i=1}^{N} P_i R_i \tag{7.3}$$

where P_i is the probability of outcome i occurring; and R_i is the rate of return associated with outcome i.

expected rate of return the forecast rate of return from holding a security expressed as a percentage per annum

Numerical example 2

Calculation of expected rate of return

Consider an example of the expected rate of return on a security whose asset returns and subjective probabilities are given below.

Outcome	Asset return	Subjective probability
1	30%	0.20
2	20%	0.25
3	10%	0.30
4	0%	0.15
5	−10%	0.10

$$E(R_i) = P_1R_1 + P_2R_2 + P_3R_3 + P_4R_4 + P_5R_5$$
$$= 0.2(30\%) + 0.25(20\%) + 0.3(10\%) + 0.15(0\%) + 0.1(-10\%)$$
$$= 13\%$$

Hence the expected rate of return is 13%.

7.4 The variance and standard deviation of the rate of return

The variance of return is the weighted sum of squared deviations from the expected return. Squaring deviations ensures that positive and negative deviations from the expected value contribute equally to the measure of variability regardless of sign. The formula for variance is given by:

$$\sigma_i^2 = P_1\left[R_1 - E(R_i)^2\right] + P_2\left[R_2 - E(R_i)^2\right] + \ldots + P_N\left[R_N - E(R_i)^2\right] \tag{7.4}$$

where σ_i^2 is the variance of the expected rate of return on security 1; $P_1, P_2 \ldots P_N$ is the probability of outcome 1, 2, ... N occurring; and $R_1, R_2 \ldots R_N$ is the rate of return associated with outcome 1, 2, ... N.

Equation (7.4) can be expressed as:

$$\sigma_i^2 = \sum_{i=1}^{N} P_i\left[R_i - E(R_i)^2\right] \tag{7.5}$$

The standard deviation σ_i is the square root of the variance.

Numerical example

Using the expected return calculated above, the variance is given by:

$$\sigma_i^2 = 0.2(30 - 13)^2 + 0.25(20 - 13)^2 + 0.3(10 - 13)^2$$
$$+ 0.15(0 - 13)^2 + 0.1(-10 - 13)^2$$
$$= 151$$

and $\sigma_i = 12.29$.

When we have N observations each with an equal probability of being observed, then we use the following formula to calculate the variance:

$$\sigma_i^2 = \sum_{i=1}^{N} \frac{1}{N}\left[R_i - E(R_i)\right]^2 \tag{7.6}$$

7.5   Risk on a security

risk the danger that
the rate of return
on a security will
be less than the
investor expects
when purchasing the
security, including the
possible loss of part
or all of the original
investment

Unlike return, there is no agreed definition of what constitutes risk, let alone how to measure it. The definition of risk most frequently used in the finance literature is the probability that the value of a financial asset or return will be less than its expected value. In the context of our example, if the investor on average expects his asset to make 13% at the end of the year, then the risk is the probability that the expected return will be less than 13% per year, which is 25%. Some assets such as government Treasury bills and Treasury bonds are regarded as risk-free; the investor can be sure what the return on the bill will be if it is held to maturity. Other assets, such as stocks and shares, futures and options have uncertain rates of return and investors have to attach subjective probabilities to the expected return.

In financial markets, it has frequently been observed that the returns on securities typically have a normal distribution. This means that there is an equal probability that they will lie above the mean expected return or below, and that as we move further from the mean the probability of the rate of return deviating from the expected rate of return decreases. A normal distribution is shown in **Figure 7.1**.

If expected rates of return follow a normal distribution, then the variance becomes a very useful measure of risk. The larger the variance then the greater the dispersion of values around the mean value, and therefore the greater the degree of risk facing the investor. The normal distribution has a number of useful properties:

1 The distribution is symmetric, so that the total variability of returns is twice the size of the portfolio's variability below the mean expected return. Hence, if variability of return is used as a proxy for risk in ranking alternative portfolios, the ranking will be identical to the case where variability of returns below the mean is used.

Figure 7.1   The normal distribution

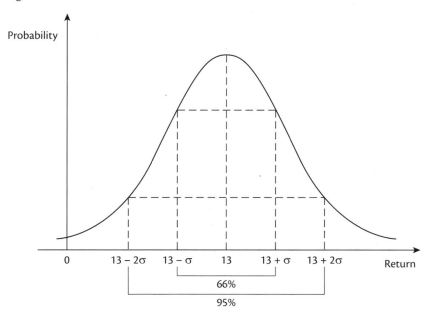

2 There is an approximately 95 per cent probability that the actual return on a portfolio will lie within two standard deviations of the expected return, and approximately 66 per cent probability that it will lie within 1 standard deviation. For example, if the mean expected return is 13 per cent and the standard deviation is 4, then there is a 95 per cent probability that the expected return will lie within the range 13% ± (2 × 4) = 5 to 21% and a 66 per cent probability that it will lie in the region of 13 ± (1 × 4) = 9 to 17%.

7.6 Covariance and correlation of rates of return

Covariance

When looking at a portfolio of securities there is an important factor in addition to the variance of the two shares that needs to be considered. This is the extent to which two shares move up or down together, and this is measured by their covariance. Consider two securities A and B that have the following distribution of returns:

Probability	Rate of return on security A	Rate of return on security B
0.2	30	15
0.2	12	13
0.2	7	7
0.2	6	0
0.2	0	−10

The expected rate of return on asset A, $E(R_A)$ = 11% and the expected rate of return on asset B, $E(R_B)$ = 5%. The covariance between A and B (σ_{AB}) is given by:

$$\sigma_{AB} = \sum_{i=1}^{N} P_i[(R_{Ai} - E(R_A))(R_{Bi} - E(R_B))] \tag{7.7}$$

$$\sigma_{AB} = 0.2(30 - 11)(15 - 5) + 0.2(12 - 11)(13 - 5)$$
$$+ 0.2(7 - 11)(7 - 5) + 0.2(6 - 11)(0 - 5)$$
$$+ 0.2(0 - 11)(-10 - 5)$$
$$= 76$$

When we have N observations each with an equal probability of being observed, then we use the following formula to calculate the covariance:

$$\sigma_{AB} = \sum_{i=1}^{N} \frac{1}{N}[(R_A - E(R_A))(R_B - E(R_B))] \tag{7.8}$$

A negative covariance implies that the returns on securities A and B tend to move in opposite directions, while a positive covariance indicates that the returns on securities A and B tend to move in the same direction. The problem with the covariance term is that we cannot easily make comparisons between two different covariances.

The correlation coefficient

An extremely useful transformation of the covariance term is an index known as the correlation coefficient, which is given by the formula:

$$\rho_{AB} = \frac{\sigma_{AB}}{\sigma_A \sigma_B} \tag{7.9}$$

In our example, $\sigma_A = 10.24$ and $\sigma_B = 9.14$, with the covariance $\sigma_{AB} = 76$. Hence the correlation coefficient ρ_{AB} has a value of:

$$\rho_{AB} = \frac{76}{10.24 \times 9.14} = 0.812$$

The correlation coefficient takes on values between +1 and −1. A positive coefficient indicates that the returns on both assets tend to rise together, while a negative value indicates that the returns tend to move in opposite directions. The closer the value is to +1, then the stronger the positive relationship and the easier it is to approximate to a positively sloped straight line. The closer the value is to −1, then the stronger the negative relationship and the easier it is to approximate to a negatively sloped straight line. If the correlation coefficient is zero then the returns on the two assets are said to be independent and randomly dispersed. The correlation coefficient shows only the extent to which the relationship is positive or negative, and the extent to which this can be approximated by a straight line; it does not say how steep such a line would be (the steepness needs to be determined by regression analysis).

7.7   Different types of investors

Consider two securities A and B which have the same rate of return, say 20 per cent, but have different degrees of risk, with A having a standard deviation of 10 and B of 15. A risk-averse investor is an investor that, given the same expected rate of return, will always choose the less risky security, in this instance security A. A risk-averse investor will only accept increased risk if there is a sufficient increase in the expected rate of return to compensate for the additional risk. A risk-neutral investor is an investor that, given the same expected return, will be indifferent towards the degree of risk. In this instance he would be indifferent between security A and security B, even though security A is more risky than security B. A risk-neutral investor will always seek to maximize the expected return from an investment and will therefore invest in the security offering the highest expected rate of return regardless of the risk. A risk-loving investor is an investor that enjoys taking on risk, and that given the same expected return will always choose the more risky security, in this instance security B. A risk-loving investor, while (presumably) longing for a high return, is prepared to accept greater risk for a lower return!

In general, it is believed that most economic agents correspond to risk-averse investors. One of the key economic principles behind this idea is that most investors suffer from a diminishing marginal utility of wealth. That is, for every £1 increase in an investor's wealth, the additional gain in utility to the investor is less and less the wealthier the investor becomes. For example, someone with a wealth of £100 will

risk-averse investor
an investor that will only take on increased risk if there is the prospect of a sufficient increase in return to compensate

get a greater increase in utility from a £1 increase in his wealth than if he already had a wealth of £1 million. An important implication of this is that, for a given level of wealth, an investor that loses £1 loses more utility than he gains if his wealth rises by £1. This being the case, an investor who has a choice between two investments, one of which is risk-free with a guaranteed return of X%, and one with an average return of X% but which may go up or down with equal probability by a given percentage, will always invest in the risk-free asset. The reason is that the extra utility that may be associated with the riskier investment is outweighed by the disutility if the investment falls short of expectations.

7.8 The indifference curves of risk-averse investors

For simplicity, we shall assume that most investors are risk-averse, that is they are only prepared to take on increased risk if there is the prospect of a sufficient increase in expected return to compensate for the increased risk. This can be summarized by saying that an individual investor prefers more expected return to less, and prefers less expected risk as measured by the standard deviation. An indifference curve shows different combinations of risk and return between which an investor is indifferent. The assumption of risk-aversion means that the indifference curves for an investor are positively sloped in the expected rate of return–standard deviation space as depicted in **Figure 7.2**.

In **Figure 7.2** we have a set of indifference curves for an individual investor, and each curve is positively sloped and becomes steeper as riskiness (measured by the standard deviation of the portfolio) increases. The positive slope reflects the fact that risk-averse investors will only accept increased risk if there is the prospect of a

Figure 7.2   Indifference curves in the risk–return space

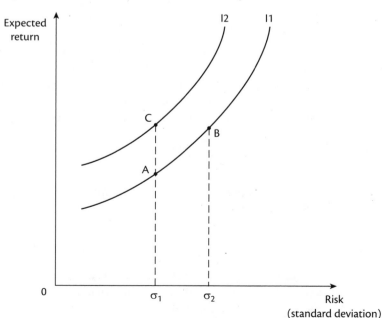

sufficient increase in expected return to compensate. The fact that an indifference curve becomes steeper as we increase risk, for example as we move from point A to B on curve I1, reflects the fact that as risk increases an investor becomes increasingly reluctant to take on more risk. The slope of the indifference curve is determined by the coefficient of absolute risk-aversion, the greater an investor's absolute risk-aversion then the steeper the indifference curve. There are a whole map of indifference curves that can be drawn for an investor, within this example indifference curve I2 being preferred to indifference curve I1 since for a given level of risk we find a higher rate of return on I2 than on I1. As we shall see, an important assumption of portfolio theory is that investors are assumed to be utility maximizers and will therefore seek to reach the highest possible indifference curve.

7.9   Portfolio theory

We now turn to an analysis of portfolio theory which was pioneered in a series of classic papers by Harry Markowitz in the early 1950s. We begin by stating the assumptions of portfolio theory:

1 Agents prefer more wealth to less.
2 Agents are risk-averse and require a higher expected rate of return for taking on more risk.
3 The rates of return follow a normal distribution. This means that the risk of an individual security can be measured by its standard deviation.
4 The wealth-holder cannot affect the probability distribution of the security held.
5 The theory considers only existing assets not new issues.

The return on a portfolio of assets is given by the expression:

$$R_p = \sum_{i=1}^{N} w_i R_i \tag{7.10}$$

where R_p is the value-weighted return on a portfolio of risky assets; w_i is the value-weighted proportion of a portfolio invested in asset i; R_i is the return on asset i in the portfolio; and N is the number of securities in the investor's portfolio.

The average expected return on the portfolio is simply the weighted average of the expected return on the individual assets in the portfolio, that is:

$$E(R_p) = \sum_{i=1}^{N} w_i E(R_i) \tag{7.11}$$

where $E(R_p)$ is the average expected return on the portfolio, and $E(R_i)$ is the average expected return on asset i.

7.10   Reducing risk through diversification

Suppose there are two securities, A and B, and that security A has a higher expected return plus a lower standard deviation than security B. Why should any risk-averse investor wish to hold asset B?

The crucial insight of portfolio theory lies in the fact that so long as the returns on security A and security B are not perfectly correlated, there are gains to be had from portfolio diversification. By portfolio diversification we mean the combining of various financial assets to reduce risks.

7.11 Measuring risk on a portfolio

portfolio diversification
the process of investing money in a range of different securities and assets with the aim of reducing risk

If the portfolio is made up of just two assets A and B, the expression for the variance of the portfolio is given by:

$$\sigma_p^2 = w_A^2\sigma_A^2 + w_B^2 w_B^2 + 2w_A w_B \sigma_A \sigma_B \rho_{AB} \tag{7.12}$$

where σ_p^2 is the variance of return on a risky portfolio; w_A is the value-weighted proportion of a portfolio invested in asset A; σ_A^2 is the variance of return on asset A; σ_A is the standard deviation of return on asset A; and w_B is the value-weighted proportion of a portfolio invested in asset B; σ_B^2 is the variance of return on asset B; σ_B is the standard deviation of return on asset B; and ρ_{AB} is the correlation coefficient of returns between asset A and asset B.

Numerical example

A portfolio contains two securities A and B. An investor's total financial wealth (W) is therefore given by $W = V_A + V_B$ where V_A is the value of holdings of asset A and V_B is the value of holdings of asset B.

If the amount of wealth held in asset A is 70% $w_A = 0.7$, and the remaining 30% of wealth is held in asset B so that $w_B = 1 - 0.7 = 0.3$. The expected rate of return on asset A is 25% and the expected rate of return on asset B is 20%. The standard deviation of the rate of return on asset A is 75% and the standard deviation of return on asset B is 50%, while the correlation coefficient of returns between A and B is −0.6.

$$R_A = 0.25 \ (25\%), \quad \sigma_A = 0.75 \ (75\%)$$
$$R_B = 0.20 \ (20\%), \quad \sigma_B = 0.50 \ (50\%), \quad \rho_{AB} = -0.6$$

Substituting these values into equation (7.12) we find that the variance of the portfolio is given by:

$$\sigma_p^2 = w_A^2\sigma_A^2 + w_B^2\sigma_B^2 + 2w_A w_B \sigma_A \sigma_B \rho_{AB}$$
$$= (0.7)^2(0.75)^2 + (0.3)^2(0.50)^2 + 2(0.7)(0.3)(0.75)(0.50)(-0.6)$$
$$= 0.2036 \ \text{ or } \ 20.36\%$$
$$\sigma_p = 0.4512 \ \text{ or } \ 45.12\%$$

whereas $\sigma_A^2 = 0.5625$ and $\sigma_B^2 = 0.25$ so that the weighted average of σ_A^2 and σ_B^2 is $0.7(0.5625) + 0.3(0.25) = 0.46875$. Hence with a portfolio variance of 0.2036 the investor has, in this example, more than halved the variability of investment without affecting the expected rate of return which is given by:

$$E(R_p) = (0.7)(0.25) + (0.3)(0.20) = 0.235 \ (23.5\%)$$

From the example, we can see that portfolio diversification has a role in reducing the risks facing an investor but not the expected return which is simply the weighted average of the return on the individual financial assets in the portfolio. This means that diversification is not a means of enhancing the return on a portfolio but is about reducing the variability of return.

Case 1: Perfect positive correlation i.e. $\rho_{AB} = 1$

In this case, the variance of the portfolio reduces to:

$$\sigma_p^2 = w_A^2 \sigma_A^2 + w_B^2 \sigma_B^2 + 2w_A w_B \sigma_A \sigma_B \times 1$$
$$\sigma_p^2 = (w_A \sigma_A + w_B \sigma_B)^2 \tag{7.13}$$

so that the standard deviation is

$$\sigma_p = w_A \sigma_A + w_B \sigma_B \tag{7.14}$$

For the portfolio used in our example:

$$\sigma_p = 0.7(0.75) + 0.3(0.50) = 0.675 \quad \text{or} \quad 67.5\%$$

In this instance, there are no gains to be had from portfolio diversification. The standard deviation is simply the weighted average of the individual standard deviations of the two assets, $[0.7(0.75) + 0.3(0.50) = 0.675$ or $67.5\%]$.

Case 2: Perfect negative correlation i.e. $\rho_{AB} = -1$

In this case the variance of the portfolio reduces to:

$$\sigma_p^2 = w_A^2 \sigma_A^2 + w_B^2 \sigma_B^2 + 2w_A w_B \sigma_A \sigma_B \times -1$$
$$\sigma_p^2 = (w_A \sigma_A - w_B \sigma_B)^2 \tag{7.15}$$

so that the standard deviation is

$$\sigma_p = \text{absolute value of } (w_A \sigma_A - w_B \sigma_B) \tag{7.16}$$

Note we cannot have a negative value for the standard deviation so in equation (7.16) we must take the absolute value should the expression be calculated directly rather than calculating the variance first then taking the square root of the variance.

For the portfolio used in our example:

$$\sigma_p^2 = [0.7(0.75) - 0.3(0.50)]^2 = 0.140625$$

so that

$$\sigma_p = 0.375$$

In this instance, the gains from portfolio diversification are at a maximum. The standard deviation is below the weighted average of the individual standard deviations of the two assets, $[0.7(0.75) + 0.3(0.50) = 0.675$ or $67.5\%]$.

Case 3: Zero correlation i.e. $\rho_{AB} = 0$

In this case the variance of the portfolio reduces to:

$$\sigma_p^2 = w_A^2 \sigma_A^2 + w_B^2 \sigma_B^2 \tag{7.17}$$

so that the standard deviation is:

$$\sigma_p = \left(w_A^2 \sigma_A^2 + w_B^2 \sigma_B^2 \right)^{1/2} \tag{7.18}$$

For the portfolio used in our example:

$$\sigma_p = \left[(0.7)^2 (0.75)^2 + (0.3)^2 (0.5)^2 \right]^{1/2} = 0.546 \quad \text{or } 54.60\%$$

In this instance, the gains from portfolio diversification are not as big as in the case of perfect negative correlation. Nonetheless, the standard deviation is below the weighted average of the individual standard deviations of the two assets, $[0.7(0.75) + 0.3(0.50) = 0.675 \text{ or } 67.5\%]$.

7.12 The two-asset efficiency frontier

efficiency frontier
a curve depicting
dominant risk–return
portfolios with
increased return
only achievable by
increasing risk

A risk-averse investor will generally be keen to select a weighted combination of shares that minimizes risk for a given return. The efficiency frontier for a combination of two risky shares shows the maximum rate of return for a given level of risk, or equivalently those portfolios with the minimum of risk for a given rate of return. The set of portfolios that dominate all other portfolios form the so-called efficiency frontier.

Total portfolio risk is given by equation (7.12) repeated below:

$$\sigma_p^2 = w_A^2 \sigma_A^2 + w_B^2 w_B^2 + 2 w_A w_B \sigma_A \sigma_B \rho_{AB} \tag{7.12}$$

while the expected return on a portfolio is given by:

$$E(R_p) = w_A E(R_A) + w_B E(R_B) \tag{7.19}$$

The investor can invest his money in either asset A or asset B, so the sum of the weight is therefore unity, that is:

$$w_A + w_B = 1 \tag{7.20}$$

There are an infinite number of investment opportunities for the investor to allocate his wealth between securities A and B. A weight of 1 to security A and a weight of zero to security B, or any other combination such as 0.7 to security A and 0.3 to security B, or 0.6 to security A and 0.4 to security B, and so on. The mapping of these alternative possibilities gives what is known as the mean-variance (or mean–standard deviation frontier). The efficiency frontier maps out the combination of the two securities that has the maximum expected return for any given level of risk, or equivalently the minimum level of risk for a given expected rate of return.

Table 7.1 shows the efficiency frontier (mean–standard deviation frontier) for different weights of assets between A and B, and different possible correlation coefficients of return.

Table 7.1   Mean–standard deviation frontier

$R_A = 0.25$ (25%), $\sigma_A = 0.75$ (75%) $R_B = 0.20$ (20%), $\sigma_B = 0.50$ (50%)							
w_A	w_B	$\rho_{AB} = 1$	$\rho_{AB} = 0.5$	$\rho_{AB} = 0$	$\rho_{AB} = -0.5$	$\rho_{AB} = -1$	Return
1.0	0	75.0	75.0	75.0	75.0	75.0	25.0
0.9	0.1	72.5	70.1	67.7	65.1	62.5	24.5
0.8	0.2	70.0	65.6	60.8	55.7	50.0	24.0
0.7	0.3	67.5	61.6	54.6	46.8	37.5	23.5
0.6	0.4	65.0	57.7	49.2	39.1	25.0	23.0
0.5	0.5	62.5	54.5	45.1	33.1	12.5	22.5
0.4	0.6	60.0	52.0	42.4	30.0	0	22.0
0.3	0.7	57.5	50.2	41.6	30.7	12.5	21.5
0.2	0.8	55.0	49.24	42.7	35.0	25.0	21.0
0.1	0.9	52.5	49.18	45.6	41.8	37.5	20.5
0	1.0	50.0	50.0	50.0	50.0	50.0	20.0

Figure 7.3 shows the expected rate of return and standard deviation for an investor for different weights of investment between assets A and B for a value of the correlation coefficient of zero derived from **Table 7.1**. At point A all the investor's wealth is in asset A and none in asset B, while at point B all the investor's wealth is in asset B and none in asset A. Other points on the efficiency frontier correspond to increasing amounts of the investor's wealth being in asset A as we move from B to A on the efficiency frontier. Point C is known as the minimum variance portfolio, and the relevant part of the efficiency frontier for an investor is between points C and A as these dominate portfolios between points B and C.

minimum variance portfolio a portfolio which minimizes the risk of a combination of risky assets

Figure 7.3   The mean–standard deviation frontier for a zero correlation coefficient

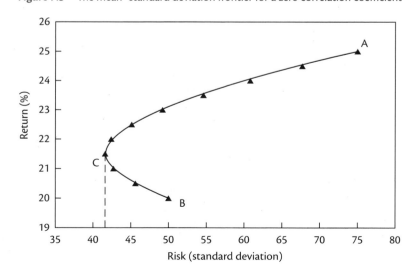

7.13   The minimum variance portfolio in the two risky asset case

When there are only two risky securities there is a straightforward solution to finding the weights of the two securities that will achieve the minimum variance (and standard deviation) portfolio. The weight that should be invested in security A to give the minimum variance in the two-security case is given by:

$$w_{A(min)} = \frac{\sigma_B^2 - \sigma_{AB}}{\sigma_A^2 + \sigma_B^2 - 2\sigma_{AB}} \tag{7.21}$$

since the covariance between A and B is given by the formula:

$$\sigma_{AB} = \rho_{AB}\sigma_A\sigma_B \tag{7.22}$$

If we take the case where the correlation coefficient ρ_{AB} between securities A and B is 0.5, then the covariance σ_{AB} between A and B is:

$$\sigma_{AB} = 0.5 \times 0.75 \times 0.5 = 0.1875$$

Hence, given the parameters $\sigma_A = 0.75$, $\sigma_B = 0.5$, $\sigma_{AB} = 0.1875$, the minimum variance share in A is given by:

$$w_{A(min)} = \frac{0.5^2 - 0.1875}{0.75^2 + 0.5^2 - 2 \times 0.1875} = 0.1429$$

The minimum variance will occur when 14.29% is invested in security A and 85.71% is invested in security B.

Note in the case when the correlation coefficient is −1, given the parameters $\sigma_A = 0.75$, $\sigma_B = 0.5$ then the covariance must be −0.375.

$$\sigma_{AB} = -1 \times 0.75 \times 0.5 = -0.375$$

$$w_{A(min)} = \frac{0.5^2 - (-0.375)}{0.75^2 + 0.5^2 - 2(-0.375)} = 0.4$$

That is, the portfolio variance is minimized when there is 40% invested in security A and 60% invested in asset B. This is readily verified by looking at **Table 7.1**, with such proportions the standard deviation of the portfolio is in this special case equal to zero! Of course, this is only possible when assets are perfect negatively correlated.

Figure 7.4 plots the values of means and standard deviation for the various possible correlation coefficients in **Table 7.1**. For each of the different possible correlation coefficients, there is a different efficiency frontier as depicted in **Figure 7.4**. We can clearly see that the less positive (and more negative) the correlation coefficient, the better the return possibilities open for an investor for a given level of risk (or the lower the risk possibility for a given rate of return). Indeed, the less positive (and more negative) the correlation coefficient is, not only is the potential return higher for a given level of risk, but also the greater the ability to reduce risk. Indeed, when the correlation coefficient is minus unity the investor has the possibility of eliminating risk entirely.

Figure 7.4   The mean–standard deviation frontier for different values of the correlation coefficient

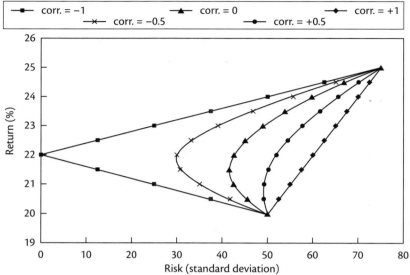

7.14   The portfolio efficiency frontier

In our previous derivation of the efficiency frontier we assumed that there are only two risky assets. In practice, investors have a large range of risky assets to choose from, which means that there is a huge number of possible portfolios containing different asset mixes that investors could choose. For example, if an investor has a choice between three risky securities (A, B, C) then it is possible to have the following sets of portfolios: portfolio 1 (A, B, C), portfolio 2 (A, B), portfolio 3 (A, C), portfolio 4 (B, C), portfolio 5 (A), portfolio 6 (B), portfolio 7 (C). For each of portfolios 1 to 4 there are separate efficiency frontiers that can be derived, and the final three portfolios constitute single points in the risk–return space.

If we have N different assets, then we can constuct numerous possible portfolios containing different mixes of assets. **Figure 7.5** shows the map of all the possible portfolios that could be constructed with N assets. The dominance principle states that a portfolio will dominate another portfolio if it has either a lower standard deviation and the same expected rate of return or it has the same standard deviation and a higher expected rate of return. Looking at the case of N securities in **Figure 7.5** we can see that portfolio A dominates portfolio B, which in turn dominates portfolios C and D. Not all portfolios marking the boundary of the portfolio opportunity set are of interest since certain combinations and weightings of shares on the boundary dominate others; for instance, portfolio A dominates portfolio C and portfolio E dominates portfolio F. This means we are interested only in the part of the efficiency frontier indicated by the arrows.

While there are an infinite number of portfolios that could be constructed, a map of all the dominant portfolios – the portfolio efficiency frontier – can be created. The portfolio efficiency frontier consists of those portfolios with the maximum rate

Figure 7.5   The portfolio efficiency frontier

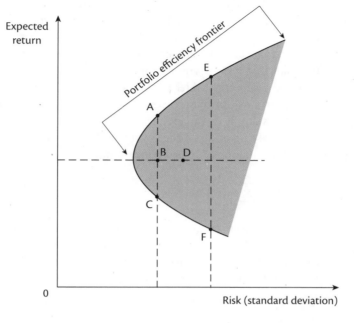

of return for a given level of risk, or equivalently those portfolios with the minimum level of risk for a given rate of return. The set of portfolios that dominates all other portfolios forms the so-called efficiency frontier. An efficient portfolio is a portfolio that for a given level of risk offers the highest possible return, and all dominated portfolios are known as inefficient portfolios.

If we have a portfolio containing N separate securities, then the expected return and variances are given by:

$$E(R_p) = \sum_{i=1}^{N} w_i E(R_i) \tag{7.23}$$

That is, the expected rate of return is simply the weighted average of the individual average expected returns on the N securities:

$$\sigma_p^2 = \sum_{i=1}^{N} \sum_{j=1}^{N} w_i w_j \sigma_{ij} \tag{7.24}$$

Thus, the variance of the portfolio with N securities is the sum of the weighted average of the individual covariances. It is important to illustrate the meaning of the double summation in equation (7.24). Imagine we have three securities 1, 2 and 3 such that:

$$\sigma_p^2 = \sum_{j=1}^{3} w_1 w_j \sigma_{1j} + \sum_{j=1}^{3} w_2 w_j \sigma_{2j} + \sum_{j=1}^{3} w_3 w_j \sigma_{3j} \tag{7.25}$$

$$\sigma_p^2 = w_1 w_1 \sigma_{11} + w_1 w_2 \sigma_{12} + w_1 w_3 \sigma_{13} + w_2 w_1 \sigma_{21} + w_2 w_2 \sigma_{22}$$
$$+ w_2 w_3 \sigma_{23} + w_3 w_1 \sigma_{31} + w_3 w_2 \sigma_{32} + w_3 w_3 \sigma_{33} \tag{7.26}$$

Each term in the double summation involves the product of the two weights times the covariance of the two securities. When we have three securities there are $3^2 = 9$ terms to be added together; in the case of four securities there are $4^2 = 16$ terms to be added together. When there are N securities then in general there will need to be N^2 terms to be added together. Here there are a couple of important points to note. The first is that $\sigma_{ij} = \sigma_{ji}$, for example, $\sigma_{12} = \sigma_{21}$, and so on. A more interesting point is when the subscripts refer to the same security, which is what happens when we have σ_{11}, σ_{22}, σ_{33}. In these cases $\sigma_1 = \sigma_1 \times \sigma_1$; that is, the covariance of a security with itself is simply its variance.

A special case occurs if the covariance between different securities is set equal to zero, when equation (7.26) simplifies dramatically to:

$$\sigma_p^2 = \sum_{i=1}^{N} w_i^2 \sigma_i^2 \qquad (7.27)$$

That is, when the covariances between the various securities are all assumed to be zero then the variance of the portfolio with N securities is simply the weighted average squared of the individual variances. For example, in the three-asset scenario the relevant equation is now:

$$\sigma_p^2 = w_1^2 \sigma_1^2 + w_2^2 \sigma_2^2 + w_3^2 \sigma_3^2 \qquad (7.28)$$

As can be seen, compared to equation (7.25) the calculation of portfolio variance is far more straightforward. In general, however, there will be non-zero covariances between securities which requires the use of equation (7.25).

A mathematical solution for the portfolio efficiency frontier can be arrived at through the Markowitz method (1959), which involves a technique known as quadratic programming. The essential element of this procedure is to calculate an obtainable target rate of return X%, and then find a set of portfolio weights wi (with the sum of these weights equal to unity) that achieves this target rate of return with the minimum of variance. Markowitz diversification reduces risk until the minimum risk for a given return is reached. It does this by minimizing the correlation between the rates of return on two or more securities.

A major problem with the Markowitz method is the amount of covariances that have to be calculated. In the case when we have only two securities, then there is only one covariance term; however, with N securities there are $(N^2 - N)/2$ covariance terms to be calculated. For 100 securities this means 4950 terms are needed, and for 500 securities the number is 124,750! Even in the N-security case, we get the same basic message as in the two-security case, that the risk of any combination of N securities will be less than the weighted average of the securities that make up the portfolio.

7.15 Market risk and specific risk

Although the risk of holding a security can be reduced by diversification so long as returns are not perfectly positively correlated, it cannot eliminate a certain degree of risk which is inherent in the market. Risk attached to holding an asset that can be

Figure 7.6   The effect on risk of increasing the number of shares in a portfolio

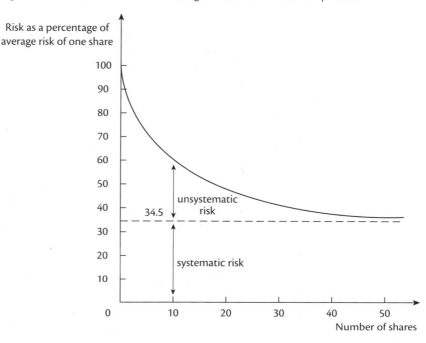

specific risk risk that is specific to a particular security (e.g. a share) and which can be reduced by increasing the number of shares since positive and negative shocks affecting individual companies and assets will tend to cancel out

market risk risk that is inherent in market fluctuations and cannot be diversified away

naïve diversification the process of investing in a variety of securities and assets in equal value-weighted proportions

eliminated by the process of diversification is known as specific risk (or unsystematic risk or diversifiable risk), while risk attached to an asset that cannot be eliminated through the process of diversification is known as market risk (or systematic risk or non-diversifiable risk), as shown in **Figure 7.6**.

If an investor has a choice of constructing a portfolio from N securities, the investor could choose a portfolio with all N securities or portfolios with less than N securities depending on the correlation between the securities. An interesting question concerns how many securities the investor should choose from the N securities.

One way of answering this question is to randomly pick out a selection of shares making no allowance for possible correlations between the shares, a process known as naïve diversification (randomly chosen securities held in equal value amounts). In a well known study, Solnik (1974) investigated the issue for UK securities. Random selections of securities were made of sizes 1 to 50 shares and the average risk as measured by the standard deviation of returns expressed as a percentage of the average risk of holding only one share were calculated. The results revealed that the gains from diversification in terms of risk reduction are quite substantial up to 20 shares, but thereafter the risk reduction achieved becomes relatively modest. As N becomes very large the investor is left with a risk level that coincides with that of the market in general. Solnik found that this measure of risk could not be reduced below 34.5 per cent of the average risk of holding one share no matter how many securities were held, as depicted in **Figure 7.6**.

We have learnt that as the number of randomly picked shares increases, the unsystematic risk component of a portfolio will be reduced. An interesting question

Table 7.2   Number of shares in a portfolio and correlation with the market

Number of shares in portfolio	Standard deviation of portfolio (% per month)	Correlation with return on market portfolio
1	7.0	0.54
2	5.0	0.63
3	4.8	0.75
4	4.6	0.77
5	4.6	0.79
10	4.2	0.85
15	4.0	0.88
20	3.9	0.89

Source: Wagner and Lau (1971)

concerns how many shares are required to dramatically reduce the unsystematic component. A well known study by Wagner and Lau (1971) investigated this question and the results of their study, reported in **Table 7.2,** are very much in line with Solnik's results.

According to the Markowitz analysis an even better method than random selection of securities (naïve diversification) is to take into account correlations between shares and to select securities. The term efficient diversification refers to the process of selecting weights to invest in securities, taking into account the covariances/correlations between securities and standard deviations of securities so as to maximize the return for any given level of risk. Efficient diversification therefore involves selecting portfolios that lie on the efficiency frontier, and this should enable smaller more efficient portfolios than a random selection method.

Since part of the risk attached to a portfolio can be eliminated through further diversification, in equilibrium there will be no need for this risk to be priced. It is only the market risk attached to a security that cannot be eliminated through portfolio diversification that will need to be priced by the market. While diversification can reduce the risks facing an investor in a given asset, it cannot eliminate some degree of risk attached to holding the financial asset, the market risk. This will vary from one security to another, and will depend upon such things as the nature of the business conducted, labour relations, the credit rating of the issuer and so forth.

efficient diversification
the process of investing in a variety of securities and assets taking into account the covariances and variances of the securities and assets to achieve optimal risk–return portfolios

7.16   The efficient set with a riskless security

riskless security
a security whose nominal rate of return is certain, often proxied by a three-month Treasury; such a security earns the risk-free rate of return

Up to this point we have included only risky securities in the selection of the efficient portfolio set. James Tobin (1958) extended Markowitz's analysis by allowing for the possibility of a riskless security to be included in asset holders' portfolios. If we allow for the inclusion of a riskless security that can be both lent and borrowed at the same risk-free rate of interest, then we obtain the striking result that the efficient set will become a straight line known as the capital market line (CML).

To demonstrate this, consider a portfolio made up of only two securities, a risk-free security with a known rate of return R^*, and a risky portfolio X with an expected rate of return $E(R_X)$. The expected rate of return on the portfolio is:

$$E(R_p) = (1 - w)R^* + wE(R_X) \qquad (7.29)$$

where w is the weight invested in the risky portfolio X.

Since the standard deviation of the rate of return on the risk-free asset σ_{R^*} is zero, then the standard deviation of the combined portfolio is simply the standard deviation of the risky portfolio X, that is, σ_X times the weight of the risky portfolio:

$$\sigma_p^2 = w_{R^*}^2 \sigma_{R^*}^2 + w_X^2 \sigma_X^2 + 2w_{R^*} w_X \sigma_{R^*} \sigma_X \rho_{R^*X} \qquad (7.30)$$

because $\sigma_{R^*} = 0$ and $\rho_{R^*X} = 0$ then:

$$\sigma_p^2 = w_X^2 \sigma_X^2 \qquad (7.31)$$

and

$$\sigma_p = w_X \sigma_X \qquad (7.32)$$

This result follows from the fact that there is no correlation between the risk-free asset and the risky portfolio X that is $\rho_{R^*X} = 0$. Equation (7.30) implies that, when there is a riskless asset, then there is a linear trade-off between risk and return.

In **Figure 7.7** there are two key points of interest. At point A the entire portfolio is invested in the risk-free security and so earns the risk-free rate of interest R^* with zero standard deviation in the portfolio. At point X the entire portfolio is invested in the risky portfolio X and so has an expected rate of return $E(R_X)$ and a standard deviation σ_X. At point L between points R^* and X, the investor has some of his money $(1 - w)$

Figure 7.7   The portfolio opportunity set with a risk-free and risky security

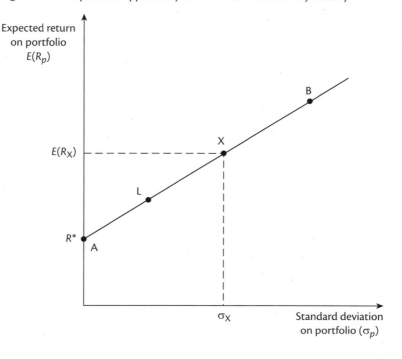

invested in the risk-free rate asset and the rest w, invested in the risky portfolio X earning $E(R_X)$; this means the expected rate of return lies between the risk-free rate of interest R^* and the expected rate of return on portfolio X, $E(R_X)$. All points between R^* and X on the capital market line represent a diversified portfolio where the weight attached to investment in the risky assets lies between zero (at R^*) and unity (at X).

If the investor can borrow at the risk-free rate of interest, then this opens up the possibility that his investment in the risky portfolio X can exceed 100 per cent of his wealth. This is done by borrowing at the risk-free rate of interest R^* and then placing all the borrowed funds in the risky portfolio X. In effect, the investor is borrowing in the hope that the investment in portfolio X will provide a sufficient excess return to compensate for the increased risk; such a position is indicated by point B.

7.17   The market portfolio

In **Figure 7.8** we have the portfolio opportunity set that we derived in **Figure 7.7** along with three capital market lines L1, L2 and L3. All the CMLs start from the risk-free rate of interest R*, but only L1 is tangential to the portfolio opportunity set at point M. When the risk-free asset is combined with portfolio Z then line L3 is the portfolio opportunity set, but this is dominated by line L2 which can be obtained by combining the riskless asset with portfolio Y. However, line L2 is dominated by line L1 which is achieved by combining the risk-free asset with the portfolio M.

Portfolio M in **Figure 7.8** is a unique set on the portfolio efficiency frontier known as the market portfolio, and provides the benchmark from which the risk–return

market portfolio
a portfolio made up of all the assets in the economy with weights equal to their relative market values

Figure 7.8   The capital market line with N securities

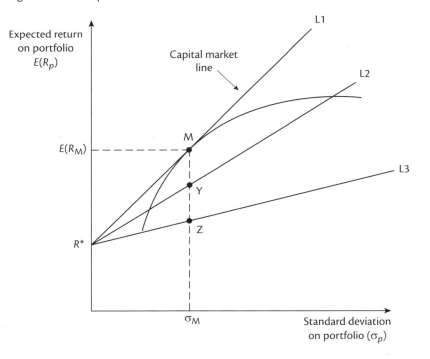

trade-off can be calculated. The market portfolio is a portfolio made up of all the assets in the economy with weights equal to their relative market values. The weight of asset i in the market portfolio is equal to its market value divided by the total value of all marketable assets in the economy. The market portfolio is the most desirable portfolio since it includes only assets which enable investors to create dominant portfolios along the capital market line.

The most diversified portfolio M is the market portfolio which in conjunction with the risk-free asset dominates all other portfolios by having a lower standard deviation for any given level of risk. Portfolio M is the only portfolio on the efficient portfolio frontier and also on the capital market line. Hence, it is a unique portfolio in that it is well diversified with no specific risk, and therefore there is no scope for further risk reduction by means of diversification. We know that some risk can be diversified away and that the standard deviation of the portfolio is reduced as the number of securities rises. As we increase the number of securities then the correlation of returns with the market rises. Highly diversified portfolios tend to have returns that are highly correlated with the market. The greater the number of securities that are added to the portfolio, the more it will start to mimic the market. Market risk cannot, however, be diversified away, it is affected by the factors that affect the economy in general such as the business cycle, macroeconomic policy and so on.

7.18 The market price of risk

The market portfolio is defined as the portfolio of all risky assets in an economy with weights equal to their relative market values. For instance, if the total value of all securities is £1000 billion and a company has a total market capitalization of £10 billion, then the company would have a weight of 1 per cent in the market portfolio. $E(R_M)$ is the average expected return with the market portfolio and σ_M the standard deviation of market returns shows the degree of market risk. Once we have calculated the expected rate of return on the market portfolio and the risk-free rate of interest, then the market price of risk is given by the slope of the capital market line, that is:

$$\text{Market price of risk} = \frac{E(R_M) - R^*}{\sigma_M} \qquad (7.33)$$

where: $E(R_M)$ is the expected return on the market portfolio; R^* is the risk-free rate of interest; and σ_M is the standard deviation of market rate of return.

The relevant equation for portfolio return along the capital market line is given by the equation:

$$E(R_p) = R^* + \sigma_p \left[\frac{E(R_M) - R^*}{\sigma_M} \right] \qquad (7.34)$$

where $E(R_p)$ is the expected rate of return of a portfolio on the capital market line; and σ_p is the standard deviation of a portfolio along the capital market line. Notice that along the capital market line, because all diversifiable risk has been eliminated through diversification, the portfolio standard deviation coincides with the market risk.

7.19   Measuring the market index

The market index should include the returns associated with all assets in the economy. This is an impractical proposition and for this reason the market rate of return and standard deviation are usually proxied by the series of returns associated with a broad index such as the FTSE 100 or Standard & Poor's 500.

Numerical example

Assume that the risk-free rate of interest is 8%, the return on the market index is 16%, and the standard deviation of the market is 40%; that is:

$$R^* = 8\%, \quad R_M = 16\% \quad \text{and} \quad \sigma_M = 0.40 \ (40\%)$$

Then the market price of risk is (16-8)/40 = 0.20 and the equation for the capital market line is:

$$E(R_p) = 8 + 0.2\sigma_p$$

If an investor is prepared to hold part of his wealth in the risk-free asset and part in the market portfolio, so that he has a risk between 0% and 40%, say $\sigma_p = 30\%$, then the expected return is:

$$E(R_p) = 8 + 0.2(30) = 14\%$$

7.20   Conclusions

The fundamental insight of portfolio theory is that in general the process of diversification enables investors to improve the risk–return trade-off. Crucial to this process is consideration of both the number of securities and the degree of correlation amongst the individual securities that make up a portfolio. A well diversified portfolio will tend to be one that is made up of securities that have a tendency to move in opposite directions or have low correlations, rather than securities that tend to move in similar directions and with high correlations. To the extent that shares are likely to move in similar directions, then shares that have low positive correlations provide better scope for diversification than shares that have a higher positive correlation.

We have seen that the correlation coefficient lies between −1 and +1. In the extreme case when securities are perfectly correlated (correlation coefficient +1) then diversification will not result in any risk reduction; whilst at the other extreme, of perfect negative correlation (correlation coefficient −1), it is possible by choice of appropriate weightings between the two securities to totally eliminate portfolio risk. While naïve diversification can lead to substantial risk reduction to a portfolio, the process of efficient diversification by taking account of correlations and standard deviations between securities can enable investors to obtain an even better risk–return trade-off.

Further reading

Cuthbertson, K. and Nitzche, D. (2008) *Investments*, Wiley.

Elton, E., Gruber, M., Brown, S. and Goetzmann, W.N. (2007) *Modern Portfolio Theory and Investment Analysis*, Wiley.

Reilley, F.K. and Brown, K.C. (2005) *Investment Analysis and Portfolio Management*, South Western College Publishing.

Sharpe, W.F., Alexander, G.J. and Baley, J. (2002) *Investments*, 6th edn, Pearson.

Chapter 7	Revision questions

1 Explain the difference between naïve diversification and efficient diversification.

2 Describe what is meant the market portfolio and how it relates to the idea of a risk premium on risky assets.

3 You have the following 6 years of data covering share A and the market portfolio:

Year	Share A	Market portfolio	Weighted yearly return
2005	7%	9%	?
2006	4%	2%	?
2007	6%	15%	?
2008	1%	5%	?
2009	−3%	−4%	?
2010	4%	15%	?

   (i)   Calculate the yearly returns of a portfolio created by allocating your money 30% in share A and 70% in the market portfolio.

   (ii) Calculate the expected return and standard deviation of stock A.

   (iii) Calculate the expected return and standard deviation (use population *N*) of the market.

   (iv) Calculate the expected return and standard deviation (use population *N*) of a portfolio made up of 30% investment in share A and 70% in the market.

4 A market portfolio is made up entirely of the following four securities:

	Total value in millions	Standard deviation		Correlation matrix A	B	C	D
Security A	$100	20%	A	1.0	0	0	0
Security B	$40	30%	B	0	1.0	0	0
Security C	$60	40%	C	0	0	1.0	0
Security D	$80	50%	D	0	0	0	1.0

   (i) Calculate the standard deviation of the market portfolio.

   (ii) If the risk-free rate of interest is 5% and the expected rate of return on the market portfolio is 12%, draw a diagram to depict the relevant capital market line.

| Chapter 7 | Revision questions – *continued* |

    (iii)   You have to advise someone seeking to obtain an expected rate of return of 19%. What investment strategy do you advise them to achieve this and what standard deviation can they expect?

5   The risk-free rate of interest is 5%. Alternatively, a risky portfolio is available that has an expected return of 11% for next year and a standard deviation of 20%.

    (i)   How could you combine the risk-free security with the risky portfolio to obtain an expected rate of return of 8%?

    (ii)   How could you combine these two portfolios to obtain a standard deviation of 17%?

    (iii)   How could you combine the two portfolios to obtain an expected return of 23%?

6   The policy-making committee of Bank ABC recently used reports from its securities analysts to develop the following efficient portfolios.

Portfolio	Expected rate of return	Standard deviation
1	8%	5%
2	10%	6%
3	15%	8%
4	20%	13%
5	25%	18%

    (i)   If the risk-free rate of interest is 3% which portfolio is best?

    (ii)   Assume that the policy-making committee would like to earn an expected rate of return of 10% with a standard deviation of 4%, is this possible?

    (iii)   If a standard deviation of 12% was acceptable to the investment committee, what would be the expected rate of return and how could it best be achieved?

    (iv)   What is the expected rate of return on a combined portfolio made up of all the above five portfolios with an equal weighting given to each portfolio? Would the standard deviation of this combined portfolio be higher or lower than that of portfolio 3 or is it not possible to say?

7   Explain what is meant by risk aversion. How might we measure risk in financial markets?

8

THE CAPITAL ASSET PRICING MODEL

Learning objectives

In this chapter you will learn about:

- the market model and the difference between systematic and unsystematic risk
- the theory behind the capital asset pricing model (CAPM)
- the empirical evidence concerning the CAPM
- the multifactor CAPM model
- criticisms of the CAPM
- the arbitrage pricing theory (APT)

8.1   Introduction

One of the problems with implementing portfolio theory is that a huge number of covariances have to be calculated when assessing the risk to a portfolio. While the Markowitz model provides a relatively straightforward solution for the two-asset case, it becomes much more complicated to solve for the efficiency frontier when there are more than two assets. In the N-securities case, it is necessary to calculate $(N^2 - N)/2$ covariances. This means with 100 securities one would need to calculate 4950 covariances, and with 500 securities this increases to 124,750 covariances. The amount of calculation required for the Markowitz method was one of the factors stimulating other approaches to investment management. The foundations for the capital asset pricing model (CAPM) were laid by portfolio theory and the introduction of a risk-free asset. Underlying the CAPM is, however, the basic idea that agents will only accept increased risk for an increased expected rate of return. The CAPM attempts to place a price on the increased risk and show that the market will only place a price on market risk, that is risk that cannot be diversified away. In its turn, the expected return tells us how any security or any portfolio should be priced.

8.2   The market model

The first attempt to simplify portfolio theory was suggested by Sharpe (1963). The basic observation behind Sharpe's market model was that shares tend to move in varying degrees in line with market itself. When the market rises, then most shares have some degree of positive correlation with the market and tend to rise as well. Sharpe postulated a linear link between a security and the market as a whole as given by:

$$E(R_i) = \alpha_i + \beta_i E(R_m) \tag{8.1}$$

where $E(R_i)$ is the expected rate of return on security i; $E(R_m)$ is the expected rate of return on the market; α_i is a constant factor which varies between securities; β_i is the security's beta which measures the sensitivity of the return on security i to the return in the market as a whole.

The Sharpe model introduces the idea via the beta coefficient that the return on a security is sensitive to fluctuations in the market as a whole. If a share has a beta of unity it would rise or fall by a similar percentage as the market rises or falls. If, however, it has a beta of greater than unity it will tend to be more volatile than the market as a whole and therefore should have a higher expected return. If the share has a beta of less than unity it will fluctuate less than the market as a whole and should therefore command a return lower than the market as a whole assuming alpha is zero. According to Sharpe's market model, the sole common factor affecting all securities is the market rate of return; influences such as dividend yield, price–earnings ratios, quality of management and industry-specific factors have no separate influence. For regression purposes the market model given by equation (8.1) becomes:

$$R_i = \alpha_i + \beta_i(R_m) + e_i \tag{8.2}$$

where R_i is the actual return of an individual security; R_m is the actual market return over the period; and e_i is a random error.

Equation (8.2) is often referred to as the characteristic line of a security as shown in **Figure 8.1**. The systematic component is $R_i = \alpha_i + \beta_i(R_m)$ and the unsystematic or specific component is picked up by the error term e_i.

The alpha term in equation (8.2) gives the constant of the regression; in this case alpha is positive suggesting that on average the security in question tends to earn a positive return even when there is no movement in the market as a whole. The beta coefficient is picked up by the slope of the regression line and it tells us how much on average the return on the security can be expected to rise for a 1 per cent rise in the market rate of return. If a security has a beta equal to 1.5, this means that if the market rises by 10 per cent, then one can expect the security to rise on average by 15 per cent; whereas, if a security has a beta of 0.7 and the market rises by 10 per cent, then the company's share would rise on average by 7 per cent.

The regression line is a fitted equation giving the line of best fit for the data. The deviation of an observation from the line of best fit is known as the error of the

Figure 8.1   The market model

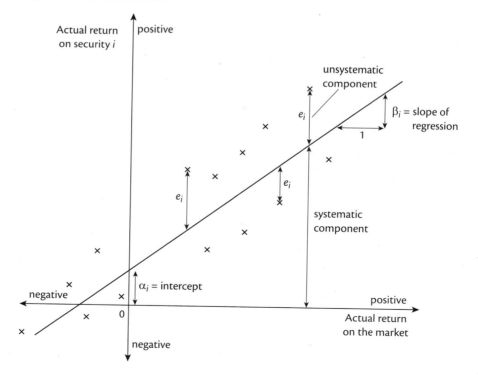

regression and in this case picks up the unsystematic risk of the security. The greater the deviation of the square of these observations, the greater the unsystematic risk of the security, other things being equal. We use the square of the error terms because the ordinary least-squares estimation technique ensures that the sum of these errors is zero (the positive and negative deviations from the regression line cancelling each other out). Squaring the errors means that positive and negative deviations are both relevant to the unsystematic risk.

The total risk factor on an individual security, since α_i is a constant, is given by:

$$\sigma_i^2 = \beta_i^2 \sigma_m^2 + \sigma_{e_i}^2 \tag{8.3}$$

Total risk = Market risk + Specific risk

If a security has a high proportion of its total risk made up of specific (diversifiable) risk, this can be easily reduced or eliminated by low-cost diversification.

8.3 Portfolio risk and return using the market model

Using the market model the expected return and variance of a portfolio are given by:

$$E(R_p) = \alpha_p + \beta_p E(R_m) \tag{8.4}$$

with

$$\alpha_p = \sum_{i=1}^{N} w_i \alpha_i \tag{8.5}$$

and

$$\beta_p = \sum_{i=1}^{N} w_i \beta_i \tag{8.6}$$

where w_i is the value weight of security i in the portfolio; α_p is the alpha of a portfolio of securities; and β_p is the beta of a portfolio of securities; N is the number of securities in the portfolio.

Note that the weights in equations (8.5) and (8.6) must sum to unity. Equations (8.4) to (8.6) say that the expected rate of return on a portfolio is given by a weighted average of all the weighted alpha and beta coefficients, where the portfolio beta is multiplied by the market rate of return.

Since the alpha coefficients are assumed to be constant and therefore have zero variance, then the total risk of the portfolio is given by:

$$\sigma_p^2 = \beta_p^2 \sigma_m^2 + \sum_{i=1}^{N} w_i^2 \sigma_{e_i}^2 \tag{8.7}$$

Total portfolio risk = Market risk + Specific portfolio risk

where σ_p^2 is the variance of the portfolio; β_p^2 is the square of the portfolio beta; σ_m^2 is the variance of the market; w_i^2 is the square of the weight of security i; and $\sigma_{e_i}^2$ is the variance of the error of security i.

The first expression on the right-hand side of equation (8.7) shows the market risk (systematic risk) of the portfolio, while the summation expression involving the error terms shows the unsystematic risk of holding the portfolio. Hence, the market model looks at total risk, both systematic and unsystematic, when evaluating a portfolio.

The effect of including a large number of securities in a portfolio is to make their random error components cancel each other out, leaving only the market risk (systematic risk) factor for investors to worry about. In the case where wealth is allocated in equal proportion over N securities, then $w_i = 1/N$ in equation (8.7) and it is clear that, as N increases, specific risk can be eliminated almost entirely since $w_i^2 = 1/N^2$ which becomes smaller more quickly than N increases.

A major advantage of the market model is that it dramatically reduces the number of variables required to evaluate a portfolio. All we need is $3N + 2$ data items; that is, for each security we need to calculate α_i, β_i and $\sigma_{e_i}^2$ and the relevant market risk and portfolio specific risk as in equation (8.7), rather than $N(N-1)/2$ covariances as required by the Markowtiz model. For 100 securities we need only 302 calculations rather than 4950 under the Markowitz method! Against this, however, a major problem with Sharpe's model is that it lacks a clear theoretical base. Such a base is provided by the capital asset pricing model (CAPM).

8.4   The capital asset pricing model

The CAPM was originally devised as an offshoot from the market model by Sharpe (1964) and Lintner (1965). It attempts to explain the relationship between the risk and return on a financial security, and this relationship can then be used to determine the appropriate price for the security.

The basic idea of the CAPM is that if a share helps to stabilize a portfolio, that is make it more in line with the market, then that share will earn a similar rate of return to the market portfolio. If a share makes a portfolio more risky as compared to the market portfolio it will be less in demand by risk-averse investors, its price will fall and its expected rate of return will be above the market rate of return. Conversely, if a share reduces the risk of a portfolio compared to the market portfolio it will be more in demand by risk-averse investors, its price will be bid up so that it earns a lower rate of return than the average market return.

Another key idea of the CAPM is that in an efficient market all diversifiable risk will be eliminated (given that there are no transaction costs), so that the only risk that will be priced by the market on a portfolio is systematic or market risk. Hence, the CAPM model concentrates only on the pricing of undiversifiable market risk. As we shall see, the CAPM provides a simple measure of the systematic risk attached to a security given by the security's beta.

8.5   Assumptions of the CAPM

The CAPM makes a number of key assumptions relating to the operation of capital markets and investors' behaviour:

1   Capital markets are perfect, there is only a single borrowing and lending rate (no transaction costs), all capital assets are perfectly divisible (one can buy fractions

of a security) and there are no taxes, investors can sell short (sell stock they do not own), and information is freely available to all market participants.

2 Investors attempt to maximize their utility, which consists of maximizing returns for a given level of risk. Investors are risk-averse and measure risk in terms of standard deviations of returns.

3 Investors use a common one-period-ahead time horizon for investment decisions. All investment decisions are made at the beginning of the period and no changes are made during the investment horizon.

4 Investors have identical expectations about the risk and return on various securities. Hence, the only reason why investors hold different portfolios is because they have different risk preferences.

5 There exists a single risk-free asset at which borrowing and lending can take place.

These assumptions set the CAPM apart from the Markowitz model. In particular, assumption 4 means that investors all have the same efficiency frontier, which is more restrictive than portfolio theory whereby investors with different perceptions can have different efficiency frontiers. The inclusion of the risk-free asset means that in the CAPM there is a linear trade-off between risk and return that is not present in the Markowitz model.

8.6 The theory behind the CAPM

Consider the efficiency frontier with N risky securities, given by the curve EF in **Figure 8.2**. Since we have assumed that all investors have identical expectations, then this efficiency frontier is the same for all investors in the economy. A straight line L1 is drawn in the figure from the risk-free rate of interest R* tangential to the efficiency frontier at point M. The question we need to consider is which out of portfolios M, A and B, or any other portfolio along the efficiency frontier, investors will choose. The striking result of the CAPM model is that in equilibrium all investors will choose to allocate their investment wealth between the same mix of securities as given by portfolio M and the risk-free asset. The only difference between investors will be the proportions in which they allocate their wealth between the portfolio of securities given by M, and the risk-free rate of interest.

First consider portfolios A and B which lie on the efficiency frontier EF. We have placed two indifference curves representing two different investors, one at A and one at B. The investor at point A is more risk-averse than the investor at B; that is, the investor at A prefers less risk for a lower expected rate of return than the investor at B. Investor 1 at A is on indifference curve I1, and investor 2 at B is on indifference curve I2. These are their optimum positions in the absence of a risk-free security.

With the possibility of lending and borrowing at the risk-free rate of interest, it is relatively straightforward to show that both investors should pick portfolio M regardless of their risk–return preference, and then borrow or lend funds at the risk-free rate of interest R*. To understand this result and the significance of the portfolio given by M, consider what happens when the risk-free asset is introduced into the picture. There is now a linear trade-off between risk and return, and the line that will enable either investor to get on the highest indifference curve is L1 which is tangential

Figure 8.2   The capital market line and the market portfolio

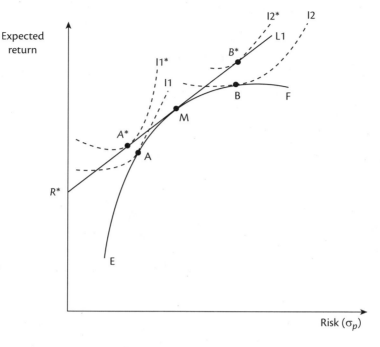

to the efficiency frontier at portfolio M, the market portfolio. Line L1 is known as the capital market line and shows that there is a linear trade-off between risk and return.

Since the standard deviation of the risk-free asset is zero, $\sigma_{R^*} = 0$, then the standard deviation of the combined portfolio is simply the standard deviation of the risky market portfolio M times the weight of the risky market portfolio.

$$\sigma_p = w\sigma_m \tag{8.8}$$

where w is the weight invested in the risky market portfolio.

When all wealth is invested in the market portfolio (that is, $w = 1$), the investor will have a portfolio with the same standard deviation as the market portfolio. However, since investors can borrow or lend money at the risk-free rate of interest R^*, they might wish to invest all their money in the portfolio M or a mixture of the two. The investor that was at A now has the option of investing a proportion of his money (w) in a risky market portfolio M, and the remainder ($1 - w$) in the risk-free asset. By doing this the investor can move onto a higher indifference curve I1*. This means that investor 1 is lending funds. The proportion of his money invested in the risk-free asset is given by ($1 - w$) or the distance $[1 - (R^*A^*/R^*M)]$. The closer A* is to M then the greater the proportion invested in the market portfolio.

Since the portfolio includes a risk-free asset, then we have already determined from equation (8.8) that $\sigma_p = w\sigma_m$. The variance is the square of this as given by:

$$\sigma_p^2 = w^2\sigma_m^2 \tag{8.9}$$

where σ_p^2 is the variance on the portfolio; and σ_m^2 is the variance on the market portfolio.

capital market line
a straight line passing through the risk-free rate of return and the expected rate of return on the market portfolio with risk measured by the standard deviation on the horizontal axis and the rate of return on the vertical axis

The investor that was at B could also reach a higher indifference curve I2*. To do this, however, the investor needs to borrow funds at the risk-free rate of interest since the investor has a w greater than 1 and therefore invests more than 100 per cent of his wealth in the risky asset. Where w is greater than 1, then $(1 - w)$ is a negative position in the risk-free asset, indicating that the investor has borrowed money at the risk-free rate of interest. By doing this he can move onto a higher indifference curve I2*. The proportion of his money invested in the risk-free asset is given by $(1 - w)$ or the distance $[1 - (R*B*/R*M)]$.

The striking result is that both investors will be content to invest in the market portfolio regardless of their risk–return preferences. The issue is not what portfolio of risky securities to invest in, but rather how much of one's wealth should be allocated to the risk-free asset and how much to the market portfolio.

We have established that M is the optimum portfolio, but why is it called the market portfolio? The answer is that since M is the only portfolio that all investors will hold, then all the risky securities in the economy that make up portfolio M must be correctly priced and willingly held by all investors. In consequence, the market portfolio is a portfolio of all the risky assets in the economy weighted by their market value over the market value of all assets in the economy. Since the market portfolio is by definition a value-weighted portfolio of all the risky assets in the economy, it is also a portfolio with no diversifiable risk. The only risk in the market portfolio is market risk; all specific/diversifiable risk has been eliminated.

The expected rate of return on a combined portfolio M is given by:

$$E(R_p) = (1 - w)R^* + wE(R_m) \tag{8.10}$$

where $E(R_p)$ is the expected rate of return on a composite portfolio of the risk-free asset and the market portfolio; and $E(R_m)$ is the expected rate of return on the market portfolio.

Equation (8.10) can be rearranged to yield equation (8.11):

$$E(R_p) = R^* + w[E(R_m) - R^*] \tag{8.11}$$

from which we can see that, when w is greater than 1 (borrowing), the expected return on the combined portfolio is greater than the market rate of return; while if w is less than 1 the portfolio earns less than the market rate of return.

By rearranging equation (8.8) we obtain:

$$w = \frac{\sigma_p}{\sigma_m} \tag{8.12}$$

and substituting equation (8.12) into equation (8.11) yields:

$$E(R_p) = R^* + \frac{\sigma_p}{\sigma_m}[E(R_m) - R^*] \tag{8.13}$$

Equation (8.13) represents the capital market line (CML) which expresses the expected return for a portfolio in terms of risk. Any portfolio on the CML is efficient since it must be perfectly positively related with the market portfolio. The expression $[E(R_m) - R^*]/\sigma_m$ gives the slope of the CML and is known as the market price of risk.

If we define the beta of a portfolio (β_p) as $\beta_p = \sigma_p / \sigma_m$, then equation (8.13) becomes:

$$E(R_p) = R^* + \beta_p[E(R_m) - R^*] \tag{8.14}$$

Equations (8.13) and (8.14) represent the CAPM for portfolios of securities. Equation (8.14) says that the average expected return on a composite portfolio made up of a risk-free asset and a portfolio of risky assets will exceed the riskless rate of interest by an amount proportional to the portfolio's beta. Furthermore, this relationship is linear.

8.7   Expressing the CAPM in risk premium form

risk premium the extra rate of return charged by investors above the risk-free rate of return to compensate for risk

The CAPM is frequently defined in terms of a risk premium. If we define the expected risk premium on a portfolio $E(RP_p)$ as the difference between the expected return on the portfolio $E(R_p)$ and the risk-free rate of interest R^*, and the expected risk premium on the market portfolio $E(RP_m)$ as the difference between the expected rate of return on the market portfolio $E(R_m)$ and the risk-free rate of interest, then:

$$E(RP_p) = E(R_p) - R^* \tag{8.15}$$

and

$$E(RP_m) = E(R_m) - R^* \tag{8.16}$$

Substituting equations (8.15) and (8.16) into equation (8.14) we obtain:

$$E(RP_p) = \beta_p E(RP_m) \tag{8.17}$$

which tells us that the excess return above the risk-free rate of interest on a portfolio is a function of the beta of the portfolio and the difference between the market rate of return and the risk-free rate of interest. When the beta of a portfolio is equal to unity, the excess return coincides with the market excess return. When beta is greater than unity, the portfolio can be expected to have a higher excess return than the market portfolio. Conversely, when beta is less than unity the portfolio can be expected to have a lower excess return than the market portfolio.

We can conclude that the correct measure of risk for an efficient portfolio, as represented by the capital market line, is the standard deviation of the return, that is the total risk. This must be so because in an efficient portfolio all diversifiable/specific risk has been eliminated, leaving only undiversifiable market risk. By definition an efficient portfolio has no diversifiable/specific risk since it has all been diversified away.

8.8   The securities market line

The capital market line is a useful expression for the pricing of efficient portfolios, that is combinations of the market portfolio and the risk-free security, but does not give a clue to the pricing of inefficient portfolios, individual securities or poorly diversified portfolios containing only a few securities. Ideally, we would like to derive an expression for the risk–return trade-off for any individual security or any portfolio, not just efficient portfolios which lie on the capital market line.

It can be shown that the appropriate measure of the risk of an individual security is given by:

$$E(R_i) = R^* + \frac{\sigma_{im}}{\sigma_m^2}[E(R_m) - R^*] \qquad (8.18)$$

where σ_{im} is the covariance of security i with the market portfolio M; and σ_m^2 is the variance of the market portfolio.

This is equivalent to:

$$E(R_i) = R^* + \frac{\sigma_i \rho_{im}}{\sigma_m}[E(R_m) - R^*] \qquad (8.19)$$

where σ_i is the standard deviation of security i; and ρ_{im} is the correlation coefficient of security i with the market portfolio.

> **securities market line** a line which measures the relationship between beta (or systematic risk) and firm's expected rate of return

Equation (8.19) is the equation for the securities market line (SML) and relates the rate of return for a security to its systematic risk as given by its beta. It looks reasonably similar to the equation for the CML, but a crucial difference is the inclusion of the correlation coefficient of the security with the market. When a new security is added to the portfolio we are concerned not only about its variance relative to the market, but also its correlation with the market. If it has a low correlation with the market it will help to stabilize a portfolio and will thus tend to receive a lower return than a security that adds to the instability of a portfolio. Equation (8.19) can be rewritten as:

$$E(R_i) = R^* + \beta_i[E(R_m) - R^*] \qquad (8.20)$$

where $\beta_i = \sigma_i \rho_{im}/\sigma_m$.

> **defensive security** a security with a beta less than 1 that is expected to earn a lower rate of return than the market

An individual stock's beta, β_i, is a function not only of its variance compared to the market, but also its covariance with the market. If a stock is perfectly correlated with the market portfolio (that is, $\rho_{im} = 1$) then its standard deviation will also coincide with the market portfolio ($\sigma_i = \sigma_m$) and therefore its beta is unity and its expected rate of return coincides with the market rate of return. Stocks with a beta of less than unity (that is, $\sigma_i \rho_{im} < \sigma_m$) help to stabilize portfolios and are referred to as defensive securities. Stocks with betas greater than unity (that is, $\sigma_i \rho_{im} > \sigma_m$) which increase the volatility of a portfolio and are expected to earn the market rate of return are known as aggressive securities. Typical defensive stocks are companies in relatively stable sectors of the economy such as food retailers, gas and electricity companies (so-called utilities), while aggressive stocks include those that are more volatile than the market such as property, luxury goods manufacturers, technology, fashion industries and so on.

> **aggressive security** a security with a beta greater than 1 that is expected to earn a higher rate of return than the market

When it comes to inefficient portfolios or single securities, total risk is no longer an appropriate measure because an inefficient portfolio is not well-diversified and so contains both diversifiable/specific and market risk. Since the specific risk could be easily diversified away, then only the systematic component of total risk as reflected in the beta of the security will be priced by the market. This undiversifiable component is correlated with the market return which represents the inherent risk of the economy in general. The return on an individual share should be based on the systematic risk rather than on total risk. All inefficient portfolios contain both systematic and unsystematic risk; no one will pay for that component of risk that can be easily diversified away at low cost, and the market will only pay for undiversifiable risk.

The CAPM suggests that the required rate of return on a security consists of three components:

1   The price of time as measured by the risk-free rate of interest (that is, the reward to the investor for delaying consumption).
2   The quantity of risk as measured by the beta of the security.
3   The market price of risk as measured by the difference between the expected return on the market and the risk-free rate of interest $[E(R_m) - R^*]$.

Once we know the market price of risk, we can calculate the required rate of return on an individual security or portfolio by looking at the beta coefficient. When measuring risk to calculate the capital market, we looked only at systematic or market risk as measured by the total risk since all specific risk can be eliminated by low-cost diversification. When calculating the securities market line we again only need to look at the systematic risk and for this reason we replace the standard deviation for the security with the security's beta coefficient on the horizontal axis as depicted in **Figure 8.3**.

If the CAPM holds, then the expected rate of return for any individual asset given its beta coefficient should lie on the SML. An asset that is not on the SML is deemed to be incorrectly priced. For example, if security Z has a return R_Z above the SML, then it is underpriced since its rate of return is greater than its expected rate of return $E(R_Z)$ as indicated by its beta would merit. Conversely, if security Y has a return R_Y which is below the SML, then it is overpriced since its return is below the expected rate of return $E(R_Y)$ that its beta would merit.

Figure 8.3   The securities market line

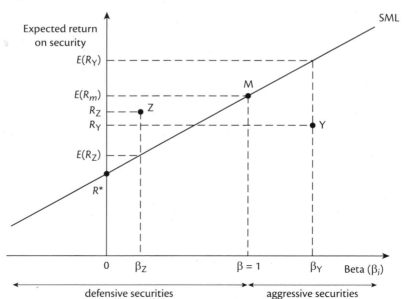

The key point about the CAPM as it relates to an individual security is that when adding a security to a portfolio an investor will only be rewarded for the covariance of the security with the market, not for its total risk as represented by the standard deviation of the security. The CAPM shows that the holder of a risky security can only expect to be rewarded for the systematic or market risk, and not for unsystematic or specific risk since the latter can be easily diversified away. Securities with betas above unity are classified as aggressive securities, while those with betas below unity are classified as defensive securities.

8.9   The CAPM in action: measuring the beta coefficient

It is possible to empirically estimate the value of a beta by using historical time-series data. A study might also estimate the beta coefficient over different time periods to examine its stability over time. The data set can consist of daily, weekly, monthly or even quarterly data; the time period and frequency of the data will determine the number of observations used, and it is important that the time period and frequency used for estimation of the beta is the same for both the portfolio and the market. For the market index, the series of returns associated with a broad index such as the FTSE 100 or the Standard & Poor's 500 are generally used. The estimated beta will be affected by a number of variables, such as the time period over which the return is calculated, the frequency of the data (daily, weekly, monthly or quarterly) and the market index used.

Various agencies conduct regression analyses of equation (8.20) to find the relevant coefficients. The analyses are usually based on monthly observations of the last five years' data. An essential prerequisite is that the estimated betas need to be stable over time (that is, exhibit stationarity).

$$E(R_i) = R^* + \beta_i[R_m - R^*] + e_i \tag{8.21}$$

where ei is the random error (representing specific risk).

Consider a regression analysis of five shares A–E that are estimated using equation (8.21) and have the following results:

Share	Beta	Specific risk e_i	Annual return (%)
A	0.6	0.25	20
B	0.8	0.35	15
C	0.7	0.55	7
D	1.1	0.30	18
E	0.9	0.40	10

Note that specific risk e_i is measured in this case by the standard deviation of the error term, that is, σ_{e_i} so we need to take the square of this to get the variance.

The risk-free rate of interest $R^* = 7\%$, the market rate of return is $R_m = 12\%$ and the standard deviation of the market is $\sigma_m = 0.20$. The question we would like to answer is does a portfolio made up equally of the five shares A to E have a good risk–return performance? We shall assume that an investor has equal amounts invested in the five shares so that wi becomes $1/N$ where N is the number of shares in the portfolio.

We need to calculate three things:

1 the portfolio's beta;
2 the total risk of the portfolio, that is, both systematic and unsystematic risk; and
3 the actual return of the portfolio against its systematic return as required by the CAPM.

The portfolio's beta is:

$$\beta_p = \sum_{i=1}^{N} w_i \beta_i \qquad (8.22)$$
$$= 0.2(0.6) + 0.2(0.8) + 0.2(0.7) + 0.2(1.1) + 0.2(0.9)$$
$$= 0.82$$

The total risk of the portfolio is made up of systematic and unsystematic risk:

$$\sigma_p^2 = \beta_p^2 \sigma_m^2 + \sum_{i=1}^{N} w_i^2 \sigma_{ei}^2 \qquad (8.23)$$

The systematic risk is given by:

$$\beta_p^2 \sigma_m^2 = (0.82)^2 \times (0.2)^2$$
$$= 0.02690$$

The specific risk is simply the weighted average of the specific risk factors:

$$\sum_{i=1}^{N} w_i^2 \sigma_{ei}^2 \qquad (8.24)$$

where $\sigma_{e_i}^2$ is the specific risk (as measured by the variance) of the portfolio. The weight for each share is 1/5 so we use $1/5 \times 1/5 = 1/25$:

$$\sum_{i=1}^{N} w_i^2 \sigma_{ei}^2 = \frac{1}{25}(0.25)^2 + \frac{1}{25}(0.35) + \frac{1}{25}(0.55)^2 + \frac{1}{25}(0.3)^2 + \frac{1}{25}(0.4)^2$$
$$= 0.0295$$

Note that the portfolio's specific risk is lower than the specific risk of any of the individual constituents; however, it is still present but diminishes rapidly as the number of assets in the portfolio increases.

The total variance of the portfolio is:

$$\sigma_p^2 = 0.0269 + 0.0295$$
$$= 0.0564$$

In the above example, $0.02690/0.0564 = 47.7\%$ of the total risk cannot be diversified away, while $0.0295/0.0564 = 52.3\%$ of the total risk can be diversified away. The standard deviation of the portfolio is the square root of 0.0564:

$$\sigma_p = 0.2375$$

The standard deviation of the portfolio, 0.2375, is greater than the standard deviation of the market, 0.2. We are now in a position to evaluate the performance of the portfolio.

The beta of the portfolio is 0.82 so, according to the CAPM, the appropriate rate of return is:

$$R_p = R^* + \beta[R_m - R^*]$$
$$= 7 + 0.82(12 - 7)$$
$$= 11.1\%$$

The return actually achieved was:

$$R_p = 0.2(20\%) + 0.2(15\%) + 0.2(7\%) + 0.2(18\%) + 0.2(10\%)$$
$$= 14\%$$

So this particular portfolio of shares has outperformed a CAPM strategy. The diversifiable (specific) risk in this instance led to a performance which beat the benchmark of investing in the risk-free asset and the market index.

8.10 Empirical testing of the CAPM

The CAPM model can be applied to both individual shares and to portfolios of shares. However, tests of the CAPM based on individual shares are not very powerful tests. This is because the estimated beta on an individual share will be vulnerable to a large number of error factors, that is, the return on an individual security typically has a large random component. This problem is considerably reduced by grouping shares with similar risk characteristics (that is, similar betas) into portfolios of shares since the measurement errors in the individual securities will tend to cancel each other out (shares with positive errors being offset by shares with negative errors). This enables a clearer picture of the relationship between systematic risk and return to emerge.

A typical empirical estimation of the CAPM involves looking at portfolio betas. Repeating equation (8.17):

$$E(RP_p) = \beta_p E(RP_m)$$

Then empirically a regression would be run such that:

$$RP_p = a + b(RP_m) + e_p \tag{8.25}$$

where RP_p is the excess return on the portfolio above the risk-free rate of interest; RP_m is the market risk premium (excess return on the market over risk-free return); and e_p is the specific (that is, unsystematic risk) risk on the portfolio. The intercept term is captured by the parameter a, and the empirical estimate of beta by b.

Box 8.1	Measuring a fund manager's performance

Risk-adjusted performance metrics (RAPM): the Sharpe ratio, Treynor ratio and Jensen's alpha

When one looks at advertisements in the press a fund will typically mention its returns – 'In the last five years our fund grew by 20% per year while the stock market rose only 10% per year' – suggesting that the fund is worthy of investing in. But there are a couple of caveats that will need to be borne in mind. The first is that the past is not necessarily a good guide to the future; just because a fund has outperformed in the past does not necessarily mean it has a greater chance of performing any better than any other fund in the future. Secondly, of course, there is something rather important missing from the advert, and that concerns the risk that the fund has been taking. Maybe it is up 20% a year on average but is extremely volatile: +60% in year 1, −20% in year 2, +60% in year 3, −40% in year 4 and +40% in year 5. Another fund might have achieved very steady returns of 12% a year fluctuating between +10% and +14%. The point is that the second fund has a lower return but also a lower risk than the first fund, which seems to have higher returns but considerably higher risk. We know from the CAPM that it is very easy for a fund to increase its expected performance by borrowing money and in so doing increase its risk. A fund manager may simply be outperforming the market and other fund managers by just using leverage (i.e. borrowing) and thereby increasing the risk. What is clear is that we need to look at risk as well as returns when evaluating a fund manager's performance. There are three well known ratios that attempt to evaluate a fund managers risk-adjusted performance measurement (RAPM). All are based upon material that we have covered in this chapter: the Sharpe ratio, the Treynor ratio and Jensen's alpha.

The Sharpe ratio or reward to variability ratio proposed by the Nobel prize winner William Sharpe (1966) is a popular measure which is defined as:

$$\text{Sharpe ratio} = \frac{R_p - R^*}{\sigma_p}$$

where R_p is the return on the portfolio, R^* is the risk-free rate of return and σ_p is the standard deviation of the portfolio. The idea of the Sharpe ratio is that the excess return in the numerator needs to be compared to the risk of the portfolio in the denominator. The idea is that a portfolio with a high Sharpe ratio can be said to be doing relatively well compared to another portfolio with a lower ratio. Imagine the market portfolio has a $\sigma_m = 10\%$ and the return on the market averages 11% while the risk-free rate of interest is 4%, then the Sharpe ratio for the market would be $(11 - 4)/10 = 0.7$. As such, a manager who achieves a 15% rate of return but with a portfolio standard deviation $\sigma_p = 20\%$ would have a Sharpe ratio of $(15 - 4)/20 = 0.55$ which is lower than the market portfolio Sharpe ratio. We can argue that although the fund manager is beating the market the extra return of 4% is not sufficient to compensate for the doubling of risk from 10% to 20%.

| Box 8.1 | Measuring a fund manager's performance – *continued* |

A great advantage of the Sharpe ratio is that it is easy to compute from observed returns. In addition, it can be useful to compare different categories of investments, for example, comparing the Sharpe ratios of various investment classes such as stocks, bonds and commodities. However, the Sharpe ratio can sometimes give very misleading signals about the risk of funds that have employed strategies that for many periods have led to steady positive return, but then eventually blow up disastrously. Also the value of the Sharpe ratio can be quite sensitive to the start and end dates used as well as the specific time periods considered.

Another ratio that can be employed to evaluate portfolios is the Treynor ratio, proposed by Jack Treynor (1965). This also looks at the excess return of a portfolio above the risk-free rate of return, but rather than divide it by the total risk as given by the standard deviation of the portfolio the Treynor ratio divides it by the systematic risk of the portfolio as given by the portfolio's beta.

$$\text{Treynor ratio} = \frac{R_p - R^*}{\beta_p}$$

The Treynor ratio can be a useful measure to compare diversified portfolios with relatively little unsystematic risk in them. A fund manager with a higher Treynor ratio than another fund manager with a similar beta is performing relatively well. A fund manager with a higher beta and lower excess return than another fund manager would be underperforming relative to one with a higher excess return and lower beta. Of the two measures, the Sharpe ratio tends to be more widely used than the Treynor ratio because the Sharpe ratio penalizes managers that have relatively undiversified portfolios and therefore high amounts of unsystematic risk.

A final measure that is has become even more popular than the Sharpe ratio is Jensen's alpha α_J, proposed by Michael Jensen (1968). It is defined as the excess return on a portfolio over that which could be predicted for the portfolio on the basis of the CAPM, that is:

$$\text{Jensen's alpha} = \alpha_J = R_p - \left[R^* + \beta_p (R_m - R^*) \right]$$

If Jensen's alpha is positive then the portfolio manager is doing better, given his portfolio's beta, than one might have predicted from the CAPM. In other words, the manager is 'beating the market' in the sense that he is achieving a higher return than the risk profile of his portfolio would merit. If Jensen's alpha is negative then the fund manager is 'underperforming the market' in the sense that he is achieving a lower return than the risk profile of his portfolio would merit. In sum, a positive alpha would show that the fund manager is doing better than one would expect given the risk profile of his portfolio, the greater the alpha the greater the outperformance.

continued overleaf

Box 8.1	Measuring a fund manager's performance – *continued*

It is important to note that we need to evaluate a fund manager's performance not over just one year but many years to determine if the manager truly has a positive alpha.

In any single year a positive performance could have been achieved purely by luck, but over a longer period the positive and negative 'luck' will tend to cancel each other out and a manager left with a positive alpha would then seem to be adding real value and have a fund that seems to be above the capital market line (see **Figure 8.4**).

Figure 8.4   Jensen's alpha

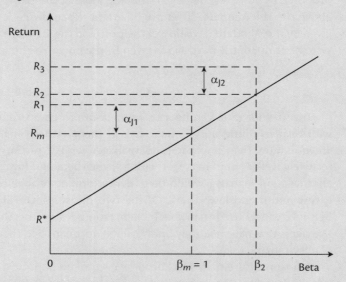

In **Figure 8.4** we know that the market has a beta equal to one and the return achieved is given by R_m. If a fund manager also has a beta equal to 1 but achieves over time a rate of return R_1 which is higher than the R_m predicted from the CAPM then the difference between R_1 and R_m is known as the manager's alpha, in this case equal to α_{J1}. Another manager may have a riskier portfolio with a higher beta than the market such as β_2, for which the CAPM tells us that the expected return over time is R_2. If the manager is achieving a rate of return of R_3 then he has a positive alpha, in this case equal to α_{J2}.

The CAPM makes the following five key predictions:

1 The intercept term in equation (8.25) should be equal to zero, that is, $a = 0$; if it were non-zero then it would mean that the CAPM model is missing something as a complete explanation of a portfolio's excess return.

2 The beta coefficient should be the sole explanation of the rate of return on the risky portfolio. The estimated slope b should be positive and not differ significantly from the risk premium on the market portfolio, $RP_m = R_m - R^*$.

3 There should be a linear relationship given by beta between the average portfolio risk premium and the average market risk premium.

4 Over time, R_m should exceed R^*, since a market portfolio is riskier than the risk-free asset.

5 Other explanatory variables such as dividend yield, firm size and price–earnings ratios should not prove to be statistically significant in predicting the required rate of return.

8.11 The empirical evidence on the CAPM

There have been numerous empirical studies of the CAPM model. Among the most important are Friend and Blume (1970), Black, Jensen and Scholes (1972), Miller and Scholes (1972), Blume and Friend (1973), Fama and MacBeth (1973), Litzenberger and Ramaswamy (1979), Gibbons (1982) and Shanken (1985). Empirical results are, generally speaking, reasonably supportive of the basic tenet of the model, but this is not to say that they constitute a full endorsement. The results of the various studies can be summarized along the following lines:

1 The estimated intercept term, a, tends to be significantly different from zero, contrary to prediction 1.

2 The estimated slope, b, while positive tends to be less than the difference between the market rate of return and the risk-free rate of interest, contrary to prediction 2.

3 The estimated relationship tends to be linear with respect to beta, and over long periods of time the return on the market portfolio exceeds the risk-free rate of interest so that predictions 3 and 4 seem valid.

4 Contrary to prediction 5, it is possible to find other factors that can explain a portfolio's excess return. For example Basu (1977) found low price–earnings-ratio portfolios have higher rates of return than predicted by the CAPM; Banz (1981) found that firm size is important, with smaller firms having higher returns than predicted by the CAPM; while Litzenberger and Ramaswamy (1979) found that equities with high dividend yields required higher rates of return than predicted by the CAPM.

The overall conclusion of the studies is that the empirical securities market line differs somewhat from the theoretical line as depicted in **Figure 8.5**. The general implication is that securities (and portfolios) with low betas tend to earn a higher rate of return than the theoretical model would suggest, while securities (and portfolios) with high betas tend to earn less.

Figure 8.5 The theoretical and empirical securities market lines

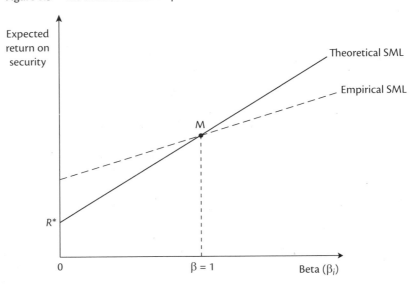

8.12 The multifactor CAPM

The CAPM model that we have looked at suggests that the only risk factor facing an investor is uncertainty concerning the future price of a security. Merton (1973) argues that investors over their lifetime also face other sources of risk that can affect their ability to consume goods and services in the future. These factors include uncertainty over future earnings, future prices of goods and future investment opportunities. Recognizing the existence of these other 'factors', Merton extended the single-factor CAPM to describe the optimal lifetime consumption for consumers facing these 'extra market' sources of risk. The Merton multifactor CAPM for an individual security is given by:

$$E(RP_i) = \beta_i E(RP_m) + \beta_{iF1}E(RP_{F1}) + \beta_{iF2}E(RP_{F2}) + \ldots + \beta_{iFk}E(RP_{Fk}) \quad (8.26)$$

where $E(RP_i)$ is the risk premium on security i, that is the expected return on the security less the risk-free rate of interest; k is the number of factors F, that is extra market sources of risk; β_{iF1}, $\beta_{iF2} \ldots \beta_{iFk}$ is the sensitivity of security i to the $1, 2 \ldots k$th factors; and $E(RP_{F1})$, $E(RP_{F2}) \ldots E(RP_{Fk})$ is the risk premium associated with the $1, 2 \ldots k$th factors, that is the expected rate of return required for each of the k factors minus the risk-free rate of interest.

Equation (8.26) says that in addition to the risk premium associated with market risk on a security, investors require compensation for all sources of extra market risk. The model does not specify either how many extra market sources of risk there are, or indeed precisely what they are. However, just as investors will diversify away unsystematic risk associated with securities, they will also attempt to reduce extra market sources of risk.

The Merton multifactor CAPM model for a portfolio of securities is given in risk premium form by:

$$E(RP_p) = \beta_p E(RP_m) + \beta_{pF1} E(RP_{F1}) + \beta_{pF2} E(RP_{F2}) + \ldots + \beta_{pFk} E(RP_{Fk}) \qquad (8.27)$$

where $E(RP_p)$ is the risk premium on the portfolio, that is the expected return on the portfolio less the risk-free rate of interest; k is the number factors F, that is extra market sources of risk; β_{pFk} is the sensitivity of the portfolio to the kth factor; and $E(RP_{Fk})$ is the risk premium associated with the kth factor, that is the expected return of factor k minus the risk-free rate of interest.

8.13   The arbitrage pricing theory (APT) critique of the CAPM

In two papers Ross (1976) and Roll and Ross (1980) argued that the CAPM model was empirically untestable. Their basic criticism was that a true 'market portfolio' needs to contain all assets, both financial and non-financial, in an economy, and many of these are not empirically observable, such as human capital and so on. Furthermore, the CAPM is based upon microeconomic foundations which require the investors' utility function to be measured in terms of expected return and risk as measured by the standard deviation of return.

The basic postulate of the arbitrage pricing theory (APT) is that market risk is itself made up of a number (k) of separate systematic factors. In other words, the single beta reflecting market risk in the CAPM is insufficient. The arbitrage pricing model is derived from a number of arbitrage conditions. In a nutshell, the APT says that the return on a security is linearly related to k systematic 'factors' without specifying exactly what these factors are:

$$E(R_i) = R^* + \beta_{iF1} E(RP_{F1}) + \beta_{iF2} E(RP_{F2}) + \ldots + \beta_{iFk} E(RP_{Fk}) \qquad (8.28)$$

where $E(R_i)$ is the expected return on security i; R^* is the risk-free rate of interest; β_{iF1}, $\beta_{iF2} \ldots \beta_{iFk}$ is the sensitivity of security i to the $1, 2 \ldots k$ factors; $E(RP_{F1})$, $E(RP_{F2})$, $\ldots E(RP_{Fk})$ is the risk premium associated with each of the systematic $1, 2 \ldots k$ factors; for example, $RP_{F1} = (R_1 - R^*)$ where R_1 is the required rate of return for factor 1 and R^* is the risk-free rate of interest.

If we move the risk-free factor to the left-hand side, equation (8.28) can be written in risk-premium form as:

$$E(RP_i) = \beta_{iF1} E(RP_{F1}) + \beta_{iF2} E(RP_{F2}) + \ldots + \beta_{iFk} E(RP_{Fk}) \qquad (8.29)$$

where $E(RP_i)$ is the risk premium of security i, that is the expected rate of return on security i less the risk-free rate of interest.

Equations (8.28) and (8.29) say that the return on a security is affected separately by all the k factors that systematically affect the return on a security. These factors might include exchange-rate and interest-rate risk, for example, which can vary from one company to another. The required compensation is equal to the quantity of risk accepted for factors $1, 2, 3 \ldots k$, which is measured by the beta of the security with respect to factors $1, 2, 3 \ldots k$ and the market price of the risk of factors $1, 2, 3 \ldots k$ as measured by the risk premium for each systematic risk factor.

Equation (8.29) contrasts with equation (8.25) of the CAPM in that it has several beta coefficients rather than just one. In addition, the CAPM deals with market risk while the APT does not have a market-risk coefficient, the whole point of the model being that market risk is unidentifiable. The proponents of the APT argue that it has two main advantages over the CAPM model:

1 The CAPM requires that the investors' utility function is based upon expected returns and the standard deviation of systematic risk. The APT does not require standard deviations to be used as a measure of risk.
2 The other main advantage is that the APT does not require an unobservable market index to be compiled.

Against this, however, the APT has its own defects. It does not say what the relevant factors are or even how many relevant factors there are! It can be argued that, although the APT gets rid of the problem of an unobservable market index, it fails to provide a solution for choosing alternative factors.

In an empirical study, Chen, Roll and Ross (1986) suggested that possible relevant factors for shares were unanticipated changes in industrial production, unanticipated changes in interest rates and the slope of the yield curve, unanticipated inflation, and unanticipated changes in the spread between high- and low-grade bonds. Nonetheless, this list is far from definitive and modelling unanticipated variables is itself far from easy.

8.14 Conclusions

The risk attached to an individual security is made up of two components: the systematic/market and unsystematic/specific risk. We have seen that the unsystematic component can be reduced or even eliminated by portfolio diversification. Since diversification is a relatively low-cost option this risk will not normally command any return. The systematic risk on the security that remains after appropriate diversification can be measured by the value of its beta times the standard deviation of the market portfolio. The value of a beta is reflected in the average expected return on the asset.

Portfolio risk is also made up of two components: the systematic and unsystematic risk. As the number of shares in a portfolio rises, the unsystematic/specific risk is reduced and eventually disappears. The systematic/market risk attached to a portfolio of shares is represented by the portfolio beta which is simply a weighted average of the individual betas in the portfolio.

The introduction of beta as a measure of risk in the CAPM dramatically reduces the number of computations necessary to construct an optimal investment portfolio. There is no need to calculate the standard deviation or the covariance of each pair of securities to calculate the variance of the portfolio. The beta of a portfolio is simply the weighted average of all the individual betas that make up the portfolio. This means that a fund manager or investor can construct 'aggressive' (beta greater than one) and 'defensive' (beta less than one) portfolios by selecting shares with relatively high or low betas as appropriate.

The great contribution of the market model and the capital asset pricing model is that they make it clear that the expected return on a security is not dependent upon the total risk embedded in the security. It is only due to that part of total risk that cannot be diversified away, that is the systematic risk. Before the development of modern portfolio analysis, such as the CAPM, it was widely believed that the risk on a financial asset could be measured by the standard deviation of its return distribution. This meant that a security's risk could be measured without reference to other securities. The crucial insight of modern portfolio theories such as the market model and CAPM is that some of the risk attached to a financial asset can be reduced by holding it in a portfolio with other assets, and the risk that cannot be eliminated by this process is the only risk that will be priced by financial markets.

The CAPM assumes that the only risk that is relevant to the pricing of a security is uncertainty over the expected future return attached to that security. The CAPM was extended into a multifactor CAPM by Robert Merton to include additional risks such as those facing investors concerning the inflation rate and so on. In the multifactor version of the CAPM the total risk on a security is measured by market risk and a number of non-market sources of risk.

In theory, the market portfolio should include all marketable assets such as works of art, property, precious stones, rare coins and the like, as well as listed securities. This has led some critics of the CAPM to argue that the true market index is unobservable and to propose alternative theories. This is the motivation behind the arbitrage pricing theory.

In practice, most investors do not hold market portfolios as predicted by the CAPM. Indeed for an individual with very limited investment funds the transaction costs involved in constructing a market portfolio would be insurmountable. However, in recent years there has been a phenomenal rate of growth in the use of index-tracking funds, and exchange traded funds (ETFs) which track general market indices such as the S&P 500 and the FTSE 100. This means that individual investors can now allocate a proportion of their wealth to index-tracking funds, in a manner required by the CAPM, without great difficulty.

Further reading

Blake, D. (2000) *Financial Market Analysis*, 2nd edn, McGraw-Hill.

Elton, E., Gruber, M., Brown, S. and Goetzmann, W.N. (2007) *Modern Portfolio Theory and Investment Analysis*, Wiley.

Sharpe, W.F., Alexander, G.J. and Baley, J. (2002) *Investments*, 6th edn, Pearson.

Chapter 8 Revision questions

1 The returns on share ABC and the market portfolio are:

Year	*Return ABC*	*Return on market portfolio*
2005	2.0%	−12.0%
2006	13.0%	18.0%
2007	10.0%	5.0%
2008	5.0%	15.0%
2009	−8.0%	10.0%
2010	−2.0%	12.0%
2011	6.0%	26.0%

(i) Calculate the average rate of return for ABC shares and the market portfolio.
(ii) Calculate the sample standard deviation of returns on share ABC and the return on the market portfolio.
(iii) Calculate the covariance between ABC shares and the market portfolio.
(iv) Calculate ABC shares' beta coefficient.
(v) Assuming that the risk-free rate of interest is 4%, what is the expected return on ABC shares? Sketch the securities market line and ABC's risk (beta) and return. Are ABC shares undervalued or overvalued?

2 Assume that the following data represent all risky securities in the economy.

Security class	*Value*	*Standard deviation*		*Correlation coefficient matrix* A	B	C	D
A	£20	5.0%	*A*	1.0	0	0	0
B	£20	10.0%	*B*	0	1.0	0	0
C	£30	20.0%	*C*	0	0	1.0	0
D	£30	30.0%	*D*	0	0	0	1.0
	£100						

(i) What is the market portfolio, that is, what percentage of each security must be invested to achieve the market portfolio? What is the standard deviation of the market portfolio?
(ii) If the risk free rate of return is 2% and the expected return on the market portfolio is 7%, what is the capital market line equation?
(iii) If the risk free rate of return is 2% and the expected return on the market portfolio is 7%, what is the security market line equation?
(iv) A pension fund that you are advising wishes to have an expected rate of return of 5%. How should the fund invest to obtain this? What would be the standard deviation and the beta of the pension fund's position?
(v) You would like to have an expected return of 10%. How should you invest your money to obtain this?

Chapter 8	Revision questions – *continued*

3   You have following investments in Securities A, B and C:

Security	Amount invested	Beta	Expected 1 year return
A	£10,000	1.15	14%
B	£8,000	1.90	20%
C	£7,000	1.72	18%

The current risk free rate of interest is 5% and you have heard that analysts are expecting a 15% return on the market portfolio over the next year. Based on your expectations for the 1 year returns of each of the securities, is your portfolio underpriced, overpriced or correctly priced?

4   Consider a regression analysis of five shares A–E which have the following results:

Share	Beta	Specific risk e_i	Annual % return
A	0.5	0.30	20
B	0.7	0.35	15
C	0.8	0.60	9
D	1.2	0.40	18
E	1.3	0.50	10

Note specific risk e_i is measured in this case by the standard deviation of the error term, that is, σ_{e_i} so we need to take the square to get the variance. The risk-free rate of interest $R^* = 5\%$, the market rate of return is $R_m = 14\%$ and the standard deviation of the market is $\sigma_m = 0.25$.

(i)   Calculate the portfolio's beta.
(ii)   Calculate the systematic risk of the portfolio.
(iii)   Calculate the unsystematic risk of the portfolio.
(iv)   Calculate the total risk of the portfolio as measured by the variance of the portfolio.
(v)   Calculate the actual return of the portfolio against its systematic return as required by the CAPM.

5   The risk-free rate of interest is 5%, the covariance of returns of share A with the market is $\sigma_{AM} = 0.2$, the standard deviation of the market σ_M is 0.5. The expected rate of return on market is 12%.

(i)   Calculate the beta of share A.
(ii)   Calculate the expected rate of return on share A.

Multiple choice questions available at **www.palgrave.com/business/pilbeam**

9

STOCKMARKETS AND EQUITIES

Learning objectives

In this chapter you will learn about:

- the relative size and importance of the major international stockmarkets
- the different types of equity
- the dividend discount model for the pricing of equities
- alternative methods to calculate the required rate of return
- the impact of primary gearing on shareholder risk and return
- the use of chartism, and technical analysis in the financial markets
- how financial ratio analysis can be used to help determine equity valuation

9.1 Introduction

Stockmarkets around the world have undergone significant changes since the 1960s, now seeming to dominate much of the financial news headlines. The 1990s bull market in the USA came to a spectacular and sudden halt on 10 October 2002, with the NASDAQ falling from its all-time high of 5132 to 1108. This decline of 78 per cent shows how shares can become spectacularly overvalued. Indeed, the US stockmarket was trading in March 2009 close to levels it had seen in 1996, some 13 years earlier.

Stock exchanges have been heavily influenced by the introduction of new technology; for instance, the stock exchanges in London, Paris and Frankfurt are now screen-based, replacing the trading-floor environment. There have also been significant regulatory changes such as London's 'big bang' in 1986 and regulatory changes in the USA following a number of scandals during the 'bubble era' of 1997–2000. In addition, the markets are increasingly dominated by institutional investors, pension funds, unit trusts/mutual funds, investment companies and trusts, insurance companies and the like which impose different demands than the traditional small investor. For example, in the late 1950s roughly two-thirds of shares on the UK stockmarket were owned by small investors, but by the early 2000s this figure had declined to less than one-fifth. Conversely, the ownership of shares by institutions rose from around one-fifth in the late 1950s to roughly two-thirds in the early 2000s.

In this chapter, we briefly review the operation of some of the major stockmarkets. We then look at the different types of equities that are traded in these markets and examine the choice between debt and equity finance. We proceed to consider the theory behind the pricing of equities, and we also look at some of the key financial ratios that are used by analysts when analyzing companies traded on stockmarkets.

institutional investors financial institutions, such as banks, pension funds, mutual funds and hedge funds, that invest pooled funds in the money and capital markets

9.2 The major international stockmarkets

The three major stockmarkets of the world are, in descending order, the USA, Japan and the UK. At any point in time a country's relative importance is influenced by the current state of its stockmarket and the performance of its currency. A depreciation of a country's currency against the US dollar will reduce the dollar value of its stockmarket, while an appreciation of its currency will raise the value of its stockmarket measured in dollars. The most useful measure of a stockmarket's importance is its capitalization. This is the total value of all the company stocks traded on the exchange. **Table 9.1** shows the seven major stockmarkets of the world as measured by the dollar value of their capitalization and as a percentage of their respective gross domestic products.

stockmarket capitalization the total value of the companies listed on the stockmarket

Table 9.1   The main stockmarkets of the world, 2009

	Stockmarket capitalization	Listings Domestic/Foreign
NYSE Euronext (USA)	9,829	5,448/792
Tokyo	3,331	2,373/16
NASDAQ	2,812	2,714/294
London	2,416	2,399/673
NYSE Euronext (Europe)	2,196	1,013/0
Shanghai	2,724	244/2
Hong Kong	2,052	2,399/673
Deutsche Borse	1,195	742/90
BME Spanish Exchanges	1,211	3,517/40
Bombay Stock Exchange	1,072	4,925/0
National Stock Exchange India	1,004	1,405/0
World	38,203	...

Figures July 2009

Source: World Federation of Exchanges

The main US stock exchange is the New York Stock Exchange (NYSE); however, it faces a high degree of domestic competition with the National Association of Securities Dealers Automated Quote System (NASDAQ). The UK stock exchange is the London Stock Exchange (LSE). Since the 'big bang' in 1986, the LSE has moved to a computer-based trading system and remains highly efficient, especially for large institutional trades. The Tokyo Stock Exchange has a very high capitalization, principally as a result of the huge postwar economic growth that occurred in Japan, but it has many antiquated trading practices such as barriers to entry for new securities firms.

While stock exchanges around the world are all predominantly concerned with the buying and selling of shares, they differ in their organizational structures and the ways in which they conduct share trades. Solnik (1991) has identified a number of ways in which stockmarkets differ.

Public versus private bourses

In countries such as France the stock exchange (bourse) was originally set up by the government which still retains a strong influence, for example via the licensing of brokers. Such government influence is also strong in Spain, Italy and Belgium. In other countries, exchanges were set up by private members for trading purposes and their stock exchanges are largely self-regulating, as in the UK, the USA, Japan, Australia, Hong Kong and Canada. In Germany, Austria and Switzerland much of the trading is done via the commercial banks.

Cash versus forward markets

In almost all exchanges there is a delay between the trade in a stock and its delivery, and this can range from 2 to 10 days. However, most of the markets are cash (spot) markets whereby the stock is delivered as quickly as the settlement procedures permit. By contrast, the Paris Bourse uses a forward delivery settlement procedure whereby all major stocks are delivered at the end of the month. The price for forward delivery differs from the spot price by the 'cost of carry' which mainly represents the foregone rate of interest.

Fixed versus continuous quotation

Most major stock exchanges such as the New York Stock Exchange, London and Tokyo have a high degree of liquidity and therefore quote most stocks on a continuous basis. In the UK this is done by market-makers, while in the USA the right to trade in a particular stock is assigned to specialists. Other countries make a distinction between brokers and jobbers to ensure continuous quoting of a stock. In some countries with less liquid share markets and thinner trading volumes share prices are determined via an auction process, the auction price applying to all transactions for that particular day.

specialist a member of an exchange that acts as a market-maker in a given stock

Computerizered versus floor trading

In many exchanges, such as London and NASDAQ, computerized trading is now the norm. Such trading has become more necessary for conducting trades in international stocks, and enables automated matching of trades and easy access to the best prices. However, floor-based trading still remains quite a popular feature in the NYSE (even though this now looks outdated) as it allows for a high degree of interaction and rapid exchange of information that is often deemed to be lacking in computerized trading.

9.3 Stockmarket participants

There are various participants in stockmarkets. Investors are the people and institutional bodies that buy and sell stock either on their own behalf or on behalf of other investors. Institutional investors such as pension funds, insurance funds and unit trusts account for the majority of trades these days. Brokers act as agents on behalf of their clients, and will attempt to execute trades at the best possible price. In addition, brokers may offer investment advice and sell research services. Market-makers provide bid–ask quotes for shares on a continual basis; if they are unable to find counterparties for a buy/sell order they have to be prepared to take an open position in the stock themselves or conduct an offsetting trade with another market-maker.

9.4 The primary and secondary market

Stockmarkets are divided into both primary and secondary markets. The primary market deals with the listing of new companies on the exchange. Companies seek a listing on the exchange to raise new finance for the company and/or its owners; for example, the new finance that is needed to assist expansion may be best raised by the sales of shares in the company rather than taking on debt finance. Alternatively, the motive for a listing may be that the existing owners wish to sell some or all of

privatization the sale of state-owned enterprises to the private sector, often through the sale of shares to the public and institutions

allotment policy the policy of distributing shares from an initial public offering to underwriters and investors

listing requirements the set of conditions and standards that a company must meet in order to gain and then maintain a stock exchange listing

their stake in the business – a good example of this is the privatization programmes pursued by many governments since the 1980s.

New share issues are normally underwritten by a syndicate of banks which will agree to buy any shares not taken up by investors at the subscription price. If a new issue is oversubscribed, then the company in conjunction with its financial advisers will determine an allotment policy which allocates the shares to applicants according to a formula based on the number of shares applied for. The allotment policy may favour large applicants over small applicants, or vice versa. In many of the heavily oversubscribed privatization issues of the UK in the 1980s and 1990s, the allotment policy tended to favour the small investor.

To be listed on an exchange a firm will need to meet certain listing requirements. It needs to have an adequate trading record, be prepared to make available certain information, produce an annual report and a set of annual accounts. The firm will be expected to hold an annual general meeting at which the management of the company is subject to approval by the shareholders who can vote according to the size of their shareholding.

The secondary market deals with the buying and selling of existing stocks and shares. It accounts for the vast majority of share-dealing with buyers and sellers attracted into the market by what they deem to be underpriced and overpriced shares. New information about a company, changes in investment sentiment, or the performance of the economy as a whole will lead to changes in the prices of the shares traded on the market.

9.5   Different types of equity

ordinary shares shares which represent partial ownership of a company, entitling the owner to vote on issues put before shareholders; the holder may or not receive dividends depending on profits

preference shares shares which entitle the holder to a given dividend; holders have priority over ordinary shareholders; they are entitled to a share of the assets if the firm goes into liquidation, but have lower priority than debt holders

Equity ownership represents an ownership interest in a corporation. Equity comes in several forms and by far the most important is ordinary shares (common stock). Ownership of shares entitles the holder to dividends and a share of the net asset value of the company once other creditors have been repaid should the company be placed into liquidation. Ordinary shareholders have voting rights and the power to change the management of the company; they also have the first right to buy new stock issued by the company.

With preference shares (or preferred stock) the holder is usually entitled to a fixed dividend payment before any dividends are distributed to ordinary shareholders. Preference shares do not confer ownership of the firm or voting privileges on their holders, the lack of which means that preferred stockholders have no vote in the event of a takeover bid being made for the company. Also, preferred stockholders, like ordinary stockholders, cannot place the firm into liquidation. If the company fails to pay dividends on preferred stock then preferred stockholders usually have the right to impose certain restrictions on the management of the company. In addition, if the company does go into liquidation then preferred stockholders have priority over ordinary shareholders in the distribution of the company's assets. Such fixed payments mean that preferred stock has more in common with debt (bonds/loans) than ordinary shares. Debt holders must be paid before any dividends are made to preferred stockholders and in the event that creditors are not paid they can force the company into liquidation.

| Box 9.1 | Initial public offerings and the dot com bubble |

An initial public offering (IPO) is an offer by a privately- or state-owned company of common stock (ordinary shares) to institutions and the public, giving the purchasers of the shares an ownership stake in the company. An IPO can be useful if the owners of a privately-owned company wish to sell some or all of their stake in the company or if they wish to raise the profile of the company by making it publicly traded. An IPO is especially useful for small fast-growing companies that need more capital to finance their expansion. Investors that buy into IPOs face a lot of risk as the company often has a limited trading record and its future profitability can be highly uncertain. The proceeds from the IPO go directly to the company and can be used to finance its future growth. When undertaking an IPO a company will usually approach one or more investment banks that will deal with the necessary legal and regulatory requirements and also arrange for the underwriting of the IPO. The underwriting means that if the IPO were to fail to attract sufficient buyers for the sale then the underwriting syndicate will pick up the remaining unsold shares and take a loss as the share price falls below its offer price.

An IPO not only raises capital for a company and gives its owners the right to sell some of their stake but it is also profitable for investment banks who receive a fee related to the size of the sums paid. A typical fee is in the region of 2 per cent to 6 per cent of the sum raised, and fees are also charged for the risk of underwriting the issue. It is not uncommon for the initial share price to be set at a level where the demand exceeds the supply of shares so that there can be high first-day returns for those able to get shares in the IPO.

While gaining shares in an IPO can prove a boon to investors in the short run, the company fundamentals will decide the fate of the shares in the long run. One of the most spectacular times for IPOs was 1998–2001 when hundreds of internet firms came to market. During a period that is now known as the 'dot com bubble' the public became aware of the potential of the internet and lots of internet companies, many funded by venture capital, were brought to the market, especially on the NASDAQ exchange. Two of the leading investment banks involved in the IPOs were Merrill Lynch, with its lead analyst Henry Blodget, and Morgan Stanley Dean Witter whose lead analyst, Mary Meeker, briefly acquired the title of 'Queen of the Internet'.

The valuations of internet and related companies went through the roof. For instance, DoubleClick.com came to the market at $8.50 a share on 20 February 1998 and rose to $85.63 a share by 25 May 1999, giving it a market capitalization of $6.73 billion based on revenue of $156 million and losses of $21 million! Another example was etoys.com which came to the market at $20 a share and peaked at $85 a share, giving it a market capitalization of $8.4 billion based on sales of $24 million and losses of $53 million! etoys eventually fell to a low of just 9 cents per share in February 2001. Webvan.com raised $375 million in its IPO, had a market valuation of $1.2 billion at its peak but went out of business in July 2001.

continued overleaf

| Box 9.1 | Initial public offerings and the dot com bubble – *continued* |

One company, netj.com, managed to raise $3 million from its IPO and its share price rose from $0.50 to $7 giving it a market capitalization of $47 million despite its IPO filing specifically stating: 'The company is not currently engaged in any substantial business activity and has no plans to engage in any such activity in the foreseeable future'. In plain English this means: 'We do nothing and we intend to continue to do nothing!'

According to an article by Ofek and Richardson (2003) entitled 'DotCom Mania: The rise and fall of internet stock prices', over the period 1 January 1998 to 31 March 2000 some 293 internet IPOs averaged a stunning 96.3 per cent first day return with a median estimate of 65.8 per cent. Even after the first day their flotation prices continued to rise dramatically. By the end of 1999 some 320 internet firms had a combined market capitalization of $942.97 billion based on sales of just $27.4 billion and net losses of $9.9 billion! Even based upon extremely optimistic future target earnings being met, Ofek and Richardson estimated the companies would have had an average price–earnings ratio of 605 with some 20 per cent of the companies having price–earnings ratios of over 1500! As such, the internet bubble must be characterized as the greatest bubble of all time because it involved so many companies, took place when investors had unparalleled access to information and happened in the USA, supposedly the country with the largest and most liquid capital markets in the world by far (although similar dot com bubbles were observed in Germany and the UK as well). The bubble burst spectacularly with the NASDAQ peaking at an all-time high of 5132 on 10 March 2000 before falling to around 1350 in February 2003.

The size and extent of the bubble is a major challenge to those that believe that stockmarkets are always efficient. Ofek and Richardson argue that the bubble occurred because overly optimistic investors overwhelmed the more rational investors that were trying to short the overvalued stocks. The problems of shorting the stocks was exacerbated by the fact that so little of the shares or 'free float' were tradable on the market due to the majority of the shares being held by insiders and CEOs who were only allowed to sell their shares after a typical lock-up period of six months' trading on the market. When the lock-up period ended the insiders tried to sell their holdings, which triggered the subsequent price collapse.

Preferred stock comes in varied forms. With cumulative preference shares the holder is entitled to any missed dividends if earnings recover sufficiently before any dividends are made to ordinary shareholders. With convertible preference shares stockholders have the right to convert their preference shares into ordinary stock at predetermined conditions if a certain number of dividend payments are missed. With redeemable preference shares the company can buy back the shares at their original price at some time in the future, which may be a specific date or an option to redeem them at any time. Another type is participating preference shares which allow for an even greater dividend in the event that profits are above certain levels.

9.6 The buying and selling of shares

short selling
the process of
borrowing a security
and selling it in the
hope of buying it
back at a lower price

Most purchases and sales of shares are made by investors who wish to own, or who already own, a stock. However, many shares are sold short, that is sold by investors that do not own the stock at the time of the sale. The ability to sell short is important to the pricing of shares as it affords investors who feel a share is overvalued the opportunity to profit from that viewpoint. If such investors were excluded from the market then there would be an upward bias in share prices, because shares would only be held by people who were optimistic about the share. There are a number of ways in which a share can be sold short – one is when an investor requests his broker to borrow the shares from an existing holder and the stock is then on-sold to a buyer. The seller subsequently 'covers' his position by purchasing the shares at some future date (hopefully at a lower price) for delivery to the party that lent the stock.

Consider the following example. Mr A believes that shares in company XYZ are currently overvalued at £10 and seeks to take advantage of an expected price fall. He instructs his broker to short sell 2000 shares at £10 on his behalf: the broker will borrow 2000 shares from Mr B to deliver to the buyer of the shares and the broker receives £20,000 on Mr A's account. The money is held in an account on Mr A's behalf but not given to him as he has sold 2000 shares short (he did not own the shares). If one week later the share has fallen in price to £8, Mr A can advise his broker to buy 2000 shares for £16,000 on his behalf for return to Mr B. Mr A is then left with £4000 profit less commissions and a fee for borrowing the shares, and any dividend payments to which Mr B may have been entitled. Obviously if Mr A is wrong and the share price rises above £10, he will incur a loss as he has to purchase the shares back for restoration to Mr B.

9.7 A rights issue

rights issue the
issuance of new
shares by a company
to raise new finance;
the shares are
offered to current
shareholders first in
proportion to the
number of shares
that they own.
Shareholders can
transfer their rights to
a third party

If a company wishes to raise further capital by some method other than the issue of debt, it can choose to issue new equity in the form of a rights issue. The aim of a rights issue may be to raise new finance to assist further development/expansion or even a takeover bid for another company. Alternatively, it might be motivated by the desire to repay some of a company's debt or even to help a company survive a temporary cash problem.

With a rights issue new shares are offered to existing shareholders in proportion to the number of shares that they already possess. For instance, in a 'one-for-two' issue, existing stock holders are offered one new share for every two that they already hold. The new shares are usually offered at a discount to the existing price to encourage take-up of the issue. If the shares are currently valued at 100 pence each, then the new stock might be priced at 70 pence. A stock holder must then decide whether to take up his rights or sell them to a third party.

If the stock holder takes up his rights then he retains the same proportion of ownership of the company as prior to the issue, but the price of his shares will normally fall to approximately 90 pence ((100 + 100 + 70)/3 = 90). Alternatively, the stock holder can sell his rights to the share for up to 20 pence to a third party; the third party then, having the right to buy shares for 70 pence, can expect them to trade around 90 pence. However, this means that the stock holder's ownership of the company will be less than prior to the rights issue and he can still expect the price of the existing stock to fall to 90 pence.

The main risk to the company is that between the time of the rights issue and the closing date for take-up, which is usually around three weeks, the share price of the existing stock will fall below the subscription price for the new stock, meaning that investors will have no incentive to take up the offer. To ensure the company of the finance that it requires, it will normally have a rights issue underwritten by a bank (or syndicate of banks) which will agree to purchase any new stock not taken up by existing shareholders. The underwriting institutions require a fee for their services and for the risk of the issue not being fully subscribed, which typically varies between 1–5 per cent of the value of the issue.

Most companies have rights issues underwritten, but on rare occasions the new shares are offered at a 'deep discount' instead. In our example, they might be offered at 40 pence rather than 70 pence, since there is little chance that the share will fall below that level. The problem, however, is that more shares have to be issued to raise the same amount of finance. Also, if the firm is to maintain the same level of dividends per share in the future, then this would imply much higher levels of dividend payments.

| Box 9.2 | Risks of shorting a share: the short squeeze |

In the popular press it is sometimes argued that stocks are falling in price because speculators are making huge profits by shorting stocks at the expense of the average investor that typically hold stocks hoping that they will appreciate in value over time. This then leads to calls for bans against short selling. However, in reality, shorting a share is a risky strategy and profits are far from certain as a share price can go up substantially in a short space of time, meaning losses for those shorting a share.

A classic case of speculators being caught out in a spectacular 'short squeeze' occurred in October 2008. The credit crunch was in play and car sales around the globe had been falling. This situation led to a lot of London hedge funds and other speculators taking large short positions on Volkswagen shares. These hedge funds and other speculators had been borrowing the stock and short selling it at around the €200 euro level, predicting a large price fall. On Friday 24 October Volkswagen shares closed at around €210. However, on Sunday 26 October Porsche announced that it held a controlling 75 per cent stake in the company – a significantly larger stake than most traders thought it had. This revelation led many traders to seek to buy the stock in order to close out their positions. The problem was that it was extremely hard to locate because 74.1 per cent was held by Porsche and 20.1 per cent by the German state of Lower Saxony, meaning that effectively around 5.8 per cent remained tradable on the market. The short position in the stock was estimated to be equal to 12 per cent of the shares so, with only 5.8 per cent available to buy, the share would be hard to purchase. The scramble to locate the stock by hedge funds seeking to close their short position led to a 147 per cent

---

Box 9.2   **Risks of shorting a share: the short squeeze** – *continued*

Figure 9.1   Volkswagen share price

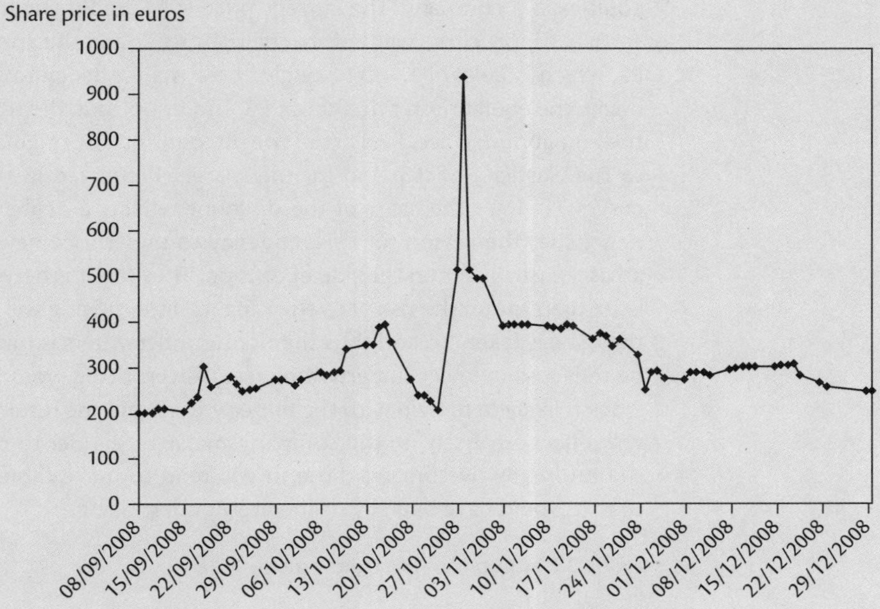

Share price in euros

rise on the Monday followed by an 82 per cent rise the next day, taking its closing share price to €945 after hitting an intraday high of €1005.

There was widespread speculation that hedge funds that had been heavily shorting the share at the €200–€300 level had lost anywhere between €20 billion and €30 billion. It appears that the huge price spike on the Monday, which occurred because some hedge funds sought to close their short position, created large losses for other hedge funds which then decided to try and close out their position on the Tuesday, leading to a second price spike in the share. Once all the short positions had been closed the share price started to fall rapidly as there was no underlying demand for the shares at the elevated price. On the Wednesday the share price dropped 37 per cent to €560 when Porsche announced it would release 5 per cent more stock to enable short speculators to close out their positions. The huge losses for the speculators of course meant huge profits for Porsche which was selling the shares at the high price to enable the hedge funds to close out their short positions.

The lesson of this episode is that shorting a stock can be a very dangerous game, especially if very little of the stock is actually tradable in the market, making it hard for short sellers to cover their short positions without a sharp spike in the share price. It also shows that share prices can suddenly rise quite sharply, even if this is not justified by a company's fundamentals, if too many market participants seek to unwind their short positions at the same time – what is commonly called a short squeeze in the market.

9.8   A simple model of the pricing of a rights issue

The price of existing stock is an important determinant of the price at which a firm can expect to raise new capital. **Figure 9.2** shows the stock demand and supply for equities in a company. The current price is P1, and if the firm issues new stock the vertical supply curve will shift to the right to S2 and the appropriate market price to P2, which is below P1. Interestingly, there is a tendency to sell new issues at a price below the equilibrium price, say at P3, and upon issue the stock tends to rise towards the equilibrium price, P2. Part of the discount on the original price P1 is attributable to the elasticity of demand for the share, as reflected in the slope of the demand curve D1. The other part of the discount reflects a deliberate underpricing of the new issue. The reason for this tendency to underprice new issues is that firms and advisers usually err on the side of caution. They feel it is better to underprice the new issue than to run the risk of overpricing it. Underpricing will help to ensure that all of the issue is taken up and thus the risk to underwriters is minimized (and this should be reflected in lower underwriting fees). Overpricing would mean that some of the stock is likely to remain with the underwriters, and the resultant fall in the share price will reflect adversely on the company, making it harder to raise additional capital in the future. By overpricing the firm will tend to make raising finance more difficult than it would have been by deliberately underpricing.

Figure 9.2   The pricing of a rights issue

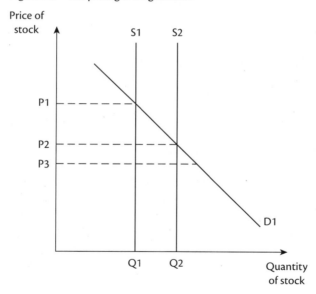

9.9   Does the performance of the stockmarket matter?

The stockmarket is predominantly a secondary market whereby investors buy and sell existing shares that have been issued by companies. Equity finance is part and parcel of the capital market in that it deals with the raising of long-term finance. On a much lesser scale it deals with new issues and the issue of new stock by existing quoted companies. Since the stockmarket is mainly a secondary market and existing firms do not have any immediate benefit or loss if their share price rises or falls, some go on to argue that the stockmarket is more akin to a casino and is of little relevance to the quoted firms and the real economy. A moment of reflection, however, reveals that such a view is flawed. The market's performance is important not only for the companies quoted on it but also for the economy as a whole.

In the first instance, the buying and selling of existing stock is important in ensuring that quoted firms remain efficient and seek to maximize their profits. If a firm is seen to be inefficient and its profitability is relatively low, then its share price will be depressed and it will be a potential takeover target. Takeovers normally result in the replacement of the management of the company that is taken over, and the threat of a takeover should encourage the management to make the firm efficient. To the extent that such forces are in play, the stockmarket encourages efficiency and profitability of firms and thereby benefits the economy in general.

takeover a situation in which an acquiring company makes a bid for a target company; a hostile takeover ensues if the acquired company resists the takeover or a friendly takeover occurs if the target company welcomes the bid

While it is true that the stockmarket is predominantly a secondary market, it is precisely because there is a healthy secondary market in shares that firms can raise finance through initial share offerings in the first instance, or via rights issues if already quoted. Investors purchase shares in newly listed companies because they know that once purchased they can sell them at a time of their choosing to other investors. A well developed stockmarket with a high degree of liquidity therefore helps to increase the volume of new issues and to reduce their cost.

The performance of the stockmarket also has both a direct wealth effect on expenditure decisions and an important confidence influence on economic agents. As the real value of shares rises the wealth and usually the confidence of economic agents is raised, which encourages greater expenditure and investment which in turn can reduce unemployment and contribute to economic growth. If the stockmarket is performing poorly this tends to lower agents' wealth and confidence, and generally has an adverse impact on the economy.

9.10 The pricing of equities

The valuation of equities is more complex than finding an appropriate price for bonds. Equities are like any other financial asset in that the price is dependent upon the market valuation of the expected future stream of income. However, unlike bonds where the income stream is generally known because of fixed coupon payments and a known maturity date, equities have an uncertain form of income stream in the shape of dividends. The precise income stream that an investor can expect will be dependent upon the success of the firm as reflected in its future profits and also the dividend policy that the company pursues.

Holders of ordinary shares expect to make a return from their investment in two ways:

1 a stream of dividends during the holding period, and
2 an increase in the value of shares (capital appreciation) during the holding period.

There are various approaches to valuing equities. One popular approach relies upon discounting the value of prospective dividends to arrive at their present value, known as the dividend pricing approach, while other methods look at earnings and various financial ratios.

9.11 The dividend pricing approach

According to this approach, the pricing of equities should be like the pricing of any financial asset. The value of the future income stream, in this case dividends, has to be appropriately discounted to yield the formula for equity prices:

$$P_E = \frac{D_1}{(1+R_1)} + \frac{D_2}{(1+R_2)^2} + \frac{D_3}{(1+R_3)^3} + \ldots + \frac{D_n}{(1+R_n)^n} + \frac{P_{E(n)}}{(1+R_n)^n} \qquad (9.1)$$

where P_E is the price of the share (equity) today; $D_1, D_2, D_3 \ldots D_n$ are the expected dividend payments per share in years 1, 2, 3 . . . n; $P_{E(n)}$ is the price of the share in year n; and $R_1, R_2, R_3 \ldots R_n$ are the rates at which future payments are discounted.

If we assume that dividend payments are fixed, that is $D_1 = D_2 = D_3 = \ldots = D_n$ and also that the rate at which dividends are discounted is fixed, that is $R_1 = R_2 = R_3 = \ldots = R_n$, then equation (9.1) simplifies to:

$$P_E = \sum_{t=1}^{n} \frac{D}{(1+R)^t} + \frac{E[P_{E(n)}]}{(1+R_n)^n} \qquad (9.2)$$

where $E[P_{E(n)}]$ is the expected price of the share in year n. Equation (9.2) says that the value of an equity is the discounted value of all the dividend payments due plus the discounted expected value of the share in year n.

9.12 The Gordon growth model

A major problem with the dividend pricing approach, expressed as equation (9.2), is that it is unrealistic to assume that the dividend payments are fixed; $D_0, D_1, D_2, D_3 \ldots D_n$ are likely to be variable. Various hypotheses can be made concerning dividends and, following a model suggested by Gordon (1962), a widely used approach is to argue that, over time, dividends will grow by a certain growth rate of g per cent per annum. This will mean that we can model the dividends in equation (9.2) as:

Dividend in previous year $= D_0$

Dividend in year 1, $D_1 = D_0(1+g)$

Dividend in year 2, $D_2 = D_0(1+g)^2$

Dividend in year 3, $D_3 = D_0(1+g)^3$

Dividend in year n, $D_n = D_0(1+g)^n$

Substituting these values into equation (9.2) yields:

$$P_E = \frac{D_0(1+g)}{(1+R)} + \frac{D_0(1+g)^2}{(1+R)^2} + \ldots + \frac{D_0(1+g)^n}{(1+R)^n} + \frac{P_{E(n)}}{(1+R)^n} \quad (9.3)$$

Having modelled dividends, we still have the problem of how to estimate the price $P_{E(n)}$, but this is merely the present value in year n of all dividends from the year n to infinity. This means that we can change equation (9.3) to:

$$P_E = \frac{D_0(1+g)}{(1+R)} + \frac{D_0(1+g)^2}{(1+R)^2} + \ldots + \frac{D_0(1+g)^n}{(1+R)^n} + \frac{D_0(1+g)^{n+1}}{(1+R)^{n+1}} + \ldots \quad (9.4)$$

Using the fact that an infinite geometric progression simplifies in the following manner:

$$ab + ab^2 + \ldots + ab^n + \ldots = \frac{a}{1-b}$$

then equation (9.4) simplifies to:

$$P_E = \frac{D_0(1+g)}{(R-g)} \quad (9.5)$$

where D_0 is the current dividend. This is equivalent to:

$$P_E = \frac{D_1}{(R-g)} \quad (9.6)$$

where D_1 is the next period dividend.

Equations (9.5) or (9.6) are known as the Gordon growth model for the pricing of equities. To have some economic sense it requires that R is greater than g to avoid the possibility of a negative or infinite share price. The model shows that there are three factors which are crucial to the price of equities:

1 The previous dividend payment made by the firm, D_0 or the forthcoming dividend D_1. This will be dependent upon the current profitability level of the firm and the dividend policy of the firm.

2 The expected growth rate of dividends made by the firm, g. One factor that may be relevant here is the rate of economic growth in the economy; the higher the economic growth rate of the economy as a whole then the higher g is likely to be. Another important factor will be the sector of the economy in which the firm operates; it may be in a low-growth or high-growth sector. Other factors that are likely to be relevant include government economic policy, especially with regard to taxation, and firm-specific factors such as the type of product, managerial competence and so on.

3 The required rate of return demanded by the market, R. A rise in the required rate of return will imply a larger discounting of future dividends for the share and a lower share price. The required rate of return will be dependent on how risky the firm is deemed to be by market participants, and the rate of return that can be obtained from alternative risk-free investments such as government bonds.

In the special case where the rate of growth of dividends is assumed to be zero, that is $g = 0$, then the Gordon model reduces to:

$$P_E = \frac{D}{R} \tag{9.7}$$

That is, shares that have a zero growth-rate factor should be priced according to the dividend divided by the rate of discount. For example, a share paying a dividend of 10 pence discounted at a rate of 10 per cent ($R = 0.1$) should be priced at $10/0.1 = 100$ pence.

Numerical example

The Gordon growth model can be used by an analyst to decide whether the current share price is fairly valued. Let us suppose that a share price in the market is currently 140 pence and the last dividend was 10 pence, and that the analyst is predicting a dividend growth rate of 8 per cent ($g = 0.08$) and the required rate of return on the share is deemed to be 15 per cent ($R = 0.15$).

Substituting these values into equation (9.5), the relevant dividend growth formula is:

$$P_E = \frac{10(1.08)}{0.15 - 0.08}$$
$$= 154.28$$

According to the analyst, at 140 pence the share would seem to be undervalued and would be recommended for a purchase. Different analysts will come to different opinions on the fair price of the share if they input different rates of growth and have different required rates of return.

9.13 A non-constant growth version of the dividend discount model

The Gordon growth model can be modified on a practical basis to measure share prices even though forecasting dividends into the future is a very hazardous task. An analyst may be confident about the next five years' dividends, but far less confident about dividends further into the future, and may wish to assess whether the current share price is favourable using different growth rates over time.

For example, the last year's dividend (D_0) was 10 pence. The analyst is predicting 12 per cent dividend growth for the next three years and 7 per cent for the following two years. Thereafter dividend growth is assumed to slow for the foreseeable future to a mere 3 per cent. The required rate of return on equity is deemed to be 15 per cent. Currently the shares are priced in the market at 125 pence. Should they be recommended for purchase?

The relevant dividend growth formula is given by equation (9.8):

$$P_E = \sum_{t=1}^{n} \frac{D_0(1 + g_1)(1 + g_2)\dots(1 + g_n)}{(1 + R)^t} + \frac{D_n(1 + g)}{(R - g)} \times \frac{1}{(1 + R)^n} \tag{9.8}$$

Substituting into equation (9.8):

$$P_E = \frac{10(1.12)}{(1.15)} + \frac{10(1.12)(1.12)}{(1.15)^2} + \frac{10(1.12)(1.12)(1.12)}{(1.15)^3}$$

$$+ \frac{10(1.12)(1.12)(1.12)(1.07)}{(1.15)^4} + \frac{10(1.12)(1.12)(1.12)(1.07)(1.07)}{(1.15)^5}$$

$$+ \frac{10(1.12)(1.12)(1.12)(1.07)(1.07)(1.03)}{(0.15 - 0.03)} \times \frac{1}{(1.15)^5}$$

$$= 113.7 \text{ pence}$$

Non-constant growth model

Future year	Yearly growth	Expected dividend	Present value at 15%
1	12%	11.2 pence	9.73
2	12%	12.5 pence	9.48
3	12%	14.0 pence	9.21
4	7%	15.0 pence	8.58
5	7%	16.1 pence	8.00
		Total	45.00 pence

At end of year 5, $P_5 = \dfrac{16.1(1.03)}{0.15 - 0.03} \times \dfrac{1}{(1.15)^5}$

$$= 68.7 \text{ pence}$$

Total value = 45 pence + 68.7 pence = 113.7 pence

Hence, at the current share price of 125 pence the share seems to be overvalued and should not be recommended for purchase.

9.14 The dividend irrelevance theorem

From equations (9.5) and (9.6) it looks as though an increase in the current dividend (D_0) or the next period dividend (D_1) must lead to an increase in the share price. Conversely, a cut in the current dividend or the next period dividend must lead to a fall in the share price. Indeed, according to equations (9.5) or (9.6), if either D_0 or D_1 were set to zero, then the share would become worthless!

retained earnings profits that are retained by a company after payment of taxes and dividends

There is a clear problem with this line of logic, however. A firm might reduce its dividend but use the retained earnings for investment, which will mean higher dividend growth in the future, that is, a higher g. This logic raises the possibility that a lower dividend will be compensated for by higher future dividend growth, thus leaving a share price unaffected. Modigliani and Miller (1958, 1961) showed that under certain assumptions reductions in dividends lead to systematically higher values of g, leaving share prices unaffected. This would mean that the market price of a share is unaffected by the dividend paid. In other words, dividends become irrelevant to the market price of the share. It is for this reason that R and g are regarded as the fundamental determinants of a share's price.

9.15   Measurement of the required rate of return

One of the crucial variables in the dividend discount model is the required rate of return on a share price. If dividends were known for certain, then the risk-free rate of interest could be applied, but dividends are not known and so some sort of additional premium needs to be added to the risk-free rate of interest. There are various ways of estimating the required rate of return R:

Judgemental risk premium basis

Here a risk premium is added to a benchmark risk-free rate of interest reflecting the investor's personal belief about the required extra return, that is:

R = real interest rate + expected inflation rate + risk premium
R = nominal rate of interest + risk premium

where the nominal rate of interest is the risk-free rate of interest on short-/medium-/long-term government bonds and the risk premium is a percentage added by the investor to reflect the extra degree of risk associated with holding the equity.

For example, the real yield on government bonds may be 3 per cent and the expected average inflation rate 5 per cent, and then the investor adds a subjective margin of say 6 per cent based on the perceived risk of the investment, giving a total discount factor of 14 per cent.

The Gordon growth model estimate of R

The required rate of return can be derived using the Gordon growth model itself since:

$$P_E = \frac{D_0(1+g)}{(R-g)}$$

Rearranging this yields:

$$R = \frac{D_0(1+g)}{P_E} + g \tag{9.9}$$

which means that R can be estimated using last year's dividend, the current share price and an assumed dividend growth rate.

For example, if Company XYZ has a current share price of 100 pence, last year paid a dividend of 10 pence and is expected to grow at 3 per cent per annum, then the estimated value for R is:

$$R = \frac{10(1+0.03)}{100} + 0.03$$
$$= 0.133 \text{ that is } 13.3\%$$

The gross dividend is used in the Gordon model to calculate the required holding rate of return, R, so that the gross holding period return can be compared with the gross yield on government bonds quoted in the financial press.

The capital asset pricing model estimate of R

We can also utilize the predictions of the capital asset pricing model to derive the appropriate value of R. According to the CAPM, the required rate of return is equal to the risk-free rate of interest plus a multiple of the market risk premium as represented by the share's beta coefficient:

$$R = R^* + \beta[E(R_m) - R^*] \tag{9.10}$$

where R^* is the risk-free rate of return; $E(R_m)$ is the market rate of return; $[E(R_m) - R^*]$ is the risk premium; and β is the share's beta coefficient.

For example, if the expected market rate of return is 14 per cent, the risk-free rate of interest 8 per cent and the firm has a beta of 1.5, then the required rate of return would be 17 per cent.

In general, a rise in the risk-free rate of interest R^* will raise R and hence cause the share price to fall. A change in the required risk premium will also affect the share price; if the market risk premium rises then so too will R, and thus the firm's share price will fall. The final factor to consider is the firm's beta; if the beta rises then the share is deemed to be more risky and R will rise, and other things being equal the share price will fall.

9.16 The subjectivity of share pricing

It should be clear by now that there is bound to be a high degree of subjectivity in the valuation of shares. The expected stream of dividends is highly subjective and will vary from investor to investor. The values of R and g are usually viewed as a share's fundamental factors, and a change in the market estimate of either will cause the share price to change. It should be noted that neither R nor g can be found scientifically, it is the market estimated values of R and g that are relevant. If these estimates change, for whatever reason, then the share price will change accordingly. A rise in R will depress the share price, while a rise in g will raise it.

The estimated values that different individuals attach to the rate of return and dividend growth will vary and this will lead to different valuations of a share price. Some investors may find the current price overvalues the share, while others may feel that it undervalues the share. If, holding other things constant, we raise the share price the proportion of investors that think the share price is overvalued will rise and this will lead to a fall in the demand for shares. For this reason, the demand for a share is inversely related to its price. We should also remember that we have been assuming that the rate of discount is assumed to be constant, but this may vary over time, further complicating the picture.

9.17 Forecasting future dividends: business risk and the effects of gearing

Forecasting prospective dividends is an extremely hazardous and complex task, but two particularly important factors here are business risk and the level of gearing.

Business risk

business risk the risk that company profits will fall by more than sales

Business risk refers to the fact that the profits of firms tend to be even more variable than their sales figures. This is because most businesses have fixed costs to cover as well as variable costs. For example, if a company has fixed costs of £1 million (regardless of whether any sales are generated) and variable costs of £10 for each

| Box 9.3 | Technical analysis and chartism in the financial markets |

In this chapter we have argued that we should use fundamentals such as prospective dividends and required rates of return to decide whether or not to buy or sell a share. However, in the financial markets many traders use technical analysis to decide whether or not to buy or sell. Technical analysis, sometimes referred to as chartism, uses purely past changes in a security's price to determine whether to buy or sell a share. Chartists claim to be able to spot buying or selling opportunities purely from recent charts of the share price, while technical analysts tend to use a variety of statistical data from the past share price, sometimes supplemented by the volume of trading in the share to determine buy and sell decisions. The point of technical analysis is that there is no need to study the fundamentals of the company as that is already contained in the share price. Technical analysis can be used to examine individual shares, stock market indices and foreign exchange, as well as other financial and even commodity markets.

According to chartists there are some patterns that are typical of market tops and market bottoms. For example, a market top can be signalled by a 'head and shoulders' pattern while a market bottom may be signalled by a 'double bottom' (see **Figure 9.3**).

In a 'head and shoulders top' there has been a significant rise in the share price, followed by a price fall and then a rise to an even higher share price (the head) followed by a share price fall to a similar level as the previous price fall, then a further rise to a similar level as the left shoulder followed by a price fall towards a 'neckline'. Once the neckline, given by the two recent lows, is broken then a substantial price fall can be predicted. In a 'double bottom' a sharp fall in price following a bearish trend in the share is suddenly reversed by a fairly large price rise, but this reversal is then also fairly sharply reversed, although the share quickly recovers again a similar low is reached. The second low and the sharp price rise from that level can be taken as a sign that the share has reached its lowest point and thereafter it is likely to resume a significant upward trend. Other concepts that are relevant to chartists are support and resistance levels – a stock may trade in a channel as depicted in **Figure 9.3**(c). Once it breaks out of the upper channel (resistance) or the lower channel (support) then a substantial upward or downward price movement is predicted to follow. **Figure 9.3**(d) shows a similar pattern but the support level increases so that it converges with the resistance level in an ascending triangle shape.

Technical analysts tend to use statistical properties of past share prices. For example, the 50-day moving average and 200-day moving average are very important. So long as a share remains above its 50-day and 200-day moving average in a rising market it is a bullish signal, but once it falls below its 50-day moving average for a few days then the next point of interest becomes the 200-day moving average. If that is broken for a few days this is generally taken as a bad sign and further price falls can be expected.

Technical analysis sometimes combines price movements with volumes traded. For example, a share price rise based on decreased market volumes is generally not

| Box 9.3 | **Technical analysis and chartism in the financial markets** – *continued* |

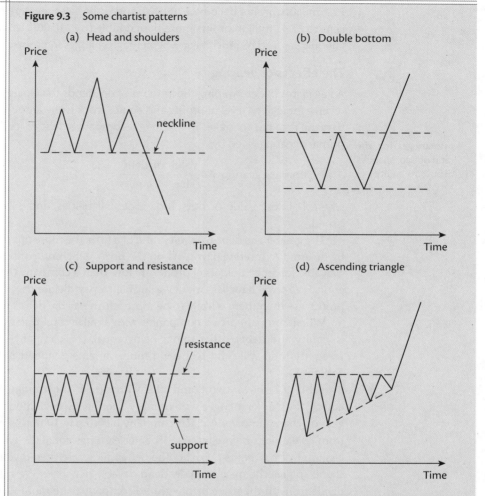

Figure 9.3   Some chartist patterns

trusted to continue, whereas a share price rise based on increased steady trading volumes confirms continued interest in the stock and is viewed as less likely to be reversed. Another commonly used indicator is the relative strength index (RSI) which is based on looking at average price rises and average price falls to give an index number. An index of 70 or above indicates that a share is overbought while a RSI reading of less than 30 indicates that the share is oversold in the short term.

Both chartism and technical analysis can be used to analyze hourly, daily, weekly and monthly data. There are many chart patterns and indicators that are used by chartists and technical analysts. Although chartism and technical analysis are quite extensively used there are unfortunately no golden rules and the different indicators and charts can give conflicting signals. Some people have likened them to the art of reading tea leaves, while some critics argue that chartists have long rulers and small brains! The reader is referred to John Murphy's (1999) book *Technical Analysis of the Financial Markets* for further reading.

unit produced and sold at £20, then it will break even on sales of 100,000 units when the sales revenue equals £2 million. If the sales revenue rises by 10 per cent to £2.2 million, profits become £100,000, and if the sales revenue rises a further 10 per cent to £2.42 million profits more than double to £210,000. Small percentage rises or falls in sales lead to much bigger percentage changes in profits.

The effects of gearing

A key factor in determining the amount of dividends that shareholders can expect to receive for a given level of profits and equity stock is the amount of debt repayments that the firm has to make. The ratio of a company's debt to its equity is known as its primary gearing given by:

primary gearing the ratio of a company's debt to its equity

$$\text{Primary gearing} = \frac{\text{Value of debt}}{\text{Value of equity}} = \frac{D}{E} \qquad (9.11)$$

where D is the value of outstanding debt liabilities, and E is the value of equity issued.

The greater the debt-to-equity ratio of a firm, the more of a firm's earnings have to be devoted to interest payments on the firm's debt, and consequently less money is available for stock holders. If profits are low, then a company that has a high debt-to-equity ratio will have less money available to pay dividends. Conversely, if company profits rise then there is likely to be more left to pay dividends to equity holders.

When comparing two companies with similar total outstanding liabilities (that is, equity and debt), other things being equal, the company with the higher debt-to-equity ratio will tend to have a more variable dividend policy, as illustrated in **Table 9.2**.

Table 9.2 shows two companies with similar outstanding liabilities (debt plus equity) but different levels of primary gearing, with company B having a higher gearing than company A. Each company has to pay 10 per cent interest on its debt from its earnings before interest. The net earnings equal the earnings before interest less interest payments on debt. The net earnings are then divided by the number of shares to give the maximum dividend payable per share. We can see that maximum dividends with the more highly-geared company B are more variable (0 to 20 pence) than for the lower-geared company A (2.5 to 17.5 pence). Companies that are more highly geared therefore tend to be regarded as more risky for investors than companies with a lower gearing, other things being equal.

To consider more formally how the expected return on equity is affected by a company's gearing, let us suppose that a company has an expected rate of profit given by p (that is, earnings before interest expressed as a percentage of debt plus equity) and has to pay an interest rate r on its debt. The expected rate of return on equity $E(R_E)$, is equal to the profits on assets (equivalent to liabilities) less interest payments divided by the value of equity as given by:

$$E(R_E) = \frac{p(E + D) - Dr}{E} \qquad (9.12)$$

where $E(R_E)$ is the expected rate of return on the equity; E is the value of the equity; D is the value of outstanding debt; p is the rate of profits (before interest payments) on combined debt and equity; and r is the rate of interest payable on debt.

Table 9.2   The effect of primary gearing on net earnings

Company A		Company B	
	£millions		£millions
Debt	100	Debt	200
Equity (£1 a share)	400	Equity (£1 a share)	300
Earnings before interest'	20	Earnings before interest	20
Interest (10% of debt)	10	Interest (10% of debt)	20
Net earnings	10	Net earnings	0
Maximum dividend	2.5 pence	Maximum dividend	0 pence
	£millions		£millions
Earnings before interest	50	Earnings before interest	50
Interest (10% of debt)	10	Interest (10% of debt)	20
Net earnings	40	Net earnings	30
Maximum dividend	10 pence	Maximum dividend	10 pence
	£millions		£millions
Earnings before interest	80	Earnings before interest	80
Interest (10% of debt)	10	Interest (10% of debt)	20
Net earnings	70	Net earnings	60
Maximum dividend	17.5 pence	Maximum dividend	20 pence

Equation (9.12) simplifies to:

$$E(R_E) = p + \frac{(p - r)D}{E} \qquad (9.13)$$

Most firms will not consider a project unless the expected rate of profit (p) is above the interest rate payable on debt (r), since they require a positive expected return from borrowing. This means that with ($p > r$) the expected rate of return on equity varies positively with the company's gearing (D/E). In other words, highly geared companies will tend to offer equity holders a higher rate of return since profits will tend to rise as expected profits are greater than the cost of servicing the debt. However, against this, the higher gearing implies a greater volatility of expected return and a greater risk of bankruptcy.

Equation (9.13) can be rewritten as:

$$E(R_E) = \left(1 + \frac{D}{E}\right)p - \left(\frac{D}{E}\right)r \qquad (9.14)$$

If we assume that r is fixed (so the standard deviation of interest rates is zero), then the only cause of variability in the expected rate of return on equity is changes in the rate of profit, hence:

$$\sigma_{E(R_E)} = \left(1 + \frac{D}{E}\right)\sigma_p \qquad (9.15)$$

where $\sigma_{E(R_E)}$ is the standard deviation of the expected rate of return on equity; and σ_p is the standard deviation of the rate of profit.

Table 9.3   The effect of primary gearing on equity returns

Debt/equity ratio (gearing)	Rate of return on equity					
	$p = 0\%$	$p = 5\%$	$p = 10\%$	$p = 15\%$	$p = 20\%$	$p = 25\%$
0.5	−5	2.5	10	17.5	25	32.5
1.0	−10	0	10	20.0	30	40.0
1.5	−15	−2.5	10	22.5	35	47.5
2.0	−20	−5.0	10	25.0	40	55.0
2.5	−25	−7.5	10	27.5	45	62.5

Note: Assuming a fixed interest rate of 10 per cent on debt, i.e. $r = 0.1$.

Equation (9.15) shows that the variability of expected return on equity varies positively with the level of gearing. Thus, highly-geared companies will have a higher variability of return on equity making them more risky, a point borne out in **Table 9.3** which provides numerical simulations of the rate of return on equity for different levels of profit and gearing.

Table 9.3 is based upon substituting the appropriate values for r and p and D/E into equation (9.14), and shows that the variability of the expected rate of return on equity grows with the debt–equity ratio. The rate of return on equity is less variable for different rates of profit the lower the level of primary gearing. Although higher gearing increases the return on equity with good profitability, it also has the effect of increasing losses on equity if the rate of profitability is low.

Another problem with having high gearing is that, if interest rates rise, then the proportion of profit absorbed by interest payments on debt will increase. The relevant formula for the proportion of profits absorbed by interest is:

$$\text{Proportion of profits absorbed by interest} = \frac{\left(\dfrac{D}{E}\right)r}{\left(1 + \dfrac{D}{E}\right)p} \qquad (9.16)$$

The effect of applying this formula for different levels of gearing and different rates of interest is shown in **Table 9.4**, which assumes an initial rate of profit of 15 per

Table 9.4   The effect of interest rates and primary gearing on profits

Debt/equity ratio (gearing)	Proportion of profit absorbed by interest						
	$r = 5\%$	$r = 7.5\%$	$r = 10\%$	$r = 12.5\%$	$r = 15\%$	$r = 17.5\%$	$r = 20\%$
0.5	11.1	16.7	22.2	27.8	33.3	38.9	40.4
1.0	16.7	25.0	33.3	41.7	50.0	58.3	66.7
1.5	20.0	30.0	40.0	50.0	60.0	70.0	80.0
2.0	22.2	33.3	44.4	55.6	66.7	77.8	88.9
2.5	23.8	35.7	47.6	59.5	71.4	83.3	95.2
3.0	25.0	37.5	50.0	62.5	75.0	87.5	100.0

Note: Assuming that the return of profit on equity and debt is 15%, i.e. $p = 0.15$.

cent. As the level of gearing rises, then so too does the proportion of profit taken up by interest payments. **Table 9.4** also reveals that highly-geared companies are more vulnerable to interest-rate rises than lower-geared companies. For example, if the rate of interest changes from 5 per cent to 15 per cent, then the proportion of profits taken in interest rate payments rises from 11.1 per cent to 33.3 per cent for a company with a gearing of 0.5; however, for a company with a gearing of 3 the proportion rises from 25 per cent to 75 per cent.

In general, companies with a low gearing in their balance sheets are said to have stronger balance sheets. In particular, they are less exposed to the risk of a simultaneous rise in interest rates and/or a fall in profitability than highly geared companies.

9.18 Debt or equity finance?

A crucial question for any major company concerns whether it should raise its finance primarily by issuing equity or debt. As we have seen, this choice will impact upon a company's gearing and this will affect investors' perception of the firm. The expected cost of equity finance is the stream of dividend payments that the firm will expect to pay in the future, which as we have seen is given by the dividend yield and expected annual rate of dividend growth.

Over time, a firm must expect to pay more for equity finance than debt finance since equity holders require a premium to compensate for their exposure to the additional capital risk and greater uncertainty over future payments. However, with equity finance the firm is not obliged to make any payments. This can make equity finance quite attractive for dynamic fast-expanding companies that prefer to pay no or low dividends in their early growth years. This means that profits can be mainly devoted to further expansion, the idea being that shareholders will be attracted by the prospect of capital gains in the early years and high prospective dividends in later years. Sometimes a firm might regard an investment project as potentially highly attractive, but financing it via debt would be too risky, so equity finance is preferred.

Debt finance can prove to be an attractive way of raising finance, particularly as it is generally easier to obtain than equity finance for a lot of companies. Many small to medium-sized enterprises are also not listed on a stock exchange and so do not have easy recourse to equity finance. They may also be reluctant to seek a listing because of the disclosure requirements or their trading record may be too short, or the owners may be reluctant to give up the degree of control in their company which a public listing entails.

There is a need to distinguish between short-term, medium-term and long-term debt when considering its attractiveness. Short-term debt usually involves bank overdraft facilities or the sale of commercial bills. Overdraft facilities are a very flexible means of obtaining finance, especially when the amount of borrowing required and its duration may be unknown. Nonetheless, most companies do not like to become too reliant on short-term finance because they could be placed in severe difficulty if the finance facility is not renewed or if interest rate movements are adverse upon renewal. For this reason, most companies keep an eye on the maturity structure of their debt.

Medium-term finance includes the use of bank loans, often secured against assets of the firm, and the use of medium-term bond finance. Long-term finance is usually obtained by the sale of corporate bonds, typically with 10 to 20 years until maturity, at fixed rates of interest. However, on average, long-term finance is more costly than short-term finance because of the need to pay investors a liquidity premium. Since holders of long-term bonds face great uncertainty about the fate of the company over periods of up to 20 years, they usually require some security should the firm run into difficulties. Hence, most long-term debt is normally secured against company assets such as land or buildings which can be expected to maintain their value. Many long-term loan agreements have covenants designed to protect debt holders' interests; for example, they might place a maximum on the amount of primary gearing (so as to ensure the firm does not become overburdened with debt), with lenders having the right to immediate repayment should the covenant be breached.

covenant a clause in a bond contract requiring a firm to do certain things and also not do some other things

9.19　Other approaches to equity valuation: financial ratio analysis

The main approach that we have used in this chapter is to value equities by their prospective dividends using variations of the dividend discount model. However, there are a number of other valuation methods which do not explicitly include dividends in the model.

As an alternative to the dividend approach, many analysts take account of various financial ratios to arrive at an opinion concerning the value of a company. These ratios look at both the return and risk characteristics of a company using both the balance sheet and cash-flow statements. **Table 9.5** provides a hypothetical set of data for company XYZ.

From Table 9.5 the following ratios can be calculated:

　　Earnings per share = 10 pence
　　Dividend per share = 5 pence
　　Dividend yield = 5%
　　Earnings yield = 10%
　　Price–earnings ratio = 10

Table 9.5　Analyzing a company's financial performance

1	Shares in issue	400 million
2	Market price	100 pence
3	Market capitalization	£400 million
4	Debt	£100 million
5	Gross profit	£54 million
6	Earnings	£40 million
7	Distributed profit	£20 million

Notes:
(a)　Debt includes borrowing, bonds and preference shares.
(b)　Earnings and profits are net of tax, depreciation and interest.

Some of the terms used in the table may need further explanation as follows:

- Shares in issue is the total number of ordinary shares issued by the company; some shares may be retained by the original owner(s) of the company and this is included in the total.
- Market price is simply the current price of each share issued.
- Market capitalization is the number of shares issued multiplied by the market price of the shares; in effect the market capitalization is the current market value of the company.
- Distributed profit is simply the amount of earnings that the company intends to distribute by the way of dividends to shareholders.

Financial ratios

Earnings per share/return on equity is the profit of a company after corporation tax and interest have been paid; that is, net earnings divided by the number of shares. In **Table 9.5** that is £40m/£400m = 10 pence per share. The advantage of this measure is that companies with high- and low-dividend policies are on a more equal footing; low-dividend payers tend to have higher share prices and high payers tend to have lower share prices; the earnings per share figure is unaffected by the dividend policy.

Return on capital employed (ROCE) is the profit net of tax and interest divided by the total capital, where capital employed is defined as the value of equity plus debt (bonds plus preference shares). In our example it is £40 million/£500 million = 0.08 or 8%. This is a commonly used ratio looking at the percentage return on total capital used by the firm. A firm that is earning less than, say, the risk-free rate of interest would be regarded as a very poor performing company since it would do better to exit the industry and invest its capital in Treasury bonds.

Dividend per share is the distributed profit divided by the number of shares issued, in our example £20 million/400 million = 5 pence per share.

Dividend yield is the dividend per share divided by the price of the share, in this case 5p/100p = 0.05 or 5 per cent. The dividend yield is viewed as important since it shows the income accruing to the investor during the holding period. Dividend yields are normally reported before income tax is applied so that the investor can make comparisons with the yield on alternative investments such as government bonds. The major problem with the dividend yield is that it ignores the capital gain accruing to the investor as a result of any price rise in the share. Another factor that has to be borne in mind is that dividend yields are very much a function of the dividend policy pursued by the company's management; some companies pay out a higher ratio of dividends as a proportion of earnings than others. Also, the dividend yield reported in the *Financial Times* is based on the last year's dividend, whereas investors are generally more interested in prospective yields.

Earnings yield is the earnings divided by the market capitalization of the firm, in our case £40m/£400m = 0.1 or 10 per cent. The numerous problems associated with the dividend yield measure mean that many analysts use the earning yield measure instead. Since shareholders earn money from their shareholding, both in the form of dividends and in the form of capital appreciation, then the dividend payout of firms

---

market capitalization
the market value of a company, found by multiplying the number of shares by the price of the share

earnings per share
the earnings net of taxation, interest payments (and dividends on preference shares) divided by the number of outstanding ordinary shares

return on capital employed the gross earnings before interest and taxes divided by the total capital of a company as reflected in the sum of its equity and debt values

dividend yield
the annual dividend per annum as a percentage of the share price

earnings yield
the ratio of earnings per share to the share price

is not necessarily the most interesting figure. If the firm pays out less in dividends and instead uses more of its profits for higher investment, this may lead to bigger profits in the future and in consequence a larger capital appreciation of its shares in the future. For this reason analysts like to know the earnings yield.

The dividend payout ratio is the total value of dividends paid out divided by earnings, in this case £20 million/£40 million or 50 per cent. The higher this ratio then, generally speaking, the better regarded is the company over time by investors, since it is seen as a sign of management confidence. However, on occasions the ratio is high because management personnel are keen to maintain dividends even when earnings are depressed – a poor dividend payout may lead to the loss of their jobs.

Price–earnings ratio (P/E) is the current price of the shares divided by the earnings per share. In our example it is 100 pence/10 pence or a P/E of 10. The price–earnings ratio can be calculated in various ways; for instance it can be based on the last 12 months' data or calculated on an average basis over, say, 5 years. Some analysts attempt to calculate the prospective P/E ratio using regression analysis, for example based on sales and predicted profit margins. The ratio derives its importance from the fact that it shows the degree to which investors value a company as a multiple of last years' earnings. A price–earnings ratio of 10 means that anyone contemplating a takeover would have to pay at least 10 times the last reported earnings. A high ratio in relation to other companies in the sector means that the firm is being highly valued by the market for some reason other than its current earnings, possibly strong future earnings growth is expected, making its shares popular. Conversely, a low price–earnings ratio in relation to other companies in the sector means that the firm is relatively cheap, possibly because its future earnings performance is expected to be relatively poor. Such a company may be vulnerable to a takeover bid.

While the P/E ratio has its uses, it needs to be remembered that reported earnings can be subject in any year to one-off factors or events that could make the reported profit figure abnormally high or low. To correct for this, some analysts calculate a P/E ratio based on 'normalized' earnings, which supposedly reflects the profits of the company after allowing for such temporary/one-off factors.

In addition, great caution has to be taken in using price–earnings ratios to compare companies, especially those in different sectors of the economy. Different companies use different accounting methods that affect reported earnings; for instance the way they treat depreciation on capital assets can be different. Also, different companies have different reporting dates, company A may report its earnings at the beginning of the year when the performance of the economy has been good, while company B may report its results later in the year when the economy has slowed and so has relatively poor reported earnings. Companies in different sectors of the economy may have very different P/E ratios, those with lower risk tend to have more expensive shares than higher-risk companies even though their earnings may be similar. Similarly, the growth potential of companies can be widely divergent, companies with high growth potential having higher-priced shares than low growth potential companies. In some sectors, such as mining, the tax treatment and accounting methods employed make price–earnings ratios so meaningless they are not reported. There is also the problem that if the company is making a loss then it is not possible to calculate a P/E ratio.

dividend payout ratio the proportion of earnings net of taxation and interest paid out in dividends

price–earnings ratio the price of a share divided by the earnings per share after payment of tax and interest

Risk ratios

In addition to the various financial ratios it is important for investors to be able to assess the riskiness or otherwise of a company. For this reason analysts will look at various risk ratios to assess the possibility that it could get into serious financial difficulty which would then adversely affect the share price. Three of the most important ratios are:

current ratio
current assets divided by current liabilities

- Current ratio: current assets divided by current liabilities. Current assets are liquid assets such as cash, securities and inventories, while current liabilities include short-term borrowing, tax liability, salaries and short-term creditors. The higher the ratio the lower the financial risk facing the firm.
- Liquid asset ratio: current assets minus inventories divided by current liabilities. This is a more conservative ratio than the current ratio since stocks are excluded from assets. The higher the ratio the lower the financial risk facing the firm.
- Interest coverage: profit before interest and taxes divided by total interest payments. The idea of this ratio is that a firm with a high ratio has more chance of meeting its obligations with respect to financing debt than a firm with a low ratio. Hence firms with good interest coverage are deemed to be at lower risk of being placed into receivership. This ratio is sometimes referred to as debt coverage.

Other comparative valuation ratios

In addition to the use of P/E and risk ratios there are other valuation measures that analysts will use to value a company or for comparative evaluation measures:

price to book ratio
the market value of a company in relation to the net asset value of a company, i.e. the value of tangible assets less intangible assets and less liabilities

- Price-to-book ratio: the ratio of the price per share divided by the book value of the company per share as recorded in its balance sheet statement. The book value of the company is the net worth of the company after allowing for current liabilities (e.g. wages, short-term creditors), tax liabilities and debt liabilities (including preference shares). Companies with high price-to-book values are being valued more aggressively than low price-to-book values.
- Price-to-liquidation ratio: the liquidation value of a share is the cash value that the shareholder could expect to receive if the company were to cease trading, sell off all its assets and pay off its liabilities. Since liquidation is the extreme course of action it represents the minimum value of the share. In practice, of course, calculating a liquidation value requires an assumption about the liquidation value of the company's assets which may not be easy to calculate.

free cash flow
a measure of operating cash flow less money set aside for future capital expenditures; it is measured as net profits plus depreciation less changes in working capital less capital expenditures

- Price-to-cash flow: Since earnings can be easily manipulated in the short term, some analysts focus on the price to cash flow coming into or out of the company. The price-to-cash-flow ratio is simply the price of the share divided by cash flow per share. The issue then is whether to use operating cash flow or free cash flow, which is operating cash flow less new investment.
- Price-to-sales ratio: Many new firms do not have profits, so analysts sometimes look at the ratio of the price per share to sales per share. This ratio can differ quite substantially between different industries and the profit margins can also vary substantially.

9.20   The usefulness of financial ratios

Financial ratios are a useful way of looking at key company information, and having certain standard measurements enables useful comparative assessments to be made between firms. Such comparisons tend to be more useful between firms in the same industry than between firms in different industries. Financial ratios provide a useful summary of key financial data and enable a particular firm to be compared to other firms in the same industry as well as with the industry average. An analyst can use financial ratios as a means of identifying above-average companies as well as those which are below average and, other things being equal, should have lower-priced shares. Ideally the selected financial ratios should show separate facets of a company's performance; if two ratios X and Y are highly correlated, then there is little additional information contained in the second ratio and one could be discarded without great loss. Financial ratio analysis can be used as an additional tool along with formal pricing models of shares to determine if a company's stock is over- or undervalued.

Although financial ratios are widely used by analysts when trying to evaluate the health and appropriate share price of a company, one has to be very careful when making comparisons between companies. Different companies use different methodologies to calculate their net profits and have different reporting years, making valid comparisons quite difficult. Some allowance also needs to be made for firm size; it can be unreasonable to expect firms of differing sizes to conform to similar financial ratios. For instance, it is well known that small firms face a bigger risk of financial failure than larger firms. On the other hand, many small but potentially fast-growing companies have quite unhealthy-looking financial ratios but strong future prospects.

Another limitation of financial ratio analysis is that one can use many different financial ratios and as yet no scientific weighting system exists to suggest which are the most important in determining the likely success or failure of a company. The ratios we have mentioned are among the most commonly used, but many others exist and can provide additional useful information. Looked at from the viewpoint of some financial ratios a firm may be viewed as healthy, while others may indicate it is less healthy. Many analysts tend to focus more on trends in a company's financial ratios than its current financial ratios. It should also be remembered that many quoted companies often have a number of subsidiaries and the overall set of accounts may disguise problems in some of the subsidiaries. Another important factor that needs to be borne in mind is that the past is not necessarily a guide to the future. Some of the most successful stocks are those that respond to their poor financial ratios by rationalizing their business and changing their ways of doing things!

9.21   Conclusions

The stockmarket plays an important part in a modern economy by matching firms that require capital with risk-taking investors seeking an expected rate of return above the risk-free rate of interest. Companies have a choice between debt and equity finance and most firms settle on a mixture of the two. The main advantage of equity finance is that the firm does not have to make a payment should it not perform adequately, while against this the cost of equity finance tends to be higher than debt finance to compensate investors for the risk of non-payment.

There is no scientific formula that gives an appropriate price for the share of a company, and the main problem is that future dividend payments are inherently difficult to predict. Nonetheless there are certain fundamental factors that drive share prices; these are the expected rate of return, the potential growth rate of earnings/dividends, and the current dividend. So long as perceptions about these differ between investors and are subject to change, then stocks will be perceived as overvalued by some and undervalued by others. Formal pricing models such as the Gordon growth model can be usefully supplemented by financial ratio analysis which can be used to compare the performance of firms in the same industry and to a lesser extent in different industries. However, financial ratio analysis is an art rather than a science, and a good deal of caution needs to be exercised in using such analysis as an appropriate guide to the relative value of companies.

Further reading

Bodie, Z., Kane, A. and Marcus, A. (2008) *Investments*, 6th edn, McGraw-Hill.

English, J. (2008) *Applied Equity Valuation: Models from Leading Investment Banks*, Wiley.

Murphy, J. (1999) *Technical Analysis of the Financial Markets: A Comprehensive Guide to Trading Methods and Applications*, New York Institute of Finance.

Poddig, T. and Varmaz A. (2008) *Equity Valuation: Models from Leading Investment Banks*, Wiley.

Stowe, J., Robinson, T., Pinto T. and McLeavey D. (2007) *Equity Asset Valuation*, Wiley.

Chapter 9	Revision questions

1   A share last year paid a dividend of $2, the company is expected to have a constant rate of growth of dividends of 5%. The required rate of return is 14%. What according to the Gordon constant growth model is a fair price for the share? What would be a fair price for the share if the forecast growth rate of dividends was to be raised to 6%?

2   Company A has introduced a new product. As a result, you expect earnings and dividends to grow at 20% for the next 3 years. After that the growth rate will fall to 5% indefinitely. The beta on Company A's stock is 1.5, the risk-free rate of interest is 6% and the market risk premium is 7%.

   (i)   Calculate the fair value of the stock if the last dividend (D_0) was 50 pence.
   (ii) Calculate the fair value for the stock at the end of year 3 and at the end of year 4.
   (iii) If your projections prove wrong and the stock grows only at 10% per year but for 5 years and then falls to 5% indefinitely will you have overpaid or underpaid for the stock, if you pay the fair value calculated from part (i)?

Chapter 9 ‖ **Revision questions** – *continued*

3   You are given the following data on companies A and B:

Company A		**Company B**	
	(£ millions)		*(£ millions)*
Debt	100	Debt	200
Equity (£1 a share)	400	Equity (£1 a share)	300
Earnings before interest	50	Earnings before interest	50
Interest (6% of debt)	6	Interest (6% of debt)	12

   (i)   What is the maximum dividend per share payable by Company A and Company B respectively?

   (ii) If the interest rate was not 6% on debt but 12% on debt what is the maximum dividend payable per share?

4   Complete the following table for the expected rate of return on equity for different rates of profit (*p*) and levels of primary gearing assuming that the rate of interest on debt is 5%.

Debt/equity ratio	Expected rate of return on equity			
(gearing)	*p* = 0%	*p* = 5%	*p* = 10%	*p* = 15%
0.5	?	?	?	?
1.5	?	?	?	?
2.5	?	?	?	?

   What can you conclude about the impact of primary gearing on the variability of return on equity?

5   Assume that the rate of profits (*p*) on combined debt and equity is fixed at 20%. Complete the following table for the proportion of profits absorbed by interest.

Debt/equity ratio	Proportion of profits absorbed by interest				
(gearing)	*r* = 5%	*r* = 10%	*r* = 15%	*r* = 20%	*r* = 25%
0.5	?	?	?	?	?
1.5	?	?	?	?	?
2.5	?	?	?	?	?

   What can you conclude about the impact of primary gearing on the vulnerability of a company to rises in interest rates?

6   Briefly discuss four disadvantages of the constant growth dividend discount model as a tool for valuing the fair price of shares.

7   (i)   What is the meant by 'short selling' of a stock?

   (ii) What are the risks of short selling a stock? What alternatives to short selling are open to hedge funds?

10

THE EFFICIENCY OF FINANCIAL MARKETS

Learning objectives

In this chapter you will learn about:

- the difference between operational efficiency and market efficiency
- the differences between weak, semi-strong and strong forms of market efficiency
- the difference between passive and active fund management
- the various types of tests that have been conducted to test for market efficiency
- the behavioural finance challenge to market efficiency

10.1   Introduction

One of the largest areas of research and interest in finance concerns the efficiency of financial markets. There have been studies of the efficiency of bond markets, the foreign exchange market, the stockmarket and more recently of derivative markets such as the options and futures market. In this chapter we restrict ourselves to examining the efficiency of stockmarkets.

One could consider market efficiency from a variety of viewpoints. For instance, we could consider the allocative efficiency of capital markets; that is, how good are they at allocating scarce capital resources among competing uses? In an ideal world, capital would be allocated to the firms that can achieve the best marginal returns. Alternatively, we could consider the operational efficiency of the capital market. In an ideal world, the costs of raising capital would be minimized and viable long-term projects would be able to raise capital as easily as short-term ones. Furthermore, investors would be faced with minimal transaction costs, such as negligible bid–ask spreads on securities, and competition between brokers would ensure only normal profits in the securities industry.

While allocative and operational efficiency are clearly desirable, the finance literature has concentrated on another type of efficiency relating to the pricing of securities. According to this definition, financial markets are informationally efficient if the current market price of a security instantly and fully reflects all relevant available information. In this chapter we focus on various types of informational efficiency according to a classic classification suggested by Fama (1970) that distinguishes between weak-form efficiency, semi-strong-form efficiency and strong-form efficiency. We also review some of the empirical investigations into the question of efficiency in relation to the pricing of shares.

The question of whether markets are informationally efficient is of more than academic interest. If they are, this can help to ensure that scarce capital is efficiently allocated amongst its alternative uses. Firms with the best prospective profitability profiles should see this reflected in rises in their share price, and should find that they can raise new capital more easily and at less cost than firms with poor profit potential. Furthermore, firms that fail to use their capital efficiently will find that their share price is depressed and they may well become takeover targets. This usually results in a new management team that hopes to use the capital base more productively. Hence, informational efficiency is not entirely divorced from the idea of allocative efficiency.

---

allocative efficiency the efficiency with which the capital markets allocate scarce capital funds to the most productive uses

operational efficiency the cost efficiency of the financial markets and financial institutions described in terms of charges to investors

informational efficiency the extent to which market prices of securities fully incorporate information and react to changes in information so that abnormal returns cannot be made on a consistent basis

10.2   Three levels of efficiency

Following Eugene Fama, an efficient market is conventionally defined as one 'in which prices always "fully reflect" available information' (1970, p. 383). This definition implies that market participants use all relevant available information bearing on the appropriate values of securities to produce a set of security prices which is such that unusual ex ante profits cannot be made on a consistent basis using a given known information set.

In connection with this broad definition, there are two key concerns: (i) Is new information instantaneously and fully absorbed into a share's price? and (ii) What is relevant and what is irrelevant information? Fama provided an operational base for testing market efficiency by distinguishing between three types of efficiency; weak-form efficiency, semi-strong-form efficiency and strong-form efficiency:

- *Weak-form efficiency*. A market is said to be weak-form efficient if the current prices of securities instantly and fully reflect all information of the past history of security prices. In other words, it should not be possible to make consistent excess returns on securities by looking at the past history of their price movements and using this as a basis for future trading. Note that this definition restricts the information data-set to the past price history of security prices.
- *Semi-strong-form efficiency*. A market is said to be semi-strong-form efficient if the current prices of the securities instantly and fully reflect all publicly available information. In other words, it should not be possible to make consistent excess returns on securities by using publicly available information as a basis for future trading. The publicly available information set includes not only the past history of security prices, but also all publicly available relevant information such as earnings, details in company reports, announcements made by the firm, information about the state of the economy and so on.
- *Strong-form efficiency*. A market is said to be strong-form efficient if the current prices of securities instantly and fully reflect all information, both public and private. In other words, even traders, directors or analysts with access to privileged inside information should not be able to make consistent excess returns on securities by using inside information as a basis for future trading.

10.3   The efficient market hypothesis and a random walk

efficient market hypothesis (EMH) a theory that says security prices reflect all available information thus making it difficult for investors to make abnormal returns

The hypothesis that security prices instantly and fully reflect all available information is commonly referred to as the efficient market hypothesis (EMH). If the EMH were to hold, then it would not be possible on an ex ante basis for an investor to expect to make consistent excess profits. The concept is very similar to that of a 'fair game'. In a fair game there is no systematic difference between the actual return on the game and the expected return on a game. In the context of the EMH there should be no systematic difference between the actual return on a portfolio of securities given its risk profile and that expected from the portfolio of securities on the basis of its risk profile (the risk profile being determined, for instance, by the portfolio's beta).

More formally, we can write down the return on a security that corresponds to the EMH as:

$$R_{it+1} = E(R_{it+1/I_t}) + u_{t+1} \qquad (10.1)$$

where: R_{it+1} is the actual rate of return on security i in period $t+1$; $E(R_{it+1/I_t})$ is the expected rate of return on security i in period $t+1$ at time t given the information available at time t (that is I_t); u_{t+1} is the prediction error, that is the difference between the actual return on security i at time $t+1$ and the expected return on security i at time t.

Equation (10.1) says that the actual return on a security corresponds to the expected return plus a random error which may be positive or negative. The error term has certain properties that establish its randomness:

1. it should have an expected value of zero with the positive and negative errors cancelling each other out in sufficiently large samples;
2. it should be independent of the expected rate of return on the security, that is the correlation between u_{t+1} and $E(R_{it+1/I_t})$ should be zero; and
3. it should not be predictable on the basis of any information available at time t. For instance, the prediction error on forecasting the return on security i should not be correlated with past errors in predicting the return on security i. Alternatively, the prediction error on forecasting the return on security i one period ahead should not be predictable as a result of information on the current prediction error on another security j.

If the EMH as given by equation (10.1) holds, then the expected rate of return one period ahead will be the same as the actual return today, that is:

$$E(R_{it+1/I_t}) = R_{it} \qquad (10.2)$$

Substituting equation (10.1) into equation (10.2) yields:

$$R_{it+1} = R_{it} + u_{t+1} \qquad (10.3)$$

Equation (10.3) defines what is known as a random walk. The return on security i one period hence is equal to the current rate of return plus some random error, and this error cannot be predicted on the basis of information available at time t.

The idea of a random-walk process was first mooted by a French economist Louis Bachelier in 1900 in relation to the price of commodities traded on the French commodities market. A random-walk process is quite simple; if a security price follows a random walk, then at the start of each period there is a 50 per cent chance that its price will go up by a given amount, and a 50 per cent chance that it will fall by a given amount. Predicting its path is essentially a matter of chance, and the best forecast of the future price is in fact the current price. Equation (10.3) relates to the expected rate of return of a security, and in terms of the price of securities the idea of a random walk can be formalized as:

$$P_{it+1} = P_{it} + v_{t+1} \qquad (10.4)$$

where P_{it+1} is the security price one period hence; P_{it} is the current price, and v_{t+1} is the prediction error.

Equation (10.4) says that the future price of the security is equal to the current price plus a random error, and represents a true random-walk forecast. However, there is a tendency for share prices to rise over time so a strict random-walk forecast for shares is not ideal since there is a slightly greater chance of the share going up than down. This means that a modified random-walk equation with a positive drift component is usually used, that is:

$$P_{it+1} = G_{it+1} + P_{it} + w_{t+1} \tag{10.5}$$

where w_{t+1} is the random prediction error. G_{it+1} is the expected rate of growth of the security price given by $R_{it+1}P_{it}$ which is presumed to be positive. Equation (10.5) differs from the simple random-walk model of share prices in that the price of the share has some positive trend given by G_{it+1}.

10.4   Implications of various forms of efficiency tests

Before we proceed to analyze the various types of tests that have been conducted on the EMH and the results of these studies, it is worthwhile thinking about some of the implications of the efficiency hypotheses. If the weak form of market efficiency were to hold, then this would suggest that chartists and technical analysts who make their living by analyzing historical price data and using this to forecast future security prices will produce forecasts that are on average of no profitable use!

Chartists claim to be able to successfully predict the future behaviour of a security's price merely by examining a chart of its recent behaviour. Chart analysis is frequently backed up by looking at data relating to the volume of transactions undertaken. Chartists claim that certain patterns of behaviour repeat themselves and that, by detecting the relevant pattern in play, considerable success can be had in predicting the future price of a security. Many of the patterns are given names such as 'head and shoulders', 'triple bottom', 'ascending triangle', and 'double top'. Feeny (1989) provides an excellent summary of chartist methodology. Technical analysts also make use of past data as the basis for future forecasting but adopt a statistical approach to analyzing the data-set. The important point about both chartists and technical analysts is that they only require information on securities' past behaviour in order to predict their future prices; fundamental information such as management changes, future earnings growth, the degree of competition and so on are not required.

If the semi-strong form of market efficiency were to hold then this would suggest that investment and research analysts that make their living by analyzing publicly available information such as company reports, company announcements, industry reports and economic forecasts will not be able to produce forecasts that yield excess profits. Any new publicly available information gets instantaneously incorporated into securities' prices and there is no chance to profit from the information. The type of methods used by investment analysts vary in their degree of sophistication. Some prefer to use simple models based upon looking at data such as earnings per share and simple models such as the Gordon growth model, others resort to the use of complex econometric models. The important thing about investment analysts is their belief that it is the prospectives for economic fundamentals that indicate future

chartist a person that uses chart patterns on past prices of a security to forecast future price changes in financial markets

technical analyst a person that uses statistical analysis of past price behaviour, sometimes supplemented with volumes traded, to predict future price change in financial markets

security prices. The semi-strong form of market efficiency leaves open the possibility for those with privileged inside information to make abnormal profits.

The strong form of market efficiency implies that even those with access to privileged inside information will not be able to profit from that information since it is already incorporated into a security's prices. If this theory were to hold, then there would be no need for securities houses to have Chinese walls to keep price-sensitive information in one part of the business from the dealing/brokerage arm of the organization, and there would also be no need for governments to have 'insider-trading' laws.

Chinese wall
a barrier put in place by a financial institution to prevent conflicts of interest within the institution

10.5   Active versus passive fund management

Active fund management is the process of looking for 'undervalued' and 'overvalued' securities, and shifting the composition of a portfolio to buy those stocks which are perceived to be undervalued and sell those stocks which are perceived to be overvalued. Active fund management should help to ensure that stocks are priced around their intrinsic value, with buying pressure leading to a rise in the price of undervalued stocks and selling pressure leading to a fall in the price of overvalued stocks.

active fund management the use of fund managers' skills and experience to buy and sell selected securities; it can involve frequent buying and selling of shares

With passive fund management, the underlying belief is that the EMH holds so there is no real need to engage in active fund management. The process of spotting and trading truly overvalued or undervalued securities is both time-consuming and results in high transaction costs for the fund. The philosophy behind passive management is to select a portfolio of securities with the appropriate risk characteristics desired by the fund management and, once selected, by and large to leave the fund alone and wait to see the results. The popularity of passive fund management has grown in recent years, with so-called index tracking funds that follow stockmarket indices such as the S&P 500 and the FTSE 100. The fund managers buy the same stocks that make up the index in the value-weighted proportions within that index, and maintain those proportions more or less as the index moves so that it is properly tracked. Passive fund management has the advantage that a key well known index is usually being tracked and the transaction costs/management fees tend to be quite low.

passive fund management
a strategy of buying and holding shares, usually to track a market index; it leads to very low transaction charges

index tracking funds funds set up to match the performance of a market index such as the S&P 500 or FTSE 100

10.6   Testing for weak market efficiency

Numerous tests have been conducted to see if weak market efficiency holds, including tests to see if security prices follow a random walk, filter-rule tests and other statistical tests that seek to find consistent patterns in data.

10.7   Tests of the random-walk hypothesis

Tests of the random-walk hypothesis have been extensively used as a test for weak-form efficiency. The basic idea of weak-form efficiency is that the best forecast of the future price of a security is the current price, and that adding details of past security price movements will be of no use in predicting the future course of the security's price. The vast majority of academic studies show that share prices do indeed follow a random walk, or a random walk with a positive drift component, and that there is no information on past prices that can be added that improves the forecasting ability. Hence, tests of the random-walk hypothesis are strongly supportive of weak-form market efficiency.

10.8   Filter-rule tests

According to the weak form of the efficient market hypothesis, it should not be possible to make abnormal returns from looking at past movements in a security's price. This idea is investigated in filter-rule tests which simply apply a mechanical trading rule based on recent price movements as shown in **Figure 10.1**. Filter rules are designed to catch significant trends in securities prices, and can be based on any percentage. **Figure 10.1** shows the operation of a 5 per cent filter rule. Once a share has fallen by 5 per cent below its previous high (point A), this is taken as an indication of a significant shift and an investor sells the share until it rises 5 per cent from any low. This occurs at B, at which point the security is bought since a significant rise is expected. Once the share falls 5 per cent from any new high (at point C) then the share is again sold until it is once again 5 per cent above any new low obtained. If such a simple mechanical trading rule produced excess profits over a simple 'buy and hold' strategy in the security, it would be indicative of weak-form inefficiency. This is because, in an efficient market, prices would move too rapidly to new highs and lows for such a strategy to work, and the best thing would be for the investor to buy the security and hold it so as to avoid the transaction costs implied by the filter strategy.

The question arises: what size of filter should be adopted? With a very small filter, for example 1 per cent, real trends will be picked up and traded on earlier than with a larger filter. However, there is an increased risk of trading on transitory movements that quickly reverse themselves, which means that any gains could quickly be offset by higher transaction costs with the underlying security failing to move. On the other hand, if the filter is set too high, for example 15 per cent, then, while transaction costs will be lower, many potentially profitable trading opportunities will have been lost.

Figure 10.1   Filter rule tests

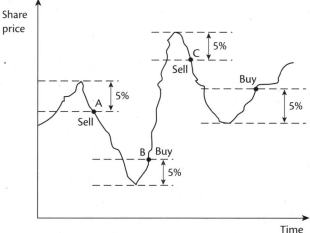

buy-and-hold strategy a passive investment strategy of holding shares through market fluctuations believing that they will perform well in the long term

To overcome the problem of the correct filter size, most studies use a range of filter sizes. The overwhelming evidence from filter tests, for example Fama and Blume (1966) and Sweeny (1988), is that whatever size of filter is chosen, there are no excess profits to be made compared to a simple buy-and-hold strategy once due allowance has been made for transaction costs. The results of filter-rule tests also provide support for the weak form of market efficiency, since recent movements in the price of a security do not seem to provide profitable trading opportunities.

10.9 Other statistical tests

A variety of other statistical tests have tried to predict future security prices on the basis of their past prices. These vary in their degree of complexity from simple run tests, to the use of relatively sophisticated time-series techniques. In a run test, the qualitative direction of share movements is examined using + for a rise, − for a fall and 0 for no change. If the share price is unpredictable, then runs with too many consecutive pluses or minuses or repeating patterns should not appear more or less frequently than one would expect from a set of random numbers. Fama (1965), using such run tests for a wide range of stocks, found that there was no significant difference between the number of runs detected and the expected number of runs from a set of random numbers.

Despite the strong evidence that day-to-day, week-to-week and even month-to-month stock movements are largely random, a few data anomalies have been uncovered that cause us to question whether share prices really do incorporate all historical data. We look briefly at three of these anomalies: (i) the day-of-the week effect, (ii) the January effect, and (iii) the winner–loser problem.

10.10 The day-of-the-week effect

Both Cross (1973) and Gibbons and Hess (1981) have found statistically significant evidence that share prices tend to fall on Mondays and rise on Fridays. There is no obvious reason why this should happen and it is certainly a result that seems to contradict the weak form of EMH. However, the results do not necessarily have an economic significance; once allowance is made for transaction costs, a strategy of buy at the close of Monday and sell late on Friday does not seem to yield excess profits. Furthermore, in a more recent study Connolly (1989) found that the weekend effect had disappeared, which is what one would expect according to the EMH as traders sell on Friday and buy on Monday to try and profit from the effect.

10.11 The January effect

One of the biggest challenges facing the EMH has been the discovery of the so-called January effect, noted by Keim (1983) from a study of the US stockmarket covering the years 1963 to 1979. The January effect is the finding that not only are returns on stocks in January relatively high compared to other months of the year, but more importantly the returns on small company stocks appear to significantly outperform the market as a whole in January. This difference is significant even if one controls for risk factors as measured by firms' betas, small firms tending to be more risky with high betas. For example, a study by Fama (1991) covering the period 1941 to 1981 found not only that January is the month with the highest average return, but also that small stocks rose by an average 8.06 per cent in January while large stocks averaged a return of only 1.34 per cent. Fama found that the January effect persisted for the period 1981 to 1991 when small capitalization stocks rose on average by 5.32 per cent while large capitalization stocks rose by 3.2 per cent. The effect is not confined exclusively to the US market; in fact Gultekin and Gultekin (1983) found the effect to be even more pronounced in 16 other countries. Haugen (1997) reported that, despite its discovery, the January effect had persisted and remained pronounced.

The January effect poses a significant problem for the EMH since it seems to point to a simple opportunity for investors to make excess profits; that is, to buy small company stocks towards the end of December and sell them at the end of January. If this were to happen in sufficient numbers, as required by the EMH, then the stock prices of smaller companies would rise in December reducing the return in January to more normal levels. The persistence of the effect seems to imply that the market is not making the best use of known publicly available information. One way that the EMH could explain the effect is to argue that risks on smaller stocks rise at the beginning of the year, but there seems to be no obvious reason to suppose that this is the case. One other possibility is to argue that, although the anomaly exists, the higher transaction costs involved in dealing in smaller company stocks means that it cannot be profitably exploited. However, this too seems to be inadequate since transaction costs for fund managers are relatively low, and the effect could still be exploited by using futures contracts on smaller stocks.

Several explanations for the January effect have been put forward. One of the most plausible is that it represents the effects of 'window-dressing' by fund managers at the end of the year. Most fund managers are obliged to report their year-end positions to their clients, and the argument is that, towards the end of the year, they switch out of lesser-known small stocks and into larger better-known stocks to make their portfolios look more 'respectable'. In January they increase the proportion of smaller company stocks in the portfolio because they offer the prospective for higher fund growth, accounting for the pronounced rise in smaller company stocks that month. There is quite a lot of anecdotal evidence for this. For instance, most of the January effect appears to occur in the first five days of trading in January, suggesting that fund managers are going back into smaller company stocks. There is a tendency for smaller stocks to underperform in December, suggesting that fund managers are selling smaller company stocks as part of a window-dressing exercise.

10.12   The winner–loser problem

In two controversial papers, De Bondt and Thaler (1985 and 1987) have argued that investors tend to over-react to moving share prices. They find that stocks that have fallen most in price during the previous three to five years will tend to yield excess returns over the following three to five years. Conversely, stocks that have been the best performers in the preceding three to five years will tend to underperform in the subsequent three to five years. Their results imply that past price information can be potentially useful for a longer-term investment strategy, posing a challenge to the weak market efficiency hypothesis at least at the longer-term horizon. Nonetheless, the results of their studies have not gone unchallenged, with some researchers arguing that the results are sensitive to the method used to calculate the expected rate of return. One further problem is that the companies examined must survive the whole sample period, therefore the results of the study will have an upward bias by excluding the worst performing companies that went bankrupt during the study period! Investors adopting a longer-term strategy may well not make excess profits once this is taken into account. In a further study, however, Jegadeesh and Titman (1993) also found that 'winners' seem to do better than 'losers' in the seven months following quarterly earnings announcements, but do significantly worse at the 8–36-month horizon, when the 'losers' actually become the 'winners'!

We can conclude this survey of weak-form efficiency tests by summarizing that the majority of the evidence indicates that financial markets are weak-form efficient. The use of past prices to forecast future security prices has been shown in the academic literature to fail to yield excess profits. Nonetheless some anomalies have been uncovered, suggesting the possibility that there may be some useful past price information around that could yield potential excess profit opportunities.

10.13   Testing for semi-strong market efficiency

When it comes to testing for semi-strong market efficiency, the information set available increases dramatically from the past history of share-price data to all publicly available information. The public information set includes earnings data, changes in dividend policy, announcement of stock splits, news of takeover bids, newspaper column tips and so on.

It is important to emphasize at this point that according to the EMH the market will only react to the 'news' element of information. For example, if a company announces that earnings are 50 per cent higher than in the previous period, this may only be 'good news' to the extent that the market was expecting a lower figure, say 20 per cent. The news element is not the 50 per cent announced improvement but the difference between what the market was anticipating, 20 per cent, and the actual announced figure of 50 per cent. The share price prior to the announcement already incorporates the expectation of a 20 per cent improvement and therefore only reacts to the news element of the announcement, that is the results are 30 per cent better than expected. If the announced figure was a 20 per cent improvement, this would be in line with what the market was expecting and the share price should not move. Finally, if the announced figure had been only a 5 per cent growth rate this would be lower than the market was expecting, and although an improvement on the previous year, would be regarded by the market as bad news and, according to the EMH, the share price should fall.

When testing to see if various pieces of publicly available information can be used to generate abnormal excess returns, careful account needs to be taken of the risk characteristics of the shares analyzed. For instance, according to the CAPM a share with a high beta should have a higher rate of return than shares with low betas. Any study of semi-strong market efficiency should subtract the expected

stock split
a situation in which a company replaces its existing shares with a greater number of shares to lower the price of each share; for example, in a 4 for 1 stock split investors are given four shares to replace each existing share that they own, if the original share price was $200 then after a 4 for 1 stock split, each new share should be worth $50

| Box 10.1 | The behavioural finance challenge to the efficient market hypothesis |

In recent years there has been a rapid growth in a branch of economics known as behavioural finance. The field of behavioural finance seeks to explain why and how financial markets can be inefficient by bringing in insights from human psychology to explain the behaviour of financial market participants. As long ago as 1912 G.C. Selden wrote a book entitled *Psychology of the Stock Market* which was based 'upon the belief that the movements of prices on the exchanges are dependent to a very considerable degree on the mental attitude of the investing and trading public'. But it was not until the publication of a paper entitled 'Does the Stock Market Overreact?' by De Bondt and Taylor in 1986 that the study of behavioural finance began. However, cognitive psychologists Daniel Khaneman and Amos Tversky are considered to be the fathers of behavioural economics/finance, having published over 200 papers. Khaneman was awarded the Nobel Prize in Economics in 2000 for his contribution.

In their papers, Kahneman and Tversky reported on a series of experimental studies in which subjects answered questions that entailed making judgments between two monetary decisions. These decisions involved prospective losses and gains, and an example of two questions is given below:

Question 1 You have $1,000 and you must pick one of the following choices:
Choice A: You have a 50 per cent chance of gaining $1,000, and a 50 per cent chance of gaining $0.
Choice B: You have a 100 per cent chance of gaining $500.

Question 2 You have $2,000 and you must pick one of the following choices:
Choice A: You have a 50 per cent chance of losing $1,000, and a 50 per cent of losing $0.
Choice B: You have a 100 per cent chance of losing $500.

There is no correct answer to the above questions. If the subjects answer the questions logically then they should give the same answer to both – with people answering 'B' being more risk-averse than those answering 'A'. However, in their study a large majority of people chose 'B' for question 1 and 'A' for question 2. The implication is that people are willing to settle for a reasonable level of gain even if they have a reasonable chance of earning more, but are willing to engage in risk-seeking behaviour where they can limit their losses. The conclusion is that losses are weighted more heavily by economic agents than an equivalent amount of gains. Kahneman and Tversky created prospect theory to explain this 'disposition effect'. The disposition effect is also observed in real-life situations; for example, people tend to cash in winning stocks for too little and yet hold losing stocks for too long, when a more logical approach would be to hold onto winning stocks for further gains whilst selling losing stocks to prevent mounting losses.

Another concept is that of anchoring, whereby economic agents tend to focus, or anchor, on a piece of irrelevant information, even though that information is of no particular relevance to the share price. In their 1974 paper 'Judgment Under Uncertainty: Heuristics and Biases', Kahneman and Tversky spun a wheel showing

| Box 10.1 | **The behavioural finance challenge to the EMH** – *continued* |

the numbers 1 to 100. Once the wheel was spun, subjects were asked whether the percentage of African countries making up United Nations membership was greater or lower than the number on the wheel. They were then asked to estimate the actual percentage. Kahneman and Tversky found that the value of the subjects' estimate was heavily influenced by the random value from the wheel spin. For example, if the wheel spin read 60 then the estimates tended to be high, like 50 per cent, whereas if the wheel spin read 20 the estimates might be only 16 per cent. The value given by the wheel spin was acting as an anchor to the response given, even though it was irrelevant to the question in hand. Anchoring can occur in financial markets. For instance, people tend to look at the year high of a share, and if the current price is well below that high they think they are getting a bargain. This perception endures even if the share has been falling in value so that the recent high is of no relevance to whether it is undervalued.

Another concept is that of herd behaviour whereby people tend to mimic the actions of a large group, although they might act differently if they acted individually. Herd behaviour can be explained by people not wanting to appear as outcasts or by a belief that a large group must be 'in the know'. During the dot com bubble many people bought internet stocks at extremely inflated prices because they observed others doing so, even though in normal times they would have avoided such stocks.

In 1985 Werner De Bondt and Richard Thaler published a paper in the *Journal of Finance* entitled 'Does the Market Overreact?'. The authors examined stock returns on the New York Stock Exchange over a three-year period. Stocks were separated into two portfolios, the 35 best-performing stocks were placed into a 'winners portfolio' and the 35 worst-performing stocks were placed into a 'losers portfolio'. The authors then tracked both portfolios against a representative market index for three years. They found that the losers portfolio consistently outperformed the market index while the winners portfolio consistently performed worse than the market index. The cumulative difference between the losers portfolio and the winners portfolio was a significant 25 per cent. As such the original losers became the future winners while the original winners became the future losers. De Bondt and Thaler's study suggested that the price of winning stocks rose too much in the winning years while the price of losing stocks fell too much, suggesting that market participants pushed the prices too high and down too low to begin with. One possible reason for over-reaction could be availability bias whereby people tend to attach too much importance to recent news and fail to take a longer-term perspective. For instance a company may report a very good quarter and so its share price increases rapidly in the short term, but had a longer-term perspective been taken the quarter might be viewed as a one-off and share price would not rise as much or as quickly.

Another problem is that of overconfidence. In a 2006 study entitled 'Behaving Badly' James Montier found that 74 per cent of professional fund managers

continued overleaf

Box 10.1	The behavioural finance challenge to the EMH – *continued*

believed they had delivered above-average performance, with the vast majority of the remaining 26 per cent classifying themselves as average performers. In other words, nearly 100 per cent believed that their performance was average or better, suggesting that a degree of overconfidence prevails in the industry. In addition, there is confirmation bias and hindsight bias to consider. Most of us have preconceived ideas about things and we tend to seek out information that confirms our preconceived ideas while ignoring, or not fully taking on board, evidence to the contrary. The confirmation bias can result in poor decision making because the one-sided view of the investment decision means that the downside and risks have not been fully considered. For instance, you might think that biotech stocks are the next big thing and worth investing in. You might then look for all the positive information about how they have the potential to produce new medical cures, generate huge potential revenues and profits, but ignore negative information that suggests only 1 in 10 biotech companies actually succeeds in generating a profit for its shareholders.

Obviously there is a lot more to behavioural finance than we can cover here and it is a rapidly growing area of finance. There now exist funds that seek to make money out of known behavioural patterns. While behavioural finance has provided many useful insights it has not yet been fully accepted as a new paradigm by the finance profession. Indeed, the father of the efficient market hypothesis, Eugene Fama mounted a robust defence of the EMH in a 1998 article entitled 'Market Efficiency, Long Run Returns and Behavioural Finance'. He argued that behavioural finance is riddled with contradictions and that many so-called anomalies can disappear if a proper methodology is applied. For instance, the winner–loser anomaly could be due to differences between the risk premium for losing shares going up, resulting in higher future returns, and the risk premium for winning stocks going down, resulting in lower future returns. Fama argued that some anomalies are really the result of chance and that markets are as likely to under-react as they are to over-react to new information.

rate of return, given the riskiness of the shares considered, from the actual return generated by trading on the information available, to see if true excess returns are being generated. By necessity, this makes the test of semi-strong EMH a joint test. A finding of abnormal profits may constitute a rejection of semi-strong EMH, but there remains the possibility that the model used to calculate normal rates of return may be deficient and underestimates the true risks facing investors. In other words, there is a possibility that the result is spurious and so-called excess returns are nothing of the sort, they are merely the additional return required for risks that have been underestimated in the study and in fact the EMH holds.

The very fact that investment houses and fund managers analyze and process information and that stock prices seem to move swiftly when 'news' reaches the market are at first suggestive that the semi-strong-form of market efficiency is valid.

Figure 10.2   The impact of news according to EMH

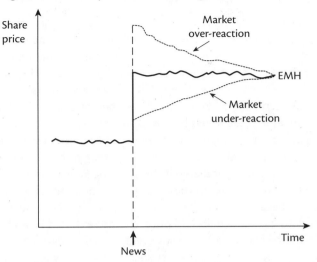

One of the most popular means of testing for semi-strong efficiency is to analyze the impact of an announcement on stock prices, and such studies are known as event studies. The idea behind event studies is to see how quickly and accurately news is incorporated into the share price. If the EMH holds, then the effect of news will be immediately and instantaneously impacted into the market price of a security, which will jump on the announcement of the new information to a new fundamental value, as shown in **Figure 10.2**.

If the EMH holds, then information that is newly released to the market, for instance a substantially higher than expected earnings growth, should lead to a sharp rise in the share price upon announcement of the news, as depicted by the EMH line. Thereafter, assuming no further news, the share should continue to trade at the new higher equilibrium price. If the market was inefficient then a variety of other scenarios are possible. The market may have a tendency to over-react to news, and this is illustrated by the path marked 'market over-reaction'. Upon announcement of the news the stock is enthusiastically purchased such that it rises too far in relation to its fundamental value, but thereafter it moves towards its fundamental value. Alternatively, the market may under-react to the news, as shown by the path marked 'market under-reaction'. Following announcement of the news, the stock rises, but only slowly, towards its new fundamental value, suggesting that the information has not been fully priced into the stock.

If there was a consistent tendency in the market to over-react or under-react to new information this would imply excess profit opportunities. If the market consistently over-reacts to new information then it would pay investors to go short on stocks which were affected by good news, and buy stocks adversely affected by bad news. Conversely, if the market consistently under-reacts to news then it would pay investors to buy stocks affected by good news and sell or go short in stocks adversely affected by bad news. In the case where the market is efficient there are no subsequent gains to be made from trading after the news since the stock will move instantaneously to the appropriate rate.

event study analysis of the impact of a particular type of announcement (e.g. takeover bid, merger, earnings announcement, change in dividend policy, profit warning, dissemination of a buy recommendation in the press) on the share prices of a group of firms for a period prior to the announcement and after the announcement (e.g. 30 days before and 30 days after)

10.14   The results of event studies

An event study analyzes the impact of a particular type of announcement (for example, a takeover bid, merger, earnings announcement, a change in dividend policy, profit warning, dissemination of a buy recommendation in the press and so on) on the share prices of a group of firms for a period both prior to the announcement and after the announcement. The returns for a period both before and after the announcement (for example, 30 days before and 30 days after) are then compared to the return that would be expected on the basis of a model such as the CAPM. On the day of the announcement one should expect to see a jump in the share price to its new appropriate value. In the days prior to the announcement there should be no excess return since, even if the announcement is expected, it should already be in the share price, while in the days after the announcement there should be no excess return because in an efficient market the announcement should swiftly move the stock to its new equilibrium price, and there should be no lagged effect.

There have been numerous event studies analyzing the impact of different types of announcement. While most such studies show a significant price movement on the day of announcement, which is in line with semi-strong efficiency, the results concerning the possibility of lagged effects are more mixed. Firth (1975), in an analysis of the effects of announced stockbuilding which often results in a subsequent takeover bid at a premium price, found that the semi-strong efficiency argument was supported. In studies of the news content of dividend policy announcements, Watts (1973) and Pettit (1972) found that the market price movements and returns were consistent with the semi-strong form of the EMH. However, like the weak form of efficiency there are some anomalies that pose a challenge for the semi-strong form. We look at three of the better known anomalies: (i) the size effect, (ii) the price–earnings effect, and (iii) the earnings-announcement effect.

10.15   The size effect

One of the most quoted studies on the size effect was undertaken by Banz (1981), who found that, for New York-quoted stocks during the period 1936–77, the excess return from holding stocks in the lowest quintile (made up of the smallest quoted companies) compared to those of the top quintile (representing the largest firms) was 19.8 per cent. He also found that the firm-size effect was as significant as the firms' betas in explaining the excess return. The results of Banz's study can be taken as either a rejection of the EMH or the CAPM as the appropriate pricing tool for small companies. However, some authors have argued that estimated betas for small firms are in fact too low; for instance, small firms are more likely to change their characteristics than larger firms or have lower survival probability in recession which makes them a greater risk than suggested by their historical betas.

10.16   The price–earnings effect

Another anomaly that seems to contradict the semi-strong EMH is the price–earnings (P/E) effect. Basu (1977) examined the performance of various portfolios on the basis of their price–earnings ratios for the period 1957–71, and found that the return on company stocks with low P/E ratios is significantly higher than the return on companies with relatively high P/E ratios. The study made due allowance for the fact that companies with low P/E ratios may well be poorly priced because the market expects such companies to have a higher bankruptcy rate. The EMH has problems dealing with the P/E effect, but could still explain the anomaly if it could be shown that companies with lower P/E ratios are riskier as measured by their betas or some other measure. The empirical evidence, however, is contrary to this; it is generally growth stocks with higher than average P/E ratios (since they are largely priced on the prospect of strong future earnings growth) that tend to be riskier, exhibiting a greater average volatility of returns than stocks with low P/E ratios.

10.17 The earnings-announcement effect

Not surprisingly, stock prices react to earnings announcements from corporations as the EMH suggests that they should. However, studies such as Rendleman, Jones and Latane (1982) show that the reaction of stock prices is not entirely consistent with what one would expect from the semi-strong EMH. These researchers separated firms into 10 groups according to the degree of good or bad news contained in the quarterly earnings announcements. They found that in the 20 days prior to the announcement the stock prices tended to move in anticipation of the announcement, with the return on good-news firms' stock rising and the return on bad-news stock declining, suggesting that a degree of inside knowledge was being priced into the stock prior to the announcement. More interesting, however, was their observation that, while there was a discernible stock price movement on the day of the announcement as one would expect according to the EMH, there were also significant and predictable returns to be made in the 90 days following the announcement, which is contrary to the EMH. More specifically, buying stock in companies with good results and selling stock in companies with poor results, even on the day after the announcement, would yield excess profits over the following 90 days. The results seem to strongly suggest that all news is not properly priced into the market at the time of the announcement as would be expected from the EMH. If anything, markets seem to under-react to good and bad news.

While the anomalies that we have looked at pose a challenge to the concept that the market is semi-strong efficient, we nonetheless have to be careful when interpreting discovered anomalies as a rejection of semi-strong EMH. With enough researchers looking at the data and enough plausible-looking information variables it should prove possible to find some statistically significant excess profit opportunities. There is a tendency for researchers to submit only statistically significant results and for academic journals to publish only significant anomalies, so that all the academic research that reveals no significant anomalies gets no publicity. Another problem is that the discovered anomalies may be time-specific and not carry over into different time periods. There is also a distinct possibility that some of the anomalies are highly correlated with some of the other anomalies and therefore do not constitute separate anomalies. For instance, Keim (1983) showed that the January effect and size effect are strongly related, while Reinganum (1981) argued that the size and price–earnings effects are also strongly correlated.

10.18   Stockmarket crashes

Between January and October 1987 most stock indices around the world had experienced a bull market; the UK market was up 75 per cent in the year, the US market up 30 per cent, the Japanese market up some 60 per cent and the Hong Kong index up 70 per cent. Then, on 19 October 1987 – otherwise known as 'black Monday' – there was a dramatic collapse in markets around the world. The US stockmarket fell by 23 per cent on 'black Monday', the UK market fell 30 per cent over three days and the Hong Kong Index fell some 50 per cent over the week. Only the Japanese market avoided the worst of the crash, falling back a relatively modest 15 per cent. At first sight, crashes of this kind, although very infrequent, suggest that stockmarkets are inefficient, with stock prices being bid up and up until there is a sudden collapse. It is argued that such crashes represent the effects of irrational market speculation, or so-called speculative bubbles; there is too much self-fulfilling speculation which is detached from company fundamentals. It is argued that stockmarkets are sometimes subjected to speculative manias during which the market gets pushed well out of line with fundamental valuations. Speculators start to believe that a price rise signals a further future price rise and consequently they purchase more shares, and for a while speculation becomes a self-fulfilling prophecy. Eventually, however, there is a change of sentiment and the market crashes back into line with the economic fundamentals.

There are, nonetheless, two arguments that have been put forward to rationalize the apparent stockmarket collapses with the EMH. One is the rational bubble argument and the other is the news argument. The rational bubble argument is that investors realize a stockmarket is overvalued, but they are nevertheless willing to continue to hold/buy shares because they believe that the market will continue to rise for a while longer and that there is only a limited risk of a collapse during a given holding period. Consequently, investors expect to be able to eventually sell shares at a value that will provide them with a sufficient capital gain to compensate them for running the risk of a collapse. Another argument put forward by proponents of the EMH is that stockmarket crashes can still be consistent with market efficiency if sufficient bad news arrives to alter future expectations, enough to justify sharply lower stock prices. Although there was bad news for investors to think about over the weekend of 17/18 October 1987 – the ever-widening US current account and budget deficits, the Iran–Contra affair, a tightening of German monetary policy and the Gulf war – most of this was already known and it seems most unlikely that this type of news was sufficient to explain the sudden and dramatic change in sentiment. The crash is even more of a challenge to the EMH because at the time there was quite a lot of evidence and market comment suggesting that many stockmarkets were overvalued in relation to fundamentals.

speculative bubble
a term used to describe fast dramatic price rises of shares or something else that is likely to prove unsustainable

rational bubble
a speculative bubble in which many speculators believe that a security or asset is significantly overpriced and likely to collapse in price at some time in the future. However, they are rationally willing to hold and even buy the security in the short term as they believe the prospects for a continued capital appreciation are sufficient compensation for the risk of a sudden price collapse

10.19   Testing the strong-form of market efficiency

Testing for strong market efficiency is more difficult than testing for weak-form and semi-strong efficiency because obtaining an appropriate proxy for inside information or inside-traders is a difficult task since insider-trading is generally outlawed. At the casual observation level, the enormous illegal profits made by insider-traders such as Ivan Boesky are highly suggestive that the market is not strong-form efficient. Furthermore, the existence of laws against insider-trading makes it hard for the market price to reflect price-sensitive information before it is made public.

10.20 Directors'/managers' share purchases

One way of testing for strong market efficiency is to look at the effects of share purchases by the directors and managers of companies which they run. All such sales and purchases have to be registered publicly and directors and managers are not permitted to trade on price-sensitive information. Nonetheless, they have a better feel for the likely prospects of the company and, although they are not allowed to trade on price-sensitive information, purchases or sales in their companies might therefore yield excess profits. One would expect insiders to purchase shares before any price rises and sell shares in advance of price falls. In a well known study, Jaffe (1974) found such a pattern in connection with registered trades. He also found that managers and directors earn excess returns from their purchases/sales, suggesting that the strong-form of market efficiency can be rejected. It seems that those with privileged information can gain from access to that information, contrary to the strong-form EMH.

10.21 Information content of analysts' forecasts

Another means of indirectly testing for strong-form efficiency is to see whether the recommendations of analysts, who presumably have a greater access to inside information about a company and whose tips are not necessarily disseminated to the wider public, could yield excess profits. Dimson and Marsh (1984) analyzed 4000 forecasts, covering 200 different UK stocks from 35 different firms of analysts that were made to the Prudential insurance company, the largest single investor in UK equities. They found some degree of positive correlation (an average correlation coefficient of 0.08) between the analysts' forecasts of excess return and the actual excess return through acting on the recommendations. The range of the forecasts' correlation coefficients was from −0.19 to + 0.26, with past predictive performance having no relation to future predictability. On the basis of these recommendations, the fund could earn an additional 2.2 per cent after due allowance for transaction costs by looking at the consensus forecast of the analysts compared to investing in the market index.

In a study of recommendations by 34 US brokerage firms and 720 analysts, Elton, Gruber and Grossman (1986) divided recommendations into five categories (best-buy, buy, hold, and two sell categories), and found evidence that excess returns could be earned once due allowance had been made for risk by buying upgraded stocks or stocks that were in a higher classification and selling downgraded stocks or stocks in a lower classification. Even more interestingly, the excess returns were found in both the month of the classification and for two months following the classification, with the greater excess returns to be found by trading on the change in classification rather than the classification itself.

Taken at face value, both the Dimson and Marsh study and the Elton, Gruber and Grossman study show that the market is not strong-form efficient. However, some caution is warranted before trading on a broker's recommendations. Firstly, both studies showed that there was not one broker/analyst that consistently outshone any other broker/analyst in terms of predictive forecasting ability. Secondly, both studies seemed to show that it is generally better to trade on the basis of aggregate or consensus forecasts and that the excess profits do not last for very long, so investors need to execute their trades reasonably quickly once recommendations are made.

There have been other authors, such as Jensen (1969), who argued that mutual fund managers/analysts, because they operate on a daily basis and have wide-ranging contacts with business and the financial community, in effect have access to privileged information and that they should therefore be able to make excess risk-adjusted profits. However, his comprehensive study involving 115 different mutual funds over a period of 10 years (1955–64) revealed that once allowance is made for the risk factor the funds underperformed by around 1 per cent a CAPM-type strategy of investing in a mix of the market index and a risk-free bond. This underperformance is taken as 'striking evidence in favour of the strong form' of the EMH.

10.22   Conclusions

The general consensus on the literature on market efficiency that we have reviewed in this chapter is suggestive that weak market efficiency holds. This poses a significant challenge to technical analysts and chartist forecasters that claim to be able to spot excess profit opportunities from looking at the past history of share prices. The plain fact is that, when subjected to rigorous academic scrutiny and with proper testing over a sufficient data-set, technical analysis and chartism make claims that are not substantiated by the available evidence. The reasons why chartism and technical analysis seem to continue to prosper despite this evidence is something of a puzzle. A few possible explanations include (i) the academic message is just not getting through, (ii) professional traders like the charts produced, and (iii) chartist and technical analysts are sufficiently convincing that they survive with their day-to-day views regardless of their long-term inability to predict prices.

The evidence in support of semi-strong market efficiency is quite strong (semi-strong!), but not as solid as for weak-form efficiency. The evidence overwhelmingly shows that share prices do seem to react to new information speedily as predicted by the theory. However, against this there are a number of puzzling anomalies such as the January effect and time lags before certain information seems to get fully priced into shares, suggesting that all information is not instantly priced into shares as required by the semi-strong EMH.

Finally, the evidence for strong-form efficiency is relatively weak! While obtaining an adequate proxy for inside information is far from easy, the *prima facie* evidence suggests that informed managers and directors can obtain excess returns from their trades. The well publicized prosecutions of insider-traders who have made fortunes as a result of dealing from inside knowledge is, at the end of the day, perhaps the most significant evidence against the strong form of market efficiency.

Further reading

Campbell, J.W., Lo, A.W. and MacKingley, A.C. (1997) *The Econometrics of Financial Markets*, Princeton University Press.

Fox, J. (2009) *The Myth of the Rational Market: A History of Risk, Reward and Delusion on Wall Street*, Harper Business.

Malkiel, B.G. (2004) *A Random Walk Down Wall Street: The Time Tested Strategy for Successful Investing*, W.W. Norton & Company.

Shiller, R.J. (2001) *Irrational Exuberance*, Princeton University Press.

Chapter 10	Revision questions

1 Explain the difference between 'weak form', 'semi-strong form' and 'strong form' concepts of market efficiency.

2 Would evidence that a fund manager whose portfolio has a beta of 1 has performed better than the stockmarket 8 years in a row be evidence against the semi-strong form concept of market efficiency? Explain your reasoning.

3 New information hits a company share such that the share price rises from 100 pence to 120 pence and then the share price rises gradually over the following 6 months to 150 pence despite any further news. Is this evidence of market efficiency? Explain your reasoning.

4 Briefly explain what is meant by the January effect and discuss its relevance to the weak form of market efficiency.

5 The stock market falls by 33 per cent in one day: is this necessarily inconsistent with the efficient market hypothesis? Explain your reasoning.

6 What is meant by behavioural finance? Give two examples of behavioural effects and their implications for market efficiency.

 Multiple choice questions available at www.palgrave.com/business/pilbeam

11

THE FOREIGN EXCHANGE MARKET

Learning objectives

In this chapter you will learn about:

- the difference between the spot and forward exchange rate
- how arbitrageurs, speculators and hedgers use the foreign exchange market
- the difference between fixed and floating exchange rate regimes
- how to calculate the forward exchange rate using the covered interest rate parity formula
- how to calculate and interpret the nominal and real exchange rate index
- how to calculate and interpret the nominal and real effective exchange rate indices

11.1   Introduction

foreign exchange market a global marketplace made up of banks and dealers/brokers where differing national currencies are bought and sold in spot markets and derivatives markets such as forwards and futures and other derivative markets

The foreign exchange market is where the various national currencies are bought and sold. In this chapter we examine the various participants in the market and the basic forces that operate within it. We examine the basic determinants of exchange rate behaviour and in particular look at the crucial role played by exchange rate expectations in the determination of exchange rates. We then look at the operational differences between fixed and floating exchange rate regimes, concluding with an examination of the relationship between the spot and forward exchange rates.

One of the most fascinating things about the foreign exchange market is the huge sums of money that are exchanged on a daily basis, and **Table 11.1** shows the result of surveys carried out by the Bank for International Settlements (BIS). The main centre for foreign exchange trading is London with some $1,359 billion worth of foreign exchange traded on a daily basis in 2007, which is quite a lot when one considers that the annual gross domestic product of the UK is less than twice that amount. The global total is nearly $4 trillion per day.

Table 11.1   Foreign exchange market turnover (daily average in billions of US dollars)

	April 1992	April 1995	April 1998	April 2001	April 2004	April 2007
UK	291	464	637	504	753	1,359
USA	167	244	351	254	461	664
Japan	120	161	136	147	199	238
Singapore	74	105	139	101	125	231
Hong Kong	60	90	79	67	102	175
Switzerland	66	87	82	71	79	242
Germany	55	76	94	88	118	99
France	33	58	72	48	64	120
Other	210	287	368	339	507	860
Total	1,076	1,572	1,958	1,619	2,408	3,988

Notes: These are net figures adjusted to allow for double counting.

Source: Bank for International Settlements

11.2   Exchange rate definitions

The exchange rate is simply the price of one currency in terms of another, and may therefore be expressed in either of two ways:

1   Foreign currency units per unit of the domestic currency; taking the pound sterling as the domestic currency, on 25 August 2009, 1.6212 dollars were required to obtain one pound, that is $1.6212/£1.

2   Domestic currency units per unit of foreign currency; for example, taking the pound sterling as the domestic currency, on 25 August 2009 approximately 0.6168 of a pound was required to purchase one US dollar, that is £0.6168/$1.

Obviously the second method is merely the reciprocal of the first. While it is not important which method of expressing the exchange rate is employed, it is necessary to be careful when talking about a rise or fall in the exchange rate because the meaning will be very different depending upon which definition is used. A rise in the pounds per dollar exchange rate from say £0.60/$1 to £0.80/$1 means that more pounds have to be given to obtain a dollar, which means that the pound has depreciated in value, or equivalently the dollar has appreciated in value. If the first definition is employed, a rise in the dollars per pound exchange rate from $1.60/£1 to $1.80/£1 would mean that more dollars are obtained per pound, so that the pound has appreciated or equivalently the dollar has depreciated. **Table 11.2** shows the exchange rates of a variety of currencies as at 25 August 2009 against the major three currencies: the US dollar, the euro and the pound.

In **Table 11.2** we have listed only the mid-point quotations of the currencies. In reality there are bid–offer spreads to consider. For sterling, for example, the mid-point is $1.6212/£1 but in the market itself two prices will be quoted, for example, $1.6214/£1 (offer) and $1.6210/£1 (bid), a spread of 4 pips. ('Pip' stands for 'price interest point' and is the smallest movement that a currency pair can move; for the dollar per pound rate, one pip = 0.0001.) The bid rate is the rate at which a bank will buy pounds (i.e. sell dollars) while the offer rate is the rate at which the bank will sell pounds (i.e. buy dollars). The bid–offer spread represents the gross profit margin of the bank, and in the sterling example is $100[(1.6214 - 1.6210)/1.6212] = 0.025$ per cent. The spread will vary from bank to bank, from currency to currency and according to market conditions. Thinly traded currencies tend to have the largest spread and the spread usually increases if the risks of trading in a particular currency are perceived to have risen.

11.3   Characteristics of and participants in the foreign exchange market

The foreign exchange market is a worldwide market made up primarily of commercial banks, foreign exchange brokers and other authorized agents trading in most of the currencies of the world. These groups are kept in close and continuous contact

Table 11.2 Exchange rate quotations at close of business, 25 August 2009 (closing mid-points)

	Foreign currency per $	Foreign currency per €	Foreign currency per £
Argentina	3.8488	5.4774	6.2400
Australia	1.2059	1.7162	1.9552
Brazil	1.8690	2.6598	3.0302
Canada	1.0979	1.5624	1.7800
China	6.8311	9.7217	11.0753
Czech Republic	17.9043	25.4805	29.0282
Denmark	5.2295	7.4424	8.4786
Euro	0.7026	1.0000	1.1393
Hong Kong	7.7511	11.0309	12.5668
India	48.9250	69.6277	79.3221
Japan	94.350	134.267	152.962
Kenya	76.2500	108.515	123.624
Mexico	13.1135	18.6625	21.2609
New Zealand	1.4654	2.0855	2.3759
Poland	2.8905	4.1136	4.6863
Russia	31.6000	33.9716	51.2331
Singapore	1.4462	2.0582	2.3447
South Africa	7.8799	11.2002	12.7596
Sweden	7.1212	10.1345	11.5456
Switzerland	1.0689	1.5212	1.7330
UK	0.6168	0.5471	1.0000
USA	1.0000	1.4231	1.6212

Source: *Financial Times*, 26 August 2009

with one another and with developments in the market via telephone, computer terminals, telex and fax. Among the most important foreign exchange centres are London, New York, Tokyo, Singapore and Frankfurt (see **Table 11.1**). The net volume of foreign-exchange dealing globally was estimated in April 2007 to be close to $4000 billion per day, the most active centres being London with a daily turnover averaging $1359 billion, followed by New York with $662 billion, Tokyo $238 billion, Singapore $231 billion, Paris $120 billion and Frankfurt $99 billion.

Easily the most heavily traded currency is the US dollar, which is known as a vehicle currency because it is widely used to denominate international transactions. Oil and many other important primary products such as tin, coffee and gold all tend to be priced in dollars. Indeed, because the dollar is so heavily traded it is usually cheaper for a French foreign exchange dealer wanting Mexican pesos to first purchase US dollars with euros and then sell the dollars to purchase pesos, rather than directly purchase the pesos with euros. The main participants in the foreign exchange market can be categorized as follows:

- Retail clients – these are made up of businesses, international investors, multinational corporations and the like which need foreign exchange for the purposes of operating their businesses. Normally, they do not directly purchase or sell foreign currencies themselves, rather they operate by placing buy/sell orders with the commercial banks. Some multinational corporations these days have sufficient foreign exchange needs that they have their own foreign exchange dealing rooms.
- Commercial banks – the commercial banks carry out buy/sell orders from their retail clients and buy/sell currencies on their own account (known as proprietary trading) so as to alter the structure of their assets and liabilities in different currencies. The banks either deal directly with other banks or more usually through foreign exchange brokers.
- Foreign exchange brokers – normally banks do not trade directly with one another, rather they offer to buy and sell currencies via foreign exchange brokers. Operating through such brokers is advantageous because they collect buy and sell quotations for most currencies from many banks. By going through a broker the most favourable quotation is obtained quickly and at very low cost. Each financial centre normally has just a handful of authorized brokers through which commercial banks conduct their exchanges.
- Central banks – normally the monetary authorities of a country are not indifferent to changes in the external value of their currency, and even though exchange rates of the major industrialized nations have been left to fluctuate freely since 1973, central banks sometimes intervene to buy and sell their currencies in a bid to influence the rate at which their currency is traded. Under a fixed exchange rate system the authorities are obliged to purchase their currencies when there is excess supply and sell the currency when there is excess demand.

proprietary trading trading that occurs when a bank or financial institution risks its own capital to take speculative trading positions in financial markets in the hope of making a profit

Figure 11.1   The organization of the foreign exchange market

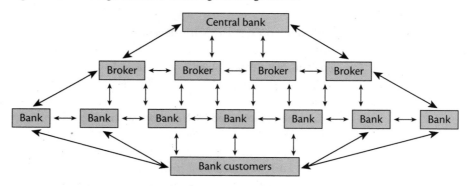

Note: The boxes represent foreign exchange market participants and the lines are the business connections between them. Bank customers place buy/sell orders with their respective banks who balance the buy/sell orders that they receive and if they have insufficient or surplus funds they then place buy/sell orders with other banks or more usually with their brokers. The central bank keeps a daily watch on exchange-rate developments and intervenes to buy or sell its currency from time to time by placing buy/sell orders with its brokers.

Box 11.1	**Bid–offer spreads in the forex market: which bank will trade with which bank?**

Some banks are keen to buy a currency because they are short of it and others are keen to sell a currency because they have too much of it. This means that banks will quote slightly different bid–offer quotes on a currency in the interbank market. Imagine we have three banks, A, B and C, which make the following bid–offer quotes on the pound.

$/£ bid–offer quotes

Bank A	1.5998–1.6002
Bank B	1.5957–1.6001
Bank C	1.5999–1.6003

The first quote is the bid rate, which is the price at which the bank will buy pounds in exchange for dollars, so, for example, Bank A is willing to buy sterling at $1.5998 per £1. The second quote is the offer rate, which is the rate at which a bank will sell sterling in exchange for dollars, so Bank A is willing to sell pounds in exchange for $1.6002 per £1. If you are a dealer working with another bank, D, then you will be keen to be matched with the bank offering you the best possible deal. This is where foreign exchange brokers' services are vital. Foreign exchange brokers provide the best possible quotes for immediate execution by collecting quotes from many banks and then executing a trade at the best possible price for the banks that use their services.

If you are a trader working for Bank D and wish to buy £10 million then you wish to give as little in dollars as possible. Therefore the broker will match you with Bank B at $1.6001/£1 so you will be required to give $16,001,000 to get £10 million; this is much better than handing over $16,003,000, which is what Bank C requires. So although the difference between Bank B and Bank C is only 0.02 of a cent it means nearly $2,000 on a £10 million trade – well worth saving. If, however, Bank D wishes to sell £10 million pounds then its broker will match it with the bank offering the most dollars in return, which is Bank C at $1.5999/£1. This amounts to receipts of $15,999,000, which is much better than Bank B with its quote of $1.5997/£1, equivalent to receipts of $15,997,000 – $2,000 less than Bank C. Given that exchange-rate quotes are constantly changing on a second-by-second basis, then the ability to deal via a broker at the best possible rate is a valuable service. The effective bid–offer quote facing Bank D is $1.5999–$1.6001 which is only 2 pips. In the world of finance a small difference in quotes can be quite significant in monetary terms given the sums of money involved. Competition between banks means that bid–offer spreads for major currencies are kept down to very low levels

11.4   Arbitrage in the foreign exchange market

One of the most important implications deriving from the close communication of buyers and sellers in the foreign exchange market is that there is almost instantaneous arbitrage across currencies and financial centres. Arbitrage is the exploitation of price differentials for riskless guaranteed profits. To illustrate what is meant by financial centre and cross-currency arbitrage, we shall assume that transaction costs are negligible and that there is only a single exchange rate quotation, ignoring the bid–offer spread.

- *Financial centre arbitrage.* This type of arbitrage ensures that the dollar–pound exchange rate quoted in New York will be the same as that quoted in London and other financial centres. If the exchange rate is $1.61/£1 in New York but only $1.59/£1 in London, it would be profitable for banks to buy pounds in London and simultaneously sell pounds in New York, thereby making a guaranteed 2 cents for every pound bought and sold. The act of buying pounds in London will lead to a depreciation of the dollar in London, while selling pounds in New York will lead to an appreciation of the dollar in New York. Such a process continues until the rate quoted in the two centres coincides at, say, $1.60/£1.
- *Cross-currency arbitrage.* To illustrate what is meant by currency arbitrage let us suppose that the exchange rate of the dollar against the pound is $1.65/£1, and the exchange rate of the dollar against the euro is $1.50/€1. Currency arbitrage implies that the exchange rate of the euro against the pound will be €1.10/£1 (1.65/1.50 = 1.10). If this were not the case, say the rate was 1.20 euros per pound, then a UK dealer wanting dollars would do better to first obtain 1.20 euros per pound which would then buy $1.80 (1.2 x 1.5) making nonsense of a $1.65/£1 quotation. The increased demand for euros would quickly appreciate its rate against the pound to the €1.10/£1 level and then selling 1.1 euros would only obtain $1.65 (1.1 x 1.5). **Table 11.3** shows a set of cross rates for the major currencies.

Table 11.3   Foreign exchange cross rates on close of business, 25 August 2009

		C$	DKr	€	Yen	NKr	SKr	SFr	£	US$
Canada	C$	1	4.763	0.640	85.94	5.534	6.486	0.974	0.562	0.911
Denmark	DKr	2.099	10	1.344	180.4	11.62	13.62	2.044	1.179	1.912
Euro	€	1.562	7.442	1	134.3	8.646	10.13	1.521	0.878	1.423
Japan	¥	1.164	5.543	0.745	100	6.440	7.548	1.133	0.654	1.060
Norway	NKr	1.807	8.608	1.157	155.3	10	11.72	1.759	1.015	1.646
Sweden	SKr	1.542	7.343	0.987	132.5	8.531	10	1.501	0.866	1.404
Switzerland	SFr	1.027	4.893	0.657	88.27	5.684	6.662	1	0.577	0.936
UK	£	1.780	8.479	1.139	153.0	9.850	11.55	1.733	1	1.621
US	$	1.098	5.229	0.703	94.35	6.075	7.121	1.069	0.617	1

Note: The exchange rate is the units of the currency in the top row per unit of the currency listed in the left hand column. The following multipliers apply to the units on the left hand column: Yen 100, Danish Krone 10, Swedish Krone 10, Norwegian Krone 10.

Source: *Financial Times*, 26 August 2009

11.5   The spot and forward exchange rates

Foreign exchange dealers not only deal with a wide variety of currencies, but they also have a set of dealing rates for each currency which are known as the spot and forward rates.

spot exchange rate
the exchange rate between two currencies for immediate delivery

- The spot exchange rate is the quotation between two currencies for immediate delivery. In other words, the spot exchange rate is the current exchange rate of two currencies vis-à-vis each other. In practice, there is normally a two-day lag between a spot purchase or sale and the actual exchange of currencies to allow for verification, paperwork and clearing of payments.

forward exchange rate the exchange rate between two currencies quoted for a given date in the future; a variety of forward rates may be quoted, e.g. 1 month, 3 months, 6 months and 1 year

- The forward exchange rate refers to a quotation that will apply at some time in the future. It is possible for economic agents to agree today to exchange currencies at some specified time in the future, most commonly 1 month (30 days), 3 months (90 days), 6 months (180 days), 9 months (270 days) or 1 year (360 days) hence. The rate of exchange at which such a purchase or sale can be made is known as the forward exchange rate. Exactly why economic agents may engage in forward exchange transactions and how the forward exchange rate quotation is determined is a subject we shall look at later in the chapter.

11.6   A simple model for determining the spot exchange rate

Since the adoption of floating exchange rates in 1973 there has developed an exciting new set of theories attempting to explain exchange rate behaviour. We shall start by looking at a model of exchange rate determination which was widely used prior to the development of these new theories. Despite its shortcomings the model serves as a useful introduction to exchange rate determination. The basic tenet of the model is that the exchange rate (the price) of a currency can be analyzed like any other price by using the tools of supply and demand. The exchange rate of the pound will be determined by the intersection of the supply and demand for pounds on the foreign exchange market.

The demand for foreign exchange

The demand for pounds in the foreign exchange market is a derived demand; that is, the pounds are not demanded because they have an intrinsic value in themselves, but, rather, because of what they can buy. **Table 11.4** illustrates the derivation of a hypothetical demand for pounds schedule with respect to changes in the exchange rate. As the pound appreciates against the dollar – that is, moves from $1.40/£1 towards $2/£1 – the price of UK exports to US importers increases, which leads to a lower quantity of exports and with it a reduced demand for pounds. Hence, the demand curve for pounds shown in **Figure 11.2** slopes down from left to right.

In this simple model, the demand for pounds depends upon the demand for UK exports. Any factor which results in an increase in the demand for UK exports, that is, column 4 in **Table 11.4** will result in an increased demand for pounds and the demand curve for pounds will shift to the right. Among the factors that could result in a rightward shift of the demand schedule for pounds are a rise in US income, a

Table 11.4   Derivation of the demand for pounds

Price of UK export good	Exchange rate $/£	Price of UK export good in dollars	Quantity of UK exports	Demand for pounds
£10	$1.40	$14	1,400	14,000
£10	$1.50	$15	1,200	12,000
£10	$1.60	$16	1,000	10,000
£10	$1.70	$17	900	9,000
£10	$1.80	$18	800	8,000
£10	$1.90	$19	700	7,000
£10	$2.00	$20	600	6,000

Figure 11.2   The demand for pounds

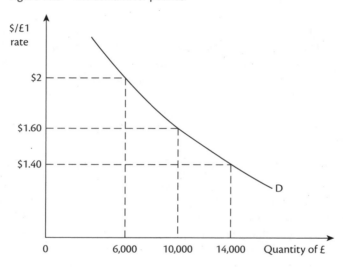

change in US tastes in favour of UK goods, or a rise in the price of US goods. All these factors would result in an increased demand for UK exports and hence pounds. The effect of an increase in the demand for pounds is to shift the demand schedule to the right.

The supply of foreign exchange

The supply of pounds is in essence the UK demand for dollars, and **Table 11.5** sets out the derivation of a hypothetical supply of pounds schedule. As the pound appreciates, the cost of US exports becomes cheaper for UK residents. As such, they demand more US exports and this results in an increased demand for dollars, which are purchased by increasing the amount of pounds supplied in the foreign exchange market, and this yields an upward-sloping supply of pounds (**Figure 11.3**).

The supply of pounds schedule depends upon the UK demand for US exports. The position of the schedule will shift to the right if there is an increase in UK income,

Table 11.5   Derivation of the supply of pounds

Price of US export good in dollars	Exchange rate $/£	Price of US export good in pounds	Quantity of US exports	Demand for dollars	Supply of pounds
20	$1.40/£1	14.29	600	12,000	8,571
20	$1.50/£1	13.33	700	14,000	9,333
20	$1.60/£1	12.50	800	16,000	10,000
20	$1.70/£1	11.76	950	19,000	11,176
20	$1.80/£1	11.11	1,100	22,000	12,222
20	$1.90/£1	10.53	1,225	24,500	12,895
20	$2.00/£1	10.00	1,350	27,000	13,500

Figure 11.3   The supply of pounds

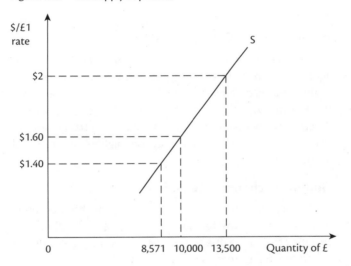

a change in British tastes in favour of US goods or a rise in UK prices. All these factors would imply an increased demand for US goods and dollars which would be reflected in an increased supply of pounds.

Since the exchange market is merely a market which brings together those people that wish to buy a currency (which represents the demand) with those that wish to sell the currency (which represents the supply), then the spot exchange rate can most easily be thought of as being determined by the interaction of the supply and demand for the currency.

Figure 11.4 shows the determination of the dollar–pound exchange rate in the context of such a supply and demand framework. The supply and demand for pounds in the foreign exchange market have been plotted, with the equilibrium exchange rate determined by the intersection of the supply and demand curves to yield a dollar–pound exchange of $1.60/£1. When the exchange rate is left to float freely it is determined by the interaction of the supply and demand curves.

Figure 11.4   Determination of the dollar–pound exchange rate

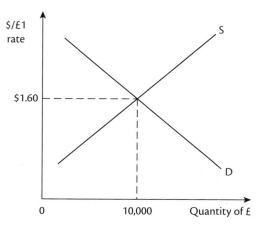

11.7   Alternative exchange rate regimes

At the Bretton Woods conference of 1944 the major nations of the Western world agreed to a pegged exchange rate system, each country fixing its exchange rate against the US dollar with a small margin of fluctuation around the par value. In 1973 the Bretton Woods system broke down and the major currencies were left to be determined by market forces in a floating exchange rate world. The basic differences between the two regimes may be highlighted using the supply and demand framework.

floating exchange rates a system whereby the exchange rate of a currency is left to be determined by market forces

Floating exchange rate regime

Under a floating exchange rate regime the authorities do not intervene to buy or sell their currency in the foreign exchange market. Rather, they allow the value of their currency to change due to fluctuations in supply and demand of the currency. This is illustrated in **Figure 11.5**.

Figure 11.5   Floating exchange rate regime

(a)   Increase in demand

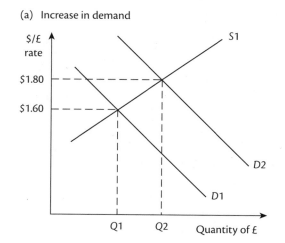

(b)   Increase in supply

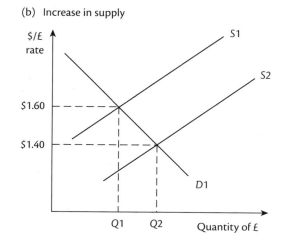

In **Figure 11.5**(a) the exchange rate is initially determined by the interaction of the demand (D1) and supply (S1) of pounds at the exchange rate of $1.60/£1. There is an increase in the demand for UK exports which shifts the demand curve from D1 to D2, leading to an appreciation of the pound from $1.60/£1 to $1.80/£1. **Figure 11.5**(b) examines the impact of an increase in the supply of pounds due to an increased demand for US exports and therefore dollars. The increased supply of pounds shifts the S1 schedule to the right (S2), resulting in a depreciation of the pound to $1.40/£1. The essence of a floating exchange rate is that the exchange rate adjusts in response to changes in the supply and demand for a currency.

Fixed exchange rate regime

For various reasons, governments can intervene to try and fix the exchange rate around certain levels. For example an appreciation of the exchange rate might be considered undesirable as it would hit the economy's exports, while a depreciation might be considered undesirable since it would lead to a rise in the cost of imports and endanger the central bank's inflation target. Indeed many countries around the world continue to maintain fixed exchange rates against currencies such as the US dollar since it is perceived to be vital for economic stability. The Hong Kong dollar, for instance, has been pegged to the US dollar at HK$7.80/$1 for nearly 30 years.

We now examine the implications of foreign exchange intervention to fix the exchange rate using a hypothetical example of the Bank of England attempting to peg the exchange rate of the pound against the US dollar. In so doing we make a crucial distinction between non-sterilized intervention and sterilized intervention. With non-sterilized intervention the buying/selling of sterling in the foreign exchange market affects the UK money supply and interest rates. Frequently, however, authorities will attempt to restore domestic money supply and interest rates back to their levels before the foreign exchange market intervention took place, and this is known as sterilized foreign exchange market intervention. As we shall see, while non-sterilized intervention is likely to be effective in moving the exchange rate in the desired direction, there is good reason to doubt that sterilized intervention can have much of an impact.

In **Figure 11.6**(a) the exchange rate is assumed to be fixed by the authorities at the point where the demand schedule (D1) intersects the supply schedule (S1) at $1.60/£1. If there is an increase in the demand for pounds which shifts the demand schedule from D1 to D2, there is a resultant pressure for the pound to appreciate. To avert an appreciation it is necessary for the Bank of England to sell Q1 – Q2 of pounds in the foreign exchange market by purchasing US dollars, these sterling sales shifting the supply of pounds from S1 to S2. Such an intervention weakens the pound exchange rate back to $1.60/£1, increasing the Bank of England's reserves of US dollars while increasing the amount of pounds in circulation from M1 to M2 and lowering the UK interest rate from r1 to r2 as shown in **Figure 11.6**(b).

The effect on the UK money market of the Bank of England selling pounds in the foreign exchange market is to increase the UK money supply from M1 to M2 and consequently lower the UK short-term rate of interest from r1 to r2 in **Figure 11.6**(b). Since the sale of pounds has increased the UK money supply the intervention is of the non-sterilized type. Such an intervention is likely to be very effective in weakening

fixed exchange rates a system whereby the exchange rate is fixed against another currency at a given target exchange rate (with small deviations usually allowed); the central bank of that currency commits itself to buy or sell the currency as appropriate to maintain the fixed rate

non-sterilized intervention foreign exchange intervention by the authorities to buy or sell the domestic currency which is allowed to affect the domestic money supply

sterilized intervention foreign exchange intervention by the authorities which is not allowed to affect the domestic money supply; this is because an offsetting open market operation is used to negate the money supply consequences of the foreign exchange intervention

Figure 11.6   Fixed exchange-rate regime: demand shock

(a) Forex market

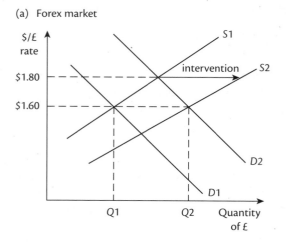

(b) UK money market

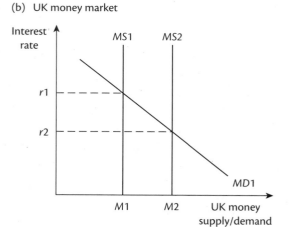

the pound from $1.80/£1 because it increases the amount of sterling in circulation and lowers the UK interest rate, both of which will reinforce the effect of selling pounds in the foreign exchange market in weakening the pound to the desired level. Non-sterilized intervention of this type that directly affects the money supply and short-term interest rate is very effective in moving the exchange rate in the desired direction.

The Bank of England could just do as above and allow the foreign exchange market intervention to increase the UK money supply and lower the UK interest rate, but this would risk overshooting the Bank's inflation target. In such circumstances, the Bank might try to sterilize the effects of the increased money supply by selling Treasury bills to the public in an open-market operation that would reduce the money supply. This is shown in **Figure 11.6**(b) as a move from $M2$ back to the original level of $M1$. However, the Treasury bill sales would reduce the price of Treasury bills and raise the UK interest rate from $r2$ back to $r1$ in **Figure 11.6**(b). The reduction in the amount of pounds and the rise in interest rates resulting from the sterilization policy would then tend to increase the attractiveness of pounds in the foreign exchange market and start shifting the demand for sterling ($D2$) to the right. The pound would then head back towards $1.80/£1, as the UK money supply and interest rates return to their levels $M1$ and $r1$ prior to the foreign exchange market intervention. As such, it is highly unlikely that a sterilized foreign exchange market intervention would be effective in achieving the weaker pound desired by the Bank of England.

This begs the question as to why the central bank would wish to sterilize their foreign exchange market interventions, as this would undermine its ability to achieve the desired exchange rate. Part of the answer is that the central bank may hope to have a psychological impact on market participants whilst sticking to its monetary and interest-rate targets. The fact that the Bank of England has been selling pounds in the foreign exchange market, even though sterilized, might reduce the demand for pounds in the foreign exchange market in the very short run. Having said this, most traders will tend to ignore central bank intervention unless they see it is of the non-sterilized type leading to changes in money-market interest rates.

Figure 11.7   Fixed exchange-rate regime : supply shock

(a) Forex market

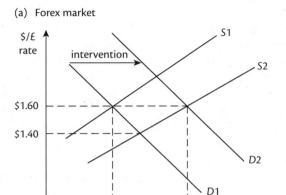

(b) UK money market

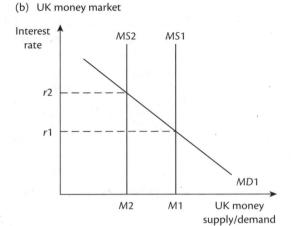

In **Figure 11.7**(a) the exchange rate is assumed to be fixed by the authorities at the point where the demand schedule (D1) intersects the supply schedule (S1) at $1.60/£1. If there is an increase in the supply of pounds in the foreign exchange market the supply schedule shifts from S1 to S2 and there is a resulting pressure for the pound to depreciate to $1.40/£1. To avert a depreciation, it is necessary for the Bank of England to buy Q1 – Q2 pounds with dollars from its foreign exchange reserves in the foreign exchange market, these purchases shifting the demand for pounds from D1 to D2. Such an intervention, by raising the demand for pounds, enables the exchange rate to remain fixed at $1.60/£1, decreases the Bank of England's reserves of US dollars and decreases the amount of pounds in circulation.

The effect on the UK money market of the Bank of England buying pounds in the foreign exchange market is to decrease the UK money supply from M1 to M2 and consequently to raise the UK short-term interest rate from r1 to r2. Since buying pounds in the foreign exchange market has reduced the UK money supply from M1 to M2, the intervention is of the non-sterilized type. It is likely to be very effective in strengthening the pound back to $1.60/£1 because it decreases the amount of sterling in circulation and raises the UK interest rate, both of which reinforce the effect of buying pounds in the foreign exchange market to strengthen the pound to the desired level.

Again, the Bank of England could do as above and allow the foreign exchange market intervention to decrease the UK money supply and raise the UK interest rate, but this would risk the Bank undershooting its inflation target, possibly leading to an unwanted slowdown in the UK economy. In such circumstances the Bank might try to sterilize the effects of the decreased money supply by buying Treasury bills from the public in an open-market operation, raising the money supply in **Figure 11.7**(b) from M2 back to the original level M1. The problem with doing this, however, is that the Treasury bill purchases will raise the price of Treasury bills and thereby lower the UK interest rate from r2 back to r1. The increase in the amount of pounds and the fall in interest rates resulting from the sterilization policy would then tend to decrease the attractiveness of pounds in the foreign exchange market and therefore

Box 11.2	The foreign exchange rate policy of the People's Bank of China

The People's Bank of China (PBOC) is the central bank of the People's Republic of China. Since the mid 1990s the Chinese economy has been growing very rapidly, in large part fuelled by a rapid increase in exports and investment. In 1995 exports were around 20% of GDP but by 2007 exports were 40% of GDP. For many years the Chinese authorities pegged the renminbi exchange rate at RMB8.25/$1. Since there was a massive demand to buy renminbi in order to purchase Chinese exports and a high demand by foreign companies to undertake foreign direct investment in China the PBOC had to sell renminbi to buy US dollars. It was only on 22 July 2005, under pressure from the USA with a huge current account deficit of $750 billion, that the Chinese changed their foreign exchange policy such that the renminbi would be pegged to a basket of five currencies, thus enabling a gradual appreciation to occur over time against the US dollar. Following the adoption of the new foreign exchange policy the PBOC continued to sell renminbi and buy dollars to prevent the renminbi appreciating too rapidly. The foreign exchange intervention of the PBOC was by and large of the non-sterilized type, resulting in a rapid growth of the Chinese money supply and producing low interest rates which stimulated a property and stockmarket boom. In addition, there was an unprecedented rise in the foreign exchange reserves of the PBOC from $165 billion in 2000 to over $2132 billion by the middle of 2009, making them by far the largest foreign exchange reserves of any country in the world. The reserve increases suggest that the PBOC had been buying the equivalent of over $200 billion a year over that period.

We can represent the Chinese foreign exchange intervention diagrammatically in **Figure 11.8**. In **Figure 11.8**(a), we have the renminbi–dollar exchange rate starting at RMB 8.25/$1. There is heavy selling of dollars, represented by a shift to the right of the supply curve for dollars from S1 to S2, and left to a free market the exchange rate would change from 8.25/$1 to say 5/$1. However, the PBOC buys dollars (Q2, Q3) through its foreign exchange interventions, shifting the demand curve for dollars from D1 to D2. The effect of the intervention is that the appreciation of the renminbi is limited to only RMB 6.80/$1 rather than the RMB 5/$1 that would occur in a free market. In **Figure 11.8**(b) we depict the rise in the Chinese money supply from M1 to M2 as a result of the sales of the renminbi to purchase US dollars, along with an accompanying fall in the short-term interest rate.

Table 11.6   Chinese foreign exchange reserves (excluding gold holding)

Year	$ billions	Year	$ billions	Year	$ billions
1995	75.4	2003	403.3	2007	1,528.2
2000	165.6	2004	609.9	2008	1,946.0
2001	212.2	2005	818.9	2009	2,132.0
2002	286.4	2006	1,066.3		

Note: The 2009 figure refers to June, all others are end of year.

| Box 11.2 | The foreign exchange rate policy of the People's Bank of China – *continued* |

Figure 11.8 Chinese foreign exchange intervention

(a) Forex market

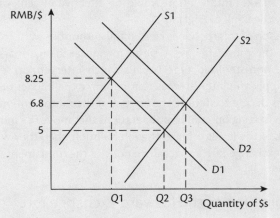

(b) Chinese money market

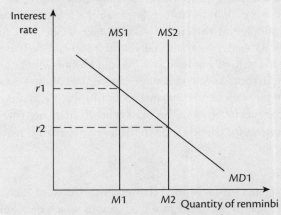

Table 11.6 shows the rapid rise in the Chinese foreign exchange reserves over the period 2000 to 2009. The Chinese invested the dollars they bought in the foreign exchange market into foreign currency bonds such as US Treasuries and Euro-denominated Treasury bonds and also sterling- and yen-denominated bonds. Without the Chinese purchases of US Treasuries over this period, the US government would have struggled to finance its large fiscal deficits at relatively low yields. As the level of foreign exchange reserves have increased, the Chinese authorities have become increasingly concerned about the fact that approximately 65 per cent of its reserves were in US dollars, making it vulnerable to a large depreciation of the dollar. In response to these concerns, in September 2007 the Chinese set up a sovereign wealth fund called the China Investment Corporation (CIC), with an initial endowment of $200 billion, to invest in alternatives to US Treasury bonds such as foreign companies, commodities and other overseas investments.

induce further selling pressure which, by shifting the supply from $S2$ further to the right, would mean that the pound would tend to go back towards $1.40/£1 as the UK money supply and interest rates return to their levels $M1$ and $r1$ prior to the foreign exchange market intervention. Again, it is highly unlikely that a sterilized foreign exchange market intervention would be effective in achieving the stronger pound desired by the Bank of England.

The lesson of this section is clear: if the authorities want to influence the exchange rate then the most effective type of foreign exchange market intervention would be of the non-sterilized type because such intervention leads to changes in the money supply and interest rates that reinforce the impact of the intervention. If the authorities decide to sterilize the impact of their interventions on the money supply through offsetting open-market operations that move the money supply and interest rates back to the levels prior to the intervention, then they will most likely have only a limited exchange rate impact since none of the fundamentals change.

11.8   Determination of the forward exchange rate

In the forward exchange market buyers and sellers agree to exchange currencies at some specified date in the future. For example, a UK trader who has to pay $15,500 to his US supplier at the end of August may decide on 1 June to buy $15,500 for delivery on 31 August of the same year at a forward exchange rate of $1.55/£1. The question that naturally arises is: Why would anyone wish to agree today to exchange currencies at some specified time in the future? To answer this question we need to look at the various participants in the forward exchange market. Traditionally, economic agents involved in this market are divided into three groups, distinguished by their motives for participation in the foreign exchange market.

Hedgers

exchange rate risk the risk of losses due to an adverse movement in the exchange rate

These are agents (usually firms) that enter the forward exchange market to protect themselves against exchange rate fluctuations which entail exchange rate risk – the risk of loss due to adverse exchange rate movements. To illustrate why a firm might engage in a forward exchange rate transaction, consider the example of a UK importer who is due to pay for goods from the USA to the value of $15,500 in one year's time. Let us suppose that the spot exchange rate is $1.60/£1, while the one-year forward exchange rate is $1.55/£1. By buying dollars forward at this rate the trader can be sure that he only has to pay £10,000. If he does not buy forward today, he runs the risk that in one year's time the spot exchange rate may be worse than $1.55/£1, for example $1.50/£1, which would mean having to pay £10,333 (15,500/1.50). Of course, the spot exchange rate in one year's time may be more favourable than $1.55/£1, for example $1.80/£1, in which case he would only have had to pay £8,611 (15,500/1.8), which would ex post have been better than engaging in a forward exchange contract. However, by engaging in a forward exchange contract the trader can be sure of the amount of sterling he will have to pay for the imports, and as such can protect himself against the risk entailed by exchange rate fluctuations.

We might ask why the importer does not immediately buy US $15,500 dollars spot at $1.60/£1 and hold the dollars for one year. One reason is that he may not at present have the necessary funds for such a spot purchase and is reluctant to borrow the money knowing that he will have sufficient funds in one year's time from sales of goods. By engaging in a forward contract he can be sure of getting the dollars he requires at a known exchange rate even though he does not yet have the necessary sterling. In effect, hedgers avoid exchange risk by matching their assets and liabilities in the foreign currency. In the above example, the UK importer buys $15,500 forward (his asset), but will have to pay $15,500 for the imported goods (his liability).

Arbitrageurs

These are agents (usually banks) that aim to make a riskless profit out of discrepancies between interest-rate differentials and what is known as the forward discount or forward premium. A currency is said to be at a forward premium if the forward exchange rate quotation for that currency represents an appreciation for that currency compared to the spot quotation. It is said to be at a forward discount if the forward exchange rate quotation for that currency represents a depreciation compared to the spot quotation.

The forward discount or premium is usually expressed as a percentage of the spot exchange rate, that is:

$$\text{Forward discount/premium} = \frac{F - S}{S} \times 100$$

where F is the forward exchange rate quotation, and S is the spot exchange rate quotation.

The presence of arbitrageurs ensures that what is known as the covered interest parity (CIP) condition holds continually. CIP is the formula used by banks to calculate their forward exchange quotation, given by:

$$F = \frac{(r^* - r)S}{(1 + r)} + S \tag{11.1}$$

where F is the one-year forward exchange rate quotation in foreign currency per unit of domestic currency; S is the spot exchange rate quotation in foreign currency per unit of domestic currency; r is the one-year domestic interest rate; and r^* is the one-year foreign interest rate.

The formula in equation (11.1) has to be amended by dividing the one-month interest rate by 12 to calculate the one-month forward rate, the three-month interest rate by 4 to calculate the three-month forward exchange rate quotation, and dividing the six-month interest rate by 2 to calculate the six-month forward exchange rate. **Table 11.7** shows how the calculation works using the dollar–pound exchange rate and relevant annualized interest rates at different time horizons.

The one-month forward exchange rate is calculated as:

$$\frac{[(0.02 - 0.045)/12]1.60}{[1 + (0.045/12)]} + 1.60 = \$1.5966/£1$$

forward discount
a measure expressed as a percentage per amount of the spot rate by which a currency is weaker in the forward market than in the spot market

forward premium
a measure expressed as a percentage per annum of the spot rate by which a currency is stronger in the forward market than in the spot market

covered interest rate parity a formula used by banks to calculate a forward exchange rate quotation

Table 11.7   Calculation of the $/£ forward exchange rate

	Dollar–pound exchange rate	Sterling eurocurrency interest rate	Dollar eurocurrency interest rate
Spot rate	1.60		
One-month	1.5966	4.50	2.00
Three-month	1.5889	5.00	2.20
Six-month	1.5785	5.25	2.50
Twelve-month	1.5621	5.50	3.00

Notes:
The data source is hypothetical calculations using hypothetical exchange rates and interest rates. The spot sterling exchange rate is assumed to be 1.60 dollars per pound.

The three-month forward exchange rate is calculated as:

$$\frac{[(0.022 - 0.05)/4]1.60}{[1 + (0.05/4)]} + 1.60 = \$1.5889/£1$$

The six-month forward exchange rate is calculated as:

$$\frac{[(0.025 - 0.0525)/2]1.60}{[1 + (0.0525/2)]} + 1.60 = \$1.5785/£1$$

The one-year forward exchange rate is calculated as:

$$\frac{[(0.03 - 0.055)]1.60}{[1 + 0.055]} + 1.60 = \$1.5621/£1$$

Example calculations of the forward exchange rate

Suppose that the one-year dollar interest rate is 5%, and sterling interest rate is 8% and spot rate of the pound against the dollar is $1.60 per pound. Then the one-year forward exchange rate of the pound is:

$$F = \frac{(0.05 - 0.08)1.60}{1.08} + 1.60 = \$1.5555/£1$$

since

$$\frac{F - S}{S} = \frac{1.5555 - 1.60}{1.60} \times 100 = -2.78,$$

the one-year forward rate of sterling is at an annual forward discount of 2.78 per cent.

    To understand why CIP must be used to calculate the forward exchange rate, consider what would happen if the forward rate was different from that quoted in the example, say $1.70/£1. In this instance, a US investor with $100 could earn the US interest rate and at the end of the year have $105. However, by buying pounds spot at ($1.60/£1) and simultaneously selling pounds forward (at $1.70/£1) he would have

£62.50 earning the UK interest rate of 8 per cent. At the end of one year he would have £67.50 (£62.50 × 1.08), which he would sell at a forward price of $1.70 giving $114.75. Clearly, it pays a US investor to sell pounds forward. With sufficient numbers of investors doing this, the forward rate of the pound depreciates until such arbitrage possibilities are eliminated. With a spot rate of $1.60/£1, the guaranteed yields in US and UK time deposits will only be identical if the forward rate is $1.5555/£1 since £67.50 times $1.5555 equals $105. Only at this forward exchange rate are no riskless arbitrage profits to be made.

Since the denominator in equation (11.1) is typically very close to unity (for interest rates of say 8% or lower), equation (11.1) can be simplified to yield an approximate expression for the forward premium/discount:

$$\frac{F - S}{S} = r^* - r \tag{11.2}$$

Equation (11.2) says that if the domestic interest rate is higher than the foreign interest rate, then the domestic currency will be at a forward discount by an equivalent percentage; while if the domestic interest rate is lower than the foreign interest rate the currency will be at a forward premium by an equivalent percentage. In the example above, the US interest rate of 5 per cent less the UK interest rate of 8 per cent gives an annual forward discount on the pound of 3 per cent, which is approximately the same as the 2.78 per cent of the full CIP formula.

Speculators

Speculators are agents that hope to make a profit by accepting exchange rate risk. They engage in the forward exchange market because they believe that the future spot rate corresponding to the date of the quoted forward exchange rate will be different than the quoted forward rate. Consider, if the one-year forward rate is quoted at $1.55/£1 and a speculator feels that the pound will be $1.40/£1 in one year's time, he may sell £1000 forward at $1.55/£1 to obtain $1,550, hoping to change them back into pounds in one year's time at $1.40 to obtain £1107.14 making £107.14 profit. Of course, the speculator may be wrong and find that in one year's time the spot exchange rate is above $1.55/£1, say $1.70/£1, in which case his $1,550 would be worth £911.76, implying a loss of £88.24.

A speculator hopes to make money by taking an open position in the foreign currency. In our example, he has a forward asset in dollars which is not matched by a corresponding liability of equal value.

open position
a speculative position held by a trader or an institution that has not yet been closed, leading to the possibility of future losses or gains depending on movements in market prices

The interaction of hedgers, arbitrageurs and speculators

The forward exchange rate is determined by the interaction of traders, hedgers and speculators. One of the conditions that must hold in the forward exchange market is that for every forward purchase there must be a forward sale of the currency so that the excess demand for the currency sums to zero:

$$ED_H + ED_A + ED_S = 0$$

where ED_H is the excess demand of hedgers; ED_A is the excess demand of arbitrageurs; and ED_S is the excess demand of speculators.

Figure 11.9   The joint determination of the spot and forward exchange rate

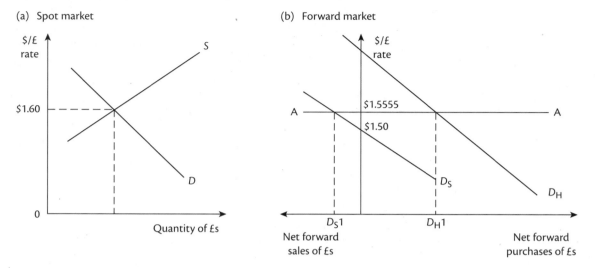

(a) Spot market

(b) Forward market

The forward exchange rate and the volume of forward transactions are determined jointly by the actions of arbitrageurs, traders and speculators, and the forward exchange rate is jointly determined with the spot exchange rate. This is illustrated in **Figure 11.9**.

Figure 11.9(a) shows the supply and demand situation in the spot market and **Figure 11.9**(b) the net supply and demand schedules in the forward market. The AA schedule reflects the forward exchange rate consistent with CIP. In effect, this is the supply and demand of forward exchange of arbitrageurs for a given interest differential. Since the pound is at a forward discount, the interest rate in the UK is above that in the USA. The D_H schedule is the net demand for pounds of hedgers in the forward exchange market. As the pound depreciates in the forward market then hedgers' net demand for pounds rises.

The D_S schedule is the net demand schedule for forward exchange of speculators which cuts the vertical axis at $1.50/£1. This means that $1.50/£1 represents the average forecast of speculators since at this rate they would be neither net purchasers nor sellers of forward pounds. However, because speculators on average expect the pound to depreciate more than is indicated by the forward exchange rate, they are net sellers of pounds forward if the rate is above $1.50/£1 and net purchasers of pounds forward if the rate is below $1.50/£1 (because they then expect to be able to sell in the future at a better rate than they purchased).

At the end of the day, the arbitrage formula as given by CIP is crucial to the forward rate, which is determined along the arbitrage schedule AA at $1.5555/£1. At this rate hedgers happen to be net purchasers of pounds given by D_H1 while speculators happen to be net sellers of pounds given by D_S1. Since the net purchases of hedgers exceed the net sales of speculators, then there is pressure for the forward rate to rise above $1.5555/£1 which induces arbitrageurs to be net sellers of pounds forward (constituting net sales equal to $D_H1 - D_S1$) so as to clear the forward exchange market.

Speculators are at work in both the spot and forward exchange markets. If they decide that the current spot rate is overvalued they may sell spot so that the currency depreciates; if interest rates do not change then both the spot and forward exchange rates depreciate. Similarly, if speculators feel that the currency is overvalued forward then they will sell forward and both the forward and spot exchange quotations will depreciate. Hence, arbitrage ties the spot and forward exchange market quotations together via the CIP condition. Speculation may be thought of as determining the level of the spot and forward exchange quotations.

11.9　Nominal, real and effective exchange rates

Policy-makers and economists are very much concerned with analyzing the implications of exchange rate changes for the economy and the balance of payments. The exchange rate itself does not convey much information, and to analyze the effects and implications of changes in the exchange rate economists compile indices of the nominal, real and effective exchange rates. Since most national and international authorities quote these rates as foreign currency per unit of domestic currency, we shall compile some hypothetical nominal, real and effective exchange rates using this definition. This means that a rise in these indices will represent an appreciation of the currency being indexed.

The nominal exchange rate

nominal exchange rate index an index which tracks the movements of a currency against another currency; it is usually constructed so that a rise represents an appreciation, while a fall represents a depreciation of the indexed currency

The exchange rate that prevails at a given date is known as the nominal exchange rate, for example the amount of US dollars that will be obtained for one pound in the foreign exchange market. Similarly, a euro quotation of €1.50/£1 is again a nominal exchange rate quotation. The nominal exchange rate is merely the price of one currency in terms of another, with no reference made to what this means in terms of the purchasing power of goods/services. The nominal exchange rate is usually presented in index form. If the base period for the index is $1.60/£1 and one period later the nominal exchange rate is $1.80/£1, the nominal index of the pound will change from the base period of 100 to 112.5. A depreciation or appreciation of the nominal exchange rate does not necessarily imply that the country has become more or less competitive on international markets. For such a measure we have to look at the real exchange rate.

The real exchange rate

real exchange rate index an index which tracks the changes in economic competitiveness of one country's currency against another country's currency; it is usually constructed so that a rise represents a loss of competitiveness, while a fall represents a gain in competitiveness of the indexed currency

The real exchange rate is the nominal exchange rate adjusted for relative prices between the countries under consideration, and is normally expressed in index form algebraically as:

$$S_r = S_I \frac{P_I}{P_I^*}$$

where S_r is the index of the real exchange rate; S_I is the nominal exchange rate (foreign currency units per unit of domestic currency) in index form; P_I the index of the domestic price level; and P_I^* is the index of the foreign price level.

Table 11.8 illustrates the compilation of hypothetical nominal and real exchange rate indices for the pound, and what exactly changes in the real exchange rate

Table 11.8   Construction of nominal and real exchange rate indices

Period	Nominal exchange rate	Nominal exchange index of £	UK price index	US price index	Real exchange index of £
1	$2.00/£1	100	100	100	100
2	$2.20/£1	110	120	100	132
3	$2.40/£1	120	120	120	120
4	$1.80/£1	90	130	117	100
5	$1.50/£1	75	150	125	90

Note: The real exchange rate index is constructed by multiplying the nominal $/£ index by the UK price index and dividing the result by the US price index.

measure. In the first period the real exchange rate index is set equal to 100. A basket of UK goods priced at £100 will cost a US resident $200, while a basket of US goods priced at $100 would cost a UK resident £50. Between period 1 and period 2 there is an appreciation of the pound by 10% to $2.20/£1 and the UK price index rises while the US index remains the same. This means that there has been a real appreciation of the pound, UK goods now become relatively more expensive for US residents. They have to use $264 dollars to purchase the original bundle of UK goods which now cost £120, while the bundle of US goods costs a British citizen only £45.45. This decreased competitiveness is picked up by the real exchange rate appreciation from 100 to 132. Clearly, since the nominal exchange rate has only appreciated by 10% to 110, it has failed to pick up the loss in UK competitiveness of 32% which is picked up by the real exchange rate index.

Between periods 2 and 3 UK prices remain unchanged while US prices increase 20% while the pound appreciates only 10% so that the UK gains an improvement in competitiveness. Between periods 3 and 4 UK prices rise and US prices fall but the competitive disadvantage to the UK is offset by a substantial depreciation of the pound, so that there is a real depreciation of the pound, meaning an improvement in UK competitiveness. Finally, between periods 4 and 5, although UK prices rise much more than US prices making the UK less competitive, this is offset by a large nominal depreciation of the pound and overall there is a real depreciation of the pound.

From this example it is clear that the real exchange rate monitors changes in a country's competitiveness. Real exchange rate indices, unlike nominal exchange rate indices, are not publishable on a daily basis because the price indices used are normally only published monthly.

Figures 11.10, **11.11** and **11.12** show the evolution of the dollar–pound and the yen–dollar nominal and real exchange rate indices between 1973 and 2010, and the euro–dollar rates for 1999–2010, compiled using monthly data and consumer price indices. They show that there have been very substantial movements in both nominal and real exchange rates since the commencement of generalized floating in 1973.

The effective exchange rate

Since most countries of the world do not conduct all their trade with a single foreign country, policy-makers are not so much concerned with what is happening to

Figure 11.10 The evolution of the dollar–pound nominal and real exchange rate, 1973–2010

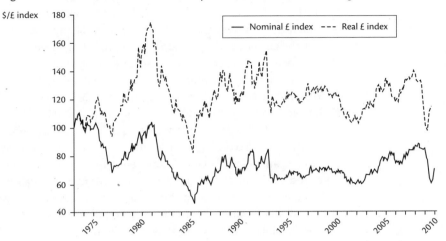

Figure 11.11 The evolution of the yen–dollar nominal and real exchange rate, 1973–2010

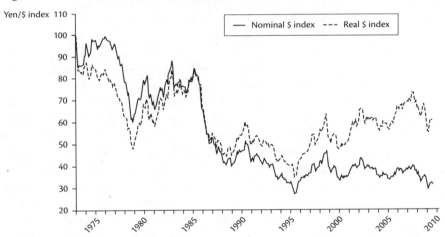

Figure 11.12 The evolution of the dollar–euro nominal and real exchange rate, 1999–2010

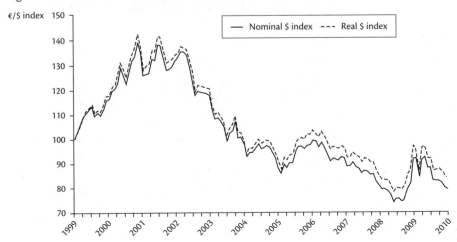

their exchange rate against a single foreign currency but rather what is happening to the exchange rate against a basket of foreign currencies from the countries with which that country trades. The effective exchange rate is a measure of whether or not the currency is appreciating or depreciating against a weighted basket of foreign currencies. In order to illustrate how an effective rate is compiled, consider the hypothetical case of the UK conducting 30% of its foreign trade with the USA and 70% of its trade with Europe. This means that a weight of 0.3 will be attached to the bilateral exchange rate index with the dollar and 0.7 with the euro.

Table 11.9 shows the movements of a hypothetical effective exchange rate index for the pound, based upon movements in the bilateral nominal exchange rate indices against the dollar and euro. Between periods 1 and 2 the pound appreciates 10 per cent against the dollar but depreciates 10 per cent against the euro. Since the euro has a greater weight than the dollar, the effective exchange rate index indicates an overall depreciation of 4 per cent. Period 3 leads to further appreciation against the US dollar and no change against the euro, and the resulting appreciation of the effective exchange rate is consequently less marked than the appreciation against the dollar. In period 4, the pound depreciates against both the dollar and the euro and consequently there is a depreciation of the effective exchange rate. Finally, in period 5 the pound depreciates against the US dollar and appreciates to a lesser extent against the euro; however, the effective exchange rate depreciates only marginally because more weight is attached to the appreciation against the euro than to the depreciation against the dollar.

While the nominal effective exchange rate is easy to compile on a daily basis and normally provides a reasonable measure of changes in a country's competitive position for periods of several months, it does not take account of the effect of price movements. In order to get a better idea of changes in a country's competitive position over time we would need to compile real effective exchange rate indices. For this, we would first of all compile the real exchange rate against each of the trading partners' currencies in index form and then use the same procedure as for compiling the nominal effective exchange rates. **Table 11.10** shows the nominal effective exchange rate indices for the major industrialized countries since 1980, derived from the Bank for International Settlements, while **Table 11.11** shows the real effective exchange rate indices for the same countries using consumer price indices for calculation purposes.

Table 11.9   Construction of an effective exchange rate index

Period	Nominal exchange rate index of $/£	Nominal exchange rate index of €/£	Effective exchange rate index of the pound
1	100	100	100
2	110	90	96
3	120	90	99
4	90	80	83
5	75	85	82

Note: The effective exchange rate index is constructed by multiplying the $/£ index by 0.3 and the €/£ index by 0.7.

Table 11.10   Nominal effective exchange rate indices 1980–2008, annual averages

	USA	Canada	Japan	UK	Germany	Italy	France
1980	100.0	100.0	100.0	100.0	100.0	100.0	100.0
1981	108.1	100.0	112.0	102.4	95.6	90.6	93.4
1982	118.6	100.5	106.3	98.0	100.6	84.5	86.4
1983	123.5	101.7	116.0	91.7	105.4	82.4	81.2
1984	130.8	98.7	122.4	88.2	104.6	78.7	77.9
1985	135.9	94.4	125.8	87.6	105.0	75.0	78.8
1986	115.2	87.3	161.6	81.2	114.7	76.1	81.7
1987	102.4	88.0	175.1	78.7	121.8	76.3	82.0
1988	94.5	92.7	191.6	83.3	121.2	73.6	80.3
1989	96.6	97.7	181.6	81.0	119.4	73.8	79.0
1990	93.6	98.3	164.7	79.1	125.3	75.4	82.9
1991	91.9	99.5	177.7	80.0	124.4	74.4	81.7
1992	90.5	94.1	186.9	77.2	127.6	72.2	84.0
1993	93.1	88.4	222.3	70.2	131.8	60.7	86.5
1994	91.9	83.0	240.8	70.4	131.9	57.7	87.2
1995	87.1	80.9	253.5	67.3	138.7	52.5	89.9
1996	90.6	82.5	222.3	68.1	135.9	56.8	90.1
1997	97.4	83.0	210.2	78.9	129.3	57.4	87.0
1998	105.2	79.0	206.4	82.9	130.6	57.6	87.9
1999	102.6	77.8	235.6	81.9	127.5	56.3	86.4
2000	105.9	78.9	258.9	84.0	120.6	53.9	82.5
2001	112.9	76.9	238.6	82.9	121.2	54.1	82.8
2002	112.1	75.3	225.5	83.2	122.9	54.7	83.7
2003	100.2	93.1	223.7	79.4	131.3	57.5	88.1
2004	92.2	86.8	232.0	82.0	131.5	57.6	88.2
2005	89.6	93.0	224.4	81.4	131.4	57.5	88.2
2006	88.7	99.4	208.8	81.8	131.6	57.6	88.3
2007	84.2	103.6	198.6	83.5	134.6	58.6	89.8
2008	80.8	104.3	202.2	73.5	138.1	59.8	91.8

Notes: Annual average based on monthly averages. Calculated using a moving average trade weight system. Author has rebased the series to 1980 = 100.

Source: Bank for International Settlements, rebased by author

Table 11.11   Real effective exchange rate indices 1980–2008, annual averages

	USA	Canada	Japan	UK	Germany	Italy	France
1980	100.0	100.0	100.0	100.0	100.0	100.0	100.0
1981	107.0	101.8	105.5	103.9	91.2	98.3	95.6
1982	118.5	107.0	96.1	100.3	92.5	99.0	91.3
1983	122.6	111.2	102.0	92.7	93.6	104.9	88.2
1984	128.7	108.0	105.3	88.9	89.3	105.6	86.3
1985	133.2	103.5	106.3	89.6	86.8	105.2	88.2
1986	115.8	98.2	134.7	84.2	92.1	110.9	91.7
1987	105.2	100.3	141.9	83.0	95.3	114.0	92.7
1988	97.3	105.8	150.4	88.8	92.9	112.5	90.6
1989	99.4	111.8	139.0	87.3	90.1	115.3	88.4
1990	96.9	112.0	123.3	87.1	92.5	120.1	91.4
1991	94.3	114.5	130.8	90.7	90.9	120.3	88.5
1992	92.5	106.6	135.0	88.4	94.6	118.2	89.3
1993	94.9	99.1	157.3	80.0	98.8	100.5	90.6
1994	94.7	91.0	166.7	79.8	99.2	97.0	90.3
1995	94.2	88.9	171.3	76.6	103.6	90.9	92.4
1996	97.7	89.5	146.1	77.7	100.6	100.4	92.3
1997	102.9	89.2	137.0	90.1	95.7	101.5	88.4
1998	110.3	84.3	133.1	94.9	96.3	102.5	88.7
1999	107.7	82.7	149.1	93.9	93.2	100.7	86.4
2000	111.0	83.5	158.5	95.1	87.4	96.8	82.1
2001	117.4	81.2	141.4	92.8	87.5	97.7	81.8
2002	116.9	80.1	130.4	92.7	88.5	99.5	82.8
2003	108.4	99.0	120.8	88.1	93.3	106.2	87.5
2004	102.5	93.2	128.9	90.6	94.0	106.4	87.9
2005	100.8	98.9	121.3	89.7	93.5	106.4	87.6
2006	101.1	104.8	110.4	90.3	93.1	106.6	87.3
2007	97.5	108.8	102.7	92.5	95.6	108.2	88.3
2008	95.1	108.3	105.2	81.6	97.1	110.6	89.8

Notes: Annual average based on monthly averages. Calculated using a moving average trade weight system. Author has rebased the series to 1980 = 100.

Source: Bank for International Settlements, rebased by author

11.10   Conclusions

The need for a foreign exchange market arises because international trade in goods/ services and financial assets almost always involves the exchange of differing national currencies. The modern foreign exchange market is truly a global market and is characterized by a huge volume of daily transactions. When conducting an economic analysis of the effects of exchange rate changes, it proves useful to distinguish between the real and nominal exchange rate and between bilateral and effective exchange rates, depending upon the purpose of the particular analysis being undertaken.

Governments are not indifferent to movements in the value of their currencies in the foreign exchange market, and on occasions they intervene in an attempt to influence the rate of exchange at which their currencies are traded. Indeed, many governments for various reasons have decided to peg their exchange rates to one another, such as the Hong Kong dollar which is tied to the US dollar at HK$ 7.80/$1.

Although exchange rates may move quite substantially at times, this is not necessarily disruptive to international trade as traders can protect themselves against exchange risk by hedging in the forward exchange market. For many countries, the depreciation or devaluation of their currencies is an important mechanism for maintaining their international competitiveness and trade volumes.

Further reading

Chen, J. (2009) *Essentials of Foreign Exchange Trading*, Wiley.
Shamah, S.A. (2008) *Foreign Exchange Primer*, Wiley.
Walmsley, J. (2000) *The Foreign Exchange and Money Markets Guide*, 2nd edn, Wiley.

Chapter 11	Revision questions

1   The $/£ spot rate is $1.60/£1. The UK interest rate is 9% and the US interest rate is 6%. Calculate the one year forward rate using the covered interest parity formula and state whether the dollar is at a forward premium or discount.

2   Fill in the missing values for nominal and real $/£ indexes in the table below.

Period	$/£ rate	Nominal $/£ Index	UK price index	US price index	Real $/£ index
1	$2.00/£1	?	100	100	?
2	$2.10/£1	?	120	110	?
3	$2.50/£1	?	120	120	?
4	$2.00/£1	?	130	140	?
5	$1.70/£1	?	160	150	?

Chapter 11 | Revision questions – *continued*

3   Fill in the missing values for effective (trade weighted) pound index in the table below. Assuming that the UK does 40% of its trade with the USA and 60% of its trade with Europe.

Period	Nominal $/£ index	Nominal €/£ Index	Nominal (effective) £ trade weighted index
1	100	100	?
2	140	120	?
3	110	100	?
4	80	120	?
5	100	90	?

4   The spot dollar-pound rate is $1.80/£1 and the one year forward rate is also $1.80/£1. You expect the spot dollar-pound rate will be $1.65/£1 in one year's time. You have £1 million to speculate with.

  (i)   Do you buy or sell £1 million in the forward market?

  (ii)   What is your profit in pounds if you are correct and the spot dollar–pound rate is $1.65/£1 in one year's time?

  (iii)   What is your loss in pounds if you are wrong and the spot sterling rate is $2/£1 in one years' time?

5   The pound is very strong against the US dollar due to increased demand for yen in the foreign exchange market and has moved from $1.60/£1 to $1.80/£1, so the Bank of England decides to intervene to sell the pound and buy US dollars to move the rate back to $1.60/£1. Illustrate all of this using the supply and demand for pounds in the foreign exchange market diagram. Clearly indicate the amount of intervention undertaken by the Bank of England. Briefly comment on the implications of the intervention for the UK money supply, UK interest rate and the Bank of England's foreign exchange reserves (assume the intervention is non-sterilized).

   Multiple choice questions available at **www.palgrave.com/business/pilbeam**

12

THEORIES OF EXCHANGE RATE DETERMINATION

Learning objectives

In this chapter you will learn about:

- the difference between the absolute and relative versions of purchasing power parity (PPP)
- the empirical evidence regarding PPP
- expected future spots rates and the uncovered interest rate parity theory
- what is meant by the 'carry trade' and whether such trades are likely to generate excess returns
- the flexible price and sticky price monetary models
- the Dorbusch 'overshooting' model and its importance
- the Frankel real interest rate differential model

12.1   Introduction

One of the key questions confronting international investors concerns what moves exchange rates? In this chapter, we look at a variety of alternative exchange rate theories. Firstly, we look at purchasing power parity (PPP) theory which has been advocated as a satisfactory model of exchange rate determination in its own right. Having looked at PPP theory, we proceed to examine how well suited this theory is to explaining actual exchange rate behaviour since the adoption of generalized floating in 1973. As we shall see, PPP theory does not provide an adequate explanation of some of the observed features of floating exchange rates. Some possible explanations for this failure are then discussed.

We then proceed to look at some more recent and sophisticated exchange rate models that have been developed in an attempt to model exchange rate behaviour more successfully. The models we examine are known as monetary models. They bring macroeconomic factors into the picture, emphasizing the important role of relative money supplies in explaining the exchange rate. A variety of monetary models have been put forward in an attempt to explain exchange rate behaviour, and we deal with three of the most important: the 'flexible-price' monetary model, the 'sticky-price' monetary model and the 'real-interest-rate-differential' model.

Important note

Throughout most of this chapter we shall be defining the exchange rate as domestic currency per unit of foreign currency. Taking sterling as the domestic currency and the US dollar as the foreign currency we are talking of pounds required to purchase one US dollar. Hence a depreciation of sterling is represented by a rise in the exchange rate, that is, more pounds have to be given to purchase one dollar; for example a move from £0.50/$1 to £0.60/$1 per dollar represents a depreciation of sterling. Conversely, an appreciation of sterling is represented by a fall in the exchange rate.

12.2   Purchasing power parity theory

Purchasing power parity (PPP) theory is one of the earliest and best-known models of exchange rate determination. It has been advocated as a satisfactory model in its own right and also provides a point of reference for the long-run exchange rate in many of the modern exchange rate theories which we examine later in this chapter. PPP relies heavily upon the concept of goods arbitrage and argues that the exchange rate will adjust to ensure that goods prices are equalized once they are measured in the same currency.

Goods arbitrage occurs where economic agents exploit price differences so as to provide a riskless profit. For example, if a car costs £10,000 in the UK and the identical model costs $20,000 in the USA, then, according to the law of one price, the exchange rate should be £10,000/$20,000 which is £0.5/$1. If the exchange rate were higher than this, at say £0.6666/$1, then it would pay a US resident to purchase a car in the UK because with $15,000 he would obtain £10,000, which could then be used to purchase a car in the UK, thus saving $5,000 compared to purchasing in the USA. According to the law of one price, US residents will exploit this arbitrage possibility and start purchasing pounds and selling dollars. Such a process will continue until the pound appreciates to £0.50/$,1 at which point arbitrage profit opportunities are eliminated. Conversely, if the exchange rate were £0.4/$1, then a UK car would cost a US resident £10,000 = $25,000 while a US car would cost a UK resident $20,000 × 0.4 = £8000. In this case we would say that the pound is overvalued. US residents will not buy UK cars and UK residents will buy US cars, so the pound will depreciate on the foreign exchange market to its PPP value of £0.5/$1.

The proponents of PPP argue that the exchange rate must adjust to ensure that the 'law of one price', which applies only to individual goods, also holds internationally for identical bundles of goods.

12.3   Absolute PPP

The absolute version of PPP holds that if one takes a bundle of goods in one country and compares the price of that bundle with an identical bundle of goods sold in a foreign country converted by the exchange rate into a common currency of measurement, then the prices will be equal. For example, if a bundle of goods costs £100 in the UK and the same bundle costs $200 in the US, then the exchange rate defined as pounds per dollar will be £100/$200 = £0.5/$1. Algebraically, the absolute version of PPP can be stated as:

$$S = \frac{P}{P^*} \qquad\qquad (12.1)$$

where S is the exchange rate defined as domestic currency units per unit of foreign currency; P^* is the price of an identical bundle of goods in the foreign country expressed in terms of the foreign currency; and P is the price of a bundle of goods expressed in the domestic currency.

According to absolute PPP, a rise in the domestic price level relative to the foreign price level will lead to a proportional depreciation of the home currency against the foreign currency. In our example, if the price of the UK bundle rises to £160 while the price of the US bundle remains at $200, then the pound will depreciate to £0.8/$1.

12.4   Relative PPP

The absolute version of PPP is, even proponents of the theory generally acknowledge, unlikely to hold precisely because of the existence of transport costs, imperfect information and the distorting effects of tariffs and protection. Nonetheless, it is argued that a weaker form of PPP, known as relative purchasing power parity, can be expected to hold even in the presence of such distortions. Put simply, the relative version of PPP theory argues that the exchange rate will adjust by the amount of the inflation differential between two economies. Algebraically this is expressed as:

$$\%\Delta S = \%\Delta P - \%\Delta P^* \qquad\qquad (12.2)$$

where $\%\Delta S$ is the percentage change in the exchange rate defined as domestic currency units per unit of foreign currency; $\%\Delta P$ is the domestic inflation rate; and $\%\Delta P^*$ is the foreign inflation rate.

According to the relative version of PPP, if the inflation rate in the UK is 15 per cent whilst that in the USA is 5 per cent, the pounds per dollar exchange rate should be expected to depreciate by approximately 10 per cent. The absolute version of PPP does not have to hold for this to be the case. For example, the exchange rate may be £0.6666/$1 ($1.50/£1) while the UK bundle of goods costs £100 and the US bundle of identical goods costs $200, so that absolute PPP is not holding (this would require a rate of £0.5/$1). But if UK prices go up 15 per cent to £115 and the US bundle goes up 5 per cent to $210 the relative version of PPP predicts the pound will depreciate 10 per cent to £0.7333/$1 (even though absolute PPP requires £0.5476/$1 = £115/$210).

12.5   Measurement problems in testing for PPP

Many of the proponents of PPP argued prior to the adoption of floating exchange rates that exchange rate changes would be in line with the predictions of purchasing power parity theory. Before examining some of the empirical evidence on PPP theory, it is worth considering some of the practical problems involved in testing for PPP.

One of the major problems is to decide whether or not the theory is supposed to be applicable to all goods or whether a distinction should be made between traded and non-traded goods. Traded goods are goods that are susceptible to the rigours of international competition, be they exports or import-competing industries, such as most manufactured goods. Non-traded goods are those that cannot be traded internationally at a profit; examples include houses and certain services such as a haircut, or restaurant food. The point of the traded/non-traded goods distinction is that on *a priori* grounds PPP is more likely to hold for traded goods than for non-traded ones. This is because the price of traded goods will tend to be kept in line by international arbitrage, while the price of non-traded goods will be determined predominantly by domestic supply and demand considerations. For example, if a car costs £10,000 in the UK and $20,000 in the USA, arbitrage will tend to keep the dollar/pound rate at £0.5/$1. However, if the price of a house costs £150,000 in the UK and $80,000 in the USA and the exchange rate is £0.5/$1, arbitrage forces do not easily come into play (unless sufficient numbers of UK citizens emigrate to America, pushing up US house prices and lowering UK prices!). Similarly, if a haircut costs £15 in the UK but $20 in the USA and the exchange rate is £0.5/$1, i.e. $2/£1, only insane people in the UK will travel to the USA to save £5 on a haircut because of the time and transport costs involved. At first sight, PPP theory seems more readily applicable to traded goods. However, some argue that the distinction between the two categories is fuzzy and there are mechanisms linking both traded and non-traded goods prices. For example, some traded goods are used as inputs into the production of non-traded goods and *vice versa* (for example, shop rents differ in price between the USA and, say, Mexico).

The argument over whether or not PPP should be applied to traded or non-traded goods or whether a more general price index should be used, made up of both traded and non-traded goods, is important for the empirical testing of PPP theory. If the theory is supposed to be applicable to traded goods only, then the price index used for testing the theory must be made up only of traded goods. Conversely, if the theory is applicable to both traded and non-traded goods then a more general price index should be employed. In practice, researchers who test PPP theory for traded goods typically use wholesale or manufacturing price indices which are normally dominated by traded goods, while if the test involves both traded and non-traded goods then consumer price indices which weight both classes of goods are generally used. An overall problem facing researchers, whichever price index they decide to employ, is that PPP is only expected to hold for similar baskets of goods but national price indices typically attach different weights to different classes of goods. For instance, consumer price indices in underdeveloped economies typically have a high weighting for food, while those in developed countries have a lower weighting for food and a higher weighting for consumer goods.

Another statistical problem in testing for PPP is that the base period for the test should ideally be one where PPP held approximately. In addition, there are divergences of view over the time span during which PPP can be expected to assert itself; a strong version of PPP would suggest it holds on a monthly basis whereas progressively weaker versions would argue that it can be expected to hold only quarterly, six-monthly or yearly and beyond. Bearing in mind some of these practical problems we proceed to look at some of the empirical evidence on PPP theory.

Box 12.1	The hamburger standard

In 1986 *The Economist* magazine launched a Big Mac index. The 'McDonald standard' is based upon the concept of PPP, the price index for measuring PPP being simply the price of a Big Mac hamburger. In July 2009 the average price of a Big Mac in the US was $3.57 and in Mexico the price was 33 pesos. Dividing the peso price by the US dollar price yields an implied PPP of 9.24 pesos per dollar compared with an actual exchange rate of 13.80 pesos per dollar, yielding a 33 per cent undervaluation of the peso. **Table 12.1** presents the measurements of over/undervaluation of the dollar in terms of PPP against various other currencies using hamburger prices. According to **Table 12.1** the second most undervalued currency is the Chinese Yuan – a Beijing Big Mac costs only $1.83 – while the Hong Kong dollar is the most undervalued currency – a big Mac costs $1.72 – and the most overvalued currency is the Swiss Franc – a Zurich Big Mac costs a beefy $5.98.

Box 12.1	The hamburger standard – *continued*

Table 12.1 Hamburgers and purchasing power parity

Country		Big Mac prices		Implied PPP of the dollar*	Actual $ exchange rate	Local currency under/over (−/+) valuation (%)
		In local currency	In dollars			
USA		$3.57	$3.57	–	–	
Argentina	Peso	11.50	3.02	3.22	3.81	−15
Australia	A$	4.34	3.37	1.22	1.29	−6
Brazil	Real	8.03	4.02	2.25	2.00	+13
Britain	£	2.29	3.69	1.56**	1.61	+3
Canada	C$	3.89	3.35	1.09	1.16	−6
Chile	Peso	1750	3.19	490	549	−11
China	Yuan	12.50	1.83	3.50	6.83	−49
Czech Rep.	CKr	67.92	3.64	19.00	18.70	+2
Denmark	DKr	29.50	5.53	8.26	5.34	+55
Egypt	Pound	10.00	1.62	3.45	6.17	−44
Euro Area	€	3.31	4.62	1.08***	1.39	+29
Hong Kong	HK$	13.30	1.72	3.73	7.75	−52
Hungary	Forint	720	3.62	202	199	+1
Indonesia	Rupiah	20,900	2.05	5,854	10,200	−43
Japan	Yen	320	3.46	89.6	92.6	−3
Malaysia	M$	6.77	1.88	1.90	3.60	−47
Mexico	Peso	33.00	2.39	9.24	13.80	−33
New Zealand	NZ$	4.90	3.08	1.37	1.59	−14
Peru	Sol	8.06	2.66	2.26	3.03	−25
Philippines	Peso	99.00	2.05	27.8	48.4	−42
Poland	Zloty	7..60	2.41	2.13	3.16	−33
Russia	Rouble	67.00	2.04	18.8	32.8	−43
Singapore	S$	4.22	2.88	1.18	1.46	−19
South Africa	Rand	17.95	2.17	5.03	8.28	−39
South Korea	Won	3,400	2.59	952	1,315	−28
Sweden	SKr	39.00	4.93	10.9	7.90	+38
Switzerland	SFr	6.50	5.98	2.17	1.09	+68
Taiwan	NT$	75.00	2.26	21.0	33.2	−37
Thailand	Baht	64.49	1.89	18.1	34.2	−47
Turkey	Lire	5.65	3.65	2.45	1.55	+2

Euro area is a weighted average price based on the price in the 13 Eurozone countries.
*PPP = local price divided by price in USA, ** Dollars per Pound, *** Dollars per Euro

Source: The Economist July, 2009.

12.6   Empirical evidence on PPP

There are a variety of methods of testing for PPP, including graphical evidence, simplistic data analysis and more sophisticated econometric evidence. We look in particular at some graphical evidence.

Graphical evidence on PPP

Figures 12.1 to **12.7** plot the actual exchange rate and the exchange rate that would have maintained PPP, using 1973 as the base year, and show that the exchange rate has diverged considerably from that suggested by PPP for the major currencies. That is, PPP has not worked well for the dollar–pound, dollar–deutschmark or yen–dollar rates. However, it was somewhat better for countries that are geographically close and have high trade linkages; for example it tracked the deutschmark–pound parity reasonably well and did even better at tracking the French franc–deutschmark and lira–deutschmark parities.

In **Figure 12.1** it can be seen that PPP did not do at all well in tracking the dollar–pound rate – it performed reasonably well up to 1977, but between mid-1976 and mid-1981 there was a dramatic appreciation of the pound while PPP would have predicted a depreciation (due to higher UK inflation). A massive dollar appreciation after 1981 led to the restoration of PPP in early 1984. Thereafter the pound had a brief period of undervaluation in relation to PPP and from late 1985 to 2005 the pound became rather overvalued in relation to PPP. Looking at **Figure 12.2**, the deutschmark–dollar rate is not explained by PPP either, with the dollar generally undervalued in relation to PPP up to early 1981. Thereafter the dollar became substantially overvalued up until mid-1986 when it once again became undervalued in relation to PPP. Again with the yen–dollar rate (**Figure 12.3**) there are sustained and marked departures from PPP.

When it comes to tracking the lira, French franc and pound against the deutschmark (**Figures 12.5** to **12.7**), the plots reveal that, although there were deviations from PPP, the order of magnitude of the deviation was much smaller than against the dollar, and that PPP did a reasonable job. This is not that surprising

Figure 12.1   The actual exchange rate and the PPP dollar–pound rate

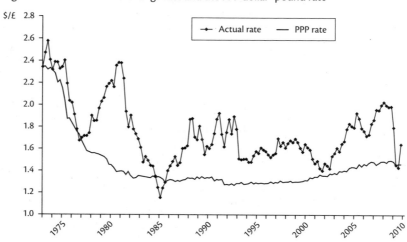

Figure 12.2   The actual exchange rate and the PPP deutschmark–dollar rate (equivalents post 1 January 1999)

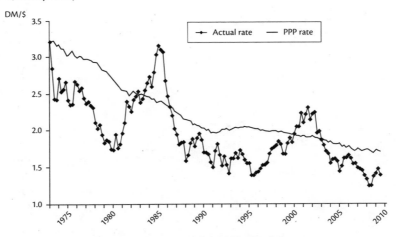

Figure 12.3   The actual exchange rate and the PPP yen–dollar rate

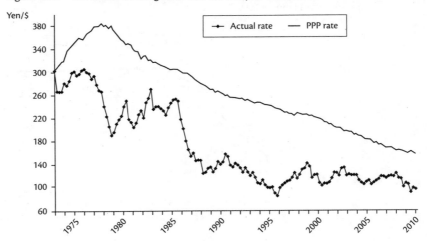

Figure 12.4   The actual exchange rate and the PPP dollar–euro rate

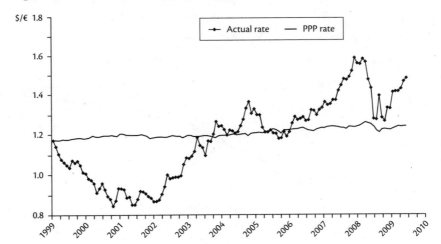

Figure 12.5   The actual exchange rate and the PPP deutschmark–pound rate (equivalents post 1 January 1999)

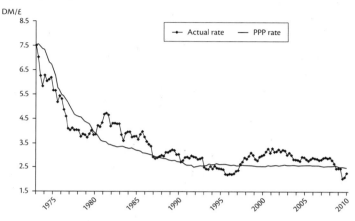

Figure 12.6   The actual exchange rate and the PPP French franc–deutschmark rate (equivalents post 1 January 1999)

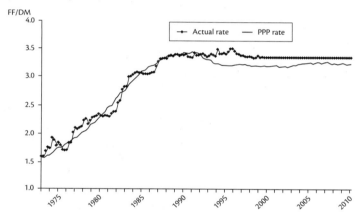

Figure 12.7   The actual exchange rate and the PPP lira–deutschmark rate (equivalents post 1 January 1999)

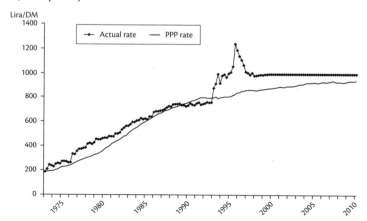

since transport costs and trade barriers between France, Italy and Germany are small because of their geographical proximity, and membership of the European Union prohibits the use of trade barriers between member countries. These conditions facilitate the goods market arbitrage that PPP is so heavily dependent on.

It is noticeable in most of the plots that, although the exchange rate is frequently far from PPP, it does have a tendency to go back towards the PPP rate over the longer run. This provides some evidence that PPP may be a useful guide for the determination of the long-run exchange rate.

12.7 Summary of the empirical evidence on PPP

Before moving on to examine in more detail the poor performance of PPP, the main findings from the empirical evidence are summarized below:

1 Frenkel (1981) showed that PPP performs better for countries that are geographically close to one another and where trade linkages are high. This is also borne out in the graphical plots – the biggest divergences between the actual and PPP exchange rates were for the pound, deutschmark and yen against the dollar, while the lira and French franc rates against the deutschmark were quite accurately tracked by PPP. Not only are France, Italy and Germany in close proximity to one another, minimizing transport costs, but they are also members of the European Union so that there exist no tariff impediments to restrict trade among them.

2 The plots of the exchange rates and PPP rates show that there have been both substantial and prolonged deviations from PPP which have frequently been reversed.

3 Empirically, PPP holds better in the long run than the short run. Many authors, such as Ardeni and Lubian (1991), have shown that, although PPP holds in the long run, there can be prolonged and substantial deviations in the short run. The longer run over which PPP tends to hold can be anything from 5 to 15 years.

4 Overall, PPP holds better for traded goods than for non-traded goods, and this is confirmed in a study by Officer (1976). In addition, a striking and major empirical regularity is that non-traded goods tend to be more expensive in rich countries than in poor countries once the prices are converted into a common currency. This point is quite important because the reason why a dollar buys less in the USA than in a developing country is predominantly that non-traded goods are much cheaper in developing countries than in developed countries.

5 The currencies of countries that have very high inflation rates relative to their trading partners tend to experience rapid depreciations reflecting their relatively high inflation rates. This suggests that PPP is the dominant force in determining their exchange rates.

6 Exchange rates have been much more volatile than the corresponding national price levels; see Frenkel and Mussa (1980) and MacDonald (1988). This again is contrary to the PPP hypothesis in which exchange rates are only supposed to be as volatile as relative prices. This point is quite important. Because exchange rate volatility seems to be considerably greater than that justified by volatility in relative national price levels, this suggests that the goods and foreign exchange markets are to some considerable extent detached from each other.

12.8   Explaining the poor performance of purchasing power parity

There have been many explanations put forward to explain the general failure of exchange rates to adjust in line with the suggestions of PPP theory, and in this section we proceed to look at some of the most important.

Statistical problems

We have seen that PPP theory is based upon the concept of comparing identical baskets of goods in two economies. An important problem facing researchers in this respect is that different countries usually attach different weights to various categories of goods and services when constructing their price indices. This means that it is difficult to compare 'like with like' when testing for PPP. This factor is probably very significant when testing for PPP between developed and developing economies which have vastly different consumption patterns. People in developing countries usually spend a high proportion of their income on basics such as food and clothing, while these take up a much smaller proportion of people's expenditure in developed economies.

Differing consumption baskets are not of such significance when comparing most industrialized economies since consumers have fairly similar consumption baskets in these economies. Even between developed economies, however, there is a problem posed by the differing quality of goods consumed. Although British and German consumers both spend roughly the same proportion of their incomes on cars, the Germans tend to drive German makes like BMW while the British tend to drive Japanese cars. We do not necessarily expect PPP to hold in terms of cars between the two countries because, once again, we are not comparing like with like.

Transport costs and trade impediments

Studies such as Frenkel (1981) which note that PPP holds better when the countries concerned are geographically close and trade linkages are high can partly be explained by transport costs and the existence of other trade impediments such as tariffs. If a bundle of goods costs £100 in the UK and $200 in the USA, PPP would suggest an exchange rate of £0.5/$1. If transport costs are £20 then the exchange rate could lie anywhere between £0.4/$1 and £0.6/$1 without bringing arbitrage forces into play. Nonetheless, since transport costs and trade barriers do not change dramatically over time they are not sufficient explanations for the failure of the relative versions of PPP.

Imperfect competition

One of the notions underlying PPP is that there is sufficient international competition to prevent major departures of the price of a good in one country from that in another. However, it is clear that there are considerable variations in the degree of competition internationally. These differences mean that multinational corporations can often get away with charging different prices in different countries. In fact, the conditions necessary for successful price discrimination – namely, discrepancies in different sets of consumers' willingness to pay, the ability to prevent resale from the low-cost to high-cost market, and some degree of monopoly power – are for the most part more likely to hold between rather than within countries.

Differences between capital and goods markets

Purchasing power parity is based upon the concept of goods arbitrage and has nothing to say about the role of capital movements. In a classic paper which we shall be looking at in section 12.13, Rudiger Dornbusch (1976) hypothesized that in a world where capital markets are highly integrated and goods markets exhibit slow price adjustment, there can be substantial prolonged deviations of the exchange rate from PPP. The basic idea is that in the short run goods prices in both the home and foreign economies can be considered as fixed, while the exchange rate adjusts quickly to new information and changes in economic policy. This being the case, exchange rate changes represent deviations from PPP which can be quite substantial and prolonged.

12.9   Modern theories of exchange rate determination

The PPP theory just considered is far from a satisfactory explanation of observed exchange rate behaviour. In particular, it is very much concerned with goods arbitrage and has nothing to say about capital movements internationally. In today's financial markets it is possible for international investors to switch huge amounts of money out of one currency into another very speedily. In particular, speculators will tend to move their money between currencies based on the expected rate of return from one currency compared to another. What people expect to happen to the exchange rate will play a crucial role in determining which currencies to buy and sell – if a currency is expected to depreciate, then agents will tend to switch out of that currency into currencies that they expect to appreciate. We now proceed to look at some more recent and sophisticated exchange rate models that have been developed in an attempt to model exchange rate behaviour more successfully than the PPP model.

The common thread to the modern exchange rate models is that they all emphasize the important role of relative money supplies in explaining the exchange rate. The monetary models start from the observation that the exchange rate is the price of one money in terms of another. However, the monetary models go beyond this simple observation to argue that exchange rate movements can be explained by changes in the supply and demand for national money stocks. A variety of competing models have been put forward to explain exchange rate behaviour, and we shall deal with three of the most important: the 'flexible-price' monetary model, the 'sticky-price' monetary model, and the 'real-interest-rate-differential' model. However, we need to introduce the important concept of uncovered interest parity.

12.10   Uncovered interest rate parity

Imagine an international investor that has the option of investing his money in UK bonds or US bonds of similar risk and maturity. If he regards the bonds as equally risky and can switch between the two assets instantaneously, the only difference between the bonds is their currency of denomination and the interest rate attached to them. International investors will bear in mind two factors when considering whether to purchase, say, UK bonds or US bonds; these are the rates of interest on UK bonds and

US bonds and what they expect to happen to the dollar–pound exchange rate. This idea is captured in an equation known as uncovered interest parity given by:

$$E\dot{s} = r_{uk} - r_{us} \qquad\qquad (12.3)$$

where $E\dot{s}$ is the expected rate of appreciation (−)/depreciation (+) of the exchange rate of the pound, defined as pounds per dollar; r_{uk} is the UK interest rate; and r_{us} is the US interest rate.

The uncovered interest parity condition (UIP) says that the expected rate of depreciation of the pound–dollar exchange rate is equal to the interest rate differential between US and UK bonds. For example, if the interest rate in the UK is 10 per cent per annum, while the interest rate in the US is 4 per cent per annum, then on average international investors expect the pound to depreciate by 6 per cent per annum.

With an initial pound per dollar exchange rate of £0.5/$1, investing £1,000 in UK bonds will yield the investor £100 return (10 per cent) at the end of the year. If he expects the pound to depreciate by 6 per cent during the year he expects the pound–dollar exchange rate to be £0.53/$1. Hence, he could purchase £1,000-worth of dollars today at £0.5/$1, which gives him $2,000 which will earn the US interest rate of 4 per cent. At the end of the year he will have $2,080 which he expects to convert back into pounds at £0.53/$1, giving him £1,102.40. This implies an expected return of £102.40 (approximately 10 per cent of $100 \times (£102.40/£1,000) = 10.2$ per cent) from investing in US bonds, which is approximately equal to the expected return on UK bonds. Hence, the UIP condition implies that the expected rates of return on domestic and foreign bonds are equal. In other words, the UIP condition says people are happy to hold dollars at 4 per cent because they are expecting a 6 per cent appreciation of the dollar (that is a 6 per cent depreciation of the pound), so that being in dollars gives a total expected yield of 10 per cent which competes with the UK interest rate of 10 per cent.

If the expected rate of depreciation of the pound was 8 per cent, then according to UIP the UK interest rate would have to be 8 per cent higher than the US interest rate to ensure the equalization of expected yields on UK and US bonds. Crucially, the condition for the uncovered interest rate parity condition to hold continuously is that capital is perfectly mobile so that investors can instantly alter the composition of their international investments. In addition, they have to regard UK and US bonds as equally risky – were this not the case then investors that are risk-averse would require a higher expected return on the riskier asset. For example, if risk-averse UK investors viewed the risk on UK bonds as being greater than the risk on US bonds, they would require a higher expected rate of return on UK bonds than US bonds so that the UIP condition no longer holds.

12.11   Monetary models of exchange rate determination

Having provided the basic background to the monetary models of exchange rate determination, we now proceed to examine the specific characteristics and predictions of three of the major monetarist models: the 'flexible-price', 'sticky-price' and 'real-interest-rate-differential' monetary models. A common characteristic of these models is that the supply and demand for money are the key determinants of exchange rate determination. Another common starting point is that all the models employ the UIP condition; that is, they assume that domestic and foreign bonds are equally risky so that their expected returns are equalized.

Beyond these similarities there are some significant differences between the models. The flexible-price model argues that all prices in the economy – be they wages, prices or exchange rates – are perfectly flexible both upwards and downwards in both the short and the long run. This model also incorporates a role for the effect of inflationary expectations. The sticky-price model which was first elaborated by Rudiger Dornbusch (1976) argues that in the short run wages and prices tend to be sticky and only the exchange rate changes in response to changes in economic policy; only in the medium to long run do wages and prices adjust to changes in economic policy and economic shocks. In the Dornbusch model, inflationary expectations are not explicitly dealt with. Finally we look at the real-interest-rate-differential model that combines the role of inflationary expectations of the flexible-price monetary model with the sticky prices of the Dornbusch model.

12.12 The flexible-price monetary model

The flexible-price monetary model was developed by Frenkel (1976), Mussa (1976) and Bilson (1978a and 1978b) and assumes that PPP holds continuously. However, it represents a valuable addition to exchange rate theory because it explicitly introduces relative money stocks into the picture as determinants of the relative prices which in turn determine the exchange rate.

We start by assuming that there is a conventional money demand function, given by:

$$m = p + \eta y - \sigma r \qquad (12.4)$$

where m is the log of the domestic money stock; p is the log of the domestic price level; y is the log of domestic real income; and r is the nominal domestic interest rate. Equation (12.4) says that the demand to hold real money balances is positively related to real domestic income due to increased transactions demand, and inversely related to the domestic interest rate.

A similar relationship holds for the foreign money demand function which is given by:

$$m^* = p^* + \eta y^* - \sigma r^* \qquad (12.5)$$

where m^* is the log of the foreign nominal money stock; p^* is the log of the foreign price level; y^* is the log of foreign real income; and r^* is the foreign interest rate.

It is assumed that PPP holds continuously, and this is expressed as:

$$s = p - p^* \qquad (12.6)$$

where s is the log of the exchange rate defined as domestic currency units per unit of foreign currency.

Box 12.2	The carry trade does not make sense according to UIP

In a carry trade investors borrow money in a low interest-rate currency and place it into a higher interest-rate currency in the hope that the high interest-rate currency will either appreciate or not depreciate more than the interest-rate differential, enabling an excess return to be made. The carry trade has been increasingly used in recent years by hedge funds, speculators and banks despite the fact that UIP theory suggests that it will not produce excess returns in the long run. Remember, the UIP condition predicts that over the long run the low interest-rate currency will on average appreciate by the interest-rate differential so as to make the carry trade a break-even strategy. Nonetheless, if UIP does not hold then the carry trade might work in the short run or even for several years (just as it can also fail at both time horizons). The carry trade will prove unprofitable if the currency with the high interest rate depreciates by an amount greater than the interest-rate differential over the relevant time horizon.

A simple example of the carry trade will suffice. Imagine the yen–euro rate is 130 yen per euro, the Japanese interest rate is 1% and the euro interest rate is 5%. A hedge fund might decide to borrow 10 million yen for one year knowing it will have to pay back 10,100,000 yen in a year's time. The hedge fund then sells the yen in the spot market to gain €76,923.08 which will earn 5% in euros and so become €80,769.23. So long as the euro has not depreciated to below 125.06 yen/€1 then the carry trade will be profitable. For example if the euro actually appreciates to 135 yen/€1 then the hedge fund will make 803,046 yen profit (or €5,954.41). Even if the exchange rate remains at 130 yen/€1 the hedge fund will be able to convert the €80,763.23 and obtain 10,500,000 and so make a 400,000 yen profit (or €3,076.92).

Figure 12.8   The profit/loss associated with a carry trade

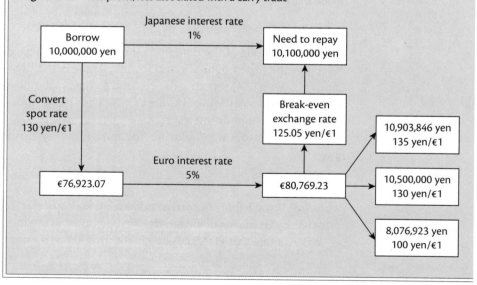

| Box 12.2 | **The carry trade does not make sense according to UIP** – *continued* |

The carry trade strategy will break even if the euro depreciates approximately 4% to 125.06 yen/€1 when €80,769.23 converts to 10,100,000 yen, just sufficient to repay the borrowed 10,000,000 yen plus 100,000 yen interest. However, there are risks with the carry trade. The real danger is if the yen appreciates by substantially more than 4%. Say the yen were to appreciate sharply to 100 yen per euro by the end of the year, the €80,769.23 will then be worth 8,076,923 yen, leaving the hedge fund with a shortfall (loss) of 2,023,077 yen of the required 10,100,000 yen that it needs to repay, which is equivalent to a loss of €20,230.77. The various scenarios are depicted in **Figure 12.8**.

According to UIP, on average we can expect the Japanese yen to appreciate to 125.05 so that the expected profit from the carry trade is zero. The carry trade therefore implies that markets on the average lead to a smaller depreciation of the currency than would be predicted by the interest differential. During the early part of this century the carry trade proved to be very profitable as the yen–euro rate started at 100 yen/€1 and moved all the way to 170 yen/€1 even though the European interest rate was above that of Japan through the period depicted in **Figure 12.9**. However, starting in July 2008 there was a very abrupt depreciation of the euro – from 170 yen/€1 to 115 yen/€1 in the space of just three months – so that anyone doing the carry trade at that point would have lost very substantially in a very short space of time!

Figure 12.9   The yen–euro exchange rate 2001–2010

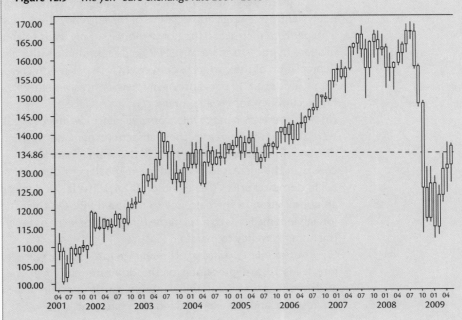

The monetarist models make a crucial assumption that domestic and foreign bonds are perfect substitutes. This being the case, the uncovered interest parity condition holds:

$$E\dot{s} = r - r^*$$ (12.7)

where $E\dot{s}$ is the expected rate of depreciation (if positive) of the domestic currency.

Equation (12.7) says that the expected rate of depreciation of the domestic currency is equal to the interest-rate differential between domestic and foreign bonds. We can rearrange equations (12.4) and (12.5) to give solutions for the domestic and foreign price levels:

$$p = m - \eta y + \sigma r$$ (12.8)
$$p^* = m^* - \eta y^* + \sigma r^*$$ (12.9)

and then substitute equations (12.8) and (12.9) into equation (12.6) to obtain:

$$s = (m - m^*) - \eta(y - y^*) + \sigma(r - r^*)$$ (12.10)

Equation (12.10) is known as a 'reduced-form' exchange rate equation. The spot exchange rate (the dependent variable) on the left-hand side is determined by the variables (explanatory variables) listed on the right-hand side of the equation.

What does equation (12.10) predict about the effect of a change in one of the right-hand variables on the exchange rate?

(a) *Relative money supplies affect exchange rates*. A given percentage increase in the home money supply leads to an exactly equivalent depreciation of the currency, while a given percentage increase in the foreign money supply leads to an exactly equivalent percentage appreciation of the currency. The rationale behind this is that a 10 per cent increase in the home money supply leads to an immediate 10 per cent increase in prices, and because PPP holds continuously this also implies a 10 per cent depreciation of the currency. Conversely, a 10 per cent increase in the foreign money supply leads to a 10 per cent rise in foreign prices, and for PPP to hold this means the home currency appreciates 10 per cent.

(b) *Relative levels of national income influence exchange rates*. If the domestic income were to rise, this increases the transactions-demand for money, and the increased demand for money means that if the money stock and interest rates are held constant, the increased demand for real balances can only come about through a fall in domestic prices (see equation (12.4)). The fall in domestic prices then requires an appreciation of the currency to maintain PPP. On the other hand, an increase in foreign income leads to a fall in the foreign price level and therefore a depreciation of the home currency to maintain PPP.

(c) *Relative interest rates affect exchange rates*. An increase in the domestic interest rate leads to a depreciation of the domestic currency. The rationale behind this assumption is that the nominal interest rate is made up of two components, the real interest rate and the expected inflation rate, that is:

$$r = i + P\dot{e}$$ (12.11)

where i is the real rate of interest; and $P\dot{e}$ is the expected rate of price inflation.

Similarly, the foreign nominal interest rate is given by:

$$r^* = i^* + P\dot{e}^* \qquad (12.12)$$

Assuming that the real rate of interest is constant and identical in both countries ($i = i^*$), an increase in the domestic nominal interest rate is due to an increase in domestic price-inflation expectations. Such increased inflation expectations lead to a decreased demand for money and increased expenditure on goods, which in turn leads to a rise in domestic prices. The rise in domestic prices then requires a depreciation of the currency to maintain PPP. Conversely, a rise in the foreign price level reduces foreigners' money demand leading to increased expenditure on foreign goods and a rise in the foreign price level, requiring an appreciation of the home currency to maintain PPP.

Equation (12.10) can be rewritten using price-inflation-expectations differentials instead of interest-rate differentials as:

$$s = (m - m^*) - \eta(y - y^*) + \sigma(P\dot{e} - P\dot{e}^*) \qquad (12.13)$$

The flexible price monetary model is based upon the premise that all prices in an economy are fully flexible, bonds are perfect substitutes and what matters for exchange rate determination is the demand for money in relation to the supply of money. In such circumstances, countries with high monetary growth rates will have high inflationary expectations, which leads to reduction in the demand to hold real money balances, increased expenditure on goods, a rise in the domestic price level and a depreciating currency in order to maintain PPP.

Despite its shortcomings and reliance on PPP, the flexible-price monetarist model is an important addition to exchange rate theory because it introduces the role of money supplies, inflationary expectations and economic growth as determinants of exchange rate changes.

12.13   The Dornbusch sticky-price monetarist model

One of the major deficiencies of the flexible-price monetarist model is that it assumes that purchasing power parity holds continuously and that prices are as flexible upwards and downwards as exchange rates. Indeed, it is price changes that are supposed to induce exchange rate changes via the PPP condition. As such, the model is of no use in explaining the observed prolonged departures from PPP since the adoption of floating exchange rates. In a classic article, Rudiger Dornbusch (1976) proposed a monetary exchange rate model that could explain large and prolonged departures of the exchange rate from PPP.

The model outlined by Dornbusch is termed the sticky-price monetarist model and introduces the concept of exchange rate overshooting. The basis underlying the model is that prices in the goods market and wages in the labour market are determined in sticky-price markets and they only tend to change slowly over time in response to various shocks such as changes in the money supply. Prices and wages are especially resistant to downward pressure. However, the exchange rate is determined in a 'flex-price' market, and can immediately appreciate or depreciate in response to new developments and shocks. In such circumstances, exchange rate changes are

exchange rate overshooting
the phenomenon that a currency may appreciate or depreciate following an economic shock in the short run by a greater percentage than required in the long run, so that it 'overshoots' its long-run value

not matched by corresponding price movements and there can be persistent and prolonged departures from PPP.

As the Dornbusch overshooting model represents such an important contribution to exchange rate theory and understanding exchange rate behaviour, we shall first consider a simple explanation of the model without recourse to the use of mathematics. Only when the essential ideas have been grasped shall we proceed to a more formal presentation of the model, which can be omitted from less advanced courses.

12.14   A simple explanation of the Dornbusch model

In the Dornbusch model the UIP condition is assumed to hold continuously; that is, if the domestic interest rate is lower than the foreign interest rate then there needs to be an equivalent expected rate of appreciation of the domestic currency to compensate for the lower domestic interest rate. This is because there is perfect arbitrage of expected returns in capital markets. By contrast, goods prices adjust only slowly over time to changes in economic policy, partly because wages are only adjusted periodically and partly because firms are slow to adjust their prices upwards or downwards, so we have 'sticky' domestic prices.

In such an environment, imagine that everyone believes that the long-run exchange rate is determined by PPP. Also, that the economy is initially in full equilibrium with a domestic interest rate $r1$ equal to the world interest rate, so that there is no expected appreciation or depreciation of the currency. Such a situation is depicted in **Figure 12.10**. The domestic money stock is given by $M1$ which gives a domestic price level of $P1$ and an exchange rate $S1$ which, given the foreign price level, corresponds to PPP. Let us now suppose that at time $t1$ the authorities unexpectedly expand the domestic money supply by 20 per cent from $M1$ to $M2$. In the long run everyone knows that a 20 per cent rise in the domestic money supply will lead to a 20 per cent rise in domestic prices from $P1$ to $P2$, and therefore a 20 per cent depreciation of the domestic currency from $S1$ to $\bar{S}$ to maintain long-run PPP. However, in the short run the Dornbusch model shows that things will be very different.

In the short run, because domestic prices are sticky they remain at $P1$. The unexpected increase in the domestic money supply will mean that at price level $P1$ there is now an excess supply of money that will only willingly be held if the domestic interest rate falls from $r1$ to $r2$. As the domestic interest is now lower than the world interest rate, this means that speculators will require an expected appreciation of the domestic currency to compensate. For this reason, the domestic currency jump depreciates at time $t1$ from $S1$ to $S2$ overshooting its long-run equilibrium value $\bar{S}$. The exchange rate has to 'overshoot' its long-run equilibrium value because it is only by depreciating by more than 20 per cent that there can be an expected appreciation of the domestic currency to compensate for the lower rate of interest on domestic bonds.

After the initial response of the exchange rate and interest rate to the increase in the money stock, there are a number of forces that come into play to move the economy to its long-run equilibrium. As a result of the fall in the domestic interest rate and the depreciation of the domestic currency, there is an increase in the demand for

Figure 12.10 The dynamics of the Dornbusch overshooting model

(a) Money supply

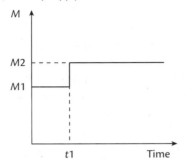

(b) Exchange rate

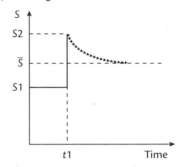

(c) Domestic prices

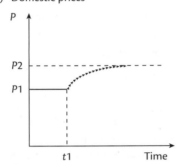

(d) Domestic interest rate

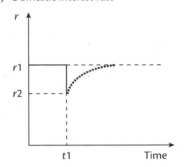

domestic goods. As output is assumed to be fixed, this excess demand for domestic goods starts to drive up domestic prices from P1. The increased demand for domestic goods by foreigners leads to an exchange rate appreciation from S2 towards $\bar{S}$ (thus the expected appreciation is matched by an actual appreciation). At the same time, the rise in the domestic price level leads to an increase in domestic money demand and a rise in the domestic interest rate to maintain money market equilibrium. Over time the domestic price level rises from P1 to P2 by the same percentage as the increase in the money supply, and the exchange rate appreciates from S2 to $\bar{S}$ which corresponds to a restoration of PPP. Meanwhile, the domestic interest rate rises from r2 to its original level r1, so that once again there is neither an expected appreciation or depreciation of the domestic currency.

Having outlined the principal idea we now proceed to a more formal exposition of the Dornbusch model of exchange rate overshooting.

12.15 A formal explanation of the Dornbusch model

In the model outlined, we focus upon a 'small country' in the sense that it faces a fixed world interest rate r^* which it cannot influence. The demand to hold money in the home country is given by a conventional money demand function:

$$m - p = \eta y - \sigma r \tag{12.14}$$

where m is the log of the domestic money stock; p is the log of the domestic price level; y is the log of domestic real income; and r is the nominal domestic interest rate.

We again assume that domestic and foreign bonds are perfect substitutes, so that the UIP condition holds, that is:

$$E\dot{s} = r - r^*\qquad(12.15)$$

where $E\dot{s}$ is the expected rate of depreciation of the home currency.

The major difference between the sticky-price and flexible-price monetary models is that the sticky-price model assumes that PPP holds only in the long run, not continuously as assumed in the flexible-price model. The hypothesis that the long-run exchange rate is determined by PPP yields:

$$\bar{s} = \bar{p} - \bar{p}^*\qquad(12.16)$$

where $\bar{s}$ is the log of the long-run equilibrium exchange rate; $\bar{p}$ is the log of the long run domestic price level; and $\bar{p}^*$ is the log of the long-run foreign price level.

Since the model allows for departures from PPP, it is necessary to specify an equation for the expected rate of change of the exchange rate. The Dornbusch model specifies a regressive exchange given by:

$$E\dot{s} = \Theta(\bar{s} - s) \text{ where } \Theta > 0\qquad(12.17)$$

Equation (12.17) says that the expected rate of depreciation of a currency is determined by the speed of adjustment parameter Θ, and the gap between the current exchange rate s and its long-run equilibrium value $\bar{s}$. If the current exchange rate s is below its long-run equilibrium rate $\bar{s}$, then it can be expected to depreciate towards its long-run value (that is, $E\dot{s}$ will be positive); while if the current exchange rate s is above its long-run equilibrium rate it can be expected to appreciate (that is, $E\dot{s}$ will be negative).

We now proceed to derive the two schedules vital to the Dornbusch model: the goods market equilibrium schedule which shows equality of aggregate demand and supply for goods, and the money market equilibrium schedule which shows equality between the demand and supply of money.

Derivation of the goods market equilibrium schedule

The goods market equilibrium schedule shows the equality of demand and supply for goods in the price–exchange rate plane. The model postulates that the rate of price inflation in the model is determined by the gap between aggregate demand and aggregate supply. That is:

$$\dot{p} = \pi(d - y)\qquad(12.18)$$

where $\dot{p}$ is the rate of domestic price inflation, π is the speed of adjustment of prices, d is the log of aggregate demand and y is the log of domestic income.

Aggregate demand is assumed to be a function of exogenous expenditure β, a positive function of the real exchange rate expressed in log form as $(s - p + p^*)$, a positive function of domestic income and a negative function of the domestic nominal interest rate; this yields:

$$d = \beta + \alpha(s - p + p^*) + \varphi y - \lambda r\qquad(12.19)$$

Substituting equation (12.18) into equation (12.19) we obtain:

$$\dot{p} = \pi[\beta + \alpha(s - p + p^*) + (\varphi - 1)y - \lambda r] \qquad (12.20)$$

Along the goods market equilibrium schedule (GG in Figure 12.8) the equality of supply and demand for goods means that there is zero inflation, that is $p = 0$. To find the slope of the goods market schedule we must substitute the solution for r from equation (12.14) into equation (12.20) to obtain:

$$\dot{p} = \pi[\beta + \alpha(s - p + p^*) + (\varphi - 1)y - \lambda/\sigma(p - m + \eta y)] \qquad (12.21)$$

Then by setting equation (12.21) to zero, we find the slope of the GG schedule in the price level–exchange rate plane. Along the GG schedule aggregate demand equals aggregate supply, implying zero price inflation. The slope of the GG schedule is given by:

$$\left.\frac{dp}{ds}\right|_{\dot{p}=0} = \frac{\alpha}{\alpha + \lambda/\sigma} \qquad (12.22)$$

From equation (12.22) we can see that the GG schedule is upward-sloping from left to right, and has a slope of less than unity as depicted in **Figure 12.11**.

The rationale behind the GG schedule is that a depreciation (rise) of the exchange rate leads to an increased demand for exports, and this increase in demand can only be offset by a rise in the domestic price level which negates the competitive advantage of the depreciation. However, because the rise in the price level increases money demand, it is accompanied by a rise in interest rates which further reduces demand. This means that the percentage depreciation of the exchange rate has to exceed the percentage rise in the price level to keep aggregate demand in line with aggregate supply.

To the left of the GG schedule there is an excess supply of goods due to the fact that, assuming output to be fixed for any given price level, an exchange rate appreciation (fall) reduces aggregate demand. The excess supply of goods will put downward pressure on prices. Conversely, to the right of the GG schedule, for any given price level, the exchange rate depreciation (rise) leads to an excess demand for domestic goods, causing an upward pressure on prices.

Figure 12.11   The goods market equilibrium schedule

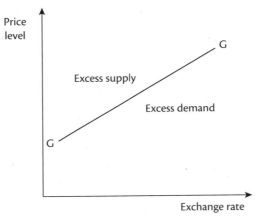

Derivation of the money market equilibrium schedule

The money market schedule shows different combinations of the price level and exchange rate that are consistent with equilibrium in the money market; that is, equilibrium of the supply and demand for money. To derive the money market schedule we first of all invert the money demand function equation (12.14) to solve for the domestic interest rate, which yields:

$$r = \frac{m - p + \eta y}{\sigma} \tag{12.23}$$

We then substitute the solution for $E\dot{s}$ in equation (12.16) into equation (12.18) and replace the solution for r in equation (12.23) to obtain:

$$s = \bar{s} - \frac{1}{\sigma \Theta} [p - m + \eta y - \sigma r^*] \tag{12.24}$$

This means that the slope of the money market schedule is given by:

$$\frac{dp}{ds} = -\sigma \Theta \tag{12.25}$$

Hence the money market schedule (MM) is shown to have a negative slope in the price level–exchange rate plane as shown in **Figure 12.12**.

The explanation is that for a given money stock, a fall in the price level implies a relatively high real money stock, and high real money balances will only be willingly held if the domestic interest rate falls. A fall in the domestic interest rate requires an expected appreciation of the currency to compensate holders of the domestic currency. Given that exchange rate expectations are regressive, such an expected appreciation can only occur if the exchange rate depreciates.

Equilibrium of the model occurs when both the goods and money markets are in equilibrium and the exchange rate is at its PPP value as shown in **Figure 12.13**. The PPP line is depicted as a ray from the origin, indicating that if the domestic price level increases by x per cent then the exchange rate must also depreciate by x per cent to maintain PPP. The GG schedule as we have seen is less steep than the PPP line because an x per cent rise in the price level needs to be accompanied by a greater-

Figure 12.12   The money market equilibrium schedule

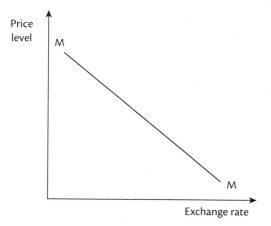

Figure 12.13   Equilibrium in the Dornbusch model

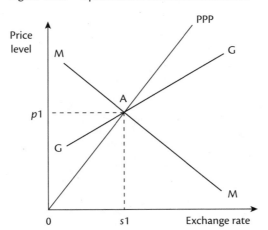

than-x per cent depreciation of the exchange rate. The money market schedule is given by MM, and it is assumed that the money market is in continuous equilibrium so that the economy is always somewhere on the MM schedule. The economy is in full equilibrium when the exchange rate corresponds to PPP, aggregate supply equals aggregate demand and there is asset–market equilibrium. This occurs where all three schedules intersect at point A.

We are now in a position to consider the effects of an economic shock such as an increase in the domestic money supply in the Dornbusch model.

12.16 A money supply expansion and exchange rate overshooting

The effects of an x per cent increase in the money supply in the context of the Dornbusch model are illustrated in **Figure 12.14**. Initially the economy is in full equilibrium at point A where the G1G1 schedule intersects the M1M1 schedule. Let us now suppose that the authorities unexpectedly expand the money supply by x per cent. Before examining the short-run effects of the money expansion it is worth considering what will be the long-run effects. In the long run, we know that domestic prices will rise by the same percentage as the rise in the money stock, and this gives a long-run price of $\bar{p}$ which is x per cent above $p1$. As PPP holds in the long run, a rise in the domestic price level of x per cent requires a depreciation of the exchange rate by x per cent, which gives a long-run exchange rate $\bar{s}$. Bearing this in mind, we can now consider the short-run effects of the monetary expansion.

In the short run, the x per cent increase in the money supply results in a rightward shift of the M1M1 schedule to M2M2. We know that the M2M2 schedule must pass through the long-run equilibrium price $\bar{p}$ and the long-run exchange rate $\bar{s}$ at point C. The major feature of the Dornbusch model is that domestic prices are sticky in the short run, while money markets are in continuous equilibrium as indicated by the UIP condition. In the context of **Figure 12.14** this means the economy is always on the new money market equilibrium schedule M2M2. As domestic prices do not initially change, the price level remains at $p1$ and this is consistent with a jump in the exchange rate from $s1$ to $s2$ on the money market equilibrium schedule M2M2. The

Figure 12.14   Exchange rate overshooting

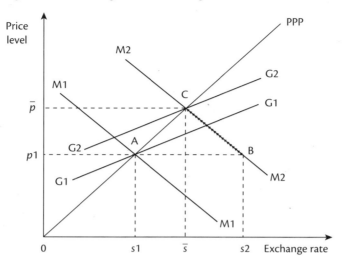

fact that the short-run equilibrium exchange rate $s2$ exceeds the long-run equilibrium rate $\bar{s}$ is known as the phenomenon of exchange rate overshooting.

The reason why in the short run the exchange rate overshoots its long-run equilibrium value is as follows. Given that domestic prices are fixed in the short run, the money supply expansion creates an excess of real money balances which (given a fixed output level) are only willingly held at a lower domestic interest rate. According to the UIP condition, a fall in the domestic interest rate means that international investors will require an expected appreciation of the domestic currency to compensate for the lower domestic interest rate. An expected appreciation of the domestic currency is only possible if the exchange rate depreciation in the short run exceeds the required long-run depreciation. This is shown in **Figure 12.11** by the fact that the exchange rate depreciates from $s1$ to $s2$, overshooting the long-run equilibrium exchange rate $\bar{s}$. The exchange rate is then expected to appreciate from $s2$ to $\bar{s}$.

Having had a short-run jump in the exchange rate to point B on the M2M2 schedule, forces come into play to move the economy along the M2M2 schedule over time from point B to the long-run point C. There are two factors at work in the movement from B to C, during which time the currency appreciates from $s2$ to its long-run equilibrium value $\bar{s}$ and the price level rises from $p1$ to its long-run value $\bar{p}$. First, the reduced domestic interest rate will encourage increased expenditure; second, the undervaluation of the currency in relation to its PPP value will mean that domestic goods become relatively cheap as compared to foreign goods and this leads to a substitution of world demand in favour of domestic goods which Dornbusch identifies as the 'arbitrage effect'. These two factors work to shift up the goods market expenditure schedule from G1G1 to G2G2, and drive up the domestic price level and appreciate the exchange rate until the long-run equilibrium is established at point C. During the transition, the rise in the price level reduces real money balances, requiring a rise in the domestic interest rate until at $r1$ the original interest rate is restored and there is no expected change in the exchange rate.

12.17   Importance of the Dornbusch overshooting model

The Dornbusch overshooting model represented a major advance in the exchange rate literature and it has had lasting appeal. The major innovation of the model is its emphasis on capital-market rather than goods-market arbitrage, being the major determinant of exchange rates in the short run. Goods-market arbitrage is viewed as relevant to exchange rate determination only in the medium to long run, while the desire of investors to equalize expected yields on their international portfolios is viewed as the major determinant of the short-run exchange rate.

The model provides an intuitively appealing explanation of why exchange rate movements have been large relative to movements in international prices and changes in international money stocks. Furthermore, it explains such movements as the outcome of a rational foreign exchange market that produces an exchange rate that deviates from PPP based on economic fundamentals not in isolation from them. Most economists find it hard to accept the notion that observed divergences of exchange rates from PPP have been due to irrational speculation. The existence of models such as Dornbusch's that explain such deviations as the result of rational speculation provide considerable comfort.

Another important point coming from the Dornbusch model is that it helps explain why observed exchange rates are usually even more volatile than supposed determinants such as the money supply. Since the exchange rate initially depreciates by more than x per cent in the short run in response to an x per cent increase in the money supply, it follows that the exchange rate will be more volatile than domestic monetary policy.

12.18   The Frankel real interest rate differential model

The Dornbusch sticky-price monetary model represents a major advance on the flexible-price monetary exchange rate model but, unlike the former, the Dornbusch model does not explicitly take into account inflationary expectations. However, the 1970s period of floating exchange rates was dominated by inflation. In a bid to combine the inflationary expectations element of the flexible-price monetary model with the insights of the sticky-price model, Frankel (1979) developed a general monetary exchange rate model that accommodates the flexible-price and sticky-price monetarist models as special cases.

As in the other monetarist models, there is a conventional money demand function:

$$m - p = \eta y - \sigma r \tag{12.26}$$

where m is the log of the domestic money stock; p is the log of the domestic price level; y is the log of domestic real income; and r is the nominal domestic interest rate.

Similar relationships are postulated for the rest of the world as represented by the foreign country:

$$m^* - p^* = \eta y^* - \sigma r^* \tag{12.27}$$

where an asterisk represents a foreign variable.

For simplicity it is also assumed that elasticities (η and σ) are identical across countries. Combining (12.26) and (12.27) yields:

$$(m - m^*) = (p - p^*) + \eta(y - y^*) - \sigma(r - r^*) \tag{12.28}$$

Like the other monetarist models, the theory assumes that domestic and foreign bonds are perfect substitutes so that the uncovered interest parity condition holds:

$$E\dot{s} = r - r^* \tag{12.29}$$

where $E\dot{s}$ is the expected rate of depreciation of the home currency.

As in the Dornbusch model, it is assumed that the expected rate of depreciation of the exchange rate is a positive function of the gap between the current (spot) rate s and the long-run equilibrium rate $\bar{s}$. In addition, it is also a function of the expected long-run inflation differential between the domestic and foreign economies. This yields:

$$E\dot{s} = \Theta(\bar{s} - s) + P\dot{e} - P\dot{e}^* \tag{12.30}$$

where Θ is the speed of adjustment to equilibrium; $P\dot{e}$ is the expected long-run domestic inflation rate; and $P\dot{e}^*$ is the expected long-run foreign inflation rate.

Equation (12.30) states that in the short run the spot exchange rate as given by s is expected to return to its long-run equilibrium value $\bar{s}$ at a rate Θ. In the long run, since $s = \bar{s}$, the expected rate of depreciation of the currency is equal to the difference of the domestic to foreign inflation via the relative PPP condition. Combining equations (12.29) and (12.30) yields:

$$s - \bar{s} = -\frac{1}{\Theta}[(r - P\dot{e}) - (r^* - P\dot{e}^*)] \tag{12.31}$$

Equation (12.31) states that the gap between the current real exchange rate and its long-run equilibrium value is proportional to the real-interest-rate differential as given by the term in brackets. Thus, if the expected real rate of interest on foreign bonds is greater than the expected real rate of interest on domestic bonds, there will be a real depreciation of the domestic currency as capital flows from domestic to foreign bonds until the real interest rates are equalized in the long-run steady state.

By invoking long-run PPP, the long-run equilibrium exchange rate $\bar{s}$ can be expressed in log form as the difference between the long-run price levels:

$$\bar{s} = \bar{p} - \bar{p}^* \tag{12.32}$$

In the long run the expected real rates of interest are equalized so that any long-run nominal-interest-rate differentials are explained by differences in the steady-state inflation rates:

$$(r - r^*) = (P\dot{e} - P\dot{e}^*) \tag{12.33}$$

By combining (12.33) and (12.32) with equation (12.28) we can obtain an expression for the long-run steady state equilibrium exchange rate given by:

$$\bar{s} = (m - m^*) - \eta(y - y^*) + \sigma(P\dot{e} - P\dot{e}^*) \tag{12.34}$$

Equation (12.34) states that the long-run equilibrium exchange rate is determined by the relative supply $(m - m^*)$ and relative demands as given by $\eta(y - y^*) + \sigma(P\dot{e} - P\dot{e}^*)$ of the two national money stocks. The reader will note that equation (12.35), which refers to the long-run exchange rate, is identical to equation (12.13) of the flexible-price monetarist model for the short-run exchange rate. However, the solution for the short-run exchange rate in the Frankel model differs because of sticky prices in the short run. We now proceed to find the solution for the short-run exchange rate in the Frankel model.

In the Frankel generalization of the Dornbusch model, the speed of adjustment of the goods market is relevant to the determination of the short-run exchange rate, so that equation (12.31) has to be taken into account when solving for the short-run exchange rate. Combining equations (12.34) and (12.31) and rearranging terms yields the following solution for the short-run exchange rate:

$$s = (m - m^*) - \eta(y - y^*) + \sigma(P\dot{e} - P\dot{e}^*)$$
$$- \frac{1}{\Theta}[(r - P\dot{e}) - (r^* - P\dot{e}^*)] \tag{12.35}$$

The Frankel formulation makes clear that if there is a disequilibrium set of real interest rates, then the real exchange rate will deviate from its long-run equilibrium value. If the real domestic interest rate is below the real foreign interest rate then the real exchange rate of the domestic currency will be undervalued in relation to its long-run equilibrium value, so that there is an expected appreciation of the real exchange rate of the domestic currency to compensate.

The fully-flexible-price monetarist school argues that all markets clear instantaneously, so that the speed of adjustment parameter Θ in equation (12.35) is infinite and the solution for the short-run exchange rate is given by equation (12.13). In the real-interest model, as portrayed by equation (12.35), the goods and labour market prices are assumed to be slow to adjust to shocks so the speed of adjustment parameter Θ is finite. Thus, rational expectation holds for the foreign exchange market but not for domestic markets. In such circumstances, an unanticipated monetary expansion leads to a fall in the real domestic interest rate relative to the real foreign interest rate, while the domestic price level is initially unchanged but expected to rise. The result according to equation (12.35) is that the short-run exchange rate overshoots its long-run equilibrium value, depreciating proportionately more than the increase in the money stock so that there are expectations of a future real appreciation of the currency to compensate for the lower real rate of return on domestic bonds.

12.19   Conclusions

At the time of the adoption of floating exchange rates it was widely believed that they would adjust in line with changes in national price level as predicted by PPP theory. However, the experience with floating rates has shown that there can be substantial and prolonged deviations of exchange rates from PPP. A clear conclusion is that in the short to medium term, international goods arbitrage is nowhere near as powerful as proponents of PPP had presupposed.

One of the most plausible explanations for these deviations from PPP is that the theory relies too heavily on goods arbitrage and has no role for the international capital movements which have grown enormously in scale since the end of the Second World War. Such capital movements are heavily influenced by prospective returns and therefore agents' expectations about the future. As expectations change, then so will exchange rates, regardless of whether goods prices are changing.

Nonetheless, the fact that PPP does not hold very well in the short to medium term does not mean that it has no role to play in exchange rate determination. Over- or undervaluation of currencies in relation to PPP induces changes in current-account positions which will eventually lead to exchange rate changes. It is the case that deviations from PPP do have a habit of reversing themselves over the longer run. Furthermore, although exchange rates may diverge substantially from PPP, if the break in this link becomes too large the forces of goods arbitrage do start to come into play and move the exchange rate towards its PPP value.

The most important factor in determining the short-run value of a currency is expectations about the future value of the currency. What people expect to happen to the exchange rate will play a crucial part in determining which currencies to buy and sell; if a currency is expected to depreciate then agents will tend to switch out of that currency into currencies that they expect to appreciate. The monetary models start from the observation that the exchange rate is the price of one money in terms of another. However, the monetary models go beyond this simple observation to argue that exchange rate movements can be explained by changes in the supply and demand for national money stocks. Expectations are heavily influenced by the current and prospective future monetary policy and in the sticky-price monetary models there are fundamental differences between 'sticky'-price goods markets and 'flexible'-price foreign exchange markets. In such circumstances, changes in monetary policy and interest rates can lead to rapid changes in expectations and thereby result in substantial rational movements in exchange rates.

Further reading

McDonald, R. (2007) *Exchange Rate Economics: Theories and Evidence*, Routledge.

Moosa, I. and Bhatti, R. (eds) (2009) *Theory and Empirics of Exchange Rates*, World Scientific Publishing.

Pilbeam, K.S. (2006) *International Finance*, Palgrave Macmillan.

Rosenberg, M. (2003) *Exchange Rate Determination: Models and Strategies for Exchange Rate Forecasting*, McGraw-Hill.

Sarno, L. and Taylor, M.P. (2002) *The Economics of Exchange Rates*, Cambridge University Press.

Chapter 12	Revision questions

1   A computer costs $1,500 in the USA and the same computer costs €1,800 in Europe. The spot exchange rate is $1.30/€1. What is the appropriate dollar per euro exchange rate according to absolute PPP? Is the US dollar spot rate overvalued, undervalued or correctly valued according to absolute PPP?

2   The US inflation rate is predicted to be 9 per cent and the UK inflation rate is predicted to be 4 per cent. The current dollar–pound exchange rate is $1.70/£1. What is the expected dollar per pound rate in one year's time according to relative PPP?

3   The UK interest rate is 4 per cent, the US interest rate is 7 per cent and the spot exchange rate is $1.70/£1. Is the pound expected to appreciate or depreciate? What is the expected dollar per pound rate in one year's time according to UIP?

4   Briefly explain what happens in the flexible price monetary model if there is an increase in the domestic money supply.

5   Briefly explain what will happen in the Dornbusch overshooting model if there is an increase in the domestic money supply.

 Multiple choice questions available at www.palgrave.com/business/pilbeam

13

FINANCIAL FUTURES

Learning objectives

In this chapter you will learn about:

- different types of financial futures contracts including stock index futures, interest rate futures and currency futures
- differences between futures and forward contracts
- initial and variation margin payments
- how to measure open interest and reversing trades
- how futures can be used for speculative and hedging purposes
- how to manage risk exposure on futures contracts
- how different futures contracts are priced

13.1 Introduction

futures contract
a standardized
agreement between
two parties to buy/
sell something at a
predetermined price
at a predetermined
date in the future

A financial futures contract is an agreement between two counterparties to exchange a specified amount of a financial security (bond, bill, currency or stock) at a fixed future date at a predetermined price. The contract specifies the amount of the asset to be traded, the exchange on which the contract is traded, the delivery date and the process for delivery of the asset and funds. Financial futures contracts were first traded on the Chicago Mercantile Exchange (CME) in the USA in 1972. A decade later London opened the London International Financial Futures Exchange (LIFFE) which in 2001 was merged with the Amsterdam, Paris and Belgium exchanges to create Euronext.LIFFE. Since then Euronext has also merged with the Lisbon Stock Exchange.

Futures contracts have proved very popular for both commodities and financial assets. Among the most popular commodity contracts are futures in gold, oil, cotton and coffee, and for financial futures contracts the most popular are short-term and long-term interest rate contracts, currency contracts and stock-index contracts.

Like other financial instruments, futures and forward contracts can be used for both managing risks and assuming speculative positions. We shall examine three different types of futures contract: (i) short-term interest rate futures, (ii) currency futures, and (iii) stock-index futures. We shall consider how each contract can be used for both speculative and hedging purposes and the pricing of each contract.

13.2 The growth of futures exchanges

There has been an astonishing growth of futures markets as illustrated in **Table 13.1**.

Table 13.1   Turnover of futures contracts traded on international exchanges (numbers of contracts in millions)

Instruments	1990	1995	2000	2005	2008
Interest rate	219.1	561.0	781.2	2,110.4	2,582.9
Currency	29.7	99.6	43.6	143.0	433.8
Equity index	39.4	114.8	225.2	918.7	2,467.9
All markets	288.2	775.4	1050.0	3,172.1	5,485.6

Source: Bank for International Settlements

Reasons for the rapid growth of futures markets

The volatility of foreign exchange markets and interest rates following the collapse of the Bretton Woods system of fixed exchange rates which operated between 1949 and 1972, combined with greater freedom of movement of capital internationally, has created a large demand on the part of companies, investors, fund managers and the like for a means to cope with the greater volatility and risk. As we shall see, futures markets for interest rates, currency and stock indices provide a cheap and flexible means of managing risk exposure. The main reasons for the popularity of futures contracts are:

1   Futures markets offer a low-cost means of managing risk exposure. Many futures markets are more liquid than the spot market in the underlying asset. For example, there are an enormous amount of outstanding UK government bond issues but only one UK bond futures contract; the high degree of liquidity in the bond futures contract keeps transaction costs for trading in bonds down.

2   Futures markets enable traders to take speculative positions on price movements for a low initial cash payment (see Section 13.6).

3   Futures contracts enable traders to take short positions, that is, sell something they do not own, with considerable ease. This means that taking positions on price falls is made as easy as taking positions on price rises. For example, if a speculator feels the stockmarket will fall below the futures price of 4,200 he can sell a future contract on the stockmarket index; if the future index subsequently falls to 4,000 he will receive a cash profit based on the difference of 200 index points. Without the futures market only participants who currently own a portfolio of stocks that make up the index, or who are able to borrow stock, will be in a position to take advantage of expected price falls.

4   Unlike forward contracts where there is a degree of counterparty risk, all futures contracts are guaranteed by the exchange on which they are traded.

> **counterparty risk**
> the risk that a counterparty to a contract will fail to settle the contract

13.3   Comparison between futures and forward contracts

Financial futures and forward contracts are basically very similar financial instruments; they are both agreements to make an exchange of an underlying asset between two parties at an agreed price at some time in the future. One party agrees to sell the underlying asset (go short) and the other party agrees to purchase the asset (go long). **Table 13.2** summarizes the main similarities and differences between currency forwards and currency futures contracts. However, despite their high degree of similarity there are some practical differences between forward and futures contracts.

1   A futures contract is a standardized notional agreement between two counterparties to exchange a specified amount of an asset at a fixed future date for a predetermined price. For example, a currency futures contract may specify £62,500 per contract being bought or sold. With a forward contract, the amount to be exchanged is negotiable between the two parties, for example the two parties can agree to buy/sell say £73,160 forward.

Table 13.2   Similarities and differences between currency forwards and futures

Forwards	Futures
An agreement to exchange currencies at some time in the future	An agreement to exchange currencies at some time in the future
Large range of delivery dates	Limited range of delivery dates
Amount to be exchanged is negotiable	Contracts are for standardized amounts
Each party faces some counterparty risk	Contracts are guaranteed by the futures exchange
No margin is required	Initial margin required Variation margin may be called for
Obligation cannot be easily sold on to a third party	Obligation can be easily sold on to a third party
Buying and selling via screen-based market	Buying and selling mostly around the pit on an open outcry system
Usual contract size of at least $5 million	Smaller contract sizes usually around $50,000–$100,000
Covers over 50 currencies	Covers only major currencies
Profit/loss only realizable on maturity of contract	Profit or loss can be realized prior to maturity
Contract is completed by actual delivery of the underlying asset	In around 99% of cases there is no actual delivery since traders enter into reversal trades

2   Futures contracts are traded on an exchange while forward contracts are over-the-counter instruments with the exchange being made directly between two parties.

3   Futures contracts are guaranteed by the exchange whereas forward contracts are not. The fact that the contract is guaranteed by the exchange on which it is traded removes the counterparty risk inherent in forward contracts. With a forward contract each counterparty needs to carefully consider if the losing party will be capable of seeing through their commitment which may involve quite substantial losses. This credit risk tends to limit the forward market to only very high-grade financial and commercial institutions.

4   Futures contracts have greater liquidity than forward contracts. Because of their standardized nature futures contracts can easily be sold to another party at any time up until maturity at the prevailing futures price, with the trader taking a profit or loss. Since forward contract obligations cannot be transferred to a third party they are relatively illiquid assets. The only way for a trader to get out of a forward contract is to take out a new offsetting forward position. For example, if a trader is committed to buying £1 million of sterling forward at $1.50/£1, then the only way out of the forward contract is to take out another forward contract to sell £1 million sterling with another party. However: there are two problems with this: (i) the trader is now exposed to two counterparties (doubling his counterparty risk) and (ii) the maturity date of the second forward contract may not be perfectly matched with that of the first forward contract (for example,

the original forward contract may be for 90 days and, if the trader tries to take an offsetting position 20 days later, the nearest available forward contract would be 60 days, leaving 10 days' open exposure).

13.4   Exchange-traded derivative contracts versus the over-the-counter market

One of the major advantages of exchange-traded futures and options is that the exchange guarantees every contract, thus relieving the parties to a contract of the risk of default. This means that the parties are relieved of the burden of evaluating the creditworthiness of the other party. To protect themselves against the risk of default by the parties to futures and options contracts, exchanges impose substantial capital and stringent margin requirements. Membership requirements and standards are high and members' positions are constantly monitored by the futures exchange. In addition, a futures exchange will maintain a large clearing fund to meet unforeseen circumstances.

Major international banks have for many years marketed the advantages and flexibility of futures and options contracts to their multinational corporate clients. Since multinational corporations have varied demands, not all of which can be matched by exchanges, banks have found it worthwhile to offer tailor-made futures and options contracts to meet the specific needs of their clients. This tailor-made market, which allows for negotiation of the terms of the contract between the buyer and seller of an option, is known as the over-the-counter (OTC) market. The OTC market is dominated by major banks and securities houses, and contrasts with the standardized contracts on offer at the futures and options exchanges. The major advantage of the OTC market is that a client's specific needs with regard to the size, exercise price and expiration date of the contract can be met. However, the OTC market has a number of disadvantages:

> **over-the-counter market** a market where trading does not take place in an organized exchange; contracts are typically tailor-made by a bank or financial institution to meet the specific needs of the buyer

> **exchange clearing house** a separate part of a derivatives exchange which is responsible for settling contracts, monitoring and reporting on trading positions and collecting margin payments; it will also guarantee to fulfil a contract should one party default on its obligations

1   the relatively small number of buyers and sellers means that the contract could be mispriced;
2   the lack of standardization of contracts in the OTC market means that there is only a severely limited secondary market for OTC contracts, that is, OTC instruments lack the liquidity that is a vital part of exchange-traded futures and options; and
3   each party to a contract runs the risk of default on the part of the other party whereas exchange-traded contracts are guaranteed by the exchange. For this reason, only high-quality financial institutions tend to be involved in the OTC market.

13.5   Trading in exchange futures contracts

Exchange-based futures contracts were traditionally sold in a central exchange by an open outcry system. Under this system, traders congregate around a 'pit' on the trading floor of the exchange and contacts are bought and sold within hearing distance of all other traders. Once a contract price is agreed, the traders fill out trading slips which are then matched by the exchange clearing house. Once the clearing house confirms the deal, a futures contract is in existence, and the contract is guaranteed by the exchange. This means that if one of the parties fails to fulfil its obligations then the exchange will assume the defaulting party's obligations, the only credit risk involved is that of the exchange. These days most exchanges use a mix of computer screen-based futures trading and the open outcry system.

13.6 The role of the clearing house

initial margin
the initial deposit paid to an exchange/broker when opening a futures contract or writing an option contract

variation margin
the margin payments required of the losing party to a futures contract to maintain their open position

marking to market
the process of monitoring the profit and loss positions of each party by using the prevailing market price

When a futures contract is taken out between trader A and trader B, the contract is placed through the clearing house of the exchange which guarantees the contract. The clearing house is usually separately incorporated and independent from the exchange. To limit its exposure, exchange regulations require that each counterparty makes an initial deposit with the exchange known as the initial margin (usually between 2 and 10 per cent of the value of the contract). Once the contract involves a party making a loss greater than the initial margin, further deposits are required on a daily basis from the losing party, known as the variation margin, to reflect the potential loss associated with the contract. The marking to market, that is calculation of variation margins, is carried out at the end of each day on the basis of the settlement price (usually this is the closing price). The other party has its profit position credited to its margin account. Since all potential losses have to be paid on a daily basis this limits the exposure of the exchange. In the rare event that a trader fails to settle a margin payment, the exchange has the right to close the trader's position by taking an offsetting contract limiting its potential exposure to that trader's position. A further means by which the exchange limits its exposure is to restrict dealing to members of the exchange who are usually representatives of well established financial institutions.

13.7 Open interest and reversing trades

open interest the outstanding number of futures or options contracts obligated for delivery, i.e. the number of contracts that have not yet been closed

Two important but linked terms that crop up in connection with futures trades are the open interest in a contract and the concept of reversing trades. Open interest is the outstanding number of contracts obligated for delivery. Consider four traders A, B, C and D, none of whom has any current position in a futures contract. If trader A takes a long position in a new contract with trader B taking a short position, then the open interest rises by one contract. Similarly, if trader C takes a long position in a futures contract with trader D taking the short position, then open interest rises by a further one contract.

reversing trade
a trade that closes out a trader's open position at a profit or loss by reversing the original trade at the prevailing market price

For most futures contracts, especially those that involve physical commodities such as gold, cotton and so on, the physical delivery of the commodity would be a cumbersome process. To avoid getting involved in the actual delivery process most traders enter into what is known as a reversing trade prior to the maturity of the contract. That is, they will liquidate their position at the clearing house so that they neither have to actually deliver or actually receive the underlying commodity. In our example, traders A and C are committed to buying the underlying commodity upon expiry, while traders B and D are committed to delivering it upon expiry. Trader A may not actually wish to receive the underlying commodity and trader D may not

Figure 13.1   Typical open interest profile

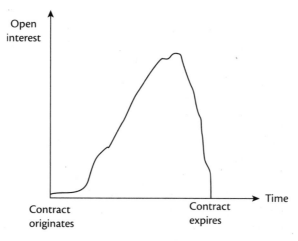

wish to actually deliver it, and hence at some date prior to expiry trader A and trader D will take out reversing trades to liquidate their positions. Trader A will take out a contract to sell the underlying commodity (at the then prevailing market price). As far as the clearing house is concerned, then A will have no net position in the futures market since it has an identical futures contract to both receive and deliver the underlying instrument. If trader A sold his contract to a new party, E, then the open interest would have been left unaffected by A's trade. If, however, trader A had sold his position to trader D who was also undertaking a reversing trade, then open interest would have declined by one since both A and D have effectively negated their positions with the clearing house.

Figure 13.1 shows the typical profile of open interest on futures contracts from the day that trading in the contract is started (contract originates) to the time that the contract expires.

Each contract starts with zero open interest and during the early days of the opening of a futures contract open interest in the contract slowly builds up as the number of new contracts increases. However, eventually open interest in the contract peaks. Thereafter, as the expiry date of the contract nears, the number of traders involved in trade reversals increases so that open interest rapidly declines until the expiry date when open interest falls to zero.

Financial futures contracts cover interest rates, currencies and stock indices. Interest rate futures are used by investors and borrowers of funds to protect themselves against interest-rate fluctuations. We now proceed to examine examples of these various types of contracts and how their prices are derived from arbitrage relationships.

13.8   Stock index futures

A particularly popular type of futures contract is stock-index futures, which are notional commitments to buy or sell a given amount of stock on a specified date in the future at a predetermined price. The amount of stock is a weighted basket of

Table 13.3   S&P 500 index futures, $250 per index point

	Open	Settlement price	Change	High	Low	Estimated volume	Open int.
September	998	1005	+8	1008	995	12,372	375,374
December	991	1000	+8	1002	990	1,640	13,315

(a) Futures settlement prices on 19 August were September: 997, December: 992

(b) The cash S&P 500 on close of business 20 August was 1007 up 9 points on the day. Hence the September futures settlements price is at a discount of 2 points and the December contract at a discount of 7 points.

(c) There is an S&P 500 mini futures contract that trades with much higher volumes and very similar prices but at only $50 a point.

Source: Chicago Mercantile Exchange, 20 August 2009

cash settlement
a method of settling futures or options contracts via a cash transfer between the losing and winning party, rather than actual delivery of the underlying asset/security

opening price the price at which a derivatives contract is trading once the exchange officially opens for business

settlement price
the price at which a security is settled (usually the closing price). For derivatives, it is an important price since the daily settlement price will determine the amount of variation margin that may be required

estimated volume
the daily estimated volume of trades in a security or derivatives contract

nearby contract
the date of the next futures contract due for expiration

shares, and the best-known stock futures indices include the Standard & Poor's 500 in the USA, the Nikkei 225 in Japan, the Financial Times Stock Exchange 100 (FTSE 100), the DAX in Germany, the CAC 40 in France and the Hang Seng index in Hong Kong.

It should be noted that actual delivery of the stock is not required for stock-index futures since this would be impractical. Imagine the cost and hassle of actually delivering in the appropriate value-weighted proportions the 500 stocks that make up the S&P 500 or the 100 shares that make up the FTSE 100 index! For this reason, stock-index futures are settled on a cash settlement basis after due allowance for any variation margin payments that have been made. **Table 13.3** shows typical stock-index futures contracts for the S&P 500 index.

The S&P index is a value-weighted, real-time index made up of 500 of the largest US companies. The weighting system operates on the basis of capitalization so that higher-capitalized companies are given higher weights and on the size of the free float in shares. The index itself is calculated every 15 seconds throughout the trading day which starts at 9:30 am and ends at 4:00 pm.

There are a number of terms in **Table 13.3** that require some explanation. The months listed are the expiration months of the contract, usually the third Friday of each month; in the case of the S&P 500 these are March, June, September and December. The opening price is the price at which contracts began trading in the morning, which is not necessarily the same as the previous day's closing price. The settlement price is the price used for 'marking to market', normally based on the last trade of the day and is the price used to make daily adjustments to the margin accounts. If there were little trade at the end of the day then the settlements committee can set a settlement price that differs from the closing price. The change is the change in price compared to the previous day's settlement price. The high/low figures show the trading range of the contract throughout the day. Estimated volume is the estimated number of contracts exchanged during the day, and open interest is the number of contracts open as of the previous trading day.

The next contract due for delivery is known as the nearby contract (in this case the September contract), and for stock-index futures it is usually the contract that has the largest open interest. However, this will not be the case when it is about to expire since many trade reversals will lead to a rapid decline in the open interest. The other contracts are known as distant or deferred contracts (in this case the

distant contracts
the futures contracts
with longer terms to
expiration than the
nearby contract

most distant contract is the December contract). A tick is the smallest possible price movement on a contract, and in the case of the S&P 500 futures this is 0.01 of a point, with each whole point being worth $250. Each one-point movement in the index is worth $250 and the smallest movement allowed in the contract is 0.01 which is equivalent to $2.50. Since each S&P 500 contract is valued at $250 per index point, then each contract has an equivalent value of $250,000 if the index reads 1000. For a long position on the S&P 500 index each one-point movement of the futures index represents a gain of $250, while for each point the index falls the loss is $250. The settlement of the S&P 500 futures is based on the settlement price on the third Friday of the month of expiration of the contract.

Examples of the use of stock-index futures

Stock-index futures can be used either as a hedge against adverse stock movements or for speculative purposes. Because they are composed of a basket of well known shares they are attractive as a means of hedging for pension funds, mutual funds and other institutional investors that hold a wide variety of shares.

One of the big advantages of a futures contract is that an investor is able to speculate on the movement of 500 companies without having to engage in a substantial cash outlay (other than the initial margin payment). Indeed, for many investors the futures contract enables a large variety of trading positions to be taken on the overall movement of a large number of shares, positions that would otherwise be impractical.

Example 1 Using the S&P 500 for speculating

Imagine that we have two speculators, Mr Bull and Ms Bear, who hold no previous positions in the futures market. It is 20 August, the cash S&P 500 index is 1007 and the December futures is 1000. Mr Bull, having looked at the current position of the US economy, is convinced that the cash S&P 500 index will be considerably higher in three months' time (December), rising from 1007 to say 1200 well above the December futures price of 1000. On the other hand, Ms Bear feels that the market is overvalued and is headed for a fall and predicts that the cash market will fall to 800. As a result Mr Bull buys the futures contract at 1000 and is said to be long futures while Ms Bear will sell the futures at 1000 and is said to be short futures. Both parties will now have to make an initial margin deposit against potential losses. If the initial margin on the contract is set at 50 points then the initial margin deposit by each party will be 50 points × $250 per point = $12,500.

long futures the
position of the buyer
of a futures contract

short futures the
position of the seller
of a futures contract

In **Table 13.4** we show various possible values for the S&P 500 cash index on expiration of the futures contract on the third Friday of December. On the date of expiration of the futures contract the cash and futures index will be identical. In general, the futures premium or discount will narrow over the life of the futures contract and, importantly, on expiration of the future's contract the cash price of the index will be identical to the futures price. This is an important rule with all futures contracts – the cash and futures on expiration will be identical at the time of expiration. Let us assume that Mr Bull and Ms Bear keep open their contracts all the way through to expiration on the third Friday of December when the cash index and futures index will have the same price. If the cash and futures indices have risen

Table 13.4   The profit and loss from speculation on S&P 500 futures

Cash S&P 500 index*	Profit/loss long futures	Profit/loss short futures
700	−$75,000	+$75,000
750	−$62,500	+$62,500
800	−$50,000	+$50,000
850	−$37,500	+$37,500
900	−$25,000	+$25,000
950	−$12,500	+$12,500
1000	$0	$0
1050	+$12,500	−$12,500
1100	+$25,000	−$25,000
1150	+$37,500	−$37,500
1200	+$50,000	−$50,000
1250	+$62,500	−$62,500
1300	+$75,000	−$75,000

* Cash S&P 500 index on third Friday of December equals futures price on expiration.

to expire at 1150 then Mr Bull will have made a profit since he agreed to pay Ms Bear 1000 on the futures contract which is now worth 1150; that is, a profit of 150 points × $250 a point which equals $37,500. Alternatively, if the cash and futures index have risen to expire at 1300 then Mr Bull will have a profit of 300 points × $250 a point which equals $75,000. In the case where Mr Bull makes a profit he is credited with his profit (as we shall see this is equivalent to Ms Bear's loss) and will be returned his initial margin of $12,500.

Of course, Mr Bull might have got it badly wrong and the market has fallen to 800 by expiration, in which case he will pay Ms Bear 1000 even though its market value is 800. In this case he loses 200 points × $250 per point = −$50,000. The more the market falls the more Mr Bull will lose; if the market falls to 700 he will lose 300 points × $250 a point = −$75,000. It should be noted that once the market has fallen so that Mr Bull is facing losses greater than his initial margin the futures exchange will ask him to make variation margin payments approximately equivalent to his losses. For instance, if at the end of October the cash market is reading 854 and the December futures is reading 850, then the exchange will ask Mr Bull to make variation margin payments based on the 150 points fall in the futures. He will be asked to make variation payments of approximately 150 points × $250 = $37,500. The more the market falls the more the variation margin payments Mr Bull will be expected to make. Failure to meet variation margin calls would mean that the exchange or broker responsible for monitoring Mr Bull's position would have the right to close his position at the prevailing market price of the futures contract. This would realise Mr Bull's loss and prevent him from reducing his loss or even making a profit should the market rise.

Trading futures is a 'zero-sum game' in that the profits of one party are equivalent to the losses of the other party. If the futures expires at 1150 then Mr Bull will make 150 points × $250 = $37,500, but his profit is Ms Bear's short futures loss. She sold when the market was at 1000 but it is now worth 1150 so she is selling the contract for less than it is worth and so she loses −150 points × $250 = −$37,500. The more the market rises the more she will lose; if the market rises to 1300 by expiration she will lose −300 points × $250 = −$75,000. Of course, as the market rises, the exchange or broker managing the contract will have chased her for variation margin payments that were approximately equal to her losses. If the futures has risen to 1300 by expiration and if the exchange has $72,000 in variation margin payments, then they will deduct a further $3,000 from Ms Bear's initial margin account so as to have the $75,000 with which to credit Mr Bull, and will return her the balance of $9,500 left in her initial margin account. If they were to have received $75,000 in variation margin payments from her, then they will return the $12,500 of initial margin.

Things could, of course, be much better for Ms Bear if the market falls. Should the futures (and cash) market be reading 800 on expiration then she will make a profit of 200 points × $250 = $50,000, and will also receive back her initial margin deposit of $12,500. Her profit arises because she is selling the market at 1000 to Mr Bull when it is worth only 800, so she is selling it for 200 points more than it is worth. The more the market falls the greater her profits; if the market falls to 700 then she will make 300 points × $250 = $75,000 and will receive all of her initial margin back.

So far we have assumed that both Mr Bull and Ms Bear hold their long and short positions through to expiration on the third Friday of December when they will automatically be closed out at the prevailing futures price. However, let us suppose that we have moved from 20 August to 30 October and that there has been a big upward movement in the market such that the cash S&P 500 index reads 1154 and the December futures reads 1150 (note the futures discount has narrowed from 7 to 4 points). Mr Bull will be quite happy, he bought the futures at 1000 and it is now worth 1150 so he has a potential profit of $37,500. If Mr Bull thinks the market will continue to rise he will probably wish to keep his futures position open and hope to make even more profits. On the other hand, he may be concerned that the market might start to fall back and the futures will move lower, reducing his profits. In such a case he may decide to lock in his profits by closing his position. Since he is long futures, having originally bought the futures contract to close his position, he needs to sell the futures at 1150 (so that he is neither a net buyer nor seller overall). If he sells at 1150 then he will be credited with $37,500 (financed by the variation margin/initial margin payments made by Ms Bear) and returned his initial margin deposit of $12,500.

The next issue is the impact of Mr Bull's sale on the open interest. Since Mr Bull and Ms Bear were new to the market when opening their positions on 20 August then the original buy and sell orders increased the open interest by one contract and the volume traded that day by one contract. If on 30 October Mr Bull closes his position by selling a futures contract and a new party, Mr Stag, with no previous position enters the market to be the buyer then the open interest will not be affected. Ms Bear is still short futures and Mr Stag has replaced Mr Bull as the long futures, so while the trade will increase the trading volume by one contract on 30 October, it will not affect the open interest. If, however, Mr Bull decides to sell on 30 October and on the same day Ms Bear decides to close her position by buying the futures at 1150 (and realising her loss), then, while the volume of trade will have increased by one contract on 30 October, the open interest will fall by one contract. The open interest falls by one contract since both Mr Bull and Ms Bear have closed out their positions, Mr Bull has realised his profit of $37,500 and Ms Bear her loss of -$37,500. Both have reversed their long and short positions by selling and buying respectively, making them each neither a net buyer nor a net seller. In sum, an increase in trading volume by one contract can increase the open interest by one contract, leave the open interest unchanged or decrease the open interest by one contract depending upon the original positions of various traders in the market.

Another point worth emphasizing is that either party to the futures contract can close their position at any time, they do not have to wait for the expiration of the contract or for the other party to close their position. Ms Bear can remain open even if Mr Bull decides to close or *vice versa*. The market price adjusts to ensure buyers and sellers are continually matched, if buyers exceed sellers the futures price rises until an equal number of sellers emerge, while if sellers exceed buyers then the futures price falls until an equal number of buyers emerge.

A final issue worth mentioning is the possibility of taking a futures position with a stop-loss order. Say Mr Bull is bullish on the market but does not wish to risk losses of more than $25,000. When he buys the futures at 1000 he can put in a stop-loss order with his broker to automatically close him out by selling a futures contract if the price of the futures ever hits 900. There is usually a small fee for this service but it means that the loss Mr Bull will face is now limited to approximately $25,000 since the second the market hits 900 or slightly below, such as 899, then the broker will execute an automatic sell order to close Mr Bull's position, so ensuring a loss of $25,000 (futures price 900) or $25,250 (futures price 899). As such, the stop-loss automatically protects Mr Bull from further losses – if the futures price falls to 800 Mr Bull need not worry since he has automatically been stopped out at around 900. While the stop-loss will limit the losses that Mr Bull can suffer, it has one disadvantage: if the futures price temporarily dips to 899 and then swiftly rises to 1050 Mr Bull will not be able to make a profit of $12,500 because his broker will have stopped him out at a loss of $25,000! Normally traders do not set a stop-loss too close to the current market price of the futures for fear of being stopped out at a loss too quickly.

From this example we can see that one of the great things about futures markets is that they enable you to bet on markets falling as well as markets rising. You could be a European investor who thinks the US markets are headed for a fall and can take a bet on that happening by taking a short futures position in the S&P 500 stock-index futures. Alternatively, if you think the Japanese market is going to rise then it is easy to take a long position in the Nikkei 225 futures and if the Nikkei 225 rises then the Nikkei futures will rise with it (pretty much by a similar percentage) and a profit can be made. Stock-index futures give investors and traders quick exposure to a basket of well known stocks speedily and at very low cost.

Stop-loss an order to close out a futures position (or trading position) at a loss when the price of a contract hits a predetermined level

13.9   The symmetry of profits/losses on futures/forward positions

An important point about futures and forward contracts is that the gains or losses of the two parties engaged in the contract are symmetrical around the difference between the future spot price on expiry of the contact and the futures price at which the contract was taken out. This is illustrated for the case of the stock-index futures for the S&P 500 in **Figure 13.2**.

Figure 13.2   The profits/losses on a forward/futures contract

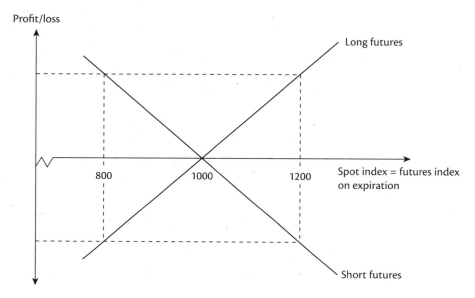

In **Figure 13.2** the December S&P 500 futures contract is taken out at a price of 1000. Mr Bull, the long futures, has agreed to buy the market at 1000 and Ms Bear, the short futures, has agreed to sell the market at 1000. On the horizontal axis we have the future spot price of the S&P 500 upon expiration, which is the same as the futures price at that time, and the vertical axis depicts the corresponding profit or loss. If the futures price on expiration is above 1000 the long futures makes $250 per point, so at 1200 the long futures makes $50,000. If, however, the spot price on maturity is 800 the long futures will lose $50,000. The gain (or loss) of the long futures party is mirrored by the corresponding loss (or gain) of the short futures party. One party to a forward/futures contract is always likely to lose in the sense that the future spot price on expiration will generally differ from the price agreed in the futures contact. From **Figure 13.2** we can see that the payoff to both parties is very symmetrical around the original 1000 futures price.

Example 2 Using the S&P 500 for hedging

Consider the case of a pension fund manager in August that has a $50 million pension fund mainly invested in S&P 500 shares. The fund manager fears the pension fund could be adversely affected by a fall in the S&P 500 index in the period up to December. The value of the fund tends to move very much in line with the S&P 500 index. The current level of the S&P 500 is 1007 and the December S&P 500 futures index is reading 1000, with the fund manager fearing that by December the S&P 500 index could be around the 800 level.

The fund manager fears that if the S&P 500 index falls from 1007 to 800 then the $50 million pension fund may be worth only:

$$\frac{800}{1007} \times \$50 \text{ million} = \$37,721,945$$

Hence the fund could lose potentially $10,278,055 of its value. In this instance, the fund manager could protect his fund by selling December futures contracts at 1000 and then buying them back at 800, thus making a profit of $200 \times \$250 = \$50,000$ per contract sold. To calculate the number of contracts that need to be sold to hedge against the risk of stockmarket fall we take the potential loss and divide it by the corresponding profit per contract, that is:

$$\frac{\$10,278,055}{\$50,000} = 206 \text{ contracts}$$

In this instance, the fund manager needs to sell approximately 206 S&P 500 futures contracts. If the S&P 500 index has fallen in December to 800, then the value of the shares held by the fund will be worth approximately $39,721,945 ($50 million × 800/1007). However, the fund manager will be able to close the S&P 500 contract by buying 206 contracts at 800 (on expiry the futures and cash market indices coincide), thus gaining $206 \times \$50,000 = \$10,300,000$. This will mean that his total portfolio is worth $39,721,945 + $10,300,000 = $50,021,945 and the fund will have been protected from a fall in the S&P 500 index.

We should note that in the above example the fund manager, having taken a short position in the futures index, is still entitled to dividends on the underlying fund in the interim, and hence the fund will be worth more than we have suggested. Also, the fund manager is not necessarily achieving a perfect hedge by using stock-index futures. His portfolio may differ from the S&P 500 index and changes in the dividend–yield and interest-rate relationship may mean that the forward index does not move exactly in line with the underlying cash market. Of course, we should also note that if the S&P 500 index actually rises to say 1,200 by December, then the fund manager will have a loss on the futures contracts sold ($206 \times -\$50,000 = -\$10,300,000$). However, against this the value of the shares held by the pension fund will have risen to approximately $(1200/1007) \times \$50$ million $= \$59,582,219$ enabling virtually all the losses on the futures contract to be covered and giving a net position of approximately $49,282,915. Of course, the fund will not then have participated in the rise of the stockmarket.

Example 3 The use of stock indices for asset allocation

A UK fund manager holds UK equities, UK bonds and cash in a ratio of 60:30:10. He has decided to adjust the position as quickly as possible to 70:20:10 in order to take advantage of a perceived likely rise in the stockmarket and a rise in long-term interest rates. The simplest thing to do is to take a long position on the FTSE futures and a short position on the bond futures. If all goes to plan there will be a gain on both the long futures and short bond positions. Over time, the underlying fund can be changed and the futures positions unwound at a profit.

13.10 The pricing of stock index futures

In a normal futures contract, the futures price exceeds the spot price by the rate which is equivalent to the cost of financing a position in the cash market. In the case of the futures index we have to look at the net financing cost. Holders of the underlying stock receive dividends which reduces the cost of financing a position in the underlying stocks. Hence, it is possible for a futures stock index to be priced at a discount to the cash price when the expected dividend yield on holding the stock is less than the cost of financing the cash position as represented by the rate of interest on borrowing.

The appropriate arbitrage model for the pricing of the futures index is given by:

$$FSI_{t,T} = CSI_{t,T} + \left[CSI_{t,T} \times (r_{t,T} - d_{t,T}) \times \frac{T-t}{365} \right] \qquad (13.1)$$

where $FSI_{t,T}$ is the stock-index futures price at time t with a settlement date T; $CSI_{t,T}$ is the price of the cash stock index at time t; $r_{t,T}$ is the annualized cost of finance for the period between t and T; and $d_{t,T}$ is the expected average dividend yield on the stocks that make up the cash index during the holding period.

Equation (13.1) indicates that when the annualized cost of finance exceeds the expected dividend yield ($r_{t,T} > d_{t,T}$) then the futures index price will exceed the cash index; that is, it will be at a premium to the cash index. When the annualized cost of finance is less than the expected dividend yield ($r_{t,T} < d_{t,T}$) then the futures index price will be less than the cash index; that is, it will be at a discount to the cash index. Since interest rates are usually higher than dividend yields, the futures index usually trades at a premium to the spot index.

Another point to note is that as the time to maturity approaches, that is $T - t$ reduces, then the difference between the cash price and the futures price reduces (assuming the interest rate and dividend yield are unchanged) and on the day of expiry the futures price will coincide with the cash price.

Numerical example of pricing of futures

On 20 August 2009 the S&P 500 cash index was 1007, the borrowing cost of funds based on the three-month Treasury bill rate was approximately 0.2 per cent. The expected annualized dividend yield was approximately 2.5 per cent based upon the historical dividend yield and the carrying period ($T - t$) is 120 days:

$$FSI_{t,T} = CSI_{t,T} + \left[CSI_{t,T} \times (R_{t,T} - d_{t,T}) \times \frac{T-t}{365} \right]$$

$$= 1007 + \left[1007 \times (0.002 - 0.025) \times \frac{120}{365} \right]$$

$$= 999.38$$

The actual December futures price of 1000 is very close to the results we would expect. In the above example, the stock-index futures is below the cash index because the assumed rate of interest is less than the dividend yield. Normally interest rates are higher than the dividend yield so stock-index futures are normally higher than the related cash index. (The extraordinarily low US interest rate of 0.2 per cent in this example results from the Federal Reserve's monetary easing in response to the credit crunch (see Chapter 17).)

13.11   Short-term interest rate futures

interest rate future
an agreement between two parties to lend/borrow a certain amount of money at a predetermined rate of interest for a specified period of time at a predetermined date in the future

An interest rate future is a commitment to borrow or lend a predetermined sum of money at a specified future date at a predetermined rate of interest. Short-term interest rate futures contracts are quoted on an index basis, and **Table 13.5** shows a Euro interest futures contract traded on Euronext.LIFFE. The contract size is for €1 million. The index is quoted as 100 minus the annualized rate of interest.

For example, the December 2011 contract is quoted as settling at 97.00, which means that at the close of business on 25 August 2009 the contract was specifying that the buyer is lending €1 million to the seller of the contract (the borrower) for three months from the contract date in December 2011 at 100 − 97.00 = 3.00 per cent.

In the case of the Euribor futures contract, the smallest tick movement is 0.005 which means that each 0.005 point movement on the contract is worth €12.50, that is €1,000,000 × 0.00005 × 0.25 = €12.50. So each basis point movement, that is 0.01 movement is worth €25 (0.01 = 2 × 0.005). A movement in the price of a three-month futures contract from say 97.00 to 97.20 represents a change of 20 basis points or equivalently 20 × €25.00.

Table 13.5   Three-month Euribor (LIFFE), €1 million

	Open	Sett.	Change	High	Low	Est. vol.	Open int.
Dec 2009	99.085	99.095	+0.010	99.100	99.075	63,438	537,550
Mar 2010	98.880	98.885	+0.010	98.895	98.845	58,747	446,878
Jun 2010	98.520	98.540	+0.010	98.550	98.475	73,596	382,776
Sep 2010	98.140	98.180	+0.030	98.185	98.095	68,654	270,093
Dec 2010	97.795	97.845	+0.045	97.850	97.750	67,834	253,662
Mar 2011	97.540	97.585	+0.055	97.595	97.495	24,519	163,632
Jun 2011	97.315	97.355	+0.050	97.365	97.270	22,616	147,424
Sep 2011	97.140	97.175	+0.050	97.185	97.100	7,385	87,563
Dec 2011	96.965	97.000	+0.050	97.020	96.935	8,590	59,613
Mar 2012	96.865	96.905	+0.050	96.915	96.840	3,544	47,126
Jun 2012	96.760	96.790	+0.045	96.800	96.730	4,980	32,406
Sep 2012	96.655	96.690	+0.040	97.700	96.655	2,582	10,757
Dec 2012	96.550	96.580	+0.035	96.580	96.550	570	6,724

Notes: Estimated volumes and open interest refer to previous trading day.

Source: Euronext.Liffe, 26 August 2009

Numerical example of Euribor futures used for hedging

Imagine that a corporate treasurer is expecting to have €1 million in December 2011 for three months but is fearful that interest rates will be only 2 per cent in December 2011 and would therefore like to take advantage of the 3.00 per cent from the December 2011 futures contract. The treasurer will be able to guarantee an interest rate of 3.00 per cent for three months by buying the December 2011 Euribor futures contract. The selling party is agreeing to borrow €1 million in December 2011 for three months at 3.00 per cent. The purchase of the Euribor futures contract guarantees the corporate treasurer an interest rate of 3.00 per cent for three months from December 2011, even if the annualized three-month interest rate happens to be only 2 per cent in December 2011.

Imagine that the treasurer's fears are realized and in December 2011 the euro three-month interest rate is 2 per cent. Then he can only deposit €1 million at 2 per cent in the cash markets for 3 months, which will become $0.25 \times 0.02 \times €1,000,000$ which is €5,000 of interest (remember only one-quarter of the 2 per cent is obtainable after three months). But the treasurer will have a profit by selling the futures contract at 98 (100 − 98 = 2 per cent − recall that cash equals futures so if cash interest rates are 2 per cent in December 2011 then the futures price must be 98 on expiration). As such, the treasurer will make 100 basis points (1 basis point = 0.01 per cent) by selling the futures previously purchased at 97.00 for 98. Since each basis point is worth €25 he will make a profit of $100 \times €25 = €2,500$. So in total the treasurer will get €7,500 (€5,000 interest + €2,500 profit from the futures contract), which is what €1,000,000 would earn after three months at 3.00 per cent ($€1,000,000 \times 0.25 \times 0.03 = €7,500$). By buying a futures contract the treasurer is hedging against the risk of a downward fall in interest rates.

Numerical example of Euribor futures used for speculating

Imagine that a speculator believes that interest rates on the euro in December 2011 will be only 2 per cent, which is lower than the implied 3.00 per cent rate of interest of the December 2009 futures contract. This means that the speculator is predicting that the value of the Euribor futures contract will be 98 in December 2011. Hence the speculator will buy a December 2011 futures contract. If the speculator is proved right and the annualized three-month euro interest rate is 2 per cent in December 2011 then the futures contract will be valued at 98 (cash = futures on expiration so futures expires at 100 − 2.00 = 98.00). The speculator will make a profit by having bought the contract at 97.00 and closing out the contract by selling at 98.00, making 100 basis points or $100 \times €25 = €2,500$. If however the speculator is badly wrong and in fact the annualized three-month euro interest rate is 5 per cent in December 2011 then the futures contract will be valued at 95.00 and the speculator will make a loss by having bought the contract at 97.00 and closing out the contract by selling at 95.00, making a loss of 200 basis points or $200 \times €25 = €5,000$.

There is another way of looking at the speculator's profit/loss potential in the above example. Since the speculator, by buying the December 2011 contract, is effectively agreeing to lend €1 million at 3.00 per cent for three months then the speculator is effectively expecting to receive funds equivalent to receiving €1,07,500 in March 2012 (that is, €1 million plus 3.00 per cent/4 = 0.75 per cent since only one-quarter of 3.00 per cent will be earned over three months). If the annualized three-month interest rate on the euro in December 2011 is only 2 per cent as the speculator predicts then €1 million would only have become €1,005,000 in March 2012 (that is, €1 million plus 2%/4 = 0.5 per cent since only one-quarter of 2 per cent will be earned over three months). By taking out a long position in the futures contract the speculator makes a profit of €2,500 (€1,007,500 − €1,005,000).

If, however, the annualized three-month interest rate on euros in December 2011 is 5 per cent, contrary to the speculator's prediction, then the speculator has pre-committed to earning only 3.00 per cent; that is, to have only £1,007,500 in March 2012. Whereas if the speculator had not taken out the contract with euro interest rate at 5 per cent, €1 million would have become €1,012,500 in March 2012 (that is, €1 million plus 5%/4 = 1.25 per cent since only one-quarter of 5 per cent will be earned over three months). By taking out a long position in the futures contract the speculator makes a loss of €5,000 (€1,012,500 − €1,007,500).

13.12 The pricing of a Euribor interest rate futures contract

The pricing of interest rate futures contracts is based on arbitrage conditions. In particular, the price of a futures interest-rate contract is determined by the so-called forward/forward rate, given by:

$$Z\% = \left[\left(\frac{1 + [r_d \times (t_d/365)]}{1 + [r_n \times (t_n/365)]} \right) - 1 \right] \times \frac{365}{t_d - t_n} \qquad (13.2)$$

where Z per cent is the interest rate implicit in the futures contract; r_d is the interest rate on the distant forward/forward period; r_n is the interest rate on the near forward/forward period; t_d is the number of days remaining to the distant forward/forward period; and t_n is the number of days remaining to the near forward/forward period.

Numerical example

Assume the three-month interest rate is 4 per cent per annum while the six-month interest rate is 5 per cent per annum. The three-month contract has 91 days to expiry and the six-month contract 182 days to expiry. The forward/forward rate is given by:

$$Z\% = \left[\left(\frac{1 + [0.05 \times (182/365)]}{1 + [0.04 \times (91/365)]} \right) - 1 \right] \times \frac{365}{182 - 91}$$

$$= 0.0594 \quad \text{or} \quad 5.94 \text{ per cent}$$

Therefore the appropriate three-months-ahead futures price is 100 − 5.94 = 94.06.

To fully understand why this forward/forward rate is the appropriate price for the futures contract let us consider the cash flows. At an interest rate of 5.94 per cent, investors would not be able to find any arbitrage possibilities. Suppose that a trader invests €1,000,000 for six months at 5 per cent per annum; this means that he will receive €1,025,000 at the end of six months. Alternatively, he could invest the money for three months at 4 per cent, which means he would receive €1,010,000 in three months' time. He could then lend the money by selling a euro futures contract at 5.94 per cent for three months so that the €1,010,000 becomes €1,025,000, which is identical to leaving the funds on deposit for six months. If three-months-ahead futures prices were different, say below the forward/forward rate at 92, then it would pay arbitrageurs to borrow long and lend short by buying a futures contract to guarantee the future interest rate of 8 per cent. By borrowing €1,000,000 at 5 per cent for six months the arbitrageur would have to eventually repay €1,025,000. At the same time, he could lend money for three months at 4 per cent so would receive €1,010,000, and also buy a three-month futures contract at 92 so he would earn 8 per cent and so would receive €1,010,000 × 1.02, that is €1,030,200. The guaranteed profit is €5,200, and such an arbitrage opportunity would mean there would be excess demand for the futures contract until the price was bid up to 94.06.

If futures prices were above the forward/forward rate, for example at 95, then it would pay an arbitrageur to lend long and borrow short by selling a futures contract to guarantee the future interest rate of 4 per cent. By lending at 5 per cent for six months the arbitrageur would receive €1,025,000. By borrowing €1,000,000 at 4 per cent for three months the arbitrageur would have to repay €1,010,000; he would then borrow the equivalent money for three months (by selling the futures at 95) at 5 per cent so having to repay €1,022,625 (€10,010,000 × 1.01485, that is 5.94 per cent for 3 months). This means he receives €1,025,000 and pays out only €1,022,625, guaranteeing a profit of €2,375. Such an arbitrage opportunity would mean there would be excess selling of the futures contract until the price fell to 94.06. Having examined how a Euribor futures contract is priced, we now proceed to look at some practical examples of how interest rate futures contracts can be used.

13.13   Using interest rate futures

There are basically two strategies for hedging against adverse interest-rate movements using interest rate futures. We take an example of Eurodollar interest rates (that is, offshore dollar interest rates – recall that a Eurodollar is a dollar deposit or loan outside of the USA and is nothing to do with the euro):

1   A borrower of funds who wishes to protect himself against a rise in the Eurodollar rate should sell Eurodollar contracts. If Eurodollar interest rates rise he will gain as the Eurodollar contract falls in price.
2   A lender of funds who wishes to protect himself against a fall in the Eurodollar rate should buy Eurodollar contracts. If the Eurodollar interest rate falls he will gain as the Eurodollar contract rises in price.

Example 1   Hedging using a Eurodollar interest future

Assume that it is June and a company currently has a loan for $1,000,000 at a variable interest rate, which is currently 3 per cent and is subject to review in three month's time in September, and the company wishes to protect itself against a rise in interest rates.

The firm can sell a September Eurodollar three-month futures contract with a face value of $1,000,000. Assume the price is currently 97, implying a 3 per cent interest rate. Each basis point, that is 0.01 movement in the price of the contract is worth $1/4 \times 0.01 \times \$1,000,000 = \$25$.

What would happen if dollar interest rates rise to 4 per cent by September? The company will have to pay an extra 1 per cent on its borrowing costs, equivalent to $2,500 per quarter. However, in September the firm will close its position by buying back the September futures contract for 96 (since this will be the price of the futures contract now that interest rates have risen to 4 per cent). This will leave the company with a profit on its Eurodollar futures contract of $1.00 \times 1/4 \times \$1,000,000 = \$2,500$. The company has been able to offset its higher borrowing costs with the gain from closing out its short position on the September futures contract.

Example 2 Speculating using a Euribor future

It is September and a speculator observes that the December Euribor futures contract is at 98, that is, 2 per cent. The speculator feels that by December the three-month euro interest rates will be 3 per cent. The speculator can sell a December Euribor futures contract today at 98 and if the speculator is proved correct, and in December the three-month euro interest rate is 3 per cent, then the futures contract will be valued at 97. Each basis point movement in the contract is worth $0.01 \times 0.25 \times 1,000,000 = €25$. The Euribor contract can be closed out at 97 implying a profit of 100 basis points or $100 \times €25 = €2,500$ per contract sold.

13.14 Bond futures contracts

Government bond futures contracts are among the most popular financial futures contracts. In particular, futures based on US Treasury bonds, US Treasury notes, UK government gilts, German bunds and Japanese bonds are especially popular, as are futures in other major government bonds such as Italian government bonds. **Table 13.6** shows the contract specifications for some popular bond contracts traded on LIFFE.

A bond futures contract is a commitment to buy or sell a long-term government bond at a predetermined price at some future date. The precise bond to be delivered is chosen by the seller from a range of deliverable bonds set out in the futures contract. Unlike short-term interest rate futures, bond futures contracts are not settled via a cash payment; rather they are settled by delivery of one of a range of government bonds specified in the contract. The reason for having a range of deliverable government bonds is to eliminate the possibility of price manipulation which could occur if a bond fund/speculator cornered the market in a particular

Table 13.6 Contract specifications of LIFFE government bond futures contracts

	UK gilts	German bunds	Japanese government bonds
Nominal value	£100,000	€100,000	Yen 100,000,000
Maturity range in years	8.75–13	8.5–10	7–11
Notional coupon	7%	6%	6%
Tick size	0.01	0.01	0.01
Tick value	£10	€10	Yen 10,000

Source: LIFFE

bond issue. The bond that would actually be delivered is known as the cheapest-to-deliver bond, and calculating which bond is cheapest to deliver is quite complex and is not dealt with here. Like most other futures contracts, the vast majority of government bond contracts are closed out prior to maturity so actual delivery does not usually take place. We shall not cover the pricing of bond futures since this is quite complex compared to other futures contracts. We shall, however, see how they can be used by bond managers to hedge against changes in long-term interest rates and also for speculative purposes.

Example of bond futures contract for hedging

Say a fund manager with €10 million of long-term German government bonds (known as bunds) in his portfolio fears that there will be a rise in long-term European interest rates (on the euro) over the next couple of months that will lower the value of the bund holdings. The fund manager can protect the value of his German bund holdings by taking a short position in the futures contract which will provide an offsetting gain if the feared rise in long-term interest rate occurs, since it will lower both the cash and futures price of bonds.

For example, consider the bund futures contract which is traded on LIFFE. The bund futures contract is for €100,000 (the minimum price movement for the futures contract is 0.01, meaning each tick movement is worth 0.0001 × €100,000 = €10). The bund futures contract traded at LIFFE is based upon a notional bond with a 6 per cent coupon which is priced at €1000. The fund manager with €10 million may sell 100 futures contracts at a price of 100.00 based upon a current interest rate of 6 per cent. If the interest rate rises to 7 per cent the value of the government bonds in his portfolio may have fallen to say €9,000,000 (depending upon the term to maturity of the bonds). The bund futures contract will have fallen to 90.94 (and will be sold at 100.00) so this will give a gain of 916 ticks × €10 × 100 contracts = €916,000 which nearly fully offsets the €1,000,000 loss on his bond portfolio. In this case, the forward hedge is not perfect because the duration of the fund manager's portfolio is greater than that of the long bond futures contract and has consequently fluctuated more in price.

Example of a long gilt speculation using an interest future

Imagine that the current interest rate on UK gilts is 8 per cent and a speculator feels that long-term interest rates are likely to rise over the next three months. The speculator, might sell a gilt futures contract trading at 102.50. (The minimum price movement for the futures contract is 0.01, which means each tick movement is worth 0.0001 × £100,000 = £10.) If interest rates do subsequently rise then the value of the gilt futures will fall to say 101. The speculator will then be able to close the position by buying the gilt futures for 101 and make 150 ticks × £10 = £1,500 profit .

13.15 Currency futures

A currency futures contract is an agreement between two parties to buy/sell specified amounts of a currency at a predetermined price at a given date in the future. To a large extent currency futures are very similar to forward currency purchases, but,

Table 13.7 $–€ (dollar–euro) currency futures (CME), €125,000

	Open	Sett. price	Change	High	Low	Est. vol.	Open int.
Sept	1.4347	1.4287	–0.0085	1.4390	1.4281	229,045	130,843
Dec	1.4350	1.4286	–0.0085	1.4388	1.4280	2,398	5,883

Spot rate $1.4310/€1

Source: CME, 28 August 2009

as **Table 13.2** shows, there are some significant differences between the two types of contract. **Table 13.7** shows the dollar–euro contracts offered by the Chicago Mercantile Exchange (CME).

Since futures are quite similar to forward contracts, they are extensively used for hedging and speculative purposes. Unlike forward contracts they do not always provide a perfect hedge but they have some advantages. Let us consider a simple example of how a currency futures contract can be used for hedging purposes.

Example of a currency futures contract used for hedging

currency futures contract
an agreement between two parties to buy/sell a specified amount of an underlying currency at a predetermined price at a predetermined date in the future

Suppose a US exporter has made export sales to Europe and is due in six months' time to receive €1 million. The firm wishes to protect itself and ensure that the sale is profitable when translated back into dollars. The exporter is able to obtain a six-month futures quotation of $1.40/€1 and, because US and European interest rates at the six-month time horizon are equal, the spot rate also happens to be $1.40/€1. The exporter is concerned that the dollar will appreciate over the next six months to say $1.25/€1 and wishes to protect the company against the adverse currency movement (which would mean his €1 million would only be worth $1,250,000). The trader could take out 8 contracts to sell €125,000 at $1.40/€1 and therefore be guaranteed $1,400,000 with the €1,000,000.

Suppose that in six months' time, when in receipt of the €1,000,000, the exporter has been proved right: the dollar–euro parity is $1.25/€1 and, because interest rates have remained unchanged, the futures contract is valued at $1.25/€1. In these circumstances, the exporter will now be in a position to close his futures contract by buying 8 euro contracts at $1.25/€1. The exporter has therefore closed out his futures contract position at a profit of 15 US cents (selling euros at $1.40 and buying them at $1.25), so his profit from the futures contract is ($0.15 × 125,000 × 8 = $150,000). The hedger therefore has a total of €1,000,000 which can be converted at $1.25/€1 in the spot market which gives $1,250,000 plus the $150,000 profit from the futures contracts, and so he obtains a guaranteed $1,400,000.

Suppose that in six months' time, when in receipt of the €1,000,000, the exporter has been proved wrong: the dollar–euro parity is $1.55/€1 and, because interest rates have remained unchanged, the futures contract is valued at $1.55/€1. In these circumstances, the exporter will now be in a position to close his futures contract by selling 8 euro contracts at $1.55. The exporter has therefore closed out his futures contract position at a loss of 15 US cents (selling euros at $1.40 and buying them at $1.55), so the loss from the 8 futures contract is ($0.15 × 125,000 × 8 = –$150,000). The hedger therefore has a total of $1,550,000 from converting the €1 million at $1.55/€1 in the spot market less the $150,000 loss from the futures, and he therefore has obtained a guaranteed $1,400,000. Either way, whatever the dollar–euro parity turns out to be, the futures market has been successfully used for hedging purposes. Indeed, in this example the hedger has achieved a perfect hedge.

In the example above, the spot and forward rates move exactly in tandem. However, if they do not, there is still some residual risk for an investor. For example, if the spot rate moves from $1.40/€1 to $1.25/€1, and if the futures rate only moves from $1.40/€1 to $1.27/€1, then the profit on closing out the futures contract would only have been 13 US cents, so yielding $0.13 × 125,000 × 8 = $130,000 in profit from the futures contract. This would give the hedger $1,250,000 when selling €1million plus $130,000 from the futures contract, totalling $1,380,000 which is $20,000 short of a perfect hedge. The risk of an adverse change in the spread between the spot and futures rate is known as basis risk. Despite the existence of basis risk, it is usually considered to be a relatively minor risk compared to having an open position.

Another reason why futures contracts do not provide a perfect hedge is the fact that they come in standardized amounts. In the example we considered, the €1 million conveniently equates to exactly 8 contracts (€1,000,000/€125,000 = 8). If the firm was expecting to receive €1,050,000, then at $1.40/€1 it could sell 8 contracts corresponding to $1,400,000 but there would be a residual of €50,000 that would be unhedged.

> **basis risk** the risk that a hedging strategy using futures contracts will provide an imperfect hedge due to differences in the movement of spot and futures prices

13.16   The pricing of currency futures

The appropriate futures price is given by:

$$F = S \times \left[\frac{1 + [r_{us} \times (T - t)/360]}{1 + [r_{eu} \times (T - t)/360]} \right] \tag{13.3}$$

where F is the futures price (dollars per euro); S is the spot exchange rate (dollars per euro); r_{us} is the interest rate of the US dollar; r_{eu} is the interest rate on the euro; T is the number of days of duration of the contract, e.g. 30, 60, 90, 180; t is the number of days into the contract; and $T - t$ is the number of days remaining to delivery of the contract.

Numerical example

The US interest rate is 4 per cent, the euro interest rate is 2 per cent and the dollar–euro rate is $1.40/€1. What is the price of a six-month (180-day) Euro futures contract which is 100 days into the contract? (Use a 360-day year.)

$$
\begin{aligned}
F &= S \times \left[\frac{1 + [r_{us} \times (T - t)/360]}{1 + [r_{eu} \times (T - t)/360]} \right] \\
&= \$1.40/€1 \times \left[\frac{1 + [0.04 \times (180 - 100)/360]}{1 + [0.02 \times (180 - 100)/360]} \right] \\
&= \$1.40/€1 \times \frac{1.008888}{1.004444} \\
&= \$1.4062/€1
\end{aligned}
$$

Notice that the dollar is at a discount on the futures market; this is because the holder of dollars benefits from a higher interest rate. To compensate for the lower interest on holding euros, the Euro is a forward premium enabling euro holdings to be converted back into dollars at a favourable rate. If an investor had $1,000 he could hold it in the USA and earn 4 per cent for 80 days so that it becomes $1,008.89. Alternatively, he could sell dollars spot at $1.40/€1, so obtaining €714.39. Knowing that it will earn 2 per cent over 80 days to become €717.46, he will take out a simultaneous forward contract to sell €717.46 at $1.4062, thus returning $1008.89. In other words, the price of the futures contract ensures that there are no arbitrage profits to be made.

13.17 Conclusions

Financial futures are now a well established tool for risk management in a whole range of financial markets. The key to the successful use of futures contracts for hedging purposes is to offset the adverse implications of any change in the underlying cash position by a profit from an appropriate futures contract. A futures contract enables an investor to hedge against price risk by buying (selling) a futures contract at a guaranteed price in the future regardless of what the corresponding future spot price turns out to be. The range of financial futures contracts now available means that the risk facing companies and fund managers of adverse movements in interest rates, currencies and equities can generally be considerably reduced at least up to the 12–18-month horizon.

In addition to hedging, futures contracts are useful instruments for taking speculative positions. For example, if a speculator feels that the stockmarket is likely to fall, it is remarkably easy to take out a short position on the appropriate futures stock index. This contrasts with the immense difficulties he would have in short-selling a large amount of shares using the spot market. The low margin requirements also make speculation relatively easy.

Financial futures contracts are examples of derivative instruments; that is, the price of the contract is partly derived from the price of the underlying asset in the cash or spot market. Futures prices are determined by arbitrage conditions between the cash and future markets.

Further reading

Chisholm, A. (2004) *Derivatives Demystified: A Step by Step Guide to Forwards, Futures and Options*, Wiley.
Hull, J.C. (2008) *Options, Futures and Other Derivatives*, Prentice-Hall.
Kolb, R.W. and Overdahl J. (2007) *Futures, Options and Swaps*, 5th edn, Blackwell.

Chapter 13	Revision questions

1 You are given the following data on the three-month sterling interest rate futures contract. The contract has a notional size of £1 million.

Sterling futures contract

June 2012   97

  (i) Explain what the sale of such a contract implies.

 (ii) If you think three-month interest rates in June 2012 will be 2 per cent would you buy or sell the contract? Explain your reasoning and the profits you can expect if you are correct.

(iii) Briefly explain how a corporate treasurer who is looking to lend £1 million of funds for 3 months from June 2012 might use the above contract to hedge interest-rate risk.

2 The March FTSE 100 stock index futures contract is reading 4300 while the cash index is reading 4250. The futures contract is worth £10 per point.

  (i) Explain why the FTSE futures contract is at a forward premium.

 (ii) You have £10 million of funds invested in FTSE 100 stocks under management and are concerned about a fall in the market by March expiration to 3800. Describe the hedging strategy that you may adopt to protect your fund against such a fall.

(iii) You are pessimistic about the market prospects and predict that the FTSE 100 index will be reading 3800 by expiration. Describe the speculative strategy that you would adopt and the risks that you run.

3 You are given the following data on the three-month Euribor interest rate futures contract. The contract has a notional size of €1 million.

Euribor futures contract

June   96.0

  (i) Explain what the sale of such a contract implies

 (ii) If you think the three-month interest rate in June will be 3 per cent would you buy or sell the contract? Explain your reasoning and the profits you can expect if you are correct.

(iii) Briefly explain how a corporate treasurer who is looking to borrow £2 million of funds for three months from June might use the above contract to hedge interest-rate risk.

4 The dollar/pound ($/£) exchange rate is currently $1.82/£1 and the following futures price exists for June.

Futures (contract size £50,000)

June $1.80/£1

You work for an American travel company and are due to pay in June, £100,000 for hotel bookings to the UK Hotel chain. Discuss how you may use the future's contract to hedge the exchange rate risk. In your answer consider a range of possible future spot rates for dollar–sterling.

| Chapter 13 | Revision questions – *continued* |

5   The US interest rate is 6 per cent per annum, the interest rate on the pound is 3 per cent and the spot exchange rate is $1.80/£1. What is the price of a nine month (270 days) dollar–pound futures contract which is 150 days into the contract? (Use a 360-day year.)

6   Explain the difference between initial margin and variation margin. Is the margining process similar for futures and options contracts?

Multiple choice questions available at www.palgrave.com/business/pilbeam

14

OPTIONS

Learning objectives

In this chapter you will learn about:

- the difference between call and put options
- individual stock options, stock index options, interest rate options and currency options
- how options can be used for speculative and hedging purposes
- differences between using futures and options for hedging and speculative purposes
- different option strategies such as straddles and strangles
- different types of exotic options

14.1 Introduction

Options are a special type of financial asset that give the holder the right but not the obligation to buy or sell an underlying security at a predetermined price. Options were first traded in Chicago in 1972, and a decade later the London International Financial Futures Exchange (LIFFE) opened. LIFFE is currently the largest options exchange in Europe. Options contracts have proved very attractive for both commodities and financial securities, and among the most popular contracts traded on LIFFE are interest rate, currency and stock-index contracts.

Like futures, options contracts are derivative instruments; that is, the price of the contract is derived from the price of the underlying asset in the cash or spot market. In this chapter we illustrate various types of options contracts covering individual stock options, interest rate options, currency options and stock index options. We shall consider how options contracts can be used for both speculative and hedging purposes. We shall also discuss the economic role that option contracts can fulfil and emphasize the differences between futures and options contracts.

14.2 The growth of options markets

There has been a massive growth in the use of options markets as illustrated in **Table 14.1**.

As with futures contracts, options are traded on exchanges, and as tailor-made contracts in the over-the-counter instruments offered by leading banks and securities houses to their clients. Also, as with futures contracts, an exchange will protect itself against the risk of default by the writer and will impose capital and stringent margin requirements on option writers.

Table 14.1   Turnover of options traded on international exchanges
(numbers of contracts in millions)

Instruments	1990	1995	2000	2005	2008
Interest rate	52.0	225.5	107.6	430.8	617.7
Currency	18.9	23.3	7.1	19.4	59.8
Equity index	119.1	187.3	481.4	3,139.8	4,174.1
All markets	190.0	436.1	596.1	3,590.0	4,851.6

Source: Bank for International Settlements

14.3   Options contracts

writer the person
who sells a call or put
option contract

holder the person
who buys a call or put
option contract

call option
a contract that
gives the holder
the right but not
the obligation to
buy an underlying
asset/security at
a predetermined
exercise price at some
time in the future

put option
a contract that
gives the holder
the right but not
the obligation to
sell an underlying
asset/security at
a predetermined
exercise price at some
time in the future

exercise price
the price at which
an option holder has
the right to sell or
buy an underlying
asset/security; often
referred to as the
strike price

option premium
a fee that is paid by
an option holder to
the option writer in
return for the right
to buy or sell an
underlying asset/
security at a given
exercise price

An option contract involves two parties, the writer who sells the option and the holder who purchases it. The holder of an option contract has the right but not the obligation to either buy or sell the underlying asset at a predetermined price in the future. If the contract gives the holder the right to purchase the underlying asset at a predetermined price from the other party the contact is known as a call option. If the contract gives the owner the right to sell the underlying asset at a predetermined price to the other party the contact is known as a put option.

An option contract that can be exercised at any time up until its maturity date is known as an American option, whilst one that can only be exercised on the expiration date is known as a European option. The options traded on LIFFE are all of the American variety. The rules relating to European options facilitate certain trading strategies, such as strangles and straddles (see Section 14.13), and also facilitate arbitrage between the options and futures markets by guaranteeing traders that the positions they take will not be upset by premature exercise. The price at which the underlying security can be bought or sold is known as the strike price (or exercise price), and the date at which the contract expires is known as the expiry date or maturity date.

Table 14.2 shows the price of put and call options on British Petroleum shares traded at LIFFE for differing expiry dates. The bracketed price underneath the share (*525 pence) is the current price of the share on the market. The two strike prices published are at 520 and 540 pence; other strike prices are obtainable but only the ones closest to the current price of the share are published in the financial press. The limited number of strike prices and contract maturity dates, in this case September, December and March, while restricting the potential range of investments for investors, are crucial to ensuring there is a sufficient market to guarantee investors the liquidity that they require. Two sets of prices are quoted: for call options and for put options. Consider the March 2010 call price of 18 pence at a strike price of 540 pence. The price paid for the call option of 18 pence is known as the option premium, and the buyer of such a call option would have the right but not the obligation to buy 1,000 British Petroleum shares at a price of 540 pence in March 2010 for a cost of 18 pence per share (that is, a total cost of £180). Alternatively, an investor could, for 38 pence per share, have the right but not the obligation to sell 1,000 (that is, a total cost of £380) British Petroleum shares at a price of 540 pence in March 2010.

Table 14.2   LIFFE equity options

British Petroleum	Strike price	Calls			Puts		
		Sep	Dec	Mar	Sep	Dec	Mar
(*525)	520	16.0	23.0	28.0	10.0	17.0	27.0
	540	7.0	13.5	18.0	21.0	27.0	38.0

Note: 525 pencce is the current BP share price.

Source: Euronext.LIFFE, 27 August 2009

There are basically four positions that can be taken on an options contract:

1   Buying a call option – known as being long call.
2   Selling a call option – known as being short call.
3   Buying a put option – known as being long put.
4   Selling a put option – known as being short put.

14.4   A call option contract

Consider the underlying asset as 1,000 shares in British Petroleum which are currently priced at 525 pence. Mr A buys a call option with a strike price of 540 for March 2010 for an option premium of 18 pence a share (a total of £180, that is £0.18 × 1000). Mr A has purchased the right to buy from the writer of the option 1,000 shares in British Petroleum at a price of 540 per share. The maximum amount that the option holder can lose is £180, while the maximum profit the option writer can make is £180.

If the price in March is below 540 pence, the holder will not exercise the option as the shares can be bought more cheaply on the spot market and the option holder will have lost the £180 premium paid, with the writer making £180. If the price of the shares at the expiration date in March is above 540, then the holder will exercise the option, since it will pay him to buy the shares at 540 pence and sell them spot at a higher price. If the price rises above 540 pence but to less than 558 pence, it pays the holder to exercise the option. However, since he has paid 18 pence for the option he will make an overall loss. For example, if the price has risen to 550 pence he will exercise the right to buy the shares at 540 pence and sell them spot at 550 pence making 10 pence per share; but taking into account the 18 pence option premium he paid, he will make a loss of 8 pence per share or £80 in total. A future spot price of 558 pence will mean the option holder breaks even as the gain from exercising the option of 18 pence per share just matches the option premium paid of 18 pence per share. If the price rises above 558 pence the holder will exercise his option at a profit. For example, if the price has risen to 580 pence he will exercise the right to buy the shares at 540 pence and sell them spot at 580 pence making 40 pence per share, but taking into account the 18 pence option premium paid he will make a profit of 22 pence per share or £220 in total. **Table 14.3** shows the profit and loss profile per share for the March call option for different possible spot prices of British Petroleum shares in March 2010.

An important point about an option is that the most the option holder can lose is the option premium, that is 18 pence per share or £180 in total premium, while the maximum that the option writer can make is the option premium received. However, the option holder has a potentially unlimited up side; for instance, if the share goes up to 800 pence the option holder makes a net profit of 242 pence a share or £2,420 in total and the share could possibly go well above this level. Likewise the option writer faces a potentially unlimited down side; for instance, if the share goes up to 800 pence the option writer makes a loss of 242 pence per share or £2,420 in total, and the share might go well above this level, so increasing his losses.

Table 14.3 Profit and loss profile on a call option

Details:	
Option premium	18
Strike price	540
Expiration	March 2010
Contract	1000 shares

Price of BP shares on expiration date	Holder profit/loss on long call	Writer profit/loss on short call
200	−£180	+£180
300	−£180	+£180
400	−£180	+£180
500	−£180	+£180
540	−£180	+£180
550	−£80	+£80
558	£0	+£0
560	+£20	−£20
580	+£220	−£220
600	+£420	−£420
650	+£920	−£920
700	+£1,420	−£1,420
800	+£2,420	−£2,420
900	+£3,420	−£3,420

Figure 14.1 The profit and loss profile of a call option

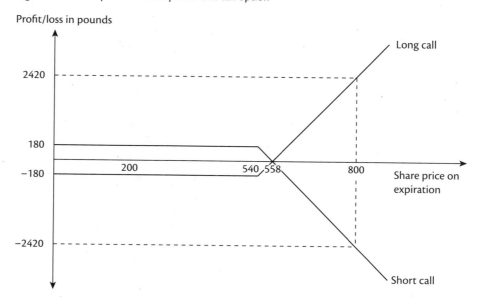

Hence, the holder of the option has a substantial upside potential profit with limited maximum downside (that is, the option premium), while the writer of the option has a maximum gain (the option premium) and a substantial loss potential. The asymmetrical profit and loss profile facing the option writer and holder is depicted in **Figure 14.1**.

In **Figure 14.1** we can see that the holder of the option has a maximum loss per share of 18 pence and has unlimited upside potential if the future spot price is above 558 pence. Conversely, the writer of the option can only make 18 pence a share at most and has an unlimited downside risk if the future spot price is above 558 pence.

14.5   A put option contract

Let us now consider the profit and loss profiles associated with a put option. As an example we take a put option on the shares of British Petroleum March 2010 at a strike price of 540 pence and a put option premium of 38 pence (see **Table 14.2**). The total premium payable is £0.38 × 1000 = £380, for which the holder is acquiring the right to sell 1,000 shares to the writer for £5.40 a share. Let us consider the profit and loss profiles of the buyer and writer of the option.

If in March 2010 the price of the shares is 540 pence or more, the holder will not exercise the put option and will make a loss of 38 pence per share or £380 in total. The writer will make a profit of £380. If the share is priced at less than 540 pence but greater than 502 pence then the holder will exercise the option but still make a loss. For example, if the stock is priced at 520 pence it will pay the holder to buy the stock at 520 pence and exercise the right to sell it at 540 pence, thereby making 20 pence a share. However, since he paid 38 pence for the put premium, he is left with a net loss of 18 pence a share, or £180 in total. If the share price is below 502 pence then the holder of the put option will make a profit from exercising the option. For example, if the price of the share is 400 pence he will exercise the right to sell the shares at 540 pence so making 140 pence less the option premium of 38 pence, leaving a net profit of 102 pence a share or £1020 in total. The profit and loss profile of the put option to the holder and writer is shown in **Table 14.4**.

Table 14.4 shows that the holder of the option has a maximum loss of £380 and substantial upside potential once the share is below 502 pence. Conversely, the writer of the option can only make the option premium of £380 at most and has substantial downside risk if the future spot price is below 502 pence.

We have now covered the basic profit and loss profiles on call and put option contracts. There is one slight complication that so far we have ignored: when buying an option the holder pays a fee to the writer of the option at the time of the sale. This means that the holder is foregoing interest and the writer has funds that can earn interest. The effect of the interest-rate factor is to lower the profit profile for the buyer of the option and raise the profit profile for the writer of the option. However, the interest factor is usually relatively unimportant.

Table 14.4   Profit and loss profiles on a put option

Details:	
Option premium	38
Strike price	540
Expiration	March 2010
Contract	1000 shares

Price of BP shares on expiration date	Holder profit/loss on long put	Write profit/loss on short put
100	+£4,020	−£4,020
200	+£3,020	−£3,020
300	+£2,020	−£2,020
350	+£1,520	−£1,520
400	+£1,020	−£1,020
450	+£520	−£520
480	+£220	−£220
500	+£20	+£20
502	£0	£0
520	−£180	+£180
540	−£380	+£380
600	−£380	+£380
650	−£380	+£380
700	−£380	+£380
800	−£380	+£380

14.6   Stock index options

In addition to basic share options on individual companies, stock index options enable positions to be taken on the movement of a broad market index such as the FTSE 100. **Table 14.5** shows the price of stock index options traded at LIFFE.

Table 14.5   Call and put contracts on the FTSE 100 index

	FTSE 100 index options (Euronext.LIFFE), £10 per full index point													
	4750		4800		4850		4900		4950		5000		5050	
	C	P	C	P	C	P	C	P	C	P	C	P	C	P
Sep	207.0	38.5	168.5	50.0	134.0	65.5	102.5	84.0	77.0	108.5	56.0	137.5	40.0	171.5
Oct	260.5	95.5	226.0	111.0	194.5	129.5	163.5	148.5	136.5	171.5	113.0	198.0	91.5	226.5
Nov	292.5	153.0	261.0	171.5	231.5	192.0	203.0	213.5	177.0	237.5	152.5	263.0	130.0	290.0
Dec	326.0	190.0	292.5	207.0	263.5	227.5	235.0	249.5	208.5	272.5	183.0	296.5	161.5	325.0

Note: The FTSE 100 closing value of 31 August 31 2009 was 4869.

Source: Euronext.LIFFE, 1 September 2009

| Box 14.1 | The difference between writing naked and writing covered |

Writing options can seem like a very risky business. The maximum profit obtainable for the writer is the call or put premium received while the losses can be very substantial if there is a large price movement in the underlying share (security or commodity). Look at the example of British Petroleum call options. The holder has paid a premium of £180 to buy 1,000 shares at strike price of 540 pence and the writer has received £180 which is the maximum profit the writer can make. If the share price rises to 800 pence we have seen that the writer will lose £2,420. This is because we have assumed that the writer does not own any shares in British Petroleum. When you write options on a security that you do not own you are said to be 'writing naked.' Writing naked is quite risky as the share price can go up and up in value increasing the writer's loss in the process.

However, writing can be a lot less risky if the writer is 'writing covered'; that is, the writer owns a quantity of the shares on which he is writing the call option. If the writer in our example actually owns shares in British Petroleum at the time of writing the call option, then he will profit from the rise in the price of the shares and that will offset his losses from writing the call option. Suppose the writer owns 900 shares in British Petroleum at the time of writing the option contract, then they are worth $900 \times £5.25 = £4,725$ at that time. If the share rises in price to 800 pence by the time of expiration in March then the 900 shares will be worth $900 \times £8 = £7,200$. The writer thus sees an appreciation in the value of his shares of £2,475 which more than covers his loss of £2,420 from having written the call options. In this case, he is 'fully covered' because the appreciation of the shares will offset the loss from writing the call option. If the writer owned only 500 shares then the appreciation in price of £2.75 each will give him a profit of £1,375 which, although reducing his loss from writing the options, is insufficient to fully cover the loss. In this case, we say the writer is writing 'partially covered.'

From this discussion, we can see that writing naked is quite risky whereas writing covered is far less risky. Writing covered could be a useful strategy for a fund manager who owns some shares as part of his portfolio but does not expect them to do too much in the short term. If the fund manager owns 1000 shares in British Petroleum as part of his 'core portfolio' and does not expect them to change much between August and March then he could write some call options on the share. If the share remains at £5.25 between August and March then the shares he owns will still be worth £5,250, but he will have a useful profit of £180 from having written the call options which expire worthless to the holder. Indeed, if the shares fall in price to £5.15 then his shares will be worth £5,150 which is £100 less but his profit of £180 from writing the call option will mean his net position in British Petroleum is worth £5,150 plus the profit from writing the call of £180 which is £5,330.

Of course if the share rises to £8 then his shares are worth £8,000 but the loss of £2420 from writing the call options will mean his net position in British Petroleum is worth only £5,580. This is an improvement over £5,250 but far less than the £8,000 value he would have had if he had not written the call option.

stock index option
a contract giving the holder the right but not the obligation to buy or sell a stated stock index at a particular price at some time in the future

The FTSE 100 index options are valued at £10 × the FTSE 100 cash index level, with expiration on the third Friday of the month. The premium is quoted in pence per unit of the contract with each full point movement in the index being worth £10. For example, if someone buys a call contract on the FTSE 100 for December 2009 at 4900 for 235 points, or a premium of £2,350, the holder has the right between 31 August 2009 and the third Friday of December 2009 (the expiration day of the contract) to buy the index at a level of 4,900.

$$\text{Cost of December 2009 strike price of } 4,900 = 235 \times £10$$
$$= £2,350$$

Since the actual delivery of the many shares that comprise the index would be impractical and costly, index options work on a cash settlement basis. If the FTSE 100 index in our example is above the 4,900 level, then the option will be exercised and the writer has to pay the holder the difference between the spot price of the index

Table 14.6   Profit and loss profile on a FTSE 100 call index option

Details of FTSE 100	
Call option premium	235 points or £2350
Strike price	4900
Expiration	December 2009
Value of contract	£10 per index point

Possible values of FTSE 100 index in December	Holder's profit/loss on long call	Writer's profit/loss on short call
4750	−£2,350	+£2,350
4800	−£2,350	+£2,350
4850	−£2,350	+£2,350
4900	−£2,350	+£2,350
4950	−£1,850	+£1,850
5000	−£1,350	+£1,350
5050	−£850	+£850
5100	−£350	+£350
5135	£0	£0
5150	+£150	−£150
5200	+£650	−£650
5250	+£1,150	−£1,150
5300	+£1,650	−£1,650
5350	+£2,150	−£2,150
5400	+£2,650	−£2,650
5500	+£3,650	−£3,650
6000	+£8,650	−£8,650

and the exercise price of the index multiplied by £10. For example, if the index has risen to 5,200, then the holder will receive from the writer (5,200 – 4,900) × £10 = £3,000 leaving the holder with a net profit after allowance for the premium paid of £3,000 −£2,350 = +£650. **Table 14.6** shows net profit or loss per contract on the FTSE 100 index for different spot prices of the index for a range of possible closing prices in December 2009.

14.7 Interest rate options

interest rate option
a contract giving the holder the right but not the obligation to lend or borrow a stated nominal notional amount, for a given period of time at a predetermined rate of interest

Interest rate options are based upon movements in debt instruments and are especially popular in the USA, where they are referred to as options on physicals. **Table 14.7** shows hypothetical values for one of the popular LIFFE short-term interest rate (STIR) option contracts.

With interest rate options a call option gives the holder the right but not the obligation to lend from the expiry date at the implied rate of interest, while a put option gives the holder the right but not the obligation to borrow. For example, looking at the short sterling contract for 4 basis points (that is 0.04 per cent) in **Table 14.7**, the option holder would have the right to lend £500,000 at an interest rate of 5.00 per cent (100 – 95.00) for three months from November. Each tick movement on the contract is worth £12.50, calculated from the value of the contract (£500,000) times 1 basis point (0.0001) times a quarter of a year (0.25), that is £500,000 × 0.0001 × 0.25 = £12.50. The cost of the call is therefore:

$$\text{Cost of call} = 4 \text{ ticks} \times £12.50$$
$$= £50$$

Suppose that by November the contract rises in value from 95.00 to 95.50, then the holder is entitled to a gain of 50 basis points and his margin account will be credited with 50 × £12.50 = £625, implying a net profit from the contract of £625 less the £50 premium = £575. If, however, interest rates have risen to 5.50 per cent so that the contract is trading at say 94.50, then the contract will not be exercised and the holder will lose the premium paid of £50.

Table 14.7 Short sterling options (LIFFE), £500,000 points of 100 per cent

	Calls		Puts	
Strike	**Oct**	**Nov**	**Oct**	**Nov**
94.625	0.280	0.290	0.005	0.015
94.750	0.165	0.185	0.015	0.035
94.875	0.070	0.085	0.045	0.060
95.000	0.020	0.040	0.120	0.150

Estimated volume totals:
Calls 19,930
Puts 67,800.

Source: Hypothetical values

14.8   Currency options

currency option
a contract giving the holder the right but not the obligation to buy or sell a certain amount of the underlying currency at a given exchange rate

Currency options were first traded on the Philadelphia Stock Exchange in the early 1980s, but since then they have become increasingly popular instruments on other exchanges such as London, Paris and Singapore. We shall look at an example from the Chicago Mercantile Exchange (CME). The options traded on this market are American options and can be exercised at any time to maturity. **Table 14.8** shows CME options for the dollar against the pound exchange rate as at 28 August 2009.

Table 14.8   Chicago Mercantile Exchange $/£ Option £62,500 ($6.25 per tick)

Strike price ($/£)	Calls		Puts	
	Sep	Dec	Sep	Dec
1.6000	2.95	5.76	0.26	3.09
1.6100	2.30	5.17	0.44	3.49
1.6200	1.43	4.61	0.74	3.93
1.6300	0.65	4.09	1.19	4.41
1.6400	0.36	3.61	1.80	4.93
1.6500	0.24	3.17	2.55	5.48

Note: Spot exchange rate at close of business was $1.6290/£1

Source: Chicago Mercantile Exchange, 28 August 2009

American option
a contract that can be exercised at any time up until its maturity date

underlying currency
the currency that you have committed to buy or sell in a futures contract or the right to buy or sell in an option contract

Table 14.8 shows the premium measured in US cents for traded currency options of the dollar against the pound. The spot exchange rate of the dollar against the pound at the close of business on 28 August 2009 was $1.6290/£1. A trader can buy a call option (that is the right to buy pounds) at a strike of $1.65/£1 expiring in December 2009 for 3.17 US cents per pound. Similarly, a put option (right to sell pounds) for $1.65/£1 expiring in December 2009 can be bought for 5.48 US cents per pound. The contract refers to the right to buy or sell £62,500 pounds which is known as the underlying currency. It is important to know which is the underlying currency in order to correctly calculate the premium and relevant payoffs from the contract. For example, for the right to buy £62,500 at $1.6500 per pound the total premium payable is $0.0317 × 62,500 = $1981.25.

Example of profit/loss profiles for a currency call option

The profit and loss profiles for a contract on a December call will depend upon the actual exchange rate prevailing in December. Let us consider firstly the profit profile for such a call at a strike price of $1.65/£1. If the future spot exchange rate is less than $1.65/£1, then it does not pay the buyer of the option to exercise his option because it is cheaper to buy pounds in the spot market and he will lose the premium paid of 3.17 US cents per pound. If the future spot exchange rate is between $1.65/€1 and $1.6817/£1 it will pay the buyer of the option to exercise the option although he will make a loss equating to the future spot price less the strike price and option premium. If the future spot price is above $1.6817/£1, the call option will make a net profit for the holder. The writer of the option makes a profit or loss that is the mirror image of the profit and loss profile of the holder.

14.9 The uses of option contracts

Option contracts provide a cheap and flexible way for economic agents to control some significant risks and to take on highly leveraged speculative financial positions. In other words, options enable risks to be transferred from one party, that wishes to reduce its risk exposure, to another party that is willing to take on that risk for a premium. Like other financial instruments, options attract hedgers, speculators and arbitrageurs. Hedgers' basic motivation in dealing with options is to control their risk exposure. By contrast, speculators' motivation for dealing in options derivative instruments is to make profits by taking risk positions in the instruments. In many ways options are particularly attractive financial instruments for speculators since a small initial premium gives the possibility of a spectacular return. It is worth briefly looking at some examples of how various option contracts can be used for hedging and speculative purposes.

Example 1 Hedging the risk of an adverse equity price movement.

A pension fund with a portfolio of shares needs to realize £50 million of funds in three months' time. The fund is exposed to the risk that within the next three months the stockmarket will fall, thus requiring more shares to be sold to realize the necessary funds.

A possible options solution is for the fund manager to purchase put options on a stockmarket index. If the stockmarket falls by a specified amount, the pension fund will be able to exercise the right to sell at the predetermined price. The profit from the put option will mean that the fund does not have to sell extra shares to realize the £50 million of funds that it requires.

Example 2 Hedging the risk of an adverse interest rate movement.

A company requires a $20 million long-term bank loan in six months' time. Long-term interest rates are currently 5 per cent and the company wishes to protect itself against the possibility of a rise in interest rates which might be 6 or 7 per cent in six months' time.

A possible options solution is to purchase put options on a bond index. If interest rates rise then bond prices will fall and the company can exercise its right to sell bonds at a predetermined price. The resulting capital gain will compensate for the higher interest rate payments.

Example 3 Risk-averse foreign exchange movement.

A British firm is borrowing for one year $20 million at a fixed 7 per cent, which will require US dollar interest and principal repayments. The actual amount that the firm will have to pay, measured in sterling, will be dependent on movements of the dollar–sterling exchange rate. The company reports its profits in sterling, and is particularly concerned to protect itself against a depreciation of sterling which would increase the sterling cost of its dollar principal and interest rate repayments. On the other hand, it would like to take advantage of an appreciation of sterling.

A possible options solution is for the firm to buy dollar calls; that, is the right to buy dollars at a predetermined price. If the dollar appreciates then the calls can be exercised. However, if the dollar depreciates the firm will then be able to buy dollars spot.

Example 4 Speculation using a share option

A share in Company ABC is currently priced at £2 and an investor with £1,000 to invest is confident that in six months' time the share will be at approximately £3. The premium on a six-month call on the share at a strike price of £2.20 is currently 10 pence a share. One straightforward investment would be for the investor to buy the 500 shares at £2; if he is proved right and the share rises to £3 then he would make a net profit of £500 from the £1000 investment. Alternatively, the investor could invest the £1,000 in purchasing the right to buy 10,000 shares at £2.20; that is, take out 10 call option contracts of 1,000 shares. If the share price goes up to £3 then he will exercise the right to buy the shares at £22,000 and immediately sell them at £30,000, so making £8,000 less the option premium of £1,000 and leaving a net profit of £7000. A return of £7,000 on an initial investment of £1000 shows the spectacular returns that are possible with options. However, while they offer the prospect of a spectacular return this comes at a higher risk to the investor than a spot purchase of the shares. If the share only rises to £2.10 then if he had bought the shares spot he would be in profit to the tune of £50 whereas if he had taken out the options he would have lost his entire investment of £1,000!

14.10   Differences between options and futures contracts

While options and futures contracts are both examples of derivative instruments in that their price is derived in relation to the spot price, they can also both be used for hedging and speculative purposes. However, there are some significant differences in the two contracts. With an options contract the buyer of the option is not obliged to transact, whereas both parties to a futures contract are obliged to transact. The other major difference lies in the risk–return characteristics of the contract. With a futures contract, the buyer and seller have a simple pound-for-pound gain/loss scenario; for every pound the future spot price is above the futures rate on expiry of the contract the buyer makes a pound and the seller loses a pound. This is not the case with an options contract. The maximum loss of the option buyer is limited to the premium paid for the option, while the maximum gain for the option writer is limited to the premium paid for the option. However, there is considerable upside potential for an option holder and likewise considerable downside potential loss for the writer. This fundamental difference in the risk/return characteristics of futures and options is very important; futures may be useful instruments for hedging against symmetric risks, while options can prove useful for hedging against asymmetric risks. The differences between options and futures/forwards are best illustrated by means of a couple of examples: in the first we shall consider how the two contracts compare for hedging purposes, and in the second how they compare as speculative instruments.

14.11 A currency option versus a forward contract for hedging

In January a US company orders €1 million of goods from a German company which will be delivered in one year's time. Upon delivery the goods must be paid for in cash. The euro has been weak against the dollar and has depreciated from $1.70/€1 to $1.50/€1 over the last year. The company feels that the euro is likely to bounce back (that is, appreciate) and so wishes to protect itself from any rise in the euro. It would also, however, like to take advantage of any further appreciation of the dollar, should it occur. The spot rate of the euro is $1.50/€1 while the one-year forward/futures rate is $1.45/€1. Alternatively, the company can buy a one-year call option to buy euros at $1.45/€1 for 8 US cents per euro.

Table 14.9 (overleaf) compares the costs of obtaining the €1 million using an options contract versus a forward contract. A forward contract would mean that the company has to give $1,450,000 regardless of the exchange rate in one year's time. The call option will be exercised so long as the dollar/euro is above $1.45/€1 in one year's time. Table 14.9 also looks at what would happen if the position is left unhedged, and the company simply purchases the €1 million spot in one year's time at whatever the exchange rate then happens to be.

With the options contract, the position can be hedged for a premium of $80,000 which will give the holder the right to buy €1 million at a rate of $1.45/€1. If the dollar–euro parity is above $1.45/€1, then the option will be exercised and the US company will have to pay only $1,450,000 to obtain €1,000,000 which, given that the option has cost $80,000, gives a total cost of $1,530,000. If the dollar–euro rate is below $1.45/€1 then the option contract will not be exercised and the US firm will instead take advantage of the strong dollar to buy euros spot at the prevailing rate. For example, if the rate is $1.30/€1 then the firm will obtain €1,000,000 for $1,300,000 which, given that the option has expired worthless, implies a total cost of $1,380,000. An alternative means of hedging would be for the firm to take out a one-year forward contract to buy €1 million at $1.45/€1, which means the firm is guaranteed to obtain the required euros for $1,450,000 no matter what the spot rate is in one year's time. Finally, with an unhedged position the firm will have to pay whatever the spot exchange rate is one year hence.

Overall, Table 14.9 shows very clearly the advantages and disadvantages of hedging using an option or futures contract. The option contract enables the firm to fix a maximum payable price and also to take advantage of a favourable movement in the exchange rate. The forward rate provides the firm with full certainty over the future cost of obtaining €1 million but, unlike the options contract, does not permit the firm to take advantage of a favourable movement in the exchange rate. Both futures and options contracts help reduce the risk to the firm as compared to taking an unhedged position.

14.12 A currency option versus a forward contract for speculating

The spot exchange rate is $1.50/€1, while a year ago the rate was $1.70/€1. A speculator feels that the euro is likely to appreciate to $1.70/€1. He has two speculative choices: (i) take out a forward contract at $1.45/€1, or (ii) buy a call option on euros giving him the right to buy at $1.45/€1, the premium of the call being 8 US cents. The profit

Table 14.9 Comparison of hedging using futures and options

Spot exchange rate on expiry of the contract	Cost with option contract	Cost with forward contract	Cost with spot
2.00	$1,530,000	$1,450,000	$2,000,000
1.90	$1,530,000	$1,450,000	$1,900,000
1.80	$1,530,000	$1,450,000	$1,800,000
1.70	$1,530,000	$1,450,000	$1,700,000
1.60	$1,530,000	$1,450,000	$1,600,000
1.55	$1,530,000	$1,450,000	$1,550,000
1.54	$1,530,000	$1,450,000	$1,540,000
1.53	$1,530,000	$1,450,000	$1,530,000
1.52	$1,530,000	$1,450,000	$1,520,000
1.51	$1,530,000	$1,450,000	$1,510,000
1.50	$1,530,000	$1,450,000	$1,500,000
1.49	$1,530,000	$1,450,000	$1,490,000
1.48	$1,530,000	$1,450,000	$1,480,000
1.47	$1,530,000	$1,450,000	$1,470,000
1.46	$1,530,000	$1,450,000	$1,460,000
1.45	$1,530,000	$1,450,000	$1,450,000
1.44	$1,520,000	$1,450,000	$1,440,000
1.43	$1,510,000	$1,450,000	$1,430,000
1.42	$1,500,000	$1,450,000	$1,420,000
1.41	$1,490,000	$1,450,000	$1,410,000
1.40	$1,480,000	$1,450,000	$1,400,000
1.39	$1,470,000	$1,450,000	$1,390,000
1.38	$1,460,000	$1,450,000	$1,380,000
1.37	$1,450,000	$1,450,000	$1,370,000
1.36	$1,440,000	$1,450,000	$1,360,000
1.35	$1,430,000	$1,450,000	$1,350,000
1.30	$1,380,000	$1,450,000	$1,300,000
1.20	$1,280,000	$1,450,000	$1,200,000

and loss profile of an $80,000 open position in the option versus the forward contract is shown in **Table 14.10**.

In **Table 14.10** a speculator is assumed to have $80,000 available for speculative purposes and he feels that the euro is likely to appreciate from $1.50/€1 to $1.70/€1. He could choose between taking out a forward contract to buy euros at $1.45/€1 or buy an option to purchase euros at $1.45/€1 for 8 US cents per €1. Let us first consider the options contract: an $80,000 investment gives the right to purchase €1,000,000-worth of euros at $1.45/€1, that is $1,450,000 at a premium of 8 US cents per euro. If the spot rate in one year's time is above $1.45/€1, then the option will

Table 14.10 A currency option versus a currency forward for speculation

Spot exchange rate 1 year ahead	Per €1 option	Per €1 forward	Open position	
			Option	Forward
2.00	0.47	0.55	+$470,000	+$30,344.83
1.90	0.37	0.45	+$370,000	+$24,827.59
1.80	0.27	0.35	+$270,000	+$19,310.34
1.70	0.17	0.25	+$170,000	+$13,793.10
1.60	0.07	0.15	+$70,000	+$8,275.16
1.55	0.02	0.10	+$20,000	+$5,517.24
1.54	0.01	0.09	+$10,000	+$4,965.52
1.53	0.00	0.08	0	+$4,413.79
1.52	−0.01	0.07	−$10,000	+$3,862.07
1.51	−0.02	0.06	−$20,000	+$3,310.34
1.50	−0.03	0.05	−$30,000	+$2,758.63
1.49	−0.04	0.04	−$40,000	+$2,206.90
1.48	−0.05	0.03	−$50,000	+$1,655.17
1.47	−0.06	0.02	−$60,000	+$1,103.45
1.46	−0.07	0.01	−$70,000	+$551.72
1.45	−0.08	0	−$80,000	0
1.44	−0.08	−0.01	−$80,000	−$551.72
1.43	−0.08	−0.02	−$80,000	−$1,103.45
1.42	−0.08	−0.03	−$80,000	−$1,655.17
1.41	−0.08	−0.04	−$80,000	−$2,206.90
1.40	−0.08	−0.05	−$80,000	−$2,758.63
1.39	−0.08	−0.06	−$80,000	−$3,310.34
1.38	−0.08	−0.07	−$80,000	−$3,862.07
1.37	−0.08	−0.08	−$80,000	−$4,413.79
1.36	−0.08	−0.09	−$80,000	−$4,965.52
1.35	−0.08	−0.10	−$80,000	−$5,517.24
1.30	−0.08	−0.15	−$80,000	−$8,275.86
1.20	−0.08	−0.25	−$80,000	−$13,793.10

be exercised. If the speculator is correct then he will buy €1,000,000 at $1.45/€1 for a total cost of $1,450,000 and immediately convert the €1,000,000 back at $1.70/€1 to receive $1,700,000, so leaving a profit of $1,700,000 − $1,450,000 − $80,000 (the option premium paid) = $170,000. So long as the future spot rate is above $1.53/€1, so that the 8 US cents cost of the option premium is covered, then the option can be profitably exercised. Between $1.45/€1 and $1.53/€1 the option will still be exercised but an overall loss made. If the rate is below $1.45/€1 then the option will not be exercised and the speculator will lose the entire $80,000 premium!

As an alternative to the options contract, the speculator could take an $80,000 position in the forward market, that is contract to buy $80,000/1.45 = €55,172.41 forward. If the speculator is proved right, and the future spot rate turns out to be $1.70/€1, then on delivery of the forward contract he will give $80,000 and receive €55,172.41, and can then immediately sell the €55,172.41 at $1.70 and receive back $93,793.10, implying a profit of $93,793.10 − $80,000 = $13,793.10. For each cent that the spot rate in one year's time is above $1.45 he makes a profit of $551.72, and for each cent the rate is below $1.45 he makes a loss of $551.72. For instance, if the future spot rate is $1.40/€1, then on delivery of the forward contract he will give $80,000 and receive €55,172.41, and can then immediately sell the €55,172.41 at $1.40 and receive back $77,241.37, implying a loss of $77,241.37 − $80,000 = −$2,758.63.

We can see from this example that an options contract offers a very different risk–return profile for speculative purposes than that offered by the forward/futures contract. The options contract offers an asymmetric profit and loss profile: on the one hand it offers potentially huge gains but the speculator runs the risk of losing all of his $80,000, although he cannot lose more than the option premium paid. The forward market offers a symmetric and far less dramatic speculative profit/loss profile.

14.13   Option strategies

Because of their special risk–return profiles, options can be used in numerous ways for risk management. They can be used on an individual basis or combined with other option positions or even futures contracts to achieve a desired risk–return profile. To illustrate this we consider two well known strategies using option contracts – the straddle and the strangle. The rules relating to European options facilitate these two strategies.

The straddle

The fact that the downside risk is limited while the upside potential is unlimited can be exploited by an investor that thinks a share is about to move but is unsure of the particular direction in which it may move. In such circumstances, an investor can buy both a call and a put on a share with the same strike price and the same expiration date, and such a position is known as a straddle.

Consider the share price of British Petroleum, currently at 525 pence, with the price of a call at 540 being 18 pence and the price of a put at 540 being 38 pence. **Table 14.11** shows the profit and loss profile if the position is held to maturity.

The maximum loss for a straddle position is the sum of the call and put option premiums paid, in this example 56 pence. This maximum loss from the position occurs when the future spot rate coincides with the exercise price of the call and put options. The more that the spot price of the underlying share on expiry deviates from the strike price, then the smaller any loss or the greater any profit from the straddle position. The beauty of the straddle position is that it enables a trader to bet on the volatility of the share. If he does not think the share will move much then he could write (that is sell) call and put options. If, however, he thinks the share is likely to move substantially then a straddle position may be deemed appropriate.

straddle an option strategy that involves the simultaneous purchase of call and put options on a share at the same strike price and the same time to expiration

strangle an option strategy that involves the simultaneous purchase of call and put options on a share at different strike prices and the same time to expiration

European option a contract that can only be exercised on the expiration date

Table 14.11 Profit/loss profiles from a long straddle

Details:				
Option premiums				
Call	18	Strike price	540	
Put	38	Strike price	540	
Current share price	525			
Expiration	March 2010			
Contract	1000 shares			

Price of BP shares on expiration date	Holder profit/loss on long call	Holder profit/loss on long put	Net profit/loss on straddle
200	−£180	+£3,020	+£2,840
300	−£180	+£2,020	+£1,840
350	−£180	+£1,520	+£1,340
400	−£180	+£1,020	+£840
450	−£180	+£520	+£340
480	−£180	+£220	+£40
484	−£180	+£180	£0
500	−£180	+£20	−£160
502	−£180	£0	−£180
520	−£180	−£180	−£360
540	−£180	−£380	−£560
550	−£80	−£380	−£460
558	£0	−£380	−£380
596	+£380	−£380	£0
600	+£420	−£380	+£40
650	+£920	−£380	+£540
700	+£1,420	−£380	+£1,040
800	+£2,420	−£380	+£2,040

The strangle

A strangle is a combination of a call and a put option on a security with the same expiry date but different exercise prices. Consider the share price of British Petroleum, currently 525 pence, when the price of a call at 540 is 18 pence and the price of a put at 520 is 27 pence. **Table 14.12** shows the profit and loss profile of the strangle if the position is held to maturity.

With the long strangle position there is a price range between the call option strike price and the put option strike price where maximum losses are made; in our

Table 14.12   Profit/loss profiles from a long strangle

Details:			
Option premiums			
Call	18	Strike price	540
Put	27	Strike price	520
Current share price	525		
Expiration	March 2010		
Contract	1000 shares		

Price of BP shares on expiration date	Holder profit/loss on long call	Holder profit/loss on long put	Net profit/loss on strangle
200	−£180	+£2,930	+£2,750
300	−£180	+£1,930	+£1,750
350	−£180	+£1,430	+£1,250
400	−£180	+£930	+£750
450	−£180	+£430	+£250
475	−£180	+£180	£0
493	−£180	£0	−£180
500	−£180	−£70	−£250
520	−£180	−£270	−£450
525	−£180	−£270	−£450
530	−£180	−£270	−£450
535	−£180	−£270	−£450
540	−£180	−£270	−£450
550	−£80	−£270	−£350
558	£0	−£270	−£270
585	+£270	−£270	£0
600	+£420	−£270	+£150
650	+£920	−£270	+£650
700	+£1,420	−£270	+£1,150
800	+£2,420	−£270	+£2,150

example, these losses are capped at £450. Then as we start to deviate either below the call or above the put price, losses are reduced or profits rise in a symmetrical fashion on either side of the strike prices. This occurs because when the price is below the call strike price, while the call premium is wasted, the profits on the put are increasing. If, however, we are above the put strike price, while the put premium is wasted, the profits on the call are increasing.

There are numerous other well known strategies that can be pursued using combinations of options to change the profit/loss profile, such as a 'strap' (two calls and one put with the same expiry date, although exercise prices can differ) or a 'strip' (one call and two puts with the same expiry date, although exercise prices can differ). In addition to taking only long or only short positions in call and put contracts, there are also numerous strategies whereby an investor can have both a long and a short position in two or more option contracts. For example, in a 'long butterfly' strategy the investor has a long call with a low exercise price (X1), two short calls with a middle exercise price (X2) and a long call with a high exercise price (X3), where we have X1 < X2 < X3 and all options contracts have the same expiry date. A 'long butterfly' has a similar risk–return profile to a short straddle, but caps the potential downside losses.

Other option strategies, known as 'horizontal spreads' or 'calendar spreads', involve using similar strike prices but different expiry dates, while 'diagonal spreads' are strategies using both different expiry dates and different strike prices.

14.14   Exotic options

Securities houses and banks have devised a number of so-called 'exotic options' to meet particular needs of their clients. The main problem with these options is that their non-standard nature means there is not an active secondary market. However, their main advantage is that they may be better suited to a client's particular needs than the standard product. Besides the basic put and call options there are a wide variety of other options available today, some of which are listed below:

- *As you like it option*. An option that allows the holder to convert from one type of option to another at a certain point before expiration, normally from a call to a put option or *vice versa*. Also called a 'call or put' option or a 'chooser' option.
- *Average rate option*. An option on which settlement is based upon the difference between the strike price and the average price of the stock or index on certain dates. The average feature makes it less volatile and hence cheaper than a spot price option. Sometimes called an 'Asian Option'.
- *Barrier options*. A number of different options whose payoff pattern and even survival depend not only on the underlying price of the security, but also on whether the security reaches a predetermined barrier at any time during the life of the option. For example, knock-in options are first activated by the underlying security reaching a predetermined level, whereas knock-out options are 'killed off' if the underlying security hits a predetermined price.
- *Compound option*. An option on an option. The holder has the right to buy an option at a preset date at a preset premium.
- *Lookback option*. An option on which the payout is determined by using the highest intrinsic value of the underlying security or index over the life of an option. For a lookback call the highest market price would be used, whereas for a lookback put the lowest market price would be used.
- *Quanto option*. An option in which the foreign exchange risks in an underlying security have been eliminated.

- *Warrant.* A special type of option normally attached to a newly issued security (for example, a Eurobond) which gives the holder of the warrant the right to buy or sell an underlying instrument at a given price and time, or at a series of prices and times. Normally issued for more than a year.

14.15   Conclusions

The options market is now established as one of the most important growth areas of financial markets. Options can help investors to hedge positions at relatively low cost and can prove more suited to hedgers' needs than futures contracts. While buying a futures contract guarantees the price to be paid in the future regardless of what the corresponding future spot price turns out to be, hedging with a futures contract means that the investor also gives up the opportunity to benefit from a favourable price movement. It is here that options contracts can provide an important alternative. By hedging with an options contract the hedger can ensure a maximum price to be paid in the future and yet still be able to take advantage of a favourable price movement. Properly used, options contracts are extremely useful hedging tools. The symmetric risks involved in forwards and futures contracts contrasts with the asymmetric risks of options contracts, and for this reason options tend to be more costly hedging instruments to purchase. In order to induce a party to write an option the purchaser must be prepared to pay a fee that reflects the increased exposure of the writer.

Options contracts can also provide extremely attractive, and at times spectacular, speculative returns compared to taking speculative positions in the cash or forward market. However, against this, it must be borne in mind that many options contracts lapse without being exercised and the speculator thereby risks losing all of the option premium paid. Also, in this chapter we have ignored the issue of option pricing which is dealt with in the following chapter; the more likely an option is to be exercised the higher will be its price and the lower the consequent profit profile. One of the features that makes options so attractive is their asymmetrical profit/loss profile which means that investors can combine downside protection with significant upside potential. This contrasts with the symmetric profit/loss profiles offered by futures/forward contracts.

Another attractive feature of options is that they can be combined with other options, futures and spot positions to devise numerous innovative speculative and hedging strategies. Overall, therefore, options contracts enable investors, hedgers and speculators to take positions which are more suited to their risk–return preferences.

Further reading

Chisholm, A. (2004) *Derivatives Demystified: A Step by Step Guide to Forwards, Futures and Options*, Wiley.

Hull, J.C. (2008) *Options, Futures and Other Derivatives*, Prentice-Hall.

Kolb, R.W. and Overdahl, J. (2007) *Futures, Options and Swaps*, 5th edn, Basil Blackwell.

Chapter 14	Revision questions

1 You are given the following data on call and put premiums in pence per share for Company ABC shares which are currently priced in the market at 311 pence. Each contract refers to 1000 shares.

Strike price	September call premium	September put premium
300 pence	61	44
330 pence	48	60

(i) You expect the share price to rise to 400 pence. Discuss a speculative strategy and the profits/losses at a range of different prices for the underlying share in September.

(ii) You own 1000 shares in Company ABC and fear that the share price might fall to 200 pence. Discuss a partial hedging strategy using one of the above contracts and the approximate value of your net hedged position at a range of different prices for the underlying share in September.

2 Company XYZ shares are priced in June at 250 pence a share. You believe that they are currently considerably overvalued and are worth only 150 pence a share. September put options on a strike price of 230 pence a share are currently valued at 25 pence. Each call option contract is based on 1000 shares.

(i) What is the break-even XYZ share price in September that will yield the option holder zero profits from the put option contract?

(ii) What is the total net profit (+) /net loss (−) in pounds to the put holder if the shares are priced at 150 pence in September?

(iii) What is the net profit (+)/ net loss (−) in pounds to the put holder if the shares are priced at 300 pence in September?

3 Briefly explain with a simple numerical example a 'long straddle' position in the options market.

4 It is January and you are missing data on June FTSE 100 index options which are valued at £10 per full index point. The cash value of the FTSE 100 index is reading 4800.

FTSE 100 index value	5000		5100	
	Call	Put	Call	Put
June	?	?	?	?
Dec	?	?	?	?

Complete the above table by placing some plausible looking index points premiums where there are question marks and explain your reasoning.

5 It is January, the dollar/pound ($/£) exchange rate is currently $1.72/£1 and the following options and futures prices exist for June

June futures (contract size £100,000): $1.70/£1
June options: The underlying contract is to buy/sell £100,000 at $1.70/£1

Strike price	Call option premium	Put option premium
$1.70/£1	$0.05	$0.03

| Chapter 14 | Revision questions – *continued* |

You are a speculator and expect the spot rate on expiry in June to be $1.85/£1. Discuss the relative merits of using the futures or options contracts to speculate on your predicted currency movement . In your answer consider a range of possible future spot rates for sterling and the resulting profits/losses.

6   State which of the following statements are TRUE and which are FALSE.

   (i)   The maximum gain from writing a call option is limited but the maximum loss is not.

  (ii)   For an option writer the risk of writing a call option is reduced if the writer has a short position in the underlying stock.

 (iii)   The writer of a call option will make a profit once the share price falls below the strike price.

 (iv)   Both parties to a put option contract will have to make margin payments.

 Multiple choice questions available at www.palgrave.com/business/pilbeam

15

OPTION PRICING

Learning objectives

In completing this chapter you will learn about:

- the difference between intrinsic value and time value
- the factors that determine call and put premiums
- how to price call options using the Black–Scholes option pricing formula
- how to calculate historical volatility and the difference between historical, expected and implied volatility
- importance of the 'Greeks' in measuring the sensitivity of option prices

  how to price put options from call option premiums using put–call parity

15.1 Introduction

Black–Scholes formula a model used to price a European call option premium which was published in 1973 by Fisher Black and Myron Scholes

In the previous chapter we examined some of the basic issues relating to options and looked at possible return profiles. In this chapter we look at the more complex question of option pricing. In particular we examine the factors that determine the price of an option, first intuitively and then analytically using the famous Black–Scholes option pricing formula which was put forward in a classic paper by Black and Scholes (1973). Although there have been many refinements to the Black–Scholes formula it has become one of the most famous equations of economics and is widely used by practitioners to determine appropriate option premiums. We also consider the relationship between call and put premiums via the put–call parity condition.

15.2 Principles of option pricing

When considering the price of an option we need to bear in mind exactly what the buyer of an option is purchasing. An option offers the purchaser limited downside loss as given by the option premium paid, combined with unlimited upside potential. An option that has no chance of ever being exercised would be worthless; however, if an option has a high probability of being exercised then one should expect to pay more for it. A fundamental principle underlying the pricing of an option is that the greater the probability of an option being exercised, the higher will be the option premium, other things being equal.

Bearing this basic principle in mind, let us consider conceptually the factors that are likely to influence the price of a European call option in company ABC. Payment for a European call option gives the buyer the right but not the obligation to buy shares in company ABC at a predetermined price at a given date in the future. There are five crucial factors that determine the likelihood of the call option being exercised and hence influence the price to be paid for the call option:

1 The current price of the share – the higher the current price of the stock the more likely the option is to be exercised for any given exercise price and consequently the higher the price of a call option.
2 The strike price – the higher the strike price of a call option the less likely it is that it will be exercised and hence the lower its price.
3 The time left to expiration – the longer the time left to expiration then the more the chance of the option being exercised and hence the higher its price.
4 The volatility – the more volatile an option is the more likely that its price will exceed the strike price at expiration and hence the higher the price of the option.

5   The risk-free rate of interest – the purchaser of a call option is paying the issuer cash for an option that can be exercised to buy an underlying security at a future date. The option holder is thus benefiting from the fact that the difference between the option premium and actually buying the underlying security can be invested at a risk-free rate of interest until the option expires. A rise in the risk-free rate of interest makes it more attractive to buy the option rather than the underlying security. For this reason, other things being equal, a call option premium needs to be priced more highly when interest rates are high than when interest rates are low. The higher the risk-free rate of interest the higher a call option price. Note, however, that changes in the risk-free rate of interest are usually only a marginal factor in the pricing of options.

Table 15.1 summarizes the relationships between each of the five determinants of an option's price and the price of a European call and put option.

Table 15.1   Summary of factors affecting an option's price

Factor a rise in:	European call	European put
Current price	+	–
Strike price	–	+
Time to expiration	+	+
Volatility	+	+
Risk-free interest rate	+	–

Note: The above assumes that there are no dividends due during the life of the option.

15.3   Intrinsic value and time value

intrinsic value the value that would be realized if an option were exercised immediately. For a call option it is the amount by which the current price of the underlying exceeds the exercise price; for a put option, it is the amount by which the current price of the underlying is below the exercise price

An option premium is made up of two components, the intrinsic value and the time value. The intrinsic value is the gain that would be realized if an option was exercised immediately. For a call option, this is simply the cash price less the strike price of the underlying asset, while for a put option it is the strike price less the cash price:

Intrinsic value for a call option = cash price − strike price

Intrinsic value for a put option = strike price − cash price

If an intrinsic value for an option exists, then the option is said to be 'in-the-money'. A call option will be in-the-money if the strike price is below the cash price. If the strike price is above the cash price the call option will have zero intrinsic value and is said to be 'out-of-the-money'. If the strike price is equal to the cash price it is 'at-the-money' with zero intrinsic value.

time value the remainder of an option premium after deducting its intrinsic value

Table 15.2   In-the-money, at-the-money and out-of-the-money options

	Call	Put
In-the-money	current price above exercise price	current price below exercise price
At-the-money	current price equals exercise price	current price equals exercise price
Out-of-the-money	current price below exercise price	current price above exercise price

Table 15.2 summarizes the various possible states for both call and put option contracts. The intrinsic value reflects the price that would be received if the option were 'locked in' today at the current market price, and is either positive or zero.

The time value of an option is the option premium less the intrinsic value, and reflects the fact that an option may have more ultimate value than the intrinsic value alone:

Time value = option premium − intrinsic value

An option buyer, even if the option is out-of-the-money will still have some hope that at some time prior to expiration changes in the spot price will move the option into the money or further increase the value of the option if it is already in-the-money. This prospect gives an option a value greater than its intrinsic value.

Numerical examples

Example 1

Consider a call option valued at 18 pence in the stock of Company ABC with a strike price of 90 pence and a cash price for the underlying share of 100 pence. The option is in-the-money to the tune of 10 pence and so has an intrinsic value of 10 pence; the other 8 pence represents the time value.

Example 2

Consider a call option valued at 11 pence in the stock of Company XYZ with a strike price of 85 pence and a cash price for the underlying share of 80 pence. The option is out-of-the-money and so has no intrinsic value, the whole value of the option, that is, 11 pence is time value.

15.4 The distribution of the option premium between time and intrinsic value

One of the crucial assumptions underlying the theory of option pricing as set out in the Black–Scholes option pricing formula is that the natural logarithm of the cash price of the underlying asset is normally distributed, that is it follows a log-normal distribution. A variable that has a log-normal distribution can have any value between zero and infinity as shown in **Figure 15.1**.

Figure 15.1   A log normal distribution

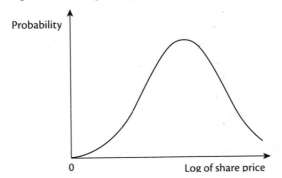

The time value for a given expiry date will get closer to zero the more in-the-money or out-of-the-money the contract is. This is illustrated in **Figures 15.2**(a)–(e) that show the various probability factors behind the intrinsic and time-value components of an option. There is a log-normal distribution around the spot price such that the spot price may go up or down by a given amount with equal probability; however, the larger the move in any direction the smaller the probability.

Figure 15.2(a) shows a deep-in-the-money option, with the spot price exceeding the exercise price. This option has a roughly 50 per cent chance of rising further, giving good upside potential. However, there is also a lot of intrinsic value that could easily be reduced or even lost entirely if the security were to fall in price. The time value is then given by the potential upside area minus the potential loss of the intrinsic value, which is quite high, leaving a small amount of time value.

Figure 15.2(b) shows a slightly-in-the-money option, with the spot price exceeding the exercise price. This option has a roughly 50 per cent chance of rising further, giving good upside potential, but there is less intrinsic value that could be wiped out or reduced than in case **Figure 15.2**(a). Therefore, the time value, which is given by the potential upside area minus the potential loss of the intrinsic value, is higher than in the deep-in-the-money case due to the lower intrinsic value.

Figure 15.2   Intrinsic and time values

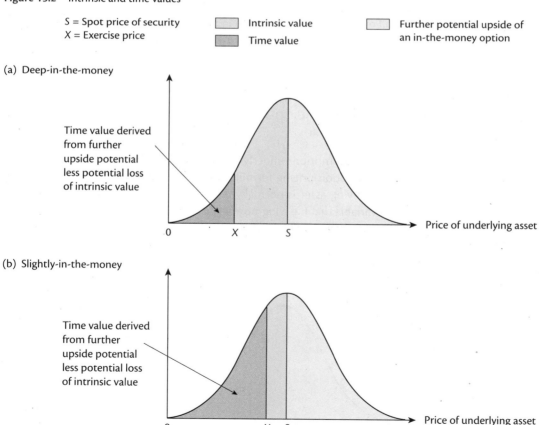

Figure 15.2 Intrinsic and time values – *continued*

(c) At-the-money

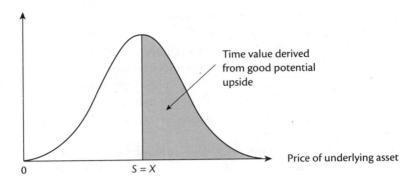

Time value derived from good potential upside

Price of underlying asset

0   S = X

(d) Slightly-out-of-the-money

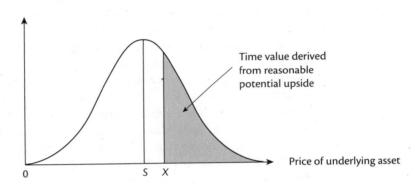

Time value derived from reasonable potential upside

Price of underlying asset

0   S   X

(e) Deep-out-of-the-money

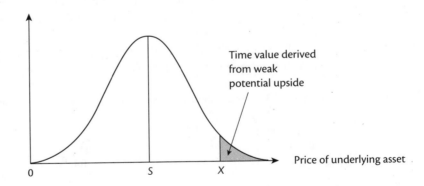

Time value derived from weak potential upside

Price of underlying asset

0   S   X

Figure 15.2(c) shows an at-the-money option, with the spot price being equal to the exercise price. The time value of the option is at its maximum, reflecting the fact that any upward movement in the price of the underlying security will place the option in the money, while there is no intrinsic value to be lost.

Figure 15.2(d) shows a slightly-out-of-the-money option, with the spot price not too far below the exercise price. The option has no intrinsic value but there is a good chance that the spot price may exceed the exercise price prior to maturity, although less than in the at-the-money case. For this reason, the option will have a lower time value than in Figure 15.2(c), other things being equal.

Figure 15.2(e) shows a deep-out-of-the-money option, with the spot price well below the exercise price. The option has no intrinsic value and there is only a relatively small chance that the spot price will exceed the exercise price prior to maturity. For this reason, the option has only a small time value which is lower than in the slightly-out-of-the-money case (**Figure 15.2**(d)), other things being equal.

An important point about these examples is that, as we move from **Figure 15.2**(a) to (e), the value of the option falls, other things being equal (that is, for a given exercise price, volatility, risk-free rate of interest and term to maturity) because the probability of the option being exercised – the area to the right of the exercise price – decreases.

In **Figure 15.3**, the distribution of the total option premium between time value and intrinsic value is shown for a variety of spot prices (S1, S2, S3, S4 and S5), other things being equal, and for a given strike price (X). A deep-out-of-the-money option with price S1 has zero intrinsic value and a small amount of time value. If the spot price were higher (S2), so that the option is only slightly out-of-the-money, the option premium has zero intrinsic value but more time value, reflecting the greater probability of being exercised than at S1. When the spot price (S3) is equal to the exercise price – that is, the contract is at-the-money – the entire premium is made up of the time value which is at its maximum. Above the exercise price, the option premium starts to have a positive intrinsic component which increases by 1 unit for each 1 unit that the spot price exceeds the exercise price. However, time value starts to fall because, although there is further upside potential, there is the risk that some (or all) intrinsic value can be lost, so at S4 the time value is smaller than at S3 although the total option premium is higher. At the spot price S5 the option is deep-in-the-money with a large component of intrinsic value and continued upside potential, and only a slight risk that the option will end up worthless, which is reflected in a small amount of time value.

The lesson is that the more in-the-money the contract, the greater the probability that the option holder will be able to exercise the contract and therefore the lower

Figure 15.3   The distribution of a call premium between time and intrinsic value

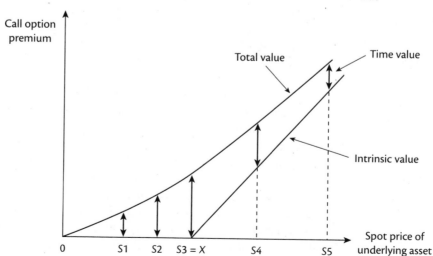

Table 15.3 Intrinsic value and time value

Option status	Intrinsic value	Time value	Reason for time value
Deep-in-the-money (Figure 15.2(a))	S – X	Low	Small downside protection
Slightly-in-the-money (Figure 15.2(b))	S – X	High	High downside protection High upside potential
At-the-money (Figure 15.2(c))	Zero	Maximum	Maximum upside potential Maximum downside protection
Slightly-out-of-the-money (Figure 15.2(d))	Zero	High	High upside potential High downside protection
Deep-out-of-the-money (Figure 15.2(e))	Zero	Low	Small upside potential

Note: S = cash or spot price of the underlying asset and X is the exercise price of the call option.

the time value on the contract. Similarly, the more out-of-the-money the contract the greater the probability that the contract will not be exercised and therefore the lower the time value of the options contract. **Table 15.3** summarizes the division of the option premium between intrinsic and time value for various option statuses, and the reason for the time value.

15.5 The Black–Scholes option pricing formula

In a famous paper, Fischer Black and Myron Scholes (1973) derived a formula for the pricing of options. The formula only applies to European options, although more sophisticated versions exist to deal with the pricing of American options. For the purpose of our analysis we will deal with the pricing of a call option. The Black–Scholes formula is based upon a number of simplifying assumptions:

1 The underlying asset being analyzed pays no dividends or interest during its lifetime.
2 The option is a European option, that is, it cannot be exercised prior to maturity.
3 The risk-free rate of interest is fixed during the life of the option.
4 The financial markets are perfectly efficient with zero transactions costs, no bid–ask spread and no taxes.
5 The price of the underlying asset is log-normally distributed, with a constant mean and standard deviation.
6 It is possible to short-sell the underlying asset and utilize the proceeds obtained without restriction.
7 The price of the underlying asset moves in a continuous fashion.

The basic idea underlying the derivation of the Black–Scholes option pricing model is that a long position in the underlying stock is neutralized by a short position in options (appropriately priced) such that the stock holder with such a combined position will only have a return equal to the risk-free rate of interest. When the stock price rises, the premium on the option rises (implying a loss for a short position) so as to offset any gain from the rise in the price of the stock.

The starting point for the Black–Scholes formula is that the intrinsic value of a call option on expiration is the spot price (S) less the exercise price (X) if the option is in-the-money, or zero if the option is at or out-of-the-money. Imagine that we knew today with 100 per cent certainty the intrinsic value on expiration, and that this was above the exercise price, then the value of the call premium on expiration would be:

$$C = S - X > 0 \qquad (15.1)$$

where C is the call premium; S is the cash or spot price of the underlying asset; and X is the exercise price.

The holder of such a call option will be able to set aside less money than the actual exercise price (X) prior to maturity, since during the time remaining to maturity (T) he can obtain a rate of interest r on such funds that when continuously compounded will give him the sum X when the exercise is due. The sum of money that needs to be set aside to achieve the exercise price is given by:

$$Xe^{-rT} \qquad (15.2)$$

where X is the exercise price; e is the natural number 2.7182 . . .; r is the risk-free rate of interest; and T is the time left to maturity expressed as a fraction of a year.

The term Xe^{-rT} is simply the present value of the exercise price when continuous time discounting is used. Hence, the call option would actually be worth more than suggested by equation (15.1). At any time up to maturity, the value of such an option would be given by:

$$C = S - Xe^{-rT} \qquad (15.3)$$

which says that the value of the call would be equal to the price of the share on expiration less the present value of the exercise price.

In reality, the assumption that the share price will close above the strike price is unrealistic. Hence, the actual present value of $S - Xe^{-rT}$ is uncertain, so equation (15.3) needs to be modified to be based upon the expected value upon expiration. The expected value involves use of cumulative normal distribution tables, leading to:

$$C = SN(d1) - Xe^{-rT}N(d2) \qquad (15.4)$$

where $SN(d1)$ is the expected value of the underlying security upon expiration (assuming that the option is exercised), while the term $Xe^{-rT}N(d2)$ is the expected present value of the strike price on expiration (assuming that the option is exercised).

The $d1$ and $d2$ terms are given by:

$$d1 = \frac{\ln(S/X) + (r + \sigma^2/2)T}{\sigma\sqrt{T}} \qquad (15.5)$$

and

$$d2 = d1 - \sigma\sqrt{T} \qquad (15.6)$$

where C is the price of the call; S is the current spot price; X is the exercise price; σ^2 is the variance of the price of the underlying asset on an annual basis; σ is the standard deviation of the price of the underlying asset on an annualized basis; and T is the time to expiry in a fraction of a year (e.g. one quarter = 0.25, 6 months = 0.5).

The Black–Scholes formula therefore states that the current value of a call option is the present value of the expected cash price less the expected value of the strike price.

Interpretation of the N(d1) and N(d2) terms

The N(d1) and N(d2) terms involving the cumulative probability function are the terms which take into account the risk of the option being exercised.

The N(d1) term reflects the cumulative probability relating to the current value of the stock, and its value shows the amount by which the option premium increases for each one unit rise in the price of the underlying security. The value of N(d1) lies between 0 and 1. If a stock is deeply out-of-the-money then any unit rise in the stock price will have little effect on the value of the call since it remains unlikely that the option will be exercised, so that N(d1) will be low, for example 0.2. If the option is currently at-the-money, then there is a 50 per cent chance it will end up in-the-money and a 50 per cent chance it will end up out-of-the-money, so N(d1) will be 0.5; that is, if the underlying stock rises by one unit then the option price will rise by 0.5 of a unit. If the option is already deep-in-the-money, each one unit rise in the share price will be increasingly reflected in the price of the call so that N(d1) will get closer to 1, for example 0.9. The higher the stock price in relation to the exercise price, the higher the value of N(d1).

The N(d2) term is an approximate measure of the probability that the call option will actually be exercised; for example, if N(d2) is 0.60 then there is an approximately (though not exactly) 60 per cent chance that the option will be exercised.

The value of N(d1) is always greater than N(d2) except in the special case when the option is certain to be exercised. In this case, N(d1) = N(d2) = 1. When N(d1) and N(d2) are equal to 1 then the Black–Scholes option pricing formula becomes:

$$C = S - Xe^{-rT} \tag{15.7}$$

One of the most notable features of the Black–Scholes option pricing formula is that expected volatility is a key factor in determining the price of an option. The formula does not depend upon the level of the future price of the underlying asset to determine the appropriate option price.

A numerical example of the Black–Scholes formula

Let us consider the pricing of a call option for shares in Company ABC. For simplicity, we ignore complications posed by the possibility of dividend payments. Let us assume that the current spot price of a share is 100 pence and an investor buys a call option to purchase the share at 90 pence. The risk-free rate of interest is 6 per cent and the relevant measure of historical volatility given by the variance is 49 per cent. The option has 90 days to expiry. Hence:

$$S = 100p$$
$$X = 90p$$
$$r = 0.06$$
$$T = 90/365 = 0.25 \text{ (approx)}$$
$$\sigma^2 = 0.49 \text{ so that } \sigma = 0.7$$

We firstly calculate the value of $d1$:

$$d1 = \frac{\ln(S/X) + (r + \sigma^2/2)T}{\sigma\sqrt{T}}$$

that is;

$$d1 = \frac{\ln(100/90) + (0.06 + 0.7^2/2)0.25}{0.7\sqrt{0.25}}$$

$$= 0.52$$

From the cumulative normal distribution **Table 15.8** at the end of the chapter we find:

$$N(d1) = N(0.52)$$

$$= 0.6985$$

Note: If the value we find for $N(d1)$ or $N(d2)$ is negative then when we look up the value in the normal distribution table we must subtract the value we find in the table from 1. For example, if we need to look up the value $N(d1) = N(-0.12)$ in the table, we first look up $N(0.12)$, which is 0.5478, and then subtract this value from 1, so that $N(d1) = N(-0.12)$ is given by $1 - 0.5478 = 0.4522$. For positive values of $N(d1)$ and $N(d2)$ we use the value listed in the table.

We next calculate the value of $d2$:

$$d2 = d1 - \sigma\sqrt{T}$$

that is,

$$d2 = 0.52 - 0.7\sqrt{0.25}$$

$$= 0.17$$

and

$$N(d2) = N(0.17)$$

$$= 0.5675$$

With these calculations we are now in a position to calculate the price of the option.

$$C = SN(d1) - Xe^{-rT}N(d2)$$

Substituting the appropriate values yields:

$$C = 100(0.6985) - 90(2.718)^{-0.06(0.25)}(0.5675)$$

$$= 19.35$$

Of the 19.35 premium 10 pence is intrinsic value and 9.35 pence is time value.

The above calculations are based upon a current share price of 100 pence and a strike price of 90 pence. **Table 15.4** shows how the values of $N(d1)$ and $N(d2)$ change as the value of the current share price changes, and the resulting call price in pence.

Table 15.4   The values of N(d1) and N(d2) for different current share prices

Share price in pence	d1	N(d1)	d2	N(d2)	Call price in pence
70	−0.50	0.3085	−0.85	0.1977	4.07
80	−0.12	0.4522	−0.47	0.3192	7.88
90	0.22	0.5871	−0.13	0.4483	13.08
100	0.52	0.6985	0.17	0.5675	19.35
110	0.79	0.7852	0.44	0.6700	26.97
120	1.04	0.8508	0.69	0.7549	35.18
130	1.27	0.8977	0.92	0.8212	43.93

Notes: T = 3 months (0.25 in formula), r = 6 per cent (0.06 in formula), standard deviation = 0.7, X = 90 pence.

15.6   Different measures of volatility

> **historical volatility**
> the volatility obtained by using actual historical data

The intrinsic value of an option is easily calculated, and the time left to expiration and the risk-free rate of interest are all measurable; the most contentious thing to measure is volatility. Ideally, the efficient pricing of options would contain a measurement of volatility that is likely to reflect the volatility that will occur in the future. Historical volatility may be a useful measure for this purpose, but it could prove to be defective as the past is not necessarily a good guide to the future. In addition, should an appropriate measure of historical volatility be based on the last month, the last three months, the last six months or the last year? Another problem with historical volatility is that it usually fails to pick up the possibility of large discrete shifts. Expected volatility will differ from one market participant to another and therefore the view of the appropriate market price of an option will vary between market participants. Implied volatility is the volatility implicit in the current option price, which is found by taking the current price of the option and finding a volatility that, when plugged into the option-pricing formula, gives the current market price of the option. (This is easily calculated using a spreadsheet.)

> **expected volatility**
> the volatility expected by an option trader which varies from trader to trader based upon their individual forecasts

15.7   The calculation of historical volatility

> **implied volatility**
> the volatility implicit in the current option price. It is found by taking the current price of the option and finding a volatility that when plugged into the option-pricing formula gives the current market price of the option

Volatility in the Black–Scholes option pricing formula can be measured by historical volatility, the most common method of calculation being the annualized standard deviation of daily, weekly or even monthly changes in prices. The annualized price volatility is obtained by multiplying the calculated sample standard deviation by the square root of the number of periods:

For daily data (based on 252 trading days per annum)

$$\sigma = \sqrt{252} \times \text{daily standard deviation}$$

For weekly data

$$\sigma = \sqrt{52} \times \text{weekly standard deviation}$$

For monthly data

$$\sigma = \sqrt{12} \times \text{monthly standard deviation}$$

Table 15.5   Example calculation of volatility

Week	Share price (S_t)	Relative price ($S_t/S_t - 1$)	Log of relative price i.e. $\ln(S_t/S_t - 1)$
1	91		
2	102	1.1209	0.1141
3	95	0.9314	−0.0711
4	101	1.0632	0.0612
5	116	1.1485	0.1385
6	101	0.8707	−0.1385
7	108	1.0693	0.0670
8	95	0.8796	−0.1283
9	102	1.0737	0.0711
10	107	1.0490	0.0479

Note: The standard deviation of the log of relative prices is 0.0975

The volatility used is therefore the annualized standard deviation of the changes in prices, which are most easily calculated by taking the natural log of relative prices as in **Table 15.5**.

From **Table 15.5**, the annual standard deviation $0.0975 \times \sqrt{52} = 0.7$ and the annual variance $= 0.7 \times 0.7 = 0.49$. The correct variance estimator in the Black–Scholes model is the annual variance of relative log prices.

Box 15.1   **The Chicago Board Options Exchange Volatility Index: VIX – 'the fear index'**

In 1993, the Chicago Board Options Exchange (CBOE) introduced the CBOE Volatility Index – the VIX – which was originally designed to measure the market's expectation of 30-day volatility implied by at-the-money S&P 100 index option prices. Following its introduction, the VIX (ticker ^VIX) was regularly reported in the financial press and on financial news television as Wall Street's 'fear index' or 'fear gauge'. In 2003 the calculation of the VIX was updated so that it was based on a wide range of put and call premiums at different strike prices on the S&P 500 index. The new method of calculation made the VIX even more popular. The VIX measures the 30-day expected volatility in the S&P 500 index expressed as an index value between 0 and 100. If expected volatility in the stockmarket rises, then so do call and put premiums and so too will the calculated VIX. By contrast, if expected volatility in the stockmarket falls, then so too will call and put premiums and the calculated VIX.

Box 15.1	The VIX – *continued*

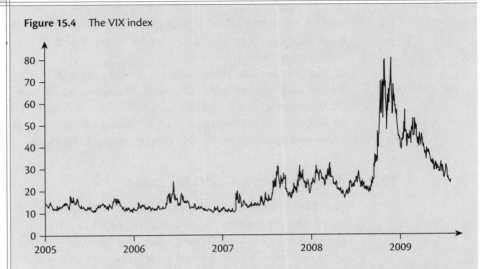

Figure 15.4 The VIX index

The CBOE has backdated calculations of the VIX, so that historical data for the VIX exists from 1990 onwards. Historically, the VIX on average has traded around the 20 level, with periods of low volatility bringing its value down towards to 10 and periods of high volatility taking it to around 30. During the credit crunch however, particularly after the collapse of Lehman Brothers and large falls and volatility in the stockmarket, the VIX rose to unprecedented levels. It reached a peak of 80.06 on 27 October 2008, with a further all-time high of 80.26 on 20 November 2008. By December 2009 the worst of the financial crisis seemed to be nearing an end as the VIX recorded a more normal measurement of 20–22. The fluctuations in the VIX between January 2005 and July 2009 are depicted in **Figure 15.4**.

The VIX index is so popular as a measurement of market volatility that it has led to the creation of new financial instruments based upon the VIX itself. Since 24 March 2004 there has been a futures contract on the VIX that enables investors to buy or sell volatility, and also call and put options with various strike prices on the VIX. In addition, there are similar volatility indices based on calculations for the NASDAQ-100 (VXN) and the Dow Jones Industrial Average (VXD) and a 3-month rather than 30-day volatility index for the S&P 500 (VXV).

Using a similar methodology to estimate expected volatility on the S&P 500 the CBOE has recently introduced volatility indices to estimate the expected volatility of certain commodities and foreign currencies; for example, the CBOE Crude Oil Volatility Index (OVX); CBOE Gold Volatility Index (GVZ) and CBOE EuroCurrency Volatility Index (EVZ). Trading volatility is one of the world of finance's latest products!

15.8   Problems with the Black–Scholes option pricing formula

The formula we have looked at is only applicable to European options. American options are usually priced slightly higher than European options because of the extra advantage that they give to the holder of being able to exercise the option at any date prior to maturity.

Another consideration is that the formula assumes that the log of the share price follows a log-normal distribution, whilst real-world distributions tend to be leptokurtic. They have fatter tails than a normal distribution, implying that there are better chances of an option being exercised than suggested by the Black–Scholes formula. Hence, real-world option prices tend to exceed the Black–Scholes formula price.

15.9   The sensitivity of options prices

The Black–Scholes option pricing formula shows that the price of options is determined by the time left to maturity, the strike price, the risk-free rate of interest, the volatility of the underlying share and its price. Any fund manager or investor using options will be interested in how the price of an option is affected by changes in any of these factors, so we will briefly mention these measures:

- **Option theta** (θ). An option's theta measures its sensitivity to the passing of time. The longer an option has until expiry the greater the possibility of time value being realized. The time value of an option will fall over time according to the square root of time.
- **Option delta** (δ). An option's delta measures the sensitivity of its price to the price of the underlying share. The formula for a call option is given by:

$$C = SN(d1) - Xe^{-rT}N(d2)$$

and the delta for a call option is given by:

$$\delta C = \frac{\partial C}{\partial S} = N(d1) \leq 1$$

The value of delta on a long call or short put option will lie between 0 and 1. Delta is a particularly important measure because its inverse yields what is known as the riskless hedge ratio, which is a ratio of calls that need to be sold to protect a position in the underlying stock. For example if delta is $N(d1) = 0.6985$, then the hedge ratio $h = 1.432$. Given that a standard option contract is for 1,000 shares, to hedge these 1,000 shares it would be necessary to write 1.432 option contracts.

From our example, for a share currently priced at 100 pence with a strike price of 90 pence and a current premium of 19.35 pence per option, each time the share rises by 1 pence the holder of the underlying share makes 1 pence on holding the underlying share. On the other hand, the holder will lose $1.432 \times 0.6985 = 1$ pence from a loss on writing the call option contract.

- **Option gamma** (γ). This a measure of the rate at which an option's theta is changing. It is given by the change in delta divided by the change in the share price. If a share price moves from 100 pence to 101 pence and this causes the delta on the 90 pence call option to move from 0.69 to 0.70 then the gamma on a 90 pence call is $0.01/1 = 0.01$.

- **Option lambda (λ) (or Option kappa (κ)).** An option's lambda measures the sensitivity of an its price to changes in the underlying volatility of the share; that is, the change in the call premium divided by the change in the variance of the share price.
- **Option rho (ρ).** An option's rho measures the sensitivity of its price with respect to a percentage change in the interest rate; that is, the change in the call premium divided by the percentage change in the interest rate.

15.10   Put–call parity

put–call parity
an arbitrage formula published by Hans Stoll in 1969 that shows how to price a European put premium given the relevant call premium, the strike price, time to expiration parameters and risk-free rate of interest that were used to price the call premium

Call and put options, while they offer very different rights, are nonetheless linked together via a fundamental arbitrage relationship. This relationship, described by Stoll (1969), is known as the put–call parity. The relationship holds only for European options.

The basis of the put–call parity relationship is that combining a long position in the security with both a short call and a long put contract with the same exercise price X and expiry date T creates a riskless hedge portfolio, that is, a portfolio with a known guaranteed value in the future. Since the portfolio will have a known guaranteed value, then the return on the portfolio should be no greater than the current risk-free rate of interest.

If the put contract expires in-the-money, then the investor will have:

$$
\begin{aligned}
\text{value of security} \ &= S \\
+\ \text{value of long put} \ &= X - S \\
-\ \text{value of short call} &= 0
\end{aligned}
$$

Hence, the value of the portfolio is X.

If on the other hand the put contract expires out-of-the-money then the investor will have:

$$
\begin{aligned}
\text{value of security} \ &= S \\
+\ \text{value of long put} \ &= 0 \\
-\ \text{value of short call} &= S - X
\end{aligned}
$$

Hence, the value of the portfolio is X.

Table 15.6 illustrates how a combination of the underlying security and a short call and long put position at a given strike price will result in a riskless hedge portfolio with a known guaranteed future value equal to the exercise price regardless of what happens to the price of the security. Since such a portfolio is riskless, the value of the portfolio at the time of its construction must be X discounted by the riskless rate of interest, that is Xe^{-rT}.

$$S + P - C = Xe^{-rT} \tag{15.8}$$

where S is the spot price (i.e. value of the security); P is the put premium; and C is the call premium. So that:

$$P = C - S + Xe^{-rT} \tag{15.9}$$

Table 15.6　Creation of a riskless hedge portfolio

Price	Value of short call position at expiry	Value of long put position at expiry	Value of security + short call + long put
70	0	20	90
80	0	10	90
90	0	0	90
100	−10	0	90
110	−20	0	90
120	−30	0	90
130	−40	0	90

This means that once we have calculated the call premium via the Black–Scholes option pricing formula, then it is simple to also calculate the relevant put option price.

In our example, given the following parameters:

$$S = 100, X = 90, r = 0.06, T = 90/365 = 0.25 \text{ (approx.)},$$
$$\sigma^2 = 0.49 \text{ so that } \sigma = 0.7$$

We have previously calculated that the call price is 19.35 pence. The appropriate put price is therefore:

$$P = C - S + Xe^{-rT}$$
$$= 19.35 - 100 + 90(2.7182)^{(-0.06 \times 0.25)}$$
$$= 8.01 \text{ pence}$$

The put premium in this case is below the call premium. To check that this is an appropriate price the investor should be left with the discounted strike price regardless of what happens to the price of the share, as depicted in **Table 15.7**.

Since a portfolio with a current share price of 100 pence, a strike price of 90 pence, a short call option of 19.35 pence and a long put of 8.01 pence is entirely riskless whatever happens to the share price, the future value of this portfolio should be equal to the riskless rate of interest of 6 per cent (0.06). The holder of a share which is currently priced at 100 pence should end up with a portfolio worth only 1.5 per cent

Table 15.7　Creating a risk-free portfolio

Price of security	Profit on short call at expiry	Profit on long put at expiry	Net value of security + short call + long put at expiry
70	19.64	11.87	101.51
80	19.64	1.87	101.51
90	19.64	−8.13	101.51
100	9.64	−8.13	101.51
110	−0.36	−8.13	101.51
120	−10.36	−8.13	101.51
130	−20.36	−8.13	101.51

more upon expiry (i.e. 6 per cent per annum for three months); that is the security would have risen to 101.50, and this is the case as shown in **Table 15.7**.

In **Table 15.7**, the profit on a short call (that is, writing the call option) is calculated as the option premium (19.35) plus the risk-free rate of interest receivable by investing the premium at the end of three months (19.35 × 1.015 = 19.64 pence) less the value of the call at expiry. For example, if the price of the security on expiration is 70 pence, the profit on the short call is 19.35 pence plus 1.5 per cent interest minus zero = (19.35 × 1.015) = 19.64 pence, whereas if the current price of the security is 120 pence, the profit on the call is 19.35 pence plus 1.5 per cent interest minus 30 pence = (19.35 × 1.015) − 30 = −10.36 pence. The profit on the long put is the value of the put at expiry less the put premium paid 8.01 less foregone interest on the put at the end of three months (8.01 × 1.015 = 8.13 pence). For example, if the price of the security on expiry is 70 pence, the profit on the long put is 20 pence minus 8.13 pence (8.01 × 1.015), that is 11.87 pence, whereas if the price of the security at expiry is 120 pence the profit on the long put is 0 pence minus 8.13 pence (8.01 × 1.015). As we can see in **Table 15.7**, whatever the price of the security upon expiry the combination of the underlying share at 100 pence and the short call position and long put leaves the portfolio worth 101.51 pence regardless of the share price at expiry.

15.11 Conclusions

Option pricing is a relatively complex area and there are some crucial assumptions that need to be made for a valid application of the Black–Scholes option pricing formula; in particular, the expectation that the underlying asset on which the option is based has a log-normal distribution. In the market, the formula also needs to be amended to take account of problems such as dividend payments. Perhaps the biggest problem facing the Black-Scholes formula concerns the appropriate volatility to be used; there is no guarantee that any historical volatility measure will be a fair approximation of the likely future volatility of the underlying asset. The model also makes a crucial assumption that the volatility is fixed over the life of the option, but in financial markets volatility is observed to change over time, with periods of low volatility suddenly being followed by periods of high volatility. The market price of an option can be used to solve for the implied volatility, and participants that think that the implied volatility is inappropriate can write or hold options accordingly in the hope a making a profit. This ability to take a position on the likely volatility of a financial asset (for example, a straddle position) is just one of the innovative strategies that options permit for financial market participants.

There are many factors that interplay in the appropriate pricing of an option, including the risk-free rate of interest, the strike price, the spot price of the underlying instrument, its volatility, and the time left to expiry of the option. The beauty and significance of the Black–Scholes option pricing formula is the way that all these factors are brought together, and it is no exaggeration to say that it is one of the most important and most widely applied economics formulas in the real world! The put–call parity formula shows that there is a clear arbitrage relationship between the call and put premiums, and any divergence from this relationship will lead to arbitrage on the part of market participants.

Table 15.8   The cumulative distribution function for the standard normal random variable

	.00	.01	.02	.03	.04	.05	.06	.07	.08	.09
0.0	.5000	.5040	.5080	.5120	.5160	.5199	.5239	.5279	.5319	.5359
0.1	.5398	.5438	.5478	.5517	.5557	.5596	.5636	.5675	.5714	.5753
0.2	.5793	.5832	.5871	.5910	.5948	.5987	.6026	.6064	.6103	.6141
0.3	.6179	.6217	.6255	.6293	.6331	.6368	.6406	.6443	.6480	.6517
0.4	.6554	.6591	.6628	.6664	.6700	.6736	.6772	.6808	.6844	.6879
0.5	.6915	.6950	.6985	.7019	.7054	.7088	.7123	.7157	.7190	.7224
0.6	.7257	.7291	.7324	.7357	.7389	.7422	.7454	.7486	.7517	.7549
0.7	.7580	.7611	.7642	.7673	.7704	.7734	.7764	.7794	.7823	.7852
0.8	.7781	.7910	.7939	.7967	.7995	.8023	.8051	.8078	.8106	.8133
0.9	.8159	.8186	.8212	.8238	.8264	.8289	.8315	.8340	.8365	.8389
1.0	.8413	.8438	.8461	.8485	.8508	.8531	.8554	.8577	.8599	.8621
1.1	.8643	.8665	.8686	.8708	.8729	.8749	.8770	.8790	.8810	.8830
1.2	.8849	.8869	.8888	.8907	.8925	.8944	.8962	.8980	.8897	.9015
1.3	.9032	.9049	.9066	.9082	.9099	.9115	.9131	.9147	.9162	.9177
1.4	.9192	.9207	.9222	.9236	.9251	.9265	.9279	.9292	.9306	.9319
1.5	.9332	.9345	.9357	.9370	.9382	.9394	.9406	.9418	.9429	.9441
1.6	.9452	.9463	.9474	.9484	.9495	.9505	.9515	.9525	.9535	.9545
1.7	.9554	.9564	.9573	.9582	.9591	.9599	.9608	.9616	.9625	.9633
1.8	.9641	.9649	.9656	.9664	.9671	.9678	.9686	.9693	.9699	.9706
1.9	.9713	.9719	.9726	.9732	.9738	.9744	.9750	.9756	.9761	.9767
2.0	.9772	.9778	.9783	.9788	.9793	.9798	.9803	.9808	.9812	.9817
2.1	.9821	.9826	.9830	.9834	.9838	.9842	.9846	.9850	.9854	.9857
2.2	.9861	.9864	.9868	.9871	.9875	.9878	.9881	.9884	.9887	.9890
2.3	.9893	.9896	.9898	.9901	.9904	.9906	.9909	.9911	.9913	.9916
2.4	.9918	.9920	.9922	.9925	.9927	.9929	.9931	.9932	.9934	.9936
2.5	.9938	.9940	.9941	.9943	.9945	.9946	.9948	.9949	.9951	.9952
2.6	.9953	.9955	.9956	.9957	.9959	.9960	.9961	.9962	.9963	.9964
2.7	.9965	.9966	.9967	.9968	.9969	.9970	.9971	.9972	.9973	.9974
2.8	.9974	.9975	.9976	.9977	.9977	.9978	.9979	.9979	.9980	.9981
2.9	.9981	.9982	.9982	.9983	.9984	.9984	.9985	.9985	.9986	.9986
3.0	.9987	.9987	.9987	.9988	.9988	.9989	.9989	.9989	.9990	.9990
3.1	.9990	.9991	.9991	.9991	.9992	.9992	.9992	.9992	.9993	.9993
3.2	.9993	.9993	.9994	.9994	.9994	.9994	.9994	.9995	.9995	.9995
3.3	.9995	.9995	.9995	.9996	.9996	.9996	.9996	.9996	.9996	.9997
3.4	.9997	.9997	.9997	.9997	.9997	.9997	.9997	.9997	.9997	.9998

Further reading

Haug, E.G. (2007) *The Complete Guide to Option Pricing Formulas*, 2nd edn, McGraw-Hill.
Hull, J.C. (2008) *Options, Futures and Other Derivatives*, 7th edn, Prentice-Hall.
Kolb, R.W. and Overdahl J. (2007) *Futures, Options and Swaps*, 5th edn, Basil Blackwell.
Natenberg, S. (2009) *Basic Option Volatility Strategies: Understanding Popular Pricing Models*, Marketplace Books.

Chapter 15	Revision questions

1 You are given the following data on call and put premiums in pence per share for Company ABC shares, which are currently priced at 311 pence. Each contract refers to 1000 shares.

	Call premiums in pence			Put premiums in pence		
Strike prices	April	June	September	April	June	September
300 pence	31	49	61	20	33	44
330 pence	18	35	48	36	50	60

Which of the following statements is FALSE?

A The time value for the September 300 pence call premium is higher than for the September 300 pence put premium.

B The intrinsic value for the June 300 pence call premium is the same as for the September 300 pence call premium.

C The intrinsic value for the June 300 pence call premium is higher than for the June 330 pence put premium.

D The time value for the April 300 pence put premium is higher than the intrinsic value for April 330 pence put premium.

2 You are given the following data on call and put premiums in pence per share for Company ABC shares, which are currently priced at 425 pence. Each contract refers to 1000 shares.

	Call premiums in pence			Put premiums in pence		
Strike prices	April	June	September	April	June	September
420 pence	22	31	34	14	20	27
460 pence	6	12	15	39	42	48

(i)   List all the call and put premiums that are 'out of the money'.

(ii)   Explain the intuition as to why the premiums rise between April and September.

(iii) Which of the above options has the lowest time value?

(iv)   Explain what you would do using any one of the above premiums if you expect the share price to fall to 300 pence by expiration and the total profit you will make measured in pounds if you are proved correct.

| Chapter 15 | Revision questions – *continued* |

3 You are given the following information about the stock of Company A:

Share price $60, risk-free rate of interest is 8%, time to expiration is 3 months, annualized standard deviation is 0.4 and exercise price is $65.

   (i)   Calculate the appropriate call value of the stock according to the Black–Scholes option pricing formula. Show your workings in full.

   (ii)   Calculate an appropriate put premium. Show your workings in full.

4 Briefly discuss the relationship between a call premium and the five determinants of the call premium according to the Black–Scholes option pricing model.

5   (i)   Explain the difference between historical volatility and expected volatility and their potential significance for option pricing.

   (ii)   Explain why an option writer is prepared to 'write' call options even though the potential losses are large compared to the potential premium to be received.

   (iii)   What does a rise in implied volatility potentially signify?

4 State which of the following statements are TRUE and which are FALSE.

   (i)   A call premium for a strike price of 200 pence is 15 pence and the share is currently priced at 190 pence. The time value for the call premium is greater than the intrinsic value.

   (ii)   The Black–Scholes model provides an estimate of the price of an American option on a dividend paying stock.

   (iii)   If implied volatility rises, other things being equal, both call and put premiums will rise.

   (iv)   If, on a newly issued option, the share price is 100 pence and the strike price is 100 pence then time value will be at its maximum.

 Multiple choice questions available at www.palgrave.com/business/pilbeam

16

SWAP MARKETS

Learning objectives

In completing this chapter you will learn about:

- the potential situations that may lead to a mutually beneficial swap
- how swaps can arise from both absolute and comparative advantages in the capital markets
- the difference between an interest rate swap and a currency swap
- the crucial role played by intermediaries in the swap market
- how to interpret swap rates published in the financial press
- innovations in the swap market

16.1   Introduction

A swap is an agreement between two parties to exchange two differing forms of payment obligations. There are basically two types of swap: an interest rate swap and a currency swap. In an interest rate swap the exchange involves payments denominated in the same currency, while in a currency swap the exchange involves two different currencies.

The first well documented swap was a currency swap between the World Bank and International Business Machines (IBM) in 1981, whereby the World Bank committed itself to financing some of IBM's deutschmark/Swiss franc debt in return for a commitment by IBM to finance some of the World Bank's dollar debt. Since the early 1980s there has been an enormous growth in the swap market, and **Table 16.1** shows the value of interest rate swaps and currency swaps for the period 1998–2008.

Like many other financial instruments, swap agreements are used to manage risk exposure; however, as we shall see, one of the main reasons for the rapid growth of the swap market has been that they enable parties to raise funds more cheaply than would otherwise be the case. The swap market is used extensively by major corporations, international financial institutions and governments, and is an important part of the international bond market. The swap market is currently organized by the International Swaps and Derivatives Association (ISDA) which, since 1985, has been responsible for standardizing documentation and dealing terms.

In this chapter we look at both interest rate and currency swaps, and in particular we focus on the economic advantages of swaps and the reasons for the existence of swap opportunities. We also focus attention on the role played by intermediaries in arranging swaps, and finally look at some of the innovations that have occurred in the swap market.

16.2   Potential swap scenarios

We shall first consider a few scenarios where companies might use the swap market.

Scenario 1   Restructuring debt

Company A might have, in the past, issued debt at a floating rate of interest but subsequently decided that it would like to convert this debt into a fixed interest payment debt. Conversely, Company B might have issued fixed rate debt but would now prefer floating debt. In such a scenario, then, there may be potential for a mutually beneficial exchange of interest rate obligations between the two companies;

Table 16.1   Currency composition of notional principal value of outstanding interest rate and currency swaps (in billions of US dollars)

Interest rate swaps

	1998	2000	2002	2004	2006	2008
US dollar	13,763	19,421	34,399	61,103	97,430	146,249
Japanese yen	9,763	13,107	14,650	24,209	38,113	56,419
Euro	na	21,311	38,429	76,161	111,791	154,773
Pound sterling	3,911	4,852	7,442	15,289	22,238	29,593
Other	22,578	5,977	6,738	13,739	22,010	31,644
Total	50,015	64,668	101,658	190,501	291,582	418,678

Currency swaps

	1998	2000	2002	2004	2006	2008
US dollar	15,810	14,073	16,500	25,726	33,755	42,170
Japanese yen	5,319	4,254	4,791	7,076	9,490	12,128
Euro	na	5,981	7,818	11,900	16,037	20,969
Pound sterling	2,612	2,391	2,462	4,331	6,135	5,606
Other	12,261	3,993	5,349	9,545	15,125	18,633
Gross total	36,002	31,322	36,920	58,578	80,542	99,506
Net total	18,001	15,666	18,460	29,289	40,271	49,753

Notes:
1 Figures for currency swaps are gross and have not been adjusted for double counting as each currency swap involves two currencies. To obtain the net figure the quoted currency swap figures need to be halved.
2 The notional principal amount, while giving an idea of market size, should not viewed as the amount potentially at risk, since it is the interruption of the cash flows between parties to a swap agreement that is at risk and this is a very small fraction of the above figures.

Source: Bank for International Settlements.

that is, Company A swaps some or all of its floating rate debt with Company B for some or all of its fixed rate debt. It may be easier, quicker and cheaper for the two companies to exchange interest obligations than to repay the outstanding debt and reissue debt in their preferred forms.

Scenario 2 Hedging interest rate risk

Another use of swaps is for companies to hedge interest rate risk. Consider the case where the Treasury bill (TB) rate is currently 9 per cent. Bank A may have lent out £100 million at a fixed rate of interest of 10 per cent for five years and be financing this from the issue of six-month certificates of deposit paying the Treasury bill rate plus 60 basis points. On the other hand, bank B may have raised £100 million at a fixed rate of finance of 9 per cent and lent out the funds at the Treasury bill rate plus 90 basis points (that is, 9.9 per cent). Bank A is currently raising funds at 9.60 per cent so making a spread of 40 basis points, while bank B is raising funds at 9 per cent and has lent out the funds at 9.9 per cent so making 90 basis points.

The fear at bank A is that the Treasury bill interest rate will rise to 9.40 per cent or higher, so that it would have to pay at least 10 per cent on new deposits. Conversely, bank B fears that Treasury bill rates will fall to 8.1 per cent or below so that its 90 basis point spread disappears. A swap would enable both banks to lock in their current spreads regardless of what happens to Treasury bill interest rates. Consider what happens if bank A agrees to pay bank B a fixed rate of 9.80 per cent and in return bank B agrees to pay bank A a floating rate of Treasury bill + 80 basis points. As **Table 16.2** shows, on this basis both banks will be locked into their current spreads regardless of what happens to Treasury bill interest rates.

Table 16.2   Managing interest rate risk

Pre-swap	
Bank A	
Annual income received fixed	10%
Annual income paid floating	TB + 60 basis points
Profit at current TB interest of 9%	40 basis points
Profit if TB interest rate 7%	240 basis points
Loss if TB interest rate 11%	−160 basis points
Bank B	
Annual income received floating	TB + 90 basis points
Annual income paid fixed	9%
Profit at current TB interest of 9%	90 basis points
Loss if TB interest rate 7%	−110 basis points
Profit if TB interest rate 11%	290 basis points
Post-swap	
Bank A	
Annual income received fixed	10%
Annual income paid floating	TB + 60 basis points
A receives from B floating	TB + 80 basis points
A pays to B fixed	9.80%
Profit at current TB interest of 9%	40 basis points
Profit if TB interest rate 7%	40 basis points
Profit if TB interest rate 11%	40 basis points
Bank B	
Annual income received floating	TB + 90 basis points
Annual income paid fixed	9%
B receives from A fixed	9.80%
B pays A floating	TB + 80 basis points
Profit at current TB interest of 9%	90 basis points
Profit if TB interest rate 7%	90 basis points
Profit if TB interest rate 11%	90 basis points

Scenario 3 Reducing the cost of raising finance

A currency swap might prove attractive for two companies that have differing abilities to raise funds in different markets. A Chinese company might wish to raise dollar funds at a floating rate of interest, while a US company might wish to raise yen at a fixed rate of interest. It might be the case that Japanese investors are not too keen on US companies, but are keen to invest in Chinese companies, while US investors are not too keen to lend to Chinese companies. In such circumstances, there may be a swap opportunity, with the Chinese company raising yen funds at a fixed rate of interest while the US company raises dollar funds at a floating rate of interest. In the swap, the US company would raise dollar funds on the US capital market at a floating rate of interest and the Chinese company would raise yen funds at a fixed rate of interest in Japan, the companies then swap the funds raised and the corresponding obligations. The net result is that the Chinese company gets the dollar funds it needs at a fixed rate of interest, cheaper than it could have raised the funds itself, while the US company would get the fixed rate yen funds at a cheaper cost than if it had raised those funds itself.

Having looked at some potential swap scenarios, we now proceed to examine some specific numerical examples of swaps. In the first instance, to concentrate on the basic issues we shall assume that the two parties to a swap do not require the services of an intermediary to arrange the swap.

16.3 An interest rate swap

An interest rate swap is an agreement involving two parties to exchange periodic interest rate payments. The value of the interest rate payments to be exchanged is based upon a specified amount of principal known as the notional principal amount. In a typical interest rate swap one party agrees to pay the other party a fixed interest rate payment at specified dates, while the other party agrees to pay a floating rate of interest based upon a reference rate of interest such as LIBOR, Treasury bill rates or certificate of deposit rates. The party paying the fixed rate of interest is known as the fixed rate payer while the party making the floating payments is referred to as the floating rate payer.

notional principal amount the pre-specified amount of money upon which a swap agreement is based

Example 1 An absolute advantage swap

One of the most common types of swap agreements involves a fixed rate party and a floating interest rate party, and such a swap is commonly referred to as a plain vanilla swap.

A simple demonstration of the potential gains from an interest rate swap is when Company A can borrow at a fixed rate of interest cheaper than Company B, while Company B can borrow in the floating interest rate market at a cheaper rate than Company A. Assume Company A would like to borrow £100 million for 10 years at a floating rate of interest, while Company B would like to borrow £100 million for 10 years at a fixed rate of interest. **Table 16.3** shows the borrowing options open to each company.

Table 16.3 shows that Company A can borrow at a fixed rate of interest at 50 basis points cheaper than Company B. Conversely in the floating rate market Company

plain vanilla swap a simple interest rate swap in which one party swaps a fixed coupon payment for a floating rate payment with another party

Table 16.3   An absolute advantage swap

	Fixed rate	Floating rate
Company A	Treasury bond + 1%	LIBOR + 1.0%
Company B	Treasury bond + 1.5%	LIBOR + 0.6%

B can borrow at a rate of interest linked to LIBOR that is 40 basis points cheaper than Company A. Company A is said to have an absolute advantage in the fixed rate market and Company B is said to have an absolute advantage in the floating rate market. In a swap arrangement, Company A would borrow £100 million at a fixed interest rate of Treasury bond plus 1 per cent, while Company B would borrow £100 million at a floating rate of interest of LIBOR plus 0.6 per cent. With a swap between the two companies, there would be no need to exchange principal since both have raised £100 million; however, Company A will be obligated to pay LIBOR plus 0.6 per cent to Company B to finance its debt and Company B will be obligated to pay Treasury bond plus 1.0 per cent to Company A to finance its debt. The result of the swap is that Company A effectively obtains floating rate finance at LIBOR plus 0.6 per cent, while Company B obtains fixed rate finance at Treasury bond plus 1 per cent. The net result of the swap is that Company A obtains floating rate finance 40 basis points (0.4 per cent) cheaper than if it had raised floating finance itself, while Company B obtains fixed rate finance at 50 basis points (0.5 per cent) cheaper than if it had raised fixed rate finance itself.

Example 2   A comparative advantage swap

In the previous example, Company A had an absolute advantage in the fixed rate market and Company B had an absolute advantage in the floating market. In the following example of a swap, we shall see that an interest rate swap can still be mutually beneficial even if one of the companies can borrow more cheaply in both the fixed interest market and floating interest market compared to another company.

Assume that Company A can borrow £100 million for 10 years at a fixed interest rate of 1 per cent over the UK 10-year Treasury bond rate, or alternatively that it could borrow at a margin of 0.4 per cent over LIBOR at a floating rate of interest. Company B can borrow £100 million for 10 years at a fixed interest rate of 1.5 per cent over the UK 10-year Treasury bond rate or borrow at a margin of 0.6 per cent over LIBOR at a floating rate of interest. In this example, Company A can borrow at a cheaper interest rate compared to Company B in both the fixed and floating rate capital markets. However, its advantage is 0.5 per cent in the fixed rate market but only 0.2 per cent in the floating market. **Table 16.4** shows the borrowing options open to each company.

Table 16.4   A comparative advantage swap

	Fixed rate	Floating rate
Company A	Treasury + 1.0%	LIBOR + 0.4%
Company B	Treasury + 1.5%	LIBOR + 0.6%
Difference	0.5%	0.2%

**comparative
advantage swap**
a swap between two
parties in which one
of the parties has an
absolute advantage at
raising funds at both
fixed and floating
rates of interest
but its advantage is
greater in one of the
markets

Table 16.4 shows that Company A can borrow funds at both fixed and floating rates cheaper than Company B but its greatest advantage is in the fixed interest rate market. Company A is said to have a comparative advantage in the fixed rate market and Company B, because its absolute disadvantage is least in the floating rate market, is said to have a comparative advantage in the fixed rate market. Assume that Company A wishes to borrow £100 million at a floating rate of interest, while Company B wishes to borrow £100 million at a fixed rate of interest. In such circumstances, both companies can benefit from a swap as illustrated in **Figure 16.1**.

In the swap scenario, Company A wishes to borrow funds at a floating rate of interest and Company B wishes to borrow funds at a fixed rate of interest. In the prelude to the swap, Company A borrows £100 million of funds at a fixed rate of interest (the market in which its absolute advantage is greatest) at Treasury bond plus 1 per cent, while Company B borrows £100 million at a floating rate of interest of LIBOR plus 0.6 per cent.

Figure 16.1 A comparative advantage swap

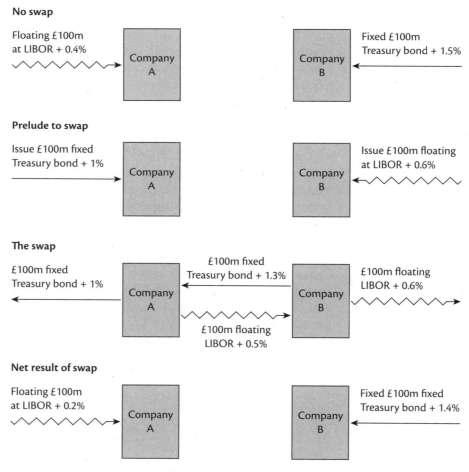

Notes: A squiggly line indicates a floating rate of interest while a straight line indicates a fixed rate of interest.

In the swap agreement, Company A agrees to pay Company B floating LIBOR plus 0.5 per cent, while Company B agrees to pay Company A Treasury bond plus 1.3 per cent. We now need to establish that both companies benefit from the swap agreement. Company A is receiving Treasury plus 1.3 per cent from Company B, of which it only has to pay Treasury plus 1 per cent to finance its fixed rate borrowing which represents a gain of 30 basis points; however, it is paying Company B LIBOR plus 0.5 per cent whereas it could have borrowed at LIBOR plus 0.4 per cent itself, so it is losing 10 basis points on this aspect of the swap. Overall, Company A is a net gainer of 20 basis points from the swap arrangement; it is effectively able to borrow at a floating rate of interest of LIBOR plus 0.2 per cent compared to LIBOR plus 0.4 per cent if it had raised the floating rate funds itself.

Company B also gains from this arrangement, as it is effectively paying Treasury plus 1.3 per cent for a fixed rate loan, whereas if the Company Borrowed at a fixed rate itself it would have to pay Treasury plus 1.5 per cent. Company B saves 20 basis points from this aspect of the swap arrangement; however, it is receiving LIBOR plus 0.5 per cent from Company A but having to pay LIBOR plus 0.6 per cent to finance its debt, so it is losing 10 basis points on this aspect of the swap. Overall, Company B is a net gainer of 10 basis points from the swap arrangement; it is effectively able to borrow at a fixed interest of Treasury bond plus 1.4 per cent compared to Treasury bond plus 1.5 per cent if it had raised the fixed rate funds itself.

The total gain from the swap to both parties is 30 basis points; in this example, 20 basis points for Company A and 10 basis points for Company B. It is no coincidence that 30 basis points is the difference between Company A's advantage in the fixed rate market (50 basis points) and its advantage in the floating rate market (20 basis points). The swap is basically an arbitrage transaction designed to exploit this differential; the swap has enabled both parties to reduce their borrowing costs. It is important that the terms of the swap deal are set between the differing borrowing rates of the two parties in the two markets; that is, between Treasury bond plus 1 per cent to Treasury bond plus 1.5 per cent in the fixed rate part of the agreement, and between LIBOR plus 0.4 per cent and LIBOR plus 0.6 per cent in the floating rate market. The closer the fixed interest payments made by Company B to Company A are to Treasury bond plus 1.5 per cent, the less it gains (and the more Company A gains), while the closer its receipts from Company A are to LIBOR plus 0.6 per cent the more it gains (and the less Company A gains).

A swap agreement can be viewed as equivalent to the two parties engaging in a forward contract. Company A has agreed to buy (take a long position on) a floating rate LIBOR plus 0.5 per cent payment on a notional principal amount of £100 million in return for a fixed payment of Treasury bond plus 1.3 per cent, while Company B has agreed to sell (take a short position on) a floating rate LIBOR plus 0.5 per cent payment on a notional principal amount of £100 million while making a fixed payment of Treasury bonds plus 1.3 per cent.

If a swap is no more than equivalent to a forward contract arrangement, then one must ask whether there are any advantages compared to a forward contract? One obvious advantage is that a swap agreement can be arranged for a period of 10 years or more for which there are no corresponding forward markets. Forward and futures markets have reasonable liquidity for up to 18 months, but beyond this offer little in the way of hedging potential. Another advantage is that one swap agreement between the two parties can prove transactionally more efficient than negotiating a series of forward contracts every year. In our example, a single swap agreement replaces the need for 10 separate annual forward contracts. Another advantage of a swap is that there is an active secondary market in which a party to the agreement can on-sell their obligations to a third party.

16.4   A currency swap agreement

In a currency swap, unlike an interest rate swap, differing currencies are involved. Consider the following example of two companies: one is a British company wishing to raise $150 million for 10 years at a floating rate of interest for investment in the USA, and the other a German company wishing to raise £100 million for 10 years at a fixed rate of interest for investment in the UK. For convenience we assume that the spot exchange rate is $1.50/£1.

The UK company can borrow $150 million at a floating rate of interest but is advised that it will have to pay LIBOR plus 0.75 per cent. The German company could borrow £100 million of funds directly at a fixed rate of interest of 8.50 per cent. A swap dealer that has both these clients on its books may spot a swap opportunity. The dealer knows that market conditions would permit the UK company to borrow

Table 16.5   A currency swap

	UK sterling Fixed rate	US dollar Floating rate
British company	8%	$LIBOR + 0.75%
German company	8.5%	$LIBOR + 0.25%

£100 million on the London market at a fixed rate of interest of 8 per cent, while a current US investment bias for German companies would enable the German company to borrow $150 million at LIBOR plus 0.25 per cent. The borrowing opportunities open to the two companies are illustrated in **Table 16.5**.

If the companies were to exchange debt obligations, the UK company would be able to gain dollar finance at LIBOR plus 0.25 per cent, saving 50 basis points, while the German company would be able to gain sterling finance at 8 per cent saving 50 basis points. The mechanics of the currency swap can be summarized using swap boxes as shown in **Figure 16.2** (see p. 404).

Figure 16.2 firstly indicates the position of each company without a swap: the UK company would raise $150 million in the USA at a floating rate of interest 75 basis points over LIBOR, while the German company would raise £100 million at a fixed rate of interest of 8.5 per cent. As a prelude to the swap, since the UK company can raise fixed rate funds in the UK market cheaper than the German company, it will issue £100 million at a fixed rate of interest of 8 per cent (straight arrows in the figure indicate fixed), while the German company will raise $150 million in the USA at a floating rate of LIBOR plus 0.25 per cent (squiggly arrows indicate floating). We then

Box 16.1	Swap rates in the financial press

Although swaps are over-the-counter instruments most of the features of the contracts, such as terms and conditions, settlement procedures and the terms and conditions, are pretty much standardized, resulting in a large and liquid market. The *Financial Times* publishes a daily table of swap rates for major currencies as set out in **Table 16.6**.

Table 16.6   Swap rates, US$

	Bid	Ask
1 year	5.40	5.42
2 year	5.30	5.34
3 year	5.26	5.30
4 year	5.21	5.26
5 year	5.15	5.20
6 year	5.10	5.15
7 year	5.05	5.10
8 year	5.00	5.05
9 year	4.95	5.00
10 year	4.91	4.96
12 year	4.81	4.88
15 year	4.70	4.79
20 year	4.52	4.65
25 year	4.39	4.52
30 year	4.29	4.42

Source: *Financial Times*

The rates in **Table 16.6** refer to swaps of differing time horizons. For example, at the 10-year horizon there are two rates: the bid rate of 4.91 per cent and the ask rate of 4.96 per cent. The rates refer to fixed rates of interest that banks involved in the swap market would charge if engaged in a swap contract with a highly rated (typically AA) counterparty and a notional principal amount of around $8 million (or £5 million). The 4.91 per cent bid rate refers to the rate the bank would be willing to pay if it was the fixed rate payer in return for a floating rate based on floating three-month $LIBOR from the highly rated counterparty. The 4.96 per cent ask rate refers to the rate that a bank would expect to receive if it was the fixed rate receiver in return for paying a floating rate based on three-month $LIBOR.

Figure 16.2   A currency swap

No swap

Floating $150m
at LIBOR + 0.75%

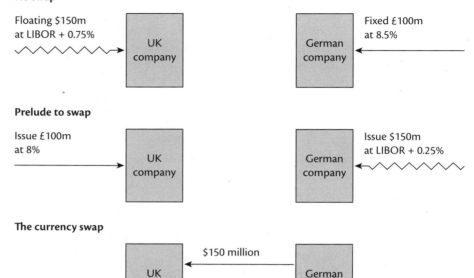

Fixed £100m
at 8.5%

UK company   German company

Prelude to swap

Issue £100m
at 8%

Issue $150m
at LIBOR + 0.25%

UK company   German company

The currency swap

$150 million

£100 million

UK company   German company

Periodic exchange of coupon payments

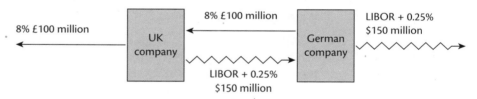

8% £100 million

8% £100 million

LIBOR + 0.25%
$150 million

LIBOR + 0.25%
$150 million

UK company   German company

Final exchange redemption of principal

£100 million

£100 million

$150 million

$150 million

£100 million

UK company   German company

Result of swap

Floating $150m
at LIBOR + 0.25%

Fixed £100m
at 8%

UK company   German company

have the initial exchange of principal; the UK company gives the German company the £100 million, while the German company gives the UK company the $150 million it requires (a fair exchange at the $1.50/£1 parity). Next we have the periodic exchange of interest payments by the two; the UK company pays dollar LIBOR plus 0.25 per cent to the German company which is used to repay holders of its bonds, while the German company pays the UK company 8 per cent sterling which is used to pay its bond holders. Finally, after 10 years we have the final exchange of principal, the UK company pays the German company $150 million so that it can pay back its US bond holders upon maturity, while the German company will pay the UK company £100 million so that it can pay its UK bond holders upon maturity.

In effect the currency swap has enabled the UK company to raise the $150 million it required at dollar LIBOR plus 0.25 per cent, thus saving itself 50 basis points (or $750,000 per year) over what it would cost to raise the funds itself in the USA. The German company manages to raise the £100 million it requires at 8.0 per cent, thus saving itself 0.5 per cent (or £500,000 per year) over what it would cost to raise the funds itself in the UK. Strictly speaking the initial and final exchange of principal is unnecessary since the UK company could convert the £100 million it raises at the spot rate of $1.50/£1 into the $150 million it needs, and the German company could convert the $150 million it raises into £100 million. The main feature of the swap is the interest rate exchange.

Effectively the swap arrangement exploits an arbitrage opportunity enabling the UK company to obtain US funds at the same rate as the German company, and the German company the opportunity to raise funds at a similar cost to the UK company.

Prior to the development of swap markets, such arbitrage opportunities were undertaken by hedging the position in the forward exchange market. The UK company would raise funds at floating rates of interest in the UK, convert these into dollars and then use the forward exchange rate to hedge the foreign exchange risk. However, most forward markets for foreign exchange are for less than two years. In order to hedge a 10-year position each party would have to take out an annual forward contract for each of the next 10 years. Furthermore, the forward rate contracts it takes out may still not be ideal if the forward rate is moving against the company. With the swap agreement each party is achieving a perfect 10-year hedge in one contract.

16.5 The role of the intermediary in the swap

Intermediaries play an important part in both identifying potential swap arrangements and arranging them. In cases where the two parties are interested in different notional principal amounts, say Party A is interested in £100 million and Party B is interested in £80 million, then the intermediary will frequently balance the transaction by undertaking £20 million to make up the difference between the two parties. It will then normally reduce its risk exposure by undertaking a hedge position in another market.

Figure 16.3   The role of an intermediary in a swap

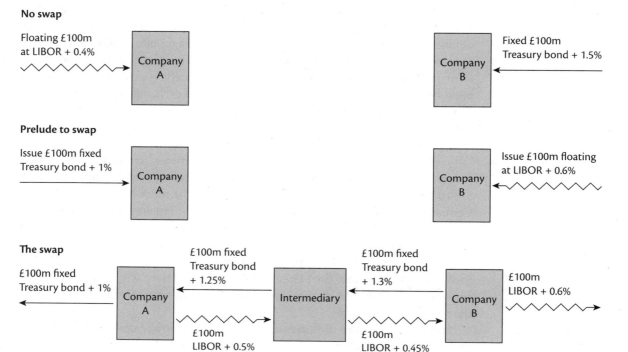

No swap

Floating £100m
at LIBOR + 0.4%

Company A

Fixed £100m
Treasury bond + 1.5%

Company B

Prelude to swap

Issue £100m fixed
Treasury bond + 1%

Company A

Issue £100m floating
at LIBOR + 0.6%

Company B

The swap

£100m fixed
Treasury bond + 1%

Company A

£100m fixed
Treasury bond
+ 1.25%

£100m
LIBOR + 0.5%

Intermediary

£100m fixed
Treasury bond
+ 1.3%

£100m
LIBOR + 0.45%

Company B

£100m
LIBOR + 0.6%

Net result of swap

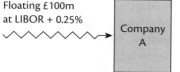

Floating £100m
at LIBOR + 0.25%

Company A

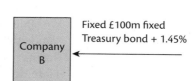

Fixed £100m fixed
Treasury bond + 1.45%

Company B

A major concern for both parties to the swap is that the other party will default on its interest payments. A default would not mean any principal is lost, since the notional principal amount is retained by both parties, but it could involve losses on the interest side of the swap. For this reason, an intermediary, for an appropriate fee, will often guarantee the swap payments should one party fail to honour its obligations. In many swaps, the intermediary itself becomes the counterparty to the transaction. This feature is especially important in today's swap market; many swap users such as multinationals require swaps to be made speedily, and this is often most easily achieved when the financial intermediary itself becomes the counterparty rather than waiting for the intermediary to achieve a brokered arrangement with another party.

Consider our previous comparative advantage swap, whereby Company A raised fixed rate funds at Treasury plus 1 per cent and Company B raised floating rate funds at LIBOR plus 0.6 per cent. Company A paid Company B LIBOR plus 0.5 per cent and Company B paid Company A fixed Treasury bond plus 1.3 per cent. If the deal was arranged by an intermediary, then the intermediary could take a fee; Company A would pay the intermediary LIBOR plus 0.5 per cent and the intermediary would pass on LIBOR plus 0.45 per cent to Company B (so making 5 basis points) and company B would pay the intermediary Treasury plus 1.3 per cent and the intermediary would give Company A Treasury plus 1.25 per cent thus making a further 5 basis points. The intermediary would therefore make 10 basis points and companies A and B have net gains compared to the no-swap scenario of 15 and 5 basis points respectively. In effect, the intermediary would be gaining 10 of the 30 basis points as a reward for arranging the swap as shown in **Figure 16.3**.

16.6   The secondary market in swaps

swap reversal a deal whereby a party to a swap contract enters a new swap arrangement with a new counterparty that cancels out its arrangements with its original counterparty

A party that has agreed to a swap transaction may, for one reason or another, wish to end its obligations. Although there is no formal secondary market, there are several ways in which a party can terminate its swap obligations.

One method is to enter a new swap arrangement with a new counterparty that will effectively cancel out its arrangements with its original counterparty, and such an arrangement is known as a swap reversal. For example, consider the case when Party A is in a swap arrangement for a notional principal amount of £100 million and is paying a fixed 10 per cent and receiving LIBOR plus 0.5 per cent for 10 years and has six years remaining. To cancel its swap, it could arrange a new swap with another Party C for a £100 million notional principal amount for six years for which it pays LIBOR plus 0.5 per cent and receives a fixed rate of interest. The fixed rate of interest it will be able to arrange will depend upon the market conditions at the time and might involve it in a loss/profit. The swap reversal effectively cancels out a party's swap obligations. However, a potential problem with the swap reversal is that Party A is now dealing with two counterparties and has thereby increased its default risk exposure.

swap sale a deal whereby a party to a swap contract pays money to or receives money from another party to take over its obligations

As an alternative to a swap reversal, Party A might be able to find another party that is willing to undertake its swap obligation; that is, Party A conducts a swap sale with Party D. Since Party A is paying a fixed 10 per cent and receiving LIBOR plus 0.5 per cent, if fixed interest rates are currently 12 per cent it could sell its swap position to another party for a profit since that party will be getting LIBOR plus 0.5 per cent and paying only 10 per cent. If, however, the current fixed interest rate is only 7 per cent, Party A would have to pay Party D to take on its swap position since Party D would have to pay a fixed 10 per cent, which is above the current fixed rate of interest, whilst receiving LIBOR plus 0.5 per cent. A difficult problem with a swap sale is that it requires the consent of Party B, and whether Party B grants this consent may well depend upon the credit rating of Party D. If this is superior or similar to Party A, then Party B may consent, but if it is inferior then Party B may not consent or will require some form of payment for the increased risk.

buy-back a deal whereby one party to a futures contract pays or receives a sum of money from the other party to cancel the future obligations inherent in the contract

quality spread the difference between the advantages held by one party at fixed and floating interest rates. For example, if it can borrow fixed at 0.75% less than the other party and floating at 0.25% less then the quality spread is 0.5%

A final alternative for Party A is to conduct a buy-back with the original counterparty. That is, Party A will pay to, or receive money from, Party B to cancel the swap arrangement. Whether Party A receives from or pays to Party B will depend upon the state of interest rates at the time of the buy-back and any movements in the quality spread since the swap was initiated.

16.7 Distinguishing characteristics of the swap market from the forward and futures markets

A swap agreement is basically the same as a forward/futures contract in that both parties are committing themselves to a stream of future obligations just as participants do in a forward/futures contract. There are, nonetheless, significant differences between exchange-traded futures contracts and the obligations entered into in a swap contract, the most obvious being that exchange-traded futures contracts are of a much shorter duration than the vast majority of swap contracts. While futures contracts are usually for a year or less, most swap contracts cover periods ranging from 5 to 20 years and possibly longer. This factor is particularly important in explaining the popularity of swap contracts to business; the hedging opportunities offered by forward and futures contracts are usually for two years at most, whilst swaps offer hedging possibilities that meet the longer time frames within which many businesses have debt obligations.

Futures contracts are also highly standardized contracts that may not meet the specific needs of a firm because of their limited time horizon and few fixed expiration dates each year. By contrast, with a swap agreement a party is able to obtain a highly specific agreement with a time horizon and payment schedule matched closely to its needs.

Another significant difference between futures and swaps is that futures contracts are highly regulated contracts that come under the control of the futures exchange and relevant authorities, and the exchange guarantees the obligations should one of the parties default on its obligations. By contrast, the swap market is virtually free of regulation and unless the counterparties ensure the agreement is underwritten by a third party, there is the risk that one of the parties will not fulfil its obligations.

A significant advantage of futures contacts over swaps is that there is an active secondary market in futures contracts, so that obligations can be easily be terminated by selling the contract to another party. By contrast, swap agreements because of their non-standardized nature have a far less active secondary market and a swap agreement can only be cancelled with the consent of both parties. A party that wishes to end its swap obligations will either have to enter a swap buy-back, a swap sale, or a swap reversal with another counterparty that reverses (as closely as is possible) the cash flows inherent in its original swap agreement or a buy-back.

16.8 Reasons for the existence of the swap market

The fundamental reason for the existence of the swap market is that it is transactionally efficient and enables firms to exploit arbitrage opportunities resulting from imperfections in the credit market. There are a number of credit-market imperfections that enable firms with similar credit ratings to borrow at different rates of interest, and among the more important are:

- *Differing time horizons of floating and fixed markets.* The market for floating rates of interest is predominantly a short-run market, while that for fixed interest is more a medium- to long-term market. There is no real reason why spreads should be the same as they are two separate markets.

- *Home country preference.* Domestic firms may be able to raise funds in their domestic market cheaper than foreign firms with similar credit ratings due to a preference on the part of domestic investors for domestic company debt. There are several possible sources of this advantage. Domestic investors may prefer to invest with companies with which they are familiar and which have a history that can be checked easily. In addition, it is usually cheaper and easier to obtain information on and to monitor domestic firms than it is foreign firms.
- *Regulatory considerations.* There may be regulations about the holding of debt that mean more domestic debt is held by domestic debts holders (banks, investment funds and so on) than would otherwise be held. This enables domestic firms to issue debt at a lower rate of interest than would otherwise be the case.
- *Differing preferences between banks and the rest of the capital market.* The bond market tends to have a much higher preference to hold debt of firms with a very high credit rating, such as AAA and AA companies, which means that lower-grade companies generally find the risk premium that they are charged in the bond market to be quite high. However, banks are traditionally willing to charge a lower risk premium for lower-grade companies than the bond market, which means that lower-grade companies tend to have a comparative advantage in the bank loan market, while higher-grade companies tend to have a comparative advantage in the capital market. The result is that there is potential for swaps, even though higher-grade companies are likely to be able to raise funds in both markets at a cheaper rate than lower-grade companies.

16.9 Innovations in the swap market

zero coupon swap
a swap in which the fixed-rate payer makes one final lump sum interest payment, while the floating-rate payer makes regular periodic payments at a higher rate

forward rate swap
an agreement between two parties to do a swap which will take place at a predetermined date

basis swap a swap in which both parties exchange floating interest rate payments, but the base contract is different

The swap market has been a major source of financial product innovation in recent years. Apart from the basic plain vanilla interest rate and currency swaps that we have looked at, there are numerous other types of innovative swap contracts aimed at meeting specific customer needs. In a zero coupon swap the fixed-rate payer makes only one lump sum interest payment at the end of the agreement, while the floating-rate payer makes regular quarterly/semi-annual/annual payments. This means the floating-rate payer requires an additional payment to reflect the increased risk of default. With a forward rate swap the two parties agree today to a swap which will take place at a predetermined date in the future. In a basis swap both parties to the swap exchange floating rate of interest payments, but the base contract is different; for example, one may be based on dollar LIBOR and the other on US Treasury bill rates. With a roller-coaster swap the notional principal amount is varied in a predetermined manner over the life of the contract. With an index swap the payments between the two parties are determined by movements in an index such as the consumer price index or stock index.

Other innovations include the emergence of so-called swaptions, contracts in which the buyer has the right but not the obligation to enter into a swap contract with the other party. With a call swaption the buyer has the right but not the obligation to enter into a swap contract whereby it pays a floating rate of interest and receives a fixed rate of interest. With a put swaption the buyer has the right but not the obligation to enter into a swap contract whereby it receives a floating rate of interest and pays a fixed rate of interest. Some swap contracts have embedded options; a callable swap allows one of the parties the right to extend the contract for a specified period, whilst a putable swap allows one of the parties the right to terminate the agreement.

16.10 Conclusions

The swap market has grown enormously since the first swaps took place in the early 1980s (see **Table 16.1**). The market has matured so much that the potential gains to be had from swaps has fallen from around 50 basis points to 5–10 basis points. The evolution of the swap market has been one of the most significant developments in the bond market since it has enabled firms to obtain lower-cost financing and also to hedge risks at far longer-term horizons than is possible with futures and options.

Arranging swaps and even becoming a counterparty to swap arrangements has generated a source of fee income for banks, but has also meant that they have had to adopt new risk-management techniques and procedures. Underwriting a swap deal involves some 'off-balance-sheet' exposure for a bank should one of the counterparties default on its obligations. Hence, a bank needs to keep a careful eye on its potential swap exposures and the creditworthiness of the parties with which it deals.

It should also be remembered that the swaps that we have looked at in this chapter have been major simplifications of actual swaps carried out in the real world. In practice, swap agreements involve more complexity in that the two swap parties may wish to exchange different notional principal amounts, have different payment dates and, in the case of currency swaps, an intermediary has to take into account different interest-rate conventions such as different day counts used in different countries.

> **callable swap** a swap which allows one of the parties to extend the swap contract for a specified period

> **putable swap** a swap which gives one of the parties the right to terminate the swap contract prior to maturity

Further reading

Das, S. (2006) *Swaps/Financial Derivatives: Products, Pricing, Applications and Risk Management*, 3rd edn, Wiley.

Flavell, R. (2002) *Swaps and Other Derivatives*, 2nd edn, Wiley.

Kolb, R.W. and Overdahl, J. (2007) *Futures, Options and Swaps*, 5th edn, Basil Blackwell.

Sadr, A. (2009) *Interest Rate Swaps and their Derivatives: A Practitioner's Guide*, Wiley.

| **Chapter 16** | **Revision questions** |

1   Explain the difference between an absolute advantage swap and a comparative advantage swap.

2   Explain the difference between an interest rate swap and a currency swap.

3   Explain with the aid of a numerical example why in a plain vanilla swap the total potential gain from a swap is limited to a certain amount.

4   Explain what is meant by a swap reversal and discuss an alternative way of ending a swap obligation.

5   Explain how a swap may prove a useful way for a firm to hedge interest-rate risk when the firm has a lot of floating-rate debt on its books.

17

FINANCIAL INNOVATION AND THE CREDIT CRUNCH

17.1   Introduction

In this chapter you will learn about: financial innovations such as CDOs and CDSs, the causes of the credit crunch, the failure of Lehman Brothers and AIG, the financial cost of the credit crunch, the measures taken by the authorities in response to the crisis and the policy lessons and implications of the credit crunch.

A number of financial innovations have been developed since the 1990s through to the present. These new financial instruments such as collateralized debt obligations and credit derivatives including credit default swaps played a significant role in the so-called credit crunch which is generally considered to have started on 9 August 2007. On that date when BNP Paribas warned investors that they would not be able to withdraw money from two of its funds due to a 'complete evaporation of liquidity' in the market. In addition, the European Central Bank pumped €95 billion of liquidity into the markets, followed a few days later by a further €108.7 billion. Up until the outbreak of the credit crunch financial innovation had generally been viewed as a good thing for financial markets and the economy. It was believed that risk could be divided up into various tranches and transferred from market participants wishing to reduce their risk exposure to other participants prepared to take on greater risk exposure. However, the credit crunch showed that rather than reduce risk exposure much of the financial innovation had in fact built up the level of risk to such a high level that there was a major breakdown in the banking and financial systems. In April 2009, the International Monetary Fund (IMF) estimated that there would be close to $4.1 trillion dollars of losses in financial institutions worldwide. The scale of the financial crisis was unprecedented in modern times and comparisons were made with the global depression of the 1930s.

The chapter begins with a look at two of the key financial instruments linked to the credit crisis, (i) collateralized debt obligations (CDOs) and (ii) credit derivatives with a particular emphasis on credit default swaps (CDSs). As we shall see, these two financial securities played a pivotal role in the crisis, so an understanding of these instruments is essential to understanding how the credit crunch impacted so heavily upon the banking sector and, in the case of credit default swaps, was directly related to the failure of American International Group (AIG). Prior to the outbreak of the crisis AIG was the world's largest insurance firm, but it had to be bailed out to the tune of approximately $180 billion by the US taxpayer in September 2008. We then proceed to look at the credit crunch, analyzing the role played by the financial innovations and the responsibilities of the different players involved in the crisis. These players include individuals such as the former chairman of the Federal Reserve, Alan Greenspan, heads of banks and financial companies such as Freddie Mac, Fannie Mae and Citigroup, and organizations including financial regulators such as the Securities Exchange Commission (SEC) and the Financial Services Authority (FSA), the rating agencies, Governments, financial institutions, and ultimately households and companies that took on unserviceable debt levels.

---

credit derivative
a financial contract under which an agent buys or sells risk protection against the credit risk associated with a specific reference entity (or entities). For a periodic fee, the protection seller agrees to make a contingent payment to the buyer on the occurrence of a credit event (usually default in the case of a credit default swap)

credit crunch
a steep reduction in the volume of funds available for loans and credit in the economy; even cuts in official interest rates failed to return credit to more normal levels

---

CREDIT CRUNCH TIMELINE CREDIT CRUNCH TIMELINE CREDIT CRUNCH TIMELINE CREDI

27 February 2007 HSBC sacks two of its top chiefs due to large losses on subprime lending. ▶ **2 April 2007** New Century Financial, which specialized in subprime mortgages, files for Chapter 11 Bankruptcy and cuts half its workforce. ▶ **3 May 2007** UBS announce the closure of its Dillon Reed hedge fund following $125 million of subprime losses. ▶ **22 June** Bear Stearns announces a $3.2 billion bailout of two of its hedge funds. ▶ **June/July 2007** Rating agencies announce significant downgrades on some subprime mortgage ▷

17.2   Financial innovation: collateralized debt obligations and credit default swaps

collateralized debt obligation (CDO) an asset-backed security that is divided up into to different tranches with each tranche having a different risk–return characteristics; the junior tranches having higher risk and higher rates of return than the senior tranches

In this section we look at some of the key financial innovations that played a significant role in laying the foundations for the credit crunch. As we shall see, to some extent these financial innovations were linked to each other during the financial crisis. In theory each of these instruments has clear benefits in helping to manage risk and transfer it to those willing to take on the risk. In practice, however, they did not work as well as they should have. In large part the failure lay in the fact that CDOs and other structured finance products were 'misunderstood, misrated, mis-sold and mispriced'.

Collateralized debt obligations

A collateralized debt obligation (CDO) is a security that bundles together a range of different debt obligations and/or a package of bank loans into a financial security that is divided up into various tranches, with each tranche having different risk and return characteristics. The best way to illustrate a CDO is via a simple example.

subprime mortgages mortgages made to people with a poor credit rating; they have a higher rate of interest than conventional mortgages to compensate for the higher risk of default

Example of a CDO

Imagine that a series of mortgage loans equivalent to $500 million has been made to various borrowers. Some of these borrowers are high-risk (for example, loans to subprime borrowers) and some are medium- to lower-risk (for example, Alt-A and prime borrowers). If fully serviced the interest payable on the loans is equivalent to 10 per cent, resulting in an interest cash flow of $50 million plus principal repayments each year. A possible CDO that can be formed is illustrated in **Figure 17.1**.

The original set of bank loans with a zero default rate would yield $50 million per annum of interest income. The bank that made the loans may try to offload a large part of the risk on the loans by bundling the various loans and packaging them into a CDO. The first tranche (Tranche 1) is known as the equity tranche and is the riskiest part because, if there is a default on the first $25 million of principal and interest, then the holders of the equity tranche would be wiped out. Since this is the riskiest part of the CDO it attracts the highest rate of interest, in this example 30 per cent. Typically the equity tranche is not assigned a rating as it is understood to be high risk. If the default rate goes above $25 million then Tranche 2 – the junior tranche is next at risk. The value of the junior tranche in the example is $100 million, so if losses/defaults on interest and principal increase to $125 million this tranche would also be wiped out. Since the junior tranche is the next in line after the equity tranche, it will have a relatively low credit rating, for example BBB, and attract a lower yield of say 15 per cent. This yield is lower than that of the equity tranche but higher than the next tranche at risk, which is Tranche 3 – the mezzanine tranche. Holders of the

Alt-A mortgage a mortgage with a risk profile between prime and subprime mortgages

equity tranche the riskiest slice of a CDO offering the highest prospective rate of return

junior tranche a high-risk slice of a CDO

backed securities previously rated AAA to A+. ▶ July 2007 Investment Bank Bear Stearns warns that two of its hedge funds are in major financial difficulties and that investors in the funds have lost most of their investment. ▶ 19 July 2007 Federal Reserve Chairman Ben Bernanke warns that losses in the subprime market could total $100 billion. ▶ 31 July 2007 Credit market turmoil – shares in American Home Mortgage Investment plummet 90 per cent after the US lender said it could no longer fund home loans. Australian ▷

Figure 17.1   The creation of a CDO

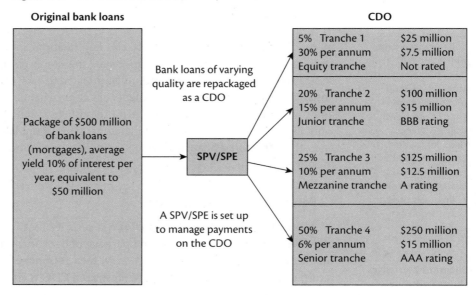

mezzanine tranche
a medium-risk slice of
a CDO

senior tranche
the safest slice of a
CDO

mezzanine tranche will only incur losses if defaults rise above $125 million, but they will be wiped out if losses hit $250 million. The safest tranche, which was frequently given a AAA rating, is Tranche 4 known as the senior tranche. It is only once losses exceed $250 million that losses will be suffered by owners of this tranche. Since it is the safest tranche it attracts the lowest rate of return; in the example, this is set at 6 per cent per annum.

Since the various tranches of a CDO have different risk–return characteristics the credit rating agencies such as Moody's and Standard & Poor's play a pivotal role in assigning credit ratings to them. When assigning its credit ratings, Moody's applies a methodology that looks at the default correlations between the various securities in the pool, the average credit quality of the pool of securities, the structure of the CDO and expected losses to each tranche. The fact that the CDO was sliced up into various tranches makes it an attractive security for different types of investors – for example, pension funds would be attracted to the AAA tranche, hedge funds to the junior tranche and other banks to the mezzanine tranche.

Although the above example gives a good idea of what a CDO is, there are a number of additional important points that need to be made. The first is that each CDO is a unique package, the quality of the CDO and the credit rating attached to each of its tranches will depend upon the quality of the original bank loans and how these have been packaged in the CDO. Another point is that even if some of the borrowers default on their bank loans there is likely to be some recovery against the assets owned by the defaulting borrower. For example, if one of the loans in the CDO

Macquarie Bank announces that two of its fortress funds, which invest in securitized loans, could lose up to a quarter of their value, or more than A$300 million. MSCI Asia index excluding Japan falls 4%. ▶ 2 August 2007 German Bank IKB announces $12 billion in subprime exposure. ▶ 6 August 2007 American Home Mortgages, the 10th largest home lender in the US which specializes in prime or near prime mortgages, files for Chapter 11 bankruptcy. ▶ 9 August 2007 BNP Paribas warns investors that they will not be able to   ▷

is for $500,000 against a house purchase then if the borrower defaults the bank will still be able to foreclose on the home and this will have some value, say $300,000 after recovery expenses, that can be used to repay the CDO holders. There are likely to be some covenants in the CDO that make it hard for the originating bank to reschedule and renegotiate loans with the original borrowers if they are having difficulty making payments.

All of these factors make the pricing of a CDO a very complex issue as the cash flows of each CDO are highly uncertain. Assumptions about timings of defaults, default rates, recovery rates, the impact of covenants and the fact that each CDO is unique combine to make designing the correct pricing structure a difficult task. As we shall see later in the chapter, the complexity of the CDOs and difficulties of determining their secondary market values ultimately became quite crucial in the evolution of the credit crunch.

It should be noted that many CDOs were issued by banks to free up capital that the bank would otherwise be forced to hold against those loans. If loans are made and then the risks of the loans sold off to other investors, then banks have new capital to make further loans, undertake share buy backs or develop new products while freeing themselves of the credit risk of the loans they have made. In our example, suppose that the bank has a loan book worth $500 million and is required to hold regulatory capital of 8 per cent (that is $40 million) to cover potential losses. By selling the CDO the bank sells 95 per cent of its loan book, retaining the equity piece worth 5 per cent of the $500 million – it is required to hold 100 per cent of the equity piece, that is $25 million, for regulatory capital purposes. As such the bank has managed to reduce its regulatory capital holding from $40 million to $25 million, a saving of $15 million. In addition it has raised $475 million from selling the CDO. Of course, the debt repayments on the loans are now used to make payments to the holders of the various tranches of the CDO rather than accrue to the bank. As such, the returns the bank gets on its $475 million cash received from the CDO become crucial to determining the overall profitability of creating the CDO.

There are variations in CDOs. One of the most notorious is the CDO squared (CDO²), which is a CDO based upon a package of existing CDOs or tranches of differing CDOs. A collateralized loan obligation (CLO) is simply a CDO based upon a package of loans, such as a package of auto loans or student loans or credit card loans. A collateralized bond obligation (CBO) is a CDO based upon a pool of bonds, such as a pool of corporate bonds. One issue of concern with a CDO is the asymmetric information involved – the bank creating the CDO is more likely to understand the quality of the loans behind the CDO than outside investors. This problem is partially solved by the bank retaining the risky equity tranche of the CDO, so that it suffers the first loss before outside investors. Also by holding the equity tranche, the bank is more likely to monitor and enforce the loan than if the entire loan has been sold off to a third party.

CDO squared
a CDO whose underlying assets are slices of other CDOs

collateralized loan obligation (CLO)
a CDO whose underlying assets are the cash flows from non-mortgage-related loans such as auto loans, student loans, consumer bank loans etc

collateralized bond obligation a CDO whose underlying assets are the cash flows from a variety of bonds such as corporate and government bonds

withdraw money from two of its funds due to a 'complete evaporation of liquidity' from the market. The ECB pumps €95 billion of liquidity into the markets, followed a few days later by a further €108.7 billion. ▶ 13 August 2007 Goldman Sachs injects $3 billion into one of its hedge funds which has been hit by falls in global equity markets. ▶ 16 August 2007 Countrywide Financial, America's largest mortgage provider, calls on $11.5 billion lifeline from 40 of the world's largest banks. ▶ 17 August 2007 The Federal Reserve cuts ▷

17.3   Special purpose vehicle/special purpose entity

special purpose vehicle (SPV) a legal entity set up for a specific purpose such as administering the cash flows from a CDO to the buyers of the various tranches; the American term is special purpose entity

When a CDO or other securitized product is sold onto the market it is usual for a bank to sponsor the formation of a special purpose vehicle (SPV) or special purpose entity (SPE) in the USA. An SPV/SPE is a legal entity set up for a specific limited purpose by another entity or a sponsoring firm. An SPV/SPE can take on one of three forms – a trust, a partnership, or a limited liability company. The SPV/SPE may be a subsidiary of the sponsoring firm, or it may be an 'orphan' SPV/SPE, one that is not consolidated with the sponsoring firm for tax, accounting, or legal purposes (or may be consolidated for some purposes but not others). An SPV/SPE is normally incorporated in an offshore centre such as the Cayman Islands.

In the context of a typical securitization, the SPV/SPE takes the form of a trust which is 'demonstrably distinct' from the sponsoring bank in that the sponsoring bank cannot unilaterally dissolve the SPV. In addition, the SPV/SPE must be 'bankruptcy remote', which means it will not be dissolved if the sponsoring bank were to go bankrupt, and the SPV/SPE is structured in such a way that it cannot itself become legally bankrupt. The fact that the SPV/SPE is bankruptcy remote provides some comfort for investors in the SPV/SPE since it cannot go under if the sponsoring bank were to get into trouble. An SPV/SPE is set up for a specific purpose or circumscribed activity or a series of such transactions. SPVs/SPEs have no other purpose than the transaction(s) for which they were created. The SPV/SPE can make no substantive decisions since the rules governing them are set down in advance and carefully circumscribe their activities. An SPV/SPE is merely a legal/accounting entity with no employees or even physical location. A typical SPV is thinly capitalized, its assets are serviced by a servicing department, its administrative functions are performed by a trustee that follows pre-specified rules with regard to the receipt and distribution of money.

A bank transfers loans or mortgages to the SPV/SPE, which then securitizes the pool of assets into a securitized product such as a CDO or an asset backed security (ABS) and manages the cash flows from the assets to ensure payments to investors in the CDO or ABS. By sponsoring the transfer of assets to the SPV/SPE, the parent bank can in theory eliminate its risk because write downs on the assets due to non-payment by borrowers will be suffered by the SPV/SPE and not the parent bank. In this sense an SPV/SPE is different from a subsidiary company because losses by the subsidiary would hit the profitability of the parent company. By setting up a separate company to manage the securities the bank is able to isolate the itself from the financial risks. However, it is important to understand that the sponsoring bank often makes implicit commitments to the SPV/SPE, known as 'implicit recourse' or 'moral recourse', whereby it is expected to provide credit and other support beyond its contractual obligations. This is widely recognized by regulators, credit rating agencies and the sponsoring bank such that the sponsoring parent bank will suffer a loss even though, from a legal/accounting perspective, it is not required to do so.

its Federal Funds rate from 6.25% to 5.75%, its first rate cut in 4 years ▶ 22 August 2007 Bank of America injects $2 billion of capital to rescue Countrywide Financial. ▶ 4 September 2007 (3-month) £LIBOR rises to 6.80% above the Bank of England's base rate of 5.75% as banks show increased reluctance to lend to each other on the interbank markets. ▶ 6 September 2007 The Federal Reserve provides $31.25 billion of loans to its banks and the ECB follows with €42 billion of liquidity for banks in the Eurozone area. ▷

17.4   A structured investment vehicle

structured investment vehicle (SIV) a legal entity that is financed by borrowing short-term and investing the borrowed funds in medium- to long-term securities

The first structured investment vehicle (SIV) was set up in 1988 by Citigroup, and SIVs have since become part of what is popularly known as the 'shadow banking system'. A SIV is a pool of assets and liabilities that attempts to exploit the difference between short- and long-term interest rates. The basic idea of a SIV is in essence quite simple – to raise funds at the short end of the market at relatively low rates of interest and invest those funds in longer-term securities at higher yields. The aim of the SIV is to capture the spread between the low funding costs of their short-term liabilities and higher returns on their longer-term assets. A typical SIV would raise money from the money markets primarily through the issuance of short-term commercial paper of say 90 and 180 days and medium-term notes with a maturity of 1 to 2 years. The funds are then invested in a variety of longer-term securities such as corporate bonds, Treasury bonds and structured finance products including ABSs and CDOs made up of things like mortgages, credit card receivables and student loans. The typical spread income for a SIV is 20 to 30 basis points. A typical SIV has some basic equity funding (initial capital) and usually employs a large degree of leverage, typically between 10 and 20 times the equity funding. One motivation for banks to set up SIVs is that they are far less regulated than the bank itself, and the requirements for capital against losses are usually much lower than that required by regulators.

One obvious risk of SIVs is that in a liquidity crisis they would be unable to roll over their short-term liabilities (that is, refinance them once they mature). As such, a SIV would typically seek a backstop facility from a parent bank or group of banks, enabling it to cover some of its issuance in the event of market disruption that prevented it successfully issuing some of its commercial paper. It is important to note that a SIV is a separate legal entity and its commercial paper issuance would be given a credit rating from the one or both of the major credit rating agencies (Standard & Poor's and Moody's). In certain cases, SPVs/SPEs sell their assets to a SIV which is mainly financed by the issuance of asset backed commercial paper (ABCP).

There are a number of differences between SIVs (shadow banking) and the traditional banking model. Under the traditional banking model the bank acts as an intermediary, dealing directly with depositors and borrowers and a lot of effort is put into screening the credit worthiness of the borrowers in particular. In contrast, the SIV is dependent on the short-term wholesale markets for funding and is therefore reliant on the work of the credit agencies to establish the credit worthiness of the securities it invests in. Another key difference is that in the traditional banking model the providers of funds (the depositors) are to some extent protected by the deposit guarantee provided by, for example, the Federal Deposit Insurance Corporation (FDIC) in the USA or the Financial Services Authority in the UK. This is not so in the case of buyers of the commercial paper and medium-term notes that fund the SIV who are subject to the risk of substantial losses if the SIV were to get into trouble.

▶ 13 September 2007 It is revealed that the British bank Northern Rock has funding problems and is to be granted emergency support from the Bank of England. ▶ 14–16 September 2007 Worried depositors in Northern Rock cause the first run on a British bank since 1866 as they queue to withdraw their funds. ▶ 17 September 2007 The UK government guarantees all deposits in Northern Rock to end the bank run. ▶ 18 September 2007 The Federal Reserve cuts its Federal Funds rate from 5.25% to 4.75%. The Dow Jones index   ▷

liquidity risk the risk that the market in a security will dry up so that it is difficult to turn it into cash without taking a substantial loss

solvency risk the risk that a creditor will lose all or part of his investment if a debtor fails to repay in full; traders call it **counterparty risk**

The SIVs were badly affected by the credit crunch. As it became apparent that a lot of the banks were in trouble, banks stopped lending to each other. The SIVs also found themselves in trouble as they had invested heavily in CDOs and subprime mortgages. The SIVs quickly found themselves unable to refinance their commercial paper except at very high rates of interest, and also had to start selling some of their assets, such as CDOs, at heavily discounted prices into a distressed market. The credit rating agencies also started to downgrade the ratings of the SIVs during the crisis, which either made funding themselves with commercial paper prohibitively expensive or made them reliant on bank credit lines to continue operating. Hence, the SIVs were badly hit by a combination of liquidity risk, because they were unable to roll over their commercial paper, and solvency risk, because the value of their assets fell below the value of their liabilities. One result of the credit crunch is that SIVs became unviable and by the end of 2008 there were no SIVs in operation.

17.5   Credit derivatives and credit default swaps

credit default swap (CDS) a credit derivative with a payout which is triggered by a 'credit event', typically a default. Settlement is either physical – the seller buys a defaulted reference asset from the buyer at its face value – or by cash – the seller pays the buyer the the face value of the reference asset less the current secondary market price of the defaulted asset

reference entity the entity whose debt is being insured against default in a CDS

credit event an event that impacts adversely upon a borrower's credit rating

Another significant financial innovation that played a crucial role in the credit crunch was the development of credit derivatives and in particular credit default swaps (CDSs). A credit derivative is a contract between two parties – a protection buyer and a protection seller – in which the seller sells credit protection to the buyer against the credit risk of a third party. The third party is known as the reference entity and may be a company or a government that has issued debt. Credit derivatives fall into two categories: unfunded credit derivatives and funded credit derivatives.

1   With an unfunded credit derivative the contract between the two parties means that payments are cash settled. For instance, the protection buyer will pay premiums in cash and receive a cash settlement from the seller of the credit risk protection if a credit event occurs.

2   With a funded credit derivative the party that assumes the credit risk, that is the protection seller, will make an initial payment that can be used to settle a credit event. This feature makes a funded credit derivative a lot safer since the protection buyer does not need to concern themselves with the counterparty risk of the protection seller.

The meaning of a credit event is crucial and will be specified in a credit derivative contract. It may include the bankruptcy of the reference entity, a restructuring of payments by the reference entity, a failure by the reference entity to make a scheduled payment or a moratorium on payments by the reference entity (see **Box 17.1**).

Credit default swaps

The most common credit derivative is a credit default swap (CDS), which is similar to an insurance product. In theory there are good reasons to believe that insurance against a default is a good idea. However, the uncontrolled writing of CDS contracts

rises 2.51% on the news to 13,759. ▶ 19 September 2007 The Bank of England announces it will inject £10 billion into the money markets to try and reduce the £LIBOR 3-month rate. ▶ 1 October 2007 UBS announces $3.4 billion of losses from its subprime exposure. Citigroup announces losses of $3.1 billion. ▶ 5 October 2007 Merrill Lynch announces $5.6 billion of subprime losses. ▶ 15 October 2007 Citigroup announces a further $5.9 billion of losses from subprime and other exposures. ▶ 30 October 2007 ▷

Box 17.1	What constitutes a credit event?

The International Swaps and Derivatives Association specifies five things that could constitute a credit event. A credit default swap will specify one or more of the five as constituting a credit event, and so trigger payments from a protection seller to a protection buyer.

Bankruptcy

A corporate becomes insolvent or is unable to pay its debts. The bankruptcy event is, of course, not relevant for sovereign issuers.

Failure to pay

Failure of the reference entity to make due payments greater than the specified payment requirement (typically $1 million), taking into account some grace period to prevent accidental triggering due to an administrative error.

Obligations acceleration/obligations default

Obligations that have become due and payable earlier than they would have been because of default or similar condition or obligations have become capable of being defined due and payable earlier than they would have been because of a default or similar condition. The latter description is the more encompassing definition and is generally preferred by the protection buyer. The aggregate amount of obligations must be greater than the default requirement (typically $10 million).

Repudiation/moratorium

A reference entity or government authority rejects or challenges the validity of the obligations.

Restructuring changes

Restructuring changes in the debt obligations of the reference creditor, excluding those that are not associated with credit deterioration, such as a renegotiation of more favourable terms.

by the leading insurance company American International Group (AIG) ultimately led to its failure and resulted in it being taken over by the US government. In 2007 the International Swap and Derivatives Association (www.isda.org) reported that the total amount of credit derivatives outstanding was $62.2 trillion, up from $0.5 trillion in 2000 (see **Table 17.1**). The main centre for trading in credit derivatives is London and the vast majority of trading in such contracts is conducted by insurance companies, commercial and investment banks, securities firms, hedge funds, pension funds, speculators and corporations in the over-the-counter market.

Merrill Lynch announces $7.9 billion of losses and its Chief Executive Officer resigns. ▶ 1 November 2007 Credit Suisse announces a £1 billion write down on structured finance, mortgages and leveraged loan-related losses. ▶ 2 November 2007 Citigroup announces further losses of $8 to $11 billion and its Chairman/CEO Chuck Prince resigns. ▶ 7 November 2007 Morgan Stanley announces a $3.7 billion subprime-related write down. ▶ 13 November 2007 Bank of America announces a $3 billion write down. ▷

Table 17.1   The value of CDSs in $ trillions

Year	Notional value
2000	0.5
2001	0.9
2002	2.2
2003	3.8
2004	8.4
2005	17.1
2006	34.4
2007	62.2
2008	38.6

Source: ISDA

A CDS is a credit derivative contract in which one party (the protection buyer) pays a periodic fee to another party (the protection seller) in return for a payout in the instance of a credit event by a reference entity. It is important to understand that the reference entity is not a party to the CDS, and it is not necessary for the protection buyer to suffer an actual loss in order to be eligible for a payout if a credit event occurs.

When a credit event occurs, the protection buyer will issue the protection seller a credit event notice making the basis for a claim against the protection seller. In effect, a CDS enables the protection buyer to short the credit risk of the reference entity, while the protection seller is taking a long position on the credit risk of the reference entity. Each contract sets out the specific terms of the agreement including identification of the underlying asset (loan or bond), what constitutes a credit event and the settlement process. The vast majority of CDS contacts have a non-bank corporate as the reference entity, followed by CDS contracts with banks as the reference entity. Trading in sovereign CDS contracts, contracts in which the reference entity is government debt, has been growing over the years. The growth has been especially strong in bonds issued by emerging market economies where the risk of a credit event is, generally speaking, significantly higher than for developed market economies. A typical credit default swap is set out in **Table 17.2**.

Table 17.2 shows the details of a straightforward CDS on company ABC. The duration of the contract is 3 years and the notional size of the contract is $10 million of debt. The contract is to be settled by means of physical delivery of bonds with a face value of $10 million and a maturity of 5 years to the protections seller, who will pay the difference between the secondary value of the debt and the face value of the debt in the event of a bankruptcy filing by company ABC. The possible payout profiles are depicted in **Figure 17.2**.

CREDIT CRUNCH TIMELINE CREDIT CRUNCH TIMELINE CREDIT CRUNCH TIMELINE CRED

▶ 15 November 2007 Barclays Bank announces a £1.3 billion write down. ▶ 20 November 2007 Freddie Mac announces a $2.2 billion quarterly loss after a $4.8 billion charge due to bad debts and write downs. ▶ 6 December 2007 President George W. Bush announces a plan to help more than 1 million homeowners facing foreclosure and the Bank of England cuts its base rate by 0.5%.

▶ 10 December 2007 UBS announces a $10 billion write down while Société Générale launches a $4.3 billion bailout of one of its SIVs. ▷

Figure 17.2   Cash flows on a CDS

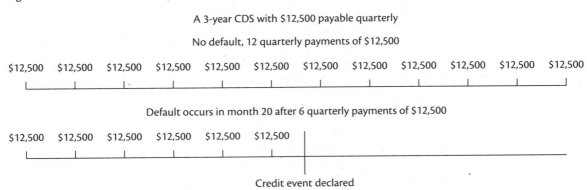

Table 17.2   A CDS contract

Reference entity	Company ABC
Specified currency	US dollar
Duration of the CDS	3 years
Notional value	$10 million
Default swap spread premium payable per annum	50 basis points
Frequency of premium payments	Quarterly
Conditions for payoff	Upon physical settlement of the reference entity's bonds with a minimum of 5 years to maturity
Credit event	Bankruptcy

The quarterly premium which is typical for corporate CDOs is simply determined by the face value of the contract times the basis points per annum times 0.25 to reflect the quarterly premium payable. In this case therefore the quarterly premium is:

$$\$10,000,000 \times 0.005 \times 0.25 = \$12,500$$

so that the annual premium is $50,000 to insure against the risk of default on $10 million of debt, payable in quarterly instalments of $12,500.

It is important to understand that the contract lasts for three years (in this example) and the premium payable is set by the protection seller for the lifetime of the contract. There is, however, a secondary market for the CDS premiums once issued. If the credit worthiness of the reference entity deteriorates then this will be reflected in a rise in the basis points payable in the secondary market. For instance, if the likelihood of company ABC filing for bankruptcy rises after one year then the basis points charged will rise from say 50 to 80 basis points. The premiums payable

RUNCH TIMELINE CREDIT CRUNCH TIMELINE CREDIT CRUNCH TIMELINE CREDIT CRUNCH

▶ 12 December 2007 The Federal Reserve cuts the interest rate from 4.50% to 4.25%. ▶ 13 December 2007 The Federal Reserve, the European Central Bank, Bank of England, Swiss and Canadian central banks coordinate to offer a combined $110 billion of loans to troubled banks. ▶ 17 December 2007 A $20 billion injection is announced by the Federal Reserve ▶ 18 December 2007 The European Central Bank announces a $500 billion injection to see banks through the Christmas/New Year period. ▶ 19 December 2007 Standard ▷

on the secondary market would then rise from $50,000 per year to $80,000 per year, meaning a potential profit of $30,000 a year for the remaining two years of the contract, or $60,000 in total, for a protection buyer. Note that the maturity of the CDS does not need to correspond to the maturity of the underlying debt of the reference entity – it is quite usual for the CDS to specify a debt instrument (for example, bonds with 10 years to maturity) with a longer term to maturity than the CDS (for example, three years).

Although CDS contracts are like an insurance product in many ways there are some characteristics that make them quite different. The protection buyer does not need to have any interest in the reference entity or to have suffered an actual financial loss to make a claim if a credit event occurs. In other words, the protection buyer may or may not hold any debt issued by the reference entity. By contrast, with a normal insurance product you need to have an 'insurable interest' in the item you insure; for example, you can insure your own house as you will suffer a loss if it burns down, but you will not normally be allowed to insure a stranger's house and benefit if it burns down. Also, an insurance contract pays out a buyer if a loss has actually been sustained, whereas a CDS contract is more akin to a bet on whether a 'credit event' will or will not occur. Furthermore, since CDSs are over-the-counter products, they do not involve the same actuarial analysis as a typical insurance product. Instead, the analysis is based upon the financial strength of the reference entity issuing the underlying credit asset (loan or bond). Unlike insurance products which require regulatory capital to be set aside to meet prospective claims, there are no regulatory capital requirements imposed on the protection seller. In addition, since the protection seller has no relationship with the reference entity then the seller cannot make a claim against or sue the reference entity.

Once a credit event occurs either one or both parties issues a credit event notice to the other party, based upon publicly available information such as specified news sources, which if validated will the trigger settlement of the CDS. There are two ways in which a CDS can be settled: cash or physical settlement. With a physical settlement the protection buyer delivers the face value of the underlying security or comparable securities specified in the CDS contract (*pari passu* or equivalent securities) to the protection buyer in exchange for the face payment on the security. The protection seller will then own the security and will be able to claim against the reference entity or sell the security on to another party at the then prevailing secondary market price. With cash settlement, the protection buyer will be entitled to a cash payment equal to the difference between the par value of the security and a secondary market price of the security. The secondary market price is normally obtained from five dealers some 14 to 30 days after the occurrence of the credit event. In instances where no reliable secondary market price can be determined, then cash settlement will be based upon other instruments of similar quality and characteristics, such as maturity,

& Poor's downgrades the credit rating of some monoline insurers which repay the bond holder if a bond issuer defaults. This increases concerns about future bank losses and the health of the financial system. ▶ 8 January 2008 Bear Stearns' Chief resigns. ▶ 11 January 2008 Bank of America buys Countrywide Financial for $4 billion. ▶ 14 January 2008 Citigroup announces $9.8 billion loss following $18.1 billion of write downs due to subprime exposure. ▶ 17 January 2008 Merrill Lynch announces a further write ▷

outlined in the contract. It should be noted that the protection buyer will stop all premium payments once a credit event has occurred, and this also needs to be factored into the appropriate premium charged by the protection seller.

fixed recovery CDS
a CDS that fixes the amount of the payoff to be made should a credit event occur; it removes uncertainty over the payoff for both the protection buyer and protection seller

Rather than have a payoff based upon the difference between the face value of the security and its secondary market price or recovery price, a fixed recovery CDS (or binary swap or digital swap) fixes the amount of the payoff to be made should a credit event occur. The fixed recovery CDS therefore removes uncertainty over the payoff for both the protection buyer and protection seller. The fixed recovery CDS can be used to speculate on the recovery rate. For instance, say the protection seller assumes that there will be a 50 per cent recovery rate in the event of a default. If he sells protection on a CDS with a fixed payment of 40 per cent of the face value of the bonds, that is $4 million for a $10 million contract, and the recovery rate is 50 per cent then he will receive $5 million upon recovery and make $1 million of profit plus the premiums received. If the actual recovery rate is below 50 per cent, say only 30 per cent, then the protection seller would make a loss of $1 million less the premiums received.

contingent CDS
a CDS for which a payout requires both a credit event and an additional trigger which could be a credit event by another reference entity or a specified price movement in some market security

There are variations on the basic CDSs that we have outlined. For example, it is possible to have a CDS contract that is based upon a basket of reference entities and a payment is made when one of the reference entities incurs a credit event. Some CDSs require an upfront fee to be paid in addition to the quarterly premiums. Such upfront fees can be particularly high if the reference entity is close to bankruptcy; for example, an upfront fee could be $2 million to $3 million (on a notional value of $10 million) if a company has a high likelihood of filing for bankruptcy. Some CDSs are based upon a credit reference asset rather than a credit reference entity. In such contracts, the recovery rate on the underlying asset is important to the payout; for example, senior secured debt in the reference entity will have a higher recovery rate than junior unsecured debt in the reference entity. With a contingent CDS, a payout requires both a credit event and an additional trigger. The additional trigger could be a credit event by another reference entity or a specified price movement in some market security. In a dynamic CDS the notional amount determining the payout is linked to the mark to market value of a portfolio of swaps.

mark to market the monitoring of the profit and loss positions of each party to a contract by using the prevailing market price

One problem with CDS contracts is that they are bought and sold as individual contracts and appear not to be subject to securities laws. There is no regulatory body that governs the buying and selling of CDS. While the International Swaps and Derivatives Association provides recommended CDS documentation guidelines it is not a regulatory body that issues regulations which are legally enforceable. Also, since the protection seller does not have to set aside capital against a credit event, the buyer of credit protection is subject to noticeable counterparty risk.

The first CDS products were developed in the mid 1990s and the market expanded rapidly from around $631 billion in the first half of 2001 to an estimated

down of $14.1 billion of subprime losses. ▶ 21 January 2008 Global stockmarkets suffer their biggest fall since the 11 September 2001 terrorist attacks. ▶ 22 January 2008 The Federal Reserve cuts the Federal Fund rate by 0.75% to 3.5%, its biggest cut in 25 years. ▶ 30 January 2008 The Federal Reserve announces a 0.5% cut on Federal Funds rate from 3.5% to 3%. ▶ 31 January 2008 MBIA, a bond insurer, announces a quarterly loss of $2.3 billion due to subprime exposure. ▶ 7 February 2008 The Federal Reserve Chairman Ben   ▷

$62 trillion in the second half of 2007. In the early 2000s the CDS market changed in three substantive ways:

1   A secondary market developed and new parties became involved in the CDS market. This development made it more difficult to determine the financial strength of the protection seller.
2   CDSs were issued for SIVs, ABSs, mortgage backed securities (MBSs) and even CDOs. These investments no longer had a known entity by which to determine the strength of a particular loan or bond, unlike the case for commercial loans, corporate bonds or municipal bonds.
3   The CDS market became used far more for speculation rather than hedging. Rampant speculation in the market meant that buyers and sellers of CDS contracts were no longer owners of the underlying asset (bond or loan), but were just 'betting' on the possibility of a credit event of a specific asset.

17.6   The pricing of credit derivatives

The pricing of credit derivatives is an enormously complex area and the level of modelling required is well beyond the scope of this book. However, it is clear that there are two crucial factors that need to be borne in mind when calculating the appropriate price of a credit derivative:

1   The likelihood of default.
2   The payment or payoff to be made in the event of a default.

The likelihood of default will depend upon the credit rating of the reference entity, it being less likely to default if it is a AA rated issuer than if it is a BBB rated issuer. The payment to be made in the event of a default will depend upon recovery rates if the issuer defaults. The recovery rate will crucially depend on whether the debt is senior (unsubordinated) or junior (subordinated). In addition, there is a difference in recovery rates for senior secured bonds than for senior unsecured bonds and likewise between junior secured and unsecured bonds. Traditionally, secured bonds have quite good recovery rates, in the region of 60 to 90 cents per dollar, while junior unsecured bonds have much lower recovery rates, in the region of 10 to 25 cents per dollar.

Under certain highly restrictive conditions, the annual premium payable for a CDS is approximately equal to the yield of a Corporate bond, less the risk-free rate of interest, of the same length to maturity as the reference entity. For example, if a five-year Treasury bond yields 6 per cent and the reference entity issues a bond with five years to maturity at 6 per cent then the credit premium will be equal to 100 basis points or $100,000 per annum on a notional principal amount of $10,000,000. Unfortunately, the calculation of the actual premium payable is far more complex

Bernanke expresses concern over monoline insurers. The Bank of England cuts it interest rate by 0.5% to 5.25%. ▶ 10 February 2008

Leaders from the G7 economies estimate losses from subprime mortgages at $400 billion. ▶ 17 February 2008 Bear Stearns, the fifth

largest investment bank in the USA, is rescued through an acquisition by JP Morgan for a mere $240 million (one year earlier its market

capitalization had been $18 billion) and the deal is backed by $30 billion of central bank loans. Northern Rock is nationalized by the UK ▷

| Box 17.2 | Credit derivatives and the fall of American International Group |

American International Group (AIG) was the world's largest insurance group, dealing with all types of insurance including commercial, health, residential and life insurance. It was ranked as the tenth largest company in the *Fortune* 500 list of American companies in April 2007, and was, generally speaking, a very profitable company. On 28 February 2008 it announced annual profits of $6.2 billion and had a market capitalization of $95.8 billion with its shares trading at $50.50. However, by October 2008 its share price had collapsed below $1 following a dramatic rescue by the American taxpayer on 16 September .

In 1998 AIG Financial Products Division (AIGFP) made the fateful decision to get involved in selling protection in CDSs, especially on mortgage backed securities and collateralized debt obligations which were often made up of bundles of subprime mortgages. Things went well during the period 1998–2006 as AIG was picking up premiums from selling the CDSs and making virtually no payouts. Insurance is a great business to be in when you are collecting premiums and not having to make any payouts! The Financial Products Division employed around 430 staff, mostly in London, and had written some 44,000 complex, often long-term contracts with a notional value of $2 trillion. Over time, AIGFP had become a multistrategy hedge fund engaged in a variety of businesses. In addition to CDSs, it wrote and traded equity, currency and commodity derivatives.

According to Gerry Pasciucco, who was given the job of unwinding AIG's exposures following its collapse, it was AIG's exposure to fewer than 200 insurance contracts that were sensitive to its credit ratings and the value of the underlying CDOs that led to its collapse. There were several features of AIG's contracts on CDOs that made them potentially dangerous. Firstly, they were mostly unhedged and the contracts required AIG to post billions of dollars of collateral if its credit rating was downgraded. Secondly, AIG agreed to post collateral if the market value of the CDOs it insured fell, even if there were no credit downgrades or defaults on the CDOs. As the credit crisis developed, the price of CDOs that AIG had insured began to collapse and on 15 September 2008 the ratings agencies downgraded its rating: Moody's cut AIG's rating from Aa3 to A2, Standard & Poor's and Fitch both reduced its rating from AA– to A–. The downgrades and fall in price of CDOs forced AIG to post tens of billions of dollars of collateral with its counterparties, but the amount of collateral required soon exceeded its resources. On 16 September 2008, the American government intervened, with an $85 billion credit line in

continued overleaf

government. ▶ 6 March 2008 Carlyle Group, a private equity firm, announces a $22 billion write down in its bond fund, Carlyle Capital Corporation. ▶ 16 March 2008 Bear Stearns is sold to JP Morgan for $240 million (less than 1% of its market valuation a month earlier) in an emergency takeover. As part of the deal the Federal Reserve agrees to underwrite $30 billion of Bear Stearn toxic subprime exposure. ▶ 1 April 2008 UBS Chief Marcel Ospel resigns following a £10 billion write off. ▶ 8 April 2008 IMF estimates that ▷

| Box 17.2 | **Credit derivatives and the fall of American International Group** – *continued* |

exchange for a 79.9 per cent stake to prevent AIG's collapse. The US government deemed that AIG was 'too big and too interconnected' to fail. The failure of AIG would have led to severe financial problems in dozens of other major financial institutions that had paid premiums to AIG to protect themselves against defaults in CDOs they owned.

In March 2009 AIG announced the largest ever loss in corporate history of $61.7 billion for its final quarter of 2008, and it is estimated that its total losses could eventually be in excess of $180 billion dollars. The government was forced to reveal payouts from AIG to some of its major counterparties. From late 2007 through 2008 Société Générale received $16.5 billion, Goldman Sachs received $14 billion, Deutsche Bank received $8.5 billion and Merrill Lynch $6.2 billion. Had the US Treasury not made these payouts then the problems facing some of these financial institutions would have been greatly exacerbated.

AIG caused a massive public storm in January 2009 when it revealed that it had set aside $450 million in retention bonuses to pay some 400 of its staff who were in the process of unwinding its complex trades. Many of these staff had been involved in writing the very contracts that led to AIG's failure but were deemed to be essential to successfully unwinding the complex trades that ruined the company. Not surprisingly, in March 2009 Ben Bernanke the Chairman of the Federal Reserve stated:

> If there is a single episode in this entire 18 months that has made me more angry, I can't think of one other than AIG. AIG exploited a huge gap in the regulatory system, there was no oversight of the financial products division, this was a hedge fund basically that was attached to a large and stable insurance company.'

On 6 August 2009 the *Wall Street Journal* reported that Wall Street banks and lawyers could benefit from up to $1 billion in fees for managing the break up and winding down of AIG. It was being reported that Morgan Stanley could collect as much as $250 million, with other beneficiaries being the private equity firm Blackstone Group, the law firm Davis Polk & Wardwell, accounting firm Ernst & Young, with Goldman Sachs and JPMorgan Chase all in line for large fees for helping to sort out the AIG mess.

potential losses from the credit crunch could exceed $1 trillion. ▶ 14 April 2008 Wachovia announces $4.4 billion of write downs. ▶ 18 April 2008 Citigroup announces a further $15.2 billion write down and 9,000 job losses. ▶ 21 April 2008 Bank of England announces a new Special Liquidity System £50 billion swap facility scheme to aid banks. ▶ 22 April 2008 The Royal Bank of Scotland announces the biggest-ever rights issue in UK corporate history of £12 billion. It also announces £5.9 billion of write downs. ▷

than this simplification. Nonetheless, the basic idea generally holds that the higher the corporate bond spread the higher the CDS premium payable.

Having looked at the various financial instruments such as CDOs, CDSs and investment vehicles such as SPVs/SPE and SIVs, we are now in a position to proceed to an analysis of the credit crunch.

17.7   The credit crunch

The credit crunch which started on 9 August 2007 is generally viewed as the most significant crisis to affect the financial markets and the global economy since the 1930s. The term 'credit crunch' refers to the sudden and very significant tightening of lending conditions in the financial system which happened independently of official interest rates. In particular, there was a pronounced fall off in lending, both between banks on the interbank market and between banks and their clients. Many other features also came into play, such as an increase in risk aversion combined with declines in the price of risky assets such as equities and corporate bonds and a flight to quality assets such as Treasury bonds. In the remainder of this chapter, we consider the causes of the credit crunch, the issues raised by the crisis, the policy response to the crisis, its economic impact and some of the lessons to be learned from it.

The dimensions of the credit crunch

The 2007 credit crunch is generally considered to have been triggered by losses on subprime mortgages in the USA, but its impact was too wide and too deep to be explained by losses in that sector alone. The crisis led to the two mortgage financing giants Fannie Mae and Freddie Mac, with combined loans totalling $5.5 trillion, being placed under the control of the US government, and in March 2008 Bear Stearns had to be rescued through a merger with Bank of America. Shares in most of the top banks around the world plunged dramatically in value, as depicted in **Table 17.3.**

The crisis took a particularly nasty turn on 29 September 2008 when the investment bank Lehman Brothers was placed into bankruptcy (see **Box 17.3**). The Lehman bankruptcy set off significant falls in global stockmarkets around the world. In order to survive the crisis major commercial and investment banks like Citigroup, Bank of America, Goldman Sachs and Merrill Lynch became heavily reliant on funds and other support provided by the Federal Reserve and US Treasury. Another institution that found itself drawn into the crisis was American International Group (AIG) that, due to losses from its London-based Financial Products Division, had to be taken over by the American government with estimated losses in excess of $180 billion.

bank run a situation in which many of a bank's customers rush to withdraw their deposits, placing the bank in jeopardy since its reserves may not be sufficient to meet the withdrawals

While the crisis started in the USA, it quickly spread itself throughout the world. In the UK, during September 2007 the Northern Rock bank found itself unable to fund its mortgage book, and it was subjected to the first bank run since 1866 as depositors

▶ 25 April 2008 UK housebuilder Persimmon announces major cutbacks.   ▶ 29 April 2008 HBOS announces a £4 billion rights issue.   ▶ 30 April 2008 The first fall in UK house prices year on year is announced by Nationwide and followed later in the week by Halifax's announcement of a 0.9% annual fall.   ▶ 2 May 2008 The Federal Reserve and European Central Bank inject $82 billion into the money markets.   ▶ 14 May 2008 Bradford & Bingley announces an emergency £300 million rights issue.   ▶ 22 May 2008 UBS announces a ▷

Table 17.3   The effects of the credit crunch on stockmarket capitilizations of the banking system

Country	Bank stockmarket capitalizations 1 Jan 2007 ($ billions)	Bank stockmarket capitalizations 31 March 2009 ($ billions)
China	667.4	525.3
USA	1560.5	352.1
Japan	651.3	248.8
UK	714.4	163.3
Australia	225.7	139.7
Canada	236.7	135.1
Hong Kong	345.8	131.5
Spain	306.2	112.0
Italy	338.1	99.3
France	372.8	97.8
Switzerland	281.9	81.3
India	60.4	41.1
Sweden	108.4	39.3
Germany	151.6	37.0
Singapore	68.3	34.5
South Africa	48.2	33.0
Indonesia	30.9	24.8
Russia	126.0	23.9
Belgium	184.6	17.0
Poland	51.2	20.2
Portugal	38.3	10.4
Argentina	9.2	3.7
Netherlands	22.7	1.8
Ireland	53.9	1.2

Source: *Financial Times*

queued to withdraw their money. The bank run was only halted after the government guaranteed all its deposits. By February 2008 it became evident that Northern Rock could not survive and it had to be nationalized. The Bradford & Bingley building society was also caught out in the crisis and had to be rescued and taken over by the Treasury in September 2008. The demise of Northern Rock was later eclipsed by the problems at the Halifax Bank of Scotland (HBOS) which was rescued through a merger with Lloyds TSB bank. The rescue proved to be fateful to Lloyds TSB as losses

CREDIT CRUNCH TIMELINE CREDIT CRUNCH TIMELINE CREDIT CRUNCH TIMELINE CRED

$15.5 billion rights issue with its subprime losses having increased to $37 billion. ▶ 19 June 2008 Research shows that 190 hedge funds have been wound up in the previous 3 months. ▶ 25 June 2008 Barclays announces a £4.5 billion rights issue and sells a £1.7 billion stake in itself to the Qatar Investment Authority. ▶ 10 July 2008 Fannie Mae and Freddie Mac shares fall in value by 50% during the trading day. ▶ 11 July 2008 Indymac Bank is seized by the Federal Deposit Insurance Corporation following a run on the bank. ▷

in HBOS led to Lloyds itself being drawn into the crisis and having to be rescued by the UK taxpayer who took a 45 per cent stake in the bank. In March 2009 the stake was raised to 65 per cent. Another major bank drawn into the crisis was the Royal Bank of Scotland (RBS) which over several years had become the largest bank in the UK. In December 2007 it made the fateful decision to take over the Dutch bank ABN Amro. The acquisition proved ill timed and was not subjected to the same degree of scrutiny that such an acquisition would normally attract. The huge losses that later emerged on the ABN deal (estimated to be as much as €22 billion), coupled with the problems on its own loan book, meant that RBS had to be rescued by the UK government, which took a majority 70 per cent holding in the bank.

The UK financial sector was heavily hit by the crisis in general with the fall off in mergers and acquisitions, underwriting activity, IPOs, commercial paper and corporate bond issues leading to tens of thousands of job losses. Globally, estimates put job losses in the financial services sector at 350,000 during 2008 and the first half of 2009, which is approximately 20 per cent of the pre-crisis workforce.

While a great deal of the crisis was concentrated in the USA and the UK, it had a significant effect on both commercial and investment banks in many other nations. In Switzerland the Union Bank of Switzerland (UBS) had losses on its subprime exposure in excess of 40 billion dollars. In Germany, although the property market had been stagnant for many years, many German banks had losses from CDOs and SIVs amounting to tens of billions of euros. Banks in other countries such as Belgium, the Netherlands and even Australia also had large losses resulting from their holdings of subprime securities. More dramatically, banks in Iceland and Ireland which had boomed in the preceding years were brought to the point of collapse. A timeline of the key events during the credit crunch runs through this chapter.

17.8   Causes of the credit crunch

In the following analysis we shall argue that the credit crunch had multiple causes, many of which interacted with one another in creating unsustainable levels of household debt and house prices. This was especially true in the USA and the UK, although housing bubbles were also evident in Ireland, Spain, Australia, Dubai and even parts of China.

17.9   Legislative changes and deregulation

Long before the credit crunch took place, there were background forces that encouraged banks to get more heavily involved in the mortgage loan market. The Basel Accord of 1988 required banks to hold less capital for loans made for mortgages, which were regarded as relatively safe, than for consumer loans, which were regarded as relatively risky. This undoubtedly increased the incentive for banks to increase

▶ 14 July 2008 The US authorities announce that they are stepping in to support Fannie Mae and Freddie Mac which have a combined $5.5 trillion of mortgage-related assets. ▶ 23 July 2008 President George W. Bush backs a plan to save Fannie Mae and Freddie Mac. ▶ 30 July 2008 Lloyds Bank announces £1.09 billion write down on structured finance holding and investments. ▶ 8 August 2008 Royal Bank of Scotland announcees a write off of £5.9 billion on assets affected by the credit crunch. ▷

Box 17.3	The Lehman Brothers bankruptcy

On 15 September 2008 Lehman Brothers Holdings, the fourth largest investment bank on Wall Street, filed for Chapter 11 bankruptcy. It was the largest bankruptcy in US history sparking large falls in stockmarkets around the globe. The collapse of Lehman Brothers and the downfall of its CEO Dick Fuld became one of the biggest stories of the credit crunch, and set off the most complex bankruptcy in history. Prior to its collapse, Lehman was a global investment bank dealing with a huge range of interests covering investment banking, equity and bonds trading, derivatives, securitization and wealth management. It had offices around the world, including New York, London, Tokyo, Hong Kong, the Middle East and Latin America. Lehman Brothers had a long and distinguished history, having originally been formed as a cotton brokerage in 1850. Just prior to its collapse it was employing some 28,600 staff worldwide.

The losses that brought Lehman down were primarily due to its large exposure to subprime mortgages through its CDO holdings. The precise reasons as to why Lehman had accumulated such a large exposure to the subprime sector are unclear: it was either holding the risky tranches of CDOs willingly or holding them unwillingly because it could not find buyers. In the second quarter of 2008 Lehman announced losses of $2.4 billion and its stock, which had been falling since the collapse of Bear Stearns in March, began to decline dramatically. In a bid to protect shareholders the CEO Dick Fuld looked around for interested parties which would be willing to buy Lehman, including Korea Development Bank (KDB). However, on 9 September KDB made it clear that it was not going ahead with a deal, leading to a continued collapse of Lehman's shares. As things became critical, an attempt was made to sell the company over the weekend of 13–14 September to Barclays or Bank of America, but a deal could not be reached, and the Federal Reserve Chief, Ben Bernanke, and Treasury Secretary, Hank Paulson, made it clear that they would not step in to save Lehman. So on 15 September Lehman filed for bankruptcy, citing assets of $639 billion and liabilities made up of bank debt and bond debt of $768 billion – a gap of $129 billion.

The Lehman's collapse created great uncertainty in the financial markets because it was a counterparty to tens of thousands of contracts around the globe. Many hedge funds and financial institutions for which Lehman was acting as broker/money manager found their accounts frozen and had problems executing trades. The Dow Jones Industrial Average fell 504 points, interbank interest rates rose significantly and there was a rush to withdraw funds from money markets around the globe.

CREDIT CRUNCH TIMELINE CREDIT CRUNCH TIMELINE CREDIT CRUNCH TIMELINE CRED

▶ 1–6 September 2008 Stockmarkets around the world have one of their worst weeks. ▶ 7 September 2008 The US government announces the biggest rescue in US corporate history as Fannie Mae and Freddie Mac are placed into 'conservatorship' (nationalization by any other name). ▶ 10 September 2008 Lehman Brothers announces a $3.9 billion loss for the quarter. ▶ 15 September 2008 Lehman Brothers files for Chapter 11 bankruptcy and Merrill Lynch agrees to be taken over by Bank of America for $50 billion. ▷

| Box 17.3 | The Lehman Brothers bankruptcy – *continued* |

The rise and fall of Lehman Brothers became inextricably linked to the rise and fall of its CEO Dick Fuld, who had presided over the company since 1994. He joined the firm in 1969 and became a formidable fixed income trader, eventually rising to CEO. During the years to 2006, profits at Lehman rose dramatically and in 2006 *Institutional Investor* placed Dick Fuld as number one CEO in its Brokers and Asset Managers category. In the eight years prior to Lehman's collapse he earned an estimated $300 million. From press accounts, it appears that Dick Fuld was an authoritarian leader and did not listen to his risk managers who were warning of potential trouble from the bank's exposure to the subprime sector. The CDOs and CDSs being traded on Wall Street were very different instruments from those he had traded in his days as a trader. This, combined with his staff's reluctance to give him a full picture of the risks Lehman Brothers faced, probably contributed to the bank's demise. The bankruptcy of Lehman and news of his earnings made Dick Fuld a figurehead for Wall Street's excesses. In December 2008, Dick Fuld was the inaugural winner of the *Financial Times*' 'Lex Overpaid CEO' award for having received $40.5 million in 2006 and $34m in 2007, the two years preceding Lehman's collapse. CNBC.com named Dick Fuld at the top of its list of 'Worst American CEOs of All Time' stating that he was 'belligerent and unrepentant'

Glass Steagall Act
a piece of legislation passed by Congress in 1933 prohibiting commercial banks from engaging in investment banking activities

conduit
a government or private sector entity that pools mortgages and other loans enabling banks and other financial institutions to on-sell their mortgages or loans to investors

their mortgage exposure. The rescue of Long Term Capital Management in 1998 exacerbated the moral hazard in the financial system. In 1999 the repeal of the Glass-Steagall Act and the setting up Federal Deposit Insurance Corporation (FDIC) were key reforms. The Glass-Steagall Act of 1933 had separated the US banking system into two distinct types of banks: the commercial banking sector and the investment banking sector. Its repeal followed heavy lobbying from the banking industry which argued that the distinction was not necessary in the modern era, that it was hampering the competitiveness of the US banking system and that repeal of the Act would bring greater stability to the financial system via diversification. The repeal was important in that it enabled major commercial banks like Citigroup to get involved in the issuance of CDOs and mortgage backed securities, and in establishing SPVs/SPEs, SIVs and other conduits that would ultimately play such a significant role in the crisis. In addition, some believe that the investment banks' risk-taking culture started to permeate to the commercial banking sector following the repeal of the Act. The other key reform was the setting up of the Federal Deposit Insurance Corporation (FDIC) to protect deposits in the commercial banking sector.

These background factors combined with lax and irresponsible lending by banks and financial institutions, who overestimated the ability of the process of financial

▶ 16 September 2008 The US government announces an $85 million rescue of the world's biggest insurer American International Group which has heavy losses in credit default swaps in return for an 80% stake in the company. ▶ 17 September 2008 Lloyds TSB announce a £12 billion takeover of Halifax Bank of Scotland (HBOS), the UK's largest mortgage provider. The regulatory authorities allow the takeover which would normally have been referred due to the combined group having close to a 1/3 share of the UK savings ▷

innovation to manage and control their risks, were the proximate causes of the crisis. Other contributing factors were the actions of the Federal Reserve following the dot com bust and generally lax regulation of the financial system, the regulatory authorities having become convinced that financial markets were engines of economic growth and were in general best left to develop without excessive interference from regulators. We shall argue that while the immediate trigger for the credit crisis was problems in the subprime market, the magnitude of the eventual losses and the extent of the crisis strongly suggest that other factors played a significant role in the crisis. In its 'Declaration of the Summit on Financial Markets and the World Economy,' dated 15 November 2008, leaders of the Group of 20 pinpointed a variety of causes:

> During a period of strong global growth, growing capital flows, and prolonged stability earlier this decade, market participants sought higher yields without an adequate appreciation of the risks and failed to exercise proper due diligence. At the same time, weak underwriting standards, unsound risk management practices, increasingly complex and opaque financial products, and consequent excessive leverage combined to create vulnerabilities in the system. Policy-makers, regulators and supervisors, in some advanced countries, did not adequately appreciate and address the risks building up in financial markets, keep pace with financial innovation, or take into account the systemic ramifications of domestic regulatory actions.

17.10   Deterioration in bank lending standards and adverse selection

originate-and-hold a traditional banking model in which banks lend to their customers and then hold the resulting risk on their own balance sheets

originate-and-distribute a banking model in which banks lend to their customers and then on-sell the resulting loans and risks to outside investors

Another key factor behind the credit crunch was a deterioration in the quality of bank lending, especially the rapid growth of lending to the subprime sector. In 1994 subprime loans were a mere 5 per cent of total mortgage originations and totalled $35 billion. By 1999 this had risen to 13 per cent of originations and $160 billion of lending, but by 2006 this had risen again to 20 per cent of mortgage lending and $600 billion. By March 2007 the total exposure amounted to $1.3 trillion. It seems that banks had moved from an originate-and-hold model – meeting customers directly and screening them out – to an originate-to-distribute model whereby they originated the loans, repackaged them into ABSs and CDOs and sold them to investors. This was very different from the traditional 'originate-and-hold' banking model, whereby banks originate the loans and keep them and the risks on their own balance sheets. The 'originate-to-distribute' model paid mortgage brokers an upfront fee for each mortgage they arranged, and this encouraged them to emphasize quantity over quality because no penalties were payable if the mortgagee later went into default or foreclosure. The originator of the loan also had less incentive to monitor the loan since the risk of the loan was ultimately going to be securitized and passed on to investors in the form of a MBS or CDO.

and loan market. ▶ 18 September 2008 The Federal Reserve announces a $180 billion increase in swap facilities with the European Central Bank, Swiss National Bank, Bank of England, Bank of Canada and Bank of Japan. ▶ 25 September 2008 Washington Mutual with assets of $307 billion is closed down by regulators (Office of Thrift Supervision) and sold off for $1.9 billion to JP Morgan following a run on its deposits, with $16.9 billion being withdrawn in the preceding 10 days. ▶ 28 September 2008 Fortis, a European Banking ▷

adjustable rate mortgage
a mortgage on which the interest payable is reset periodically in line with changes in a predetermined benchmark plus a spread; the initial rate of interest is normally fixed for the first few years

adverse selection
a market process in which 'bad' customers who present themselves to financial institutions are more likely to be accepted because of asymmetric information; if a bank raises its interest rate it will tend to attract more poor quality customers who do not intend to repay

Most of the subprime mortgage loans were adjustable rate mortgages (ARMs) with low initial interest rates which would rise significantly after one or two years. Since the subprime mortgages were viewed as risky the interest rate charges were significantly higher than for Alt-A or prime loans. This in itself also meant that subprime mortgages had a significant adverse selection problem in that the high interest rate charges tended to attract a larger proportion of borrowers who would default on payments than would be expected for traditional mortgages. It seems that another problem with subprime mortgages was that banks failed to screen out the higher-risk loans. The job of granting the mortgages was left to mortgage brokers that obtained significant commissions from the banks when a mortgage loan was made, and this led to predatory lending practices in which mortgage brokers encouraged people to take on bigger loans at higher rates of interest than they could afford. The extent of the lax lending practices was typified by the so-called popularity of NINJA loans, which stood for 'No verified INcome, Jobs or Assets.' In the UK there was also plenty of evidence of lax lending standards. Northern Rock, which had to be rescued by the government, had a 'Together' package which granted mortgages and loans equivalent to 125 per cent of the value of the property being purchased. These loans were being marketed aggressively to customers that in the past would have only been extended mortgages of around 80 per cent of the value of the property. Some commentators believe that the origins for the subprime crisis can be blamed in large part on the Clinton Administration which encouraged mortgage providers like Fannie Mae and Freddie Mac to engage in increased mortgage lending to low- to moderate-income groups and neighbourhoods which were much riskier than their traditional markets.

17.11 Increase in household indebtedness

There was an increase not only of mortgage debt but also other forms of debt such as student loans, auto loans and credit card debt. US household debt as a percentage of disposable income rose from 60 per cent of disposable income in 1974 to 134 per cent of disposable income in mid 2008. The savings rate in the USA declined from 6 per cent in 1993 to under 1 per cent by 2006, while the ratio of total debt to disposable income rose from 75 per cent to 120 per cent over the same period in the OECD area. Much of the build up of debt was securitized as CDOs or MBSs and bought by banks, fund managers, pension funds, insurance companies and hedge funds.

The Federal Reserve also played a significant part in creating the credit bubble by reacting to the fall in the stockmarkets following the dot com bust in 2000 and the 9/11 terrorist attacks with an unprecedented loosening of American monetary policy. It cut the Federal Funds rate from 6.5 per cent in May 2000 to an all-time low of just 1 per cent in June 2003. In retrospect, many commentators regard this as an over-reaction to the bust in the internet sector which accounted for less than 2 per cent

and Insurance group, is rescued through part-nationalization (49% stake) in return for a capital injection of €11.2 billion from the central banks of Belgium (€4.7 billion), Netherlands (€4 billion) and Luxembourg (€2.5 billion). The Bank had made major losses after taking a €24 billion stake in the Dutch bank ABN Amro, which had huge losses on its books from its subprime exposures. US law makers announce that they have agreed on a $700 billion bailout fund designed to purchase distressed assets from US banks. ▷

mortgage equity withdrawal (MEW) the borrowing of funds against the equity stake that consumers have in their homes

of the American economy. The low interest rates contributed to a rapid expansion of mortgages and a rapid rise in house prices over the period. Indeed, the lower cost of finance contributed to a high degree of speculative activity in the housing market; for example, in areas like Miami there was 'flipping' of condos by speculators who quickly on-sold properties they had bought for short-term profits. Also there was a growth in bank lending based on mortgage equity withdrawals whereby people were able to take out new loans based on the higher value of their house.

17.12   Financial innovation and the credit rating agencies

Financial innovation undoubtedly played a significant role in the crisis – in particular many of the banks that had increased their mortgage book, particularly in the subprime area, believed they could reduce their risk exposure and save on regulatory capital through securitizing the mortgage loans they had made by issuing MBSs and CDOs. It is essential to realize that the banks could not have sold on the CDOs and MBSs without ratings on the securities being issued by the credit rating agencies. Crucially, the credit rating agencies gave the securities credit ratings that in retrospect clearly under-rated the risks involved. Securities that should have merited BBB and lower ratings were issued with AAA and AA ratings. The precise reasons why the credit rating agencies got their ratings so wrong is a matter of dispute, it has been argued that they had big financial incentives to rate the securities generously in return for generous fees. Also, the assumptions they made when rating the securities were found to be wanting. They assumed continued house price rises and unrealistically low default rates when making the ratings. The fact that the securities were given investment grade ratings is absolutely crucial. If they had been rated below BBB then far fewer loans and mortgages would have been made, and many banks and financial institutions would not have bought the securities and suffered catastrophic losses. In addition to the growth of CDOs and MBSs a key financial innovation that contributed directly to the downfall of AIG and Lehman Brothers and created problems for many hedge funds was their exposure to the CDSs. The notional value of CDSs grew from $500 billion in 2000 to $62 trillion by 2007.

17.13   Increased leverage in the financial system

Another key factor that played a prominent role in the credit crunch was the increased use of leverage, defined as the ratio of total debt to shareholder capital being employed by investment banks and other financial institutions. For instance, Merrill Lynch increased its leverage from 15 to over 30 times capital between 2003 and 2007, Lehman Brothers increased its leverage from around 22.7 to 29.7 times capital, Goldman Sachs from around 17.7 to 25.2 and Morgan Stanley from around 23.2 to 32.4 while Bear Stearns increased its leverage from around 27.2 to 32.5. The

▶ 29 September 2008 The Dow Jones index falls 770 points (its biggest ever points fall) or 7.7% following rejection of the proposed $700 billion bailout plan by Congress. Bradford & Bingley, a British mortgage provider, is nationalized. Its £50 billion of mortgage-loan book is taken over by the British government and its savings business sold to the Spanish bank Santander. Iceland's government takes a 75% controlling interest of its third largest bank, Glitner, with a €600 million capital injection. ▶ 30 September 2008 Dexia Bank is ▷

investment banks were not alone in increasing their leverage ratios as many hedge funds were also highly leveraged, ratios of 20 to 30 times capital being common. The problem of increased leverage is that, although it increases returns during the good times, it also increases the risk level and therefore the dangers facing financial institutions during periods of negative returns. In the period 2003 to 2007 the increased leverage became even more problematic because many of the funds raised by investment banks were used to purchases tranches of CDOs and MBSs. In the view of some commentators the investment banks were guilty of both producing and consuming toxic securities.

17.14   Mispricing of risk

There is a lot of evidence that there was widespread mispricing of CDOs by market participants and credit rating agencies who were using David Li's Gaussian copula model which based the price of CDOs on the price of related CDSs. However in an article in wired.com Felix Salmon (2009) reported:

> Li's formula, known as a Gaussian copula function, looked like an unambiguously positive breakthrough, a piece of financial technology that allowed hugely complex risks to be modeled with more ease and accuracy than ever before. With his brilliant spark of mathematical legerdemain, Li made it possible for traders to sell vast quantities of new securities, expanding financial markets to unimaginable levels.
>
> His method was adopted by everybody from bond investors and Wall Street banks to ratings agencies and regulators. And it became so deeply entrenched – and was making people so much money – that warnings about its limitations were largely ignored.
>
> Then the model fell apart. Cracks started appearing early on, when financial markets began behaving in ways that users of Li's formula hadn't expected. The cracks became full-fledged canyons in 2008 – when ruptures in the financial system's foundation swallowed up trillions of dollars and put the survival of the global banking system in serious peril.

In sum, the pricing of the CDOs did not properly reflect the risks of the securities and the pricing formula underpriced the risks involved.

David Li's paper, 'In Default Correlation: A Copula Function Approach', was published in 2000 in the *Journal of Fixed Income*, and was very quickly adopted by Wall Street and the financial community. Li had come up with an ingenious way to model default correlations without looking at historical data, but instead by using prices of CDSs. Li's copula function led to a rapid growth of both the CDO and CDS markets; for example, at the end of 2001 there was $920 billion of CDSs outstanding

rescued by the Belgian, Dutch and French governments with a €6.4 billion package. The Irish government announces a decision to protect all Irish bank deposits for the next two years. ▶ 3 October 2008 The $700 billion bailout package is passed by the House of Representatives. The Financial Services Authority raises the limit on insured deposits from £35,000 to £50,000, which protects 98% of retail deposits. ▶ 6 October 2008 Germany announces a €50 billion rescue package of Hypo Real Estate, one of its biggest banks, and ▷

and by the end of 2007 this had grown to a staggering $62 trillion. Similarly the CDO market which was $275 billion in 2000 had grown to $4.7 trillion by 2006. The flaw in the formula was that it was used in a period when house prices rose rapidly, and this led to extremely low default rates and also low correlations between defaults. However, if house price rises turned to house price falls and default correlations were to rise rapidly then the CDO yields predicted by the model were too low and CDS contracts seriously underpriced. To quote Kai Gilkes who worked for 10 years at the ratings agencies:

> Everyone was pinning their hopes on house prices continuing to rise ... When they stopped rising, pretty much everyone was caught on the wrong side, because the sensitivity to house prices was huge. And there was just no getting around it. Why didn't rating agencies build in some cushion for this sensitivity to a house-price-depreciation scenario? Because if they had, they would have never rated a single mortgage-backed CDO.

17.15   Incentive structures and risk management practices in the banks

The creation of new securities such as CDOs and CDSs and the boom in lending and house prices made banking and the financial services industry very profitable. During the period 2000–2006 financial sector earnings accounted for nearly 40 per cent of the earnings of S&P 500 companies. As profits boomed so did the paypackets of traders and top level bankers. However, in retrospect it is clear that the level of risk being taken was excessive and that the markets were underpricing the risks involved in the housing and construction boom. The rewards being generated during the good times meant that bankers and traders were more interested in continuing the boom than monitoring the risks that were being accumulated in the system.

There were clearly problems with the incentive and reward structure of the banks, which were biased to the generation of short-term profits and not the long-run viability of the banks. As many commentators have pointed out, the annual system of bonuses in Wall Street and London meant that bankers and traders could get large bonuses when times were good which would not be clawed back in bad times. Indeed, even in the disastrous year of 2008 when banks were reporting unprecedented losses of over $500 billion and banking share prices collapsed, Wall Street bankers received bonuses in excess of $70 billion. It seems that much of the remuneration and bonus packages offered to investment bankers was dependent on revenues earned rather than profits earned. With such a system large bonuses were payable even if huge losses were being incurred. In retrospect, it is clear that many of the profits reported during the 2002 to 2007 period were 'illusory profits' as they were in fact the foundations for the massive losses reported once the credit crunch started.

gives an unlimited guarantee on German bank deposits. A similar bank deposit guarantee is announced by the Danish government. Iceland announces a package to rescue its banking system. ▶ 7 October 2008 The Icelandic government takes control of its second largest bank, Landsbanki, which owns Icesave bank in the UK, causing concerns for UK depositors who have their accounts frozen.

▶ 8 October 2008 The UK government announces a £50 billion rescue of its banking system in return for preferred shares, along with ▷

Table 17.4   'The dirty dozen' – worst bank losses in 2008 ($millions)

1	Royal Bank of Scotland	$59,281
2	Citigroup	$53,055
3	Well Fargo & Co	$47,788
4	Fortis Bank	$28,248
5	Union Bank Switzerland	$19,636
6	HBOS	$15,780
7	Credit Swiss Group	$14,010
8	Deutsche Bank	$7,990
9	Hypo Real Estate Holding	$7,841
10	Bayerische Landesbank	$7,190
11	Dresdner Bank	$6,543
12	Merrill Lynch	$6,330

Source: *The Banker*

It is also clear in retrospect that the banks' risk management systems were not up to the job. In particular, banks lent too much money to people that were likely to default on their payments, placed too much faith in the credit rating agencies' ratings of highly dangerous securities, and their risk management models underestimated the risks they were taking. Most banks were using sophisticated value at risk modelling techniques to manage their day-to-day risk exposure, but these models were deeply flawed by the assumptions they were making, especially about house prices and the behaviour of macro variables. In addition, they were clearly not prepared for the drying up of liquidity in the financial system, and failed to manage their counterparty exposures. There can be little doubt that many more financial institutions would have been in even greater difficulty if the American government had not stepped in to make good the payments due from AIG.

17.16   The response to the credit crunch

When the credit crunch started on 9 August 2007, market participants and the authorities clearly failed to understand the full extent of the crisis that was to ensue. Indeed, in June 2007 the Head of the Federal Reserve Ben Bernanke made a speech arguing that subprime losses would be contained and limited to $100 billion. It took more than a year – a time that saw the collapse of Lehman Brothers and AIG, the taking over of Fannie Mae and Freddie Mac and a collapse in the prices of banking sector shares – for the full scale of the crisis to become evident for all to see. In particular, the collapse of Lehman Brothers and takeover of AIG by the US government showed the huge amount of counterparty risk that had built up

£100 billion of lending support from the Bank of England and £250 billion of loan guarantees on interbank lending. The Federal Reserve, European Central Bank (ECB), Bank of England, and the central banks of Canada, Sweden and Switzerland make a coordinated 0.5% interest rate cut, making the Federal Funds rate 1.5%, the ECB rate 3.75%, and the UK base rate 4.5%. ▶ 10 October 2008 Large falls in stockmarkets in the UK, Germany and France of 7% to 9%, with Wall Street having fallen 20% in the preceding 10 days. ▷

Box 17.4	The bonus culture in banking: no rhyme or reason

The massive losses in American banks as a result of the subprime crisis led to an intense debate about rewards in the financial services industry, and especially in banks where huge pay packages have been awarded to CEOs and bank traders. Stories abound about individual pay packages, such as Hank Paulson earning $700 million while working at Goldman Sachs, Charles Prince, the head of Citigroup, earning over $30 million a year while the bank's share price collapsed, and in Britain Sir Fred Goodwin, the CEO of the Royal Bank of Scotland, was granted a £700,000 per annum pension at the age of 50 despite his bank having racked up enormous losses.

The extent of the bonus culture in the banking system was investigated by Andrew Cuomo the Attorney General of New York as a direct result of the financial crisis and his report was released in August 2009. Entitled, 'No rhyme or reason: The heads I win, tails you lose bonus culture', the report is extremely critical of the bonus culture in banking. It argues that the bankers' claim that high pay is related to high performance is spurious and that the link between pay and performance is in practice virtually non-existent. The report states:

> In many ways, the past three years have provided a virtual laboratory in which to test the hypothesis that compensation in the financial industry was performance-based. But even a cursory examination of the data suggests that in these challenging economic times, compensation for bank employees has become unmoored from the banks' financial performance.
>
> Thus, when the banks did well, their employees were paid well. When the banks did poorly, their employees were paid well. And when the banks did very poorly, they were bailed out by taxpayers and their employees were still paid well. Bonuses and overall compensation did not vary significantly as profits diminished.

The report looks at the 2008 bonuses and earnings at nine banks that received bailouts totalling $55 billion. Two firms, Citigroup and Merrill Lynch, suffered massive losses of more than $27 billion each but nonetheless Citigroup paid out $5.33 billion in bonuses and Merrill paid $3.6 billion in bonuses. So, despite losing a combined $54 billion, they still paid out nearly $9 billion in bonuses! A look at historical filings further supports the view that there is no link between pay and performance. Pay increased greatly during the bull-market years of 2003 to 2006; for example, at Bank of America gross pay increased from $10 billion to $18 billion but in 2008 remained at $18 billion despite huge losses. A similar pattern occurred at Citigroup where gross pay rose from $20 billion to $30 billion during 2003–2006

▶ 11 October 2008 Finance ministers from the G7 industrialized nations announce a five-point plan to unfreeze the credit markets, protect savers, provide liquidity, strengthen financial institutions and restore confidence by taking an appropriate regulatory response. ▶ 13 October 2008 The UK government announces a £37 billion package to inject capital into three of its biggest banks: Lloyds TSB, HBOS and the Royal Bank of Scotland. ▶ 14 October 2008 The US government announces a $250 billion programme to buy stakes in ▷

| Box 17.4 | The bonus culture in banking: no rhyme or reason – *continued* |

Table 17.5   TARP recipients' bonus pools (2008)

	Earnings (Losses)	Bonus pool	Employees	Earnings/ employee	Bonus/ employee	TARP funds	Number of bonuses		
							$3m+	$2m+	$1m+
Bank of America	$4.0bn	$3.3bn	243,000	$16,461	$13,580	$45bn	28	65	172
Bank of New York Mellon	$1.4bn	$945m	42,900	$32,634	$22,028	$3bn	12	22	74
Citigroup	($27.7bn)	$5.3bn	322,800	($85,812)	$16,512	$45bn	124	176	738
Goldman Sachs	$2.3bn	$4.8bn	30,067	$77,228	$160,420	$10bn	212	391	953
JP Morgan	$5.6bn	$8.7bn	224,961	$24,893	$38,642	$25bn	200+	1626	
Merrill Lynch	($27.6bn)	$3.6bn	59,000	($467,797)	$61,017	$10bn	149	696	
Morgan Stanley	$1.7bn	$4.5bn	46,964	$36,347	$95,286	$10bn	101	189	428
State Street Corp	$1.8bn	$470m	28,475	$63,600	$16,055	$2bn	3	8	44
Wells Fargo & Co	($42.9bn)	$977m	281,000	($152,786)	$3,479	$25bn	7	22	62

Source: Cuomo (2009)

and remained at $30 billion in 2007 even though the firm ran into major financial difficulties. At Merrill Lynch gross pay was nearly $16 billion in 2007 while losing $7 billion and was still close to $15 billion in 2008 despite the bank facing collapse. **Table 17.5** shows the bonus pools of the first nine US banks to receive funds from the Trouble Asset Relief Programme (TARP). It shows each bank's earnings/losses, bonus pool, number of employees, earnings per employee, bonus per employee, amount of TARP funds received and the amount of bonus payments in excess of $3 million, $2 million and $1 million.

Cuomo's report concludes that:

In sum, as we seek to learn lessons from this economic crisis and repair the damage it has wrought, it will be vital to develop and implement sound principles and rationales for executive compensation and bonuses that promote sustainable and rational economic growth. The repeated explanation from bank executives that bonuses are tied to performance in a manner designed to promote such growth does not appear to be accurate. Indeed, our investigation suggests a disconnect between compensation and bank performance that resulted in a 'heads I win, tails you lose' bonus system. In other words, bank compensation structures lacked consistent principles and tended to result in a compensation system that was all 'upside.'

the form of preference shares in US banks and to insure newly issued debt by the banks on a temporary basis. ▶ 15 October 2008 The Dow Jones falls 733 points or 7.87%, its biggest one-day percentage fall since the stockmarket collapse of 26 October 1987. ▶ 30 October 2008 The Federal Reserve cuts the Federal Funds rate from 1.5% to 1%. European governments agree a €1 trillion facility to guarantee interbank lending in the Euro area. ▶ 6 November 2008 The International Monetary Fund (IMF) announces a ▷

in the system. While institutions like Fannie Mae, Freddie Mac, Citigroup and Bank of America were deemed to be 'too big to fail', the world's largest insurer AIG was considered to be both 'too big and too interconnected' to fail. Although the financial crisis started in August 2007 the effects on the real economy took some time to take a grip. It was really only in the second half of 2008 that economic growth and international trade started to collapse and the full cost to taxpayers of the financial bailout and economic recession became evident.

As can be seen from the timeline, the authorities in the USA and the UK in particular responded with unprecedented actions, with similar responses in countries such as China, Japan and Germany. We shall divide our discussion of the official policy response to the crisis into the following:

1   Cuts in official short-term interest rates
2   Liquidity provision
3   Quantitative easing
4   Fiscal stimulus packages to stimulate the economy
5   Official bailouts of troubled financial institutions
6   Bank stress tests

17.17   Cuts in official short-term interest rates

In the first instance, the Federal Reserve and the Bank of England made a series of interest-rate cuts that led to record low short-term interest rates in the two economies. The Federal Reserve reduced the Federal Funds rate from 5.25 per cent in June 2007 to a record low target range of 0 to 0.25 per cent in December 2008, while the Bank of England cut its rate from 5.25 per cent in July 2007 to a mere 0.5 per cent in March 2009.

The interest-rate cuts seem to have had three roles:

(i)   to reduce the interest payments of heavily indebted consumers and firms, which was especially important in helping those with variable rate mortgages to continue to service their mortgage payments;

(ii)   to increase banks' profit margins which are positively related to the spread between short-term and longer-term rates of interest;

(iii)   to stimulate consumer expenditure and economic activity.

The cuts in short-term interest rates, particularly after the collapse of Lehman Brothers, were unprecedented in size – the UK base rate of 0.5 per cent was the lowest in the history of the Bank of England which had started operations in 1694, and the indicative range of 0–0.25 per cent of the Federal Reserve was its lowest ever Federal Funds rate.

UK base rate
the rate of interest used by banks to determine the rate of interest that they will charge to their safest customers

Federal Funds rate
an overnight interest rate at which one US bank lends funds to another; the Federal Reserve Open Market Committee sets a target for such interest rates at its FOMC meeting

---

CREDIT CRUNCH TIMELINE CREDIT CRUNCH TIMELINE CREDIT CRUNCH TIMELINE CREDI

$16.4 billion loan rescue package for Ukraine. The Bank of England cuts its base rate from 4.5% to 3%, the lowest level since 1955. The ECB also cuts its rate from 3.75% to 3.25%. ▶ 9 November 2008 China announces a $568 billion stimulus package for its economy. ▶ 12 November 2008 The USA abandons its plan to use the $700 billion to buy distressed assets from the banks and instead decides to concentrate the funds on improving the flow of consumer credit. ▶ 14 November 2008 G20 meeting of developed and developing ▷

Table 17.6   Cuts in official interest rates

Federal Reserve		Bank of England		European Central Bank	
Date	Federal fund rate	Date	Bank rate	Date	Refinancing rate
29 Jun 2006	5.25%	11 Jan 2007	5.25%	15 Jun 2006	2.75%
11 Sep 2007	4.75%	10 May 2007	5.50%	9 Aug 2006	3.00%
31 Oct 2007	4.50%	5 July 2007	5.75%	11 Oct 2006	3.25%
11 Dec 2007	4.25%	6 Dec 2007	5.50%	13 Dec 2006	3.50%
22 Jan 2008	3.50%	7 Feb 2008	5.25%	14 Mar 2007	3.75%
30 Jan 2008	3.00%	10 Apr 2008	5.00%	13 Jun 2007	4.00%
18 Mar 2008	2.25%	8 Oct 2008	4.50%	9 Jul 2008	4.25%
30 Apr 2008	2.00%	6 Nov 2008	3.00%	15 Oct 2008	3.75%
8 Oct 2008	1.50%	4 Dec 2008	2.00%	12 Nov 2008	3.25%
29 Oct 2008	1.00%	8 Jan 2009	1.50%	10 Dec 2008	2.50%
16 Dec 2008	0–0.25%	5 Feb 2009	1.00%	21 Jan 2009	2.00%
		5 Mar 2009	0.50%	11 Mar 2009	1.50%
				8 Apr 2009	1.25%
				13 May 2009	1.00%

17.18   Liquidity provision

As the financial markets froze, many banks found it very difficult to raise money by issuing short-term commercial paper, to borrow from other banks on the interbank markets or even to find buyers for some of their assets. The shortage of liquidity was exacerbated by the phenomenon of 'liquidity hoarding' whereby banks decided to hoard whatever liquidity they had to ensure they could see themselves through the crisis. So central banks stepped in to buy many of the securities that banks and other financial intermediaries were attempting to sell. This was in some ways merely fulfilling their traditional duty as 'lender of the last resort', but the sheer size of the liquidity injections was unprecedented in scale. Also, the central banks increased the maturity of the lending and the range of assets that they were prepared to accept as collateral for providing liquidity. For instance, the US Treasury in September and December 2007 increased the term of loans it allowed through its discount window and in March 2008 agreed to accept less liquid securities such as MBSs as collateral for loans. Following the collapse of Bear Stearns in March 2008 the US Treasury created a primary dealer credit facility so that primary dealers could gain access to Federal Reserve facilities. In addition, the Federal Reserve set up a temporary arrangement to ensure unlimited liquidity for Fannie Mae and Freddie Mac if required.

primary dealer
a pre-approved broker, dealer, bank or other financial institution that is able to make bids for newly issued government debt; such a dealer is expected to meet certain liquidity and other requirements

nations discusses the financial crisis and longer-term reform issues. ▶ 20 November 2008 The IMF extends a $2.1 billion loan to Iceland following the collapse of its banking system ▶ 23 November 2008 The US government announces a $20 billion rescue package for Citigroup following a 60% collapse in its share price in the preceding week. ▶ 24 November 2008 The UK government announces a one-year cut in value added tax from 17.5% to 15% to stimulate consumer demand, as part of a £25.6 billion stimulus package   ▷

In April 2008 the Bank of England introduced a Special Liquidity Scheme (SLS) for eligible financial institutions to swap less liquid securities for UK Treasury bills. The SLS was extensively used in its nine-month existence – to the tune of £185 billion. In May 2008 the Bank of England raised the ceiling on the deposits banks were allowed to hold at the Bank of England from 1 per cent of sterling eligible liabilities or £1bn, whichever was higher, to 2.5 per cent of eligible liabilities or £5 billion – more than doubling the amount lenders could hold on deposit at the Bank of England. Lenders use the facility because it provides them with risk-free interest, at the same time as giving them instant access to the funds. In the USA, on 18 September 2008, following the bankruptcy of Lehman Brothers and the rescue of AIG, the Federal Reserve agreed to a $180 billion expansion of its temporary reciprocal currency arrangements (swap lines) with the Bank of Canada, Swiss National Bank, Bank of England, Bank of Japan and European Central Bank. This increased capacity, ensuring that these central banks would have sufficient dollar funding for both term and overnight operations.

In sum, central banks increased liquidity by providing large increases in the funds they provided, by extending the maturity of their credit operations, significantly expanding the range of eligible collateral as well as the list of counterparties to include broker-dealers and special swap facilities allowing participants to swap temporarily their high quality mortgage-backed and other securities for highly liquid government bills and bonds. Finally, an increase in swap lines between central banks ensured that central banks and their counterparties had sufficient access to foreign currency liquidity.

17.19   Quantitative easing

Traditionally central banks intervene through open market operation to influence short-term interest rates, as outlined earlier. During the credit crunch short-term interest rates reached record lows. However, during the crisis they also became concerned about the relatively elevated levels of long-term interest rates facing corporations, and thus engaged in a new practice of 'credit easing' as it was called in the USA or quantitative easing as it was called in the UK. The basic idea of quantitative easing was to purchase existing government and even corporate/mortgage backed bonds from financial institutions and market participants with the hope of raising their prices and thereby lowering the yields on such assets. Another motive of quantitative easing was to avert the risk of deflation; that is, a period of falling consumer prices as a result of excess capacity and rising unemployment rates that were occurring in the real economy as a result of the crisis. Finally, another hope of quantitative easing was that the increased cash holdings of the banks would encourage them to increase lending to consumers and businesses, so easing the effects of the credit crunch.

> **quantitative easing**
> the creation of new money by the central banks to purchase a range of financial assets on both the primary and secondary markets

equivalent to 1.1% of UK GDP. ▶ 25 November 2008 The US Federal Reserve announces it will inject a further $800 billion of support to the financial system: $600 billion to purchase mortgage backed securities (including $100 billion from Fannie Mae and Freddie Mac) and $200 billion to encourage consumer lending (by buying up securitized debt in credit cards, auto loans and credit card debt). ▶ 26 November 2008 The European Commission announces a coordinated €200 billion economic recovery plan financed by ▷

An important aspect of the quantitative easing policy is the expectation that purchases of longer-term securities would be accompanied by an increase in the monetary base and a lowering of longer-term interest rates, as the additional demand for the longer-term securities raised their prices and thus lowered their yield. However, since quantitative easing effectively involves the printing of new money it also brings with it the potential to raise inflation expectations and inflation risk premiums, so that in the medium- to long-term it could actually raise longer-term yields rather than lower them. The inflationary dangers of quantitative easing ultimately depend on the amount of quantitative easing and whether it creates a permanent or temporary increase in the monetary base. In the UK the Bank of England set aside £125 billion for quantitative easing, and in the USA some $300 billion was set aside. While these were large absolute figures they represented less than 8 per cent of the GDP of the UK and 3 per cent of the GDP of the USA. Even the European Central Bank in May 2009 announced that it would undertake a policy of credit easing to the tune of €60 billion of covered euro bonds (mostly backed by mortgage repayments).

17.20 Fiscal stimulus

fiscal stimulus
the use of increases in government expenditure and/or cuts in taxes to increase aggregate demand in an economy

Another response involved the extensive use of fiscal stimulus packages to try to cushion the effects of the credit crunch on the real economy. In the USA a combination of economic stimulus packages increased government expenditure and tax concessions, which resulted in a rise in the fiscal deficit from 2.1 per cent of GDP in 2007 to 13.6 per cent of GDP in 2009. Initially, under President Bush, the economic stimulus package was relatively muted. In February 2008 a $168 billion economic stimulus package was announced, consisting mainly of tax cuts and rebates.

On 10 February 2009 the Obama administration passed a $789 billion economic 'recovery package' made up of $502 billion of expenditure and $287 billion of tax relief, with a plan to spend 70 per cent of it within the first two years. There was a noticeable change in the stimulus packages offered by the two administrations. The initial Bush plan based on tax cuts was not deemed to be a great success because much of the tax cuts and rebates were just saved or used to pay down debt rather than increase expenditure. As a result, President Obama's much larger stimulus package aimed to directly boost aggregate demand through government expenditure on infrastructure. On 9 November 2009 China announced a $586 billion stimulus package equivalent to nearly 15 per cent of its GDP. Even the European Union agreed a €200 billion package, which was around 1.5 per cent of its GDP, on 12 January 2009. On 24 November 2008 the UK announced a £25.6 billion stimulus plan, including a temporary cut in value added tax (VAT) from 17.5 per cent to 15 per cent. Germany announced a €31 billion stimulus package in November 2008, followed by a €50 billion plan in February 2009; while Japan presented a $50 billion stimulus package in October 2008 and a further $150 billion package in April 2009.

the member states and designed to stimulate the European economy with a targeted 1.2% fiscal stimulus. ▶ 4 December 2008 President Sarkozy announces a €25 billion package to stimulate public sector investment and loans to the French car industry.

▶ 11 December 2008 Bank of America announces 35,000 job losses. The Bank of England cuts its base rate from 3% to 2%, its lowest for 57 years. The ECB cuts it policy rate from 3.25% to 2.5%. Sweden cuts its policy rate from 3.75% to 2%. ▶ 16 December 2008 The ▷

Table 17.7   Fiscal deficits and national debts as percentages of GDP

Year	USA		UK		Japan		Germany	
	Fiscal deficit	National debt	Fiscal deficit	National debt	Fiscal deficit	National debt	Fiscal deficit	National debt
2007	−2.1	63.1	−2.6	44.1	−2.5	187.7	−0.5	63.6
2008	−6.9	70.5	−5.4	51.9	−5.6	196.3	−0.1	67.2
2009	−13.6	87.0	−9.8	62.7	−9.9	217.2	−4.7	79.4
2010	−9.7	97.5	−10.4	72.7	−9.8	227.4	−6.1	86.6

Source IMF, *World Economic Outlook*, April 2009.

The net result of the bank bailout packages, economic recession and economic stimulus packages was a massive increase in the actual and projected fiscal deficits and corresponding increases in the national debt, especially in countries like the USA and the UK. **Table 17.7** shows the actual and projected fiscal deficits and the national debt projections for the USA, UK, Japan and Germany for 2007–2010.

17.21   Bailouts of financial institutions

The US response

> **Troubled Asset Relief Program (TARP)**
> a $700 billion US government programme, created in October 2008, to buy MBSs from financial institutions

Although the economic stimulus packages were among the biggest ever undertaken, their scale was dwarfed by the amount of funds used to bail out the financial sector through capital injections and guarantees. The US set the ball rolling when a $700 billion Troubled Asset Relief Program (TARP) was passed, allowing the US Treasury to buy up or insure up to $700 billion of troubled assets (primarily residential and commercial mortgage related securities issued prior to 14 March 2008) from the banking and financial sector. The aim was to provide some liquidity and pricing to these securities, which had proved very difficult to trade following the onset of the crisis. Any bank selling securities to the TARP was expected to grant the government warrants, equity or senior debt to the Treasury, giving the taxpayer some potential upside should the bank's shares recover. The first $350 billion was released on 3 October 2008 and the second instalment of $350 billion on 15 January 2009. On 14 October 2008 there was a change in the TARP, enabling the Treasury to buy senior preferred shares and warrants in the banks under a Capital Partnership Programme (CPP). Subsequent changes to the TARP permitted the funds to be used to enhance consumer credit and mitigate the financial crisis more generally, thus enabling TARP funds to be allocated to bailing out the big three car makers, Ford, Chrysler and General Motors. In February 2009 the Treasury Secretary Timothy Geithner announced that $50 billion of TARP funds would be used to mitigate mortgage foreclosures.

Federal Reserve cuts its Federal Fund rate from 1% to a 0–0.25% target range, the lowest in its history. ▶ 19 December 2008 George W. Bush announces that $17.4 billion of the $700 billion TARP fund will be used to bail out the big three auto companies: Chrysler, General Motors and Ford. ▶ 29 December 2008 The US Treasury announces a $6 billion rescue package for General Motors Acceptance Corporation, the financing arm of General Motors. ▶ 8 January 2009 The Bank of England cuts its base rate to 1.5%, the lowest in its ▷

Term Asset Banked Loan Facility (TALF) a November 2008 programme announced by the Federal Reserve to support the issuance of ABSs; under TALF the Federal Reserve Bank of New York would lend up to $1 trillion (originally $200 billion) to holders of certain AAA-rated ABSs.

On 25 November 2008 the Term Asset Backed Securities Loan Facility (TALF) was announced by the Federal Reserve, enabling financial institutions to borrow funds to purchase distressed securities. Under the scheme some $200 billion (later changed to $1 trillion) of funds was made available to holders of certain AAA-rated ABS on a non-recourse basis. A non-recourse loan is a loan secured against collateral but for which the borrower is not responsible if he defaults; the lender can seize the collateral but he cannot chase the borrower if the collateral is insufficient to cover the value of the loan. The idea of the TALF was to inject liquidity into the ABS market, which was viewed as important in financing consumer credit and small business loans.

On 23 March 2009 a Public-Private Investment Program (P-PIP) was established to use $75–$100 billion of TARP funds to buy troubled legacy loans and securities in conjunction with the private sector. The Federal Deposit Insurance Corporation would make non-recourse loan guarantees for up to 85 per cent of the purchase price, effectively limiting private markets participants' possible loss to 15 per cent of the price paid for the securities. It was envisaged that the P-PIP would lead to the purchase of some $500 billion of troubled assets in total.

Another part of the policy response was the takeover or purchase of stakes in some of America's best known financial institutions. In particular, the government takeover of Fannie Mae and Freddie Mac, which had combined assets totalling $5.5 trillion on 7 September 2008, was pivotal, and merely a confirmation of the widely held view that they were too big to fail. The government's takeover of AIG on 16 September 2008 due to losses on its CDSs was instigated because AIG was deemed both too big and too complex to be allowed to fail on top of the collapse of Lehman Brothers. The bailout of AIG totalled over $180 billion, and was also important because the government made good on $93 billion of CDS contracts that it had entered into with Goldman Sachs ($12.9 billion), Société Générale ($11.9 billion), Deutsche Bank ($11.8 billion) and Barclays ($8.5 billion). If the US Treasury had not honoured those contracts then these institutions would have been in much greater difficulty.

Stress tests

In February 2009 the US government announced that the 19 largest US banks would be subject to 'stress tests' by the Federal Reserve to see if they could survive a 'worst case scenario' consisting of 8.9 per cent unemployment in 2009 rising to 10.3 per cent by 2010, a further 22 per cent fall in property prices and a fall in real GDP of 3.2 per cent in 2009 with only 0.5 per cent growth in 2010. The results of the stress tests were announced on 7 May 2009, with 10 of the 19 banks being required to raise $74.9 billion of new capital by November 2009. In the event of a failure to raise the capital then the banks would get the required capital from the US government in return for equity stakes. It was made clear to market participants before the tests that further bank failures among the top 19 would not be permitted.

315-year history. ▶ 9 January 2009 US jobless rate rises to 7.2%, its highest in 16 years. ▶ 12 January 2009 Angela Merkel announces a €50 billion stimulus package for the German economy including investment in railways, roads and schools, tax cuts and tax relief. China announces the largest drop in exports for a decade. ▶ 14 January 2009 The UK government announces £14 billion in loans to small and medium-sized businesses. ▶ 15 January 2009 The ECB cuts its key interest rate to 2%. The Irish government nationalizes ▷

The UK response

The UK's response to the financial crisis was initially much tougher than that of the USA. The first institution requiring a bailout was Northern Rock, which in September 2007 was facing a bank run. The government initially failed to make any guarantee to protect depositors beyond the statutory commitment to protect the first £20,000. However, as queues formed outside bank branches the Bank of England was forced to step in as lender of last resort and guarantee all Northern Rock deposits. Eventually in February 2008, when it became clear that Northern Rock was unable to refinance itself, the bank was nationalized and its shares became worthless. Another nationalization took place on 28 September 2008 when the government took over Bradford & Bingley's £50 billion mortgage and loan book and sold its branch network off to Spanish banking group Santander.

The full extent of the crisis in British banking really became apparent when the government was forced to bail out the largest bank in the UK, the Royal Bank of Scotland (which included the well known NatWest franchise), and the newly merged Lloyds TSB and HBOS banks. On 8 October 2008, in what Robert Peston the BBC business editor characterized as 'perhaps the most extraordinary day in British banking history', the UK government announced an unprecedented £500 billion bank rescue scheme. The main aims of the scheme were to restore market confidence and to stabilize the British banking system. The package provided for £200 billion of short-term loans through the Bank of England's Special Liquidity Scheme, £250 billion of government guarantees on interbank lending and up to £50 billion of state investment in the UK banking sector. Two major banks took part in the Bank Recapitalisation Fund scheme, the Royal Bank of Scotland (RBS) and Lloyds TSB with its new acquisition, HBOS. RBS took £20 billion with £5 billion in preference shares and £15 billion in ordinary shares, giving the government a 60 per cent holding, while Lloyds TSB-HBOS took £17 billion with £8.5 billion in preference shares and £8.5 billion in ordinary shares, giving the government a 40 per cent holding. On 6 March 2009, after it became clear that the HBOS losses were far bigger than expected, the British government announced a further injection which increased its stake in Lloyds TSB to 65 per cent, or 77 per cent including non-voting preference shares.

Despite its huge scale, the October 2008 bailout was not sufficient to stabilize the British banking system or the UK financial markets. Therefore, on 19 January 2009 the government announced a second bank rescue package designed to increase the ability of British banks to lend to business and their customers. The January package was made up of an initial £50 billion of funds which were available for large corporates and an Asset Protection Scheme (APS), an insurance scheme designed to limit participating UK banks' future losses on their 'toxic assets'. On 26 February 2008

Asset Protection Scheme (APS)
a UK government scheme announced in February 2009 whereby, in return for an insurance premium, participating banks could insure a large part of their loan books against future losses

Anglo Irish Bank.　▶ 16 January 2009 The US government lends $20 billion to Bank of America following losses from its takeover of Merrill Lynch.　▶ 19th January 2009 The UK government announces a further bailout of the UK banking system, with £50 billion being set aside for lending to large corporations and an Asset Protection Scheme to insure around £600 billion of toxic bank assets.

▶ 24 January 2009 President Obama announces an economic recovery package including expenditure on electricity power lines.　▷

the basic idea of the scheme was announced by the UK Treasury. In return for an insurance premium participating banks would be able to insure a large part of their loan books against future losses. RBS announced its intention to participate in the scheme in respect of £325 billion of assets, paying a participation fee of £6.5 billion (in the form of B shares giving the Treasury the right to dividends but not voting rights) to the Treasury in capital and agreeing to bear a first loss of up to £19.5 billion, As part of the deal RBS agreed to make 2009 lending commitments totalling £25 billion comprising £9 billion of mortgage lending and £16 billion of business lending. For its part the UK Treasury made a capital injection of £13 billion into RBS and made a commitment to subscribe for an additional £6 billion at RBS's option. The other major participant was Lloyds-HBOS, which on 27 March 2009 announced an agreement with the UK Treasury to place £260 billion of assets into the APS for a participation fee of £15.6 billion with the bank being responsible for a first loss of £25 billion. As part of the deal Lloyds-HBOS agreed to make additional lending commitments totalling £14 billion over the following year comprising £3bn of mortgage lending and £11bn of business lending.

| Box 17.5 | The nationalizations of Northern Rock and Bradford & Bingley |

The concept of nationalization was becoming a distant memory for many British citizens, with some one of the last major nationalizations being the car company British Leyland in 1976 and the Bank of England rescue of Johnson Matthey Bank in 1984. An even more distant event was a bank run – one had not occurred in Britain since 1866. However, the credit crunch reintroduced the British public to both concepts with the nationalizations of its third largest mortgage lender Northern Rock (6,000 employees) in February 2008, followed by its eighth largest mortgage provider Bradford & Bingley (3,200 employees) in October 2008.

The reasons for the problems at Northern Rock and Bradford & Bingley were somewhat different from subprime mortgages losses that created havoc with the US banking system. The seeds for the demise of the two institutions dated back to legislation, passed by the Thatcher government in 1986, enabling building societies to become banks. Northern Rock took advantage of the legislation in October 1997 and Bradford & Bingley in December 2000. The principal problem for both companies was the funding mechanism that they used to finance the expansion

continued overleaf

▶ 28 January 2009 The International Labour Office forecasts 51 million job losses worldwide as a result of the credit crunch.
▶ 2 February 2009 France announces a €33.1 billion economic stimulus package. ▶ 5 February 2009 The Bank of England cuts its base rate from 1.5% to 1%. ▶ 10 February 2009 US Treasury Secretary Tim Geithner announces that stress tests will be conducted on 19 of the largest US banks with assets over $100 billion each. ▶ 13 February 2009 Germany passes its €50 billion stimulus package.

| Box 17.5 | The nationalizations of Northern Rock and Bradford & Bingley – *continued* |

of their mortgage books. Traditionally banks and building societies funded their mortgage books by using their customers' deposits. However, with their new-found bank status, both organizations borrowed money, quite a lot of it short-term from international financial markets, to supplement their deposit-based funding in order to aggressively grow their mortgage businesses. The business model was badly disrupted by the subprime crisis when interbank lending dried up and the banks could not roll over their short-term paper as the credit markets froze. Both banks also made the mistake of increasing their mortgage business by aggressively lending high amounts of mortgage compared to property values, often requiring little or even no deposit from borrowers. Bradford & Bingley was particularly aggressive in lending to landlords in the 'buy-to-let' market, often requiring only self-certification of their income.

A bank run on the Northern Rock bank started on 14 September 2007 after the bank announced that it was seeking emergency assistance from the Bank of England. This sparked queues of its customers to form outside its branches and three days later the Bank of England, afraid that other banks might face a bank run, decided to step in to guarantee all deposits at the bank. During the next few months Northern Rock's share price continued to fall and attempts to find a private buyer failed. On 22 February 2008 the Northern Rock was nationalized. Bradford & Bingley became increasingly exposed as speculators realized that its funding model was similar to that of Northern Rock. Despite initial denials that it needed new capital, the bank was forced to raise £400 million in June 2008. However, this was not sufficient to restore confidence in the bank and it was nationalized on 29 September 2008 after customers started to queue to withdraw their money and it became clear it could not roll over its short-term debt. Bradford & Bingley's mortgage business was taken over by the government and its branches and deposits were taken over by the Spanish bank, Santander Group.

The nationalization of Northern Rock and Bradford & Bingley required Acts of Parliament, as well as permission from the European Commission whose competition rules generally forbid direct state support for a company. As a result of the nationalizations the British government injected £25 billion into Northern Rock and £8.2 billion into Bradford & Bingley. The nationalizations meant the government had a mortgage book exposure totalling £140 billion (£90 billion from Northern Rock and £50 billion from Bradford & Bingley) at the end of 2008. The investments in Northern Rock and Bradford & Bingley are managed on behalf of the taxpayer by the newly formed UK Financial Investments (UKFI).

▶ 17 February 2009 President Obama signs a $787 billion economic stimulus programme aimed at saving/creating 3.5 million jobs, calling it 'the most sweeping recovery package in our history'. ▶ 26 February 2009 The Royal Bank of Scotland announces its participation in the Asset Protection Scheme by insuring some £325 billion of its assets against future losses in return for a £6.5 billion premium to the government. ▶ 2 March 2009 AIG announces a $61.7 billion loss for the third quarter of 2008, the largest in US   ▷

Other countries' responses

While US and UK banks were the most heavily affected by the credit crunch, the crisis had severe impacts on other countries' banking systems. German banks had bought US subprime-related securities and were heavily impacted by the collapse of Lehman Brothers, but had also overlent to Eastern Europe. On the 6 October 2008, the German government was forced to step in with a €50 billion rescue of Hypo Real Estate (HRE), taking a 90 per cent stake in return for its capital injection. HRE's viability was threatened when its Irish-based subsidiary bank Depfa faced severe funding problems following the Lehman Brothers collapse. As it became apparent that more German banks were facing problems, on 17 October 2008 the German government announced a €500 billion Special Fund for Financial Market Stabilization, with $400 billion available for guaranteeing interbank loans, $80 billion available for capital injections and €20 billion set aside to cover potential losses. In January 2009 the German government also set aside €100 billion for guarantees and loans to assist German companies adversely affected by the recession.

On 27 September 2008, Fortis, a European banking and insurance group, was rescued through a part-nationalization, surrendering a 49 per cent stake in return for a capital injection of €11.2 billion from the central banks of Belgium (€4.7 billion), Netherlands (€4 billion) and Luxembourg (€2.5 billion). The bank had made major losses through taking a €24 billion stake in the Dutch bank ABN Amro, which had huge losses on its books following its subprime exposures. A few days later on 30 September 2008 Dexia Bank was rescued by the Belgian, Dutch and French governments with a €6.4 billion package. Another country drawn, perhaps inevitably, into the crisis given its well established banking sector was Switzerland. The Swiss banking sector had a reputation for conservative banking principles and secrecy. However, it seems that during the boom years its two largest investment banks, the Union Bank of Switzerland (UBS) and Credit Suissse, had departed from this tradition of cautious money management. In particular, UBS under former Chairman Marcel Ospel had set itself the goal of becoming the world's number one investment bank. In so doing it had abandoned its traditionally conservative strategies to leap into US subprime-backed investments and other high-risk instruments. In particular, its hedge fund Dillon Read Capital had built up a large exposure to the US subprime mortgage sector. As credit-related losses mounted to over $40 billion and worried depositors withdrew tens of billions of dollars from the bank, on 17 October the Swiss National Bank (SNB) stepped in with a $59.2 billion rescue package made up of a $5.3 billion capital injection and a commitment to buy $53.9 billion of UBS securities and assets to be transferred to a separate entity controlled by the SNB. Credit Suisse decided to seek capital from the Sovereign Wealth Fund Qatar Investment Authority which injected $8.75 billion of capital.

Two of the more surprising countries to be heavily drawn into the crisis were

corporate history. ▶ 5 March 2009 The Bank of England reduces its base rate from 1% to 0.5% and announces a £75 billion policy of quantitative easing. ▶ 14 March 2009 The G20 meeting in London pledges a sustained effort to pull the global economy out of recession. ▶ 18 March 2009 The Federal Reserve announces it will buy approximately $1.2 trillion of debt in a bid to boost lending and economic recovery: $300 billion in Treasury purchases, $750 billion in mortgage backed securities and $100 billion in debt issue by   ▷

Ireland and Iceland. The Irish economy had boomed for many years and property prices had risen more dramatically in Ireland than in any other country. The trouble was that the Irish banks became heavily exposed to the property market and property developers, so that when house prices began to fall the Irish economy went into a steep recession. On 2 October 2008 following a run by depositors, the Irish government announced that it would protect all deposits in its six largest banks, a protection guarantee in the region of €400 billion. In December the Irish government announced that it would pump €7.7 billion into three of its largest banks, taking control of Anglo Irish Banking group with a 75 per cent stake. In the end even that proved insufficient to save Anglo Irish Bank which was nationalized in January 2009. In April 2009 the IMF estimated that the Irish bank bailouts would be equivalent to 13.9 per cent of Ireland's GDP, or €24 billion.

In the case of Iceland, a small country with a mere 300,000 population, its banks had grown dramatically since 2000 and had combined assets equivalent to 8 times its GDP. The massive expansion of its banks was financed by borrowing in foreign currencies, so when the Icelandic crown started to collapse the viability of its banks became questionable. In late September 2008 the Icelandic government took a 75 per cent controlling interest in its third largest bank Glitner, with a €600 million capital injection, as it became clear the bank was on the brink of collapse. In October 2008 it was forced to step in and rescue three of its largest banks. One of its banks, Icesave, a subsidiary of Landsbanki, had attracted significant deposits of up to £5 billion from the UK. When its accounts were frozen there were major problems for British companies, local authorities and individual depositors that held accounts with Icesave. In the end Iceland had to go to the IMF for an emergency $2.1 billion loan, with Finland, Sweden, Norway and Denmark lending an additional $2.5 billion.

17.22   Conclusions

The credit crunch has many lessons for regulators, financial market participants, policy makers and financial institutions. It will take many years before we can properly assess the lessons to be learnt from the crisis and judge the longer-term consequences and appropriateness of the policy response. At the heart of the crisis was an unprecedented increase in debt levels of the private sector, misunderstood, mis-sold, mispriced and misrated financial innovations, a housing bubble and inadequate management of risk by banks, along with regulation that was too lax. The credit rating agencies also played a pivotal role because, had CDOs and MBSs been properly rated, there would have been far less build up of bad debt and the resulting losses would have been far lower.

One clear lesson for regulators is that they need to analyze and quantify systemic risk in the financial sector in a much better way. While regulators were concentrating on looking at risks in individual institutions, the build-up of systemic risk in the sector

Fannie Mae and Freddie Mac. ▶ 27 March 2009 Lloyds HBOS announces its participation in the Asset Protection Scheme by insuring some £260 billion of its assets against future losses in return for a £25.6 billion premium to the government. ▶ 2 April 2009 Meeting of the G20 in London pledges measures totalling $1.1 trillion to stave off recession in the global economy. ▶ 5 April 2009 Japan announces a $100 billion stimulus package. ▶ 22 April 2009 The IMF predicts financial losses from the credit crunch could total   ▷

| Box 17.6 | The total global cost of the credit crunch |

The total costs of the credit crunch are impossible to calculate since we need to also know what would have happened if there had not been a credit crunch. Furthermore, the boom that preceded the credit crunch meant higher employment and higher tax revenues for governments that to some extent helped to offset the lower levels of employment and tax revenues that followed the onset of the credit crunch. In its April 2009 report the IMF estimated that banks faced $2.5 trillion in losses between 2007 and 2010, insurers $300 billion and other financial institutions $1.3 trillion, a total of $4.1 trillion.

In July 2009 the IMF put the cost of government support packages at over $10 trillion, with rich countries providing $9.2 trillion of support for the financial sector and emerging economies $1.6 trillion. Of this, some $1.9 trillion is upfront costs and the remainder is made up of guarantees and loans. The financial bailout costs include:

Capital injections	$1.1 trillion
Purchase of assets	$1.9 trillion
Guarantees	$4.6 trillion
Liquidity provision	$2.5 trillion

The fiscal and financial costs of the policy reponse to the credit crunch are given in **Table 17.8**.

Table 17.8   Fiscal and financial costs of the policy response to the credit crunch

	Gross government debt		Percentage change 2008–10	Financial stabilization costs as a percentage of GDP
	2008	**2010**		
Canada	64	77	20.3	4.4
France	67	80	19.4	1.8
Germany	67	87	29.9	3.1
Italy	106	121	14.2	0.9
Japan	196	227	15.8	1.7
UK	52	73	40.4	9.1
USA	71	98	38.0	12.7

Notes
Debt-to-GDP estimates are from the IMF, *World Economic Outlook*, April 2009.
Financial stabilization costs are estimates by the IMF Fiscal Affairs Department based on support measures announced through mid-February 2009. This is the net cost, which is gross support minus recovery over the next five years.

£4 trillion with $2.7 trillion of losses for banks and $1.3 trillion for other financial institutions. ▶ 7 May 2009 The Federal Reserve announces the results of its stress tests on 19 leading US banks. Ten out of the 19 banks are required to produce plans to raise $74.6 billion in capital by 8 June 2009 and complete the capital raising by November. The capital could be raised by issuance of new equity or asset sales. In the event of failing to raise the capital then the banks would receive funds from the Treasury in return for stakes in the

had clearly not been appreciated prior to the outbreak of the crisis. Clearly, neither the regulatory authorities nor the banks had understood the linkages between the house price bubble, financial innovation, the growth of leverage in the financial system and the degree of globalization of the financial sector.

Another lesson is that prior to the outbreak of the crisis there had been too much focus on the capital adequacy of banks and not enough focus on liquidity issues. Once the crisis began, the drying up of liquidity of many financial instruments made them virtually untradeable. For example, the secondary and new issuance markets for CDOs and other MBSs virtually dried up at points during the credit crunch. In addition, many financial institutions that were reliant on commercial paper or the interbank lending market for funding found themselves in major financial difficulties when these sources of funding suddenly ceased to be available. Many of the financial services intermediaries that failed during the crisis met capital adequacy requirements but were unable to function due to a lack of liquidity. This lack of liquidity meant that it became very hard to establish the prices of the CDOs and MBSs which banks and financial institutions held on their trading books, and in turn created uncertainty over banks' viability and share prices.

Another issue requiring close attention is the role played by the credit rating agencies. In retrospect, it is clear that the credit rating agencies applied too high a credit rating to both banks and the securities that they were issuing. The models that they were using to rate new financial products such as CDOs were faulty and underestimated the risks involved. Without such high ratings the amount of securitization of subprime and other loans would have been greatly reduced, as would have been the extent of the crisis. It should also be remembered that the credit rating agencies were assigning a rating based on the potential for default. As such, they were not concerned with the potential price risk and liquidity issues that investors that bought these instruments might confront. Some argue that the credit rating agencies should also be regulated, and there is certainly a need to examine the potential for conflicts of interest on their part. In the run-up to the crisis it is estimated that over 40 per cent of their revenues were being generated from rating structured finance products.

Improved data collection is needed when assessing banks. In particular, the growth of off-balance-sheet exposures and risks in the form of SPVs and SIVs and other conduits undoubtedly contributed to the crisis. In addition, the growth of leverage in the financial system was not fully recognized as a source of risk, when it clearly should have been. Many investment banks and hedge funds were operating with leverage of 20 to 30 times their capital.

Another feature of the crisis was the extent to which it was concentrated in over-the-counter products such as swaps, CDOs, CDSs and the like in which there were significant counterparty risks, risks that were heavily exposed by the Lehman bankruptcy and failure of AIG. By contrast, exchange traded products such as futures

companies. ▶ 8 May 2009 The ECB announces it is to engage in €60 billion of covered euro-denominated bonds and cuts its benchmark interest rate to 1%. The Bank of England announces a further £50 billion of quantitative easing for the five months from March 2009, bringing its total to £125 billion. ▶ 1 June 2009 The world's largest car maker, General Motors, goes into bankruptcy. ▶ 10 June 2009 Ten of the largest US banks announce they are able to repay the US government $68 billion of TARP money. ▷

and options continued to trade effectively throughout the crisis. Exchange traded products are marked to market on a daily basis and initial and variation margin payments mean that the counterparty risk is kept to a very low level. By contrast, since OTC instruments do not have such stringent margining requirements, the risks and potential losses of a counterparty defaulting do not get fully recognized by market participants until disaster strikes, as happened when both Lehman's and AIG got into difficulty. In the case of Lehman Brothers, many banks and financial institutions were hit by its failure and suffered large losses due the counterparty failure. Further large losses would have been suffered by many banks had the US Treasury not stepped in to honour the CDSs that AIG Financial Products Division had written. In the future, one can expect to see a movement away from OTC products to competing products with proper margining processes as they become available on exchanges.

In retrospect, it seems that once the credit crisis started some sound financial institutions got themselves into difficulty by believing that it was an opportunity to expand their business franchise. RBS made a disastrous decision to take over ABN Amro in December 2007, Lloyds TSB acquired HBOS and Bank of America took over Merrill Lynch. These takeovers proved disastrous for the acquiring companies since the banks they took over had huge losses on their portfolios that were not fully appreciated at the time of the takeover.

Another issue that will need extensive examination is the relationship between compensation in the financial sector and profitability. It is clear that the system of annual bonuses linked primarily to revenues and short-term profits created an incentive for traders and financial institutions to take on too much risk so as to maximize short-term performance at the expense of longer-term viability and returns. Many of the profits during the boom years were in fact 'illusory profits' on which large salaries and bonuses were paid. In reality, many of the transactions at that time were to lead to unprecedented future losses and destruction of shareholder and bond holder wealth.

Tackling the moral hazard problem will become an even more important and tricky issue to address following the crisis. Central banks and treasuries came to the rescue of the financial sector on an unprecedented scale. This included massive injections of liquidity into the system, cuts in short-term interest rates, financial support for bank mergers, State guarantees on interbank loans, government guarantees on bank debt and state insurance limiting future losses from the crisis. The financial system was shown to be too important to be allowed to fail and the problem is exacerbated by the fact that bankers now know that the State will intervene to rescue key financial institutions if necessary. As such, much more thought will be required to design a system and regulatory infrastructure which encourages banks to avoid excessive risk-taking. Of course, shareholders of financial institutions suffered very significant losses and those whose financial institutions were taken over by the state were effectively wiped out. They suffered heavy losses

▶ 17 June 2009 The US Treasury announces plans for reform of the banking system, including higher capital requirements for large banks, regulation of securitized assets, consumer mortgage protection, powers to take over failing banks and global regulatory standards. ▶ 16 July 2009 Ben Bernanke talks about the 'exit strategy' of the Federal Reserve following its handling of the credit crunch. ▶ 6 August 2009 The Bank of England announces an increase in its quantitative easing policy from £125 billion to £175 billion. ▷

in other cases as share prices collapsed, but these losses would have been even higher without intervention by the authorities.

The regulators face many hard questions following the credit crunch, some commentators have accused them of being 'asleep at the wheel'. They failed to recognize the build-up of risks in the system, and generally failed to spot problems in the mortgage market and in the banks and investment houses that were at the centre of the crisis. There were clearly problems of understaffing, lack of expertise and a mistaken belief that the banks were using sophisticated modelling techniques to manage their own risks effectively. There was also a clear problem of coordination between different regulatory authorities. In the USA there are both Federal and State regulations to be considered, while the UK has a combination of FSA regulation, Bank of England responsibility for financial stability and the Treasury's involvement in the financial bailouts.

There will undoubtedly be a need to look at off-balance-sheet vehicles, such as SIVs and SPVs/SPEs that were involved in the purchase of so many of the structured finance products where losses were heavily concentrated. The lack of transparency in banks' balance sheets prior to the outbreak of the crisis and the use of off-balance-sheet vehicles meant that the build-up of systemic risk in the system was not properly recognized until the crisis started. The Basel I Accord required large US banks to maintain capital reserves equivalent to 8 per cent of the risk-adjusted assets while SPVs/SPEs were not required to hold such reserves. This created an incentive for banks to set up SPVs so as to minimize their need for capital reserves. There are clearly dangers in banks having both on-balance- and off-balance-sheet structures, since the on-balance-sheet report can give a misleading impression of financial stability when the real risks are hidden in off-balance-sheet SPVs/SPEs and SIVs. The SIVs turned to their sponsoring banks when they got into funding difficulties, and the parent banks had problems providing the necessary liquidity. To some extent the Basel II Accord overcomes this problem by requiring similar capital reserves for SPVs. The need for greater transparency in banks' balance sheets and operations will undoubtedly be one of the crucial areas for reform in the wake of the financial crisis.

The longer-term consequences of the crisis for national debts, the roles of governments in the economy, the regulatory system and the financial sector remain in a state of flux. It will take many years to understand the full implications. What is clear is that the policy response to the crisis meant that the taxpayer has ended up assuming a significant part of the losses and the financial risks that the banks took on during the boom times. In return, the public sector now has a significant stake in the form of equity or debt in many large and small financial institutions. Fannie Mae, Freddie Mac and AIG are now effectively controlled by the US government. In Britain the taxpayer has large stakes in the RBS and Lloyds TSB group, combined with ownership of Bradford & Bingley and Northern Rock which are now looked after on behalf of the UK taxpayers by UK Financial Investments (UKFI).

CREDIT CRUNCH TIMELINE CREDIT CRUNCH TIMELINE CREDIT CRUNCH TIMELINE CRED

▶ 25 August 2009 President Obama reinstates Ben Bernanke as Chairman of the Federal Reserve. ▶ 27 August 2009 FDIC announces the number of 'problem banks' has increased to 416 institutions with $300 billion of assets. ▶ 1 November 2009 CIT Group files for Chapter 11 bankruptcy wiping out the $2.8 billion stake taken out by the US government in December 2008. ▶ 5 November 2009 Fannie Mae reports net loss of $18.9 billion for Q3 2009, a total of $111 billion since Q3 2008. ▶ 2 December 2009 Bank of America   ▷

Chapter 17	Revision questions

1   Discuss what is meant by a collateralized debt obligation and the role of CDOs in the credit crunch.

2   Explain what is meant by a credit default swap and how the writing of CDSs contributed to the fall of American International Group.

3   Discuss the role played by the credit rating agencies in causing the credit crunch.

4   What is meant by quantitative easing? How is it likely to affect bond prices in the short and the long term?

5   Who was most responsible for the credit crunch – the bankers or the regulators?

6 · Discuss five of the measures implemeted by the US authorities to mitigate the effects of the credit crunch.

Multiple choice questions available at **www.palgrave.com/business/pilbeam**

announces it will buy back $45 billion of preferred stock issued to the US government under the TARP ▶ 14 December 2009 Wells Fargo and Citigroup announce they will buy back a combined $45 billion of preferred stock issued to the US government under the TARP

Credit Crunch Timeline available at
www.palgrave.com/business/pilbeam

18

REGULATION OF THE FINANCIAL SECTOR

Learning objectives

In completing this chapter you will learn about:

- the rationale for government intervention in the financial sector
- different types of government intervention
- key pieces of UK and European legislation
- the respective roles played by the Financial Services Authority (FSA) and the Securities Exchange Commission (SEC)
- the Basel I and Basel II Accords
- regulatory issues arising as a result of the credit crunch

18.1 Introduction

No analysis of financial markets and institutions can be complete without an examination of the regulatory environment in which they operate. Not only does regulation have a major impact upon the operation and developments of financial markets, regulation itself is often revised and adjusted in response to changes in market structure, financial market developments, new financial instruments and the occasional financial scandal or crisis. Effective regulation is seen by the authorities not only as a means of exerting some degree of control over the markets, but also as a means of maintaining confidence and stability in the financial system.

In this chapter, we look at the rationale for government intervention in financial markets including a brief cost–benefit analysis. Throughout, the main emphasis is on the banking sector which has traditionally been the most regulated part of the finance industry. We look at the objectives and various types of government regulation of financial markets. We then focus on three key pieces of UK legislation, followed by some analysis of European regulation and finally a look at global regulation in the form of the Basel Accords. We finish by looking at regulatory issues raised by the credit crunch.

18.2 The rationale for government intervention

Financial markets and financial institutions have a pivotal role to play in today's modern economies. Financial institutions are responsible for enormous amounts of investors' money, and they also run the payments system upon which a modern economy is crucially dependent. In addition, the financial sector is a major employer and can be a significant foreign exchange earner for a country. The financial sector is also charged with the crucial role of allocating financial capital to its most productive use. For these reasons, governments have consistently intervened to regulate and control the activities of financial institutions. The degree of regulation and control varies greatly between countries due to different historical, cultural, economic and political factors.

Usually government intervention in financial markets is rationalized on the grounds of 'market failure', that is, left to itself the market would produce a sub-optimal outcome. Four instances of market failure in the financial sector are frequently cited as requiring government intervention to correct:

1 *The externalities problem.* The financial system provides a payments mechanism for the entire economy and financial institutions play the pivotal role of linking both users and lenders of funds. This means that problems in the financial

sector can potentially have a disastrous effect on the entire economy. This kind of argument is almost unique to the financial sector of the economy; for most countries the failure of firms that produce goods or services or even whole industries is less likely to have devastating effects throughout the entire economy than the collapse of a leading bank or the financial sector.

2 *The problem of asymmetric information.* The directors and managers of companies as well as financial institutions have available to them an information set on the soundness of their company or institution and its likely policies that is superior to those that either lend or invest in the company or institution. This could lead to problems such as insider-trading and the concealment of relevant information from investors. For this reason, many countries have adopted insider-trading laws prohibiting trading in shares on information that is not publicly available. A further set of regulations imposes disclosure requirements on companies, obliging companies to make public a great deal of financial information to potential and actual investors.

3 *The moral hazard problem.* By moral hazard we mean that insurance against an event occurring will make the event more likely to occur than if the event was not insured against. For instance, a deposit insurance protection scheme will guarantee investors their funds should a deposit-taking institution get into difficulty. However, this may encourage depositors to channel more of their funds into risky financial institutions which are more likely to run into problems and thereby lead to a higher loss of deposits than if no deposit protection insurance policy existed. This will be even more the case if financial institutions take on more risk than they otherwise would, knowing that investors will be protected if the institution encounters problems.

4 *The principal–agent problem.* The directors and managers of financial institutions act as agents for shareholders and investors with the institution (the principals). There is therefore a potential problem that the directors and managers could pursue their own interests at the expense of the shareholders and investors. For example, managers may receive performance-related bonuses that encourage them to take high risks which imperil the funds of shareholders and investors. For this reason, they are obliged to disclose information on the financial performance of the company and are subjected to rules on their own dealings.

While there may be benefits from having regulation, we need to recognize that there are numerous costs. Ideally, from a societal viewpoint, the marginal benefits from additional regulation should be equated with the marginal costs imposed by the regulation. There has been a strong case made in the economics literature against government regulation of industry and many of these arguments have also been applied against government regulation of the financial sector. Regulation is not a costless exercise; there are direct costs in that the authorities need to devote resources to supervise compliance with the regulations as well as costs imposed on firms in meeting the regulations. Financial institutions tend to view regulations as imposing additional costs as well as resulting in the loss of some potentially profitable business. Further, regulations may distort the conduct of financial business by encouraging

---

asymmetric information
a situation in which one party to a transaction has superior information compared to the other party

insider-trading
the buying or selling of a security by someone who has access to privileged information not publicly available; in most countries such trading is illegal

moral hazard
the problem that the existence of insurance against an event occurring will make the insured event more likely to occur than if the event was not insured against

principal–agent problem the situation when a principal hires an agent to manage things on their behalf but the agent abuses the position and instead acts in their own interests

financial activities in areas that are favoured by the regulators rather than favoured by clients. Excessive licensing requirements can restrict competition and result in excess profits for the licensed financial institutions and higher prices for consumers. Regulations may also mean that financial innovation is reduced or limited to a nature designed to overcome the restrictions imposed by the regulations. A further danger is that over-regulation by one financial centre will merely drive business away to less-regulated foreign centres. Finally, there is the risk of inappropriate regulatory frameworks being applied.

18.3 The objectives of government regulation

structural regulation regulation of the different types of activities, products and geographical boundaries within which a financial institution can operate

Governments have many objectives when intervening in financial markets. The prime objective is usually seen as promoting financial stability, since in the absence of government regulations the financial system could be prone to periodic instability. Another motivation is to provide protection for investors against fraud or the dissemination of misleading or inadequate information. Fraud can take many forms; it might involve the deliberate manipulation of share prices, the concealment of crucial information from investors, the sale of inappropriate policies, insider-trading or the misuse of investors' funds. A further concern is a desire to promote fair and healthy competition to ensure competitive prices for consumers. A major concern of many authorities is to control the activities of financial institutions in order to exert some degree of control over the level of economic activity, particularly with respect to monetary policy.

18.4 Types of government regulation

prudential regulation measures governing the internal management of a financial institution; for example, to ensure that the institution has sufficient capital to absorb possible losses and sufficient liquidity to meet its obligations

investor-protection regulation measures designed to protect investors from mismanagement of funds, malpractice and fraud

To meet the objectives of government intervention and attempt to ensure financial stability as well as address the problems of externalities, asymmetric information, principal–agent and moral hazard, there are a number of means by which governments intervene and regulate financial markets. Regulation can be divided up into three types:

1 Structural regulation covers the different types of activities, products and geographical boundaries within which a financial institution can operate.
2 Prudential regulation covers the internal management of a financial institution, for example the setting of ratios to ensure that the institution has sufficient capital to absorb possible losses and sufficient liquidity to ensure it can meet its obligations.
3 Investor-protection regulation covers measures designed to protect investors from mismanagement of funds, malpractice and fraud.

It should be noted that there is a considerable degree of overlap in the above types of regulation; for example, structural regulation that limits the degree of risk that an institution can take on also helps to protect investors' funds. There are numerous types of regulation that fall under these classifications, and we now proceed to briefly look at some of the key measures which include licensing regulations, disclosure requirements, deposit insurance, restrictions on activities, exposure limits and various liquidity and capital requirements to ensure solvency:

- *Licensing regulations.* Most governments require financial institutions to be licensed. These licensing arrangements are partly designed to prevent undesirable individuals from running financial institutions and partly to ensure that a financial institution does not act recklessly with investors' funds. Confidence is a vital factor in the financial services industry, and this can be undermined if undesirable people and firms are in charge of investors' funds.
- *Disclosure requirements.* Many governments require public companies to disclose a large amount of information relating to their financial performance. However, some economists have argued that disclosure requirements are unnecessary, arguing that financial institutions that fail to disclose sufficient information of their own accord will fail to attract investors.
- *Deposit insurance.* One means of forestalling runs on deposits is by the authorities operating a deposit insurance scheme that will guarantee investors' funds should a financial institution run into trouble. Such a scheme has the advantage of ensuring that depositors have speedy access to funds if a financial institution is closed down. Nonetheless, there are problems with deposit insurance schemes; if investors know that their funds are protected they tend to place their funds with institutions that offer the highest interest rates. In order to pay the interest these financial institutions may then invest the funds in high-risk ventures and may well end up insolvent. This is an example of moral hazard, insuring against an event makes that event more likely to occur.
- *Restriction on activities.* Many governments restrict the range of activities that can be undertaken by a financial institution. These restrictions may cover investing, lending, borrowing and funding activities. The idea of these restrictions is to ensure that financial institutions do not take excessive risks with investors' funds and also to limit potential conflicts of interest. For example, in the UK and the USA banks have long been prohibited from holding significant stakes in companies since this could result in distorted lending to such companies should they get into financial difficulty.
- *Exposure limits.* Most authorities expect a bank to have a diversified assets portfolio to control its risk exposure. In the UK, a bank is required to notify the Bank of England if its exposure to any individual client is greater than 10 per cent of its capital base, and any exposure above 25 per cent requires the Bank of England's prior permission. Since exchange rates can move rapidly, the Bank of England also restricts a bank's currency exposure to a maximum of 10 per cent of its capital base for any individual currency, and a maximum of 15 per cent for all currencies.
- *Liquidity requirements.* Since financial institutions have liquid liabilities (deposits) and relatively illiquid assets (loans), regulation aims to ensure that unnecessary problems do not arise due to insufficient liquidity to meet depositors' demands. Most commercial banks are expected, and sometimes legally required, to maintain a prudent level of cash reserves as a ratio of their total deposits to meet withdrawal demands, known as the cash reserve ratio. This ratio generally differs according to the type of deposit liabilities, with demand deposits requiring a higher ratio

cash reserve ratio
the amount of cash held by banks in relation to their total deposits

of reserves than time deposits. Cash reserves do not earn commercial banks any return, but should a shortage occur they can borrow from the central bank at a penal rate of interest (in the USA this is the Federal Funds rate, in the UK it is the base rate). The authorities also tend to impose requirements on banks to ensure some degree of matching of the cash flows on liabilities and maturing assets.

- *Capital adequacy.* Liquidity requirements are essentially about maintaining adequate short-term cash to meet demands for deposit withdrawals. Solvency is, however, a medium- to long-term concept concerning the ability of an institution to meet its liabilities as they fall due. Some argue that a solvent institution will always be able to meet these demands by raising funds from the market, and if it is unable to do so then it is indicative that the market has concerns about the solvency of the institution. The need to maintain sufficient capital to ensure that the institution is regarded as solvent, and remains so even if there are losses on its assets, can therefore serve a useful purpose. Capital adequacy requirements have been drawn up by the Bank of International Settlements (see Section 18.17), the idea being that shareholders in a bank should make up for losses, not the depositors.

> **capital adequacy**
> the amount of capital needed by a financial institution to cover potential losses

- *Regulation of exchanges.* There are rules that govern the structure and organization of securities exchanges, and the aim here is to ensure fair play on behalf of investors. For example, there are regulations requiring that purchases and sales of securities are conducted at the best possible price for investors. Most countries have insider-trading laws designed to ensure that market participants in positions of access to privileged price-sensitive information are legally prohibited from exploiting this.

18.5   Regulation of the banking sector

The banking sector has always been more tightly regulated than any other part of the financial sector, both for historical reasons and the fact that most significant financial crises have been associated with problems in the banking industry rather than in other financial intermediaries. In the USA the regulatory environment was very much influenced by a desire to avert bank failures such as those of the period 1929–34 when some 11,000 banks failed. Prior to the outbreak of the credit crunch in August 2007 instances of bank failure had been relatively scarce. In 1974 Bankhaus Herstatt, a German bank, and Franklin National Bank of the USA failed, and in 1973–74 the Bank of England felt compelled to organize a 'lifeboat' operation to rescue a number of fringe banks which had been badly affected by a slump in the property market. A decade later, in 1984, the eighth largest US bank, Continental Illinois, failed, as did Johnson Matthey Bank in the UK. In July 1991, the Bank of Credit and Commerce International (subsequently nicknamed the 'Bank of Crooks and Criminals International'!) was compulsorily closed by the Bank of England due to large-scale fraud. The collapse of Baring's Bank in 1994 due to losses run up in derivatives trading by the infamous Nick Leeson in Singapore was a reminder of the potential for sudden failure. Of course, the credit crunch showed that banking collapses could occur on a massive scale once again, with top American and British banks such as Citigroup, Bank of America, the Royal Bank of Scotland and Lloyds TSB becoming dependent on state funded bailouts to stay in business. These failures clearly showed that the regulations had failed to achieve their aims, and seeking a new set of regulations to govern the banking and financial sector has become a high priority.

Much of the literature on financial regulation is based upon the prudential regulation of banks, that is, legislation designed to ensure that banks act prudently. There are a number of arguments that have been put forward to justify such regulation of the banking sector, in particular the special risks they face.

Much of the concern of the regulatory authorities in regard of the banking industry has been to reduce the possibility of bank runs. The fear is that if one bank were to fail this would result in a run on other more viable banks who, being unable to meet the immediate demand for funds, would be forced into insolvency and thereby place the wider economy in peril. This risk of bank runs is known as systemic risk. Most banks have very liquid liabilities (deposits) and relatively illiquid assets (loans and advances), which leaves them very vulnerable to sudden large-scale withdrawals of funds (that is, a run) by their depositors. In particular, there is a significant risk of financial contagion whereby bad news about bank A can lead to a run on other financially sound banks, because investors do not possess sufficient information (imperfect information) about which banks are sound or unsound. Unable to distinguish between sound and unsound banks, it is rational for investors to withdraw funds. Regulation has been viewed as crucial in preventing the financial system from facing such periodic bouts of financial instability. A bank has both personal and business clients and its failure could lead to the ruin of many individuals and the collapse of many businesses.

Another risk facing banks is changes in interest rates. If large loans are made at fixed rates of interest while variable rates of interest are paid on deposits, a rise in interest rates may mean that banks will end up paying more on deposits than they are receiving from their loan portfolio. Banks are also exposed to price risk when they have open positions in the foreign exchange market, when adverse currency movements could lead to significant losses. These days this risk exposure is reduced by lending at variable rates of interest, or by limiting exposure and the use of hedging techniques.

The general economic environment can also greatly affect banks. For example, a move to monetary restraint in which the authorities raise interest rates can lead to many firms and consumers defaulting on their debt obligations. A rise in interest rates raises consumers' and firms' debt-servicing bills, which invariably leads to lower expenditure which hits firms' order books and leads to a rise in unemployment. As consumers and firms find themselves in difficulty, the effects are transmitted to the banks and the commercial and residential property markets. In 1973–74 the Bank of England came to the rescue of many fringe banks that were heavily exposed to the property sector; when interest rates rose and property prices fell many of these banks found their bad debts rose simultaneously with a fall in the value of the assets against which the debt was secured.

Fraud and mismanagement can be significant causes of loss for banks. In the USA a significant number of savings and loans institutions went under for these reasons following a deregulation of the sector in the 1980s. Furthermore, there is a concern that new derivative products which are poorly understood by senior management may give scope for unscrupulous traders to misrepresent their positions.

financial contagion the transfer of an economic shock from one entity to another or one country to another

All of the above risks make the banking sector a particular cause for concern on the part of the authorities, and the result has been a plethora of regulatory controls on the sector. It should, however, be noted that both the degree and type of regulatory control of the banking sector differs greatly between countries.

18.6 Statutory versus self-regulation

statutory regulation
a government agency is responsible for regulating an industry

self-regulation an industry-sponsored agency is responsible for regulating an industry

There has been an intense debate about the merits of having statutory regulation as opposed to self-regulation by the relevant financial institutions and practitioners. Statutory regulation is part of the law and usually supervised by the authorities, whilst with self-regulation, supervision and enforcement are left to market participants/ practitioners, usually in the form of various regulatory bodies.

One of the main arguments in favour of self-regulation is that it is more flexible and can be quickly adapted to the fast changes in the financial services industry. By contrast, statutory regulation requiring government legislation is usually a time-consuming process and is often hopelessly behind the developments in the financial sector and financial markets. Another argument is that self-regulation by market practitioners who know and understand the business is likely to be more effective at spotting breaches of the regulations. Furthermore, the involvement of practitioners and professionals in the formulation of regulations may lead to higher professional standards as the market practitioners themselves should have a self-interest in maintaining standards and rooting out fraud in their sector. In addition, market professionals are better able to judge what constitutes unacceptable standards.

Against this, however, there are a number of objections to self-regulation. These include the fact that self-regulatory bodies are dependent upon their member firms for funding, which could make the regulatory body more disposed to make judgements in favour of its members rather than consumers. More generally, since self-regulatory bodies are staffed by market practitioners they tend to be sympathetic to the industry's rather than consumers' viewpoints to begin with. In addition, since such bodies are funded by existing market players they may impose too onerous requirements on new entrants that wish to do things in an innovative fashion; that is, they have a vested interest in preserving the status quo.

18.7 Regulation in the UK

The 1980s witnessed a number of important changes in the regulatory environment in the UK. The Conservative government elected in 1979 was keen to maintain and promote London's position as one of the world's leading financial centres, and to promote greater competition in the financial services industry. Following the abolition of exchange controls in 1979, the 1980s witnessed a clear trend towards deregulation of the UK financial services industry, a trend that has subsequently been followed by other industrialized countries and many developing countries.

deregulation the reduction or elimination of regulations designed to increase competition and reduce prices facing consumers

There were a number of forces at work to encourage the trend towards deregulation, one of the most important being the globalization of financial markets. Government regulations are only enforceable at the national level, and when financial institutions and markets decide that government regulations are too costly and result in the loss of too much business they frequently find ways around the legislation. This is often most easily achieved by conducting business outside of the country. In fact a significant motivation behind UK deregulation was a feeling that London was losing business to other countries such as the USA, which prompted the so-called 'big bang' in 1986. A further motivating force behind deregulation was a feeling on the part of the authorities that legislation was largely ineffective and often caused distortions in financial markets.

Before looking at some of the key pieces of UK legislation, it should be noted that the 1980s and 1990s were not completely about greater deregulation and competition. There were a number of factors requiring new regulation. One was the amount of financial innovation; the 1980s witnessed the development of a whole range of new financial products such as options, junk bonds, swaps and so forth, and legislation was required to govern trading in these products. Financial regulations have often been a response to market developments, such as the stockmarket collapse of 1987 which was in part blamed upon speculation in derivatives markets and resulted in new regulations on programme trades.

We now proceed to look at six major pieces of legislation that impacted significantly upon the UK regulatory environment; the big bang in 1986, the Financial Services Act of 1986, the Banking Act of 1987, the Bank of England Act of 1998, the Financial Services and Market Act of 2000 and the Banking Act of 2009.

18.8   Big bang, 1986

October 1986 witnessed the so-called 'big bang' of deregulation of London's Stock Exchange. Prior to the big bang, membership of the Exchange was restricted to private partnerships. Market-making in shares was done by jobbers who would quote prices at which they would buy and sell shares, and brokers acting on their clients' instructions would place buy or sell orders with the jobber offering the best price. There was a clear separation between the jobbers that quoted share prices and brokers that advised clients and placed their buy/sell orders. Charges to clients involved minimum fixed commissions based on the size of the share trade. By the early 1980s this arrangement was looking increasingly dated; the fixed commissions were regarded as a restrictive practice and the existing partnerships were poorly capitalized. The lack of capital meant that jobbers were limited in their ability to undertake large positions in stock, and in consequence the market was less liquid than was desired. Large institutional investors were increasingly dissatisfied with a system whereby large share deals had to be placed using a client base and a fee paid to a jobber for merely certifying that the price arranged was fair. The London Stock Exchange was losing business to foreign centres for both gilt and share dealing. The government being keen to maintain London's position as an important trading centre therefore initiated the package of reform which subsequently became termed the 'big bang'. The reform consisted of three elements:

1 Admission to the Stock Exchange was opened up to corporations, whereas before membership had been restricted to private partnerships.
2 The broker–jobber divide was ended and firms were permitted to be both market-makers in shares and advisers/brokers.
3 Fixed minimum commissions were abolished.

The result of the big bang was that many merchant and international banks bought up partnerships so as to exercise their newly acquired right to deal in government bonds and company shares. The new corporate membership meant that a great deal of new capital and financial resources were brought into share dealing. One visible result of this was that the new market-making firms adopted the latest computer technology to conduct share trading, and within a week of the big bang floor trading on the London Stock Exchange virtually ceased.

The ending of the jobber–broker divide, with some firms both advising clients and making markets in the shares, required the building of so-called 'Chinese walls' between various divisions of the market-making firms. Chinese walls are attempts to prevent price-sensitive information being transmitted from one division of a corporation to another. For example, the corporate finance division of a merchant bank might have Company Y as a client. The information that Company Y is interested in a takeover bid for Company X is price-sensitive, and should not be disclosed to the fund management division of the bank which would be tempted to buy shares in Company X, believing that the share price would go up as a result of the bid.

Overall, the big bang has been regarded as a success in helping to maintain London as a key financial centre. Computer technology has improved both the speed of execution of share deals and enabled a far bigger volume of trades to be conducted. The abolition of fixed commissions, increased market capacity and greater competition resulted in a halving of the transaction costs associated with large share transactions, although commissions on small trades actually rose. Indeed, gilt-trading commissions disappeared altogether and the profitability was determined purely by the bid–ask spread.

18.9 The Financial Services Act 1986

The Financial Services Act came into force on 29 April 1988. The Act was seen as important in maintaining investors' confidence in the financial system following a number of well publicized cases of fraud. The legislation imposed a number of statutory requirements upon the financial services industry, but also left the responsibility for supervision largely with the financial services industry itself; that is, the act favoured self-regulation as compared to central regulation by the authorities.

The Securities and Investment Board (SIB) was set up as the main regulatory authority to supervise the financial services industry. In turn, the SIB recognizes a number of self-regulatory organizations (SROs) which are staffed by investment professionals and practitioners. The SROs are responsible for supervising firms and individuals that fall within their domain. Originally there were four SROs: the Securities and Futures Authority (SFA), the Investment Management Regulatory Organization (IMRO), the Life Assurance and Unit Trust Regulatory Organization (LAUTRO) and the Financial Intermediaries, Managers and Brokers Regulatory Association (FIMBRA). In 1995 LAUTRO and FIMBRA were merged to form the Personal Investment Authority (PIA). In addition, the SIB recognizes a number of professional bodies which determine the standards for their members.

The Act also required investment businesses to obtain authorization from a relevant SRO, and operation of an investment business without authorization was made a criminal offence. To this end, investment firms have to pass certain capital adequacy tests. The Act also made the provision of false and misleading information by investment practitioners a criminal offence punishable by a maximum of seven years' imprisonment. A number of other standards were also imposed upon member professionals; they were required to give suitable advice to clients which involved taking reasonable steps to ascertain the client's financial position, undertake market transactions at the best possible price and satisfy themselves that clients were aware of the nature of the risks to which they could be exposed. Clients have the right to sue for losses should a firm breach an SRO rule. The SIB also recognizes a number of exchanges which become Recognized Investment Exchanges (RIEs) if they are located in the UK or Designated Investment Exchanges (DIEs) if they are located outside of the UK.

The supervisory structure set up by the Financial Services Act tried to strike a balance between some degree of statutory regulation and self-regulation by market practitioners. The structure was the subject of much criticism, however. In particular, the fact that SROs were dependent upon subscriptions from their member firms was viewed as a weakness in the system. Furthermore, the framework was perceived as being somewhat unwieldy and fragmented with a large degree of overlap between the various SROs. Some degree of competition for members meant that the SROs have been less cooperative than might be desired, and it has been argued that it led to some lowering of regulatory standards to attract members.

18.10   The Banking Act 1987

The international debt crisis which commenced with the Mexican moratorium of 1982 led to concerns about the viability of a number of major banks both in the USA and the UK. In particular, there was considerable concern about the capital adequacy of many banks, given large potential losses on their loan portfolio to Latin America. The Banking Act provided a new framework for the Bank of England to conduct its supervision of the banking sector.

The Act ended the distinction between recognized banks and licensed deposit-taking institutions to create a single class of 'authorized institutions' subject to common rules and regulation. The Act also clarified the criteria to be used to determine who constituted a 'fit and proper' person to run a bank. The Act set up a new board of banking supervision to assist the Bank of England in its supervision of the banking sector. Banks are required to report any large individual exposure and to provide certain other information to the Bank of England, and it was also made a criminal offence to knowingly and recklessly provide false information to the Bank of England. The Bank of England was empowered to seek opinions from auditors on an institution's internal control systems and to commission further advice. In addition, it was also given power of access and entry to an institution where a contravention of the Act was suspected.

As well as the Banking Act, there were a number of accompanying criteria setting out prudential rules relating to capital and liquidity ratios, the definition and measurement of capital and supervision of off-balance-sheet exposure.

18.11 The Bank of England Act 1998

The main provisions of the Bank of England Act were to make the Bank of England independent from the Treasury, giving it operational responsibility for the conduct of monetary policy. Its principal activity is to maintain price stability whilst playing a supportive role to the government's aim of achieving employment and growth, although the Treasury would have reserve powers to direct the bank with respect to monetary policy in extreme circumstances. The Act established the monetary policy committee (MPC) to be made up of nine members, including the Governor of the Bank, to set interest rates to achieve price stability. While the Act very much strengthened the independence of the Bank it lost its power of supervision over the banking sector. The Act however transferred to the new Financial Service Authority the Bank's functions in relation to supervision of banks.

18.12 Financial Services and Markets Act 2000

The Financial Services and Markets Act (FSMA) gave the Financial Services Authority (FSA) the formal power to regulate the banking, insurance and investment business. The Act outlines the key objectives of the FSA, giving it the power to authorize firms to conduct regulated activities and to make rules. The FSA was also given powers to demand information. The Act also gave the FSA powers with respect to market abuse such as insider-trading and anti-competitive practices. It established the Financial Services and Markets Tribunal (FSMT), an independent judicial body which hears cases referred to it by the FSA. The FSMT has decision-making powers and the ability to fine, revoke licences, ban certain securities from being listed and take disciplinary action such as banning people from carrying out particular functions. The FSMA also made it a criminal offence to mislead the market or investors.

18.13 Banking Act 2009

The Banking Act of 12 February 2009 was a response to the credit crunch. The Act enhanced the so-called tripartite framework, comprising the Bank of England, the Financial Services Authority and the Treasury, and strengthened its ability to deal with crises in the banking system, protect depositors and maintain financial stability. The key part of the legislation was a new, permanent special resolution regime (SRR), giving the authorities a range of tools to deal with failing banks and building societies. The SRR builds on and refines the temporary tools introduced by the Banking Special Provisions Act of 2008 (BSPA), which was used to bring Northern Rock and Bradford & Bingley and the UK subsidiaries of two Icelandic banks, Heritable and Kaupthing Singer and Friedlander, under State ownership. The Act also contained a range of other measures designed to improve the legal framework and increase the efficiency of the Financial Services Compensation Scheme, enhance the operation of regulatory frameworks for preventing firms from failing, protect consumers and strengthen the Bank of England. It also gave powers to the Treasury to lay regulations for investment bank insolvency.

| Box 18.1 | A tale of two regulatory agencies: the FSA and the SEC |

The Financial Services Authority (FSA) and the Securities Exchange Commission (SEC) are powerful regulatory bodies that oversee the financial services industries in the UK and the USA, respectively, but they have very different histories and different responsibilities. While the FSA is responsible for bank regulation this is not the case for the SEC, which is primarily responsible for securities regulation with regulation of the banking sector being primarily the job of the Federal Reserve.

The FSA was created as a replacement for the Securities Investment Board in October 1997. It gained its powers as a result of the Financial Services and Markets Act of 2000 and has around 2,750 employees. The Act gives the FSA four statutory objectives:

1 market confidence: maintaining confidence in the financial system;
2 public awareness: promoting public understanding of the financial system;
3 consumer protection: securing the appropriate degree of protection for consumers;
4 the reduction of financial crime: reducing the extent to which it is possible for a business to be used for a purpose connected with financial crime.

In pursuing these objectives, the FSA is guided by principles which include the need to ensure healthy competition, not necessarily stifle innovation, consider the costs and benefits of regulations and the need to maintain the UK's competitiveness in the financial sector. In addition to regulating banks, insurance companies and financial advisers, since 31 October 2004 the FSA has been responsible for regulating the mortgage business, from 14 January 2005 the general insurance business and since 1 January 2009 some of the travel insurance business. The FSA is accountable to Treasury ministers but is operationally independent of the government and is financed entirely by the firms it regulates through a mixture of compulsory charges, fees and fines. The FSA was subjected to quite a lot of criticism over its handling of the credit crunch. Commentators variously regarded it as having too few qualified staff, having taken too lax an approach to regulation and lacking sufficient experience in bank regulation, and thereby contributing to the credit crisis. Moreover, some have complained that it is overly influenced by the financial sector which it regulates and that it has been reactive rather than proactive in its regulation. There have been concerns also that the FSA has only successfully prosecuted a few insider-trading cases.

The SEC is an independent regulatory agency of the US government with responsibility for enforcing federal security laws and the securities industry including the US stock exchanges. However, the derivatives markets are not under its remit as these are regulated by the Commodities Futures Trading Commission (CFTC). The SEC was created by the Securities Exchange Act of 1934 partly as a response to the stockmarket collapse of 1929. The SEC is based in Washington

Box 18.1	A tale of two regulatory agencies: the FSA and the SEC – *continued*

with 11 regional offices and around 3,600 employees, and is made up of four key divisions: Corporation Finance, Trading and Markets, Investment Management, and Enforcement. At the time of writing (2009), the SEC has responsibility for administrating seven major laws governing the Securities Act of 1933, the Securities Exchange Act of 1933, the Trust Indenture Act of 1939, the Investment Company Act of 1940, the Investment Advisers Act of 1940, the Sarbanes-Oxley Act of 2002, the Credit Rating Agency Reform Act of 2006, the Emergency Economic Stabilization Act (EESA) and the Housing and Economic Recovery Act of 2008.

The objectives of the SEC include:

1 the protection of private investors
2 maintenance of fair, orderly and efficient markets
3 facilitating capital formation

The SEC oversees the key participants in the securities world, including securities exchanges, brokers and dealers, investment advisers, and mutual funds. Key to ensuring it achieves these objectives is promoting the disclosure of important market relevant information, protecting against fraud and maintaining fair dealing. To this end, the SEC enforces a statutory requirement that listed companies make quarterly and annual reports available. The SEC also actively looks at possible instances of malpractice and fraud in the securities industry and brings civil enforcement actions against individuals and companies that violate securities laws. Typical infractions include fraudulent accounting, insider-trading, theft of investor funds, manipulation of market prices, the provision of misleading information regarding securities, violation of broker-dealers' responsibility to treat customers fairly.

On a day-to-day basis, the SEC is responsible for interpreting federal securities laws, issuing new rules and amending existing rules, overseeing the inspection of securities firms, brokers, investment advisers and the rating agencies. It also oversees the inspection of private regulatory organizations in the securities, accounting and auditing fields. Finally it coordinates US securities regulations with federal, state and overseas authorities and regulators.

The SEC has been relatively successful at pursuing malpractice in the securities sector and regularly succeeds in detecting wrongdoing, frequently imposing heavy fines and ensuring large sums are returned to defrauded investors. However, it came in for heavy criticism when it failed to spot Bernard Madoff's investment scam despite having been tipped off in 2005 by Harry Markopolos who made the unequivocal statement that Madoff was 'running the world's largest Ponzi scheme'. Also some of its actions during the credit crisis, such as a temporary ban on short selling of financial stocks, were contrary to mainstream economic theory which argues that short selling is a necessary condition for efficient market prices.

18.14   European regulation

The European Union (EU) is a common market and as such is concerned not only about ensuring free trade in goods and services but also free movement of factors of production, including capital and labour. The so-called White Paper of 1985 which aimed at achieving a 'single European market' also focused attention on the need for members of the EU to assure the freedom of movement of capital throughout the Union and to create a free internal market in financial services within a common regulatory structure.

In recent years, the two keys to the EU's approach to achieving a free internal market in the financial services sector and a common regulatory structure have been: (i) the principle of mutual recognition, and (ii) agreement on what constitutes the minimum reasonable standards to be applied. Under the principle of mutual recognition, a financial institution that is authorized in one member state should be free to set up and sell its products in other member states provided that the institution meets certain minimum commonly agreed standards. In principle, once a financial institution is licensed for a particular activity in one member state it should be free to sell its services in another member state without requiring further authorization from the host country. For example, a British bank authorized in the UK should be free to sell its services in Italy, even if it does not comply fully with Italian banking requirements. The concept goes even further than this. In principle a British bank should also be able to sell a similar product/service range in Italy as it does in the UK regardless of whether Italian banks are allowed to sell these products/ services.

The drawing up of minimum acceptable standards to cover the financial services industry is a far from easy task given that member states use different accounting methods, have different regulatory environments and tax structures and so on. Pre-1986 the approach to creating free trade in the financial services sector involved trying to agree a full common regulatory structure – an approach that was doomed to failure as member states each sought to have their own model as the standard, or sought rules that would advantage their financial services sector. The great innovation post-1986 is that it is far easier to make progress and agree on minimum acceptable standards than it is to achieve full harmonization of rules! The European Commission's overall approach has been to achieve liberalization through the 'passport' principle. Provided there is common agreement on the minimum standards then a licence obtained in one EU member state should in principle be sufficient to qualify the licensee to sell its products/services in all EU countries. The two key pieces of European legislation affecting the banking sector have been the First and Second Banking Directives.

18.15   The First Banking Directive 1977

The First Banking Directive represented an attempt by the European Commission to achieve some degree of liberalization of the banking sector in Europe. In particular, it aimed to end restrictions on the setting up of foreign branches by a bank in another Community country and to ensure the principle of free establishment.

The Directive covered the coordination of national laws, regulation and administrative procedures relating to the setting up of banking activity. A bank was free to establish a branch or subsidiary in another member state provided the branch or subsidiary operated under the supervision of the host country. Significantly, the range of products that the branch could offer was limited by the host country's legislation. Overall, the Directive aimed to create equal regulation of domestic and foreign banks within a member state whilst allowing different regulations to exist between the member states.

18.16 The Second Banking Directive 1989

The Second Banking Directive was adopted in 1989 and aimed at establishing a list of banking activities which would be covered by the principle of mutual recognition as from January 1993. The Directive defines what constitutes a bank that is free to operate in all member states, and the regulatory environment covering banks with operations in more than one member state. To this purpose the Second Banking Directive established a so-called single banking licence that was valid throughout the entire EU. Once an institution is authorized to pursue banking business by one member state, then the bank may conduct similar operations and activities (provided the activities are on an approved list) in any member state. The bank would have the freedom to do this without requiring further authorization from the host state and regardless of whether the activities are allowed in the host country.

The Directive established minimum requirements as to the size of funds required of credit institutions (five million European Currency Units), eliminated the need to maintain separate capital for the operation of foreign branches, limited bank holdings of shares in other financial and non-financial firms and provided for the exchange of information between the home and host country's supervisory authorities.

The responsibility for the supervision of financial institutions with foreign branches was to be shared between the home country and the host country. However, the Directive placed most of the responsibility on the home country, although cooperation between authorities was also envisaged:

> responsibility for the financial soundness of a credit institution, and in particular for its solvency, will rest with the competent authorities of its home Member State . . . whereas, the host country authorities retain responsibility for matters relating to liquidity and the implementation of monetary policy . . . supervision of market risk should be the subject of close cooperation between the competent authorities of the home and host countries. (Steinherr, 1992, p. 11)

The Second Banking Directive represented a significant departure from the First Banking Directive with a clear shift in regulatory responsibility from the host to the home country. Furthermore, the ability of foreign branches to offer a range of products based upon what was permissible in the home country was a significant departure from being limited to offering only what was permissible in the host country.

18.17   International regulation: the Basel I Accord 1988

The growing internationalization of finance has made the question of international financial regulation a major issue. Banks and other financial institutions increasingly interact with their counterparts in other countries. This raises the possibility that the failure of a foreign bank would create significant problems for domestic banks. The failures of Bankhaus Herstaatt and Franklin National in 1974 led to an increased interest in prudential supervision at the international level. In addition, many banks have foreign subsidiaries and regulators are keen to ensure that these do not escape effective regulatory controls. The issue of whether the home country or the host country should be responsible for supervising the subsidiary is one obvious issue that is raised.

The Basel Committee on Banking Regulation and Supervisory Practice, which consists of senior central bank officials from the G10 countries, conducted a review of capital adequacy provisions of banks internationally, and the result was the Basel Accord. The Basel Accord of 1988 had the overall aim of ensuring the soundness and stability of the international banking system. The main method of achieving this was to set a minimum capital adequacy ratio on all banks so the risk and impact of the collapse of any bank on the system as a whole would be reduced. There was perceived to be a danger that, in the absence of some degree of global coordination, competition between banks for international business would lead to a dilution of national capital adequacy ratios. In turn, this could ultimately lead to a scenario where both the risks and impact of a bank failure would rise appreciably and endanger the international banking system. The specific aims of the Basel Accord were to:

1 ensure greater consistency of capital adequacy ratios between banks of different countries; and
2 try and improve capital adequacy standards to reflect the risk profile of different banks.

The resulting capital adequacy guidelines were required to be implemented from January 1994. They attempt to deal with credit risk by segmenting and weighting capital requirements. All banks were expected to maintain a capital ratio that is risk-weighted on the basis of their assets, so that if they have to write off some of their assets the bank would not be endangered.

Under the Basel Accord, bank capital is separated into two tiers. Tier 1 capital or 'core capital' consists of common stock equity, certain preferred stock, net reserves, and minority interests in consolidated subsidiaries. Tier 2 capital or 'supplementary' capital consists of loan-loss reserves, certain preferred stock, perpetual debt (that is debt with no maturity date), hybrid capital instruments, subordinated debt and equity contract notes. The guidelines established a five-category credit risk weighting for bank assets; the more risky an asset is perceived to be, the greater the weight attached to it. The five categories are 0 per cent risk, 10 per cent risk, 20 per cent risk, 50 per cent risk and 100 per cent risk. In addition, off-balance-sheet activities are converted and taken into account when assessing the risk weighting.

Tier 1 capital the core capital supporting the lending and deposit activities of a bank; it consists primarily of common stock, retained earnings and perpetual preferred stock

Tier 2 capital the additional capital above Tier 1 capital supporting the lending and deposit activities of a bank; it includes limited life preferred stock, subordinated debt and loan-loss reserves

Table 18.1   Risk weighting under the Basel Accord (£millions)

	BANK A			BANK B		
	Asset value	Risk weight	Product	Asset value	Risk weight	Product
Treasury bills and cash	1000	0	0	1000	0	0
Local authority bonds	2000	0.20	400	500	0.20	100
Mortgage loans	1000	0.50	500	1500	0.50	750
Business loans	1000	1.00	1000	2000	1.00	2000
	5000		1900	5000		2850

In **Table 18.1** the hypothetical asset structure of two banks is illustrated by banks A and B, both of which have £5 billion worth of assets. Both have £1 billion of holdings in Treasury bills and cash, but thereafter there are differences in their asset portfolios. Bank A has a less risky asset portfolio than bank B, with more of its assets in relatively safe local authority bonds and less in more risky assets such as mortgage and commercial loans. The risk-adjusted weighted assets for bank A are £1,900 million while bank B has a higher risk-adjusted asset portfolio of £2,850 million. The guidelines established a minimum Tier 1 'core-capital' requirement of 4 per cent of risk-adjusted capital, which for bank A would be 0.04 × £1,900 million = £76 million, and a minimum total, that is Tier 1 plus Tier 2, of risk-adjusted assets of 8 per cent, which would be 0.08 × £1900 million = £152 million. To reflect its higher risk profile, bank B is required to hold more capital: it must have Tier 1 capital of 0.04 × £2,850 million = £114 million and a minimum total, that is Tier 1 plus Tier 2, capital of risk-adjusted assets of 8 per cent, that is 0.08 × £2850 million = £228 million.

The Basel I Accord represented the first attempt to ensure some degree of global regulation of the banking system, and as such was a significant landmark. Inevitably, however, it was a far from perfect system and a number of criticisms were made of the guidelines:

1   The weighting system was to some extent arbitrary. It is not at all evident that a commercial loan to a triple-A-rated company should require double the risk weighting attached to mortgage loans.
2   All commercial loans are treated as equally risky; lending to a triple-A-rated company was given the same risk weighting as a loan to a triple-B-rated company, or even a new start-up company.
3   The guidelines treated banks in all economies in a similar fashion, but it is not difficult to argue that in some economies bank assets are clearly more risky than in other countries. In consequence, banks in relatively stable economies were forced to hold similar amounts of capital to those that operate in less stable economies.
4   The guidelines to some extent led some banks to sell off some of their riskier bank loans in the secondary market so as to reduce their capital reserve requirements, and lending priorities were being distorted by the regulatory requirements.

5　The guidelines dealt with certain risks such as off-balance-sheet risks, but ignored others such as currency exposure risk which occurs when a bank has a mismatch between its assets and liabilities in different currencies. Another potential risk ignored by the guidelines was exposure risk, which rises when a bank has a high proportion of its loan book concentrated on just a few major companies or over-exposure to a particular sector of the economy (for example the property sector). A poorly diversified bank is generally more at risk than one with a less diversified loan book.

6　While the guidelines tackled the question of capital adequacy they neglected the crucial question of liquidity, leaving the international banking system with potential exposure to some form of liquidity crisis.

One of the biggest problems since the Basel Accord came into operation in 1992 is what is known as regulatory arbitrage. Banks in the UK, the USA and Germany sold off assets such as credit card business for which they felt Basel I required too high a capital requirement (compared to the riskiness) and retained assets on which they felt the capital adequacy ratios of Basel I were too low relative to their assessment of the risk. The result has been that capital adequacy in the three countries actually rose from around 10–10.5 per cent in 1992 to 12–13 per cent in 2003, well above the required 8 per cent.

As a result of these problems there was a recognition that a modified framework to tackle the issue of capital adequacy was required, and starting in 1999 the Bank for International Settlements undertook a number of studies to investigate a new approach to the capital adequacy issue. The result was the adoption in June 2004 of the so-called Basel II Accord.

> **regulatory arbitrage**
> the taking advantage of differences in regulatory treatment across countries, different financial sectors and different financial instruments by financial institutions such as banks to reduce the amount of capital they are required to hold

18.18　The Basel II Accord 2004

Like the Basel I Accord, Basel II required capital to be at least 8 per cent of risk-weighted assets. The Basel II Accord allowed for some modifications to Basel I, but introduced greater flexibility by allowing approved banks to utilize their own risk-management models to ensure sufficient capital adequacy subject to certain minimum requirements. The Basel II Accord is based upon the so-called three pillars:

- *Pillar 1: minimum capital requirements.* The Accord breaks regulatory capital into three parts to match credit risk, market risk and operational risk. The market risk deals with trading losses and is essentially the same as in Basel I. The operational risk element is new and represents the risk of loss resulting from inadequate or failed internal processes, people and systems, or from external events. Essentially the bank's capital needs to reflect the risk of mistakes and wrongdoing – for example a fine levied on the bank for overcharging credit card customers or losses due to a rogue trader. The main purpose of the Basel II Accord, however, was to improve banks' stability by tying their capital more closely to the riskiness of their assets. However, to introduce some flexibility banks are given the possibility of two approaches to ensure that they meet capital adequacy requirements.

1 The standardized approach – this is the approach prescribed by the Basel I Accord with some modifications to recognize the shortcomings of that approach. For example, lending to AAA companies would require a lower risk weighting than lending to BBB-rated companies. The weights to be assigned are generally more detailed than in Basel I.

2 The internal ratings based (IRB) approach – under this system approved banks are able to use their own risk-management models to determine the riskiness of their portfolios and therefore the amount of capital they need to allocate to protect themselves against potential losses. The internal ratings-based approach is itself divided into two possibilities – the Foundation IRB (F-IRB) or the Advanced IRB (A-IRB) – and banks adopting either of the IRB approaches will nonetheless still need to run the standardized approach in parallel for comparison and consistency and checking purposes.

internal ratings based approach
a methodology for calculating the amount of capital that a bank needs to hold as reserves based upon the bank's method of calculating the riskiness of its assets and trading positions

- Pillar 2: supervisory review process. Those banks opting for the IRB approach to credit risk will be required to test their models to prove the robustness of their capital adequacy and satisfy their supervisory bodies that they are sufficiently well protected against adverse economic and market conditions. Banks need to demonstrate that they are able to cope with a variety of adverse economic conditions and provide reports and modelling that satisfy their supervisory body that they have sufficient capital. In effect, Pillar 2 means that banks and their supervisors will have to take a view on whether the bank should hold additional capital against risks not covered in Pillar I.

- Pillar 3: market discipline. This requires a comprehensive range of information on capital and risk levels to be produced, covering all relevant portfolios within the bank as well as a guide to the bank's risk-management procedures and practices. The focus of such reports is the capital adequacy of the bank in relation to its assets and risks. The hope is that such disclosure by banks and the market reaction will act as a means of discipline on banks, encouraging them to better manage themselves with respect to dealing with credit risk, market risk and operational risk.

The Accord only covers 'internationally active' banks, with the USA applying it to only around a dozen of its banks with another dozen applying to be covered voluntarily (although it is estimated that the top 24 US banks comprise some 99 per cent of American banks' foreign exposure). By contrast, the European Union has decided that Basel II should apply to all EU banks whether 'internationally active' or not. It should be noted that countries like India and China have decided to opt out of Basel II entirely.

The Basel II Accord was implemented in stages by the end of 2006, with a year extension for US banks. However, it was quickly overtaken by the events of the credit crisis which started in August 2007. In particular, the credit crunch has revealed that risk management at banks was severely flawed and that the idea that banks' internal risk-based approach would be an appropriate framework after the crisis seems entirely inappropriate. Some argue that the new Accord exacerbated the problems of the credit crunch by forcing banks to cut lending and raise capital when the global economy was in recession.

18.19   Issues for regulatory reform raised by the credit crunch

The credit crunch and the extent of the failure of the banking system and problems revealed in financial institutions around the globe have meant that reform of the banking system and financial sector is a hot topic over the next few years, especially in the USA and the UK where the problems were shown to be the greatest. It is essential that a far more robust framework for the supervision and regulation of financial institutions is put in place. The key areas for reform include:

- The issue of capital adequacy – it is quite clear that 8 per cent risk-adjusted assets is too low to ensure banks can withstand the up and downs of the economy. Higher capital requirements for banks are needed, but how high is an open question. Some commentators have suggested that capital requirements should be countercyclical; that is, raised during times of economic expansion to limit credit growth and lowered during times of economic recession to encourage credit growth. In addition, some feel that the 'too big to fail' situation with large banks means that large banks should be forced to hold more capital and smaller banks that cannot meet those conditions should be allowed to fail. Such a policy would help to limit the call on taxpayers from large bank failures and also act as a constraint on larger banks' growth.
- Liquidity of financial institutions – a number of institutions failed during the credit crunch through a lack of liquidity. There may be a case for rules on maintaining levels of liquidity that adequately reflect the degree of liquidity risk that the financial institution may face in a crisis.
- Degree of leverage employed – while this will be difficult to regulate it is clear that the degree of leverage being employed by financial institutions prior to the credit crunch was too high. It is important to ensure that major financial institutions do not take on too much leverage and leave themselves vulnerable to a fall in the markets.
- Transparency in the over-the-counter market – the OTC market was at the centre of the financial crisis with the build-up of positions in CDOs (e.g. Lehman's) and CDSs (e.g. AIG) leading to unprecedented losses. The fact that no one knew precisely who had the losses and or their net positions in these instruments meant that interbank lending, the rolling over of debt and the raising of capital became extremely difficult at the height of the crisis. There have been calls for a centralized reporting clearing system for OTC instruments so that net positions can be reported.
- The role of the credit rating agencies – it is quite clear that the credit rating agencies played a crucial role in the crisis by their over-optimistic misrating of certain securities. The system by which credit rate agencies are paid to rate securities and structured finance products may encourage them to give more favourable ratings than the securities merit. Also the fact that there are only three key players – Moody's, Standard & Poor's and Fitch – means they have monopolistic powers, which is not healthy for the economy. The integral role of the rating agencies was enhanced in Basel II because the amount of regulatory capital that banks need to

hold was in part determined by the credit rating given by the agencies on debt the banks held.

- Renumeration in the financial sector – some of the pay packages in the financial sector seem to be extraordinarily high, with the link between pay and performance far from clear-cut. There is also concern that the culture of bonuses for short-term results contributed to excessive risk-taking and ultimately huge losses for the banks and the taxpayers that stepped in to save them from financial collapse, creating a long-term disaster for public finances.

- Reducing complexity and increasing transparency in the financial system – there is no doubt that some of the new innovations in the world of finance, such as CDOs and other structured finance products, became too complex. Lack of standardization made it difficult for market participants to understand the risks they were taking on and, thus, price them appropriately. Also the creation of off-balance-sheet entities, such as SPVs/SPEs and SIVs, made it unclear which banks were holding the real risks. Measures designed to reduce complexity and increase transparency are likely to be at the forefront of the regulatory reform process. Greater standardization of financial securities and products and better reporting of banks' balance sheets and off-balance-sheet exposures are essential elements in this regard.

- The size and degree of interdependence of financial institutions – the credit crisis showed that some institutions were deemed to be too large and in some cases too interconnected with other financial institutions to be allowed to fail. There will be attempts to limit the size and degree of interdependence of financial institutions so that individual institutions can be allowed to fail without creating too much mayhem in the financial system.

- Consumer and investor protection – safeguards will need to be enhanced. In particular, deposit guarantee systems need to ensure that deposits are returned speedily to depositors. Also, the subprime crisis highlighted the problem of 'predatory lending', with consumers being encouraged to take on more debt than they could realistically expected to manage, which ultimately proved costly to all parties involved. Conversely it is important to make sure that investors are not so protected that they are insulated from risk in their financial decisions.

- Regulations on non-bank financial institutions – the problems for US and foreign banks that resulted from American International Group's writing of CDSs showed how interconnected the modern-day financial system is. Indeed, many hedge funds also bought and sold CDSs and CDOs that were at the heart of the crisis. Some hedge funds were merely subsidiaries of investment banks, and their losses hit the parent bank, as in the case of Bear Stearns and Union Bank of Switzerland. As such, there is a need to look at the systemic risks posed by non-bank financial institutions and the regulatory framework.

- The regulatory framework – there have been real question marks about the division of regulatory powers between the various agencies, the extent of their powers and the quality of their staff. In the USA the Securities Exchange Commission was heavily criticized for its faulure to detect the Madoff ponzi scheme.

It is clear that the credit crunch has raised many issues that need to be closely examined to avoid a repetition in the future. But new rules alone will not be sufficient; there will also be a need for effective supervisory bodies with strong surveillance and enforcement powers, as well as enhanced powers for risk mangers within financial institutions.

Who is responsible for regulation? The credit crisis highlighted another issue that needs to be clarified: who is responsible for regulating what? In the USA there are five key regulatory bodies: the Federal Reserve, the Federal Deposit Insurance Corporation, the Securities Exchange Commission, the Office of Comptroller of the Currency and the Office of Thrift Supervision. Insurance companies are regulated at the State level and hedge funds are largely unregulated. During the crisis, the Federal Reserve stepped in to bail out Bear Stearns and AIG, even though it was not responsible for their regulation. The decision to let Lehman go under but to rescue AIG on the following day showed a lack of consistency in the decision-making process. Similarly, in the UK, where there is a tripartite regulatory system comprising the Bank of England, the Financial Services Authority and the Treasury, the Treasury stepped in to deal with Northern Rock and Bradford & Bingley, even though the FSA was the regulator.

18.20   Conclusions

Regulation of the financial services industry is a fascinating topic. Huge regulatory issues at the domestic, European and global levels have been raised by the recent financial crisis. These affairs are very much in a state of flux and their resolution will need urgent reform and attention. At the domestic level, there are issues such as the fair treatment of different segments of the financial sector to ensure healthy competition, investor protection and to strike an appropriate balance between statutory and self-regulation. At the European level, there is the problem of opening up the financial services sector in different member states to competition from other member states, and striking an appropriate balance between home and host-country regulation. In addition, achieving a common framework for the regulation of financial services in the EU remains a quite distant ambition. At the global level, the major concern is to ensure the stability of the international banking system and a desire to promote freer global trade in financial services.

An important final point worth remembering about the regulation of financial institutions is that no amount of regulation will prevent malpractice or mismanagement unless there are adequate supervision and control mechanisms in place. In this sense, the internal control procedures and checks within a financial institution are probably as important as any statutory regulation by outside bodies. One simply cannot expect outside regulatory and supervisory bodies to be sufficiently abreast of all the developments within a financial institution to prevent all potential crises developing.

Further reading

Buckley, R. (2008) *International Financial System: Policy and Regulation*, Kluwer Law International.

Busch, A. (2009) *Banking Regulation and Globalization*, Oxford University Press.

Eatwell, J. and Taylor, L. (2001) *Global Finance at Risk: The Case for International Regulation*, New Press.

Padoa-Schioppa, T. (2004) *Regulating Finance: Balancing Freedom and Risk*, Oxford University Press.

Schooner, H. and Taylor, M. (2010) *Regulation of Global Banking: Principles and Policies*, Academic Press.

Palaez, C. (2010) *Regulation of Banks and Finance: Theory and Policy After the Credit Crisis*, Palgrave.

Spencer, P.D. (2000) *The Structure and Regulation of Financial Markets*, Oxford University Press.

Steinherr, A. (1992) *The New European Financial Market Place*, Longman.

Chapter 18	Revision questions

1 Discuss the rationale for government intervention in financial markets, making reference to the problems of externalities, asymmetric information, moral hazard and the principal–agent issue.

2 Briefly discuss the differences between structural, prudential and investor protection regulations.

3 Discuss the different types of regulations that are imposed on banks by the regulatory authorities.

4 What are the pros and cons of self-regulation compared to statutory regulation of financial institutions?

5 What were main provisions of the Second Banking Directive of 1989 and what new concept did it introduce compared to the First Banking Directive of 1977?

6 What were the main provisions of the 1988 Basel Accord and what criticisms have been levelled against the Accord?

7 What is the key thinking behind the Basel II Accord?

8 Discuss four key issues for regulatory reform in the light of the credit crunch.

Multiple choice questions available at **www.palgrave.com/business/pilbeam**

GLOSSARY

This glossary provides a set of terms that are commonly used. It is not exhaustive and some of the terms are not used in the book but provided here for information.

AAA the highest credit rating that can be issued. It implies that bonds issued by the issuer are extremely safe with a very low probability of default.

Abnormal return a return in excess of what could be expected given the risk characteristics of a security.

Active management the buying and selling of securities in a way that is designed to achieve high levels of returns compared to passive management or just tracking an index.

Adjustable rate mortgage a mortgage on which the interest payable is reset periodically in line with changes in a predetermined benchmark plus a spread. The initial rate of interest is normally fixed for the first 2 to 3 years on a 30-year mortgage.

Adverse selection a market process in which 'bad' customers who present themselves to financial institutions are more likely to be accepted due to the problem of asymmetric information. For example, if a bank raises its interest rate it will tend to attract more poor quality customers who do not intend to repay.

Allocative efficiency the efficiency with which the capital markets allocate scarce capital funds to the most productive uses.

Allotment policy the policy of distributing shares from an initial public offering to underwriters and investors.

Alpha a term used by fund managers to describe the difference between the actual returns earned on a portfolio and the return you would have expected to make on that investment given its risk, for example by using the CAPM model. A positive alpha means the manager has 'beaten the market' and a negative alpha means the manager has 'underperformed the market'.

Alt-A mortgage a mortgage with a risk profile between prime and subprime mortgages. The person taking on an Alt-A mortgage will normally have a clean credit record but the mortgage will have some characteristics that make it potentially risky, like a high loan-to-value ratio or a high loan-to-income ratio.

Alternative Investment Market (AIM) a market for smaller companies that may not meet the listing requirements of the main UK Stock Exchange. The market was set up in June 1995.

American depository receipt a security that is traded on the American stock exchange which represents an underlying share in a foreign company that is not formally listed on the US Stock Exchange.

American option an option that can be exercised at any time prior to maturity.

Annuity a policy which makes a series of fixed payments over a specified period of time.

Arbitrage the process of exploiting a pricing anomaly to make riskless guaranteed profits.

Arbitrageur a person that seeks to exploit a pricing anomaly to make riskless profits. In practice the term can be used to describe risk-taking individuals/funds that take on risky takeovers.

Asian option an option whose payoff depends upon the average price of the underlying over a specified period of time rather than a traditional option whose payoff depends upon the price of the underlying upon maturity. Also known as an average option.

Asset backed security (ABS) a security that is backed by real underlyings or cash flows. If the underlying cash flows are collateralized by real estate it is called a mortgage backed security.

Asset Protection Scheme (APS) a UK government scheme announced in February 2009 whereby, in return for an insurance premium, participating banks are able to insure a large part of their loan books against future losses.

Assurance part of the insurance business dealing with life insurance and pensions.

Asymmetric information a situation in which one party to a transaction has superior information compared to the other party.

At-the-money option an option whose strike price is the same as the price of the underlying.

Back office the part of a financial institution that deals with accounting, settlement, record maintenance etc.

Backwardation an arbitrage opportunity that occurs when one market-maker's selling (offer) price rate is less than another's buy (bid) price. In normal market conditions the selling price is above the bid price.

Backward compatibility the need for new information technology, such as computers and software, to work with existing older technology in order to service existing clients.

Balance sheet an accounting statement of a company's assets and liabilities and net worth.

Bancassurance a French term used to describe banks involved in the selling of insurance products along with traditional deposit and lending services.

Bank for International Settlements (BIS) based in Basel and known as the central banker's bank since it specializes in central banking issues and the stability of the financial system.

Bank run a situation in which many of a bank's customers rush to withdraw their deposits placing the bank in jeopardy since its reserves may not be sufficient to meet the withdrawals.

Bankers acceptance a short-term draft by a company to pay a certain sum of money in the future. It is guaranteed for payment by a bank once it has been stamped 'accepted' and can thereafter be traded on the secondary markets at a discount to its face value.

Bankruptcy a situation where an individual or company is unable to repay its debts.

Barrier option an option whose payoff depends upon whether or not the underlying price has passed a particular point.

Basel I Accord a 1988 global accord requiring major banks to hold minimum amounts of Tier 1 and Tier 2 capital equal to 8 per cent of their risk-adjusted assets.

Basel II Accord a 2004 comprehensive revision of the Basel I Accord. Pillar I of the Accord covers the minimum capital adequacy standards for banks. Pillar II focuses on enhancing the supervisory review process. Pillar III encourages market discipline through increased disclosure of banks' financial condition.

Basis point one-hundredth of one per cent, i.e. 0.01%, e.g. 5 basis points = 0.05%.

Basis risk the risk that a particular hedging strategy will not work as well as intended because the futures/options positions and cash market may not move to exactly offset the hedged risk.

Basis swap a swap in which both parties to the swap exchange floating rate of interest payments, but the base contract is different; for example, one may be based on dollar LIBOR and the other on US Treasury bill rates.

Bear a pessimist who thinks that the prices of shares/bonds or other securities/assets will fall in price.

Bear market a market in which security prices fall by a substantial amount. In the USA a fall in the S&P 500 or Dow Jones by 20 per cent or more is often classified as a bear market.

Bearer bond a bond whose coupon and principal are payable to whoever is in possession; there is no central register of the bond's ownership.

Benchmark bond usually a government bond, the interest upon which provides a benchmark to measure the performance of other bonds such as corporate bonds. For international comparisons the yield on 10-year government bonds is often used.

Beta a measure of a security's sensitivity to market movements or systematic risk. A share with a beta of 1 tends to move by a similar percentage to the market; one with a beta of 2 tends to move up or down twice as much as the market over time.

Bid–ask spread the amount by which the ask rate exceeds the bid rate, e.g. a bid rate of £10 and ask rate of £11 implies a bid–ask spread of £1.

Bid rate the rate at which a dealer buys a security, e.g. bank deposit, bonds, foreign exchange, shares; it will be lower than the offer (ask or selling) rate.

Big bang a term used to describe the deregulation of the UK Stock Exchange in October 1986.

Bill of exchange a signed promise by the receiver of goods/services to the supplier to pay a certain sum of money. The supplier may sell the bills at a discount to a third party.

Black–Scholes formula a model used to price a European call option premium which was published in 1973 by Fisher Black and Myron Scholes.

Blue chip a term used to describe the shares of a well known and well regarded company. The company will have a good track record.

Bond a security issued by a borrower in return for funds which has longer than one year to maturity. The issuer agrees to pay the bond buyer a series of cash flows over the life of the bond.

Book value the net asset value of a company, that is, the value of tangible assets (excluding intangible assets) less liabilities.

Bretton Woods a fixed but adjustable exchange rate system agreed at Bretton Woods in 1944 in which major currencies were pegged to the US dollar ± 1% either side of an assigned central parity. Also set up the International Monetary Fund and the World Bank.

Broad money supply the narrow money supply plus demand deposits held by the banking system and certain interest rate yielding deposit accounts.

Broker an agent (individual or firm) that buys/sells securities on behalf of a client in return for a fee.

Bubble a term used to describe fast dramatic price rises of shares or something else that is likely to prove unsustainable.

Bull an optimist who thinks that the prices of shares/bonds or other securities/assets will rise in price.

Bull market a market which experiences strong sustained price rises.

Bulldog a bond issued by a foreign entity on the UK market in pounds.

Bund a German government bond.

Business risk the risk that company profits will fall by more than sales.

Buy-and-hold a passive investment strategy in which one buys shares etc and holds onto them through market fluctuations in the belief that they will perform well in the long term.

Buy back a deal whereby one party to a futures contract pays or receives a sum of money from the other party to the contract to cancel the future obligations inherent in the Swap contract.

Cable a term used by dealers to describe the pound in terms of the dollar on the foreign exchange market.

Call back feature a clause giving the issuer of a security the right to redeem the security prior to maturity.

Call money money lent by banks to other banks/security houses that can be recalled at noon each day.

Call option the right but not the obligation to buy a security/commodity/asset at a predetermined price.

Call provision a clause giving the issuer of a security the right to redeem the security prior to maturity.

Callable swap a swap that allows one of the parties the right to extend the contract for a specified period.

Cap an agreement between a borrower and a lender to set an upper limit to the interest rate payable on a loan.

Capital adequacy the amount of capital needed by a financial institution to cover potential losses.

Capital adequacy ratio a ratio of a bank's capital to its weighted risk-adjusted assets.

Capital asset pricing model (CAPM) a model that is used to determine the expected rate of return on a security, based on its risk characteristics as measured by its beta.

Capital market a market where economic agents such as governments and firms raise capital for more than a year and where such financial securities are traded, such as the equity and bond markets.

Capital market line a straight line passing through the risk-free rate of return and the expected rate of return on the market portfolio with risk measured by the standard deviation on the horizontal axis and the rate of return on the vertical axis.

Capitalization the market capitalization of a company is the number of shares times the price per share.

Cash reserve ratio the amount of cash held by banks in relation to their total deposits.

Cash settlement a method of settling futures or options contracts via a cash transfer between the losing and winning party, rather than actual delivery of the underlying asset/security.

CBOE Chicago Board Options Exchange.

CBOT Chicago Board of Trade.

CDO see collateralized debt obligation

CDO squared a collateralized debt obligation whose underlying assets are slices of other collateralized debt obligations.

CDS see credit default swap

Certificate of deposit a certificate which certifies that a deposit of a certain amount has been made at a bank and specifies the interest to be paid. Usually issued by a commercial bank. Can be used as collateral for a loan.

Chartist a person that uses chart patterns on past prices of a security to forecast future price changes in financial markets.

Cheapest-to-deliver bond a bond whose price is the cheapest to deliver in fulfilment of a bond futures contract upon expiry.

Chinese wall a barrier put in place by a financial institution to prevent conflicts of interest within the institution.

Chooser option an option the holder of which has the choice of whether it is a put or call option at a given point of time.

Clean price the price of a bond excluding the accrued interest since the last coupon payment.

Clearing house a central body that clears and guarantees futures and options contracts and monitors the positions of parties to the contracts.

CME Chicago Mercantile Exchange.

Collar a contractual limit within which the interest rate on a loan or the exchange rate on a contract may lie, e.g. 8%–10% or $1.25/£1 to $1.30/£1. As such it is a combination of a cap and a floor.

Collateralized debt obligation (CDO) an asset-backed security that is divided up into different tranches with each tranche having different risk–return characteristics. The junior tranches have higher risk and higher rates of return than the senior tranches. A CDO is collateralized because the underlyings (e.g. loans, mortgage) are used as collateral to pay the buyers of the various tranches of the CDO.

Collateralized loan obligation (CLO) a collateralized debt obligation whose underlying assets are the cash flows from non-mortgage related loans such as auto loans, student loans, consumer bank loans etc.

Collateralized mortgage obligation (CMO) a collateralized debt obligation whose underlying assets are the cash flows from a variety of bonds such as corporate and government bonds.

Common equity total shareholders' equity minus preferred equity.

Commercial bank a bank that is primarily involved in the traditional line of banking, that is, taking in deposits and making loans.

Commercial paper unsecured short-term debt issued by a corporation of usually 270 days or less duration. It is sold at a discount to its face value. A major benefit of commercial paper is that it does not need to be registered with the Securities Exchange Commission.

Common stock an American term for ordinary shares which confer ownership rights of the company and entitle the owner to voting rights and a share of the profits. However, as an owner the stock holder is last in line if the company is liquidated.

Comparative advantage swap a swap between two parties in which one of the parties has an absolute advantage at raising funds at both fixed and floating rates of interest but its advantage is greater in one of the markets.

Conduit a government or private sector entity that pools mortgages and other loans enabling banks and other financial institutions to on-sell their mortgages or loans to investors.

Contingent CDS a payout on a CDS that requires both a credit event and an additional trigger. The additional trigger could be a credit event by another reference entity or a specified price movement in some market security.

Contractionary OMO an open market operation that decreases the narrow money supply and raises the short-term interest rate.

Convertible bond a bond that can be converted into either shares or some other asset at some point.

Corporate bond a bond issued by a company to investors, with the yield depending in part on the credit rating of the company.

Counterparty risk the risk that a counterparty to a contract will fail to settle the contract.

Coupon the rate of interest payable on a bond when issued. Usually paid semi-annually.

Covenant a clause in a bond contract requiring a firm to do certain things and also not do some other things.

Covered interest rate parity a formula used by banks to calculate a forward exchange rate quotation.

Credit crunch a steep reduction in the volume of funds available for loans and credit in the economy. In this situation even cuts in official interest rates fail to return credit to more normal levels.

Credit default swap (CDS) a credit derivative with a payout which is triggered by a 'credit event', typically a default. CDS payout involves either 'physical' or cash settlement. With 'physical settlement' the protection seller buys a defaulted reference asset from the protection buyer at its face value. With 'cash settlement' the protection seller pays the protection buyer an amount equal to the difference between the face value of the reference asset face and the current secondary market price of the defaulted asset.

Credit derivative a financial contract under which an agent buys or sells risk protection against the credit risk associated with a specific reference entity (or entities). For a periodic fee, the protection seller agrees to make a contingent payment to the buyer on the occurrence of a credit event (usually default in the case of a credit default swap).

Credit event a negative event that impacts adversely upon a borrower's credit rating such as a failure to make payments due to a bankruptcy filing or a violation of the borrowers obligations.

Credit rating an assessment of a company's credit worthiness, that is, its ability to repay its debt. The two main credit rating agencies are Moody's and Standard & Poor's.

Cross rate the rate of exchange between two currencies implied by their exchange rates vis-à-vis a third currency, e.g. $1.80/£1 and $1.20/€1 implies a cross rate of €1.50/£1.

Crowding out the idea that the expansionary effects of an increase in government expenditure will to some extent be offset by a decrease in private consumption and investment and possibly exports.

Cumulative dividend a limitation placed upon a company which ensures the payment of preferred dividends before making distributions to common shareholders. If a company fails to make a dividend payment to a preferred shareholder with a cumulative dividend, the company is required to catch up the payment before any other payments can be made to common shareholders.

Currency futures an agreement between two parties to buy/sell a specified amount of an underlying currency at a predetermined price at a predetermined date in the future.

Currency option an option that gives the holder the right but not the obligation to buy/sell a particular currency at a predetermined rate at a given point in time.

Currency swap a swap that involves the two parties exchanging cash flows in two different currencies.

Debenture in the UK, a bond secured against assets; in the USA and Canada, an unsecured bond backed only by the credit worthiness of the issuer.

Debt an amount of money borrowed by one party from another. Government debt is borrowed via the issue of Treasury bonds and bills while corporate debt is borrowed from financial institutions via the issue of corporate bonds or commercial paper.

Debt–equity ratio the ratio of a firm's debt to its equity.

Default the situation when an economic agent fails to meet a contractual payment of interest or principal.

Default risk the risk that an economic agent (company, government or individual) will not pay the interest and/or principal on a debt obligation.

Deficit agents economic agents (individuals, business and governments) that need to borrow funds due to their expenditure being greater than their income.

Delivery month the month in which a contract expires and delivery of the underlying is required or the contract is settled for cash.

Deposit institution an institution such as a bank or savings institution that accepts cash deposits which can be either sight or term deposits.

Deregulation the reduction or elimination of regulations designed to increase competition and reduce prices facing consumers.

Derivative a contract the price of which is derived from the price of an underlying; examples of derivatives are futures, forwards, options and swaps.

Devaluation under a fixed exchange-rate regime a situation in which a currency is devalued to a new lower value against another currency.

Dirty price the price of a bond including the accrued interest.

Discount the difference between the lower price paid for a security and its face value on issue. For example, a Treasury bill with a face value of $1,000 is sold at $970 implying a discount of $30.

Disintermediation the process of borrowing or lending by a company without going to a bank; for example, issuing a corporate bond rather than taking out a bank loan.

Distant contracts futures contracts with longer terms to expiration than the nearby contract.

Dividend a cash payout per share to shareholders announced by a company's board.

Dividend discount model a model for valuing shares.

Dividend payout ratio the proportion of earnings net of taxation and interest paid out in dividends.

Dividend yield the annual dividend per annum as a percentage of the share price.

Domestic bond a bond issued in the domestic currency by a domestic entity.

Dow Jones Industrial Average a price-weighted index of 30 major US companies. The index was originally based on 12 stocks and created by Charles Dow in 1896, the modern index of 30 companies began in 1928.

Dragon bond a dollar-denominated bond issued in Asia.

Duration a measure of the sensitivity of a bond's price to changes in bond yields.

Earnings the profits of a company over a specified period of time, usually after tax.

Earnings per share the earnings net of taxation, interest payments (and dividends on preference shares) divided by the number of outstanding ordinary shares.

Earnings yield earnings per share (net of tax) as a percentage of the share price.

Efficiency frontier a curve depicting dominant risk–return portfolios with increased return only achievable by increasing risk.

Efficient diversification the process of investing in a variety of securities and assets taking into account the covariances and variances of the securities and assets to achieve optimal risk–return portfolios.

Efficient market hypothesis (EMH) a theory that says security prices reflect all available information thus making it difficult for investors to make abnormal returns.

Emerging market the market of a country which is experiencing rapid economic growth but whose income per capita usually makes it a low- to middle-income economy.

Equity shares which represent ownership of a company.

Equity risk premium the expected excess return above the risk-free rate of interest which is required to compensate for the riskiness of investing in shares.

Equity tranche the riskiest slice of a collateralized debt obligation offering the highest prospective rate of return.

Estimated volume the daily estimated volume of trades in a security or derivatives contract.

EUREX the European Exchange which is a merger of the German DTB exchange and the Swiss SOFFEX exchange.

Euro LIBOR the London interbank offer (lending) interest rate on the euro.

Eurobank a bank that specializes in making short-term deposits and loans in a variety of foreign currencies.

Eurobond a bond denominated in a different currency to the country of issue; for example, a dollar bond issued in London is a dollar-denominated Eurobond.

Eurocurrency a short-term deposit/loan made outside of the country of that currency; for example, a three-month yen deposit/loan made in London.

Eurodollar a short-term deposit or loan made in dollars outside the United States.

Euronote a short-term promissory note issued by a high quality corporate, financial or sovereign borrower.

European option an option that can only be exercised upon maturity.

Event study analysis of the impact of a particular type of announcement (for example, takeover bid, merger, earnings announcement, change in dividend policy, profit warning, dissemination of a buy recommendation in the press) on the share prices of a group of firms for a period both prior to the announcement and after the announcement (for example, 30 days before and 30 days after).

Exchange clearing house a separate body of a derivatives exchange which is responsible for settling contracts, monitoring and reporting on trading positions and collecting margin payments. It will also guarantee to fulfil a contract should one party to a contract default on its obligations.

Exchange rate the rate at which one currency can be exchanged for another.

Exchange rate overshooting the phenomenon that a currency may appreciate or depreciate following an economic shock in the short run by a greater percentage than required in the long run, so that it 'overshoots' its long-run value.

Exchange rate risk the risk of losses due to adverse movement in the exchange rate.

Exchange traded fund (ETF) an investment vehicle made up of assets such as shares, bonds, commodities or currencies that trades on an exchange on a continuous basis with the price of the ETF trading very close to the value of the underlyings that make up the ETF.

Exercise price the price at which an option may be exercised; also known as the strike price.

Exotic option an option which has special features compared to standard put/call options.

Expected rate of return the forecast rate of return from holding a security expressed as a percentage per annum.

Expected volatility the volatility expected by an option trader. It varies from trader to trader based upon their individual forecasts.

Factoring agency usually a subsidiary of a bank that specializes in buying trade debts at a discount to the face value; this helps provide companies with cash flow more speedily.

FDIC Federal Deposit Insurance Corporation, a US corporation that insures US bank deposits up to the value of $250,000. It was created in 1933 to maintain public confidence in the banking system.

Federal Funds rate an overnight interest rate at which one US bank lends funds to another. The Federal Reserve Open Market Committee sets a target for such interest rates at its FOMC meeting.

Federal Reserve Bank the central bank of the USA; it is made up of 12 Regional Reserve Banks that carry out the monetary policy set by the FOMC.

Financial contagion the transfer of an economic shock from one entity to another or one country to another.

Financial innovation the design of new financial securities and methods of delivering financial services.

Financial intermediation the process of transferring funds from economic agents with excess funds to those that need to acquire funds.

Financial market a generic term describing a marketplace for buying and selling financial securities/assets such as equities, bonds, foreign exchange and derivative instruments.

Fiscal stimulus the use of increases in government expenditure and/or cuts in taxes to increase aggregate demand in an economy.

Fixed exchange rate a system whereby the exchange rate is fixed against another currency at a given target exchange rate (with small deviations usually allowed). The central bank of that currency commits itself to buy or sell the currency as appropriate to maintain the fixed rate.

Fixed recovery CDS a credit default swap that fixes the amount of the payoff to be made should a credit event occur. The fixed recovery CDS therefore removes uncertainty over the payoff for both the protection buyer and protection seller.

Flight to quality a term used to describe a situation in which investors decide to sell risky securities and use the proceeds to buy what are regarded as safer securities.

Floating rate note (FRN) a bond (note) that has a variable coupon or rate of interest; for example, it may be expressed at 1% above dollar LIBOR and will fluctuate according to changes in dollar LIBOR.

Footsie a term used to describe the FTSE 100 share index.

Foreign bond a bond issued in the domestic currency of the country of issue but by a foreign entity; for example, IBM (a US company) issues a sterling bond in London.

Foreign exchange market a global marketplace made up of banks and dealers/brokers where differing national currencies are bought and sold in spot and derivatives markets, including forwards and futures and other derivatives markets.

Forward contract a contract to buy/sell a security or commodity at a predetermined price and at a predetermined date in the future.

Forward/forward an agreement to lend/borrow money at a predetermined interest rate in the future for a given amount of time; for example, an agreement to lend/borrow $1 million for three months in six months' time at 4%.

Forward discount a measure expressed as a percentage per amount of the spot rate by which a currency is weaker in the forward market than in the spot market.

Forward exchange rate the exchange rate between two currencies quoted for a given date in the future. There are a variety of forward rates quoted, for example, 1 month, 3 month, 6 months and 1 year rates.

Forward premium a measure, expressed as a percentage per annum of the spot rate, by which a currency is stronger in the forward market than in the spot market.

Forward rate swap an agreement between two parties to do a swap which will take place at a predetermined date in the future.

Free cash flow the amount of net cash generated by a company after paying ongoing expenses.

Frontier markets countries with stockmarkets that are less developed than emerging markets.

FSA Financial Services Authority, a financial regulator in the UK.

FTSE 100 an index of 100 of the largest capitalization company shares listed on the UK market.

Fund manager the person responsible for investing the assets of a unit trust/mutual fund and investment strategy.

Futures contract a standardized agreement to buy/sell a security at a predetermined price at a given date in the future.

Gearing the ratio of a company's debt to equity.

Generally accepted accounting principles (GAAP) the US system of rules, procedures and conventions governing the reporting of accounts by companies.

Gilts the name used to describe bonds issued by the UK Treasury. The name comes from the fact that they used to be issued with gilt edges.

Glass Steagall Act a piece of legislation passed by Congress in 1933 prohibiting commercial banks from engaging in investment banking activities.

Global depository receipt (GDR) a security issued in a foreign country which represents ownership of shares in a foreign company. The shares are held by the issuer of the receipt and they trade like domestic shares in the market in which they are traded. See also American depository receipt.

Globalization the tendency of financial institutions and their customers to move beyond their domestic markets to other markets around the globe.

Gordon growth model a model used to value a share assuming that dividends on the share grow at a constant rate.

Grey market an informal market for a security that sets its price prior to the opening of the official market.

Growth stock a term that describes shares in a company that is expected to grow very rapidly over the next few years.

G7 the group of 7: UK, USA, France, Germany, Italy, Canada and Japan.

G20 the group of 7 plus other countries such as Brazil, Russia, India and China.

Hedge fund a term used to describe a fund which actively seeks to make high returns for its investors. It may go both long and short on securities including the use of derivatives for this purpose. The fund usually raises its capital from wealthy individuals and institutional investors.

Hedging the process of undertaking a transaction to reduce or eliminate risk.

Hire purchase a contract with a finance company that enables a consumer or business to purchase goods in return for an initial deposit and monthly payments. The good is legally owned by the finance company until the final payment is made.

Historical volatility the volatility obtained by using actual historical data.

Holder the agent that buys a call or put option.

Hostile takeover a takeover bid for a company that is strongly resisted by the target company.

Immunization a hedging strategy that matches the duration of assets and liabilities and so minimizes the impact of interest rate changes on net worth.

Implied volatility the volatility that is expected in the market implicit from the option premium.

Indenture the terms associated with a bond contract; for example, the coupon to be paid, conversion rights, call back features etc.

Index usually refers to a stock index like FTSE 100, S&P 500, CAC 40, Dax etc.

Index arbitrage a strategy which aims to make a profit at any significant departure of stock exchange futures prices from their theoretical values. It involves selling futures and buying shares if the futures premium is too big and buying futures and selling shares if the futures premium is too small. It may involve the use of programme trades.

Index tracking funds funds set up with the specific purpose of closely matching the performance of a given market index such as the S&P 500 stock index or FTSE 100 index.

Informational efficiency the extent to which market prices of securities fully incorporate information and react to changes in information so that abnormal returns cannot be made on a consistent basis.

Initial margin the initial deposit required by an exchange/broker when opening a futures contract or writing an option contract.

Initial public offering (IPO) an American term used to describe the floating of a company on the stockmarket for the first time.

Insider-trading the buying or selling of a security by someone who has access to privileged information not publicly available; in most countries such trading is illegal.

Insurance the business of collecting premiums so that policy holders can claim money if they suffer losses.

Institutional investor a bank, insurance company, pension fund, mutual fund, hedge fund, or other financial intermediary that invests funds on behalf of its clients or on its own behalf.

Interbank market the market which deals with bank lending and borrowing with other banks.

Interest rate future an agreement between two parties to lend/borrow a certain amount of money at a predetermined rate of interest for a specified period of time at a predetermined date in the future.

Interest rate option a contract giving the holder the right but not the obligation to lend or borrow a stated nominal notional amount, for a given period of time at a predetermined rate of interest.

Interest rate swap an agreement between two parities to finance part or all of each other's interest payments based upon a specified notion principal amount.

International banking facility (IBF) a facility whereby an institution based in the USA can make short-term deposits/loans in dollars in the USA without the need to meet regulatory requirements or hold reserves. This enables US banks to compete with Eurobanks but they can only conduct business with foreign residents not US residents.

International Primary Markets Association (IPMA) oversees Eurobond issues.

In-the-money option an option that would have some intrinsic value if exercised immediately. For a call option the current price of the underlying is above the strike price. For a put option the current price of the underlying is below the strike price.

Intrinsic value the value that would be realized if an option were exercised immediately. For a call option the intrinsic value is the amount by which the current price of the underlying exceeds the exercise price. For a put option the intrinsic value is the amount by which the current price of the underlying is below the strike price.

Inverted yield curve a yield curve that has a negative slope, that is short-term interest rates are higher than long-term interest rates.

Investment banking that part of banking that deals with corporations and high-end securities; for example new equity issues (IPOs), rights issues, bond issues, mergers and acquisitions, fund management, investment management etc.

Investment grade a bond that has a credit rating of BBB (Standard & Poor's) or Baa (Moody's) or better.

Investment trust (UK)/investment company (USA) a company that holds stakes in the form of shares in other companies. It can engage in takeovers and break-ups. If it is publicly owned then its shares trade on the Stock Exchange.

Investor-protection regulation measures designed to protect investors from mismanagement of funds, malpractice and fraud.

Issuer an entity, for example, a company or government, that sells a security to raise funds.

Junior tranche a high-risk slice of a collateralized debt obligation.

Junk bond a high-risk high-yield bond with a credit rating below BBB (Standard & Poor's) or Baa (Moody's).

Kangaroo bond a bond issued in Australia in Australian dollars but by a foreign entity.

Knock-in option an option that will 'kick in' only once a certain price has been reached.

Knock-out option an option contract that will no longer be valid if a certain price is met.

LBO see leveraged buy-out

Lead manager a bank that takes a lead role in the issue of a corporate bond or a syndicated bank loan.

Letter of credit a guarantee (letter) made by a bank that a buyer of a product/service will make a payment. Should they not, then the payment will be made by the bank.

Leverage a company's debt-to-equity ratio; also used to describe the use of a limited amount of capital to make large bets on the financial markets.

Leveraged buy out (LBO) a term used to describe the takeover of a company primarily financed by the issuance of debt in the form of bonds or bank loans by the acquiring company. Often the assets of the acquired company are used to finance the debt/loans.

LIBOR (London Interbank Offered (Lending) Rate) the rate of interest at which one bank will lend to another on the London interbank market. There is Dollar LIBOR, Euro LIBOR, Sterling LIBOR and Yen LIBOR according to which currency is being lent.

LIBOR–OIS spread (London Interbank Offered Rate–Overnight Interest Swap spread) measures the premium banks' charge over what traders predict the Federal Reserve Bank's daily effective federal funds rate will average over the next three months.

LIFFE London International Financial Futures Exchange.

Liquidity the extent to which a security/asset can be easily traded in large volumes without moving the price. A share or bond with high liquidity can be bought and sold quite easily and will usually have a low bid–offer spread.

Liquidity premium the extra yield required to hold securities that are less liquid than securities of otherwise similar features with respect to risk and maturity.

Liquidity ratio the ratio of a bank's liquid assets to its eligible liabilities.

Liquidity risk the risk that the market in a security will dry up such that it is difficult to turn it into cash with taking a substantial loss.

Listed security a security that receives a listing by a recognized exchange because it meets the requirements of that exchange for listing purposes. A listing usually ensures good liquidity and that the company issuing the security is committed to making certain information publicly available.

Listing requirements the set of conditions and standards that a company must meet in order to gain and then maintain a stock exchange listing.

LME London Metals Exchange.

Long futures the position of the buyer of a futures contract.

Long position the position of a trader/institution that has a positive net holding balance in financial securities or commodities. The trader/institution will benefit if the price rises.

Macaulay duration the weighted-average term to maturity of the cash flows on a bond. The weight of each cash flow is determined by dividing the present value of the cash flow by the price of the bond.

Management buy out (MBO) a buy out of shares by the management/directors of a company; usually results in the company being made private.

Margin call a demand for a cash deposit by a broker/exchange in order to bring a margin account to a required level.

Mark to market the monitoring of the profit and loss positions of each party to a contract by using the prevailing market price.

Market capitalization the market value of a company found by multiplying the number of shares by the price of the share.

Market-maker a broker/dealer that will buy/sell up to a specified amount of a security by quoting a bid–offer price.

Market portfolio a portfolio made up of all the assets in the economy with weights equal to their relative market values.

Market risk risk that is inherent in market fluctuations and which cannot be diversified away.

Matador a bond issued in Spain in euros by a non-Spanish entity.

MATIF (Marché à Terme Internationale de France) the French futures exchange.

Maturity transformation the process of transforming of short-term liabilities, such as deposits into medium- to long-term assets such as loans.

Medium-term note (MTN) a bond (note) that matures in 5–10 years; may pay a fixed or variable rate of interest.

Merchant bank a bank that deals mainly with trade finance, underwriting and medium- to long-term company loans. See also Investment Bank.

Merger a situation in which two companies agree to become one company; this involves shares in one of the companies being replaced by shares in the acquiring company.

Mezzanine finance finance that lies between debt and equity; it is less senior than debt but more senior than equity.

Mezzanine tranche a medium-risk slice of a collateralized debt obligation.

Minimum variance portfolio a portfolio which minimizes the risk of a combination of risky assets.

Modified duration a formula that measures the sensitivity of the price of a bond to changes in the rate of interest.

Money laundering the process of recycling illegal money (for example that obtained from trading illegal drugs) through the money markets so as to make it appear to be a legitimate source of funds.

Money market a market dealing with short-term securities and the transfer of funds with a time horizon of a year or less, such as Treasury bills, commercial paper and short-term bank deposits.

Moral hazard the problem that the existence of insurance against an event occurring will make the insured event more likely to occur than if the event was not insured against.

Moratorium a situation in which a debtor declares that it is suspending repayments of principal and interest on debts pending a satisfactory agreements to reschedule with its creditors.

Mortgage backed security (MBS) a security that derives its cash flows from principal and interest payments on a pool of mortgage loans. MBSs can be backed by residential mortgage loans (RMBS) or loans on commercial properties (CMBS).

Mortgage equity withdrawal (MEW) the borrowing of funds against the equity stake that consumers have in their homes.

Mutual fund an American term for a fund that pools funds from a variety of investors and invests them in shares and/or bonds. In the UK it is known as a unit trust.

Mutual recognition a concept whereby countries agree on minimum standards and then proceed to recognize the validity of each other's financial institutions and products. This enables financial institutions to enter the other country's market and sell their products without further licensing requirements.

Naïve diversification the process of investing in a variety of securities and assets in equal value-weighted proportions.

Narrow money supply cash held by the non-bank public and cash reserves held by the banking system.

NASDAQ National Association of Securities Dealers Automated Quotation system, an electronic stockmarket in the USA, which started in 1971 and tends to specialize in fast growing technology companies, although over 5000 companies are quoted on the system.

National Debt the total value of outstanding government debt.

Nearby contract the date of next futures contract due for expiration.

Nikkei 225 a well known index measuring the performance of 225 Japanese shares.

Nominal exchange rate index index which tracks the movements of a currency against another currency. It is usually constructed so that a rise represents an appreciation, while a fall represents a depreciation of the indexed currency.

Non-sterilized intervention situation which occurs when foreign exchange intervention by the authorities to buy or sell the domestic currency is allowed to affect the domestic money supply.

Notional principal amount the value of the principal in a swap agreement upon which the exchanged interest-rate payments are based.

Off-balance-sheet liability a bank liability that is not recorded on the bank's balance sheet; for example, an underwriting liability or a letter of credit.

Offer for sale a way of bringing a company to market either via an auction process or at a fixed price per share.

Offshore market a market for loans or deposits of a currency outside of the country of issue of that currency; for example, dollar loans/deposits made outside of the USA. See also Eurocurrency.

Open interest the outstanding number of futures or options contracts obligated for delivery, that is, the number of contracts that have not yet been closed.

Open market operation the buying or selling of money market securities by the central bank, aimed at expanding or contracting the money supply and influencing money market rates of interest.

Open outcry a system for setting prices on securities/commodities in a trading pit by traders shouting out buy/sell orders in a face-to-face scenario.

Open position the situation when a trader or an institution has a speculative position that has not yet been closed, leading to the possibility of future losses or gains depending on movements in market prices.

Opening price the price at which a derivatives contract is trading at once the Exchange officially opens for business.

Operational efficiency the cost efficiency of the financial markets and financial institutions in terms of charges to investors.

Option the right but not the obligation to buy/sell shares, bonds, foreign exchange, commodities and so on at a given (exercise/strike) price at or before a predetermined date in the future.

Option premium a fee that is paid by an option holder to the option writer in return for the right to buy or sell an underlying asset/security at a given exercise price.

Ordinary shares shares which represent partial ownership of a company, entitling the owner to voting rights on issues put before shareholders. The holder may or not receive dividends depending on the company's profits.

Originate-and-distribute a banking model in which banks lend to their customers and then on-sell the resulting loans and risks to outside investors.

Originate-and-hold a traditional banking model in which banks lend to their customers and then hold the resulting risk on their own balance sheets.

Out-of-the-money option an option that has no intrinsic value. For a call option the price of the underlying is below the strike price. For a put option the price of the underlying is above the strike price.

Over the counter derivatives 'tailor made' derivative contracts that are not traded on organized exchanges but rather between banks and other financial institutions/dealers with each other and their clients.

Over-the-counter market a market where trading does not take place in an organized exchange. For example, a bank might sell an option to buy or sell a currency at a given exchange rate. Contracts are typically tailor-made by a bank or financial institution to meet the specific need of the buyer.

Par value the nominal face value of a security upon issue, for example a £100 Treasury bill or a $1000 Eurobond.

Passive fund management a strategy that involves buying and holding shares, usually to track a well known market index. It leads to very low transaction charges as the composition of a passively managed fund is changed only occasionally.

Payout ratio the percentage of earnings paid out in dividends. It is calculated as dividend per share divided by earnings per share.

Pension fund a fund established by an employer which pools contributions from the company and its employees to be invested for the purposes of providing a pension to employees upon their retirement. Pension funds in the USA and the UK are among the largest institutional investors in the financial markets.

Perpetuity a security that pays out a constant stream of cash flows into the indefinite future with no redemption date.

Pit a place where futures, options and other securities and commodities are traded via an open outcry system.

Plain vanilla swap a simple interest rate swap in which one party swaps a fixed coupon payment for a floating rate payment with another party.

Ponzi scheme a fraudulent investment scheme offering a high rate of return which is financed by payments made by newly acquired investors. Eventually the scheme is destined to collapse with large losses for the late joiners.

Portfolio diversification the process of investing money in a range of different securities and assets, with the aim of reducing risk.

Preference shares shares for which the holder is entitled to a given dividend. Holders of preference shares have a priority over ordinary shareholders with regard to dividends and also entitlement to a share of the assets should the firm go into liquidation. However they have a lower priority than debt holders.

Present value the value of a future series of cash flows at today's value when discounted at a certain rate of interest.

Price-to-book ratio the market value of a company in relation to the net asset value of a company, that is, the value of tangible assets (not including intangible assets) less liabilities.

Price–earnings (PE) ratio the price of a share divided by the earnings per share after payment of tax.

Primary dealer a pre-approved broker/dealer/bank or other financial institution that is able to make bids for newly issued government debt. Such a dealer is expected to meet certain liquidity and other requirements.

Primary gearing the ratio of a company's debt to its equity.

Primary market the market where securities are sold when first issued.

Principal–agent problem the situation when a principal hires an agent to manage things on their behalf but the agent abuses the position and instead acts in their own interests.

Private banking banking which specializes in providing services for wealthy clients.

Private equity fund a private equity partnership which invests a pool of capital. Usually used to purchase majority stakes in a variety of companies.

Privatization the sale of state-owned enterprises to the private sector, often through the sale of shares to the public and institutions.

Promissory note a signed note promising to pay a specified sum of money on a given date.

Proprietary trading trading that occurs when a bank or financial institution risks its own capital to take speculative trading positions in financial markets in the hope of making a profit.

Prudential regulation rules governing the internal management of a financial institution; for example, the setting of ratios to ensure that the institution has sufficient capital to absorb possible losses and sufficient liquidity to ensure it can meet its obligations.

Purchasing power parity (PPP) a theory that exchange rates are determined by relative goods prices in two countries. For example, if the same car costs \$40,000 in the USA and £20,000 in the UK then the appropriate PPP rate is \$2/£1.

Put option the right but not the obligation to sell a security/commodity/asset at a predetermined price.

Putable bond a bond that allows the holder to force the company to repurchase the bond at par usually on certain fixed dates.

Putable swap a swap that allows one of the parties the right to terminate the contract prior to maturity.

Put-call parity an arbitrage formula published by Hans Stoll in 1969 that shows how to price a European put premium given the relevant call premium, the strike price, time to expiration and risk-free rate of interest used to price the call premium.

Quality spread the difference between the advantage that one party has at a fixed interest rate and it's advantage at a floating rate of interest. For example, if it can borrow fixed at 0.75% less than the other party and floating at 0,25% less than the other party then the quality spread is 0.5%.

Quantitative easing the creation of new money by the central banks to purchase a range of financial assets on both the primary and secondary markets.

Quantity theory of money a theory that an x% increase in the money supply will lead to an x% rise in prices.

Quanto option an option on a share price in one currency which pays out in a different currency.

Rating the credit rating assigned to a company; also, a share analyst might make a rating on whether to buy or sell a share.

Rational bubble a speculative bubble in which many speculators believe that a security or asset is significantly overpriced and likely to collapse in price at some time in the future. However, they are rationally willing to hold and even buy the security in the short term as they believe the prospects for a continued capital appreciation are sufficient compensation for the risk of a sudden price collapse.

Real exchange rate index an index that tracks the changes in economic competitiveness of one country's currency against another country's currency. It is usually constructed so that a rise represents a loss of competitiveness, while a fall represents a gain in competitiveness of the indexed currency.

Real interest rate the amount by which the rate of interest exceeds the inflation rate. For example, if the rate of interest is 6% and the inflation rate is 3.5% then the real interest rate is 2.5%.

Real option a right to do something that arises from a business investment decision. For example, an investment of £100 million in China might create the option to expand the investment in the future or provide an option to set up a factory in India as well etc.

Redeemable a security such as a share or bond that can be redeemed by the issuer in accordance with the conditions set out when the security was issued.

Red herring a preliminary prospectus that is issued by a company prior to an IPO or a bond issue outlining the basic proposed terms of issue and basic information about the company.

Reference entity the entity whose debt is being insured against default in a credit default swap.

Regulatory arbitrage financial institutions such as banks take advantage of differences in regulatory treatment across countries, different financial sectors and different financial instruments in order to reduce regulatory capital requirements.

Reinsurance the business of laying off potential insurance liabilities with a reinsurer.

Repo a sale and repurchase agreement – an agreement by the seller to buy back the security at a future date. The discount at which it is sold determines the rate of interest.

Retained earnings profits that are retained by a company after payment of taxes and dividends.

Return on capital employed the gross earnings before interest and taxes divided by the total capital of a company as reflected in the sum of its equity and debt values.

Reverse repo the same as a repo, but the deal has been initiated by the buyer of the security.

Reverse takeover the takeover of a company listed on the stock exchange by an unlisted company. The unlisted company is normally smaller but via this process can obtain a stock exchange listing in the newly merged company.

Revolving credit a commitment by a lender to lend money on a recurring basis under predefined conditions.

Rights issue the issuance of new shares by a company to raise new finance. The shares are offered to current shareholders first in proportion to the number of shares that they own. A shareholder can transfer their rights to a third party.

Risk the danger that the rate of return on a security will be less than expected by the investor when purchasing the security including the possible loss of part or all of the original investment.

Risk-averse an investor that will only take on increased risk if there is sufficient prospective return to compensate.

Risk management the process of identifying and reducing the risks facing an institution or individual. The aim is to quantify the risks and take action to achieve a target risk–return trade-off.

Risk premium the extra rate of return charged by investors above the risk-free rate of return to compensate for risk.

Risk transformation the process of transforming low-risk deposits into bundles of risky loans/assets.

Riskless security a security whose nominal rate of return is certain, often proxied by a three-month Treasury. Such a security earns the risk-free rate of return.

Russell 2000 an index of the performance of 2000 smaller size US companies shares.

Samurai bond a yen denominated bond issued in Japan by a foreign entity

Schatz a short-term German government bond of 2–5 years till maturity.

Secondary market the market for buying and selling a security that has already been issued on the primary market.

Securities Exchange Commission (SEC) a powerful US regulatory body responsible for overseeing US securities markets and investor protection.

Securities market line a line which measures the relationship between beta (or systematic risk) and a firm's expected rate of return.

Securitization the creation of a security which is backed by a stream of cash flows from a pool of pre-existing assets and receivables. For example, a CDO may be issued, the payments of which may be financed from mortgage or rental income. The cash flows are managed and placed under the legal control of investors through a special intermediary created for this purpose known as a 'special purpose vehicle' (SPV) or 'special purpose entity' (SPE).

Self-regulation the situation when an industry-sponsored agency is responsible for regulating an industry.

Senior security a security, such as a debt instrument, the holder of which must be paid before holders of other junior securities, such as equity, are paid.

Senior tranche the safest slice of a collateralized debt obligation.

Settlement date the date by which a security trade must be settled; that is, the date when a buyer of the security must pay for the security and by which the seller must deliver the security to the buyer.

Settlement price the price at which a security is settled. For derivatives, it is an important price since the daily settlement price will determine the amount of variation margin that may be required.

Share a security that signifies partial ownership of a company; the shareholder has a part claim on the company's assets and may be paid a dividend from the company's profits. The value of the share will fluctuate with the company's performance and prospects.

Short futures the position of the seller of a futures contract.

Short selling to sell a bond or share that the seller does not own in the hope that the price will fall and it can be bought back at a lower price. Traders are short on a security if they have a negative net position in that security or asset. Also the process of borrowing a security and selling it in the hope of buying it back at a lower price.

Short squeeze a situation where there has been heavy short selling of a stock but a price rise means that the short sellers find they have to buy the stock back to cover their losses, but this then forces the price further upwards.

Soft commodities coffee, sugar, orange juice, tea etc., non-metals.

Solvency risk the risk that a creditor will lose all or part of his investment if a debtor fails to repay him in full, even after the debtor's remaining assets are sold off. Traders call it 'counterparty risk'.

Sovereign risk the risk that a country will default on its debt.

Special purpose vehicle a legal entity which is set up for a specific purpose such as administering the cash flows from a collateralized debt obligation to the buyers of the various tranches. The American term is a special purpose entity.

Specialist a member of an exchange that acts as a market-maker in a given stock.

Specific risk risk that is specific to a particular security (for example, a share) and which can be reduced by increasing the number of shares since positive and negative shocks affecting individual companies and assets will tend to cancel out.

Speculation the undertaking of a long or short position in the financial markets in the hope of making a profit.

Speculative bubble fast dramatic price rises of shares or something else that is likely to prove unsustainable.

Spot exchange rate the exchange rate between two currencies for immediate delivery.

Spot market a market in which the commodity/asset/security is paid for and delivered immediately. Often used in the currency market when talking about the spot exchange rate between one currency and another.

Spread the difference between the bid and offer rates.

Stag a person that buys a newly issued share in the hope of selling it quickly after issue at a premium to the price paid for it.

Standard & Poor's 500 index (S&P 500) an index made up of 500 major US shares which are chosen by market capitalization, liquidity and industry group. The index is value-weighted and calculated on a continuous basis throughout the day. It is one of the most widely watched stock indices in the world.

Statutory regulation the situation when a government agency is responsible for regulating an industry.

Sterilized intervention the situation when foreign exchange intervention by the authorities to buy or sell the domestic currency is not allowed to affect the domestic money supply. This is because an offsetting of open market operation is used to negate the money supply consequences of the foreign exchange intervention.

Stock index option a contract giving the holder the right but not the obligation to buy or sell a stated stock index at a particular price at some time in the future.

Stock split a process of splitting up a stock into smaller parts, normally done to improve liquidity in the share. For example, a $200 share may be split into 5 shares of $40 each in a 5 for 1 stock split. In the UK it is known as scrip issue.

Stockmarket capitalization the total value of the companies listed on the stockmaket.

Stop-loss an order to close out a futures position (or trading position) at a loss when the price of a contracts hits a predetermined level.

Straddle an option strategy that involves the simultaneous purchase of call and put options on a share at the same strike price.

Straight a bond with a fixed periodic coupon payment.

Strangle an option strategy that involves the simultaneous purchase of call and put options on a share at different strike prices.

Strike price the price at which an option holder has the right to buy or sell a security.

Structural regulation rules governing the different types of activities, products and geographical boundaries within which a financial institution can operate.

Structured investment vehicle (SIV) a legal entity that is financed by borrowing in the short term and investing the borrowed funds in medium- to long-term securities.

Subordinated debt a bond or loan that, should a company go into liquidation, is less senior than other bonds, the bondholder can only expect payout once the more senior debt holders have been paid. Also known as junior debt.

Subprime mortgages mortgages made to people with a poor credit rating. The mortgages have a higher rate of interest than conventional mortgages to compensate for the higher risk of default.

Surplus agents economic agents (individuals, business and governments) with excess funds to invest due to their expenditure being less than their income.

Swap an exchange of cash-flow obligations between two parties.

Swap rate the interest rate associated with the fixed interest part of a fixed or floating swap.

Swap reversal a deal whereby a party to a swap contract enters a new swap arrangement with a new counterparty that will effectively cancel out its arrangements with its original counterparty.

Swap sale a deal whereby a party to a swap contract pays money to or receives money from another party to take over the obligations it has from a swap contract.

Swaption an option to do a swap at some time in the future.

Syndicate a term used to describe a group of financial institutions that underwrite a debt issue or undertake a joint bank loan known as a syndicated bank loan.

Syndicated bank loan a large bank loan made to a borrower by a group of banks. The syndicate is usually led by a lead bank which makes a percentage of the loan itself and then syndicates the rest to the other banks.

Takeover a situation where an acquiring company makes a bid for a target company. A hostile takeover ensues if the acquired company resists the takeover or a friendly takeover occurs if the target company welcomes the bid.

Technical analyst a person that uses statistical analysis of past price behaviour, sometimes supplemented with volumes traded, to predict future price change in financial markets.

TED spread the difference between three-month $LIBOR and three-month US Treasury bill interest rates.

Tender to make a bid to buy Treasury bills or bonds or other financial securities.

Term Asset Banked Loan Facility (TALF) a programme announced by the Federal Reserve in November 2008 to support the issuance of ABSs. Under the TALF the

Federal Reserve Bank of New York would lend up to $1 trillion (originally $200 billion) to holders of certain AAA-rated ABSs.

Term structure of interest rates the yield to maturity on Treasury bills and bonds of different terms to maturity.

Tick the smallest possible price movement in a security, for example, 0.01.

Tier 1 capital the core capital supporting the lending and deposit activities of a bank. It consists primarily of common stock, retained earnings and perpetual preferred stock.

Tier 2 capital the additional capital above Tier 1 capital supporting the lending and deposit activities of a bank. It includes limited life preferred stock, subordinated debt and loan-loss reserves.

Time value the part of an option premium that is not part of the intrinsic value.

Tombstone a formal advertisement in the financial press of a potential or successful issue of a bond, syndicated bank loan, issue of commercial bond etc.

Traded option a standardized option contract that is traded on an Exchange and which can be sold prior to maturity.

Tranche related securities that are offered at the same time but which have different risk–reward characteristics and/or different maturities. For example, one tranche of a bond issue might be partly in dollars and the other tranche in euros, or one part at 5 years to maturity and another tranche at 10 years till maturity.

Treasury bill a short-term debt instrument issued by the Treasury of 12 or less months till maturity; Treasury bills are issued at a discount to their face value.

Treasury bond a long-term debt instrument issued by the Treasury which makes fixed coupon payments to the holder and pays the principal back upon maturity. In the USA the bond is usually 10 years or over with 2–9 year bonds being called Treasury Notes.

Troubled Asset Relief Programme (TARP) a $700 billion US government programme created during the credit crunch (October 2008) to buy MBSs from financial institutions.

UK base rate the rate of interest used by banks to determine the rate of interest that they will charge to their safest customers.

Uncovered interest rate parity the theory that exchange rates are expected to change at a rate that offsets the interest rate differential. The high interest rate currency is expected to depreciate, while the low interest rate currency is expected to appreciate.

Underwriting the process of issuing an insurance policy.

Underwriting syndicate a group of banks that agree to buy any unsold part of a newly issued security.

Underlying currency the currency that you have committed to buy or sell in a futures contract or the right to buy or sell in an option contract.

Unit trust a fund that pools money from investors and then invests it in a range of securities. See also Mutual fund.

Universal banking banking that offers a broad range of financial services to consumers and businesses, such as insurance, investment services including equity and bond investments, in addition to basic banking services such as deposit taking and loan making.

Unsubordinated debt debt which is senior with respect to repayment than other debt or junior securities.

Value at risk a statistical modelling technique used to estimate the probability of portfolio losses based on an analysis of the behaviour of past prices, correlations and volatilities.

Variation margin the additional margin payments required of the losing party to a futures contract to maintain their open position.

Venture capital private capital used to finance the growth of small companies that are generally risky and lack long-term trading records, thus making it difficult for them to secure finance from banks or the capital markets.

VIX an index measuring the 30-day implied stock market volatility in the S&P 500 stock index. It is calculated from a range of call and put premiums on the S&P 500 stock index.

Volatility a statistical measure of the tendency of a security to rise or fall over a given time frame. Usually calculated by looking at a security's variance.

Warrant an option attached to a bond that gives the holder the right to buy or sell a security at a given price. It differs from a normal option in that the company issuing the bond is issuing the warrant rather than an Exchange. In addition a warrant may be exercisable in several years compared to several months as is the case with an exchange traded option. Warrants can be detached from the bond and traded separately from the bond.

Withholding tax a tax on investment income aimed specifically at non-residents (that is, foreigners).

Writer the person who sells a call or put option contract.

Yankee bond a bond issued in the USA in dollars but by a foreign entity.

Yield curve a curve that plots the yield to maturity of Treasury bills and Treasury bonds with different terms to maturity.

Yield to maturity (YTM) the rate of return on a bond expressed as a percentage per annum if it is held till maturity. The YTM takes account of all coupon payments and any prospective capital gains/losses as well as the term to maturity and assumes that coupon payments can be reinvested at the YTM.

Zero coupon swap a swap in which the fixed-rate payer makes only one lump sum interest payment at the end of the agreement, while the floating-rate payer makes regular quarterly/semi-annual/annual payments. This means the floating-rate payer requires an additional payment to reflect the increased risk of default.

REFERENCES

Chapter 4

Culbertson, J.M. (1957) The Term Structure of Interest Rates, *Quarterly Journal of Economics*, November, pp. 489–504.

Modigliani, F. and Sutch, R. (1966) Innovations in Interest Rate Policy, *American Economic Review*, May, pp.178–97.

Chapter 6

Fons, J.S. and Kimball, A.E. (1991) Corporate Bond Defaults and Default Rates 1979–1990, *Journal of Fixed Income Securities*, 3rd edn, Business One, Irwin.

Macaulay, F.R. (1938) *Some Theoretical Problems Suggested by the Movement of Interest Rates Bond Yields and Stock Prices in the US since 1856*, National Bureau of Economic Research.

Chapter 7

Markowitz, H. (1959) *Portfolio Selection: Efficient Diversification of Investments*, John Wiley.

Solnik, B.H. (1974) Why Not Diversify Internationally Rather Than Domestically?, *Financial Analysts Journal*, July–August, pp. 48–54.

Tobin, J. (1958) Liquidity Preference as Behaviour Towards Risk, *Review of Economic Studies*, vol. 56, pp. 65–86.

Wagner, W. and Lau, S. (1971) The Effect of Diversification on Risk, *Financial Analysts Journal*, July–August, pp. 48–53.

Chapter 8

Banz, R.W. (1981) The Relationship between Return and Market Value of Common Stocks, *Journal of Financial Economics*, March, pp. 3–18.

Basu, S. (1977) The Investment Performance of Common Stocks in Relation to their Price Earnings Ratios, *Journal of Finance*, June, p. 663.

Black, F., Jensen, M.C. and Scholes, M (1972) The Capital Asset Pricing Model: Some Empirical Tests, in M.C. Jensen (eds) *Studies in the Theory of Capital Markets*, Praeger.

Blume, M. and Friend, I. (1973) A New Look at the Capital Asset Pricing Model, *Journal of Finance*, March 1973 pp. 19–34.

Chen, N.F., Roll, R. and Ross, S (1986) Economic Forces and the Stock Market, *Journal of Business*, vol. 59, pp. 383–403.

Fama, E. and MacBeth, J. (1973) Risk, Return and Equilibrium: Empirical Test, *Journal of Political Economy*, May–June, pp. 607-636.

Friend, I. and Blume, M. (1970) Measurement of Portfolio Performance under Uncertainty, *American Economic Review*, September, pp. 561–75.

Gibbons, M.R. (1982) Multivariate Tests of Financial Models: A New Approach, *Journal of Financial Economics*, March, pp. 3–28.

Lintner, J. (1965) The Valuation of Risk Assets and the Selection of Risky Investments in Stock Portfolios and Capital Budgets, *Review of Economics and Statistics*, February, pp. 13–37.

Litzenberger, R. and Ramaswamy, K. (1979) The Effect of Personal Taxes and Dividends and Capital Asset Prices: Theory and Empirical Evidence, *Journal of Financial Economics*, June, pp. 163–95.

Merton, R. (1973) An Intertemporal Capital Asset Pricing Model, *Econometrica*, September, pp. 867–88.

Miller, M. and Scholes, M. (1972) Rates of Return in Relation to Risk: A Re-examination of Some Recent Findings, in M.C. Jensen (eds) *Studies in the Theory of Capital Markets*, Praeger, pp. 47–78.

Roll, R. and Ross, S.A. (1980) An Empirical Investigation of the APT, *Journal of Finance*, December, pp. 1073–103.

Ross, S.A. (1976) The Arbitrage Theory of Capital Asset Pricing, *Journal of Economic Theory*, December, pp. 343–62.

Shanken, J. (1985) Multi-Beta CAPM or Equilibrium APT?: A Reply, *Journal of Finance*, September, pp. 1189–96.

Sharpe, W.F. (1963) A Simplified Model for Portfolio Analysis, *Management Science*, January, pp. 277–93.

Sharpe, W.F. (1964) Capital Asset Prices: A Theory of Market Equilibrium under Conditions of Risk, *Journal of Finance*, September, pp. 425–42.

Chapter 9

Gordon, M.J. (1962) *The Investment, Financing and Valuation of the Corporation*, Irwin.

Modigliani, F. and Miller, M. (1958) The Cost of Capital, Corporation Finance, and the Theory of Investment, *American Economic Review*, June, pp. 261–97.

Modigliani, F. and Miller, M. (1961) Dividend Policy, Growth and the Valuation of Shares, *Journal of Business*, vol. 34, pp. 411–33.

Solnik, B.H. (1991) *International Investments*, 2nd edn, Addison-Wesley.

Chapter 10

Banz, R.W. (1981) The Relationship between Return and Market Value of Common Stocks, *Journal of Financial Economics*, March, pp. 3–18.

Basu, S. (1977) The Investment Performance of Common Stocks in Relation to their Price Earnings Ratios, *Journal of Finance*, June, p. 663.

Connolly, R.A. (1989) An Examination of the Robustness of the Weekend Effect, *Journal of Financial and Quantitative Analysis*, June, pp. 133–69.

Cross, F. (1973) The Behaviour of Stock Prices on Fridays and Mondays, *Financial Analysts Journal*, November/December, pp. 67–9.

De Bondt, W.F.M. and Thaler, R.H. (1985) Does the Stock Market Overreact?, *Journal of Finance*, July, pp. 793–805.

Dimson, E. and Marsh, P. (1984) An Analysis of Brokers' and Analysts' Unpublished Forecasts of UK Stock Returns, *Journal of Finance*, vol. 39, no. 5, pp. 1257–92.

Elton, E.J., Gruber, M.J. and Grossman, S. (1986) Discrete Expectational Data and Portfolio Performance, *Journal of Finance*, July, pp. 699–712.

Fama, E. (1965) The Behaviour of Stock Market Prices, *Journal of Business*, January, pp. 34–105.

Fama, E. and Blume, M. (1966) Filter Rules and Stock Market Trading, *Journal of Business*, January, pp. 226–41.

Fama, E. (1970) Efficient Capital Markets: A Review of Theory and Empirical Work, *Journal of Finance*, December, pp. 1575–617.

Fama, E. (1991) Efficient Capital Markets II, *Journal of Finance*, December, pp. 1575–617.

Feeny, M. (1989) Charting the Foreign Exchange Markets, in C. Dunis and M. Feeny, *Exchange Rate Forecasting*, Woodhead-Faulkner.

Firth, M. (1975) The Information Content of Large Investment Holdings, *Journal of Finance*, December, pp.1265–81.

Gibbons, M.R. and Hess, P. (1981) Day of the week Effect and Asset Returns, *Journal of Business*, October, pp. 579–96.

Gultekin, M.N. and Gultekin, N.B. (1983) Stock Market Seasonality: International Evidence, *Journal of Financial Economics*, December, pp. 469–81.

Haugen, R.A. and Jorion, P. (1996) The January Effect: Still There After All These Years, *Financial Analysts Journal*, January–February, pp. 27–31.

Jaffe, J. (1974) Special Information and Insider Trading, *Journal of Business*, July, pp. 410–28.

Jegadeesh, N. and Titman, S. (1993) Returns to Buying Winners and Selling Losers: Implications for Stock Market Efficiency, *Journal of Finance*, vol. 48, pp. 65–91.

Jensen, M.C (1969) The Performance of Mutual Funds in the Period 1945–64, *Journal of Finance*, May.

Keim, D. (1983) Size Related Anomalies and Stock Return Seasonality: Further Empirical Evidence, *Journal of Financial Economics*, vol. 12, no. 1, June, pp. 13–32.

Pettit, R.R. (1972) Dividend Announcements, Security Performance, and Capital Market Efficiency, *Journal of Finance*, December, pp. 993–1007.

Reinganum, M.R. (1981) Misspecification of Capital Asset Pricing: Empirical Anomalies Based on Earnings Yields and Market Values, *Journal of Financial Economics*, March, pp. 19–46.

Rendleman, R.J., Jones, C.P. and Latane, H.E. (1982) Empirical Anomalies Based on Unexpected Earnings and the Importance of Risk Adjustments, *Journal of Financial Economics*, November.

Sweeny, R.J. (1988) Some New Filter Rule Tests: Methods and Results, *Journal of Financial and Quantitative Analysis*, September, pp. 285–300.

Watts, R. (1973) The Information Content of Dividends, *Journal of Business*, April, pp. 191–211.

Chapter 12

Ardeni, P.G. and Lubian, D. (1991) Is there Trend Reversion in Purchasing Power Parity?, *European Economic Review*, vol. 35, no. 5, pp. 1035–55.

Bilson, J.F.O. (1978a) Rational Expectations and the Exchange Rate, in J.A. Frenkel and H.G. Johnson, The Economics of Exchange Rates, AddisonWesley.

Bilson, J.F.O. (1978b) The Monetary Approach to the Exchange Rate: Some Empirical Evidence, *IMF Staff Papers*, vol. 25, pp. 48–75.

Dornbusch, R. (1976a) Expectations and Exchange Rate Dynamics, *Journal of Political Economy*, vol. 84, pp. 1161–76.

Dornbusch, R. (1976b) The Theory of Flexible Exchange Rate Regimes and Macroeconomic Policy, *Scandinavian Journal of Economics*, vol. 84, pp. 255–75.

Frankel, J.A. (1979) On the Mark: A Theory of Floating Exchange Rates Based on Real Interest Rate Differentials, *American Economic Review*, vol. 69, pp. 610–22.

Frenkel, J.A. (1981) The Collapse of Purchasing Power Parities during the 1970s, *European Economic Review*, vol. 16, pp. 145–65.

MacDonald, R. (1988) *Floating Exchange Rates: Theories and Evidence*, Unwin Hyman.

Officer, L. (1976) The Purchasing Power Parity Theory of Exchange Rates: A Review Article, *IMF Staff Papers*, vol. 23, pp. 1-61.

Chapter 15

Black, F. and Scholes, M. (1973) The Pricing of Options and Corporate Liabilities, *Journal of Political Economy*, May/June, pp. 637–54.

Stoll, H.R. (1969) The Relationship between Put and Call Option Prices, *Journal of Finance*, December, pp. 801–24.

Chapter 18

Steinherr, A. (1992) *The New European Financial Market Place*, Longman.

BIBLIOGRAPHY

This list is intended to guide the reader to a number of texts in the field of financial markets that will prove to be useful for further study of the subject area.

Anderton, B.A. (1995) *Financial Services*. London: Macmillan.

Bain, A.D. (1992) *The Economics of the Financial System*. Oxford: Basil Blackwell.

Bain, K. and Howells, P. (2007) *Financial Markets and Institutions*. London: FT/Prentice-Hall.

Bailey, R. (2005) *The Economics of Financial Markets*. Cambridge: Cambridge University Press.

Blake, D. (2003) *Financial Market Analysis*. Maidenhead: McGraw-Hill.

Bodie, Z., Kane, A. and Marcus, A. (2010) *Investments*. New York: McGraw-Hill.

Buckle, M. and Thompson, J. (2004) *The UK Financial System: Theory and Practice*. Manchester: Manchester University Press.

Copeland, T.E. and Weston, J.F. (1988) *Financial Theory and Corporate Policy*. Reading, Mass: Addison-Wesley.

Cuthbertson, K. and Nitzsche, D. (2001) *Financial Engineering Derivatives and Risk Management*. Chichester: John Wiley.

Cuthbertson, K. and Nitzsche, D. (2004) *Quantitative Financial Economics: Stocks, Bonds and Foreign Exchange*. Chichester: John Wiley.

Cuthbertson, K. and Nitzsche, D. (2008) *Investments*. New York: Wiley.

Dufey, G. and Giddy, I. (1994) *The International Money Market*. New Jersey: Prentice Hall.

Eales, B.A. (1995) *Financial Risk Management*. Maidenhead: McGraw-Hill.

Edwards, F.R. and Ma, C.W. (1992) *Futures and Options*. New York: McGraw-Hill.

Elton, E.J., Gruber, M., Brown S. and Goetzmann, W. (2010) *Modern Portfolio Theory and Investment Analysis*. New York: John Wiley.

Fabozzi, F.J. and Modigliani, F. (2008) *Capital Markets: Institutions and Instruments*. Englewood Cliffs, NJ: Prentice-Hall.

Fabozzi, F.J., Modigliani, F. and Jones, F (2009) *Foundations of Financial Markets and Institutions*. Englewood Cliffs, NJ: Prentice-Hall.

Francis, J.C. (1993) *Management of Investments*. New York: McGraw-Hill.

Giddy, I. (1994) *Global Financial Markets*. Lexington, Mass: D.C. Heath.

Hull, J.C. (2008) *Options, Futures, and Other Derivative Securities*. Englewood Cliffs, NJ: Prentice-Hall.

Haugen, R.A. (2001) *Modern Investment Theory*. Englewood Cliffs, NJ: Prentice-Hall.

Kolb, R.W. (2009) *Financial Derivatives: Pricing and Risk Management*. Oxford: Basil Blackwell.

Kolb, R.W. and Rodriguez, R.J. (1996) *Financial Markets*. Oxford: Basil Blackwell.

Lofthouse, S. (2001) *Equity Investment Management*. Chichester: John Wiley.

Levy, H. (2002) *Fundamentals of Investments*. Harlow: Pearson Education.

Madura, J. (2008) *Financial Institutions and Markets*. Boston, Mass: South Western College.

Pilbeam, K.S. (2006) *International Finance*. Basingstoke: Palgrave Macmillan.

Redhead, K. (1990) *Introduction to Financial Futures and Options*. London: Prentice-Hall/ Woodhead-Faulkner.

Redhead, K. (1992) *Introduction to the International Money Markets*. London: Woodhead-Faulkner.

Redhead, K. (1995) *Introduction to Financial Investment*, London: Prentice-Hall/Woodhead-Faulkner.

Rees, B. (1990) *Financial Analysis*. Hemel Hempstead: Prentice-Hall.

Rutterford, J. and Davison, M. (2007) *An Introduction to Stock Exchange Investment*. Basingstoke: Palgrave Macmillan.

Sharpe, W.G., Alexander, G. and Bailey, J. (2003) *Investments*. New Jersey: Prentice-Hall.

Steinherr, A. (1992) *The New European Financial Market Place*. London: Longman.

Valdez, S. (2010) *An Introduction to Global Financial Markets*. Basingstoke: Palgrave Macmillan.

Walmsley, J. (2000) *The Foreign Exchange and Money Markets Guide*. Chichester: John Wiley.

Useful sources for data and analysis

Annual Report, Bank for International Settlements, Published annually.

Main Economic Indicators, Organisation for Economic Co-operation and Development. Published monthly.

International Financial Statistics, International Financial Statistics, Washington. Published monthly.

Economic Outlook, Organisation for Economic Co-operation and Development, Paris. Published bi-annually.

Global Development Finance, World Bank, Washington. Published annually.

World Development Report, World Bank, Washington. Published annually.

World Economic Outlook, International Monetary Fund, Washington. Published bi-annually.

International Capital Markets, International Monetary Fund. Published annually.

Financial Market Trends, Organisation for Economic Co-operation and Development. Published tri-annually.

Financial Times, daily.

The Economist Magazine, weekly.

Wall Street Journal, daily.

Internet guide

There are thousands of useful finance related sites on the web, this is only a small but useful start. Many of them contain links to numerous other sites.

Institutions and central banks

www.imf.org	International Monetary Fund
www.bis.org	Bank for International Settlements
www.oecd.org	Organisation for Economic Co-operation and Development

www.ici.org   Investment Company Institute
www.ifsl.org.uk   International Financial Services London
www.sifma.org   Securities Industry and Financial Markets Association
www.asifma.org   Asian Securities Industry and Financial Markets Association
www.worldbank.org   World Bank.
www.federalreserve.gov   the site of the Federal Reserve
www.bankofengland.co.uk   Bank of England's website
www.hm-treasury.gov.uk   UK Treasury

News sites

www.money.cnn.com   CNN's finance site
www.bloomberg.com   Bloomberg
www.businessweek.com   Business Week magazine
www.economist.com   Economist magazine.
www.reuters.com   Reuters
www.thestreet.com   a financial news website
www.ft.com   Financial Times
www.cbs.marketwatch.com   CBS financial website
www.wsj.com   Wall Street Journal
www.finance.yahoo.com   great for stock quotes and finance news
www.uk.finance.yahoo.com   great for UK stock quotes and finance news

Economic and financial data

www.economagic.com   plenty of US data
www.globalfindata.com   a commercial data provider
www.econdata.net   links to some very good datasets
www.econstats.com   free data on the US and global economy and plenty of links

Stock and derivatives exchanges

www.cbot.com   Chicago Board of Trade
www.cme.com   Chicago Mercantile Exchange
www.euronext.com   The Euronext.Liffe Exchange
www.nyse.com   New York Stock Exchange
www.nasdaq.com   NASDAQ Exchange

Education and search

www.investopedia.com   a good site with plenty of definitions and information
www.moneyextra.com   a UK website aimed at informing the small investor
www.moneyterms.co.uk   a UK website with definitions of key financial terms
www.fool.co.uk   a UK website aimed at informing the small investor
www.fool.com   a US website aimed at informing the small investor
www.bized.co.uk   a great UK site for economic data links and for economics students

INDEX